Introduction to Political Science

How to Think for Yourself about Politics

SECOND EDITION

Craig Parsons
University of Oregon

Pearson

Library of Congress Cataloging-in-Publication Data
Names: Parsons, Craig, author.
Title: Introduction to political science: how to think for yourself about politics / Craig Parsons.
Description: Second edition. | Hoboken, NJ: Pearson, 2021. | Includes bibliographical references and index. | Summary: "Politics pervades every aspect of our lives as human beings. As Aristotle said, we are "political animals"— Provided by publisher.
Identifiers: LCCN 2020006627 | ISBN 9780135710104 (paperback) | ISBN 9780136597896 (ebook)
Subjects: LCSH: Political science. | Political science—Philosophy.
Classification: LCC JA71 .P3394 2021 | DDC 320—dc23
LC record available at https://lccn.loc.gov/2020006627

2nd Edition Access Code Card:
ISBN-10: 0-13-570308-5
ISBN-13: 978-0-13-570308-3
2nd Edition Rental:
ISBN-10: 0-13-571010-3
ISBN-13: 978-0-13-571010-4
2nd Edition Instructor's Review Copy:
ISBN-10: 0-13-570668-8
ISBN-13: 978-0-13-570668-8

6 2022

Contents

8   Inside Liberal Democracy II: Power and Policymaking   244

9   Political Economies   289

10   Economic Development and Growth   320

Preface

Politics pervades every aspect of our lives as human beings. As Aristotle said, we are "political animals." Unfortunately, many people aren't very comfortable with that status. They wish they could avoid politics, often because they find it threatening and hard to understand: a shifting, conflictual space of complex ideas and hidden agendas. This book is designed to help students become more comfortable political animals. It does so by helping them to become conscious critical thinkers about a wide range of political topics. It teaches them how—not what—to think about politics.

The first step to that goal is to recognize that avoiding politics makes no sense. *Politics* is just a word for processes of collective decision making among people, and unless we live alone on a desert island, those processes always surround us. As a rough analogy, politics is an inescapable aspect of our lives like physical health. Our health can be good or bad, but having "no" health makes no sense. Politics too can be good or bad in many ways, but it cannot simply go away. We cannot live among other human beings without being bound up in processes of collective decision making. Just as neglecting our health can only have bad consequences, so avoiding politics can only bring us missed opportunities and subjugation to other people.

The second step to that goal is to identify a set of tools that students can use to sharpen their own political thinking. This is very hard for most people to do without help, because politics *is* a shifting, often-conflictual space of complex ideas and possibly hidden agendas. The set of tools must be diverse—students need to try their hands at many cuts into politics—but also organized and bounded, so that the new student is not overwhelmed.

In other words, what students need to make politics their own is a structured sense of political alternatives. Alternatives are the foundation of all critical thinking; we cannot argue coherently for or against one view without knowing something about others. For critical thinking about politics in particular, we must be aware of three kinds of alternatives:

- Alternative arrangements of political *practice*: how is politics organized and experienced differently around the world?

- Alternative beliefs in political *ideologies*: what are different views of the good and the bad in politics?

- Alternative logics of political *explanations*: what different kinds of stories can we tell about why people act politically as they do?

For these alternatives to coalesce into a tool kit that students can take away from their studies, they must be presented in systematic and cumulative ways, especially with respect to ideologies and explanations. Though the options in political practices vary widely from topic to topic—the possibilities in representation form one menu, for example, while the choices in economic policies form another—our major ideologies and the major logics of explanation in political science stretch across these areas. The core organization of this book, then, is to apply a recurring set of major ideologies and explanatory approaches as we survey political arrangements and practices across space and time: the state, forms of government, participation, representation, policymaking, political economy and development, authoritarianism and democratization, war and terrorism, and the trends of globalization.

The key strengths of this organization are that it is simultaneously more structured and more open-ended than any other introductory text on politics:

- The largest part of each chapter covers practices "on the ground" that form the empirical content of comparative politics, American politics, and international relations.

- Attention to contrasting political ideologies in every chapter creates connections to basic political theory.

- Short but substantive examples of alternative explanations in every chapter offer an accessible entry point into theoretical debates across the empirical subfields.

- Across the whole book, a consistent emphasis on alternatives within all these spaces promotes awareness of our diverse world, of our diverse discipline, and of students' freedom and responsibility to figure out what they think about politics.

The book also includes other structured and cumulative supports for learning:

- Each chapter invites students to consider how to evaluate explanations with cross-case (quantitative) and within-case (qualitative) methodological approaches and evidence.

- Evocative photos, charts, and graphic figures strengthen the text with anchors for visual learning.

- Explicit learning objectives head each section and lead students into review questions, journal-writing assignments, and end-of-chapter summaries.

Finally, it is important that this framework responds not just to pedagogical challenges but to broader challenges of our era as well. In a time of low trust in government and rising distaste for politics, we must invite students to engage these subjects in a way that is both supportive and open-minded. In a period when political science has diversified to the point that some faculty members question any connection to their colleagues,

we need a coherent but ecumenical introductory frame that emphasizes both our unity and our diversity as a field. My hope is that this book realizes these immodest goals to some small degree.

New to the Second Edition

Today's world is pretty different from the one in which this book was first written. This is most obvious at home in the United States, thanks to the election of President Donald Trump in 2016. Trump shook up the norms of the presidency, many of his own Republican Party's positions, most of America's foreign relationships, and the architecture of global trade. But other parts of the world have seen profound developments too. The British voted to leave the European Union. Chinese President Xi Jinping consolidated extraordinary control of his vast nation. Russia systematically tampered with democratic elections around the world. North Korea's Kim Jong Un simultaneously threatened nuclear war and enjoyed chummy photo shoots with President Trump. Syria, Iraq, Turkey, Iran, Saudi Arabia, and other Middle Eastern players made Machiavellian moves in entangled regional wars. Parts of Africa boomed while others languished. India and Pakistan rattled swords over the disputed region of Kashmir. And so on.

But in a world that seems to be changing so rapidly, it is all the more important to understand the fundamental and largely unchanging building blocks of thinking about politics. This book's menu of basic alternatives still provides our touchstones: big options in political practices and institutions, political ideologies, and political-science theories to explain them. While retaining that framework, this second edition includes many updates and improvements to connect it to students' evolving lives and environment:

Chapter 1 now introduces explanatory traditions in political science by discussing how to explain the long shutdown of the U.S. federal government in early 2019.

Chapter 3, on ideologies, includes new and extended treatment of strands of conservatism and how they relate to Trump, plus discussion of "democratic socialism" on the American Left.

Chapter 4, on states and nations, gives stronger attention to the roots of tension over migration.

Chapter 5, on governments, tracks the evolving varieties of illiberal democracies and authoritarianism.

Chapter 6, on political participation, includes a substantial new section on framing and identity politics.

Chapter 7, on representation, addresses the push for a "National Popular Vote," among other updates.

Chapter 9, on political economy foundations, discusses more extensively how today's Left of the Democratic Party relates to socialist ideas.

Chapter 10, on the politics of development and growth, offers a major new discussion of debates over inequality and government intervention.

Chapter 11, on political change and democratization, addresses the politics around the nuclear deal with Iran and both the centralization and vulnerabilities of Xi Jinping's rule in China.

Chapter 13, on globalization, features attention to how and why American policies on "free trade" shifted under Trump.

Just as important as any of these substantive changes, the book's charts and data have been thoroughly revised. The Revel edition also includes far more Social Explorer features—allowing students to explore data relationships and visualization—as well as a new series of supportive videos that connect strongly to the text.

Revel™

Revel is an interactive learning environment that deeply engages students and prepares them for class. Media and assessment integrated directly within the author's narrative lets students read, explore interactive content, and practice in one continuous learning path. Thanks to the dynamic reading experience in Revel, students come to class prepared to discuss, apply, and learn from instructors and from each other.

Learn more about Revel
www.pearson.com/revel

- **Current Events Bulletins** feature author-written articles that put breaking news and current events into the context of each chapter.

- **Videos** bring to life chapter contents and key moments in politics.

- **Social Explorer interactive figures** allow frequent updates with the latest data, toggles to illustrate movement over time, rollover data that students can explore, increasing students' data literacy and analytical skills.

- **Assessments** tied to primary chapter sections, as well as full chapter exams, allow instructors and students to track progress and get immediate feedback.

- **Integrated Writing Opportunities**, helping students reason and write more clearly, are offered in several forms:
  - **Journal prompts** ask students to synthesize and apply what they have learned.
  - **Shared writing prompts** encourage students to think critically about the concepts and challenges laid out in the chapter. Through these discussion threads, instructors and students can explore multiple sides of an issue by sharing their own views and responding to each other's viewpoints.
  - **Essay prompts** are from Pearson's Writing Space, where instructors can assign both automatically graded and instructor-graded prompts. Writing Space is the best way to develop and assess concept mastery and critical thinking through writing. Writing Space provides a single place within Revel to create, track, and grade writing assignments; access writing resources; and exchange meaningful, personalized feedback quickly and easily to improve results.

Learning Management Systems

Pearson provides Blackboard Learn™, Canvas™, Brightspace by D2L, and Moodle integration, giving institutions, instructors, and students easy access to Revel. Our Revel integration delivers streamlined access to everything your students need for the course in these learning management system (LMS) environments. Single Sign-on: With single sign-on, students are ready on their first day. From your LMS course, students have easy access to an interactive blend of authors' narrative, media, and assessment. Grade Sync: Flexible, on-demand grade synchronization capabilities allow you to control exactly which Revel grades should be transferred to the LMS gradebook.

Revel Combo Card

The Revel Combo Card provides an all-in-one access code and loose-leaf print reference (delivered by mail).

Supplements

Make more time to engage with your students with instructor resources that offer effective learning assessments and classroom engagement. Pearson's partnership with educators does not end with the delivery of course materials; Pearson is there with you on the first day of class and beyond. A dedicated team of local Pearson representatives will work with you to not only choose course materials but also integrate them into your class and assess their effectiveness. Our goal is your goal—to improve instruction with each semester.

Pearson is pleased to offer the following resources to qualified adopters of *Introduction to Political Science*. Several of these supplements are available for instant download on the Instructor Resource Center (IRC); please visit the IRC at **www.pearsonhighered.com/irc** to register for access.

- **Test Bank**
  Evaluate learning at every level. Reviewed for clarity and accuracy, the Test Bank measures this material's learning objectives with multiple-choice and essay questions. You can easily customize the assessment to work in any major learning management system and to match what is covered in your course. Word, PDF, and BlackBoard versions are available on the IRC, and Respondus versions are available on request from **www.respondus. com**.

- **Pearson MyTest**
  This powerful assessment generation program includes all of the questions in the Test Bank. Quizzes and exams can be easily authored and saved online, and then printed for classroom use, giving you ultimate flexibility to manage assessments anytime and anywhere. To learn more, visit **www.pearsonhighered.com/mytest**.

- **Instructor's Resource Manual**
  Create a comprehensive road map for teaching classroom, online, or hybrid courses. Designed for new and experienced instructors, the Instructor's Resource Manual includes learning objectives; lecture and discussion suggestions; activities for in or out of class; research activities; participation activities; and suggested readings, series, and films as well as a Revel features section. Available within Revel and on the IRC.

- **PowerPoints**
  In order to support varied teaching styles while making it easy to incorporate dynamic Revel features in class, two sets of PowerPoint Presentations are available for this edition: (1) A set of accessible lecture PowerPoint slides outline each chapter of the text. (2) An additional set of the lecture PowerPoint slides includes LiveSlides, which link to each Social Explorer data visualization within the Revel product. Available within Revel and on the IRC.

Acknowledgments

This book could not have been completed without contributions from many people. My first Pearson editor, Vikram Mukhija, helped me figure out what book I wanted to write. My first development editor, Angela Kao, taught me how to write a textbook. Later, development editor Barbara Smith Vargo helped clarify the writing and connect it with powerful visuals. Pearson editor Charlyce Jones-Owen shepherded the book gracefully through the final stages. For the second edition I'm especially grateful for help on charts, videos, and other supportive features from Dea Barbieri and Megan Vertucci. Crucial research assistance came from Clay Cleveland, Cary Fontana, Leif Hoffmann, Alberto Lioy, Kelly Littlepage, and Benedikt Springer. A great many colleagues helped me work through challenges along the way, among whom Burke Hendrix stands out for helping me do less damage to political theory.

Many valuable comments also came from reviewers during the various stages of developing this text, including: Jean Abshire, Indiana University—Southeast; James Allan, Wittenberg College; Ashley Biser, Ohio Wesleyan University; Ji Young Choi, Ohio Wesleyan University; David Claborn, Olivet Nazarene University; Steven Collins, Oklahoma State University—Oklahoma City; Rosalyn Cooperman, University of Mary Washington; Mark Croatti, The George Washington University; David Darmofal, University of South Carolina; Denise DeGarmo, Southern Illinois University; Mark Druash, Tallahassee Community College; Julie Hershenberg, Collin College; Will Jennings, University of Tennessee; Andrei Korobkov, Middle Tennessee State University; Mariely López-Santana, George Mason University; Jadon Marianetti, Santa Fe College; Lynn M. Maurer, Southern Illinois University; Allyn Milojevich, University of Tennessee; K.C. Morrison, Mississippi State University; Nicholas P. Nicoletti, University of Buffalo; Jonathan Olsen, University of Wisconsin—Parkside; Bobby Pace, Community College of Aurora; David Plazek, Johnson State College; Delia Popescu, LeMoyne College; David E. Sturrock, Southwest Minnesota State University; John W. Sutherlin, University of Louisiana—Monroe; Katrina Taylor, Northern Arizona University; Lee Trepanier, Saginaw Valley State University; Mark Turetzky, Gavilan College; Kimberly Turner, College of DuPage; Adryan Wallace, University of Hartford; Winn W. Wasson, University of Wisconsin—Waukesha; John P. (Pat) Willerton Jr., University of Arizona.

Lastly, I could not make it through this kind of project without the constant support of my wife, Kari, and my children, Tor, Margaux, and Gwen.

Craig Parsons

About the Author

Craig Parsons is a professor of political science and a specialist in comparative European politics at the University of Oregon. After growing up in Chico, California, he earned degrees from Stanford University, Sciences Po Paris, and the University of California, Berkeley. His authored or edited books include *A Certain Idea of Europe* (Cornell University Press, 2003), *The State of the European Union: With US or Against US* (Oxford University Press, 2005), *Immigration and the Transformation of Europe* (Cambridge University Press, 2006), *How to Map Arguments in Political Science* (Oxford University Press, 2007), and *Constructing the International Economy* (Cornell University Press, 2010). He has also published many articles and book chapters on the European Union, national-level European politics, the U.S. Congress, and a variety of theoretical and methodological issues in political science.

Chapter 1
Introduction

Office workers in Washington, D.C. rally to protest the shutdown of the federal government in January 2019. The sign asks politicians to stop political in-fighting and "just do their jobs."

 Learning Objectives

1.1 Define "politics" and explain why it is an inescapable part of human existence.

1.2 Explain the difference between the descriptive study of politics, normative engagement with political ideologies, and the focus of political science on explaining politics.

1.3 Summarize the logic of the three main approaches to explaining political

action and recognize the logics in examples of explanatory arguments.

1.4 Identify the four main methods that political scientists use to test and support their explanations.

1.5 Identify the main subfields in the study of politics.

Introduction: Is Politics to Blame?

"Politics" gets a bad rap today. Even politicians don't seem to like it. The apparent evil of politics was on full display during the fight over the U.S. federal budget in winter 2018–2019 that brought the longest government shutdown in American history. At one point, former President George W. Bush called on President Donald Trump to "put politics aside" to end the standoff. Trump—like Bush, a leader of the Republican Party—used the same terms to denounce his opponents, accusing Congresspeople in the Democratic Party of "playing politics."

Their negative characterization of politics is normal. Trump's predecessor, Democratic President Barack Obama said the same thing when he began his first term back in 2009. "I don't expect a hundred percent agreement from my Republican colleagues," he said in his inaugural address, "but I do hope that we can all put politics aside and do the American people's business right now." Citizens use this language too. During a previous battle between Democrats and Republicans that shut down the federal government in 2013, for example, one resident of Reno, Nevada, told his local newspaper, "It's all about politics, and to me that's very frustrating." Another Nevadan commented, "It's just about politicians jockeying for position to advance their own agendas in the future. That's all it is."[1]

One of the few things that Americans can agree on today, it seems, is that *politics* causes many of America's problems. We use the word to evoke an image of infighting and counterproductive power struggles. Seen from this angle, "politics" rears its ugly head when the rightful concerns of citizens get turned over to "politicians." These political creatures focus mainly on power, the perks of office, and media attention. They whip up unnecessary fights that derail the practical solution of real problems. Healthy people who want to live productive lives, meanwhile, try to avoid active engagement with the nasty political realm. A good life in a good society would be as free of politics as possible—right?

Wrong. This book starts from the idea that this conception of politics is unhelpful. The hunger for power, infighting, and media flash are certainly parts of the political scene, but they are not the essence of politics. In fact, politics is an essential part of your everyday life. Rather than seeing it as a separate arena to be blamed for unwelcome intrusions into your affairs, think of it like other basic and inescapable parts of human existence, such as health or interpersonal relationships. You can have good health or good relationships; you can have bad health or bad relationships. Neither is ever perfect; both are partly out of your control. But both are always basic parts of your life. The same is true of politics. To reject it, as the antipolitics rhetoric suggests, is to turn your back on conscious thinking about what you believe, the problems and challenges you face, and how you and others might solve them. It also discourages you from putting any effort into understanding the political world around you: a complex context, and not always pretty, but one that shapes almost every facet of your life whether you recognize it or not.

To do well in your own life, you must reclaim politics as an essential part of it. This book will help you do so. ■

Seeing Politics in the World

1.1 **Define "politics" and explain why it is an inescapable part of human existence.**

To reclaim politics, we must first define it. *Politics is the making of collective decisions*. It is what happens, in some shape or form, when people engage with each other to govern their interactions. Unless you live alone on a desert island, you are part of many political arenas. Family members make collective decisions about how to support each other's lives, like paying for a college education and what is expected in return. In a sports team, club, religious organization, or even an informal circle of friends, you are part of ongoing negotiations about what the group does together. In any job, you are part of an organization or network of people who must coordinate and govern themselves to produce results. And then, of course, there is the most explicit level of politics—what the term "politics" makes us think of most—which is government. In and around government, people interact to make collective decisions about infrastructure like roads, airports, and irrigation; a system of laws, courts, and police to maintain social order; the provision of education, medicine, and hospitals; foreign relations in trade, diplomacy, and defense; safety regulations for food, cars, or toys; rules for institutions that support a sophisticated economy, such as banking or insurance; and many other things that affect our lives. Even beyond the level of national government, your life is affected by global politics in international trade, cooperation, and conflict.

You might quickly object: "I may be surrounded by all these political processes, but that does not mean I should not try to escape them!" You may not feel like you are significantly involved in most levels of collective decision making—especially not the large-scale politics of the U.S. government or the wider world. But let's consider what "escaping politics" would actually mean.

Why Escaping Politics Is a Dead End

Most collective decision making in and around your life is certainly not entirely open, equal, and participatory. Whether the context is your family, your university, your town, or the corridors of power in Washington, D.C., some people usually play a bigger role in collective decision making than others. Many people feel like they have some of the smaller roles, which is one reason why they long for a world "without politics." They imagine that if they could just make all of their own decisions, they would feel less excluded or controlled by others. This kind of liberated life is what political philosophers like Jean-Jacques Rousseau (1712–1778) envisioned the "**state of nature**" to be—that is, the human condition in an imaginary time before the emergence of oppressive social organization and government.

state of nature
An imagined time prior to the development of society or politics.

Few Americans realize it, but this longing for a state-of-nature world without politics is even more powerful in the United States than in most other countries. This country was founded by people who left a Europe governed by kings and queens and sailed far away in pursuit of various goals: religious freedom and political liberty, in many cases, but also land and personal opportunity. Most of the founders saw overly powerful governments as the big problem in politics, and looked for ways in which a new U.S. constitution might bolster individual rights, lessen the scope of centralized decision making, and "check and balance" the collective decision making they considered unavoidable. Settlers colonized vast territories that were sparsely populated and rich in resources, leading them to believe that a tough individual or family could thrive largely on their own on that frontier. From these origins came a political discourse that criticized government and politics for obstructing and intruding on our individual pursuit of happiness. It idealized a state-of-nature existence without governmental restraints.

But the notion of escaping into a "state of nature" would not actually appeal to most people if they thought about what it would be like. The average life span in the American colonies was less than thirty years. It didn't get much over forty years for settlers on the frontier during the 1800s.[2] In today's world, not many people ship themselves off to desert islands or the Alaskan wilderness for obvious reasons: life is not easy without a fair number of other people to ease the burden of getting clean water, growing food, building shelter, making clothing, or caring for those who are ill. Nor would most people want to forgo all the things that you can gain as part of a larger society: law and order, education, roads and other infrastructure, and so on, not to mention the opportunities for trade that bring you iPhones, mountain bikes, movies, extra-soft toilet paper, haircuts, and a million other products and services.

Maintaining access to the benefits of modern life involves collective decision making to organize and govern society. Once you are in a social context, even if you feel like you have been assigned a bit part in a production dominated by others, attempts to "escape" collective decision making tend to lead to two kinds of bad outcomes. One is that other people become even more dominant because you have left the field to them. The other is that things just fall apart and the benefits of interacting begin to disappear. This can happen at any level of collective decision making, from your family on up to the U.S. government and beyond. If you feel powerless in your family and try to escape its collective decision-making process, you find yourself with a family that dissolves or is dominated all the more by other family members. By not engaging with the governance of your club or religious group, you arrive at similar results. The same is true of the big institutions of government: pursue the fantasy of a world without politics and you do not end up "free" from politics and government; you end up with *worse* politics and government. As one saying goes, "Just because you do not take an interest in politics does not mean politics won't take an interest in you."[3]

The interpretation of U.S. history suggested by an antipolitics state-of-nature discourse is similarly misleading. In many ways, it gets the story backward. The Founding Fathers did not try to escape politics. They were political thinkers who proclaimed loudly and clearly that they sought consciously to engage politics in a whole new way. They tried very deliberately and carefully to build a different *kind* of collective decision making—a different sort of politics—where individuals could have greater liberty and equality. They saw that individual freedom is not what is left when you take away politics and government; to the contrary, they needed to construct a kind of collective decision making that supported individual freedom.

To see this fundamental point in a more concrete way, speculate for a moment on why life in Arizona is so different from life in Afghanistan. Afghanistan is one of the poorest, most insecure countries in the world. Though it has hugely promising resources, its government is barely able to hold an election or administer basic services to most of its territory. Arizona's geography is no more hospitable than central Asia. Like the least-fertile parts of Afghanistan, it has a mostly desert landscape with little water and no coastline. But life in these places is radically different: Arizonans are roughly 100 times richer on average than Afghans. According to various measures of individual freedom around the world, like those from the Heritage Foundation[4] or Freedom House,[5] Arizona, like the United States in general, scores near the top while Afghanistan scores near the bottom. While Afghanistan is one of the largest sources of refugees fleeing to other countries, people are literally dying to get into Arizona across the Mexican border.[6] It is rather obvious that the difference between the two is not that Arizona represents a state of nature with "less" politics and government. In most ways that we can measure, Arizona is much "more" controlled by a coherent politics and government than Afghanistan. But "less" and "more" are not the right terms; no one would dispute that Afghanistan has exceedingly complex politics. A better way to capture the fates of these two land-locked zones is that their radically different kinds of collective decision making have given their citizens radically different life experiences. The differences, good and bad, lie in the *kind* of politics, not in the presence or absence of politics.

A first step to reclaiming politics, then, is to see that wherever there is human interaction, there are inescapable processes of collective decision making. Politics is essential to construct the kind of safe and comfortable life that most people pursue, no matter how much we might daydream of an adventurous,

Kellie L. Folkerts/Shutterstock

The U.S.–Mexico border fence near Nogales, Arizona, forces migrants to find less fortified openings into the United States. Many continue to die every year from the heat while attempting to cross long stretches of desert.

autonomous existence in a state of nature. Once you recognize the presence and impact of politics in the world, you can begin to organize it, analyze it, and understand how it matters to you. And to see and understand politics around you, you need to grasp concepts from political science and political philosophy.

From Politics to Political Ideologies and Political Science

1.2 **Explain the difference between the descriptive study of politics, normative engagement with political ideologies, and the focus of political science on explaining politics.**

Like health, relationships, and other essential parts of life, politics is often messy and complicated. Even if the antipolitics rhetoric is wrong to equate politics with "fighting for the sake of fighting," people in politics *do* argue and disagree. These disputes, whether in your family, on talk radio, in the White House, or at the United Nations, often lead people to "spin" things to fit their views. Sometimes consciously and sometimes unconsciously, they selectively use information to support their side. Overall, it may seem like there is no truth at all to be found in politics. How, you might wonder, can you study such a free-for-all collection of disagreements and spin?

It may also seem that no one can help answer that question, since even the experts on politics cannot agree on what to think about it. Although politics is a domain as essential as health, you can rely more heavily on your doctor for concrete guidance because doctors have a fairly strong consensus about how to cure an infection, set a broken bone, or deal with asthma. By contrast, experts on politics do not have much of a strong or specific consensus on anything. Political experts debate a set of strongly different views of how to understand the political world.

It is in that set of strongly different views, though, that the study of politics offers the way forward. To reclaim politics, you must become a critical thinker: someone who can understand, criticize, and defend certain views about the political world against others. *The foundation of all independent, critical thinking is the ability to imagine alternative points of view.* Once you can imagine a few different viewpoints, you can choose one or more of them and defend your choices intelligently. Studying the main views of politics thus gives you the crucial tools to reclaim politics. It will not tell you exactly *what* to think about politics—you will still have to make your own choices—but it will teach you *how* to think and talk about politics in a useful, engaged, and critical way.

The study of politics helps you become a critical thinker by imagining political alternatives from three angles:

political description
The task of grasping how political life and action are organized.

1. First, it can help you see some of the different ways of organizing and acting in politics. This is the challenge of **political description**, asking: what are some of the ways that people have set up and understood their political

lives, whether locally, nationally, or globally? You need to describe some of the different kinds of governments, constitutions, political beliefs, political parties, public policies, and so on to be able to imagine what options exist for your political choices. Political practices around the world suggest a menu of possibilities against which to compare your own experiences.

2. Second, the study of politics can help you engage the good and bad aspects of the politics around you, and to think about your political values and goals. This is the challenge of **political philosophy**, the effort to evaluate the good or bad in political life. It centers on **normative** ideas about how the political world *ought* to be, though it also builds in **analytic** or explanatory concepts about how we think it actually *is*. In everyday politics, the alternatives of political philosophy manifest themselves as **political ideologies** that structure our debates. By learning about different ideologies and the philosophical ideas behind them, you gain a set of alternatives to inform your choices.

3. Third, the study of politics can help you explain why you and people around you have ended up with certain options on the menu of political possibilities. This is the challenge of **political science**, the systematic effort to explain why politics works as it does. Explanation is the heart of what most experts on politics do, and they can provide you with useful ways to quickly, roughly imagine some alternative answers to "why" questions about politics. When political scientists look at any political situation (in your family, university, town, state, the United States, globally, and so on), they pose the same set of basic questions about why people might be acting and speaking the way they are. These questions are rooted in different views of the core of political action: different fundamental stories we can imagine about why we see certain patterns of collective decision making in the world. Though political scientists rarely agree fully on which story is right about any situation, they share this basic set of options for thinking about what lies behind political action. You can learn to use these tools to translate the messy-looking world of politics into a small, organized set of "why" possibilities.

political philosophy
The project of evaluating the good and bad in politics, addressing both how politics works and how it should work.

normative argument
Argument about how things ought to be, not about how they are.

analytic argument
Argument about how things are or how they change, not about how they ought to be.

political ideologies
The versions of political philosophies that people use to organize political debates and action, like liberalism or conservatism.

political science
The systematic effort to explain why politics works as it does.

Familiarizing yourself with these three kinds of alternatives can be deeply empowering. In learning about political description, you get a more concrete sense of what your own life is like as you contrast it to other possibilities. In learning about political ideologies, you gain the ability to quickly brainstorm the alternatives to any single judgment that is put before you. If someone tries to persuade you of a view based in one ideological approach, quick consideration of some alternatives tells you what might be wrong or incomplete about the case they are making. In learning about political science explanations, you find that the same basic approaches can apply to any political context, from interacting with your family and friends up to issues in global politics. You become able to look at a newspaper (or website, or blog, or however you get information) and roughly, quickly grasp the main things that might be going on behind a story. Wherever you find yourself tangling with collective decision making—in the policies of your university or employer, at a school board meeting, as you think about military service or donating to charities, and of course as you consider voting choices or other engagement with government—you are able to look at the people around you and guess at what is animating their political choices.

In these ways, the study of politics can carry you beyond the narrow, distant way in which people often relate to their political surroundings. Without these tools, people often peer in on the political realm through a small window of selective, semiconscious views. A broader, more critical engagement with political alternatives may or may not lead you to change any views you hold today—perhaps it will just help you to better appreciate and defend your initial leanings—but it will remove the narrow window between you and politics. It will allow you to reclaim politics as a comprehensible part of your world and to empower yourself with a better understanding of the choices you can make.

In the next section, we explore three basic approaches to the least familiar challenge in reclaiming politics: explanation. For your critical thinking, it is just as important to tackle the two other kinds of challenges addressed in this book—describing the political world and engaging with political ideologies. But the core terrain of explanatory political science is likely to be especially new to you, so it calls for a bit of introduction.

Three Explanatory Approaches in Political Science

1.3 Summarize the logic of the three main approaches to explaining political action and recognize the logics in examples of explanatory arguments.

Everyone has at least some experience in seeing and describing politics around them. You have picked up a few descriptive facts about presidents, political parties, and other things in U.S. politics, and probably a smattering of facts about other places too. There is much more to learn about how to see the political world and its menu of alternatives, but the basic notion of seeing and describing it is not a foreign one.

Everyone has also been exposed a bit to engaging with political ideologies. You are aware that some political concepts sound good to you (perhaps democracy? Human rights? Liberty? Equality? Free markets?) and some bad (maybe dictatorship? Oppression? War? Exploitation?). You may attach good or bad judgments to "Republican" or "Democrat" and other labels. You will need a deeper and broader sense of alternative ideologies to arrive at well-informed engagement, but judging also comes fairly naturally to us all.

You may not have much experience, however, with explaining politics. For most people, it is challenging enough to keep a descriptive eye on political events and an engaged eye on how events relate to their ideological views; explaining *why* things are happening is hard even to imagine. Since explanation is the least familiar piece of the study of politics, and also because it is the core of the discipline of political science, this introductory chapter gives it some special attention.

Explanation also calls for special treatment because, at first glance, it is far from obvious to know how to organize political science into a small, useful set of explanatory alternatives. If you read a selection of what political scientists write, a simple set of approaches will not jump out at you. Instead, you find a long, confusing list of academic terms that political scientists use to label the stories they tell: "structural," "institutional," "rationalist," "constructivist," "realist," "liberal," "Marxist," and many others. Fortunately, though, only a few main explanatory traditions lie underneath all the labels. Whatever political scientists call their arguments, their views sort into three main kinds of stories used to explain politics. Once you get some sense of these three ways of thinking about how politics works—three basic views that prompt you to question, "Is *that* what is going on here?"—you have the main tools that political scientists apply to any political situation. When you are comfortable with these tools, you can get a little fancier: there are variations on each kind of story, and the three stories can be combined in interesting ways. But even if you go no further than the simple versions of the main options, you will be much better equipped to understand politics and think critically about it.

These three explanatory options are built around simple thoughts (see Figure 1-1). When we see someone making certain political choices, one

Figure 1-1 Three Ways to Explain What People Do in Politics

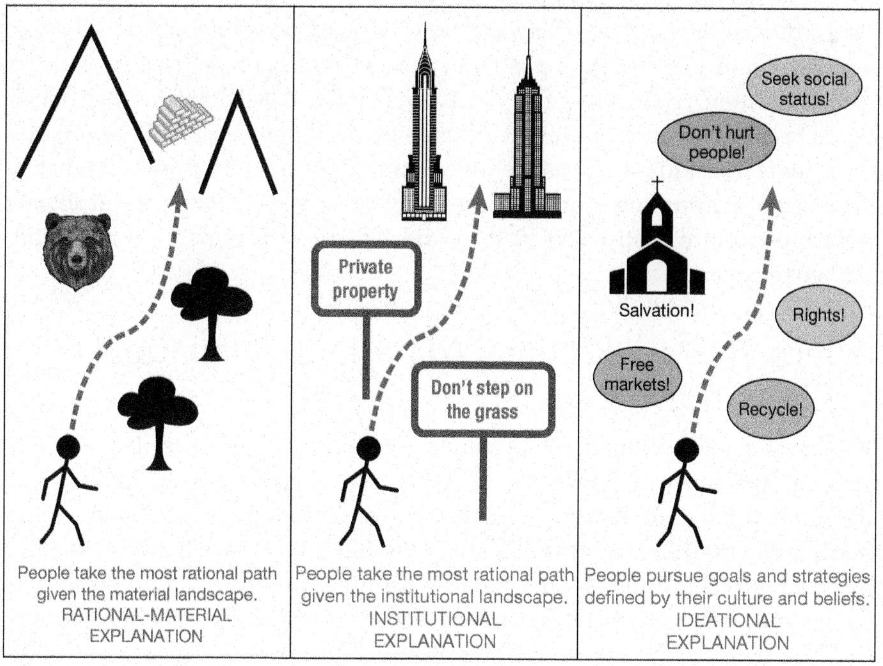

| People take the most rational path given the material landscape. RATIONAL-MATERIAL EXPLANATION | People take the most rational path given the institutional landscape. INSTITUTIONAL EXPLANATION | People pursue goals and strategies defined by their culture and beliefs. IDEATIONAL EXPLANATION |

possible explanation is that he or she is doing what anyone else would do if placed in the same place in the material landscape. Consider the figure on the left: given a forest on one side, predators on another, and rumors about gold mines through the mountain pass ahead, any rational person would head for the hills. On the other hand, his or her choices might actually be more like the figure in the middle, who is channeled in certain ways by the rules and organizations that people have built. Human-made rules and structures, often called "institutions," create obstacle courses of incentives that reward or punish us for acting in certain ways. The third major possibility is that his or her political choices are motivated and shaped by his or her culture and beliefs, like the figure on the right. This last kind of explanation suggests that a person might do many different things in his or her material or institutional surroundings, and what really shapes a person's choices is how he or she *interprets* what he or she wants and how to get it.

To introduce these three explanatory approaches more concretely, let's return to a real-world example that came up at the beginning of the chapter. From December 22, 2018 to January 25, 2019, the U.S. federal government closed nine federal departments. The shutdown followed a fight between President Trump, who mainly sought Congressional approval to spend $5 billion on a border wall with Mexico, and members of Congress—most, though not all, Democrats—who saw the wall as a bad idea. When previous deals on government spending ran out on December 22 and the two sides failed to agree on a new deal, the government had to close its doors. About 800,000 government workers were told not to come to work. Millions of private sector contractors stopped work on government-funded projects. Many businesses suffered because they depend on government services: Airlines could not put new planes in service because the Federal Aviation Administration could not certify they were safe. Alaskan fisherman faced losses because no one could issue permits to start their season. Experimental treatments for kids with cancer were put on hold. By some estimates, $11 billion evaporated from the economy overall and longer-term effects were much more costly.[7] Why? Why did American leaders shut down the U.S. government?

Alternative 1—Rational-Material Explanation: A Clash of Interests

The simplest story about the 2019 shutdown describes it as a clash between different groups in American society pursuing their own advantage. In this view, the standoff basically reflected a divide between Americans who gain or lose from President Trump's agenda. Though the fight took place between political leaders, both Trump and his adversaries were just representing fairly concrete dividing lines in society and the economy. Citizens who would benefit concretely from Trump's agenda encouraged him to push his agenda. Those who would lose pushed back. Everyone was just pursuing their own most rational strategy given their position in a landscape of resources.

More specifically, one side of the clash was a Trump-led coalition that is often understood to have two main components. His most devoted "base" are citizens who feel that their economic and social positions are not as secure as they once were. Especially among rural and racially white Americans without advanced education, many perceive that their opportunities are threatened by cheap immigrant labor at home and by "outsourcing" jobs to cheap foreign workers. They are hopeful that they will be protected by Trump's attempts to "Make American Great Again!", including his proposal for a border wall. At the same time, Trump has drawn support from many business owners. They support him mostly for other reasons: he is committed to loosening federal economic and environmental regulations, and he championed a large tax cut in 2017 that mainly benefited wealthier individuals.

On the other side are Americans who lose from Trump's agenda. One such group includes immigrants and people related to them, especially those with connections to Latin America, who do not wish to be shut off by a border wall. They may also suffer broadly from Trump's rhetoric that stigmatizes them, as may other ethnic and racial minorities. Also concerned about losses from Trump's policies are the people who benefit most from openness to the world: globalized businesses and highly educated cosmopolitan elites, who like to trade, invest, and move internationally with ease. People in these groups have thrown their support behind politicians who seek to cut back on the border wall and other aspects of Trump's plans, while the members of the Trump coalition have called for him to implement his campaign promises. The core story of the shutdown is about a battle between these social forces.

Think for a moment about the logic of this explanation. It starts by picturing a real landscape of material resources. Across this landscape, people occupy different positions. Each person controls a certain amount of wealth and some control sources of wealth, such as possessing an oil well, a farm, or a business. From their economic position, people rationally develop certain **interests**, or courses of action from which they will benefit. Those holding considerable wealth have interests in doing what they can to keep it; those without much wealth have interests in looking for ways to gain more. From these starting points, everyone chooses the most reasonable (or rational) strategy. The shutdown was a clash of such underlying interests.

interests
In political science, the courses of action that most clearly benefit someone given his or her position in the world.

A good label for this kind of explanatory story is a *rational-material explanation*. It explains what people do in politics as a rational reaction to the material landscape around them. Who the people are, or what they believe, does not matter much in this kind of story. Everyone is perceived as roughly sharing the same basic goals of personal comfort, security, and control of their surrounding environment, and their choices reflect the obstacles or incentives they encounter. Anybody else would do the same in their position.

A man at a public event in North Carolina signals his support for President Donald Trump's campaign to build a wall on the Mexican border.

We can also imagine the same basic kind of logic applying to many non-economic issues. To explain why certain people launch a war, for example, we could examine where they stood relative to tangible security threats, how much military power they held, and why their overall position in the distribution of military resources made war their best, most rational option.

This kind of story suggests that when we look at any political situation, we should ask:

1. Where do people stand in terms of controlling such tangible material resources as sources of wealth or military power?

2. How does that shape of the material landscape make certain choices beneficial and certain choices costly for specific people, depending on where they are positioned within it?

3. For each person (or similarly positioned group of people) in the story, can we imagine that anybody in the same material position would have responded similarly?

Alternative 2—Institutional Explanation: Playing by the Rules of the Game

A very different kind of story explains the shutdown as a product of American political institutions. As one political blogger put it about the previous shutdown in 2013, "It's the Constitution's fault . . . Don't hate the players. Hate the game—and think about how to change the rulebook."[8] In this view, the contending interests in American society led to an impasse due to the institutional rules inherited from the past. While many democracies in the world have only a single major election to connect citizens to their government, the U.S. federal government has three. The president, the majority in the House of Representatives, and the majority in the Senate can all claim to represent the majority of Americans, but through different kinds of elections held at different times during the voting cycle. The authors of the U.S. Constitution deliberately set these bodies to counterbalance each other, hoping to limit abuses of power by any one of them. A downside of such rules is that they encourage aggressive bargaining when competing political parties control these bodies. Stalemates and last-minute deals are common as all sides hope the others will blink first. Worsening this dynamic are unusually frequent elections—the House is the only major assembly in the world elected every two years—which makes politicians on all sides especially eager to appear to be winning the battle all the time.

This story's logic focuses our attention not on an underlying landscape of resources but on the *rules* of politics. It does not dispute that there are competing interests in society, but suggests that their interactions take very different political forms depending on how institutions organize them. The underlying logic depicts the Constitution as creating an obstacle course that channels citizens and politicians to pursue their interests in certain ways. This kind of explanation agrees with the rational-material story that people are basically rational: the Republicans and Democrats arrived at the shutdown because they were pursuing the most rational strategies available to them within the constitutional rulebook. But whereas a rational-material story analyzes political action as a raw contest between underlying interests in which all that matters is the players and their relative resources, an institutional story portrays their interaction as heavily shaped by the inherited rules of the game.

A good label for this kind of explanatory story is an *institutional explanation.* "Institutions" are the rules and organizations that people build to guide their interactions. An institutional story explains people's actions by pointing to the institutional obstacle course that surrounds them. An institutional story is not totally incompatible with a rational-material story: material positions might influence the basic agendas that people pursue in the institutional game. But a strong institutional story suggests that politics is even more heavily shaped by the institutional obstacle course than by underlying material interests. If the U.S. Constitution were different, this logic suggests, Democrats and Republicans might never have had this kind of fight.

In general, the institutional approach suggests that we think of politics as a game where everyone does what is best for him or her, given the rules. In any political situation, we should ask:

1. How are the institutional rules of politics set up?
2. How does that obstacle course of rules make some choices beneficial and some choices costly for people, depending on where they stand within the institutional game?
3. For each person (or group of people) in the story, can we imagine that anybody would have responded similarly if placed in the same position in institutional rules?

Alternative 3—Ideational Explanation: Beliefs and "Culture Wars"

The third major kind of story we hear about what caused the shutdown focuses on contending beliefs rather than material clashes or institutional games. One strength of this version is that it echoes what politicians say about their own choices. For example, neither Trump nor his critics would ever present themselves as just a mouthpiece for the interests of certain social groups, or as simple players in a political game. Instead, each sees himself or herself as a passionate champion of certain political principles. Though we should take much of what politicians say with a grain of salt, their self-images may contain a grain of truth.

Many observers saw the shutdown as a skirmish in a "culture war."[9] From this point of view, the central fight over a border wall was a battle of ideas. It wasn't clear that anyone had clear interests in actually walling off the U.S.–Mexico border. Indeed, most of Trump's statements justifying the wall were rated as misleading or false by neutral fact-checking organizations.[10] These concrete policy issues didn't matter much, though, because the fight was mostly ideological and symbolic. President Trump and his supporters shared certain ideological conceptions of national identity and security, and wanted funding for a wall to make a statement that immigration is undesirable. Other Americans with different views about national identity and security thought that this was the wrong statement to make. This helps explain why a compromise was so hard to reach. If they had really been bargaining over a budget with concrete goals in mind, they probably could have split the difference. The two sides couldn't agree because they were trying to showcase opposing values.

The logic of this story differs strikingly from the previous two alternatives because it contests that there is a clear-cut landscape within which rational people identify straightforward interests. Exactly which policies help or harm certain people overall is often hard to say, because policy choices like building a border wall have complex effects. Rather than looking out on their surroundings and simply perceiving what is best for them, people rely on ideologically informed judgment calls to make political choices. This logic also suggests that institutional rules may be interpreted in a variety of ways. The fact that the U.S. Constitution creates three centers of authority didn't simply cause the shutdown; the impasse arose because the people playing that game adopted such polarized ideologies that the divided parts of the U.S. government could not strike a deal. The main source of this political fight, then, was people's beliefs—not just the obvious strategies within material conditions or institutional rules.

A good label for this kind of explanatory story is an *ideational explanation*.[11] It explains what people do by pointing to the ideas or beliefs through which they interpret the world around them. In contrast to both rational-material and institutional stories, it suggests that not everyone sees the same situations in the same ways—and so how people *interpret* things matters even more for politics than how the material

This car, decorated with extreme political messages in Washington, D.C., suggests very directly that politics is about sharply clashing ideologies and values. Though more mainstream politics are often phrased in less openly ideological terms, they may also be shaped and driven mainly by clashing beliefs.

landscape or the institutional obstacle course is shaped around them. This kind of story suggests that when we look at any political situation, we should ask:

1. What are the particular core beliefs of the key players?

2. Do they seem to interpret their goals, capabilities, and environment in certain ways that others do not?

3. How do their particular ideas lead them to see some choices as beneficial or morally right, and other choices as disadvantageous or morally wrong?

Almost everything said and written about the 2019 government shutdown invokes one of these explanations or a combination of them. That is no accident. The same is true of almost everything written on any political event. In short, these are the three main ways to explain why people take certain political actions.

There is, admittedly, one complication to this simple set of explanations. A fourth option exists for certain kinds of political actions. When we are interested directly in individual-level political choices—such as how citizens vote, or how individual leaders make foreign policy decisions—we can also imagine explanations built on individual *psychology*. How you vote might be influenced by more than just your material positioning, the institutional rules around you, or the beliefs that you have been taught. You might also vote in certain ways because of how you are hard-wired: the genetically inherited, psychological makeup of your individual brain.[12] The psychological version of explanation is an important strand of political science. It applies more narrowly than the other three alternatives because hard-wired psychology does not vary across *groups* of people in the way that the material landscape, institutions, or ideas can; we know that in terms of genetics and hard-wired psychology, human populations overall are very similar. Many of the key questions we ask about politics are about differences across groups of people—about varying political views and practices across regions, countries, social classes, and so on—and it is not plausible to answer these questions by suggesting that these populations have different hard-wired psychology. When we look at individual-level variation in political choices, though, psychological explanation often comes in as another option.

But in most of this book, we will focus on the three most common approaches. To grasp them more concretely, try your hand at applying them to an explanatory question: why is the United States the wealthiest, most powerful big country in the world? (Only some rather exceptional, small countries are richer on average: oil-rich Qatar and Norway, and the banking city-state of Luxembourg.) This question asks about differences across large groups, so it does not make much sense to speculate that U.S. citizens have their own kind of psychological makeup. They are human beings like everyone else. That leaves three possible options: rational-material, institutional, and ideational explanations. See if you can connect the right labels to these stories:

1. The United States is wealthy and powerful mainly because Americans came to believe in limited government and "the American dream," which unleashed competition, entrepreneurship, and innovation.

2. The United States is wealthy and powerful mainly because the Founding Fathers designed a brilliant constitution with rules that balanced political conflicts, encouraged stable government, and so built a strong platform for economic growth.

3. The United States is wealthy and powerful mainly because its early European settlers (and later inhabitants) enjoyed exceptional resources, a temperate climate, and few nearby competing populations.

Hopefully, it is already easy for you to see that the first story is an ideational explanation, the second is an institutional explanation, and the third is a rational-material explanation.

As you read through this book, you will encounter many more examples that show how these three alternatives help us to hypothesize plausible explanatory stories about why people act politically as they do. Use the following three questions to analyze any political situation:

• What is the MATERIAL landscape around the players and how does it set constraints and incentives that encourage certain actions?

• What are the INSTITUTIONAL rules and organizations around the players, and how do they set constraints and incentives that encourage certain actions?

• Which IDEAS, beliefs, or culture do the players hold that lead them to interpret their options and choices in certain ways?

It takes practice to become comfortable posing these three questions about real-world political examples and brainstorming your answers to them. You will get that practice throughout the book. At this point, though, you can already see how the questions help cut through even the messiest political situation. Even when people's political choices seem hard to understand at first glance—say, joining the Nazis in Germany in the 1930s, becoming a suicide bomber in Iraq today, or (closer to home) when uninsured poor people oppose government health care programs—these three questions give you a starting point to imagine what lay behind their actions. These questions break down any political situation around you, from local politics to conflict and cooperation at the global level.

Just as important, these three questions encourage you to consider alternatives to any one view you hear. If someone complains that the government was shut down due to the sheer craziness of one side or the other, you can say, "Wait a minute: that's not obvious. What about the material interests of the groups the Republicans and Democrats were representing, or the institutional rules of U.S. politics that might have caused an impasse even given other ideological views?" And vice versa: whichever story you hear, the other questions suggest how to think critically about what it might be missing. Table 1-1

Table 1-1 Summarizing Alternative Explanatory Approaches

Explanatory Approach	Core Hypothesis	EXAMPLE		
		Why is politics different in different places and times?	Why does a U.S. citizen vote for the Republican Party instead of the Democrats?	Why would this person ever change how he or she votes?
Rationalist-materialist	People choose the most advantageous actions given their position in the material landscape.	All people are rational and similar, but their material surroundings vary.	Republican Party policies bring him or her more tangible benefits than Democratic policies.	Republicans or Democrats change policies that affect this person, or the person changes his or her own position (moving to a new place, becoming more wealthy, etc.).
Institutionalist	People choose the most advantageous actions given their position in an obstacle course of organizations and rules.	All people are rational and similar, but the organizations and rules around them vary.	The Republicans are better organized in this person's community and dominate the media and opportunities in local organizations.	The Democrats strengthen their organization in this person's community, get better media access, and perhaps offer him or her new social or career opportunities.
Ideational	People act in accordance with beliefs about how the world works and what is right.	People have different beliefs about how the world works and what is right.	This person grew up with family and friends who taught him or her that Republican values are good.	This person is exposed to new friends or ideas, or a dynamic new leader makes the Democrats appeal to him or her.
and a fourth option when explaining individual choices:				
Psychological	People have certain genetic, hard-wired personalities and dispositions.	People's personalities vary: having more or less empathy for others, favoring strong authority or not, and so on.	This person's personality inclines him or her to favor tough law and order and the "self-made man"—classic Republican themes.	Change is unlikely, but age or evolving mental health—or getting hit on the head—might alter his or her hard-wired dispositions.

summarizes these alternatives and offers another example: different explanations of why an American citizen would vote for Republican or Democratic representatives.

Alternative Methods to Test and Support Explanations

1.4 **Identify the four main methods that political scientists use to test and support their explanations.**

Because political scientists often disagree about which of these three explanatory approaches captures any particular piece of the political world, their daily work is heavily concerned with testing and supporting these alternative views against each other. That is, the three explanatory approaches form the main substance of their debates. At the same time, though, they also have debates about the best **methods** to evaluate their hypotheses and adjudicate between explanatory approaches.

methods
The ways in which scientists test or support their hypotheses.

Methods are the sets of tools that scientists use to identify, collect, and interpret evidence for their explanatory hypotheses. These tools determine the process of doing political science research. Methods are a complex subject in their own right but receive only modest attention in this book because the substance of politics and political science comes first: before you can consider the virtues of methodological tools, you first must be able to describe different political arrangements and imagine explanations for them. Still, a quick introduction here gives you basic ways to look for evidence for different explanatory stories as we move along. Political scientists organize their search for evidence mainly through four kinds of methods: quantitative methods, qualitative methods, experiments, and simulations.

Quantitative Methods: Sorting "Cross-Case" Patterns

quantitative methods
Ways to evaluate hypotheses that look for patterns in data, represented as numbers, across a large number of cases.

One way of evaluating an explanatory claim is to use **quantitative methods** to see how it relates to patterns across similar political cases. For example, we might hypothesize that the United States has enjoyed a relatively stable democracy because it has long been relatively wealthy. That claim would imply a broader rationalist-materialist theory that economic growth encourages democracy. The logic might be that economic growth tends to generate more wealthy businesspeople who desire the liberty to make and spend money as they please, so growth leads to more support for political democracy. To seek evidence for this explanatory theory, we might make a database where we score all countries on how democratic and how economically developed they were in every year since 1800. The more we see a **correlation** between democracy and a certain level of wealth—with democracy showing up in all (or almost all) wealthy countries

correlation
A patterned relationship between things that arise and change together.

and not showing up (or very rarely) in poorer ones—the more we feel confident about our explanatory hypothesis. Many explanatory claims about politics can be evaluated with similar cross-case quantitative methods. To get at complex correlations, though, we need to study statistics that help us sort through patterns that are not obvious at first glance.

Qualitative Methods: "Within-Case" Detective Work

Another way of evaluating an explanatory claim is to use **qualitative methods** to dig deeply into one or a few cases to see how well the claim fits with observable processes. To consider the economic growth/democracy hypothesis, we could look in detail at the United States and one or two other countries to trace the processes by which economic growth might have encouraged democracy. *Within* these cases, did more people call for democracy as their wealth rose over time? Did the champions of democracy emerge mostly in towns or cities where economic growth was especially advanced? Unlike quantitative methods, which try to grasp thin data about a large number of cases, these methods try to analyze richer, more complex data about one case or a small number of them. Qualitative methods instruct us to analyze the context and internal story of each case, and often to interpret how the people in the case saw their own actions. Rather than trying to get the bird's-eye view of correlations, this strategy is like detective work, looking for the smoking gun, the trail of blood, or whatever else we suspect led to the "crime" that interests us. Instead of requiring us to learn statistics, this kind of qualitative work on political processes may push us to delve deeply into history and culture, and perhaps to learn other languages to do research on the ground in other countries.

qualitative methods
Ways to evaluate hypotheses that trace evidence for how an outcome came about in particular cases.

Experiments: Manipulating Relationships

A third way to evaluate an explanatory claim is to set up an experiment. Rather than just observing cross-case patterns or within-case processes that arise in the world, we engineer a situation where we can manipulate the relationships that interest us to see what happens. This is the classic method of natural sciences like chemistry or physics—though two problems make it rarer in political science. One is that we simply can't engineer many political situations we want to study. No one can set up a country and then tweak its economic growth to explore the effects on democratization, nor can we engineer situations like elections or wars. The other is that experiments on people run into ethical problems. Even if we could vary economic conditions to study their political consequences, it seems immoral to make people poorer or richer just for a research project. Nonetheless, there are many political questions for which targeted experiments can be defensible and useful. To study housing discrimination, we might send people of different races to apply to rent the same lodging. To study political campaigns, we may be able to find a candidate or party who would cooperate with researchers to test which strategies best reach voters. To research policies for economic development, we might offer resources selectively to certain poor communities (within careful ethical guidelines) to trace effects on their opportunities. For their credibility, such experiments typically rely on strategies of "randomization" across several runs of the experiment. That is, they run the experiment many times across different settings that vary as randomly as possible. Thus, any systematic effect they see across these settings is likely to reflect the "treatment"—the main thing they manipulate—rather than something else. To employ these methods, we need to learn about the logic of experimental design and the statistics of randomization.

Game Theory and Simulations: Exploring Artificial Environments

A fourth strategy to evaluate an explanatory claim uses the same core logic as experiments—engineer a situation and manipulate it—but gets around logistical and ethical challenges by moving into a made-up context. Since it is hard to manipulate the real political world, we can turn to models to explore whether simulated people might indeed act in line with our explanatory hypotheses. One useful tool is **game theory**, in which we chart out strategic interactions by considering how a rational person might respond to other players' moves in an imaginary game with some features of real political settings. When these games become very complex, scholars often turn to **computer simulations** to play out how people might act in a modeled world, a bit like the classic video game *Sim City*. Researchers typically run many versions of the simulation while altering certain parameters—like the rate of economic growth in the growth/democracy example, or such conditions as the level of education—and then analyze which version of the simulation seems to best match real-world patterns. In principle, we can take the best-matched model as a reasonable theoretical approximation of real-world relationships. To employ these methods, we may need to study game-theoretic mathematics, psychology, or computer programming.

Each method has its own strengths and weaknesses (see Table 1-2). Quantitative methods give us the broadest pictures of patterns in politics. They usually require that our information about each case be reduced to clearly measurable numbers, however, and such a thinned-down focus on certain numbers may blind us to context and complications deeper in the cases. Qualitative methods give us the most concrete pictures of how political action takes place. They usually require focusing on only a very small number of cases, however—we never have the time and resources to gather rich data about everything—which may blind us to the ways in which any given case fits with broader patterns. Experiments give us the sharpest focus on how particular changes in the political world have certain demonstrable effects, but logistical and ethical concerns about experimenting with people's lives narrow their application. Simulations push us to develop the most explicit, logically derived versions of our theories.

game theory
The mathematical study of strategic decision making that explores how people would logically respond if placed in certain game situations.

computer simulations
The computer-based study of how people might act if placed in certain situations that can be modeled with computer programming.

experiments
In political science, the method of evaluating hypotheses by manipulating key relationships across randomized contexts.

Table 1-2 Strengths and Weaknesses of Methods for Testing and Supporting Explanations

	Logic	Main Process	Strength	Weakness
Quantitative Methods	Gather data across many cases to see what varies with what	Statistical analysis: use math to sort out correlations	Broad perspective on many cases	Cases reduced to thin data, may miss context and complexity
Qualitative Methods	Gather many kinds of data within one or a few cases to see what followed from what	Process tracing: follow trails of possible causes like a detective	Deep perspective on one or a few cases, sensitivity to context	May miss broader relationships if too focused on oddities of one case
Experimental Methods	Manipulate certain conditions to see the effects	Make same manipulations across randomized contexts	Highly focused way to highlight specific relationships	Limited to focused questions by logistics and ethics
Artificial Environments (game theory, simulations)	Create a simplified model of a situation to highlight its logic and dynamics	Use equations and computer programs to explore theorized relationships	Tightly focused like experiments and not limited by logistics or ethics	May not be sure how much artificial findings apply to real cases

Yet they always confront questions about how much their simulated examples tell us about real-world situations: college students might make certain choices in a simulated game, but do the implications transfer well to how people act in real life? Given these different strengths and weaknesses, most political scientists today agree that the best research generally uses *multiple methods* that evaluate alternative arguments in different ways.

Later chapters in this textbook touch on qualitative- and quantitative-style methods to test and support explanatory alternatives. Experiments and exploration of artificial environments are also a substantial part of political science today, but because they require learning more about formal theorizing than this book can provide, we leave them to future steps in your studies.

Conclusion and Overview of Subfields in the Study of Politics

1.5   Identify the main subfields in the study of politics.

The approach taken here can be summarized in one sentence: to reclaim politics for yourself, you must learn to see, engage, and explain alternatives in the political world. This book teaches you these skills as it leads you through the main arenas of contemporary politics.

The next two chapters join this introduction to set the background for the tour. Chapter 2 offers a quick historical survey of the emergence of political science as a discipline. This short version of the overarching story of the study of politics introduces some key political concepts, like power and authority, and displays the conceptual roots of big political debates today. Chapter 3 charts the main political ideologies that are active in our world.

The remaining chapters then lead a tour through the main political frameworks of our world, covering ground from individual and local politics up to the politics of globalization. We begin with states (meaning countries) in Chapter 4—the most basic and powerful framework that organizes our political world. Chapter 5 considers the main types of governments that run states, from democracies to dictatorships. Chapter 6 drills down further to the roots of individual and collective action. Chapters 7 and 8 then explore the kind of government inhabited by most readers of this book—liberal democracy—with a focus on representation and policymaking. Chapters 9 and 10 look at the politics of economies, first in a general sense and then with specific attention to economic growth and development. Chapter 11 looks inside nondemocratic governments around the world and considers the prospects for democracy. Lastly, Chapters 12 and 13 move out to the broad arena of international relations, addressing first war and terrorism and then the globalization of economies and governance.

To relate this introduction to other classes you may take, it is helpful to see that this tour also exposes you to the main "subfields" in the study of politics. University courses and faculty in the United States are usually organized in three conceptual divisions:

1. *Comparative politics* focuses on similarities and differences across political arenas and issues around the world. These comparisons are often between countries (comparing the power of legislatures in Japan and France, for example), but may also compare specific things like cities, regions, or economic sectors within a single country. This book often uses a comparative politics frame to help you see the varieties and common patterns of politics across countries or regions, most directly in Chapters 5 through 11.

2. *International relations (IR)* centers on the politics that operate around and between countries, like in war, international trade, international law, or international organizations. The foreign policies of national governments and relations between states is a major focus, but also important are such "transnational" actors as multinational firms; nongovernmental organizations, like Amnesty International; or some terrorist groups. IR topics appear most directly in Chapter 4 (States) and at the global level of Chapters 12 and 13.

3. *Political theory* is the label often given to political philosophy and the study of ideologies. Do not be misled by this label: theories that tell us abstractly what we should expect to see in the world are critical parts of every part of the study of politics, not just a feature of this subfield. However, this subfield does give special attention to distinctive kinds

of theories. It centers more directly than the other subfields on normative theories of the good and the bad in political life, and their related political ideologies. Every chapter from 4 to 13 touches on political theory in the section that features ideological debates about the main issues in the chapter.

Lastly, your university has another major "subfield" that is justified not by conceptual divisions but by practical considerations. *American politics* is obviously of special practical importance in American universities, and receives a large share of courses and faculty research. In Canada, there are more courses and specialists on Canadian politics, in Australia on Australian politics, and so on. In conceptual terms, these are just cases within comparative politics that get extra attention from their inhabitants, or cases within International Relations that get extra focus with respect to their foreign relations. Because most readers of this book live in the United States, American examples get an extra dose of attention throughout.

Once you have finished this tour, you will know the basics of all these subfields, some of which you may want to pursue further. More importantly, you will have skills to reclaim politics in general. You will be an active critical thinker who can dissect the political world and untangle the arguments that other people make about it. From your family, town, or university to the global arena, you will have the tools to engage in constructing the kind of politics that improves your life.

So let's get started.

Review of Learning Objectives

1.1 Define "politics" and explain why it is an inescapable part of human existence.

Politics is the making of collective decisions. Unless we live alone on a desert island—which does not appeal to most people—we are always surrounded by collective decision making at many levels, from family and friends to local groups, and from state and national to international governance. We may not always like the processes of decision making, but turning our back on them guarantees that we will neither understand nor influence them. Living a conscious life requires critical thinking to reclaim politics for ourselves.

1.2 Explain the difference between the descriptive study of politics, normative engagement with political ideologies, and the focus of political science on explaining politics.

The foundation of critical thinking about politics is awareness of alternatives. Only if we can imagine alternative points of view can we critically form our own. Critical thinking on politics is built on three kinds of alternatives:

- First is an effort of political description, or awareness of the varied ways in which people arrange collective decision making.

- Second is understanding of alternative political ideologies, that is, the packages of political philosophy that shape what people see as good and reasonable political action.
- Third is the capacity to brainstorm political science explanations of why people act politically as they do.

1.3 Summarize the logic of the three main approaches to explaining political action and recognize the logics in examples of explanatory arguments.

Almost all explanations of political action boil down to three main logics.

- Rational-material explanation hypothesizes that people occupy certain positions in a material landscape—holding certain resources and facing clear incentives and constraints—and that whatever they do politically is a rational response to their material position.
- Institutional explanation hypothesizes that the organization of politics shapes how people act, explaining what they do politically as a rational reaction to the "rules of the game" in surrounding organizations, laws, and other rules.
- Ideational explanation hypothesizes that people interpret their goals and options through particular ideas, beliefs, or culture, explaining that what they do politically reflects how they think about their political situation.

1.4 Identify the four main methods that political scientists use to test and support their explanations.

Just as important to political science as alternative explanations are the methods used to evaluate them.

- The quantitative strategy is used to consider what an explanation suggests that we should expect to see in cross-case patterns, often using statistical tools.
- The qualitative strategy is used to consider what an explanation suggests that we should expect to see in the processes leading to outcomes in specific cases.
- The experimental strategy is used to test whether a certain change to an engineered situation has the kinds of effects that our explanation would lead us to expect.
- Other options explore artificial environments that are partly like real political situations, using game theory or simulations.

1.5 Identify the main subfields in the study of politics.

The study of politics at American universities is commonly divided into four subfields.

- Comparative politics focuses on similarities and differences across political arenas and issues around the world.
- International relations centers on politics around and between countries, like in war, international trade, international law, or international organizations.

- Political theory is another label for political philosophy, which distinguishes itself from other subfields for addressing normative theories about how politics ought to be.
- American politics is justified as a special subfield for practical reasons: Americans are especially interested in understanding their own country and context.

Great Sources to Find Out More

Craig Parsons, *How to Map Arguments in Political Science* (New York: Oxford University Press, 2007). A more advanced breakdown of the ways in which we can explain political action to uncover the root causes of what people do. Also helps to organize arguments in other fields that address human action, including history, economics and business, sociology, or anthropology.

Doris Kearns Goodwin, *Team of Rivals: The Political Genius of Abraham Lincoln* (New York: Simon & Schuster, 2005). This history of the political machinations behind a great president is so gripping that it became a Steven Spielberg movie (*Lincoln*, in 2012).

Gary Goertz and James Mahoney, *A Tale of Two Cultures: Qualitative and Quantitative Research in the Social Sciences* (Princeton, NJ: Princeton University Press). Less readable, but much deeper in discussing the choices we make about how to test and support arguments. Especially helpful for understanding the logic and practices of qualitative case-study methods.

Margaret Atwood, *The Handmaid's Tale* (Toronto: McClelland and Stewart, 1985). In the near future, a religious state rules the Republic of Gilead and subjugates women. An exploration of power.

Robert Graves, *I, Claudius* (London: Arthur Barker, 1934). A British author's fictional autobiography of Roman Emperor Tiberius Claudius. Be prepared for murder, greed, lust, and other political fun. Also dramatized in an excellent BBC miniseries (availability of the series will change over time).

Robert Penn Warren, *All the King's Men* (New York: Harcourt, Brace, 1946). A riveting novel about the rise of a power-hungry Southern politician, modeled on former U.S. senator Huey Long. Also a film by the same name (Sony Pictures, 2006).

Stephen Van Evera, *Guide to Methods for Students of Political Science* (Ithaca, NY: Cornell University Press, 1997). A clear guide to methods for budding researchers.

Suzanne Collins, *The Hunger Games* (New York: Scholastic, 2008). Post-apocalyptic America is run by a dictatorship of the rich. You probably know the story from this bestseller (or from the subsequent blockbuster film trilogy).

Develop Your Thinking

Use these questions as discussion or short writing exercises to think more deeply about some of the key themes of the chapter.

1. What benefits of society would you miss most if you lived by yourself in the wilderness?

2. What single quality most defines what it means to be a good person? Thinking about yourself and your friends, what best explains why certain people have that quality?

3. Do you feel more "Democrat," more "Republican," or neither? Why? Is it mostly because of your material position in the world, how the institutions around you are organized, or your ideas and culture?

4. Describe how we could evaluate how well your university teaches political science using quantitative methods and how we could evaluate it using qualitative methods.

5. Before you started reading this book, what did "politics" mean to you?

Keywords

analytical argument 7
computer simulations 20
correlation 18
experiments 20
game theory 20

interests 11
methods 18
normative argument 7
political description 6
political ideologies 7

political philosophy 7
political science 7
qualitative methods 19
quantitative methods 18
state of nature 3

Chapter 2
Political Philosophy and Its Offshoot: Political Science

Protesters clash with riot police at the University of Athens in 2013 at the height of a deep Greek economic crisis. Though politics changes constantly, our attempts to develop coherent views about it can still draw usefully from political philosophies that trace back to ancient Greece and other civilizations.

 ## Learning Objectives

2.1 Describe the main political ideas of four key figures in ancient political philosophy.

2.2 Describe the key ideas of Machiavelli and the three strands of social contract theory.

2.3 Describe the core concepts of early rational-material, institutional, and ideational theorizing.

2.4 Identify several key shifts that clarified the explanatory alternatives in political science today.

Introduction: The Backstory to Today's Political Alternatives

What should the United States do about the tensions in the Middle East? Does rising inequality in the American economy call for more or less government action? How should you vote in the next election?

Becoming the kind of critical thinker who can think and speak with confidence on political questions like these is a major challenge. Most of this book helps you meet that challenge by looking at alternatives on the political scene today: varying political arrangements, competing ideologies, and different explanations in political science. As a starting point, though, it is helpful to know a bit about where today's alternative views came from. People have been thinking critically about politics for a few thousand years, after all. Our options today make more sense if we know some of their backstory.

In particular, it helps to see that a scientific-style focus on *explaining* politics—the enterprise of political *science*—is a fairly recent notion. It is a two-centuries-old offshoot of political philosophy—a far more ancient enterprise that remains with us very powerfully (often under the label "political theory" in American universities' programs on politics). Political philosophy, old or new, tends to offer a broad mix of normative views about how politics *should* work with analytic claims about how politics *does* work. Explanatory political science, by contrast, represents an attempt to strain out analytic claims as much as possible from normative judgments. If we trace how this agenda gradually emerged alongside political philosophy, we better appreciate the difference between explanatory political science and broader political philosophy, and we also recognize how they remain connected in many ways. Although clear thinking requires that we make an effort to distinguish analytic explanation from normative judging—being explicit about when we are analyzing how things *are* and when we are judging how they *ought to be*—the two can never be fully separated. Our judgments color how we explain the world, and our explanations affect our judgments. ∎

Political Theory in the Ancient World: Plato, Aristotle, and Contemporaries

2.1 Describe the main political ideas of four key figures in ancient political philosophy.

Our story begins, like many do, in the ancient civilizations of Greece, China, and India. Almost all of the most influential thinkers who helped invent the role of "political philosopher"—someone who thinks deeply about fundamental questions of power and governance—began by exploring normatively how politics *should* be organized in the abstract. They tended to ask, "What is the best kind of government?" or "How should good leaders act?" Their answers always involved analytic thinking about how politics actually *did* work around them, since reality as they saw it defined the problems that the best government or leaders needed to solve. Still, their analytic arguments were motivated and shaped by how they thought things ought to be.

The work of the Greek thinker **Plato** (427–347 BC) was so ambitious and influential that he is often described as the inventor not only of political philosophy but of philosophy in general. Greece in Plato's time was governed mostly as separate cities, like his native Athens, and our word *politics* comes from the Greek *politikos*, meaning "pertaining to the city." Many of his works addressed how to best organize city government, most famously *The Republic*.[1] At the core of Plato's philosophy was the strategy of first imagining the perfect version of something—what he called the "form" or the ideal—and then considering how to approximate it in our imperfect world. *The Republic* followed this strategy to define justice and the organization of a just city. Plato explored these questions through fictional dialogues between his teacher, Socrates, and various confused skeptics. Their amusing conversations are hard to sort into cut-and-dried answers, but ultimately this inventor of philosophy made a case for his own kind: he argued that the just city would be ruled by . . . philosophers.

Plato built this claim by arguing that a city was like a person. As he saw it, the human soul has three parts: reason (the rational part of the soul that seeks truth), spirit (the assertive part of the soul that seeks honor), and appetite (which lusts after things). A city, too, can be divided into philosophers who seek truth, a warrior class that seeks honor, and the ill-disciplined masses who care mainly about making money. The best way to keep everyone acting in their appropriate roles is to place the rational truth seekers in charge as **philosopher-kings**. To incentivize their focus on truth, they must live simple lives. Philosopher-kings should have no private property, thus avoiding the seductions of personal wealth. They should share wives and children to keep them from being tempted to favor their own families. Plato also added some strikingly modern notions into his ideal city: universal education, abolition of slavery, and no discrimination between men and women (though his proposal for sharing wives confuses this last idea).

Plato's equally famous student **Aristotle** (384–322 BC) shifted political philosophy a bit away from Plato's focus on the ideal and toward analysis of the world as it is. He portrayed the study of politics as the "master science" that set the rules and values of all other activities and scholarship. He also described politics in terms of causal forces that paralleled some of his other writings on the physical sciences.[2] Indeed, Aristotle invoked hints of all three of today's explanatory logics, and even included a role for the fourth option of psychological explanation. The reason cities and government arose to begin with, he wrote, was psychological: human beings are naturally "political animals" who want to live together.[3] Any city is shaped by the material elements of its natural resources and people. Its workings are directly organized, however, by the institutions of its constitution and laws. At the broadest level, any system of government is shaped by certain ideas: different systems have different aims or goals, and for Aristotle, these ideational goals are the "final cause" that animates each system.

Plato

An Athenian philosopher and author of *The Republic* who argued for a system of government led by philosopher-kings.

philosopher-kings

Leaders in Plato's *Republic* who deserved to lead because they pursued truth in the study of philosophy and kept on that path by having no private property or families.

Aristotle

An Athenian philosopher who saw the study of politics as the "master science" that guides how society in general should proceed and argued for a government balanced between the masses and an educated elite.

Thus Aristotle raised alternative explanations that later became central to political science, but he still operated in a philosophical mode that mixed normative and analytic concerns. He imagined different kinds of government and discussed what was good and bad about them. Aristotle drew two distinctions between imaginable governments that generated six options (see Table 2-1).

On the one hand, he pointed out that political control can rest in the hands of one person, a few, or many. On the other, the people in control can govern either with the interests of all in mind (producing the "genuine," good form of each option) or with only their own interests in mind (creating the "perverted," bad form). These distinctions allowed Aristotle to define six kinds of governments: kingship is rule by a benevolent person, aristocracy by a virtuous minority, and polity by representatives of all parts of society. Tyranny is rule by a bad king, oligarchy is rule by a selfish minority, and for Aristotle, democracy is the undesirable rule of the poor masses in their own crude interest. Later thinkers have often used these same terms in other ways—our modern use of "democracy," for example, is quite different—but by defining these alternatives Aristotle laid the foundations for his arguments about the best kind of government.

Aristotle's core normative principle was that a good society gives people rights and benefits in proportion to their levels of virtue. The ideal government, he suggested, would be one in which all people were equally virtuous and equally involved in government. In the real world, though, he thought poorer, less-educated people did not have the means to be virtuous and make good decisions. Thus richer, better-educated people should have at least some more influence than the average citizen. On the other hand, he thought it was also problematic to assign all power to the richer, better-educated people in a system of aristocracy. They would tend not to keep broad interests in mind and would slip toward perverted oligarchy. The best system was a mixed government that balanced the power of the rich and the poor, combining aspects of polity and aristocracy. It should ultimately aim to center power in a middle class that is rich and educated enough to understand virtue, but numerous enough to prioritize broad societal interests. Overall, then, Aristotle pulled politics a bit further out of Plato's ideal realm, and also stepped beyond philosopher-kings toward

Table 2-1 Aristotle's Classification of Governments

Rule by				
		One	**Few**	**Many**
	Genuine (reflects interests of all people)	Kingship	Aristocracy	Polity (rule by representatives of all parts of society)
Government Form	**Perverted** (reflects interests only of those in control)	Tyranny	Oligarchy	Democracy (rule of the poor masses in their own crude interest)

SOURCE: Fred Miller, "Aristotle's Political Theory," *The Stanford Encyclopedia of Philosophy* (Fall 2012 edition), Edward N. Zalta, ed., http://plato.stanford.edu/archives/fall2012/entries/aristotle-politics/.

broader-based governments. In classic philosophical style, though, he still approached the political world by holding it up against an imagined ideal.

A similar basic style characterized the greatest ancient Chinese political thinker, **Confucius** (551–479 BC). He called for individuals to pursue lives of virtue, study, and contemplation, and for government by a virtuous emperor. At the same time, he prefigured some modern concepts by hinting at rights for the people: if the emperor did not act virtuously, he suggested, the leader would lose the "Mandate of Heaven."[4] Later followers interpreted Confucius to mean that oppressed people might legitimately seek a new leader.

Confucius
A Chinese philosopher who offered rules for virtuous behavior by both subjects and emperors, but also suggested that the people could challenge tyrannical leadership.

In ancient India, on the other hand, one ancient thinker took steps toward reversing the relationship between normative and analytic arguments. A political adviser to emperors known as **Kautilya** (350–283 BC) authored a long treatise on politics with a very practical (and even bloodthirsty) bent.[5] He too set his first goal as normative counsel about how to be a virtuous ruler, but he premised his advice on an analysis of a rather bleak, harsh world in which effective leaders had to place realistic pursuit of power ahead of moral goals. To have any chance of enacting virtuous policies, he suggested, a good ruler must first do whatever it takes to hold on to power. This style of argument went beyond Aristotle in remixing analytic and normative priorities: it hinted that we must begin by asking what can work realistically, and only then can we judge which realistic actions are most virtuous.

Kautilya
An Indian philosopher who first suggested reversing the priority of analytic and normative thinking, arguing that virtuous leadership depended on understanding the roots of power and influence in the real world.

From these sources in the ancient world came rich ideas about political ideals that remain hugely influential today. In fact, they constitute the basis for the emergence of political science far down the line. As odd as Plato's philosopher-kings may sound to us today, it is not rare to hear people in this century wishing that their leaders could be more thoughtful, far-sighted, and community-minded, and less power-hungry or self-serving. Aristotle's notions of balancing the representation of different social groups inspired later thinking about the design of democracy. Confucian wisdom on personal and political virtue is still cited as a major influence on political thinking in Asia. And especially in Aristotle and Kautilya, we see the roots of the analytic views that branched off into explanatory political science.

Political Theory from the Renaissance into the Enlightenment: Machiavelli to Rousseau

2.2   **Describe the key ideas of Machiavelli and the three strands of social contract theory.**

For the next step in our story, we jump forward almost 2,000 years. Many interesting thinkers engaged with politics in the intervening centuries, but not until the European Renaissance in the 1500s did a political thinker take a major step that hinted at the emergence of a distinctively explanatory political science. Kautilya is often compared to Niccolò Machiavelli (1469–1527), another adviser to a powerful ruler who argued that stark analysis of the real world should inform our normative goals.

Like Kautilya, Machiavelli was a political actor in his own right, but in Italy rather than India. He was an important figure in the government of the **Republic** of Florence at the end of the 1400s—a city-state that had no hereditary ruler at the time. It was governed by a council elected every two months by the businesspeople of the city. In Machiavelli's later life, however, the city was taken over by the Medici family. Though he privately still preferred republican government, Machiavelli apparently wrote his greatest work, *The Prince*, in an attempt to win favor with the Medici princes.

Republic

A government that is not governed by a hereditary ruler like a king, but instead assigns power through broad public choice.

The Prince argued explicitly against the Aristotelian approach of starting from normative ideas about a morally ideal political model. He counseled that a smart person, and especially a smart prince, must focus on analyzing reality rather than an imaginary better world:

> Men have imagined republics and principalities that never really existed at all. Yet the way men live is so far removed from the way they ought to live that anyone who abandons what is, for what should be pursues his downfall rather than his preservation; for a man who strives after goodness in all his acts is sure to come to ruin, since there are so many men who are not good.[6]

The reality of politics, according to Machiavelli, was that people who tried to be good would lose out to more ruthless competitors. Politics was an arena of conflict, uncertainty, and instability. A leader who acquired raw power through strong resources and an aggressive strategy would bring stability and prosperity to his realm. It was ultimately more effective for a prince to be strong rather than good, and to be feared than to be loved. Even his fearful subjects would benefit from strong, stable government.

Clearly, these arguments carried a strong normative message as well. Indeed, Machiavelli is often remembered mainly for the notions that people tend to be wicked and that unjust actions are acceptable because they are necessary. The normative core of *The Prince*, in other words, is that the ends justify the means. One of the most prominent American political theorists of the twentieth century, Leo Strauss, argued that Machiavelli was nothing less than a "teacher of evil."[7] Today, to be "Machiavellian" means to scheme and plot in a ruthless way. In terms of how we study politics, though, Machiavelli is also remembered for distinguishing—more sharply than his predecessors—between normative judgments and explanatory analysis. More explicitly than Kautilya, Machiavelli's theories are based in claims about reality (as he saw it), and suggest that moral views must take into account how the real world works.

Over the next three centuries, as Europe's Renaissance developed into the rise of scientific thinking known as the Enlightenment, three especially influential political thinkers followed Machiavelli to lay foundations for the modern social sciences: Hobbes, Locke, and Rousseau. Each continued to mix explanatory and normative agendas, but their increasingly explicit and elaborate analyses of political reality (as they saw it) also made possible the emergence of more distinct explanatory debates.

Thomas Hobbes (1588–1679) drew on Machiavelli's theory in his great work *Leviathan*. Hobbes was writing in England during the period of the chaotic English Civil War, and was concerned above all with explaining and justifying strong, stable governance. He began with a picture of human beings in the state of nature, prior to the emergence of social organization, that was even darker than Machiavelli had imagined. People are naturally inclined to fight, threaten, and fear each other, he thought, creating a "war of all against all" in which everyone's lives would be "nasty, brutish, and short."[8] The only escape from insecurity was to form a strong government to impose order internally and protect against external attack from other groups. Even if a government claims absolute power (like the **absolutist** monarchies in some parts of Europe in his day), Hobbes thought it is still better for everyone than the chaos and anarchy of weak or no government. In arguing that everyone is better off with a strong government, Hobbes created the first version of what became known as a **social contract** theory of the rise of the state. He argued that it is rational for all individuals to sign a "contract" to consent to governance by a protective state.

absolutism
A government that assigns absolute, unchecked power to a single individual.

social contract
The notion that legitimate government is based on an agreement among the governed to accept central authority.

Dutch artist Pieter Brueghel's "The Triumph of Death" (1562) captures the long period of religious and territorial wars that formed the historical backdrop to Hobbes's writings, which emphasized the need for a protective state.

PAINTING/Alamy Stock Photo

These arguments in *Leviathan* had enormously far-reaching implications. On the one hand, Hobbes based the case for government on individual benefits for average people. A social contract view suggested that the state exists to serve the interests of the population, not just the interests of rulers. On the other hand, Hobbes explained and justified the absolute power of kings, since he thought that only a centralized, powerful government could keep the "war of all against all" at bay. Furthermore, his view of the state suggested that politics *inside* states, in what became known as "domestic politics," is profoundly different from politics *outside* them, in what later became known as "international relations." More specifically, he believed that within the social contract of the state, domestic politics operate within ordered rules and governance. Outside the state, in international relations, there is no social contract and no higher authority, and the "war of all against all" continues between states. This basic idea—that international relations may operate in a different, more chaotic kind of political space from domestic politics—is still the reason why "IR" is seen as its own subfield in political science.

John Locke (1632–1704) built on Hobbes's notion of the social contract, but took it further away from a Machiavellian view of constant strife and conflict. For Locke, basic human society in a state of nature would not be as terrifying and chaotic as Hobbes suggested. Rather than a "war of all against all," he theorized, people in a state of nature might live fairly well, but they would compete with each other for resources, and would have some problems with crime. Locke agreed with Hobbes that rational individuals would create a social contract to form a government for law and order. However, he saw the problems in the state of nature as less severe and argued for a more limited kind of government as the rational and desirable solution.[9] For Locke, repression by a highly centralized absolutist king would be worse than the state of nature. To improve on the state of nature, people needed a limited government that respected a series of individual rights. Locke's normative arguments that all people had natural rights to "life, liberty, and property" had huge political impact, inspiring the American Revolution and other calls for individual rights and limited government in the later 1700s.

The third great theorist of the social contract was Jean-Jacques Rousseau (1712–1778), who shifted this thinking another step away from a Machiavellian view. Rousseau argued that human beings are naturally good—not the conflictual and treacherous creatures pictured by Machiavelli or Hobbes—and that a pre-society state of nature would be a happy paradise. The rise of government, then, did not result from a contract that made everyone better off. Instead, the state formed mainly because certain people acquired private property, and either forced or tricked others into accepting a government that would protect their property. In other words, the whole system of government was set up to protect the rich from the poor, enshrining **inequality**: as Rousseau put it in his most famous phrase, "Man is born free, and everywhere he is in chains."[10] Government and society are the chains that serve the interests of the rich and hold down the poor. A more just society could come about only if decisions were made in the best interest of all members of society, according to what Rousseau called the "General Will." He imagined a profoundly bottom-up

inequality
In economic terms, the unequal distribution of wealth; in political terms, the assignment of rights to some people and not to others.

society, in which highly inclusive political participation would somehow identify the "General Will." Rousseau was fuzzy on how such broad participation would work, but one clear theme was that any good government would redistribute private property to achieve justice.

Though these three great social contract theorists were just as much normative philosophers as Plato or Aristotle, their work also contained more explicit development of three partly different explanatory approaches. In Hobbes's analysis, the dominant problems of society are conflict and a search for security, so rational people will organize tightly together into strong states to defend themselves. In Locke's analysis, the dominant problems of society are competing interests and scarce resources, and rational people will work out coordinating rules to respect each other's rights and property. In Rousseau's analysis, the dominant problems of society are inequality and oppression, and most people will rationally participate to work out greater equality. Table 2-2 summarizes these three views and hints, in the last line, at their explanatory legacies in today's political science. In the 1800s, these three lines of philosophy would branch off into three variants of rational-material explanatory stories that launched the explanatory social sciences: realist, liberal, and Marxist accounts.

Before we trace these legacies into the next step of our story, it is important to underscore the kind of people who dominated the story at this point (and for the next century or so). Though thinking about politics was branching into different traditions, its dominant figures were all white men who took for granted their own superiority to women and nonwhite peoples. Only much later, in the late 1900s, did the centers of political philosophy crack open to admit more diversity. In 1988, Carol Pateman wrote *The Sexual Contract*, arguing that all social contract theorizing was premised on a prior contract among men to maintain their dominance.[11] In 1997, Charles Mills extended similar arguments to racial dominance in *The Racial Contract*.[12] While the early social contract thinkers' ideas have resonated far and wide, they also buried many issues of diversity and inequality in their universalistic thinking about "mankind."

Table 2-2 The Three Dominant Traditions of Social Contract Theory

	Hobbes	Locke	Rousseau
Key concept	Conflict	Competition	Coercion/Exploitation
Problem in the state of nature	Security	Scarcity of resources	No problem
Why the state arises?	Provide security	Guarantee individual rights	Protect property rights of the rich
What kind of state is likely?	Absolute government	Limited government	Government of the rich
What kind of state is desirable?	Absolute government	Limited government	Government according to "General Will"
Explanatory legacy	Realist	Liberal	Marxist

The Emergence of Social Science in the Nineteenth Century

2.3 **Describe the core concepts of early rational-material, institutional, and ideational theorizing.**

With the ideas of the social contract theorists, especially Locke and Rousseau, came what is known as the "Age of Revolution." People around the Western world challenged absolutist monarchies and fought for some version of limited government, launching the American Revolution of 1776, the French Revolution of 1789, the Haitian Revolution of 1791, Latin America's movements for independence from Spain in the early 1800s, and waves of rebellion across Europe in the mid-1800s. At the same time, more revolutionary change entered the realm of political thought. The Enlightenment notion that science could provide useful knowledge for improving human lives was sweeping across European societies. Many thinkers began to argue that scientific inquiry should not just address physics, chemistry, biology, and other "natural sciences," but could illuminate the "social sciences" of human behavior as well. This did not cause a divorce from the normative tradition of political philosophy, since the explanatory claims that theorists increasingly asserted about the reality of society remained heavily entangled with their views of what was good and bad in society. This Enlightenment faith in science, however, did reorder the priorities for much of the study of politics, as foreshadowed by Machiavelli. Many subsequent thinkers argued that their theories analytically and scientifically captured the reality of human interactions, while sometimes hiding their normative values and judgments between the lines of "scientific" claims.

For at least the next hundred years, political science was not usually distinguished from the broader study of society, economics, or culture. Part of the reason was that the first explanatory approaches that developed from the philosophical positions of Hobbes, Locke, and Rousseau were all extremely broad rational-material theories. At their core, these theories portrayed the shape of society, the economy, politics, and culture as being collectively dictated by certain features of the underlying material landscape.

Rational-Material Beginnings: Liberal, Marxist, and Realist Variants

The most influential strand of political thinking in Europe at this time, generally known today as **classical liberalism**, followed the line of Locke's thinking. The explanatory implications of Locke's views hinted that human history was increasingly dominated by a march toward individual liberty. Humans were rational, and the main problems they encountered in the landscape around them were scarce resources and competition with others. There were some challenges of crime and disorder, but the basic arena for human existence was not

classical liberalism
A political philosophy and ideology that prioritizes individual political rights, private property, and limited government.

fundamentally conflictual. Given this kind of landscape, people were most concerned with establishing their individual liberty to do as they pleased, safeguard their possessions, and generate wealth that would help them cope with scarcity. Later thinkers who attempted to build more science-like explanatory theories on Locke's foundations expected that as history progressed, more and more people would recognize their interests in individual liberty and an open society. Then traditional societies ruled by kings, emperors, or other oppressive rulers would give way to more open, free societies with limited governments.

THE LIBERAL VARIANT OF RATIONAL-MATERIAL THINKING. A critical contribution to this liberal theory of the deep material trends to liberty came when Adam Smith (1723–1790) worked out the key economic parts of the story. In *The Wealth of Nations* (1776), not only did Smith analyze the sources of wealth, but he also grappled with a fundamental normative and analytical problem in the Lockean tradition. If individual liberty was the natural preference of all human beings, and everyone focused on pursuing his or her own individual goals, how could the narrow self-interests of individuals produce a collectively good society? Smith argued that free markets provided a way to reconcile the individual pursuit of self-interest with the collective good. In free markets, everyone could make money by selling whatever goods or services they could best provide. Competition would arise when more than one person tried to sell the same thing. The pressure of competition (and the lure of becoming wealthy for the winner of that competition) would lead people to be efficient and innovative, and would push everyone to work hard to identify their own greatest strengths. If everyone ended up developing whatever they could best offer in the market, society as a whole would become as efficient, productive, and innovative as it could possibly be. Free markets would thus deliver the best society even without anyone thinking about the collective good. As Smith put it in his most famous phrase, a good, efficient society would arise as if directed by "an **invisible hand**." This argument greatly clarified why rational human beings everywhere might ultimately be drawn—individually and collectively—toward an open society based around liberty and free markets.

In the 1800s, the connection of Locke's tradition to Smith's view of economics set the stage for a liberal, rational-material hypothesis that the spread of free markets and individual liberty was quasi-inevitable. Though no one theorist gave his name to this approach, it became especially widespread in British and American scholarship, and later gave birth to the twentieth-century school known as modernization theory. This view suggested a stage-by-stage theory of human history in which economic progress drives social and political change. Most societies start out as small, isolated populations. Because they exchange little with others, they are poor and often have their own odd local beliefs, culture, and oppressive local leaders. However, as their growing population, trade, and technology brings them more into contact with others—as larger markets emerge—people will rationally see the advantages of openness, liberty, and more free markets. Increased prosperity will encourage and empower more

invisible hand
A free market notion that competition to make money will channel everyone toward their most productive individual strengths, sorting people and resources to their best use even without any government leadership.

people to call for rights, limited government, and more open market opportunities. Economies will become ever more open and free, and liberated people will also call for a competitive "free market" for political leaders—meaning democratic government.

THE MARXIST VARIANT OF RATIONAL-MATERIAL THINKING. Not far behind the elaboration of liberal-rational-material explanatory theories, though, came a rival view that echoed some of Rousseau's points. Its main creator was Karl Marx (1818–1883), who developed a starkly different Marxist version of the quasi-inevitable material trends in human societies. For Marx, Smith was wrong to think that markets were good for everyone; instead, Rousseau was right that private property creates and reproduces inequality. Once certain people acquired some property, Marx thought that they tended to use their wealth to also acquire coercive capabilities, like gaining influence over government, the police, or the military. With coercive power behind them, the wealthy tended to manipulate subsequent economic exchanges to benefit themselves and exploit others. In particular, they paid poorer workers less than the real value of their work, skimming the "**surplus value**" of workers' labor off for "profit" and maintaining (or increasing) their wealth without doing real work themselves. Worst of all were **capitalists**: people who made money by owning businesses or investing in them. As Marx saw it, the workers in the businesses did all the actual work, while the capitalist owners or investors took most of the value created by the workers. Capitalists got richer simply because they were already rich, and used their wealth to keep everyone else down.[13]

In Marx's theory, each stage of history was built around one group or "class" of people exploiting another class. In each period, the structural distribution of wealth bonded with the coercive power in society to create conflict between the two classes. In feudal Europe, a privileged class of aristocrats had long exploited a class of peasants. But when the rise of trade gradually shifted economic power from land-owning aristocrats to business-owning **bourgeois** (which means "town dwellers"), the peasants left their villages to become workers in commerce and industry. Society thus moved from an aristocrats/peasants phase to one in which bourgeois capitalists exploited workers. Marx also called the working class the **proletariat**, from the Roman word for people without property. In this bourgeois/proletariat phase of history, Marx expected to see the rise of political democracy, but only as a fig leaf to hide the exploitations of capitalism. He saw democracy as a false competition organized by the capitalists to mislead workers into thinking that they had a real voice in the system. Eventually, Marx predicted, the workers would organize and overthrow the bourgeois capitalists in a revolution, opening the way to the abolition of private property and a happy society without exploitation.

Though a few Marxist-inspired revolutions have since taken place, most famously in Russia in 1917 and China in the 1940s, the grandest predictions of this Marxist-rational-material theory never materialized. Capitalism is still with

---

surplus value

Marx's idea that since all value came from labor, anyone who profited from selling goods besides the workers who made them (i.e., business owners) must be paying the workers less than their work was worth and taking the "surplus."

capitalists

People who make money with money rather than with labor.

bourgeois

The commercial class of people who make money by owning and investing in businesses.

proletariat

Marx's word for the working class—the people who make money by selling their labor rather than by owning or investing.

Oldtime/Alamy Stock Photo

In this 1868 etching, troops repress a riot at a Belgian coal mine. Marx developed his theories as industrialization spread rapidly in Europe, producing both massive new wealth and a harsh life for the working class in vast mines and factories.

us, and has even returned to China and Russia more strongly than ever before. Still, many serious thinkers around the world argue that Marx was substantially right about many of the dynamics of capitalist society, even if his predictions of its demise were wrong. Also, his theory has enormously influenced the social sciences. Certain currents of Marxist or Marxist-related theory remain powerful today, both in political science and in active political discourse. See Figure 2-1 for a comparison of the liberal and Marxist expectations of markets and politics.

THE REALIST VARIANT OF RATIONAL-MATERIAL THINKING.   Hobbes, lastly, also laid the foundations for an explanatory approach in which deep material conditions dictate the shape of society and politics. While liberal-rational-material and Marxist-rational-material thinkers focused mainly on economic conditions underlying society and politics, though, the Hobbesian tradition kept its emphasis on considerations of security, threats, and physical violence. Inside each country, the state created a protected political arena within which the "war of all against all" was put on hold. But in the international space between countries, the constant threat of violence remained. Therefore, the shape and dynamics of the international arena reflected how states with different capacities for violence were positioned around the landscape. Roughly speaking, international politics was driven by whoever had a big stick (or a large army, or certain military technology) and who did not. This theory expected that rational leaders of states would be forced to focus solely on this "distribution of power" around them, setting aside moral concerns in international

Figure 2-1 Liberal and Marxist Expectations about Markets and Politics

Both liberal and Marxist variants of rationalist-materialist thinking expect economic change to drive political change over time. But liberals see markets benefiting society broadly and so expect positive historical progress, whereas Marxists see markets only benefiting the rich and, therefore, expect conflict and revolution.

ADAM SMITH'S LIBERAL VIEW OF MARKETS AND POLITICS

Exchange always benefits both parties. (Otherwise, why would they exchange?)

More exchange between more people brings more benefits.

More competition forces everyone to focus on what they do best.

Free markets make each individual as productive as possible and society flourishes overall.

KARL MARX'S (MARXIST) VIEW OF MARKETS AND POLITICS

Some people start out rich, others start our poor.

More exchange and technology creates more wealth, but the rich capture most of it.

The rich use their wealth to hire muscle to keep down the poor.

The development of markets inevitably brings class conflict and revolution.

relations and building up their own power as well as they could. If they did not, their country would eventually be destroyed or taken over.

Following Machiavelli's call to focus on the reality of a nasty world, this explanatory tradition became known as **realism**. Like liberal-rational-material and Marxist-rational-material thinking, it told one main story about all of human history, and its story pictured people responding rationally to the most salient features of the hard, material landscape around them. Unlike liberal or Marxist theories, though, it did not contain a narrative of "progress" or change in history. Some states might get richer over time, and the technology of war might change, but the fundamental material reality of international relations would remain an anarchical war of all against all.

With hindsight, it is not surprising that the explanatory approaches that created the social sciences were all grand rational-material theories. These early analytic explorations of human behavior took the rather elegant, very broad, and general view that we can explain most of politics by referring to the raw shape of the material landscape and some basic conceptions of human nature. (See Table 2-3 for a summary of the rationalist-materialist theories.) On the horizon in the nineteenth century, though, were competing explanatory approaches that focused on other conditions.

realism
The theory that international relations is always dominated by an anarchical conflict between states.

Table 2-3 Early (and Still Influential) Rationalist-Materialist Explanatory Theories

	Philosophical Ancestors	What are most basic dynamics of politics?	Key Expectations
Liberal	Locke Smith	Competition for scarce resources	As societies follow the incentives to free markets, they progressively become wealthy, harmonious, and democratic.
Marxist	Rousseau Marx	Conflict over scarce resources	As exchange and technology create more wealth, the rich get richer while the poor remain poor, leading to eventual revolution.
Realist	Machiavelli Hobbes	Conflict over security	Groups of people always threaten each other; certain groups rise and fall within the global division of power, and all of history is the same story of shifting alliances and war.

Institutional and Ideational Beginnings: Tocqueville, Durkheim, and Weber

Partly in reaction to these variants of rational-material explanation, the nineteenth century also saw the first steps toward institutional and ideational explanatory approaches. One of the earliest and clearest institutional arguments came from Alexis de Tocqueville (1805–1859), an aristocratic French historian and political thinker. In the 1830s, Tocqueville took an extended trip to the young United States and wrote a two-volume study of *Democracy in America*, which analyzed why democracy had succeeded there while largely failing (at that time) in Europe.[14]

At the core of *Democracy in America* was an institutional story about how the organization of political life in the United States defined a new kind of political game, and with it a new kind of society. There was some ideational background: Tocqueville emphasized that the founders of the United States had shared ideological commitments to political equality (for white men, with huge exceptions for slavery and the treatment of women). But Tocqueville's main emphasis was not on the distinctiveness of American society's shared beliefs or culture. Rather, he stressed the notion that the strongly local organization of political life, together with a very weak and decentralized U.S. federal government, set up the political game to protect political freedoms. He saw a vibrant local **civil society**—a life organized separately from the state—in which Americans participated in clubs, religion, and every kind of association. In his view, this intermediate level of organization between individuals and separate from government

civil society
Arenas of action in a country outside direct government influence, such as associations, churches, business affairs, media, and artistic expression.

is what empowered Americans to mobilize together. It also served as a buffer against government dominance. In his native France, by contrast, Tocqueville argued that the state had penetrated or smothered the independent organizations of civil society. Individuals had few institutional shields against state power.

Tocqueville worried, however, about some consequences of American institutions. Rules that put such a thorough emphasis on equality, he thought, tended toward a society dominated by the mediocre "common man." Pervasive reliance on majority rules created the risk of **tyranny of the majority**, in which majority opinions oppressed other voices. To the eye of this French aristocrat, a strong priority on equality and majority views also discouraged excellence in intellectual life and the arts. Turning its back on the creation of knowledge and beauty by highly trained elites, Tocqueville thought, American society tended toward a crude worship of money and consumerism.

This criticism foreshadowed many later themes of debate, but in his time, Tocqueville remained an unusual thinker. It was not until the later twentieth century that institutional explanations like his became a very prominent approach. More widespread by the late nineteenth century was another kind of broad and deep reaction to rational-material thinking that centered on ideas and culture. Émile Durkheim (1858–1917) was one of its key pioneers. A French academic, Durkheim argued passionately for scientific method in the study of human society. Yet he was critical of the preceding rational-material thinkers who analyzed society as a straightforward, unambiguous landscape populated by similarly rational people. For Durkheim, human action was shaped by cultural beliefs and norms, and the study of society was necessarily the study of the forms and effects of culture. In one of his most influential observations, he argued that cultural norms or ideas were facts of life that were just as important as more tangible material things, such as the presence of mountains, gold in the ground, or a certain kind of technology. Whether or not someone believes in God, for example, was just as much a fact in their life as whether or not they live near the ocean. Culture was made up of these "**social facts**" through which people interpreted their surroundings and choices. Action was influenced by both intangible-but-real "social facts" and "material facts" in the landscape.

In his most famous study, *Suicide*, Durkheim looked at different rates of suicide between Catholic and Protestant populations in Europe.[15] He argued that lower Catholic rates reflected a stronger integration of individuals within Catholic families, while high Protestant rates resulted from more individualistic, less supportive norms in family life. In other words, culture made the difference in people's lives. Durkheim's overall view of historical change was strongly related to his specific claims about suicide. He feared that social changes linked to industrialization in Europe were undercutting previous cultural norms and ideas that had integrated society. Whether societies held together or began to break down (resulting in alienation, suicide, and social conflict) would depend on the integrative capacities of their cultures or, perhaps, the creation of new cultural ideas.

tyranny of the majority
The possibility that a democratic majority could choose to harm minorities or political opponents.

social facts
Human-created conditions of action that exist only because people believe in them.

Around the same time, the German social scientist Max Weber (1864–1920) developed similar thinking that placed culture at the center of his explanatory approach. Weber theorized that human beings are roughly rational, and tend to seek basic wealth and security much as the rational-material theorists suggested. But, he theorized, culture has a powerful impact on what exactly people see as rational and how they pursue their well-being. In one famous passage, he wrote that even if people pursue what they see as concrete, rational interests, culture plays the role of a railroad "switchman" for the tracks they follow: "Very frequently the world images that have been created by ideas, like a switchman, have determined the tracks along which action has been pushed by the dynamic of interest."[16]

Weber's most famous book, *The Protestant Ethic and the Spirit of Capitalism*, was an example of this new kind of explanation.[17] Wealthy European market economies, he suggested, did not arise naturally from the simple material incentives of trade, as liberal-structural and Marxist-structural accounts implied. The reason economic growth took off in Europe and not elsewhere, Weber claimed, was an accidental by-product of Protestant religion. Some early versions of Protestantism in the 1500 and 1600s placed a strong emphasis on the belief that people who were destined for salvation in Heaven could be recognized by their hard work and simple lifestyle in this life. In other words, the culture of early Protestants attached the ultimate motivation—eternal salvation—to living a life of hard work and saving money. Somewhat ironically (given their focus on a simple lifestyle), this was an excellent recipe for generating tremendous wealth. Following these religious instructions, many early Protestants became some of the wealthiest early capitalists, and soon their successful recipe was imitated elsewhere in Europe and beyond. Weber's main point, like Durkheim's, was that it is cultural beliefs and norms—rather than the raw material landscape— that most shape human societies and the course of history.

One of Weber's other hugely influential contributions, especially for later work in political science, was his treatment of **power** and **authority**. A widely accepted definition of *power*, both in Weber's time and today, is the ability to get someone to do something that they would not otherwise have done. Many thinkers before Weber had treated power in society as a simple set of capabilities: if someone has weapons to threaten other people, wealth to pay them off, or other simple levers of influence, they have power. As part of Weber's emphasis on the importance of culture, however, he argued that *authority* is much more important than raw power in most human interaction. Authority is the legitimate right to exercise power. An armed robber might have the power, but certainly not authority, to take your money. Government, on the other hand, can have recognized authority to collect people's money in taxes. Weber was not the first thinker to stress that authority mattered—Hobbes, Rousseau, and others had written on these subjects—but earlier thinkers tended to focus at least as much on their own normative views of legitimate power (who *should* have authority) as on analytic claims that cultural notions of legitimacy, good or bad,

power
The ability to get someone to do something they would not otherwise have done.

authority
The legitimate right to exercise power.

mattered everywhere. Weber emphasized this analytic claim: no government or other large organization can operate for long without authority. Some use brute force and repression in all eras of human history, certainly, but this cannot endure. The fundamental source of political influence is to convince people to accept certain cultural views of authority: that they should respect the decisions of elected leaders, courts, religious leaders, the elders of the clan, their parents, or whomever else. For that reason, Weber argued, we can understand and explain political interactions only if we pay attention to culture and ideas.

By the early 1900s, major elements of today's explanatory debates in political science had come onto the scene (see Figure 2-2). Prominent thinkers along the lines of Hobbes, Locke, and Rousseau had argued in different ways that to explain human action, including in politics, we should first look at the broad material landscape of geography, resources, population, and technology. Theorists like Durkheim and Weber had asserted that the main forces shaping human action, including political action, were located in cultural beliefs and

Figure 2-2 Institutional and Ideational Challenges to Rational-Material Theories

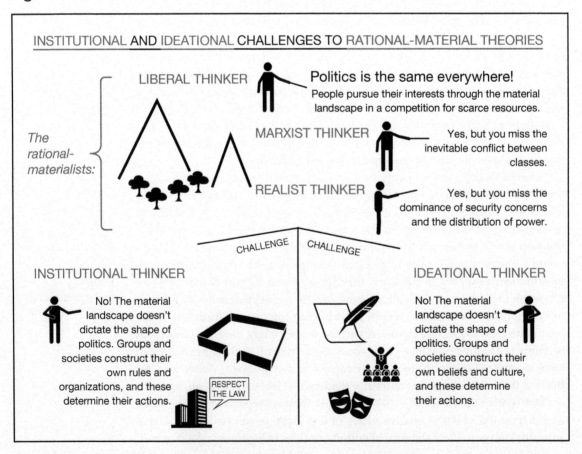

norms. Tocqueville and a few others had hinted at the importance of institutions, suggesting that society and politics should be seen as an evolving obstacle course of organizations and rules. At this time, politics and government were seen as just one piece of broader theories in the new realm of social science. The notion of a distinct "political science" would be a twentieth-century creation.

The Emergence and Diversification of Political Science

2.4   Identify several key shifts that clarified the explanatory alternatives in political science today.

By the twentieth century, the social sciences were gradually sorting out into more specialized disciplines. Economics was the first to establish itself as a distinct discipline, with its own vocabulary, famous professors, and departments at universities. It claimed a special focus on the creation of wealth and inequality and the workings of markets. Next came sociology, with such founding thinkers as Durkheim and Weber, who built the field mainly around questions of culture, identity, religion, and everyday social life. Anthropology soon developed as well: it overlapped heavily with sociology's focus on culture, but largely specialized in preindustrial societies outside the Western world. Next to follow was psychology, a study that coalesced around the study of the inner workings of the mind. Finally, political science emerged.

Why was political science so slow to develop as a distinct focus of study? Probably the main reason is that most early social scientists generally saw the political arena as a by-product of other parts of human life. This was clearest among Marxist-rational-material thinkers, who argued strongly that the political realm was just an echo of class power in the economy. For Marxists, it was (and is) foolish to study topics like political rights or democracy without addressing the real source of most social dynamics and problems: private property and capitalist markets. Even nineteenth-century liberal-rational-material thinkers tended to imply that the most important social dynamics lie in the economy: they viewed modern political rights and democracy as a rational outgrowth of flourishing trade and free markets. From a different angle, most early sociologists and anthropologists tended to see politics and government around the world as deriving from local cultures and identities. Study culture, they effectively believed, and you would understand most of politics too. For all these thinkers, politics flowed mainly from the economy on the one hand or society and culture on the other. Political science was a by-product of other disciplines.

These traditions are still powerfully with us today. Even within political science itself, an enduring debate concerns how much of politics just reflects underlying economic or social conditions. But over the twentieth century, claims about the autonomy of the political realm became better established alongside these older views. The analytic study of collective decision making, government, and public policies came into its own.

Extending Rational-Material Traditions

As explanatory political science first branched off from political philosophy, it stayed mostly within rational-material lines and sharpened rational-material approaches to explain the realm of government. Whereas European scholars had dominated nineteenth-century social science, the first scholars who started calling themselves "political scientists" were mostly at universities in the United States, which vaulted onto the world stage as a great power at the end of the 1800s. The American Political Science Association—the largest organization of political scientists in the world today—was founded in 1903.

Liberalism was the dominant normative political philosophy in the United States, and so it is unsurprising that the most influential, early explanatory approach was liberal-rational-material thinking. Scholars like Arthur Bentley (1870–1957) looked at American politics and saw something like the political "free market" that nineteenth-century liberal-rational-material theorists had portrayed as the culmination of economic development. For Bentley, the natural, rational way for people in modern societies to pursue their political inter-

interest groups
Associations in society that form around shared interests and advocate for them in politics.

ests is to form **interest groups**, and tracking these groups is the key to analyzing modern politics.[18] Each individual has his or her own package of abilities and resources, and quite rationally tends to ally with groups of other individuals who share similar positions in the economic and social landscape. Much as a market economy could be analyzed as firms competing according to their resources and strengths, so all of politics can be understood as a competitive arena of these groups:

> All phenomena of government are phenomena of groups pressing one another, forming one another, and pushing out new groups and group representatives (the organs or agencies of government) to mediate the adjustments. It is only as we isolate these group activities, determine their representative values, and get the whole process stated in terms of them, that we approach to a satisfactory knowledge of government.[19]

This approach is effectively an extension of a liberal, Adam Smith-like image of politics, with independent individuals pursuing their rights and interests in an open arena of competition and cooperation. It implies that everyone in society has roughly equal access to politics and government—it is an equal-opportunity "free market"—and politics and public policies are shaped by whichever groups attract the most resources and support. If we see new laws passed to regulate banks, for example, this view expects that there must have been a coalition of strong social groups that lobbied government for the new laws.

Liberal-rational-material thinking was also applied to other countries in the emerging subfield of comparative politics. Especially after World War II, when many colonized countries gained their independence, a school of thought arose that became known as **modernization theory**. At its core was the liberal-rational-material notion that all societies can be understood by considering where they are in a process of economic and political development that was leading to free markets and democracy. As expanding trade and markets bring dynamism and change, societies will emerge out of their traditional cultures and isolation until they display the kind of interest group competition in free markets that Bentley saw in the United States. Thus the United States and Europe display the end point of the worldwide modernization process, while poorer, less industrialized, less open and free countries stand at various stages back along the same historical path. Some of the more optimistic modernization theorists, like Walt Rostow (an adviser to President John F. Kennedy), expected that most societies would eventually follow the path blazed by Europe and the United States.[20] Other more pessimistic thinkers in this tradition, though, feared that poorer, more closed-off countries might never shake off their traditional culture and institutions and get on the road to progress.[21]

modernization theory
A rational-material theory in the liberal tradition that sees history as a march toward liberal democracy and capitalism.

If liberalism was the dominant philosophy at American universities and liberal-rational-material thinking led the way in early political science, the other rational-material traditions were also present. Marxist thinking was better represented in sociology than in early political science departments, but it produced many "political sociologists" who engaged actively in political science debates. With respect to U.S. politics, scholars like C. Wright Mills (1916–1962) criticized liberal interest group theories as naïve. There is no open, equal-access political arena in the United States, he argued; instead, it is dominated by the rich class, who constitute a "power elite."[22]

In the study of other societies in comparative politics, too, Marxist-rational-material-style thinking eventually generated a rival to modernization theory known as **dependency theory**.[23] In this view, poorer countries are not just lingering further back on the same historical path as the United States or Europe. They are poorer *because* Europe and the United States became rich. Just as the rich class exploits and dominates their poorer workers inside any capitalist country, so the rich countries exploit and dominate poorer countries around the world. American and European multinational corporations thrive on natural resources and cheap, exploited labor from poorer countries, and then take the profits back home. If need be, they call in the coercive support of their powerful militaries to keep poor countries in line.

dependency theory
The Marxist-related theory that sees all of human history in terms of dominance of poor countries by rich countries.

Realist-rational-material thinking in the Hobbesian line, lastly, also played a central role in the twentieth-century emergence of explanatory political science. As the subfield of international relations developed, especially after World War II, realism became its dominant approach. Realists like Hans Morgenthau (1904–1980) argued that the best way to understand international politics was

Cold War

A hostile stand-off in the late 1940s through the late 1980s between the communist USSR and its allies versus the capitalist-democratic United States and its allies.

to analyze it as a set of states clashing over a pursuit of security and control in a worldwide distribution of power.[24] Though Morgenthau wrote in a period when the democratic, capitalist United States was in increasing conflict with the communist Soviet Union—in the **Cold War**, from roughly 1946 to 1989—the realist theory he helped develop suggested that tension between the United States and the Soviet Union was not just about their different ideologies. These "superpowers" were the two most powerful countries in the world, to the point that no one else could threaten either of them. Given this distribution of international power—the basic shape of the material landscape—it made sense that they would realistically fixate on each other as rivals. In an even more influential

American tanks (foreground) face off against Soviet tanks in the middle of Berlin, Germany, in 1961. Realists argued that the United States and the Soviet Union fell into conflict after World War II because they were the two most powerful countries in the world—and so were the only threats to each other. Others argued that the Cold War was driven by clashing capitalist and communist beliefs, or by institutional differences between democracy and authoritarianism.

book, Kenneth Waltz (1924–2013) offered a "neo-realist" theory that the deepest lines of international politics always reflect states responding to the raw distribution of power.[25]

These three variants of rational-material thinking—liberal, Marxist, and realist—accounted for many of the best-known works in the young discipline of political science as of the mid-1900s. Their importance is reflected in contemporary arguments that claim that most political action in our world boils down to rational people running through a material landscape, with each line of thinking—liberal, Marxist, or realist—describing the main shape of the landscape differently. In the second half of the twentieth century, though, other kinds of explanatory stories became prominent as well. Some grew up within political science itself, and some reintegrated with political science from other disciplines. Overall, political science diversified into a broader debate.

Institutionalism: Human-Made Obstacle Courses

A key step in the diversification of political science came with the rise of institutional thinking in the 1970s and 1980s. Political scientists working on a wide variety of problems began to argue that politics is shaped as much or more by human-made rules and organizations as it is shaped by the raw, underlying material landscapes of economic resources or military capabilities. In studies of the U.S. Congress, scholars pointed out that the specific rules in congressional committees seemed to have a huge effect on how votes and legislation turn out.[26] In studies of economic development in poorer countries, other researchers argued that such successful countries as Taiwan or South Korea managed to "catch up" to richer countries not because of their underlying material resources, but thanks to specific institutional arrangements that encouraged growth.[27] Experts on democratization suggest that the creation and stabilization of a young democratic government depends on very careful design of institutional rules to appease or marginalize the foes of democracy.[28] In all these areas, the thinking that Tocqueville explored a century and a half earlier now developed very quickly. Politics was not shaped just by a given material landscape, said these new "institutionalists." People also constructed their own political obstacle courses on top of material conditions.

The development of institutional thinking was especially important to political science because its logic, much more than rational-material thinking, suggests that politics can be a fairly independent realm of human action with its own distinct dynamics. Such institutional thinking hints that once people design a constitution, pass a set of laws, or even set up lower-level organizations like city governments, universities, or schools, the rules of this political game exert their own influence on how people act, separately from the impact of underlying material conditions or prevailing ideas or culture. In particular, many institutional theorists argue that institutions can have **unintended consequences**

unintended consequences

In institutional thinking, this notion refers to how institutions created for one purpose may channel later politics in unforeseen ways.

long after they are set up. Take, for example, the case of the U.S. government shutdown mentioned in the introductory chapter. U.S. institutions were set up to "check and balance" each other in a time of oppressive monarchies when limiting abusive government seemed like the main problem. Centuries later, the U.S. government delivers far more services to American citizens and businesses than it did during its early years, so an impasse that shuts it down has become extremely costly. Though the initial goal of creating a self-limiting government made plenty of sense at the time (and may still have benefits, of course), this arrangement of the political game also has had unintended consequences that the founders could not have foreseen.[29]

Rational Choice: Sharpening the Logic of Material and Institutional Explanations

rational choice theory
A method for sharpening rational-material or institutional arguments that proceeds by imagining how perfectly rational people would act (and interact strategically) within material or institutional constraints.

Another important development swept across much of political science in the 1970s and 1980s, though it did not carry a new kind of explanatory story about political action. Out of the discipline of economics came a way of studying politics known as **rational choice theory**. To develop an argument about economic behavior, the first step that most economists take is to imagine that all people are perfectly rational. That is, they first imagine a world in which everyone has all the information they could need, always makes good use of information, considers all their options, connects problems to the right solutions, and thereby chooses the actions that best handle every challenge. Next, the economist analyzes how such perfectly rational people would act in something like a real-world economic context. If an economist wants to investigate how a rise in tax rates might affect people's economic choices, she or he typically begins by assuming that everyone is perfectly rational and then works out (often with mathematical theorems and proofs) how rational people will react to that given tax change. As a second step, she or he may consider how real-world people—who, most scholars agree, are not often perfectly rational—might depart from the expectations of this model. Even if the assumption of rationality is unrealistic, this process helps clarify an explanatory argument. It allows the scholar to set aside the tangle of real human thinking to get at the dynamics of a certain context. As of the 1970s, this same approach became widely used in political science to analyze how people might react in all sorts of political situations: in Congress, elections around the world, government bureaucracies, civil wars, terrorist movements, and almost every other political scenario.[30] A good example is the Nobel Prize–winning work of Elinor Ostrom, which analyzes how people cooperate (or do not) to preserve shared resources.[31]

As this description suggests, though, "rational choice theory" is not actually a new kind of explanation or *theory* in its own right; it is a tool or *method* for clarifying arguments. This tool is used with both rational-material and institutional explanations to clarify how we would expect people in a certain material or institutional position to act. Traditional rational-material thinkers of all sorts—liberal, Marxist, and realist—were often fuzzy about exactly how any particular course of action followed rationally from their description of the material landscape. Later generations of similar thinking have taken up rational choice methods to tighten up their logic, explicitly tracing how perfectly rational people would respond to a given position in markets, in exploitative class structures, or in the global distribution of power. Many institutional thinkers, too, use rational choice methods to highlight how rational people would respond to certain institutional rules of the political game. Then they typically look for evidence that real people have acted roughly like their rational models predict, even if real people are far from perfectly rational.

In effect, rational choice methods are a way of neatly imagining political arenas purely as surrounding landscapes or obstacle courses. If everyone always thought perfectly in the same, regular, predictable, rational way, there would be no need for interpretation in politics—no need for ideational or psychological stories—and all we would see would be people reacting rationally to material or institutional constraints. Thus rational choice methods have made important contributions to sharpening the older traditions of rational-material and institutional explanation.

The Return of Ideas and the Arrival of Psychology

Partly in reaction to the spread of rational choice methods, which overlooked how people perceive and interpret things, both ideational and psychological thinking became more prominent in the 1980s and 1990s. In international relations, a new ideational school of thought called "**constructivism**" arose to challenge realism. Its proponents, like Alexander Wendt, argue that the chaotic, anarchical dynamics that realists see in international politics are not the natural, obvious way for states to interact.[32] For Wendt, international anarchy itself is a constructed belief, not a material fact. He suggests that people came to believe that international politics is anarchical, and for much of history they acted as if it were—but in other eras and places people might construct different beliefs that would lead to profoundly different interactions. At the same time, scholars of public policy began to argue that to explain why governments' public policies change over time and vary across countries, it is necessary to consider the ideas and beliefs that political elites hold about how policies work and about which policies are desirable.[33] In U.S. politics, too, experts on American political development started to pay more attention to the ideologies and cultural norms that seem to have animated American politics over the country's history.[34] By the late 1990s, it was common in every corner of political science to see debates that pitted material or institutional explanations against arguments that saw ideas, beliefs, norms, and culture as the main forces shaping political action. The legacy

constructivism
A version of ideational explanation that suggests that the international arena is shaped primarily by what people believe about international politics.

of Durkheim and Weber—long shunted mainly into the disciplines of sociology and anthropology—now was strongly incorporated into a strand of political science.

The fourth logic of psychological explanation, too, saw an important expansion in political science at the same time, especially in two parts of the discipline. In the study of public opinion, political scientists became increasingly sophisticated in how they understood and studied how people form their political views. In the 1960s, the influential public opinion expert Philip Converse had famously argued that most Americans do not have any coherent political beliefs at all.[35] Later, though, other scholars argued that this could not be the whole story, since public opinion showed clear trends over time—not just randomness. Political scientists turned to elaborate models of psychology to account for how people figure out what they think, and even to the study of how genetics influences political beliefs through personality. In one study of a large set of twins (used to identify the effects of genetics), the authors argue that genetic inheritance makes some people psychologically more inclined to be politically conservative, and others more inclined to be liberal.[36]

The other area in which psychology developed a strong foothold is in the study of foreign policy, specifically in international relations. Unlike many other aspects of politics, foreign policy is frequently decided by small groups of leaders or even single individuals, such as presidents, dictators, and other top rulers. That means that the psychology of individual leaders may have a huge impact on events. If key individuals are psychologically inclined to be paranoid, or aggressive, or selective in the information they accept, that may matter a great deal for wars, diplomacy, and other important aspects of foreign policy. The individual psychology of Napoleon, Hitler, or Franklin Delano Roosevelt plausibly had real consequences in international relations. Another factor is what psychologists call "small-group psychology," which can affect policies when a set of leaders spend so much time together that they develop a kind of "groupthink" that reinforces certain views that people outside their group do not share. Just as ideas and culture have moved from sociology and anthropology into political science, so too has psychology informed some explanatory work about politics.[37]

With the consolidation of ideational and psychological strands of explanatory political science, the discipline had taken the shape it has today. Political philosophy (or "political theory") remains a major and active part of the study of politics, with leading thinkers carrying mixed normative and analytic agendas that Plato or Aristotle would recognize. Offshoots of these philosophical debates gradually branched out into the more scientific-style study of politics, focused on analytic explanation and prediction, which took the form of a debate between rational-material, institutional, ideational, and sometimes psychological alternatives. Figure 2-3 summarizes this story.

Figure 2-3 Mapping the History of the Study of Politics

Over time, analytic explanations of political science branched off from the mixed normative-analytic traditions of political philosophy, producing the very diverse study of politics we have today.

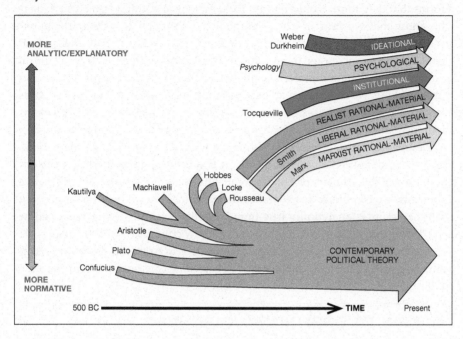

Conclusion: Putting Theories into Practice

We now can see some of the backstory to the explanatory stories introduced in Chapter 1. Although the three main kinds of explanatory stories—rational-material, institutional, and ideational—can be boiled down to simple questions to apply to the current world, those questions make more sense when we know the context in which people came up with them. We have seen where rational-material thinking came from (and its three main variants), and how institutional, ideational, and occasionally psychological stories arose to challenge or nuance its claims.

This history has also given you some sense of the back-and-forth between normative and analytic concerns or explanatory concerns in the study of politics. Most schools of thought mix these two things, offering both arguments about how the world is (and how we explain it) and arguments about how the world ought to be. This has become a bit harder to see over time as more thinkers tried to make the study of politics into a science, attempting to strain out explanatory debates from their own normative values, until the direct exploration of normative questions in political philosophy came to be seen as a subfield ("political theory") of the larger discipline. Still, the back-and-forth between explanation and normative thinking continues in all parts of the study of politics. Institutional thinkers who argue that institutions built yesterday still powerfully shape politics today, with all sorts of unintended consequences, often suggest institutional reforms that they think would be *good* for tomorrow's politics. "Constructivists" who argue that we must analyze international relations as a culturally interpreted realm of action also often advocate for people to change their ideas about global policies to encourage international cooperation and peace. When political scientists use the rational-material explanatory traditions of liberal, Marxist, and realist thinking, we can often read between the lines to see that they also endorse normative liberal emphases on individual liberty, normative Marxist concerns about inequality, or normative realist worries about insecurity and instability.

Despite—or rather *because of*—this mixing of explanatory and normative thinking, it is crucial to keep an eye on the distinction between them. Because both political leaders and scholars of politics frequently combine analytic and normative arguments, we can break down and understand their views only by sorting out what they claim is analytically true from what they claim is normatively bad or good. With practice, this gives us the ability to draw critically on others' ideas as we attempt to reclaim politics for ourselves. To relate it to Aristotle's terms, we move from being instinctual "political animals" to becoming conscious political people.

Review of Learning Objectives

2.1 Describe the main political ideas of four key figures in ancient political philosophy.

Most early thinking about politics mixed normative questions about the best kinds of political systems or leadership with analytic questions about how politics actually worked. The Greek philosopher Plato explored an ideal political system led by philosopher-kings: a group of leaders without property or families who governed in the name of truth. His student Aristotle confronted his judgments about ideal government with more elaborate arguments about what would work best in the real world, ultimately arguing that a balance between social groups would create the best possible society. The Chinese thinker Confucius more closely paralleled Plato's idealism, preaching more narrowly about virtuous behavior for the people and leaders. An Indian thinker, Kautilya, similarly advised leaders on good leadership, but suggested that good leaders had to first do whatever it took to solidify their power. Thus he pointed in the direction of prioritizing analytic claims over normative ones.

2.2 Describe the key ideas of Machiavelli and the three strands of social contract theory.

The Italian thinker Machiavelli strengthened a Kautilya-style focus on analyzing reality over seeking the ideal. In his book *The Prince*, Machiavelli argued that a successful leader must focus on the reality of politics around him, not on ideas about how they should be. He argued that reality was harsh: people were generally treacherous and only ruthless rulers did well. Similar views informed the later work of the English theorist Thomas Hobbes. Hobbes argued that the natural state of human existence was a "war of all against all" where everyone threatened everyone else. This would lead people to a "social contract." To protect themselves from threats, all would accept this contract to be ruled by a strong central state. Fifty years later, John Locke provided another social contract argument. Since he saw the state of nature as less threatening, he argued that people only needed to agree to a limited government to support societal order and respect of individual rights. Still later, Jean-Jacques Rousseau offered another social contract theory that began from a happy state of nature. For him, the emergence of government was not necessarily a good thing: it was a contract imposed by the rich to force an unequal division of property on the poor.

2.3 Describe the core concepts of early rational-material, institutional, and ideational theorizing.

The social contract theorists deeply mixed normative and analytic concepts, but over the nineteenth century, more analytic theories gradually branched out from each philosophical tradition. In Hobbes' line came a realist version of rational-material thinking, which asserted that the main patterns in politics flowed from security problems and competition for power. From Locke came a liberal variation of rational-materialism, theorizing that the spread of trade and economic growth would ultimately encourage people everywhere to adopt the kind of limited government and free-market economy that Lockean liberalism endorsed. From Rousseau-style thinking, with major additions from Karl Marx, came a Marxist variant. It agreed that economic growth would gradually lead all societies through phases of conflict and revolution until they finally abolished the underlying problem of private property. An institutional alternative first appeared clearly in the writings of Alexis de Tocqueville, who argued that that the rules of the U.S. Constitution had given rise to a new kind of society in America. Ideational alternatives grew from the work of Émile Durkheim and Max Weber, who pioneered views that ideational filters of culture and ideas lead people to interpret their surroundings in certain ways.

2.4 Identify several key shifts that clarified the explanatory alternatives in political science today.

By the early twentieth century, the social sciences divided into disciplines of economics, sociology, anthropology, psychology, and political science. Political science focused on the state and government and more generally on power, authority, and collective decision making. Liberal, Marxist, and realist strands of rational-material thinking were strong in the new discipline, but over time other options strengthened as well. Tocqueville-style institutionalism gradually became very influential. From economics came the tools of rational choice, which sharpened the logic of both material and institutional arguments. Ideational thinking entered political science from the disciplines of sociology and anthropology. Political scientists also imported approaches from psychology, especially in the study of public opinion and foreign policy.

Great Sources to Find Out More

Anthony Pagden, *The Enlightenment and Why It Still Matters* (New York: Random House, 2013). A historian's very accessible tracing of the impact of Rousseau and other Enlightenment figures' ideas.

Andrew Janos, *Politics and Paradigms: Changing Theories of Change in the Social Sciences* (Stanford, CA: Stanford University Press, 1986). A brief but remarkable overview of the early social sciences.

Graham Faiella, *John Locke: Champion of Modern Democracy* (New York: Rosen, 2006). An introduction to Locke's ideas and their political and social context.

Harvey Mansfield Jr., *Student's Guide to Political Philosophy* (Wilmington, DE: ISI Books, 2001). A lively entry point into more political philosophy.

Max Weber, *The Protestant Ethic and the Spirit of Capitalism*, Richard Swedberg, ed. (New York: Norton, 2008[1904]). The classic is far more readable than you might expect.

Mary Dietz, ed., *Thomas Hobbes and Political Theory* (Lawrence: University of Kansas Press, 1990). A collection of essays that set Hobbes in the politics of his time.

Paul Oppenheimer, *Machiavelli: A Life beyond Ideology* (New York: Continuum, 2011). An engaging biography that relates Machiavelli's political philosophy to his remarkable life.

Plato, *The Republic*, 2nd ed., Trans. Desmond Lee (New York, NY: Penguin Books, 1987). Built around the amusing character of Socrates, Plato's dialogue in quasi-story form is surprisingly readable and hugely thought provoking.

Richard Rubenstein, *Aristotle's Children: How Christians, Muslims, and Jews Rediscovered Ancient Wisdom and Illuminated the Dark Ages* (New York: Houghton Mifflin Harcourt, 2004). An accessible discussion of the rediscovery of Greek ideas in the twelfth century and its wide political effects.

Roger Boesche, *The First Great Political Realist: Kautilya and His Arthashastra* (Lanham, MD: Lexington, 2002). A well-written presentation of Kautilya's brutal philosophy.

Sheldon Wolin, *Tocqueville between Two Worlds: The Making of a Political and Theoretical Life* (Princeton, NJ: Princeton University Press, 2001). A fascinating biography by a political theorist.

Develop Your Thinking

Use these questions as discussion or short writing exercises to think more deeply about some of the key themes of the chapter.

1. What would be some advantages and disadvantages of Plato's idea of a government run by "philosopher-kings"?

2. To paraphrase Machiavelli, do you think it is more important for political leaders to be widely respected than to be widely loved?

3. Do you generally think that markets reward everyone who makes an effort, or that markets tend to reward those who are already wealthy?

4. If you stepped into the shoes of a very different person—in another material and institutional position in the world—would you gradually come to act like that person?

5. What is more important for political leaders: having a clear grasp of how the world works, or having a clear vision for how the world should be?

Keywords

Chapter 3
Ideologies

At left, demonstrators use the "fascist" label to criticize Republican President Trump and his Vice President Michael Pence. At right, a 2010 poster denounces Democratic President Barack Obama as "socialist" (and a joker to boot).

 ## Learning Objectives

3.1 Define political knowledge, political culture, and political ideology.

3.2 Identify the main principles of classical liberalism, modern liberalism, and modern conservatism.

3.3 Identify the main principles of socialism and fascism.

3.4 Identify the main principles of environmentalism and political Islamism.

The Language and Boundaries of Political Life

"One person with a belief," wrote John Stuart Mill (1806–1873), "is a social power equal to ninety-nine who have only interests."[1] Real believers in a cause, he thought, are more driven than people who are just interested in acquiring more money, comfort, or power. In more recent history, a Facebook page cited Mill's line in an exaggerated way, making one believer equal to 100,000 people with "only interests." What gave force to the quote was the owner of the page: Anders Behring Brevik, whose warped version of Christian fundamentalism led him to terrorist attacks that killed 92 people in Norway on July 22, 2011.

We do not need to look to terrorists to see the importance of the packages of beliefs we call ideologies. They generate the language, behaviors, and boundaries of mainstream political life as well. For people who do not know the American vocabulary of conservatism (and the political "Right") and of liberalism (and the political "Left"), elections and everyday political discussions in the United States are incomprehensible. To make sense of the political scene we also need to understand more radical ideological ideas and language that define the legitimate limits of mainstream politics. When Republicans see Democrats becoming especially liberal, they denounce them as "socialists" (or even "communists"). Democrats retort that the most conservative Republicans should be seen as "fascists." In both cases these labels are invoked to signal that someone has moved beyond the bounds of acceptable politics in modern America.

Learning the language of major ideologies, then, is a prerequisite to understanding politics today. These packages of political beliefs provide the most crucial part of our menu for conscious political choice and direct our possible agendas for engaging in political thinking and action. By the end of this last of the introductory chapters to this book, you will have the basic ideological and explanatory tools to set out on our tour of the political world. ■

What Is (and Isn't) Ideology?

3.1 Define political knowledge, political culture, and political ideology.

Ideologies are packages of conscious beliefs about how politics works and how, normatively, it *should* work. Just as political scientists create analytic and normative hypotheses to explain and evaluate the political world, so people in everyday life draw on analytic and normative ideas to figure out how to act. Ideologies are the rough, guiding theories of real-world action.

It may not sound appealing to dig further into ideology, since "ideological" is sometimes used as an insult: "Those people are too ideological for us to work with!" But it makes more sense to complain about specific ideologies you dislike, rather than ideologies in general, because it is impossible to think coherently about politics without ideological commitments. We cannot engage with politics without first learning its language and developing our own ideological views. That is why a dose of clear thinking about ideology is so important.

Many people's political views are, in fact, semiconscious and incoherent because they have not thought carefully about ideology. They get by with a smattering of simple facts, fragmented thoughts, common assumptions, and popular practices that do not add up to conscious positions. To highlight the critical importance of ideology, let's first look at the elements of political views that are *not* ideology but that influence the choices that people make: political knowledge, public opinion, and political culture.

What Do You Know? Political Knowledge

Many things in politics are open to diverse ideological interpretations, but some are just facts. We cannot reasonably question or debate whether or not marijuana is legal in your state, the current level of your university tuition, or the political party to which your state's U.S. senators belong. These items of political knowledge are true regardless of one's ideology.

Knowledge of such facts is critical to effective political thinking. Ignorance of basic realities can lead to odd choices and make us vulnerable to manipulation. Unfortunately, most Americans' political knowledge is sketchy. Since modern **polling** (also known as surveys) began in the 1940s, the results consistently show the same kind of picture: a small segment of people, often called the **political elite**, have high levels of knowledge. A large middle of 50 to 60 percent can answer simple questions or track very recent events. The remainder knows very little beyond hard-to-avoid factoids like the name of the current president.

Let's focus on the largest group—those in the middle. Their political knowledge mostly consists of broad facts they catch from topics that are repeatedly in the news. For example, in 2017, a majority of Americans knew who was Speaker of the House (62 percent knew that it is Republican Paul Ryan at the time) or which country was trying to leave the European Union (60 percent knew that it was the United Kingdom).[2] Beyond hot topics or the simplest background questions, though, the middle and lower groups merge into a poorly informed majority. Less than half of Americans in 2017 could identify Neil Gorsuch as a Supreme Court justice, though his appointment in January of that year had been a huge news event. Only about a quarter (26 percent) could identify the three branches of the U.S. government (executive, legislative, judicial), and more than a third (37 percent) could not name a single one of the rights in the First Amendment to the U.S. Constitution (freedom of religion, speech, press, assembly, and petition for redress of grievances).[3] Even during the famously close and intense presidential contest of 2000 between Republican George W. Bush and Democrat Al Gore, barely half of voters could identify Bush with support for a large cut in income taxes—one of his signature positions.[4] What people do know is often trivial: during the presidency of George W. Bush's, George H.W. Bush, the single most widely known fact about the elder Bush was that he hated broccoli. When we move away from presidential candidates, awareness goes still lower. In poll after poll over time, a majority of citizens cannot name their states' Senators or their own current Representative in the House.

Political facts are crucial reference points for any sort of political thinking, then, but they are only the background to conscious and coherent ideological views, not a substitute for them. Table 3-1 offers some advice on how to raise your level of political knowledge (besides reading this book).

What Are You Expected to Think? Public Opinion and Political Culture

Whether or not people know political facts, they usually have opinions on some political subjects. We might expect that to have any opinion at all people would have to draw on some ideological views. Yet this is not necessarily true. Political opinions often have less conscious and coherent sources.

polling
Survey processes that pose questions to large numbers of people to identify patterns in their views.

political elite
People who are knowledgeable about politics, actively participate in it, and are well connected to powerful organizations or groups.

Table 3-1 Good Sources to Build Your Political Knowledge

Websites on American Politics	Best for . . .	Biases?
For information:		
Politico.com	Balanced tracking of every political story for political junkies	Originally created by *Washington Post* reporters; even-handed
Realclearpolitics.com	Similarly broad political coverage, especially on polling	Owners are openly conservative; content is largely neutral
Fivethirtyeight.com	Statistics on a wide range of political issues (and other subjects too)	Run by statistician Nate Silver, hosted by ESPN; very neutral
For fact-checking:		
Politifact.com	Site that fact-checks politicians' speeches and writing, including amusing "Truth-O-Meter"	Created by Florida journalists; generally neutral
Factcheck.org	Similar to Politifact	Run by University of Pennsylvania; generally neutral
For candidate positions:		
Ontheissues.org	Nonpartisan information on issues and politicians' views	Run by ex-journalists and volunteers; very neutral
Classic Journalism		
New York Times, nyt.com	Broad and detailed coverage of U.S. and international politics	Left-leaning
Wall Street Journal, wsj.com	Especially strong coverage of business and economic issues	Right-leaning
The Economist, economist.com	Pithy coverage of major issues in the United States and abroad	Right-leaning but views are very open, not hidden
Christian Science Monitor, csmonitor. com	Thoughtful, accessible coverage of U.S. and international issues	Very neutral and professional (don't be misled by "Christian Science" in its name)
International Data		
CIA World Factbook, cia.gov/library/ publications/the-world-factbook/	Up-to-date data on all countries	From the CIA, but very focused on providing technically accurate information
Indexmundi.com	Country-based data in accessible formats	Based mainly on CIA World Factbook
The World Bank, data.worldbank.org	Rich data on many issues by country and region	Run by very technically focused statisticians
Gapminder.com	Remarkable graphics you can create from worldwide data	Based mainly on World Bank data

Indeed, to add to the bleak picture of low political knowledge in the United States, the long-dominant view of American **public opinion** is that most citizens hold a messy smattering of political ideas. In an influential study of political surveys in the 1960s, political scientist Philip Converse argued that most people's political views are so fragmented that they are hardly committed to any meaningful ideology at all.[5] One visible sign of this incoherence is when people change responses to surveys or polls depending on the wording of questions. If we ask Americans if they support "assistance for the poor," for example, we see more "yes" answers than if we ask the same question but refer to "welfare

public opinion
The patterns of views across a population that can be identified by polling.

programs."[6] In the aftermath of a big financial crisis in 2009, the Gallup polling firm found that many more Americans supported "regulating Wall Street banks" than just "regulating large banks."[7] These questions are the same—welfare programs *are* assistance to the poor, and "Wall Street" is the New York address that symbolizes large banks—and the shift hints that many respondents are not thinking consciously about the substance of the questions. Instead they just have a gut reaction to certain words like "welfare" or "Wall Street."

political culture
Ways of acting, talking and thinking about political topics that people learn to expect as normal for people like them.

Even if people cannot say consciously why a word like "welfare" provokes a gut reaction, though, such responses are not just random. Behind many patterns in public opinion stands **political culture**: ways of talking, practices of acting, and sets of justifying stories about politics that people perceive as appropriate that people perceive as appropriate for people like them. Unlike conscious ideology, however, political culture suggests background assumptions, reference points, and perceptions of how to speak and act acceptably that are not consciously justified beliefs. Such cultural expectations are especially easy to see in comparisons across countries. For example, Americans are more likely than most other peoples to say that markets reward hard work and entrepreneurialism, and so the rich deserve their wealth and the poor their poverty. In one collection of older surveys before 2000, an average of 60 percent of Europeans thought that the poor are trapped in poverty, but only 29 percent of Americans agreed. Sixty percent of Americans said that the poor are lazy, versus 26 percent of Europeans.[8] In a more recent comparison, Americans rated the importance of government policies to "protect all citizens against poverty" roughly two points lower on a 10-point scale than Europeans.[9] Such responses are not necessarily rooted in conscious ideological beliefs: many Americans and Europeans might not be able to explain coherently why they view markets and wealth this way—and they might change their responses if we reword the question! But they have learned reflexively to discuss economic issues in certain terms, and to expect each other to voice certain positions, in ways that are different from similar discussions in other countries. Americans grow up in a context where markets are often praised as a founding and central part of what it means to be American, and they may reproduce this common language about American identity even without thinking much about it.

socialization
The processes in which people learn norms, practices, and ideas from others around them.

subcultures
Groups in society that identify and interact with each other, producing distinct clusters of culture not entirely shared by others.

Expectations and practices of political culture are passed on through social interaction. This process of **socialization** can be powerful in families and peer groups, who often create their own mixes and remixes of broader cultural practices. Even attending a certain university or living in a certain town can carry distinct expectations. The University of California at Berkeley, for instance, has a tradition of activism that creates subtle expectations about how students will act. Freshmen there may feel nudged toward activism in a way that the same students would never have considered at the University of Oklahoma. Differences in political expectations also arise in wider **subcultures**: interaction among people who identify with groups like African Americans, Christian fundamentalists, or Texans can carry political expectations. Though national-level political culture has received the most attention from political scientists, political culture may also operate at higher levels. Harvard Professor Samuel Huntington provocatively argued that the twenty-first century is bringing a "clash of civilizations" between Western civilization (the United States, Europe, and Latin America), Eastern civilization in Asia, Muslim civilization, African civilization, and Orthodox civilization centered on Russia.[10] Huntington's argument attracted many critics, but it is difficult to reject the plausibility of some distinctive expectations in political culture across these regions.

Much that we hear and think about politics in everyday life, then, is not quite "ideology." Factual knowledge is a key background element to political thinking. We all absorb semiconscious expectations in political culture that give us broad political reflexes, but not conscious reasons for certain choices. It is only when we engage with politics more explicitly to criticize, defend, craft, or implement a political agenda that we begin to adopt an ideology. When we do so, we invariably find ourselves drawing on some of the dominant ideological traditions that define the language of modern politics.

The Liberal Tradition

3.2 Identify the main principles of classical liberalism, modern liberalism, and modern conservatism.

The possibilities of ideology are limitless. People have invented extremely diverse (and sometimes bizarre) ways to think about politics. Yet few ideologies have major impact. History is littered with odd political beliefs that fail to give rise to large movements or legacies. Some ideologies that do become very influential, like the fascist ideology of Italian dictator Benito Mussolini and Nazi leader Adolf Hitler or the particular version of communist ideology developed in the Soviet Union, later largely disappear as active options. This is good news for students who are new to the study of politics: a small number of ideological packages define the dominant political concepts and language in our era. People in the twenty-first century are not limited to these inherited options—ideologies are not static and surely new ones will emerge—but familiarity with just a few ideological traditions allows us to decipher much of today's political world.

Among these major traditions, one stands out for its influence in shaping contemporary politics around the world: liberalism. Before American liberals rejoice at this news, though, they must realize that they reflect only one use of the word "liberal." The broad tradition of liberalism is particularly influential because it provides major sources of both the modern "Left" *and* of the modern conservative "Right." Practically all politicians in the United States, and many elsewhere in the world, adhere to variants of liberal ideology.

Helpfully, we have already encountered some foundations of liberalism in Chapter 2, so some points here will be familiar. Like a few other ideologies, liberalism has arisen both as a broadly powerful real-world ideology and, in a narrower and more analytic form, as an explanatory approach in political science.

Classical Liberalism and Modern Liberalism

In elections over the past several decades, Republicans have often sought to "slap the L-word" on Democratic candidates characterizing them as "tax-and-spend liberals."[11] They meant someone who favors active government programs on many issues—not just health care, but poverty, the environment, and so on—and high taxes to fund them. Emphasizing the "liberalism" of politicians like Massachusetts Senator Elizabeth Warren or past President Barack Obama was intended to make them less appealing to Americans who might be leery of taxation and government intervention in these areas. The notion that individual liberties should usually trump government intervention is, after all, a founding principle in U.S. politics.

Yet the odd language of that contrast—calling for a defense of economic *liberties* by opposing *liberals*—hints at a more complex relationship between liberalism and American politics. We might expect liberals to champion liberty; the words share the same root. Related words suggest this link: to "liberalize" an economy, for example, is to *decrease* active government intervention in it. In political science, we refer to "liberal rights" to mean "individual rights." The whole U.S. system of government is often called a "liberal democracy," meaning a combination of guaranteed individual rights and democratic elections. And Democrats surely see themselves as champions of liberty.

What, then, is "liberalism" about? It was originally built mainly around two principles: a defense of individual political liberties and advocacy of open markets. From these origins, however, debates over the meaning of liberty itself led to a split within the liberal tradition between "classical liberalism" and a variant known as modern (or "social") liberalism. To understand the uses of "liberal" in America and the world today, we must grasp both these core principles and the divide over how to interpret them.

PRINCIPLE 1: POLITICAL RIGHTS.   Liberalism first arose in early modern Europe, from the 1500s to the 1700s, as a series of calls for political liberties for all individuals. At the time, the **aristocracy** held special privileges, and nonaristocrats had few protections from arbitrary abuse. Of particular concern was religious oppression. Although the Protestant Reformation of the 1500s split the dominance of the Catholic Church into many Christian churches, people in the 1600s were still expected to adopt the religion of their ruler. Early liberals began to call for a separation of church and state to allow individuals freedom of religion.

John Locke (1632–1704) helped build these arguments into the foundations of liberal ideology. He began by rejecting aristocracy and arguing that people are naturally equal. He thought disagreements over issues like religion would always arise, though, and people would be tempted to infringe on other's liberties. The solution was for free individuals to agree on a social contract to create a government that guaranteed the **natural rights** of all. Where governments failed to do so—abusing one's inherent rights to "life, liberty, and property," including religious choice —people had a right to revolt to change the government.

aristocracy
A group of people, usually hereditary, with special legal status that gives them privileges not extended to others.

natural rights
The idea that people are endowed with certain rights simply by virtue of being human beings.

These were radical arguments at the time, but they soon bloomed into the "Age of Revolution" in the late eighteenth and early nineteenth centuries. The opening event of this new age, the American Revolution of 1776, was built on Locke. Revolutionary Thomas Paine (1737–1809) based his famous pamphlet *Common Sense* on the Lockean argument that government was a "necessary evil" that was worthwhile only as long as it protected natural rights. Thomas Jefferson (1743–1826) echoed these thoughts in the Declaration of Independence, calling it "self-evident" that "all men are created equal" and that governments derive "just powers from the consent of the governed." In 1789, the same ideas were central to the French Revolution that ended the absolute monarchy of Louis XVI, as expressed in the "Declaration of the Rights of Man and of the Citizen." Over time, liberal thinkers further emphasized that they sought not just protection from abuse, but also **representation**: beyond legal equality, citizens needed the right to select their leaders through electoral democracy. The classic liberal political recipe, then, came to be defined as liberal rights and elections, or "liberal democracy." This package of ideas continues to animate revolutions in our world today, like the "Arab Spring" uprisings of 2011–2012 across the Middle East or more recent protests in Hong Kong against pressures from the communist Chinese government.

representation
Processes in which people select others to speak for them in collective decision making.

PRINCIPLE 2: OPEN MARKETS.   Economic freedoms, too, were central to the classical liberal tradition. As Locke's inclusion of "property" as a natural right suggested, liberals saw freedom to own, buy, and sell things as one of the most fundamental rights. The centrality of economic rights to liberalism further increased with the publication of Adam Smith's *Wealth of Nations* in 1776 and the development of market economics. As we saw in Chapter 2, Smith argued that economic liberties were desirable not only as inherently good for individuals, but because freedom to exchange led to the most productive society at a collective level. Given free exchange in competitive markets, each person would produce whatever he or she was most efficient at producing, being encouraged by the lure of wealth and threatened by fear of poverty. Each individual would be incentivized to perfect his or her talents, and society overall would generate as much wealth as possible. Thus the classical liberal agenda included broad support for open markets alongside liberal democracy.

THE DIVIDE: "NEGATIVE LIBERTY" VERSUS "POSITIVE LIBERTY."   By the late 1800s, the full classical liberal agenda of rights, democracy, and open markets was dominant in some of the richest countries in the world: the United States, Britain, France, and several other European countries. Once they were dominant, though, liberals began to disagree about whether they had reached their goals or not. Some thought they had: aristocratic privileges were gone, democracy was operating, markets were unleashed, and these accomplishments should be defended. These liberals had now shifted to conserving the status quo—becoming, in effect, "conservatives." On the other hand, some liberals now suggested that liberalism's victories had exposed more work to be done. British philosopher T.H. Green (1836–1882)

negative liberty

A conception of freedom centered on protection from abuse or restraint— on what should *not* be done to citizens.

positive liberty

A conception of liberty centered on the capacity and opportunity to develop one's talents—on what citizens should be empowered to do.

and other champions of "modern liberalism" (also known as "social liberalism") argued that the liberal program thus far had established only **negative liberty**, or freedom from abuse or restraint (and, moreover, mainly only for white men). They saw the real goal of liberalism as **positive liberty**: the capacity to develop one's talents and pursue opportunities. Poverty, a lack of education or health care, various kinds of discrimination, or other social problems might prevent some people from succeeding if they were left on their own; they were in such disadvantageous positions that they could never compete successfully. If the first phase of liberalism had limited abusive governments, modern liberals argued for a second phase of more active, supportive government to build a society of liberty. They called for programs like public education, health care, unemployment insurance, and old-age pensions for the poor, and supported taxing richer citizens to fund these undertakings. These modern liberals also tended to advocate liberties for less traditional ways of life— unmarried mothers, interracial marriage, and eventually homosexuality—which they saw as part of extending meaningful liberty for all.

This debate between variants of liberal ideology remains central today wherever the classical liberal agenda of rights, democracy, and markets became dominant: the United States, Europe, Japan, most of Latin America, and other

President Franklin Delano Roosevelt, one of the architects of modern liberalism in the United States, visits a Civilian Conservation Corps camp in 1933. The CCC created jobs for millions of unemployed young men to work on public projects during the Great Depression, symbolizing government action to help poorer citizens in tough times.

"liberal democracies." In these societies, a defense of negative liberties and deregulated markets now tends to be seen as part of the conservatism. A focus on active government in search of positive liberty is seen as the opposite of conservatism. Only in the United States, though, has the term "liberal" become attached to the "modern liberal" meaning of a government that actively supports social change. Americans began identifying "liberal" with the rise of a more active government under the "New Deal" of President Franklin Delano Roosevelt in the 1930s and later during the creation of a **welfare state** of social spending under President Lyndon Johnson in the 1960s. Opponents of these steps defended a more limited government and became identified as "conservative." Today, politicians in the Democratic Party are often described as liberal because they see a variety of government programs as important to help the disadvantaged. The traditional agenda of the Republican Party has been closer to that of classic liberals, seeking to cut back government programs and taxes, but they are called conservatives.

The rest of the world, by contrast, has largely continued to use "liberal" to mean classic liberalism. Outside the United States, liberalism is often a *synonym* of conservatism rather than its opposite. If members of College Democrats from an American university visited similar campuses in Australia, for example, they might be confused to find "Young Liberal" clubs in Melbourne or Sydney who represent Australian political *conservatism* and have a formal relationship with the American College Republicans! In addition to the Australian Liberal Party, there are political parties known as "liberals" in Germany, Belgium, or many other countries, all of which are opponents of government activism and champions of markets who are strongly tied to business. "**Neoliberalism**" is also the term used worldwide for the renewed movement for open markets and limited government that began in the 1970s, symbolized by British prime minister (and leader of the British *Conservative* Party) Margaret Thatcher and by the celebrated Republican President Ronald Reagan in the United States. As confusing as this use of terms can be for Americans, it makes sense in historical perspective. The ideology of liberalism defined our liberal-democratic system so powerfully that both the major political parties today are its descendants.

Fortunately, there is a parallel vocabulary that has worked somewhat more similarly across both the U.S. context and other countries since the nineteenth century: "**left**" for proponents of more social reform and "**right**" for its opponents. These labels first formed during the French Revolution. When the French National Assembly met in 1789 to consider reform, the most radical revolutionaries sat on the left of the speaker addressing the assembly. Those who wished to conserve more of the old system—conservatives, at least relatively speaking—sat on the speaker's right. Today, we use "left" and "right" as the most common identifier of political ideologies in democracies with "left" roughly meaning a continued push to extend political and social rights for all and "right" roughly meaning a conservative defense of norms and laws that are perceived as more traditional and established. American "liberals" would not be called "liberals"

welfare state
The set of policies that redistribute wealth from rich to poor in market-capitalist systems.

neoliberalism
A political movement since the 1970s to decrease active government intervention in market economies.

left
In politics, progressive groups that advocate social and political reform, usually through government action, to improve society.

right
In politics, conservative groups that seek to defend current or past political and social practices.

in Europe, but people from both places would recognize them as representing the "Left." American "conservatives" would often be called "liberals" in Europe, but people from both places would recognize them as representing the "Right."

Modern Conservatism and Its Variants

The first element of modern conservatism is clear from the preceding section: most conservatives today in the United States and other liberal democracies draw heavily on classical liberalism. But contemporary conservatism also has other sources of its own, as well as divisions among its variants. The most common version of modern conservatism combines themes of classical liberalism with arguments about the wisdom of emphasizing tradition, authority, and experience in political decision making. Some members of the conservative family also see religious revelation as a key source of conservative values. Today's variants mix these principles in different ways. The "religious Right" places especially strong emphasis on religiously founded concerns. "Libertarians" stick most closely to classical liberalism. As of 2016, President Donald Trump advanced a new mix that was very successful in political terms—it came to dominate the Republican Party—but also very contested in its labeling. Trump's strongest supporters described him as an especially devout conservative. Others insisted that he had left conservative principles behind.

PRINCIPLE 1: CLASSICAL LIBERALISM. The Republican politicians in recent history who have been seen as ideological leaders of conservatism, like

Maurice Savage/Alamy Stock Photo

The British *Daily Mail*'s coverage of the death of Margaret Thatcher, April 8, 2013. Known as the "Iron Lady" for her unapologetic conservatism, Thatcher remains a powerful symbol of the "neoliberal" movement for smaller government and less regulated markets.

Wisconsin Congressman Paul Ryan (Speaker of the House of Representatives from 2015 to 2018), present themselves above all as champions of limited government, low taxes, open markets, and economic liberty. One of their heroes is President Ronald Reagan (1911–2004), who sought to lower taxes and cut government spending (except in defense). Like his good friend Margaret Thatcher, Reagan was a proponent of liberalization and neoliberalism, calling effectively for a return to the classical liberal principles that defined the United States in the nineteenth century.

Classically conservative advocates of "small government" believe that cutting taxes and government programs is good even for the most disadvantaged people. Part of this belief is simply the view that the U.S. system, like other liberal democracies, is so open and equal that government does not need to intervene to provide "positive liberty." Groups some might call disadvantaged—the poor, women, racial minorities, gays and lesbians—enjoy adequate equality of opportunity, and it is up to individuals to succeed. Conservatives also tend to believe that even if some people *did* suffer from disadvantages, it could be counterproductive to help them with government programs. Part of Adam Smith's logic about efficient markets is that people improve themselves when incentivized by both the lure of wealth *and* the fear of poverty; helping people with government support softens the consequences of failure and can make them dependent on handouts. Addressing social ills through government programs may also have other unintended consequences that can be as bad as the problems they seek to solve. Taxing the rich to help the poor may seem generous, for example, but not only may the poor become dependent on support, the highly taxed rich may see less incentive to work hard and invest, leading to fewer jobs and fewer opportunities for poor people.

For all of these reasons, the people today who most clearly claim the conservative label are those who hold classical liberal views: if government seeks only to guarantee a clear framework of negative liberties, then individuals will be free to make the most of their lives. We must resist the temptation to intervene more actively, because even the best-intentioned interventions in markets and society skew individuals' incentives and generally do not deliver net gains.

PRINCIPLE 2: TRADITION, EXPERIENCE, AND AUTHORITY OVER RADICAL CHANGE. Classical liberalism is not the only source of conservatives' skepticism about active government. Indeed, conservatism has its own founder who sounded this theme. The British politician Edmund Burke (1729–1797) is often known as the "father of modern conservatism" for his sophisticated opposition to radical political change.

Burke was a member of the House of Commons in the British Parliament during the French Revolution in 1789. While some of his peers celebrated the fall of the French kings, Burke warned in *Reflections on the Revolution in France* (1790) that the revolutionaries' plans to reshape French society would lead to chaos. Yet he was not simply an old, aristocratic thinker who thought that kings and aristocrats deserved to keep their special privileges and power, or that individual rights were illegitimate. Instead, his core point was that society could be governed well only by tried-and-true experience. For Burke, all societies depend on experience and tradition to preserve order. People are imperfect by nature—weak and often wicked—and any revolutionary plan to leap to a new society, with untried concepts and inexperienced leaders, will soon be corrupted and succumb to unintended consequences. Only the most incremental reforms, tested carefully against past practice, can improve society. Burke did think that an aristocracy is the best form of government, but not because aristocrats inherently deserved special status. He thought aristocracies worked well because they created a class of people who were raised and trained to lead, gained leadership experience, and were wealthy enough to focus on broad social problems rather than their own welfare. Overall, Burke's conservatism emphasized respect for authority and tradition to preserve social order.

When revolutionary France fell into the chaos known as "the Terror" in 1793, under the radical regime of Maximilien Robespierre (1758–1794), many thought Burke's predictions were vindicated. Although no conservative today argues for an aristocracy, Burke's analysis of human nature and political change has influenced politics over the centuries. For many American conservatives, the notion that we might use government to reform health care, combat global warming, improve public transportation, or win greater rights and recognition for gays and lesbians seems as risky as the French attempt to establish a new society in the 1790s. Engineering social change through politics, even if well intentioned, does not respect the realities of human nature and society. Not only should we hold on to authority and social traditions, but we must also be wary of government action to "solve" problems like racial discrimination or environmental degradation. Though strong environmental regulations or "Affirmative Action" hiring preferences for minorities may mean well, the cumbersome bureaucracy of government will have difficulty implementing them without creating even more unfairness and policy problems.

CONSERVATIVE DIVIDES: RELIGION AND NATIONALISM. For many modern conservatives, but not all, their ideology has other pillars as well. Besides seeking to "conserve" a classical liberal status quo and mistrusting plans to engineer social change, some conservatives add a third theme of religious revelation. A historically important statement of this view came from another reaction to the French Revolution, by the Count Joseph de Maistre (1753–1821). For de Maistre, the Revolution had destroyed "throne and altar"—the king and the Church—in the name of "progress." The revolutionaries were mistaken, however, in thinking that human beings had the wisdom to recraft society without God's guidance. In the centuries since, religious Christians have tended to identify with conservatism out of distrust for social change based in human-made, secular plans for a better society. Other religions often support similar ties: religious Jews in Israel or religious Muslims in Turkey also tend to be politically conservative. But if religiosity often bolsters other aspects of conservatism, it sometimes does not fit perfectly with its other principles. When conservatives ask government to enforce religiously inspired norms, like opposition to abortion, they break with the limited-government spirit of classic liberalism. In this area, they want government to tell people how to behave.

Today, the "religious Right" is a major part of American conservatism. Many Americans see the Christian faith as generally opposed to abortion, gay marriage, and non-traditional sexuality or lifestyles. Especially important to their political agenda in recent years has been the appointment of judges with similar views, to head off more expansive legal interpretations of liberal rights. They have increasingly shaped Republican Party platforms ever since the leadership of Reagan, who was a key figure in combining religious-Right views with classical-liberal support for markets and limited government into a distinctive brand of conservative ideology.

In most other liberal democracies, however, conservatives focus much less on religion. Indeed, among the world's wealthy democratic countries, the United States is by far the most religious. A recent run of Pew Research Center surveys found that 53 percent of Americans said that religion was very important in their lives, compared to 11 percent in France, 10 percent in Britain, or 10 percent in Japan.[12] While the British Conservative Party is among the parties most similar to the U.S. Republicans in many respects, it is built much more on classical liberalism and Burkean traditionalism, with only a small voice for Christian values.

On the other hand, some conservatives in the United States and abroad put less emphasis on religion and stick more closely to classical-liberal views. In American politics they are known as **libertarians**. Their leading spokespeople seek the most limited possible government in all policy areas. One clear example was a Texan politician, Ron Paul, who ran several times for president. In addition to hard-line positions on limiting most government powers—like abolishing federal income tax and the U.S. Federal Reserve Bank and ending most foreign involvements, including membership in the United Nations and the NATO alliance—he long supported liberties on social issues, such as abortion rights and legalization of drugs, that religious, socially conservative Republicans opposed. A somewhat more moderate example today is William Weld, the ex-Governor of Massachusetts.

libertarianism
The strand of conservative ideology that remains the most focused on classical liberal themes of limited government and individual rights.

The other theme that both inspires and divides the conservative tradition today is **nationalism**. Nationalism is a political agenda that seeks to empower members of a perceived nation, often with special emphasis on its ethnic or racial majority. With Donald Trump's rise it became more prominent than ever in American conservatism. His main campaign slogan, "Make America Great Again," evoked for his supporters a pride in their nation's past and a call to

nationalism
An agenda that seeks political power and control for the members of a perceived cultural group.

assert American power unapologetically in the future. In endorsing Burkean or religious defenses of social traditions, many conservatives feel that they are also defending a positive narrative about their people against critics and outsiders. Unsurprisingly, this celebration of "us" tends to come with skeptical views of "them." It usually carries an image of a threatening world that requires robust national security and well-policed borders. It resonates most with demographic majorities—in the U.S. context, white people of European descent—and raises questions from minorities or more recent immigrants who can seem excluded from the imagined "us."

Like religion, however, nationalism generates tensions with modern conservatives' classical-liberal inheritance. Classical liberalism is a doctrine of openness, favoring the free flow of trade and people. It favors individual liberties over collective identity and values tolerance of differences. The contradictions are clearest on foreign economic policy and immigration. The most nationalist conservatives tend to be skeptical of classical-liberal support for wide-open international markets. Trump has radically revised longstanding Republican positions on trade, shifting a party that championed free-trade agreements to one that opposes them. On immigration, where Republicans have long been split between pro-openness and anti-immigration voices, Trump's presidency represents the victory of the latter. More classically liberal-minded conservatives have also been troubled by Trump's racist characterization of Latino immigrants as "rapists and murderers," and his unwillingness to reject ties to "white nationalist" racist groups.

These are not small changes to Republican positions since 2016—to the point that some conservatives argue that the party under Trump has left its conservative tradition behind. As conservative pundit Bill Kristol wrote in 2018, "The principles of sound conservatism compel us to criticize him, to rebut him, to resist him, and to plan to overcome him."[13] Not only has Trump opposed international openness, these critics note, he has ignored an old Republican emphasis on limited and balanced government budgets—creating a huge budget deficit by increasing spending while cutting taxes. It is also hard to see how Trump represents social-conservative or religious values, given his record of extra-marital affairs and unmistakable challenges with truthfulness.[14] Other questions surround his running fight with traditional American law-and-order institutions that conservatives usually revere, like the CIA and the FBI, and his seemingly dismissive views of the rule of law in general. On the other hand, many people who identify as conservative see much to appreciate in Trump's overall record. He has cut taxes, loosened federal regulations, appointed two unambiguously conservative justices to the Supreme Court, dismissed the idea of government action against climate change, and championed a stronger military. For these supporters, "Trumpism" is a nationalism-led improvement on conservatism, not

Table 3-2 Conservative Divisions, Ronald Reagan and Donald Trump

Conservative Themes	Libertarian	Religious Right	Ronald Reagan	Donald Trump
Limited government in economy				
Minimize regulation	★	≈	★	★
Lower taxes	★	≈	★	★
Limit spending	★	≈	★	⊘
Open trade	★	≈	★	⊘
Traditional values				
Limit abortion	⊘	★	★	★
Oppose same-sex marriage	⊘	★	★	★
Appoint traditional-value judges	⊘	★	★	★
National security and majority identity				
Prioritize national defense	≈	≈	★	★
Minimize immigration	⊘	≈	⊘	★
Oppose affirmative action	★	≈	★	★

★ Priority ≈ Less concerned ⊘ opposed.

a rejection of it. Table 3-2 illustrates some of these variants of the conservative tradition, including a comparison of Ronald Reagan and Donald Trump.

In a variety of mixes, then, conservative ideology today is founded on the negative liberties of classical liberalism and the free market, attachment to experience and tradition, religiously informed values, and nationalism. Working from these bases, conservatives try to "conserve" (and promote) a certain vision of politics and society.

Classical liberalism, modern liberalism, Burkean conservatism, the religious Right, libertarianism, "Trumpism": these concepts and terms within the broad liberal tradition allow us to grasp the main lines of mainstream politics in the United States and many other liberal democracies today. Check out your command of them by matching these sentences with the right label:

- It is only right and proper that each nation looks out for itself in a dangerous world, and avoids a naïve kind of openness that makes it vulnerable to unfair competition and abuse by others.

- On basic social values, human beings must rely on the guidance of religion, which may sometimes trump arguments for diversity and individual choice.

- Attempts to redesign politics and society too ambitiously often go wrong, so governance should stick closely to traditional wisdom and experience.

- Equality of opportunity exists only when all citizens have enough resources and opportunities to realize their potential.

- The best society is one in which government activities are kept at the minimal level necessary to ensure basic security, law and order, and protect negative liberties.

Hopefully you can see that the first sentence summarizes a key view of Trumpism, the second fits the religious Right, the third evokes Burkean thinking, the fourth captures modern liberalism, and the fifth one is a bit of a trick: it can be called both libertarianism and classical liberalism, since these are basically the same thing. Figure 3-1 offers a graphic illustration of the branchings of the liberal tradition.

Figure 3-1 Branchings and Combinations in the Liberal Tradition

Classical liberalism branched into the positive-liberty-based ideology of modern liberalism and the negative-liberty-based ideology of modern conservatism, and the latter also combined in various mixes with Burkean conservatism and religious revelation.

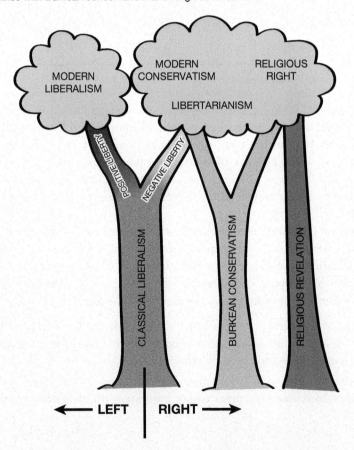

Older Alternatives to the Liberal Tradition: Socialism and Fascism

3.3 **Identify the main principles of socialism and fascism.**

The ideological labels "liberal" and "conservative" dominate American politics today and play a major role in most political arenas around the world. In the United States we are less accustomed to meeting socialists or fascists, partly for reasons that might seem obvious in light of a bit of world history. Fascism was the ideology of the losers of World War II—the German Nazis, Italian Fascists, and to some degree the Japanese military dictatorship—and few people have openly championed it since. A variant of socialism was the ideology of the Union of Socialist Soviet Republics (USSR), and it weakened when the USSR collapsed in 1992.

Yet fascism and socialism are still with us in several ways. The most common way in which an American encounters them is when politicians of Right or Left call each other "socialist" or "fascist" to suggest that their rivals have become too extreme. At the Conservative Political Action Conference (CPAC) in 2019, President Trump warned of a "socialist nightmare" if Democrats were to gain control of the government. "Fascist" is used less—its association with the Nazi Holocaust makes it very strong language indeed—but media and political commentary have increasingly used the word to warn that Trump has gone beyond the pale.[15]

Second, these labels may go beyond name-calling for a few American figures today. As American politics has become more polarized—with fewer centrist politicians and more prominent individuals toward the extremes—some political voices have come closer to real overlap with socialist or fascist positions. Trump's senior advisor in his 2016 campaign, Steve Bannon, openly admires Italian fascist leader Mussolini. Leading Left-wing Democrats like Vermont Senator Bernie Sanders or New York Representative Alexandria Ocasio-Cortez call themselves "democratic socialists."

Third, in other countries, socialists remain powerful. An odd, heavily stretched version of socialism is still the official ideology of China, Vietnam, and Cuba. In many democratic countries, especially in Europe and Latin America, socialist political parties are the major representatives of the Left in elections. People who call themselves fascists are harder to find, but European political parties of the "radical Right" echo fascist views. To understand the boundaries and extremes of American politics, to see ideologies in the rest of the world, and to appreciate ideology in history, we must consider socialism and fascism.

Socialism and Its Variants

The uses of "socialism" are not quite as complex as those of liberalism or conservatism, but socialism, too, has variants that share some basic principles but interpret them somewhat differently. Every kind of socialist ideology criticizes liberalism's view of markets and capitalism, emphasizing that "free markets" lead to unacceptable inequalities and conflict between rich and poor. What the variants of socialism disagree about is how to best resolve the conflicts that result from "free markets": is the path to a better society through revolution or peaceful reform?

PRINCIPLE 1: A CRITIQUE OF MARKETS AND CAPITALISM. At the core of socialist ideology is the notion that free-market economies cause unacceptable inequality. Markets tend to keep the rich rich and the poor poor. To redress inequality and create a just society, we must look to systems of government that somehow prioritize equality. The writings of Karl Marx (1818–1883) provided the most influential logic behind this thinking. Writing during the Industrial Revolution, Marx saw **capitalism** as generating both immense wealth for business owners and deepening poverty for workers. Capitalism, strictly defined, is a certain process within a system of private property and free markets: it exists when owners of "capital"—money—make more money not by being productive themselves, but by investing their money in activities in which other people do the work. In other words, the rich make money because they are already rich, while others work. If workers do all the productive work, Marx reasoned, the capitalists' profit must come from **exploitation** of workers, or paying them less than their work is worth. Exploitation would end, he thought, only if the system of ownership did not skim money off the workers. Therefore capitalism and private property had to be replaced by a socialist system, in which government would own and manage all production and investment.

capitalism
The making of money (or "capital") through ownership or investment in a profit-making enterprise.

exploitation
Paying workers less than their labor is worth.

PRINCIPLE 2: ECONOMIC CLASS CONFLICT. Marx's analysis suggested that any individual's chance for a good life in a market economy depends on whether he or she is born into a rich family or a poor one. Market economies are set up to increase the wealth of the "capitalist class" (also known as the bourgeoisie); their children get every advantage and later become capitalists themselves. On the other hand, the "working class" (or proletariat) is constantly exploited. These children grow up in poverty and have difficulty becoming well educated, starting a business, or otherwise ending up better off than their parents. If poor people attempt to demand more pay or change the system, moreover, the capitalists typically use their wealth to buy violent coercion, bringing in government and the police to keep order. More than anything else, then, a person's fate is tied to his or her position on one side or the other of this divide, so class conflict dominates society and politics. Other issues like religion, culture or foreign relations are less important, and just distract from the central class conflict.

THE DIVIDE: COMMUNISM (OR STATE SOCIALISM) VERSUS SOCIAL DEMOCRACY. Socialism's main divide emerged between communists who espoused revolution and social democrats who advocated reform. For Marx's most committed followers, the political agenda was clear: revolution against capitalism was the only way to improve the lives of most people in society. This revolutionary program eventually became known as **communism**, and scored its first major victory when Vladimir Lenin (1870–1924) led the Russian Revolution in 1917 and established the USSR. Many communist parties in the rest of the world created relationships with the new Soviet regime and set the goal of similar revolutions elsewhere. Notable successful takeovers later occurred in China, Vietnam, and Cuba.

It is debatable, however, how well "communist" described the government of the USSR or its related regimes. They certainly abolished capitalism, with government taking over the entire economy. But some advocates of communism maintained that their ideology called for the creation of small, local "communes" of shared living, not a huge, centralized, government-run system. They argued that even if a centralized government-run economy could, in principle, have made sense within communism, all these regimes quickly lost any clear focus on using their control of the economy to deliver equality for all citizens. Instead they became dictatorial governments that mostly served to enrich and defend the political power of members of their ruling Communist Party. Under the brutal leadership of Joseph Stalin (1878–1953) after 1924, the Soviets killed millions of their own citizens.[16] Even more people died from starvation and punitive work camps under the leadership of Mao Zedong (1893–1976) in China.[17] Because these regimes did not clearly attempt to enact the ideals of communism, a better label for their system is **state socialism**. Both countries featured a hugely dominant state that operated in the name (but often only the name) of socialist goals, and claimed the label of "communism" to suggest that this concentration of power served the common people.

As the brutal state-socialist regimes made the aggressive language of communism seem less appealing, many people who found Marx inspiring opted not to become outright revolutionaries. Such thinkers argued that socialist goals should be pursued not by Soviet-style violent revolution, but by building workers' unions and political parties with "ballots, not bullets." They thought either that capitalism could be abolished by a gradual path of reform, or that modifying capitalism—rather than destroying it entirely—was all that was needed. The groups these thinkers created were sometimes known simply as socialists, like the Socialist Party of France or Spain, but more commonly as advocates of **social democracy**, like the Social Democratic Party of Germany or Sweden. Working within liberal democracy and capitalism, these parties' most distinctively socialist goal was **nationalization** of parts of the economy: transferring major industries to government ownership. If the government ran big industries, they reasoned, better compromises could be struck between pursuing productivity and treating workers well. They also sought to improve the lot of workers by encouraging unions, boosting wages, and developing welfare state programs that redistributed money from the rich to the poor.

communism
The radical version of socialism that calls for revolutionary rejection of capitalism and private property.

state socialism
Political systems run by communist parties that abolished capitalism but then focused far more on enforcing their own power than on improving their citizens' welfare.

social democracy
The reformist version of socialism that aimed at winning democratic elections and implementing policies to moderate capitalism's inequalities.

nationalization
The shift of businesses from private ownership to public ownership under the government.

Today, Socialists or Social Democrats remain the main representatives of the Left in most European countries and in much of the rest of the world. Over time, most have become more moderate in reaction to economic challenges of global competition and to the fall or reform of state socialism in Russia and China. Although nationalization was the most distinctive goal of earlier socialist ideology, socialist or social democratic parties in France, Spain, Britain, Sweden, and other countries have now dropped it from their agendas. In this way, they have converged with modern liberals, who advocate a similar kind of active government within capitalism and markets but have never supported major nationalizations. Typically, Socialists and Social Democrats still critique capitalism more than modern liberals do, usually using stronger language that highlights class conflict and favors support for workers more than the liberal discourse of Democrats in the United States. But in recent decades, European Socialists overall have converged on modern liberalism far more than American Democrats have moved toward socialism.

That said, the Left edge of American politics has also moved in a social-democratic direction. Democrats' concerns about rising inequality have led to proposals for stronger forms of government action to address it. Senator Bernie Sanders' campaigns for the 2016 and 2020 Democratic presidential nominations advanced "democratic socialist" proposals for universal health care, free higher education, and regulation of big banks and corporations, attracting more support than similar ideas had for generations. In 2019, a newly elected Left-wing firebrand from New York, 29-year-old Latina Representative Alexandria Ocasio-Cortez, partnered with Senator Ed Markey of Massachusetts to propose major action against inequality and climate change in a "Green New Deal." Their rhetoric remained mostly in a modern-liberal line—evoking FDR's New Deal from the 1930s alongside a call to shift fully to renewable energy sources—but also openly drew inspiration from social democracy. Ocasio-Cortez argues that similar policies have "already been successful in many different models, from Finland to Canada to the UK." Dismissing President Trump's characterization of the Green New Deal as a "socialist nightmare," she insists it is about "establishing basic levels of dignity" in American society, adding, "That's what democratic socialism means in 2018."[18]

Fascism

While socialist ideology flowed from Marx's systematic philosophy, fascist ideology had no such source. As Benito Mussolini (1883–1945) crafted the first fascist movement and rose to overtake Italy in the 1920s, his ideas often seemed to reject nearly everything—liberalism, socialism, capitalism— with little coherence. The same was true of Adolf Hitler (1889–1945), who assembled the fascist-inspired Nazi Party in Germany around rantings against a host of enemies that included not only Jews, other minorities, and homosexuals but communists, socialists, big capitalism, and liberals. As hard as it is to find tightly systematic logic in fascist thinking, its agenda reflected a set of three distinctive principles: nationalism and national purity, power and authority, and defense of the "little guy."

PRINCIPLE 1: ULTRA-NATIONALISM AND NATIONAL PURITY. Fascism arose in Europe in the early 1900s, when classical liberalism became increasingly dominant and socialism was also prominent. Those ideologies of the Age of Revolution offered visions of social modernization and progress: liberalism proposed that people would live happily if they had individual rights and liberties, and socialism proposed that people would live well if they rose up to end economic exploitation. Yet not everyone was comfortable with progress. The modern, rational agendas treated everyone equally as "individuals" or "workers," neglecting tradition and history and leaving people without a distinct place or identity. A more meaningful framework for politics, some suggested, was to replace individualism with especially strong commitments to nationalism. Rather than aspiring to be free-and-equal individuals, people should engage in politics as part of a distinct, powerful, similar group of people linked by history and culture who act together for their national purposes. Rich narratives about the pride and distinctiveness of Italians, French, Germans, and other peoples were easy to construct and propagate. In many cases, these identities were actually *newly* constructed—Italy and Germany did not coalesce into countries until the late 1800s, and even the older state of France took centuries to assimilate its regions into a French identity—but nationalists usually talked as if their peoples had been united forever. With this strong emphasis on cultural identity came a strong focus on excluding nonmembers in the name of national purity, blaming problems on perceived outsiders, like Jews or immigrants.

Not all nationalism is related to fascism, as we have seen with respect to conservatism, but the fascists took nationalism to an unprecedented level. For Mussolini and Hitler, service to the homeland was the core guiding principle of politics. All outsiders or deviants deserved exclusion or even extermination. The Nazis went furthest, extending nationalism into an intense racism in which the German "Aryan master race" was destined to dominate others. These ideas produced the Holocaust, in which 6 million Jews and other "inferior" groups were systematically massacred from 1941 to 1945.

PRINCIPLE 2: FINDING MEANING IN POWER AND AUTHORITY. The service that fascists imagined providing to their homeland was not quietly building a pleasant and peaceful place to live. Part of the fascist rejection of modern rationality was a deliberately irrational call to exercise violent power. Fascists especially belittled the classical liberal vision and suggested that free individuals accomplished little on their own. They believed that the competitive elections of democracy created a weak, divisive political system. In its place, they

will to power

The philosopher Friedrich Nietzsche's phrase for a supposedly universal human need to assert and exercise power.

advocated what the philosopher Friedrich Nietzsche (1844–1900) called the **will to power**. Fascists argued that meaning in human life came from being part of a powerful, dominant nation united behind a heroic absolute leader to rule its own destiny. They also took a conservative respect for authority to an extreme. "The truth is that men are tired of liberty," said Mussolini, and he offered the slogan *credere, obbedire, combattere*: "believe, obey, fight." Hitler made clear that he totally rejected the whole line of "progress" that followed from the Age of Revolution: "If today I stand here as a revolutionary," he said, "it is as a revolutionary against the Revolution." In Italy and Germany respectively, both built regimes in which all resources were directed toward the military power and prestige of the state.

PRINCIPLE 3: DEFENDING MYTHICAL SMALL-TOWN LIFE.   It may seem contradictory that in an ideology that assigned all power to government and dismissed individual rights, fascists also viewed their agenda as a defense of the "little guy." Fascists imagined Italian or German villagers as defending a traditional, homogeneous, respectable life against outside forces. They hated classical liberals for upending the norms of traditional life in favor of rights, as well as for championing free markets and big business that threatened small business with competition. These fascists identified with the working man—and "Nazi" even stood for National Socialist Workers Party—but they also hated socialists (and especially communists) for seeking to disrupt traditional life and reshape the economy. They detested intellectuals who were part of a cosmopolitan elite. They despised diversity of any sort that threatened their idealized society. This image of defending small-town traditionalism fit uneasily with a government that invaded all aspects of life and launched total wars that disrupted all of society. But this was their belief. Only with total war and dominance could they protect their culture and compatriots.

Defeat in World War II and the Holocaust profoundly de-legitimated fascism around the world. The Nazis became the world's most recognizable symbol of evil. Even though few openly call themselves fascist today, this ideology remains active to some degree, and has undeniably become more present in the past decade. Far-right European parties like the National Front in France focus on strongly racialized national identity, exclusion of immigrants, and criticism of both socialists and big business. Alessandra Mussolini, the dictator's granddaughter, has led an Italian party that many describe as "neo-fascist." Critics of President Trump suggest that his emphasis on American "greatness," frequent dismissals of expertise and legal limits, use of clearly racist language against immigrants, and self-image as a champion of everyday "little guys" locates his political style on the edges of this space as well. Figure 3-2 illustrates the relationships between these ideological views.

Figure 3-2 The Old Alternatives to Either Side of the Liberal Tradition

Socialism and fascism define the limits of ideologies within the liberal tradition. On the left, the reformist branch of socialism moved closer to the United States' version of modern liberalism in the late twentieth century. On the right, fascism remains so illegitimate in Western democracies that no major political figures endorse it explicitly.

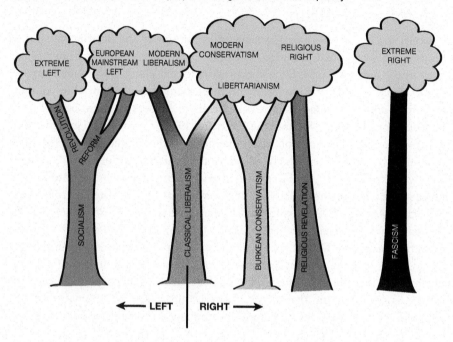

Newer Alternatives to the Liberal Tradition: Environmentalism and Islamism

3.4 **Identify the main principles of environmentalism and political Islamism.**

Old contests between liberals, conservatives, socialists, and fascists still powerfully shape our arguments and labels in politics today, but ideology is always changing. Just within their lifetime, people alive today can remember many new ideological agendas becoming politically salient: feminism, environmentalism, the African American movement of black liberation, and the pursuit of gay rights, to name a few. Recent decades are notable for religious revivals, including the emergence of a newly self-conscious political ideology of Islamism in Muslim countries. All of these newer ideologies have contributed to contemporary politics. Here, we consider two with especially broad and impactful resonance: environmentalism and Islamism. Both are also notable because they have especially distinct foundations. While feminism, black liberation, and gay rights are often seen as offshoots of the rights agenda of modern liberalism, environmentalism and Islamism spring from other sources entirely.

Environmentalism

Concern for the natural environment and criticism of the destructive side of human endeavors, like pollution, has been common in many societies as far back as the ancient world. Such concerns increased along with human capacities to impact the natural environment. In particular, the Industrial Revolution in Europe and the United States evoked calls to conserve natural beauty from rapacious humankind. Not until the 1960s and 1970s, however, did environmentalism emerge as a major political movement. In the United States—the most consumptive society ever, which today absorbs a quarter of global goods and energy with 4 percent of global population—environmentalism broke onto the political scene with the first Earth Day demonstrations in 1970. The Environmental Protection Agency (EPA) was formed in the same year. In Europe, the environmental movement went further, creating substantial political parties in many countries known as "Greens" or "Ecologists." The point of departure for the ideology they created is an attack on the narrow view of life in dominant political ideologies and a call to set human life in a broader natural context. Our natural context is so important, they argue, that we must take precautionary steps to maintain (or restore) its health before environmental problems become severe.

PRINCIPLE 1: VALUE QUALITY OF LIFE IN A BROAD CONTEXT. Environmentalists object to what they see as other ideologies' thin, human-centric and economic-centric conception of the good life. Liberalism, the most influential ideology, treated nature as largely irrelevant compared to individual freedom. Locke's *Second Treatise on Government* suggested that unless land is improved by humans, it is a "waste" that is worth "little more than nothing." Neither conservatives nor socialists brought nature more into the picture. Fascists did a bit—interestingly, the Nazis saw themselves as champions of nature and the countryside—but not very seriously.[19] But in the mid-twentieth century, as human population soared, land, water, and other resources became scarcer, and pollution spread, environmentalists increasingly argued that our lives are intimately involved with nature. They suggested that our future may depend as much on the health of the natural environment as it does on our religious liberties, precise tax rates, regulatory policies, or other details within human-made economy and society. A good human life, and a good human society, is part of nature, so environmentalists recognize natural beauty and sustainability as fundamental values.

PRINCIPLE 2: THE PRECAUTIONARY PRINCIPLE. In the 1960s and 1970s, the explosion of human population and a realization that resources like oil were finite created the perception that humankind had to moderate itself to avoid overwhelming the planet. Biologist Paul Ehrlich's widely read book *The Population Bomb* (1968) offered dire scenarios in which food and resources were exhausted. Though Ehrlich's warnings underestimated the continuing rise in food production, similar thinking remains key to environmentalists. Since the 1980s, they have placed more emphasis on the steady rise in global temperatures, which the vast majority of scientists worldwide see as linked to human-made pollution.[20] Environmentalists advise living by the **precautionary principle**: even if uncertainty remains about how much our actions are leading toward catastrophic consequences, if we wait to see if the worst scenarios are correct, it will be too late to respond. We must change behavior now as a precaution. To lessen the dangers of global warming, then, they call for limiting consumption; investing in wind, water or solar energy; phasing out nuclear power; and generally factoring environmental impacts into political decision making. Unless we "think green" now, they warn, we risk something like the bleak future portrayed in the Disney film *Wall-E*.

precautionary principle
The idea that if our actions may produce catastrophic consequences, we should act now to find solutions rather than wait until the consequences become certain.

Where, then, does environmentalism stand relative to the other ideologies? Because it equally criticizes liberals, conservatives, and socialists for ignoring the environment, it might (in principle) find opponents or allies across them. In the United States, the conservative Right has occasionally connected with environmentalism. The EPA was accepted (if not initially championed) by a conservative Republican, President Richard Nixon. In 2006, a group of church leaders tied strongly to the religious Right launched the Evangelical Climate Initiative to argue that the Bible mandates humans as stewards of the planet.[21] Yet in the United States, and also in other countries, environmentalism has almost always entered politics as an ally of the political Left, or simply as a new theme for modern liberals or socialists themselves. The main reason lies in environmentalists' receptivity to more active government. Conservatives have tended to see environmentalism and the precautionary principle as yet another argument for the government action they generally oppose. American Democrats or European Social Democrats, on the other hand, already believe that government must act to provide positive liberties, and have usually just added arguments for environmental regulation and investment to their platforms. In Europe, "Green" parties often form coalitions with Social Democrats or Socialists. In 2011, boosted by environmental outcry over of the Fukushima nuclear disaster in Japan, the German politician Winfried Kretschmann became the first Green ever to win a substantial executive office, becoming minister-president (roughly equivalent to governor of an American state) of the German state of Baden-Württemberg, in coalition with the Social Democrats.

Political Islamism

Now we shift to a very different edge of modern politics: Islamism. It is a political ideology based in a certain interpretation of the Islamic or Muslim religion. The phrase, "A certain interpretation," is the crucial part of that sentence.

Many Muslims—even religiously devout ones—are not political Islamists. Indeed, at least some Muslims live and participate in every democratic society in the world today, often identifying politically with ideological perspectives within the liberal tradition. No committed political Islamists, by contrast, participate significantly in American politics or in other stable liberal democracies. Yet political Islamists are active in places like Iraq, Indonesia, Nigeria, and Afghanistan, sometimes competing for votes in partly democratic contexts. Moreover, an especially radical subset of political Islamists have taken a prominent global role through terrorism, as vividly displayed in the events of September 11, 2001. This extreme step is not in any way a necessary part of the ideology: many political Islamists oppose terrorism specifically and violence in general. But the global significance of this strain of political Islamism, especially since 9/11, is a major reason why understanding this ideological tradition is important to people everywhere. It has three core concepts: the respect of Islamic law, a defense of the purity of Muslim communities, and the highly ambiguous notion of *jihad* ("struggle") that the most radical Islamists use as a justification for violence. Interestingly, each of these ideas has parallels in Christian tradition as well.

PRINCIPLE 1: REPLACE SECULAR LAW WITH *SHARI'A*. Islam, also known as the Muslim religion, follows the teachings of the prophet Muhammad (570–632) and the holy book he is said to have received in revelation from the angel Gabriel, the Qur'an (or Koran). The Qur'an instructs Muslims to live according to ***shari'a***, the principles and codes of conduct found in the Qur'an. Just as many committed Christians prioritize their religious values over other considerations but may not take every line of the Bible literally, so devout Muslims vary in their interpretations about how to apply a seventh-century text today. Still, political Islamism is founded on the notion that contemporary politics should map as fully as possible onto *shari'a*.

shari'a
A system of law based on the Qur'an and other foundational Islamic texts.

The key statements of this view date from the Islamic revival of the early twentieth century, led by Egyptian figures like Hassan al-Banna (1902–1949) and Sayyid Qutb (1906–1966). For Qutb, Muslim societies had been corrupted by the Western world, which he saw (like many critics inside the West!) as materialist, exploitative, alienating, power-hungry, and lacking in moral guidance. His solution—not unlike some Christian fundamentalists in the West—was to recommit more purely to religion. Like with Christian fundamentalists, individual political Islamists vary in their interpretation of exactly what a purer commitment to Islam means, but it generally includes: creating a system of religious justice, restricting interaction between the sexes, enforcing a strict female dress code, prohibiting money lending with interest, requiring tithes to the poor, barring homosexuality or blasphemy against Muhammad, and many other rules. Its implications for democracy are ambiguous—and many Muslims who are not political Islamists find support for democratic participation in the Qur'an—but political Islamists usually stand out from other Muslims in tending to see liberal rights and electoral democracy as illegitimate Western imports.

PRINCIPLE 2: DEFEND AND PURIFY THE *UMMAH*.   The *ummah* is the community of Muslims, roughly like the word "Christendom" once applied to Christians. For committed political Islamists, the division of the *ummah* into states is an aberration invented by the West. The boundaries of most states in the Muslim world were drawn by Western colonialism, and these lines artificially suggest that states govern these spaces, when in fact authority should flow from Islam. Rather than seeking to take over other places, as fascists or Soviet revolutionaries envisioned, political Islamists are focused mainly on the goal of banishing foreign influence from historically Muslim lands. This is true even for the most radical terrorist Islamists, who most frequently justify attacks outside the Muslim world as related to restoration of correct Islamic governance, without outside interference, within the *ummah*. For Osama bin Laden (1957–2011), founder of the terrorist group Al Qaeda, the main justification for attacking the United States on 9/11 was to force the United States to lessen its influence on his native Saudi Arabia.

PRINCIPLE 3: *JIHAD*.   The Qur'an assigns Muslims the duty of *jihad*, or "struggle." This struggle can be understood in multiple ways: as an internal struggle of faith, a struggle to improve Muslim society, or a defense of Islam. One of the most important questions for how we characterize political Islamism depends on how Islamists understand this commandment to defend Islam. On the one hand, classic Islamic texts prohibit killing women and children, suicide, and unprovoked attacks in general. Thus many devout political Islamists argue that terrorism has no place in their worldview. On the other hand, **martyrdom**—to be "killed while engaging in God's cause"—is strongly praised in the Qur'an. Much as medieval Christian warriors believed that the Bible justified the harsh wars of the Crusades, the most radical political Islamists draw upon these passages to justify acts of terrorism. Many authoritative Islamic scholars argue that terrorists like bin Laden are poorly trained in their own faith, but the radical wing of political Islamists has nonetheless arrived at an ideology in which terrorism is legitimate.

Where does Islamism stand relative to the other ideologies? A strong emphasis on *shari'a*, a separate and supreme *ummah*, and the particular interpretation of *jihad* that endorses terrorism set the most radical political Islamists on a collision course with the main ideologies in the United States and other liberal democracies. Once again, though, we must remember that the devotees of this strain of political Islamism are a very small minority of Muslims around the world. In Muslim countries like Turkey, Indonesia, Malaysia, Tunisia, or Egypt, millions of Muslims feel comfortable with secular governance. Even most Muslims who do endorse a form of political Islamism, whether in Egypt's **Muslim Brotherhood** or in the **theocracy** of Iran, do not accept a violent interpretation like Al Qaeda's.

martyrdom
A revered status that one obtains by dying for a cause, especially for religious reasons.

Muslim Brotherhood
The largest group of political Islamists in the world, though its Egyptian core has been repressed since 2013.

theocracy
A system of government in which most power is held by religious leaders.

Khalil Hamra/AP Images

Egyptian president Mohammed Morsi arrives to speak to a packed stadium in October 2012. A leader of the Muslim Brotherhood, Morsi was elected in June 2012 but was deposed a year later by the Egyptian military, which accused him of abusing his power. Since then the military has built a repressive regime of its own. Observers disagree over how much the Brotherhood would uphold Western-style democracy if it returned to power.

Indeed, they generally mix religious commitments with secular principles and law in ways that have rough parallels in American politics: the most devout members of the American religious Right share Islamists' core view that religious revelation should sometimes be prioritized over secular ideas. Overall, political Islamism is a diverse ideological tradition. The future relationship between its champions and the United States and its allies could go in many different directions.

Liberalism, conservatism, socialism, fascism, environmentalism, and Islamism are labels that just scratch the surface of human inventiveness in politics, but they capture the most historically significant traditions that shape political debates today in the United States, other liberal democracies, and in many more different societies. Within liberal democracy, liberalism and conservatism define the main axes of political competition around their "left-right" debate. Among their older competitors, a toned-down version of socialism remains active in much of the world outside the United States, and fascism sets the far-right boundaries of democratic politics. Environmentalism is the most globally widespread new ideology that steps beyond the left-right spectrum, though its advocates usually ally with the Left. Islamism, lastly, has many strands, of which an especially extremist version grabs global attention as the most conscious, aggressive ideological alternative to liberal democracy today. Figure 3-3 sums up these ideologies' basic relationships.

Figure 3-3 The Ideologies that Shape Modern Politics

Modern ideologies are richer and more complex than a single left-right dimension can capture, but this summary figure gives a rough overview of how they have grown and branched out over time. Environmentalism has distinct roots but has intertwined with the Left. Political Islam resembles the American religious Right in its roots in revelation.

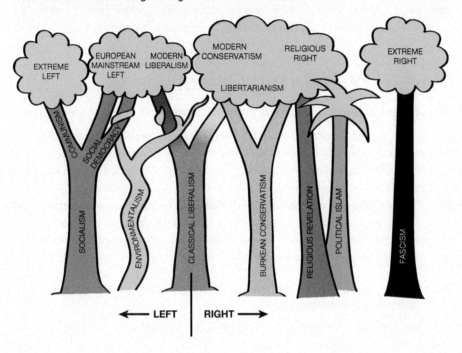

Conclusion: Putting Ideologies into Practice

These six ideologies give shape and terms to most of politics, defining our basic options to engage with the world. Perhaps some strain of one of these traditions resonates strongly with you and you want to wave its flag, pin on its buttons, and speak in its voice. In that case you will be in good company. Major political forces in our world coalesce around these ideologies. Identifying with one of them can bring you opportunities for connecting to parties, associations, marches, campaigns, and other exciting and meaningful forms of participation.

Even if this is appealing, though, you should not leap too quickly to take on a label. Only by seriously considering alternative ideologies can we have conscious reasons for declaring, "I'm a conservative," or "I'm a liberal" (or whatever else). That is one reason why socialism, fascism or political Islamism are relevant even though they are less legitimate in an American context: they rest on critiques of the other ideologies that are important and thought provoking. Moreover, these off-the-shelf ideologies are not our only options. Mixes of these traditions can be just as coherent as "pure" versions, and new visions of politics remain to be invented. To develop conscious ideological views, we need to move beyond the low political knowledge, fragmented opinions, and semiconscious political culture that regrettably characterize much political thinking around the world. Individually, you must analyze how these ideologies interpret different political issues and consider their implications for you, for the "greater good," and for the world. Every chapter in the rest of the book offers you chances to do so.

Review of Learning Objectives

3.1 Define political knowledge, political culture, and political ideology.

Ideologies are packages of conscious beliefs about politics. They define the language and concepts of political action and set the boundaries of acceptable choices. Many people do not engage enough with politics to develop an ideology, however. Their views are based on a few facts (their political knowledge, which is low on average) and a smattering of partial ideas drawn from expectations that surround them, from families, peer groups, various subcultures, national politics, and even international regions. These expectations form our political culture—the semiconscious political reflexes that "people like us" are supposed to have.

3.2 Identify the main principles of classical liberalism, modern liberalism, and modern conservatism.

Liberalism has shaped the modern world more than any other ideological tradition. It has several different strands. Classical liberalism emerged as a series of calls for political rights, economic liberties and free markets, and eventually democratic representation. By the late nineteenth century, its dominance in much of Europe and North America led its advocates to divide. Classical liberals felt they had reached a good society of freedom from interference (or negative liberty), and shifted to defending rights, markets, and democracy. A new strand of modern liberals argued, however, that liberalism's goals now required government action to promote freedom to flourish (or positive liberty). Classical liberals became modern conservatives on the political "Right," defending a status quo of limited government. Modern liberals on the "Left" argued for policies to aid the poor and bolster rights of the disadvantaged. Modern conservatives combined classical liberal principles with skepticism about active government based in a Burkean emphasis on experience and tradition. Those on the "religious Right" sought guidance from religion as well. Donald Trump's nationalism-led agenda and criticisms of open markets have introduced new debates about what conservatism means today.

3.3 Identify the main principles of socialism and fascism.

In the nineteenth and early twentieth centuries, socialism and fascism emerged as the leading competitors to liberalism and conservatism. Socialism developed mainly from the thinking of Karl Marx, who argued that free markets and capitalism create exploitation and inequality. The strong version of this ideology, which called for revolution against capitalism, became known as communism. The moderate version, which sought equality through reform, became known as socialism or social democracy. Social democracy remains influential in many societies today, though it has become more moderate and converged with modern liberalism. Fascism arose as a rejection of modern ideas of progress. Mussolini and Hitler combined defense of mythical village life and nationalism—the notion that meaning in life comes from belonging to a powerful, aggressive country—into an ideology of exclusion and conquest. Their defeat in World War II and the horrors of the Holocaust eradicated fascism from most political arenas, but it has increasingly resurfaced on the far Right.

3.4 Identify the main principles of environmentalism and political Islamism.

Among newer alternatives to liberalism and conservatism, both environmentalism and Islamism stand out for their distinctive sources and broad impact. Environmentalists argue that human quality of life is intertwined with the natural environment. We must live by the "precautionary principle" that immediate action is necessary to head off the possibilities of human-made ecological catastrophe. Political Islamists perceive the *ummah*, or Muslim community, as corrupted by intrusions from the non-Muslim world. They seek political systems based on *shari'a* law of the Qur'an, and call all Muslims to *jihad*, or "struggle." Some interpret *jihad* just as an internal struggle for faith, but the most radical Islamists believe it endorses violence and even terrorism against their opponents.

Great Sources to Find Out More

Al Gore, *An Inconvenient Truth: The Planetary Emergence of Global Warming and What We Can Do About It* (New York: Rodale, 2006). An environmental pitch by the ex-Democratic vice president.

Antonio Gramsci, *Selections from the Prison Notebooks* (London: International, 1971). Writings by the most influential Italian socialist thinker while in prison in the 1920s.

Ayn Rand, *Atlas Shrugged* (New York: Random House). The most famous novel by the favorite author of libertarians, describing an America that rejects oppressive government.

Bernard Lewis, *Faith and Power: Religion and Politics in the Middle East* (New York: Oxford University Press, 2010). An overview of Islam and politics from a famous, provocative, and conservative U.S. expert.

G. William Domhoff, *Who Rules America? Power and Politics* (New York: McGraw-Hill, 2001). A socialist-leaning account of U.S. politics.

Graham Fuller, *The Future of Political Islam* (New York: Palgrave Macmillan, 2004). A dissection of political Islam by the former vice-chairman of the National Intelligence Council at the CIA.

Mark Bauerlein, *The Dumbest Generation: How the Digital Age Stupefies Young Americans and Jeopardizes Our Future (Or, Don't Trust Anyone Under 30)* (New York: Penguin, 2008). An argument that technology has made Americans even less knowledgeable and engaged.

Paul Krugman, *The Conscience of a Liberal* (New York: Norton, 2007). A statement of modern liberal beliefs by the Nobel Prize–winning economist and *New York Times* columnist.

Rachel Carson, *Silent Spring* (New York: Houghton Mifflin, 2002[1962]). The book is often portrayed as launching the environmental movement in the United States.

Rick Shenkman, *How Stupid Are We? Facing the Truth about the American Voter* (New York: Basic Books, 2007). A sometimes-funny, often-depressing look at political knowledge in the United States.

Robert Paxton, *The Anatomy of Fascism* (New York: Knopf, 2004). A sharp essay from one of the great historians of fascism.

Roger Scruton, *Conservatism: An Invitation to the Great Tradition* (New York: St. Martin's Press, 2018). A provocative English philosopher introduces conservative thought.

Terence Ball, Richard Dagger and Daniel O'Neill, *Political Ideologies and the Democratic Ideal*, 9th ed. (New York: Pearson, 2013). An accessible, deep, and broad overview of ideological traditions.

Develop Your Thinking

Use these questions as discussion or short writing exercises to think more deeply about some of the key themes of the chapter.

1. Consider the political culture around you. What are some things that "people like you" expected to think about politics?

2. Who understands better how to achieve equality of opportunity—modern conservatives or modern liberals?

3. Do you think that individual liberties should trump broader social purposes?

4. How important do you think the "precautionary principle" should be in government policy?

5. If you had to express some sympathy for the basic views of socialism, fascism, political Islamism, or strong environmentalism, which would it be, and why?

Keywords

Chapter 4
States

An orphan boy stands next to a map of Afghanistan on the wall of his orphanage. The map's many colors show the country's provinces, which hint at the diversity and divisions in its population. Decades of war in this ethnically and religiously fragmented country have left hundreds of thousands of orphans and abandoned children.

Farzana Wahidy/AP Images

 Learning Objectives

4.1 Distinguish between states and nations and explain why the state is the dominant organizing framework for politics in the world today.

4.2 Illustrate how the historical relationship between state and nation in a country can shape its politics today.

4.3 Explain how global developments today pose new challenges to the construction of stable nation-states.

4.4 Evaluate state sovereignty from multiple ideological points of view.

4.5 Identify multiple plausible explanations for the difficulty of state building in Afghanistan.

Fitting into a World of States—Or Not

Look at any human-oriented map of our world—one that shows more than natural features—and its key framework jumps out at you. Every inch of the planet except for Antarctica is divided up into countries, or *states*. These units define much of our lives. Live on one side of a border and your government, education, economic opportunities, and culture flow through networks centered on one capital. Your neighbors over the border plug into other networks around other power centers. States form the basic architecture of political authority on Earth.

Not everyone is comfortable, though, with this boxed-in world. A few countries fit neatly into state frames: the Japanese, with their ancient shared culture inside island borders, have little trouble identifying as a unit. Yet most countries (states) do not. Even the most powerful state today, the United States, is uneasy with this model. Americans' diverse society, fragmented organization in fifty mini-"states," and ideological skepticism of central government make for a conflicted unit. If we look around the world, we find some peoples who find it nearly impossible to color themselves into state lines. In Afghanistan, after decades of U.S. intervention to forge a stable state, American leaders increasingly wonder if it will ever be possible to bring order, let alone good governance, to this divided place.

If so many people find the "state model" uncomfortable, how did it become the pervasive format for politics in the world today? We shall see that powerful dynamics of security, economics, and culture have pushed people almost everywhere into states, but the states they have formed reflect their local and ongoing challenges in different ways. To see the shape of politics in our world, we must recognize how the state forms a special, rather peculiar framework for life on Earth. ■

Organizing a World of States: Definition and Origins of State Sovereignty

4.1 **Distinguish between states and nations and explain why the state is the dominant organizing framework for politics today.**

When political scientists use the word "state," they do not mean California, Mississippi, and other subnational units that make up the United States. They mean the organization that runs a country. Countries like the United States or Japan are not just areas of land marked on maps; they are also organizations. The U.S. president, like the prime minister of Japan or other national leaders, is the head of an organization called the state that oversees a piece of land. States are the largest organizations on the planet: the U.S. federal government, not counting lower levels of government, employs more than two and a half million people and spends over $4 trillion every year. More important than their sheer size, though, is their formal supremacy over other organizations. States are the organizations that define the rules under which individuals and all other organizations—business firms, religious institutions, universities, political parties, and so on—can act on their territories.

The Principle of State Sovereignty

The most famous definition of the **state** comes from the German sociologist Max Weber (1864–1920): *the state is an organization with a monopoly on the legitimate use of violence in a fixed territory*. This sentence contains three key ideas:

- *States are territorial monopolies*, claiming exclusive ownership of a chunk of land to which they apply systematic rules. Their territories are permanently fixed, in principle; any change to state borders fundamentally challenges the state and usually means war.

- *Control of violence is at their core.* States' power is built on the use of violence. Thankfully, much of politics takes place without direct violence, but who can draw a gun or call in the police, if necessary, matters a great deal.

- *States monopolize legitimate violence.* States never fully control violence— individuals will fight or criminals may hurt their victims—but states control what is seen as appropriate or legitimate violence on their territory. States have police and military forces that catch criminals, throw people in jail, repress riots or revolts, execute criminals, or engage in wars. Any violence not endorsed by the state is typically illegal.

state
Organizations that claim a monopoly on the legitimate use of violence in a certain territory.

These ideas are often summed up as the principle of state **sovereignty**. Under this principle, a set of security-providing organizations—called states— divide all the world's territory between them, and each is supreme on its territory. Internally, each state governs its own affairs; externally, states recognize the sovereignty of other states, agreeing not to interfere across borders. It is this principle that defines the political landscape we inhabit today.

sovereignty
The principle that one organization holds supreme authority over a territory.

For most of human history, however, political responsibility was messier than today's rather neat system of territorial states. The state has come a long way and confronted a variety of challengers to wrestle politics so fully into separate boxes. The first states emerged in Europe, so our story pays special attention to its history.

The Origins of States

To understand how the world ended up as a system of states, we must see what preceded this model—how else were political units once arranged?—and how the state came to replace these alternatives. This may seem like a long-ago historical story, but it is actually very relevant today. The fact that this model evolved to solve the problems of certain European societies centuries ago helps explain why and where many societies still find it difficult to graft onto local roots. Outside of Europe in particular, where the state model was imposed more recently, local identities and institutions have often resisted this European invention.

ALTERNATIVES AND OBSTACLES TO THE STATE MODEL. From the ancient world to the 1600s, the largest and most widespread form of political organization was the **empire**. At first glance, empires looked similar to states: they were territories ruled by a central power, usually called emperor or king. But empires did not have either clearly fixed territory or highly systematic rules for the territories they possessed.

empire
A political system that claims domination over both a central, directly administered territory and other territories that it governs in other ways.

Instead, empires had a central territory that they directly controlled and more distant areas of less direct control. Populations in the latter were perceived as separate peoples from the imperial center, and were governed by some mix of imperial personnel and local leaders. Especially at their edges, empires often had different arrangements to maintain control over different peoples. In great empires like the Roman Empire, the Chinese Empire, or the Persian Empire (governed from modern-day Iran), each imperial center constantly negotiated for control in many ways with its far-flung territories. Even the later empires of **colonialism**—established by European countries, Japan, and the United States from the sixteenth to twentieth centuries— frequently governed colonies in multiple ways. The American colonies of Puerto Rico, the Philippines, Guam, and Samoa, for example, each received specially tailored governments.

colonialism
A form of empire with a state at the center that controls other territories as "colonies."

In some regions, including Europe, the rise of large organized religions added another complication and an additional competitor to the imperial patchwork of power. The pope of the Catholic Church in Rome claimed spiritual authority over all Christians. Rulers who displeased the pope could be threatened with expulsion from the Church, which believers saw as damning them in the afterlife. Similar dynamics arose within Islamic areas, with secular rulers forced to negotiate a delicate relationship with religious authorities. These religious organizations, which sometimes contested the authority even of powerful emperors, had no clear relationship to territory at all. They were spiritual shepherds wherever their flock was found.

Medieval Europe also featured another source of varied relationships underneath the competing claims of secular and religious rulers: the social rules known as **feudalism**. Feudalism organized all levels of society in a hierarchy of ties of fealty (loyalty), between families or groups of people. Each territory answered to an overlord—usually titled a king or emperor—who allowed lower-level lords (called vassals) to govern parts of the territory (called fiefs). In exchange, vassals promised to render the overlord specific services, usually delivering men and weapons to fight for the overlord whenever necessary. Marriages and successions often created overlapping commitments as fiefs, and their conditions of vassalage were renegotiated: one vassal could end up pledging fealty to multiple lords. Feudalism made the relationship between territory and political power into a complex, multilevel, messy patchwork.

feudalism
A social system of obligations in which people provide labor, produce, or service to a lord in return for land and protection.

Economic change also generated new kinds of political organization within this shifting terrain of feudalism, church authority, and variegated imperial domination. Around 1000, rising European food production, improved ships, and other technology for long-distance trade led to much larger, richer cities, which led to the creation of new centers of power known as city-states. Especially in Italy, rapidly expanding merchant wealth gave places like Venice or Genoa the resources to govern themselves and hire mercenaries for defense. City-states became independent holes that weakened the fabric of feudal ties and empires. In a few locations, city-states allied together, most notably in the Hanseatic League in northern Europe. At its height in the late fourteenth century, this flexible alliance of over 100 merchant cities was powerful enough to raise large armies and bargain with the greatest feudal lords.

Europe around 1500, then, displayed an especially messy version of the overlapping political organizations that characterized the rest of the world. Overlords' control of territories expanded and contracted in response to complex feudal ties; the Church intervened at all levels of authority; and both city-states and trading leagues asserted their autonomy. Within 200 years, though, a series of developments would cause Europe to sort into separate states.

RISE OF THE STATE. Over several centuries, a combination of religious change, warfare, and trade crafted a new kind of organization that eventually produced cleaner, territorially based lines of authority. The first obstacle to fall was the Catholic Church's claims over Christendom. In 1517, the Protestant Reformation unleashed 150 years of religious warfare. Protestants like Martin Luther and John Calvin criticized a corrupt Catholic Church and formed their own new

Holger Weitzel/Canopy/Getty Images

The city of Lübeck, Germany, still retains the shape it had as a city-state when part of the Hanseatic League from the 1200s to 1600s. Unlike modern states, which try to govern a clear territory in systematic ways, city-states were tightly defended towns with looser relationships of trade and influence to surrounding lands.

Christian denominations. The Protestant uprisings broke the political claims of the Catholic popes to supremacy across Europe. Not only did Protestant leaders reject papal power, but Catholic rulers like the French kings also took advantage of this period to become more autonomous from Rome. The pope largely dropped out of the equation of earthly authority.

Around the same time, shifts in military technology led to the emergence of larger forces of disciplined troops, helping major lords to consolidate territory. With the invention of the longbow and then firearms, foot soldiers became more deadly than armored knights. Cannons made it harder for local castles to hold out against large-scale attack. French and British kings were among the first to gain enduring control of major territories, and their formidable war-fighting machines pressed smaller units nearby to consolidate into similar units as well. As sociologist Charles Tilly famously summarized, "War made the state, and the state made war."[1]

Equally important, though, were economic developments that allowed kings to fund ever-larger armies. The French and British kings became powerful partly because they managed to acquire control of major cities and strike deals with the rising merchant class. That is, the kings would provide protection and stability within a wide economy—often awarding monopolies on the production of certain goods within their realm—in return for taxation to support wars. Central-government revenue also strengthened kings' power over local lords, increasingly replacing the patchwork of feudalism with direct rule by the monarchy.

Treaty of Westphalia

The treaty that ended the Thirty Years' War, proclaiming each territorial ruler's right to choose a religion for his or her people.

These processes culminated in the formal creation of the state system after the mid-1600s. In the **Treaty of Westphalia** of 1648, which marked the end of the long period of major religious war, European rulers agreed to recognize each other's right to choose their own religion. More generally, the treaty established that each ruler was the sovereign power for all matters, secular or religious, in their territory. The Treaty of Westphalia thus officially recognized the rule of state sovereignty: henceforth one organization had supreme authority in each separate territory.

Authority is a crucial word here. Sovereignty is not established by raw power alone. It is a claim about who has the *legitimate* right to run a territory, and so it depends just as strongly—or even more strongly—on external recognition of that right as on actual capacity to control the territory. External recognition means that states agree not to intervene on each other's territory, even if they have the raw power to do so. Some states in 1648 had quite weak control of their territory, and this remains true today. In later sections, we will see that many states rest their authority more clearly on external recognition than on strong internal power. Recognition of each state's sovereignty by other states was the key development after 1648, and it remains the linchpin of sovereignty today.

Thus the combination of warfare, trade, and religious change altered Europe's political landscape. Out of a mix of empires, religious authority, feudalism, and city-states, a simpler format of distinct states with clear territorial authority became the formal rule. Europeans who had lived in a much more fluid, complex arena now found their political and economic lives oriented increasingly inside state borders, whether they liked it or not. Later, when the state became connected to another powerful concept—the cultural idea of the nation—this model of territorial organization took on still more political significance and spread across the planet.

States, Nations, and the Nation-State

People often use the words "nation" and "state" interchangeably to mean "country," but nation actually refers to something quite different. The first states were security organizations that had little relationship to the people within them. Inhabitants of France, for example, did not necessarily identify with the aristocrats running the French state. As late as 1800, only half of the people living in French territory spoke the French language. The French state today, by contrast, is known for presiding over a powerfully united language, culture, and identity. It was a separate step for people to become a **nation**: a group who share a political identity and think of themselves as a unit that deserves to govern itself.[2] Sometimes states created nations, as in France. Sometimes nations coalesced first and then created states. Sometimes, especially where the state model was imposed from outside, states and nations never aligned at all.

nation
A group of people who share a cultural identity and think of themselves as a unit that deserves to govern itself.

WHEN STATES CREATED NATIONS.   In France, Britain, and some other cases, states developed nations to encourage loyalty, repress rebellions, and more easily build armies, collect taxes, and administer the territory. In the process, states typically stamped out other languages and subcultures and created national symbols and legends with which people could identify. For example, by drafting men from all over France to fight wars, the French state forced them to understand French and created common experiences and bonds. In the nineteenth and twentieth centuries, public schools became the primary tool for generating a shared language, culture, and identity. Thus certain states became an even more formidable kind of organization, **nation-states**. With a population that felt nationalist pride in serving and sacrificing for the national unit, states gained enormous capacity to exert power and shape their societies. They built up still stronger national identities and more integrated economies, and in times of crisis could call on very broad military mobilization. The results were not necessarily positive: warfare shifted from conflicts fought between militaries on battlefields to the kind of no-holds-barred violence on civilians that occurred in World War I and World War II. Wars between states had usually been limited, but those between nation-states often are not.

nation-states
A political model in which inhabitants of a sovereign state share a cultural identity.

WHEN NATIONS CREATED STATES.   In other cases, nations created states. When people regard themselves as a unit separate from the governing state, they often become **nationalists**: those who demand their own state and seek to increase its power. Modern-day Germany was a patchwork of small states

nationalists
Those who seek unity, recognition, and a distinct state for the members of a nation.

in the early nineteenth century until trade, the spread of printing and literacy, and religion made German the common language of this large area. Invasions by the powerful French state, especially under Emperor Napoleon Bonaparte (1769–1821) in the early 1800s, unintentionally forced German speakers together and awoke the idea that they were a nation like the French. Nationalist songs, poetry, and literature blossomed. When the brilliant statesman Otto von Bismarck (1815–1898) forged the patchwork into a single state in the 1850s and 1860s, most Germans welcomed it. A similar process happened in Italy at the same time. In Japan, too, state followed nation. The Japanese had a strongly cohesive identity and culture years for a thousand years before military pressure from the United States and European states in the late 1800s led them to construct a powerfully centralized and modern state. Japan's leaders felt they had little choice but to imitate this Western organizational innovation, and built a nation-state that was an even more unified fusion of state and nation than their European models. This process in which strong national identities led to the later creation of states had important consequences for these countries later on. In all three of these countries, a powerful sense of the need for the state to defend a shared culture was one factor behind their turn to the ultranationalist doctrines of fascism around World War II.

WHEN STATES WERE IMPOSED OVER NATIONS.   With a few exceptions, the spread of state organization and national identity outside of Europe did not align cleanly. The main mechanism for the spread of the state model beyond Europe was colonialism. Technological advances and the powerfully centralized state model allowed Europeans to conquer most of the world in the eighteenth and nineteenth centuries. They drew their colonies' borderlines to suit themselves, with little regard for the realities of language, religion, or culture on the ground. Colonial borders combined different groups or separated similar peoples in South America, Africa, the Middle East, and much of Asia. Eventually, colonial domination awakened nationalism in these regions, much like the German reaction to French invasions, and provoked movements calling for independent states. These movements led to the vast wave of **decolonization** after World War II. For the most part, though, decolonization resulted simply in the recognition of colonies as independent states that maintained their old colonial borders—creating states that mapped poorly onto local identities. Most of these former colonies had to start from scratch to build state capacity after the colonizers departed. At least initially, these new struggling states were upheld as units more by the external recognition of foreign powers than by any strong internal foundations.

decolonization
The rapid process from the 1940s to the 1960s when European states, the United States, and Japan surrendered control of their previous colonies, creating many new states.

A handful of places outside Europe, like Japan, were exceptions that took rather easily to the nation-state model. Some peoples with very long histories within established borders, as in the old kingdom of Thailand and at the cores of ancient empires like Egypt, Persia (modern-day Iran), or China, found the fusion of central organization and cultural unity fairly comfortable. Much more common, though, was that newly independent states confronted major challenges both in establishing basic internal control and in encouraging state-framed identities. Some struggled to build multinational identities, like in the ethnic and religious kaleidoscope of Nigeria. Others went through painful—often bloody—processes to rearrange colonial lines with identities, as in the separation of Britain's Indian colonies into Hindu-dominated India and Muslim-dominated Pakistan and Bangladesh around 1948. Roughly half a million people perished in conflicts surrounding this "solution."

In quite a few places, the post-colonial disjuncture of states and nations was so severe that decolonization produced states with quasi-permanent internal conflict. Such was the case with Iraq and Afghanistan—the two countries where the United States and its allies have attempted to foster the construction of nation-states in recent decades. Early twentieth-century Iraq was a British colony that lumped a large population of ethnically Arabic Shi'ite Muslims, a smaller number of ethnically Arabic Sunni Muslims, and a long-oppressed minority of Kurds in the north. Likewise, modern Afghanistan was shaped by colonial competition between Britain and Russia. It ended up combining a large area of ethnically Pashtun tribes in its south with a mix of Tajiks, Hazaras, Uzbeks, and Turkmens in the north. Of the two countries, Iraq seemed the more promising context for consolidating sovereignty, with a stronger history of central government, oil resources, and a richer and more educated society. After almost two decades of immense U.S. pressure and expenditure, though, the Iraqi state remains shaky at best. Afghanistan, meanwhile, lacks both a national identity and all foundations of a state: it is one of the poorest places in the world and has never had a government that delivered significant services to its territory. Even long deployments of American troops and over a trillion dollars in American spending largely failed to build either state or nation in this challenging territory.

Nonetheless, people everywhere continue to try to organize as states and to align nations with them as best they can. To some degree this reflects the abstract appeal of the model: the organizational format of the state is powerful, and the notion that every people should have supreme authority over its own affairs is widely appealing.

The main reason for the reproduction of the state model, though, is that the most powerful, successful states in our world insist that they will recognize and enter into relations only with other states. Only recognized states can have formal diplomatic relations, join the club of countries at the United Nations, issue passports that allow citizens to travel, legally receive loans and foreign aid, enter into treaties on trade or military alliances, or participate in other international interactions like the Olympic Games. There is no nonstate option today by which a people can organize in a different framework and still have positive relationships with the rest of the world. Like a league that accepts only certain teams, or a club that issues only family memberships, the state system does not work well with people who do not adopt the right model. Societies feel this pressure to conform no matter how poorly the model fits them. "Stateless" peoples, like the Kurds who stretch across Iraq, Turkey, Syria, and Iran, or the Palestinians in and around Israel, are systematically marginalized and excluded.

Thus the state model has spread across the globe, as we see in Figure 4-1. After the gradual emergence of the earliest states, the major leap in the number of recognized states occurred with decolonization in the mid-twentieth century. Another major wave arrived in the 1990s after communism fell in Russia and Eastern Europe. The Soviet Union and Yugoslavia had held together different national groups, and they fragmented into many new states. Nationalist movements are still demanding their own states today. The newest states are East Timor, which split with Indonesia in 2002, Montenegro, Serbia, and Kosovo, whose independence completed the breakup of Yugoslavia in 2006–2008, and South Sudan, which separated from Sudan in 2011.

In a few locations, then, the combination of state organization and coherent national identity created the powerful unit we know as the unified nation-state. Even in these places, maintenance of a cohesive nation-state has been an ongoing challenge. In most countries, a less solid alignment of state organizations and identity made those challenges more serious, sometimes to the point of the extreme instability we see in Afghanistan. The next section delves more deeply and concretely into the interaction between the spread of the state model and the

Figure 4-1 The Spread of States Worldwide in the Past 200 Years

After a slow start, the number of states leapt upward with decolonization and continues to rise as more peoples demand separate states of their own.

*Before 1920, over 500,000 population and recognized by at least two major powers; after 1920, member of League of Nations or United Nations, *or* over 500,000 population and recognized by at least two major powers.

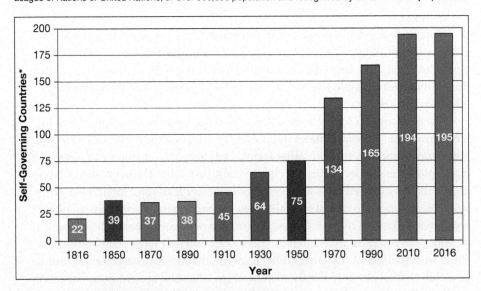

Source: Correlates of War Project, http://www.correlatesofwar.org.

construction of national identities. This relationship, compelled by a very particular political format forged in early modern Europe, continues to fundamentally shape countries today.

Variations among Nation-States

4.2   Illustrate how the historical relationship between state and nation in a country can shape its politics today.

The spread of the state model established it as the formal framework for human political organization, slicing up Earth's political map into countries. There are no more empires, city-states, or Hanseatic Leagues—just governments who each wrestle to control a discrete territory, obtain recognition from other governments, and encourage their populations to act and identify together. Some people think we may be approaching the end of the state-bound era, as we discuss in the next section, but for the moment our lives remain largely contained within state boundaries.

The state model and mobilization of national identity originated in Europe, but as it spread across the world, different people adapted it to their own political traditions, cultures, and resources. As a result, each state bears a different imprint depending on how it resolved its challenges in attempting to become a nation-state. We can see such imprints, for instance, in how much each state centralizes the internal organization of its territory, or in the varying rules by which individuals become citizens of a state. In a few places—those who have fit most poorly into the nation-state model—we see especially dramatic results in the chaos of "failed states." The next three sections survey the consequences that follow from these varying relationships with the state framework.

Unitary and Federal States

States fall into two broad categories with respect to how control of their territory is organized (see Figure 4-2). In **unitary states**, the central government holds all major political authority. Branch offices may exist across the state's territory to administer policies, but they report to the central organization or related entities that the center tolerates. People in the center can reorganize or disband these branch offices if they wish. This arrangement, in which no organization besides the central government has distinct authority of its own, is also known as political centralization. In **federal states**, on the other hand, both a central government and lower levels of government have distinct authority and responsibilities. Federal states are relatively decentralized.

Unitary states have often arisen in unified nation-states like Japan, where long historical processes suppressed or erased competing identities. The powers of Japan's forty-seven regions, known as prefectures, are defined and can be changed by national legislation. Prefectures' elected governors have some

unitary state
A state in which only one level of government has irrevocable authority.

federal state
A state in which power is shared between two levels of government with irrevocable authority.

Figure 4-2 Visualizing Unitary versus Federal Organization

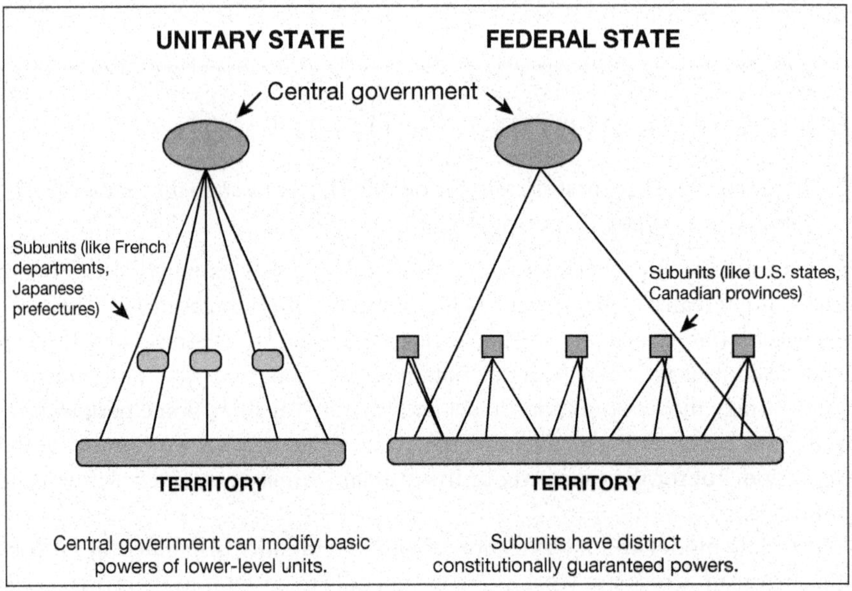

UNITARY STATE — FEDERAL STATE

Central government

Subunits (like French departments, Japanese prefectures)

Subunits (like U.S. states, Canadian provinces)

TERRITORY — TERRITORY

Central government can modify basic powers of lower-level units.

Subunits have distinct constitutionally guaranteed powers.

autonomy, but they receive most funding and policy guidance from the central government. A unitary structure is even more pronounced in the English part of Great Britain—the core of one of the very first states. Also known as the United Kingdom, Britain is not entirely unitary overall: it has exceptional regional arrangements for its outlying regions of Scotland, Wales, and Northern Ireland. Yet in its original heartland of England, which today is home to over 80 percent of the United Kingdom's population, the center holds all political power. There is no regional level of government. Central government simply establishes branch offices of its central-state departments (like for Agriculture, Commerce, Justice, and other policy areas) in several locations. At times, the center creates regional offices to coordinate particular problems, but it also erases them when this is convenient. When Prime Minister Margaret Thatcher found herself in political conflict with the city government of London in 1986, for example, she simply abolished it and shifted its powers to other entities.

Federal states can have powerful central governments, too, but other levels of government have authority that the center cannot take away. Federal states tend to arise in places where the formation of a state grouped together multiple identities. Two levels of government authority allow for some central coordination while also giving different groups some **autonomy**, or power of their own, to develop distinctive policies. Switzerland, for example, developed federalism to allow its German-speaking, French-speaking, and Italian-speaking regions some internal autonomy. It remains one of the most decentralized countries in the world. Many federations are very large

autonomy
The power or right to act independently from others.

countries that stretch across diverse populations: India, Brazil, Nigeria, Germany, Australia, Canada, and of course the United States. The U.S. federal government has offices across the territory—distributed across the landscape are federal courthouses, offices for the Department of the Interior, national forests and parks, military bases, and other federal organizations—but there are also state governments in each of the fifty states with extensive powers enshrined in the U.S. Constitution. A deep American constitutional rule is that any power not assigned specifically in the Constitution to the federal government is left to the subnational state level.

For most of U.S. history, the federal government did not dominate its territory, and even today, it has nothing like the direct authority of most unitary states. The early U.S. central government was so weak that the German philosopher Hegel (1770–1831) dismissed it as "not a real state." Even in 1900, the federal budget was smaller than spending by towns and counties alone, without counting spending by the forty-five (later fifty) states! Not until the mid-twentieth century did the federal level surpass the others. With the emergence of a huge industrial economy, federal regulation and social programs became much more important. War also continued to "make the state": the World Wars and later the Cold War competition with the Soviet Union massively increased both the powers and reach of the federal government. Still, American politics remains anchored in a decentralized mind-set, with a pervasive suspicion of central-state power in general.

Just as U.S. federalism originally arose to accommodate the demands of the thirteen colonies to retain some separate powers, unitary states may shift their territorial structure toward federalism in order to cope with internal identity conflicts. For example, in the 1990s Britain undertook a **devolution** of powers, or decentralization, in its ethnic regions of Scotland, Wales, and Northern Ireland. A few countries have shifted categories altogether. Spain was once a unitary state, but in response to nationalist movements in several regions (most importantly the powerful region of Catalonia), it has devolved enough powers to the regions to be seen today as a federal state. Federalism was also designed into Iraq's new constitution in 2005, since it was seen as one way to recognize different groups' identities. In particular, the Kurdish minority demanded a federal structure that allowed them to construct a largely autonomous region in the north. In Afghanistan, on the other hand, the central state was perceived as being so weak that the new 2004 constitution opted for a unitary structure. Because the country was already so fragmented, many felt that new institutions must focus on encouraging the emergence of central authority.

In unitary and federal arrangements, then, we can see some echoes of how states and nations aligned—or did not align—to form countries. States that are supported by a strong national identity tend toward centralization and unitary government. States that unite different peoples very often develop decentralization and a federal government. These relations are dynamic, as many states attempt to integrate, or at least balance, state control and national identities.

devolution
A transfer of authority to lower levels of government.

Citizenship: Defined by Inheritance or Residency?

Not only does the interaction of state and nation leave an imprint on the structure of government, but it shapes the relationships between states and individual citizens as well. Legal membership in a state, known as **citizenship**, is one of the most important factors in our lives, since these territorial affiliations come with hugely varying rights, benefits, and identity. Depending on how states have related to national identities, they have constructed different rules as to who can join their state and how.

In most states with strong national identities, citizenship is defined by the inheritance-based rule of *jus sanguinis*, or "right of blood." Under these rules, only children or descendants of citizens can be citizens. Germany long had a pure version of such rules. In its large population of Turkish immigrants, for example, there are people who have lived their whole lives in Germany, and whose *parents* were born in Germany, but who are not citizens. *Jus sanguinis* rules made citizenship unavailable to them no matter how long they lived in Germany. German reforms around 2000 opened a door to **naturalization**, or change of citizenship, but many long-term residents remain noncitizens. The situation is similar in Japan. Citizenship laws are based strongly on principles of Japanese parentage. A naturalization option is available after residency of five years, but very few noncitizens use this option because few people accept the notion that someone of another race or ethnicity can be a Japanese citizen. Korean and Chinese populations in Japan number over half a million each but rarely naturalize even after generations of residency.

In countries like Japan or Germany where a sense of national identity developed before a modern state, the origins of an inheritance-based view of citizenship are easy to see. "Japanese-ness" or "German-ness" were defined by culture and family ties long before they took on a coherent political framework. Even when the Japanese and German states came into existence, people continued to see membership in the group as an inherited quality.

In some of the countries where state formation preceded development of a strong cultural identity, however, another sort of citizenship emerged. The very first states of Britain and France formed before their populations shared a national identity. In the late eighteenth and nineteenth centuries, as both states tried to forge diverse regional identities into a national unit, they turned to the residency-based principle of *jus soli*, or "right of soil." Under this principle, citizenship is granted for being born on the soil of the state, no matter what "blood" one carries. *Jus soli* has often been accompanied by relatively open naturalization procedures for those who immigrate (and so live on the soil). This principle allowed the British and French states to proclaim everyone on their territory as citizens, with the implication that they should orient their loyalties and identity to that state. The same calculation also applied in the United States, Canada, Australia, New Zealand, and in most Latin American countries, where modern societies were constructed from immigrants of diverse origins.

citizenship
Legal membership in a state, typically giving full access to privileges available to other inhabitants.

jus sanguinis
Latin for "right of blood," this principle gives citizenship to those related by blood to other citizens.

naturalization
The process of acquiring citizenship in a state after having citizenship in another state or nation.

jus soli
Latin for "right of soil," this principle awards citizenship to those born on a state's territory.

Though *jus soli* is clearly a more open principle than *jus sanguinis*, countries that incorporate *jus soli* principles do not simply have easy and welcoming identities and citizenship. In fact, no country has pure *jus soli* rules; instead they tend to exist alongside "blood" pathways to citizenship, like the U.S. laws that award citizenship to children born in the United States *and* to children born abroad to parents with U.S. citizenship. The politics of citizenship and identity in these countries also tend to mix themes of openness and exclusion, as we can see very clearly in American history. Early U.S. leaders promoted *jus soli* rules and a political view of "American-ness," in which "membership in the national community demands only the decision to become American, a political decision."[3] Over time, the United States took on the image of a "melting pot" of different cultures, but this rhetoric continually clashed with reality. The enslavement of Africans before 1865 was by far the most egregious example, but almost everyone except English-Protestant settlers—Irish, Germans, Italians, Poles, Jews—long suffered from discrimination. The Chinese Exclusion Act of 1882 explicitly barred Chinese naturalizations, and nonwhites of any descent were systematically persecuted. Not until the civil rights movement of the 1950s and 1960s did U.S. practices align somewhat better with the rhetoric of "American-ness" as an open political choice. Yet tension over immigration began to rise again at the end of the millennium, and a *jus sanguinis* conception of "American-ness" became more prominent. In the 2004 book *Who Are We?: The Challenges to America's National Identity*, for example, provocative Harvard political scientist Samuel Huntington argued that the intake of so many immigrants from a single origin—Mexico—threatened to divide a nation built on an English-Protestant "core culture." Implicitly he saw Americans defined more by inherited blood and culture than by politics and "soil."

As we explore more in section 4.3, this kind of tension around citizenship and migration is an unsurprising consequence of a world composed of states. Once politics became dominated by territorial organizations, citizenship and movement between these units were sure to be major political issues. Within distinct sovereign spaces, states form the frameworks for different societies—some rich, some poor; some democratic, some not; and so on. Arguably, the most important factors for anyone's chances in life reflect which of these sovereign spaces they can access through citizenship. By blood or by birthplace, and sometimes with openings for naturalization, states assign us to different fates.

"Failed" States

In a handful of locations around the world, poor resources and enduring clashes between identities prevent the state model from taking root at all. In these **failed states**, effective political authority is absent. States depend on some allegiance from citizens in their territory, at least minimally agreeing not to fight each other and to accept some central authority. They also need some resources to support the development of central governing organizations, especially for military and

failed state
A country where the central government is entirely unable to control the territory, resulting in chaos.

police forces that give the state some control of the bottom line of violence. In the absence of both, highly unstable holes open up in the state system.

Even though it is not in complete collapse, Afghanistan is the most important example of a failing state in the news today. This Texas-sized, landlocked country of about 30 million people in central Asia has some history as a political unit, having been forged by leaders of Pashtun tribes into a short-lived Afghan Empire in the mid-1700s. However, internal ethnic challenges and external interventions have made it enormously difficult for anyone to maintain control. Ethnic Pashtuns comprise about 40 percent of the population, yet about 50 percent of Afghan citizens speak the Dari language rather than Pashto.[4] British and Russian competition to colonize the area in the nineteenth century was followed by a Soviet Union invasion and a U.S.-armed rebellion in the twentieth.

Resources for building a stable state also have been lacking. Afghanistan is one of the poorest places in the world—only a few African countries are poorer—and it is divided by immense mountains. Thus Afghanistan has never possessed an economic basis for taxes or other means to fund state organizations. In the late 1990s, it experienced a period of brief, harsh stability under the brutal rule of the Islamic fundamentalists known as the Taliban, but this period soon provoked even greater instability. Since this group provided a base for the Al Qaeda terrorist movement that launched the 9/11 attacks, a U.S.-led intervention in 2003 overturned the Taliban and began a long-running attempt to create a democratic government in its place. Today, while the current government is

Paul Avallone/ZUMA Press, Inc./Alamy Stock Photo

Women in the full veil known as the *burqa* pass by American soldiers in Paktya province of eastern Afghanistan.

recognized externally, there are few signs that it is extending control of territory beyond the capital of Kabul. A civil war with the Taliban grips much of the country, and even "peaceful" areas are run by local warlords who often ignore the central government.

The Afghan state also faces special obstacles in the organization of political and social authority because of patriarchal tribal groups called clans—a feature that it shares with the most complete example of a failed state, the East African country of Somalia. In both these societies and in some others across Africa, the Middle East, and central Asia, people identify first and foremost with the extended family of their father's bloodline. Most security and daily governance is provided by subclans numbering up to a few thousand people, who in times of major conflict or important decisions join together into larger clans. Would-be state builders in Afghanistan face a complex landscape of competition for authority that is difficult to master: overlapping clan feuds, ethnic and linguistic tensions, and the Taliban movement of radical Islamism. Somalia's beleaguered official government, which runs only the capital of Mogadishu, faces similar competition from clans and another roving Islamist army known as al-Shabaab.

The failures of state organization and unified national identity in Afghanistan and Somalia have brought tragic upheaval for their peoples and instability to their whole regions. We must be conscious, though, that the very notion of "failed states" reflects how much we take the specific nation-state model for granted. We expect each bit of the Earth to be controlled by a coherent state, and that expectation casts Afghans and Somalis as divisive people who have "failed." These expectations matter because they are held by very powerful players as well: the U.S. government, like other powerful states, will interact diplomatically and economically only with other places that organize themselves on a stable state model. Thus other places have little choice but to attempt to adopt this format. No one would argue that Afghanistan or Somalia are successes by any measure, certainly, but the failure is largely created by the imposition of a model of political authority that connects very poorly to their societies.

In other words, rather than reflecting any sort of bizarre self-destructiveness, these cases are just the most dramatic examples of tensions that we can see in many other places. Where the state model has been pushed onto ill-fitting societies amid extreme poverty, that state has sometimes disintegrated. Ongoing political fights elsewhere around immigration, citizenship, centralization, and decentralization are less striking manifestations of related tensions. Such variations and tensions, which are summarized in Table 4-1, will be with us as long as the state model remains our dominant political framework.

This last point raises a question: might there be reasons to think that the state will not be our dominant framework for much longer? Certain developments in the twenty-first century may be undercutting the state model—or perhaps just changing it in ways that make the construction of stable nation-states even more difficult, as we shall see.

Table 4-1 Variable Combinations of States and Nations

Outcome	Most Common Background	Common Features	Classic Examples
State-first nation-state	Early war-fighting state later consciously builds up national identity	Unitary structure *Jus soli* citizenship*	France, United Kingdom (though later UK devolution made it less unitary)
Nation-first nation-state	Language and/or religion generate common identity; nationalist movement then demands a shared state	*Jus sanguinis* citizenship Very strong nationalism Sometimes unitary, sometimes federal if combining strong earlier units	Germany, Italy, Japan
Fragmented nation-state	Diverse preexisting units come together for security, stability, or economic gain	Federal structure *Jus soli* citizenship*	United States, Canada, Nigeria
Failed state	Poverty + post-colonialism + ethnic or religious diversity	Institutions unable to govern	Somalia, Afghanistan, Central African Republic

*No country has pure *jus soli* citizenship rules; *jus soli* countries tend to combine citizenship rights by birth or residency with *jus sanguinis*-style pathways to citizenship by inheritance.

Challenges to the Nation-State Model

4.3 **Explain how global developments today pose challenges to the construction of stable nation-states.**

The state is a product of another era. It first arose as leaders fought to keep desta-bilizing forces out of their own territory, in a social context where most people never traveled out of their own village. National identity developed a bit later, as wider economic, social, and cultural interaction tied people together in larger groups and reinforced a logic of boundaries between "us" and "them." One running consequence of this separation of peoples into distinct political boxes was tension over migration, which has only increased over time. Additional tensions in the state system have arisen with the technological, economic, social, and political changes we call "globalization." Though we are not yet close to the end of state dominance—and perhaps that day will never come—the chal-lenges to constructing stable and successful nation-states are evolving in new directions.

Migration

Tension over migration is a common feature of the state system. States have usually permitted *some* movement across their borders—allowing trade, tempo-rary travel, and modest migration—but tend to treat large flows of people as destabilizing. This is hardly surprising: for organizations set up to manage populations within set borders, big population movements are a headache. In places where states merged with nations into nation-states, an influx of foreigners has also often been taken as a threat to identities and ways of life.

Several trends have inflamed these old tensions into major political issues today. In the historical background is the incomplete spread of industrialization in the 19th and 20th centuries. The emergence of vast economic disparities between "developed" and "underdeveloped" countries created divides in life prospects that continues to lure many migrants toward the former. Developed countries also gradually built up much more extensive public spending on education, public health, and welfare. This rendered them still more attractive as destinations—and led some rich-country citizens to resent the idea of sharing such benefits with people they perceive as outsiders. Racial, religious and ethnic differences magnify such resentments. Migrants have generally brought new diversity to Europe and North America. More visible physical or cultural differences can challenge pre-existing populations' sense of what "their" societies look like.

A related and rising tension is the fear that immigrants threaten "native" economic livelihoods because they are willing to work for lower wages. This equation has seemed increasingly compelling to many people in North America and Europe in recent decades. Roughly since the 1970s, substantial immigration has coincided with a decrease in stable, well-paid jobs for less educated people. Economists tend to find that these things are mostly unrelated: immigration has not strongly affected wages and generally benefits economic growth.[5] Economic changes trace more to technology (with automation replacing workers or making their jobs less skilled and less well paid) or to globalization (with jobs relocated to other countries; see below and later chapters).[6] Nonetheless, immigration has attracted much of the political blame.

In recent years these trends combined to produce anti-immigration political movements in most richer countries. In the United States, immigration became the issue that propelled Republican presidential candidate Donald Trump to the White House in 2016. Like similar politicians in other countries, President Trump's program sought a classic reassertion of the nation-state model. He called for reinforcing borders with physical walls, strengthening national defense, and pursuing American "national interests" unapologetically around the world. His rhetoric replaces the tale of the "melting pot" with discourse portraying a majority with shared racial and ethnic heritage.

Whether or not a Trump-style reassertion of the nation-state model is feasible in the twenty-first century—and who stands to gain or lose from it—are some of the great debates of our times. Many conditions in our "globalizing" world seem to undercut state sovereignty and control in straightforward ways. Yet that image of a states-versus-globalization clash misses some important features of today's politics. Until quite recently, the United States and other allied states have actively fostered globalization, so it does not seem quite right to say that they are undercut by it. Openness and international cooperation might challenge some states more than others.

Globalization

globalization
Rising flows of goods, services, money, people, and ideas across borders.

We live in an era of **globalization**: the increasing flows of goods, services, money, people, and ideas across state borders. Every year, we hear more loudly and frequently that it is changing our lives. Citizens' purchases, jobs, investments, personal movements, and cultural connections are no longer confined exclusively within state lines. States may be less able to regulate their own economies as they see fit, because business and investment may just move to other countries with more favorable policies. Vast movements of money in international markets make organizations as big as states look small, pressing all states to keep the favor of market investors or risk economic crisis. All these flows have increased substantially in the past few decades, and promise to keep on growing.

As we see in Figure 4-3, the trends that make up globalization are unmistakable. But do they have similarly clear implications for the state and political authority? The most common view is that globalization drains power away

Figure 4-3 Rising Global Flows

Leading into the twenty-first century, international flows of communication, trade, and cross-border investment skyrocketed. Flows of people—migration—rose more gradually.

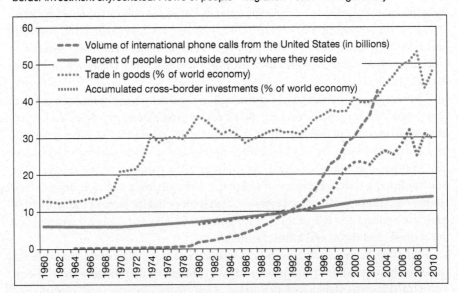

Sources: Red line (investments) from United Nation Conference on Trade and Development "Report on Inward and Outward Foreign Direct Investment Stock," Annual, 1980–2010, Available at http://unctadstat. unctad.org/; purple line (phone calls) from FCC report *Trends in the International Telecommunications Industry*, September 2005, p. 13; blue line (trade in goods) from World Bank, World Development Indicators Online; green line (percent foreign born) from UN Migration database, http://esa.un.org/unmigration/.

from states. For those states whose leaders wish to control information—most blatantly undemocratic regimes like those in China or Iran who seek to manage what their citizens know—their power is thwarted by how the Internet, and smart phones make it harder to shut out (or in) news and communication. In these and other ways, say many observers, globalization is forcing power to leak out of state boxes. To some degree, the result may simply be a net loss of political authority in which certain things that states could once control now fall under no one's control. In other respects, power is shifting away from the formal territorial authority of states into other hands: multinational corporations, financial market players, international organizations, nongovernmental organizations like Amnesty International, and other globalized players we will encounter in future chapters.

Yet as simple as it sounds—that action across borders challenges the state—globalization does not necessarily undercut the state everywhere. It challenges certain kinds of states more than others. Though today we are seeing considerable backlash against globalization in American and European politics, that is a fairly new development. Since World War II the rich states in North America and Europe have actively encouraged the development of international trade and investment, freedom of movement, and technology to support these flows of goods and services. One of the main reasons why globalization has arisen, in fact, is because these relatively open societies have worked purposely to extend some of their internal practices abroad—pushing other countries to open their markets, allow information to flow more freely, and adopt laws and governments that increase citizens' freedom to move and live as they please. Even though globalization's hard-to-control flows alter the challenges involving in managing all territories, then, it does not necessarily foretell the end of the state system itself. States that can preserve their territorial governance and fairly coherent identities amid openness seem likely to continue enjoying strong authority. States that have relied on tighter, more rigid controls may destabilize when challenged by openness. Some countries that have found it hard to build tight nation-states because of their multiethnic societies now may find their society works better with a more open model in a globalized setting. Those who have come closest to "failed states" so far, unfortunately, are likely to find the construction of stable authority even harder in a more free-flowing world. Thus, though globalization brings new challenges to all states, these evolutions will bring more opportunities than threats for some states, and for others the reverse.

Human Rights, International Law, and International Organizations

While globalization presents challenges to states by encouraging movement beyond the state's sphere of control, our era also features a more direct challenge. The principle of state sovereignty is that a state is recognized as

human rights
Rights that ostensibly apply to all people simply by virtue of being human.

international law
A set of rules that states generally accept as binding.

international organizations
Entities created by agreements between states to manage international cooperation or undertake specific tasks.

supreme within its own borders; no outsider can tell it what to do internally. In the twenty-first century, however, states face a growing number of entities that judge how they act and tell them what to do. At the broadest level, since World War II the notion of **human rights** has steadily gained influence. These are rights that individuals enjoy simply because they are human beings and that no state can legitimately ignore. Common examples are freedom of religion or the right to a fair and impartial trial. Even powerful states like China come under constant pressure to respect human rights; the United States, too, faces regular criticism as the only wealthy democracy that retains the death penalty.

Some rights are also inscribed in **international law**, which is a set of rules that states generally accept as binding. The Geneva Convention of 1949, for example, sets international law for the part of state behavior that may seem least likely to accept rules: warfare. It bans chemical and biological weapons and requires humane treatment of prisoners of war, among other things, and has a surprisingly strong record of being respected. The International Court of Justice arbitrates conflicts between states; the International Criminal Court tries individuals accused of major human rights violations who have not been prosecuted by national courts.

The most direct external pressures on some state behavior, finally, come from **international organizations** like the United Nations (UN), the World Trade Organization (WTO), or the European Union (EU). These organizations are formed through negotiated deals among states, but they then create groups of people with authority and resources "above" the states themselves. Some, including the UN, the WTO, and especially the very powerful EU, can tell their member-states what to do on many issues.

Do these explicit challenges to state sovereignty promise a future that goes beyond the nation-state to something else? They clearly qualify sovereignty, making it less absolute. Yet like global flows of currency and culture, these trends may challenge certain kinds of states (or certain political agendas within states) more than the state model itself. Many of the most powerful states in the world, especially in North America and Europe, support international organizations like the UN, which champions human rights, so we cannot simply see either human rights or international organizations as opposed to all states. In a few instances, most notably the EU—which is by far the most powerful international organization ever created—states have given so much authority to the international level that state sovereignty itself seems to have been substantially replaced by a new format for authority. Yet even in this case, leaders of these states have generally done so because they believed international organizations would make their states *stronger* rather than weaker. The UN, the EU, and other organizations have been created by states to get other states to act in certain ways. It is debatable, then, whether or not international law and organizations are forces that will gradually open up the state system to evolve into something else. Such law and organizations may be most effective as external tools for reinforcing an even tighter, more specifically defined model of state authority around the world.

The nation-state model clearly faces new challenges in the twenty-first century, but the result could just be a world of different states rather than a world of something else. We must remember that state sovereignty and the nation-state model have rarely been perfect and absolute in the past. In a few societies, they have produced relatively homogeneous, centralized, unified political units, but usually the result has been more mixed and complex. Globalization, human rights, international law, and international organizations increasingly shift the external pressures that societies face, making the challenge of building a nation-state a more complicated task of balancing political authority between internal and external demands. Some states may meet these new challenges well, while others fall into chaos or transform. Only time will tell. For now, states remain our core political architecture.

Whether the state's enduring power is a good thing, though, is another question. Do we want the state to remain dominant, or should we seek to accelerate its demise? Having seen how strongly our world is organized around this taken-for-granted framework, we can now reclaim it as an object for critical thinking. The major ideological traditions provide the concepts and language to help us personally evaluate: what is good or bad about the state?

Political Ideologies and the State

4.4 Evaluate state sovereignty from multiple ideological points of view.

As we might expect about a political model that has dominated the modern era, the state is broadly accepted by most mainstream politicians as a good thing. That acceptance is accompanied by debate about the costs and benefits of a boxed-in world of sovereignty, though, and outside the mainstream the state attracts both strong champions and aggressive critics. Our survey of ideological views runs from those who see state sovereignty as unambiguously good, to mixed positions, to its main opponents.

The State as Source of Security, Belonging, and Stability

States formed as security organizations, and the protection of citizens has long been seen as their first benefit. The principle of sovereignty aspires to give all peoples a safe dwelling place. Within spaces of security and order, nation-states also offer a sense of belonging to a group.

The more we see the world as a threatening place, the more it seems crucial to have such a physically secure space and psychologically secure place within it. Unsurprisingly, then, the political ideology that sees the outside world as most threatening—fascism—elevates the state to the source of all political good. Fascists call for a strong, militarized, aggressive state as the only way to bring security to their group of people. Belonging to a powerful nation-state with a unified identity, they believe, also gives psychological security and meaning to individuals' lives.

Though few people endorse fascism today, more mainstream ideologies include moderate versions of the same points. Most mainstream leaders would agree that the state responds to important needs for defense from external threats, some centralized provision of order, and some sense of group identity. In particular, modern conservatives place a strong emphasis on these benefits of the state. They argue that in an unstable world, a strong framework for authority and identity anchors people in time-tested values and community. Conservative politicians today in the Republican Party tend to see security, law and order, and a coherent national identity as the most worthwhile goals of state action. This is why they often favor defense spending while seeking to cut back most other areas of government activity. Donald Trump has made these views the dominant position within American conservatism.

With respect to foreign policy toward other states, conservatives also tend to see sovereignty as a stabilizing rule that is worth respecting. They often oppose interventions in the affairs of other countries for the same reason that they tend to oppose active government intervention at home: it is risky to push too much for "progress" in the world, since even the most well-meaning government interventions frequently go wrong. Even though conservatives—like other Americans—might like to press other states to reform, such as pushing for democratic governments in China or the Middle East, they tend to think that interfering in other states' affairs leads more often to instability and conflict than to positive change. Under President Trump's leadership, the main focus has been on asserting American power and leverage to get "better deals" with other sovereign states.

The State as Framework for Rights and Representation

Besides valuing the state's contribution to security and stability, modern conservatives attribute other benefits to it because of their roots in classical liberalism. In the Lockean philosophy that founded classical liberalism, the state is seen as beneficial less for providing security than for supporting individual rights and representation. By establishing supreme authority over a territory, the state makes it possible to establish and enforce individual rights within that space. Without a clear system of state sovereignty, it could be much harder to know who enjoyed which rights and who would enforce them. A single authority for each territory also offers a framework for representation, providing a clear target for popular input. With more overlapping authority, citizens might not know where to go to influence their leadership.

The combination of rights and representation that we know as "liberal democracy" emerged historically within the state, as certain peoples organized their states internally with the institutions advocated by classical liberalism. Without first being a state, it is difficult to imagine how similar liberal democracies could be created. Thus if modern conservatives typically wish to defend sovereignty for reasons of stability and security, they also see it as the foundation of rights and representation. They fear that if state control weakens—due to poor defense, inadequate internal order, uncontrolled immigration, or perhaps the rise of powerful international organizations like the European Union—rights and representation will become blurrier and will serve citizens less well.

Modern liberals, the other descendants of classical liberalism, share some of these views. They too usually perceive maintenance of state control as a key basis for delivering the benefits of rights and representation. Yet modern liberals tend to be more willing than conservatives to question how much we should focus on defending sovereignty, since they often think that this principle leaves room for improvement. The ideology of modern liberals is more optimistic about human nature and progress. They believe that active government can improve people's lives, and they typically see a less threatening world in which the state does not need to focus as much on security, order, and tight national identity. For these reasons, they tend to be open to arguments about how pure state sovereignty might not be the best and final solution for political organization, since it may have costs as well as benefits. To fully capture the modern-liberal view of states, then, we must consider what those costs might be.

The State as Source of Oppression and Exclusion

Each of the state's potential benefits has a flip side of potential costs. Sovereignty may generate areas where rights and representation can be enforced, but it also creates space for other internal rules. By declaring that each state runs its own affairs, sovereignty authorizes the Chinese government to reject liberal rights and democracy, just as it authorizes the American state to embrace them. Nondemocratic states like China, North Korea, Iran, or Syria constantly argue that sovereignty allows them to ignore other peoples' criticisms of their internal politics. When Chinese human rights advocate Liu Xiaobo was awarded the Nobel Peace Prize, China's government called the award an "obscenity" that infringed on its sovereignty.[7] The imprisoned Liu was unable to receive his prize (see photo).

Neither conservatives nor modern liberals approve of nondemocratic governments, but modern liberals are more likely to act on their disapproval. Just as modern liberals are more confident than conservatives that an active government

John McConnico/AP Images

The Nobel Prize Committee chairman sits next to an empty chair meant for the Chinese recipient of the Nobel Peace Prize in 2010, Liu Xiaobo, whose photo hangs on the left.

can improve its own society, so modern liberals tend to think that putting active pressure on nondemocratic regimes can bring about a better world. Whereas conservatives hold to sovereignty as an imperfect but stable international rule, liberals tend to seek progress even at the risk of some instability. Thus in 2011, when the Obama administration intervened to support a revolt against Libyan dictator Muammar Gaddafi, many conservatives argued that the risk of chaos in Libya meant the United States should have reluctantly respected Libyan sovereignty.

The state's benefits for belonging and security also have flip sides. Creating "us" also creates "them." States are instruments of exclusion, drawing sharp lines on the map like the increasingly fortified U.S.–Mexico border. Even states that have traditionally been relatively open to travel and immigration, like the United States, have tended to devote enormous resources to keeping out the "wrong" people: those who do not have claims to citizenship or purposes like tourism or trade that are endorsed with a passport from another state. The state's provision of security, too, can have enormous costs. Historically, states did not end security problems; they escalated them to a new level of organized violence. From this perspective, the world wars of the twentieth century were a product of the state, the destructive power of which was magnified when it connected with strong national identity and aggressive nationalism. Even in peacetime, the division of the world into states constantly hinders attempts at cooperation on problems that stretch across borders, such as international trade or pollution.

For all these reasons, ideologies that seek some vision of "progress" often question sovereignty or oppose it outright. Modern liberals are willing to consider how modest steps beyond sovereignty might deliver what they see as progress: they tend to be moderate on immigration, support more open access at borders, and favor international law and organizations to manage issues that cut across states. Moderate socialists hold similar positions, as they converge in practice with modern liberalism, but stronger socialist views are more hostile to sovereignty. For devout Marxists, states are the main tools that the rich use to divide the working class and enforce exploitation. In principle, communist ideology opposes the system of sovereignty entirely; it calls for workers everywhere to rise in a revolution across borders and recast the world economy. Environmentalism, too, follows its own vision of progress that makes it largely hostile to state sovereignty. The main environmental issue of our times, climate change, is a classic cross-state issue. The countries that most resist acting on climate change—above all China and the United States—frequently insist that their sovereignty allows them to do what they please in their territory. For environmentalists, sovereignty cannot be allowed to block a response to this global challenge. Radical Islamists, finally, believe that sovereignty must be subjugated to their own kind of "progress" to a better world: orienting the historically Muslim lands around religious authority and values. They view the state as a Western creation—as it was—that artificially fragmented the Muslim world.

Since the state defines the basic political architecture of our world, these ideological stances about its costs and benefits underlie many of our hottest issues today. For example:

- Should the United States intervene to support pro-democracy activists in China or the Middle East?
- Is immigration more about international human rights or more about each country's sovereign rights to close its doors?
- Can countries legitimately refuse to participate in international environmental cooperation?

Clashes on all these questions follow from a world in which politics is shoehorned into the state model. Fortunately, the major ideologies offer us the concepts and language to craft possible answers, as summarized in Table 4-2.

Table 4-2 Summarizing Ideological Perspectives on State Sovereignty

Political ideologies emphasize different costs and benefits of respecting state sovereignty. Starred X's indicate the most prominent themes for each ideology's view. Note that modern liberals hold the broadest (and thus most ambiguous) position, acknowledging a wide range of both benefits and costs of this principle.

IDEOLOGY (Listed in order from pro-sovereignty to anti-sovereignty ideologies)	SYMPATHY TO ARGUMENTS ABOUT SOVEREIGNTY'S BENEFITS AND COSTS							
	Sovereignty helps to provide . . .				Sovereignty's cost is . . .			
	BELONGING	SECURITY	STABILITY	REPRESENTATION	PROTECTION OF BAD REGIMES	OBSTACLES TO GLOBAL COOPERATION	EXCLUSION	OPPRESSION
FASCISM	X*	X*						
MODERN CONSERVATISM	X	X*	X*	X				
MODERN LIBERALISM	X	X	X	X*	X*	X*	X	
ENVIRONMENTALISM						X*		
SOCIALISM						X	X	X*
POLITICAL ISLAMISM							X	X*

Explaining a Case: The Whys of Afghanistan's Struggles with Statehood

4.5 Identify multiple plausible explanations for the difficulty of state building in Afghanistan.

How we ideologically judge the politics of state sovereignty is entangled with how we explain any given case of state-ness. If we explain the emergence of states mainly by pointing to geography and economic resources, for example, we can hardly blame the people who live in a mountainous desert for inhabiting a weak or failed state. If we explain states more as functions of institutions or culture, we may become more or less optimistic about people's ability to craft stable states—and assign them more or less blame for failures to do so. Afghanistan stands out as a case in which these explanations matter a great deal today. It is often perceived as being very close to a "failed state" because its central government seems unable to establish minimal authority over its territory, even after enormous assistance from American firepower and money. Why?

The three explanatory stories from the introductory chapter help us brainstorm some plausible alternatives.

Each story focuses our attention on one dynamic in Afghan politics. In the real world, all three dynamics probably matter—the material landscape, institutions, and ideas all contribute to the troubles of the Afghan state—but perhaps not equally. Thus the next step is to ask: how would we evaluate how strong the evidence is for each story?

The Rational-Material Story

The simplest explanation of Afghanistan's problems draws our attention to the material lay of the land: geography, poverty, and security threats. Landlocked and divided by mountains, Afghanistan has never developed an integrated economy and society. More powerful neighbors have constantly intervened and further weakened the state. Given these challenges, no one yet has ever established a strong and stable state over this territory. American resources might have propped up central power briefly, but unless that support were to continue indefinitely there is no sign that this will change.

The Institutional Story

An institutional approach suggests that Afghanistan's prospects are not quite so bleak. In this view, its problems mainly reflect weak central institutions and anti-state rules in society. With little history of national military, police, or administrative agencies, the central government is starting from scratch. Traditional organization of leadership in clans further impedes the state. Organizing an effective state is enormously difficult without earlier foundations to build upon, but if some basic organizational success can be found, it may gradually win over domestic support and redirect Afghan political mobilization into a new political game. The trick is to design institutions that will encourage most Afghans to play along peacefully.

The Ideational Story

From an ideational point of view, the root of Afghanistan's problems lies in conflictual identities and ideas. Both tribal identities and religious doctrines pose huge challenges to state control. The large Pashtun tribes in the south see themselves as the historical rulers of this territory. Smaller groups built around other ethnicities and languages form a majority, however, and have long resented (and fought against) a Pashtun-led state. On top of these and other tribal rivalries, a radical form of Islamism has taken root in many Afghan communities, which has created an insurgency of religious warriors ready to give their lives to enforce hard-line Islamic rules. A central state will succeed only if leaders of these various fragmented groups can be enticed into some sort of common identity.

Political scientists would look for real-world evidence with two broad research strategies (or combinations of them): quantitative research on cross-case patterns and qualitative research on within-case processes. Researchers might also design experiments or construct artificial environments to explore the plausibility of these stories, but we will focus here and in subsequent chapters on seeking observations in quantitative and qualitative evidence.

RESEARCH ON WITHIN-CASE PROCESSES. The most direct strategy is to look for evidence for each story in information about Afghanistan, the way a detective might trace evidence about plausible suspects of a crime. Just as a detective must consider carefully what evidence points to the guilty party—Who owns a gun? Whose shoes fit the bloody footprints? Who has an alibi?—so political scientists consider which detailed processes we would be able to see in Afghanistan if each story were correct. For each explanatory approach, we ask: if this story captured what was going on, *who* would we see doing *what*, and *when*? Table 4-3 sketches out some process expectations for our three plausible stories, including suggesting which kind of evidence would be like "catching the crook red-handed" for each account—the best evidence that it gets the story right.

Table 4-3 Exploring Within-Case Evidence for Explanations of Current Afghan Politics

	Rational-Material Explanation	Institutional Explanation	Ideational Explanation
Who most supports state unity?	Economic elites in cities who seek stability and development	Administrative elites in central government who seek to govern	Pashtun tribes
Who is main obstacle to state unity?	Poor, uneducated people in distant hinterlands	Organized tribes or warlords outside the central government	Other ethnic groups or competitors to Pashtun leadership (Islamic vs. secular leaders)
What is main dynamic of conflict?	The center attempts to administer public policies, fails due to lack of resources	Struggle for control between the central government and other groups	Ethnic or religious
When do we see more unity or fragmentation?	When the center gains or loses new resources (like U.S. aid)	When the center overcomes competitors or co-opts them as allies	When moderates construct cross-ethnic coalitions, or if one group dominates
Best Evidence to Support Each Explanation	We see that even the best-organized attempts at new central policies run into major problems of poverty, lack of infrastructure, geography, weather.	We see that in areas where the center is best organized (or local forces are less coherently organized) unity prevails; where local forces are stronger, the center loses control.	We find that tribal loyalties almost always trump all other considerations in support or opposition to the center.

Though Afghanistan is far off, and maybe your Pashto language skills are shaky, you can still look for evidence for these competing stories. Find a news article on the challenges of the Afghani government from a credible newspaper, magazine, or website. Then break down the way the story is presented: where do you see mentions of material resources, institutional rules and organizations in state or society, or ideas and identity that seem to fit one of these images?

RESEARCH ON CROSS-CASE PATTERNS. Another research strategy is to look at a wide set of countries to compare with Afghanistan to see what kinds of conditions appear to be associated in cross-case patterns with state success or failure. Is extreme poverty, mountainous geography, proximity of threatening societies, or some combination of these factors present in other cases of failed states? Or have some states succeeded despite these material conditions, while perhaps differing from Afghanistan in their institutions or identities? Your instructor may be able to help you find data to explore some of these possible cross-case correlations.

Conclusion: Why the State Matters to You

When we encounter someone who seems not to be from our neck of the woods, our first question tends to be, "What country are you from?" The organizations that run countries—states—define many elements of our lives, and knowing someone's home state instantly tells us quite a bit about them. For better or for worse, the territorial state is *the* key political framework for life on Earth.

If states were all the same, though, "where are you from?" would not be so interesting. We ask foreigners this question not just because states are important but because they are so different from each other. The organization of our world in states imposes similar challenges everywhere, but each state faces its own configuration of these challenges and confronts them with certain strategies and degrees of success. Few places find themselves perfectly suited to the state model, and cases those with strong state authority and unified national identities are more the exception than the rule. In most places, constructing an effective, widely accepted state and a moderately united identity are constant works-in-progress.

These works-in-progress are also changing. Globalization and the rise of international governance may increase the discomforts of the state model so much, and for so many countries, that the modern era of state sovereignty gives way to something new. More likely, though, is that the state model will persist, and peoples will simply confront different challenges to stabilize it in a more globalized world. Understanding the state model and its variations will remain crucial to grasp the politics around us.

Review of Learning Objectives

4.1 **Distinguish between states and nations and explain why the state is the dominant organizing framework for politics in the world today.**

Today, most of the politics on Earth are framed within sovereign states with supreme authority over clear territory, but this was not always the case. The state model emerged in Europe because military technology increasingly favored large armies, rising trade created resources to build stronger governments, and religious conflict broke the dominance of the Catholic Church. It became still more powerful when connected to nations, binding the state and national identity into a unified nation-state. This model spread around the world due to European colonization and by powerful states insisting that they would interact only with similarly organized entities.

4.2 **Illustrate how the historical relationship between state and nation in a country can shape its politics today.**

Depending on how state building occurred in each country, and how it related (or not) to national identities, states vary in how strongly and simply they relate to their territory and population. Where state and nation aligned strongly, we often find a unitary state today; where they did not, decentralized federal states are more common. Where national identity preceded the state, we see *jus sanguinis*, or "blood"-based citizenship rules. Where state preceded nation, or combined many nations together, we see *jus soli*, or citizenship by birth or residence on the "soil." In a few places, clashes between the state model and local identities were so sharp that we now see a chaotic "failed state."

4.3 **Explain how global developments today pose new challenges to the construction of stable nation-states.**

States today appear to be undercut by challenges from migration and from "globalization" more broadly: rising cross-border flows of trade, investment, information, and people. Another challenge comes from human rights, international law, and international organizations, which reject the notion that states can do as they please on their territory. Even if global flows and international governance pose new challenges, however, these developments have been championed by powerful states that see them as encouraging a more open, prosperous, and peaceful world. These trends may thus reinforce certain states' agendas, while challenging other states that are unwilling or too weak to go along with them.

4.4 **Evaluate state sovereignty from several different ideological points of view.**

Defenders of sovereignty see it as a system that provides security, stability, and belonging to members of nation-states. Fascists take this view to an extreme, but a milder version is important in conservatism. Conservatives and modern liberals also see the state as providing a framework within which liberal democracy can flourish. Modern liberals sympathize with some critiques of sovereignty, however, favoring international cooperation on many cross-state issues and active pressure on nondemocratic states to change their policies. Committed socialists, environmentalists, and radical Islamists are all hostile to sovereignty, respectively seeing the fight against inequality, defense of the natural environment, or Islam as trumping any state's claim to supreme authority over its territory.

4.5   Identify multiple plausible explanations for the difficulty of state building in Afghanistan.

To review for this objective, try to brainstorm rational-material, institutional, and ideational explanations of the Afghan state's troubles without looking at Section 4.5:

- If we see the construction of strong state organizations as based on the material resources and obstacles in the material landscape, what conditions in Afghanistan might impede a strong state?
- If, alternatively, we see state organizations as shaped strongly by a legacy of institutions from earlier eras, what institutions (or lack of institutions) in Afghanistan might get in the way of state building?
- If instead we see state organizations as constructed mainly around culture and ideas, what kind of a story might we tell about why state building could be difficult in this part of the world?

After brainstorming your answers to these questions, return to Section 4.5 to see if you captured the main logic of these explanatory alternatives.

Great Sources to Find Out More

Ashraf Ghani and Clare Lockhart, *Fixing Failed States: A Framework for Rebuilding a Fractured World* (New York: Oxford University Press, 2008). A hopeful but realistic discussion of how best to stabilize failed states.

Charles Tilly, ed., *The Formation of National States in Western Europe* (Princeton, NJ: Princeton University Press, 1975). A classic collection of essays on the rise of the nation-state.

Douglas Held, *Global Covenant: The Social Democratic Alternative to the Washington Consensus* (Cambridge, UK: Polity Press, 2004). A social-democratic advocate of global-level democracy makes the case for moving away from a world based on sovereignty.

Ernst Gellner, *Nations and Nationalism* (Ithaca, NY: Cornell University Press, 1983). A short, classic discussion of nationalism that is both very accessible and hugely influential.

Georg Sorensen, *Changes in Statehood: The Transformation of International Relations* (New York: Palgrave, 2001). A look at the relationship between changes inside and outside of states.

George Steinmetz, ed., *State/Culture: State Formation after the Cultural Turn* (Ithaca, NY: Cornell University Press, 1999). This book features a collection of essays that investigate the role of culture in state building around the world.

Hendrik Spruyt, *The Sovereign State and Its Competitors* (Princeton, NJ: Princeton University Press, 1994). A nuanced story of how the state replaced other organizations in Europe.

Ian Buruma, *Inventing Japan, 1853–1964* (New York: Random House, 2004). A very readable overview of the creation of a modern nation-state in Japan.

Khaled Hosseini, *The Kite Runner* (New York: Riverhead, 2003). A best-selling novel that captured life in a fractured Afghanistan.

Robert Jackson, *Quasi-States: Sovereignty, International Relations, and the Third World* (New York: Cambridge University Press, 1993). A brilliant treatment of the problems of post-colonial states.

Samuel Huntington, *Who Are We? The Challenges to America's National Identity* (New York: Simon & Schuster, 2004).

Thomas Ertman, *Birth of the Leviathan: Building States and Regimes in Medieval and Early Modern Europe* (New York: Cambridge University Press, 1997). This analysis traces how the strength and shape of early European states reflected varying prestate institutional arrangements across the continent.

T.V. Paul, John Ikenberry, and John Hall, eds., *The Nation-State in Question* (Princeton, NJ: Princeton University Press, 2003). A collection of essays on globalization and the state model.

Wendy Brown, *Walled States, Waning Sovereignty* (Cambridge, MA: Zone Books, 2010). A leading political theorist criticizes what she sees as the contradictions of exclusion and openness in a neoliberal (conservative) world through a study of border walls.

Develop Your Thinking

Use these questions as discussion or short writing exercises to think more deeply about some of the key themes of the chapter.

1. Would you rather have one state that governs all aspects of your life or multiple political authorities for different issues?
2. Should citizenship be determined by "blood" (inheritance) or by "soil" (place of birth or residence)?
3. In our globalizing world, do you think you feel less or more attached to your home state than your grandparents did to theirs?
4. Should we sometimes respect state sovereignty even if we think a certain state is not serving its citizens well?
5. Should we blame Afghanistan's troubles more on its internal conditions and people, or more on the outside world?
6. Would our world be better or worse if anyone could freely migrate across all national borders?

Keywords

Chapter 5
Governments

A Chinese boy and his mother visit Tiananmen Square in Beijing. Citizens in democracies often find it hard to believe that people in nondemocracies may genuinely support their governments—but sometimes they do.

 Learning Objectives

5.1 Explain the difference between authority and power and identify five reasons why citizens may support governments and their decisions.

5.2 Identify the two core elements of liberal-democratic government, explain their relationship, and describe how tradition and effectiveness also support such regimes.

5.3 Identify the core features of illiberal democracy and explain how some

justify this model as preferable to liberal democracy.

5.4 Identify four types of authoritarianism and their core principles and describe several sources of authoritarian support using specific country examples.

5.5 Evaluate the most important defenses and critiques of liberal-democratic government.

5.6 Identify multiple plausible explanations for China's one-party regime.

Democracy Is the Best Kind of Government . . . Right?

The citizens of most democracies tend to think their kind of government is obviously the best. By guaranteeing individual rights and making leaders accountable through representation, democracy offers "life, liberty, and the pursuit of happiness," as the U.S. Declaration of Independence puts it. Nondemocratic governments can seem, by comparison, like thugs whose power rests on guns and bribes. In China's Communist Party system, for example, the record of "forced disappearances, extralegal detentions, arrests and convictions of human rights activists, lawyers, religious leaders, and ethnic minorities" is obviously repressive.[1] Sometimes such governments kill many of their citizens, as in China's Tiananmen Square massacre in 1989 or the recent slaughter of rebels by Syria's brutal leaders.

But is democracy's superiority really so obvious? China may lead the world in executions, but the United States imprisons six times more people as a share of its population.[2] Nor is it clear where average citizens are happier with government. In 2018, only 10 percent of Americans told pollsters that they were "very satisfied" with American democracy. Another 30 percent said they were "somewhat satisfied"—leaving 60 percent in negative categories.[3] Across wealthy democracies overall, levels of reported "trust in government" have hovered around 40 percent in recent years.[4] In China, meanwhile, reputable surveys regularly find that over 80 percent of people say they have confidence or trust in their central government.[5]

This chapter investigates the roots of political authority in democracy and its main alternatives. Democracy has powerful justifications, but nondemocratic governments also construct authority beyond bribes and guns. We will also see that some similar dynamics uphold democracies and nondemocracies alike. And while such comparisons may not shake our preference for rights and representation, hopefully, they empower us to think critically about our own government in particular, as well as the multiple roots of political authority worldwide. ■

Governments, Authority, and Power

5.1 Explain the difference between authority and power and identify five reasons why citizens may support governments and their decisions.

government
The organization of political authority within a state.

legitimacy
The perception of something as rightful and appropriate, regardless of whether it is liked.

Government refers to the organization of political authority within a state. Also called "regimes" or "political systems," governments consist of rules and processes by which people gain authority to make collective decisions for a state. Different governments allocate authority in different ways and justify it according to different principles.

When we talk of political authority, we do not just mean power to impose decisions. Authority is power that claims **legitimacy**, asserting that it is rightful and appropriate. Even the most brutal, repressive governments are not quite like gangs who just force or pay off people to comply; they always try to justify their authority with principles. At the same time, even governments that are widely accepted as legitimate also employ raw incentives and force. Americans obey laws and pay taxes because the U.S. government enforces fines, jail time, and even the death penalty to incentivize acceptance of its rules. Every government mixes claims to legitimate authority with incentives to respect its power.

To set the scene for our tour of governments, this section first considers the bases of governments' claims of authority. Next, we consider how more blatant exertion of power, separate from legitimacy, can uphold governments as well. Lastly, we note that broad historical trends have favored the option of "rational-legal" authority that is associated with democratic government—but that global dominance of such authority is incomplete and its further spread uncertain.

Authority: Traditional, Charismatic, and Rational-Legal

Why might citizens feel that they should respect government rules and decisions? Sociologist Max Weber, who famously defined the state as a territorial organization with a monopoly on the legitimate use of violence, also provided the best-known breakdown of legitimate authority.[6] According to Weber, leaders assert that their authority is morally right for three kinds of reasons:

- *Traditional legitimacy* is justified by historical myths, legends, and long-standing practice, assigning authority "because that is how we do things around here." Kings and queens, for example, typically base their authority on traditional legitimacy. When practices persist for a long time, people often see respect for them as part of their identity. Traditional authority is cultivated with rituals, symbolism, appeals to old foundations, and often nationalist claims that "we" belong together and that a leader is "one of us."

- *Charismatic legitimacy* is justified by the magnetic appeal of a leader or her ideas. "Charisma" in normal conversation means attractiveness, but in a political context it refers to that peculiar quality of leaders or elegant concepts to which people are drawn. Extraordinary individuals often break with tradition and change the world due to their personal charisma: Jesus, Muhammad, Martin Luther King, or—in a darker vein—Adolf Hitler all commanded tremendous authority through charisma. People also often submit to authority in the name of beautifully charismatic ideas like equality, freedom, or salvation.

- *Rational-legal legitimacy* is justified by rules that are presented as logical, systematic, and evenly applied. It assigns authority by undertaking a process that is understood to be reasonable. Elections in democracies, for example, are mechanisms for rational-legal legitimacy. They give authority to an elected leader due to the process that selected her or him. Entrance exams or educational requirements are other mechanisms of rational-legal legitimacy, suggesting that someone can rightfully be a school principal, serve as a judge, or occupy other positions due to the fair and reasonable process that put her or him there.

Weber's categories may be easiest to grasp when we see them operating in everyday life, not just with governments. When a teenager respects a parents' curfew, traditional authority is typically at work: he or she has been taught to obey his or her parents, and may identify as part of a family that belongs together. Likewise, we have all encountered charismatic teachers, coaches, or peers who hold some authority over us, and perhaps been entranced by a beautiful cause— ending poverty, protecting the Earth, saving souls—whose champions we would follow. And finally, our daily lives are full of rational-legal processes: we follow a doctor's authority because she or he has earned degrees that signal expertise, or acknowledge universities' authority to admit or deny us because they employ exams and other fairly even-handed and transparent criteria. We have all personally experienced Weber's three options.

Analogies to these everyday situations can help us approach the more distant subject of government authority. When government leaders seek our support and compliance, do they use parental-style traditionalism, act like charismatic coaches, or command respect due to fair selection processes that put them in office? Or do they, perhaps, combine these roles?

Power: Relying on Effectiveness and Force

Besides making claims to legitimacy much like authority figures in everyday life, governments encourage compliance in ways that parents, coaches, or doctors cannot. They control the powerful organizations of states, and so hold many tools for gathering and distributing resources, plus considerable capacity for violence. Whether or not citizens recognize their authority as rightful, regimes may pay off or pressure people to accept their decisions.

effectiveness
The delivery of benefits that can convince citizens to support a regime no matter how it is legitimized.

Government power can win compliance with both carrots and sticks. For carrots, governments perform many tasks that may bring citizens wealth, security, social stability, peace, or other basic advantages. When citizens endorse a government for raw benefits, we say the government is upheld by **effectiveness**. China's extraordinary economic growth, which averaged almost 10 percent a year from the 1980s to the 2010s and remains quite high, leads many citizens to accept the regime irrespective of their moral views of it. In Russia, similarly, many citizens support President Vladimir Putin for his relative economic success, despite his blatant abuse of rights and Russian law. The American government, too, derives support from the fact that its population is well off overall. Such support is sometimes seen as a kind of legitimacy, but it is better understood in terms of power and payoffs. Quite separate from any righteous endorsement of China's Communist leadership, Putin, or U.S. government, citizens may accept these regimes—and even enthusiastically support them—for the daily benefits they provide.

Kevin Miller/Alamy Stock Photo

The skyline of Ho Chi Minh City, Vietnam (once known as Saigon), suggests that this once-impoverished country is developing a thriving economy. The Vietnamese Communist Party's lasting hold on power is supported by economic growth, which has even exceeded Chinese growth in some stretches since 1990.

When effectiveness is lacking and legitimacy claims fail to convince, governments also wield powerful sticks. States arose as security organizations, after all, and all governments possess police and military forces to enforce their decisions. Citizens who do not play by their rules end up in courts, in prisons, and in some countries in torture chambers or graveyards. Governments' sticks may be economic, too, operating through subtle elements of status: in China or Russia, uncooperative citizens might find their finances and taxes investigated, career promotions derailed, children excluded from desirable schools or universities, and so on. The worst governments rely heavily on such punishments and physical force, since they fail to deliver much of anything in the way of performance or persuasive claims to legitimacy.

Yet it is *how* governments use force, not the raw amount of force employed, that tells us whether or not it plays a distinct role in upholding a regime. Some of the most legitimate and effective governments, like Britain or Japan, also have high capabilities for force—putting sizable police forces on the streets and large militaries on bases and borders. Indeed, the United States spends almost three times more on its military than any other country,[7] ranks third in the absolute number of police personnel (after India and China), and stands out for striking use of prisons—incarcerating a larger share of its population than any other country.[8] In democracies like the United States, Japan, or Britain, however, force works in conjunction with legitimacy. Policing and imprisonment are so deeply embedded in rational-legal processes—due process of law, judges, lawyers, appeals, and so on—that leaders cannot depend on force to silence challengers. An American mayor, governor, or president cannot just have someone arrested, and prisons in the United States, Japan, or Britain do not hold political critics of the government. In places like China or Syria, by contrast, the government uses force for the direct purpose of strengthening the regime. Officials at all levels frequently employ force outside of legal processes to harass or imprison critics. Quite separately from legitimacy or effectiveness, they use physical threats to create compliance.

All governments rely on effectiveness and force, then, but relate them to legitimacy in different ways. Effectiveness supports all sorts of regimes, and that is not a bad thing: all citizens want their governments to deliver tangible benefits. It is only problematic when effectiveness compensates for weak legitimacy, buying complacency for an abusive regime. Force can be a distinct tool to support government power, scaring citizens into compliance and undercutting rivals, or force can operate within legal limits that prevent leaders from manipulating it. Governments with strong rational-legal legitimacy exert force but do not rely on it directly.

That last observation makes one major historical trend important to round out our introduction: over time, an increasing number of countries have embedded raw power in rational-legal legitimacy and its affiliated model of government—democracy.

The Spread of Democracy

Effectiveness, force, tradition, charisma, and rational-legal process: all governments choose from among these options to maintain support. Yet governments are not free to choose as they want without pressure from the outside world. At different points in history, certain options have dominated and pushed governments to justify themselves in specific ways. In our era, rational-legal legitimacy enjoys special influence, as does the democratic kind of government it supports most directly. This option sets the baseline for discussion of political authority everywhere in the world. Many robust nondemocracies remain today, but they spend time explaining why they are not legalistic and democratic, or pretending that they are.

Weber himself predicted that rational-legal legitimacy would gradually gain influence in human affairs.[9] Enlightenment ideas of rationality, he argued, would undercut traditional and charismatic authority. Prior to the Enlightenment, leaders in most places justified their authority mainly in traditional terms of ancient practices. Kings or emperors ruled because that was how it had always been done. Sometimes charismatic challengers seized power, only to soon justify their own rule as based in tradition as well. Yet traditional government confronted new pressures in the seventeenth and eighteenth centuries with the spread of Enlightenment ideas that all human beings were similarly rational. People increasingly questioned their leaders, pushing them to explain their authority as based in some sort of reasonable process. Technology like the printing press accelerated this change. Literacy, education, and the increasing flow of information encouraged more people to scrutinize how they were governed. Government was no longer taken for granted.

In Europe, where the Enlightenment emerged, a powerful new commitment to rational-legal legitimacy took hold. Enlightenment philosophers thought that if all people were similarly rational, they all deserved similar rights and treatment. Such thinking led to the notion of the **rule of law**: the idea that all people, including leaders, should be subject to the same legal rules, and that law itself—not rulers' whims—must specify how laws can be made or changed. Rather than enjoying unlimited authority, rulers should govern within the limits of reasonable processes. Kings were pressured to agree to **constitutions**, or fundamental documents guaranteeing basic rights and the processes by which laws are made. Hereditary rule itself ultimately made little sense within rational-legal processes, and many European countries moved toward selection of leaders in open elections.

The rule of law, constitutions, rights, and electoral representation—democracy, in a word—eventually spread across much of the world in several waves. Political scientists refer to the rise of these governments in North America and some of Europe as the first wave of democracy (see Figure 5-1). This wave receded somewhat during the Great Depression, and only after World War II did a second wave extend to many other states, installing democracies in places like West Germany, Italy, and Japan, and some Latin American countries. The second wave, like the first, stalled as initial attempts at democracy wavered

rule of law

The principle that laws are systematically and neutrally applied, including to top political leaders, and that law itself regulates how laws are made and changed.

constitution

A fundamental document that defines rights and processes to limit what government can do.

Figure 5-1 The Spread of Democracy in the World Since 1800

After a slow "first wave" in Europe and North America, democracy spread in successive waves in the middle and end of the 1900s.

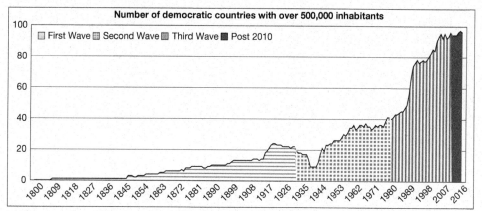

Source: Polity IV Dataset, http://www.systemicpeace.org/polity/polity4.htm.

in most Latin American countries, however, and not until a third wave began in the 1970s and 1980s did democratic government take permanent hold. That third wave began in Spain and Greece at the end of the 1970s, continued into Latin America in the 1980s, and swept into Eastern Europe in the 1990s after the collapse of communism in the Soviet Union. By the early 2000s, the majority of people in the world lived under governments based mainly on rational-legal legitimacy.

Even governments that reject the democratic trend display its pressures. Criticism from democratic governments, human rights organizations like Amnesty International, and powerful currents in international media press nondemocratic governments to explain how they justify a different system. In response, all take steps to present some façade of rational-legal legitimacy. Every nondemocratic government has adopted a constitution, though they ignore part or all of its contents. Many claim to be a special sort of democracy, like the "Democratic People's Republic of Korea"—the official name for ultra-repressive North Korea. Brutal leaders hold fake elections to claim process-based support, like when Syrian president Bashar al-Assad "won" 88.7 percent of votes in 2014—against no other serious candidates.

Yet if rational-legal legitimacy is powerful in the twenty-first century, its victory is far from complete. Even though nondemocracies feel pressure to construct rational-legal façades, many remain confident about drawing on other sources of legitimacy. Leaders in Russia, China, and other countries offer increasingly slick, modernized public relations campaigns that are based on themes of effectiveness, tradition, and charisma. And even in the world's leading democracies, we will see that rational-legal legitimacy is not fully dominant. These governments, too, boost their support using traditional appeals to history and national identity as well as arguments about effectiveness.

More importantly, perhaps, the third wave is over. In recent decades, democratic governments in Pakistan, Venezuela, and several other countries have weakened or fallen. While many people greeted the toppling of nondemocratic governments in Tunisia, Egypt, and Libya in the "Arab Spring" movements of 2011 as hopeful signs of a new expansion, so far only Tunisia has come close to maintaining a stable democracy. Just how much the wave has receded is debatable because experts disagree somewhat on which governments qualify as democracies (see Table 5-1)—but by all measures, the number has dropped. In the "Freedom in the World" measurements from the pro-democracy organization Freedom House, more countries declined than improved in each year from 2005 to 2018.[10]

Though rational-legal legitimacy has proliferated in the modern era, all three logics of authority (traditional, charismatic, and rational-legal legitimacy) still resonate loudly across our world. In complex interaction with the power dynamics of effectiveness and force, these three logics uphold several models of government. Rational-legal legitimacy and democracy enjoy a special influence, forcing advocates of other options to explain deviation from

Table 5-1 Differences in Measures of Democracy

Several different indexes of democracy combine measures of legal rights, political competition, openness, a free press, and other features to rate regimes around the world. We must be careful about using them, however, because different formulas can give different results and the studies are on different calendars. If we simply looked at recent rankings of Turkey, for example, the Polity IV Study calls it a democracy, the Economist Democracy Index calls it a "hybrid regime," and Freedom House calls it "not free."

Country	Polity IV Study (2018)	Freedom House Study (2018)	*Economist* Democracy Index (2018)
	10: Full democracy 6 to 9: Democracy 1 to 5: Open anocracy –5 to 0: Closed anocracy –10 to –6: Autocracy	Inverted scale: 1 to 2.5: Free 3 to 5: Partly free 5 to 7: Not free	8 to 10: Full democracy 6 to 8: Flawed democracy 4 to 6: Hybrid regime 0 to 4: Authoritarian
Afghanistan	Failed state	Not free	Authoritarian
Brazil	Democracy	Free	Flawed democracy
Malaysia	Democracy	Partly free	Flawed democracy
Mexico	Democracy	Partly free	Flawed democracy
Czech Republic	Democracy	Free	Flawed democracy
Turkey	Democracy	Not free	Hybrid regime
Russia	Open anocracy	Not free	Authoritarian regime
Ukraine	Democracy	Partly free	Hybrid regime
Venezuela	Open anocracy	Not free	Authoritarian

NOTE: With respect to Polity IV, "anocracy" means "neither democracy nor autocracy."
SOURCES: www.systemicpeace.org; freedomhouse.org; www.eiu.com.

their lines. Nonetheless, a closer look at today's main alternatives leaves no doubt that diverse forms of government authority will endure for the foreseeable future.

Liberal Democracies

5.2 **Identify the two core elements of liberal-democratic government, explain their relationship, and describe how tradition and effectiveness also support such regimes.**

Liberal democracy is the most widely accepted kind of government in the world today. Powerful rational-legal arguments present it as the most reasonable, fairest system of government ever devised—or at least, as British prime minister Winston Churchill called it, "The worst sort of government except all the others that have been tried."

In everyday speech, people refer to this system simply as **democracy**, which is a Greek word meaning "rule by the common people." Political scientists add "liberal" to emphasize that today's examples are a particular two-part version of

democracy
A Greek-based term for rule by the common people, combining the words *demos* (for the common people) and *kratia* (power or rule).

the broader notion of democracy. These systems use representation in elections as their main mechanism for assigning authority, and this mechanism operates within a framework of liberal rights. The relationship between representation and rights defines the model: rights support and bind the process of representation so that it assigns authority in fair and reasonable ways.

If this model's rational foundations are uniquely strong, they are also hugely demanding. Crafting plausible representation and rights is difficult and can fall apart rather easily. Where liberal democracy has succeeded, we will see, it has usually drawn support from other sources as well, strengthening a rational-legal system with tradition and effectiveness.

Representation of the People

When we think of democracy, we usually think first of people choosing leaders in elections. Yet this mechanism for assigning authority was not part of the original meaning of democracy, nor does it alone sum up the model today. To capture the logic of liberal democracy, we must first see historically how democracy came to mean representation through elections. Then we must break down how government by representatives can claim to be "rule by the common people." We will see that meaningful representation depends heavily on the other half of the formula: liberal rights.

"Rule by the common people" was first invented in the Greek city-state of Athens around 500 BC. Athenians saw all adult male citizens as legally equal and required all to attend an Assembly to enact laws ten times a year. Athens's system was thus a form of **direct democracy**: one in which the whole eligible population participates in making decisions. Its definition of "the common people" had big exceptions—women and slaves were excluded—and the system had its critics: the philosopher Aristotle, for example, thought the masses were simply too ignorant to make decisions. Yet it was still a remarkable experiment in an era dominated by traditional government, and it endured for 180 years.

direct democracy
A little-used political model in which citizens participate directly in decision making.

Around the same time and on the other side of the Aegean Sea, the Roman Republic developed another experiment in which the common people—still meaning nonslave men—had a voice. With a much larger population than Athens, and considerable sympathy for Aristotle's skepticism about the ignorant masses, the Romans opted against meetings of the whole citizenry. Instead they created an indirect system of **representative democracy** in which citizens elected representatives to assemblies that made decisions on citizens' behalf. At the time, "democracy" still meant Athens's system and they called theirs "republicanism." It lasted several centuries before giving way to the Roman Empire.

representative democracy
The much more common political model of indirect democracy in which decision-making power lies with citizens' elected representatives, also known as republicanism.

Not until the Enlightenment, almost two millennia later, did governments that were based on political equality and fair process became permanent fixtures. By the time Enlightenment thinkers finished resurrecting and reworking Greek and Roman ideas, the rise of the modern state had organized politics on such a large scale that direct democracy seemed infeasible. Modern democracy, then, came to mean the Roman model of elected representatives. Some modern democracies later restored elements of direct democracy in the form of referendums in which citizens vote directly on policy issues. Today, these direct consultations of citizens are employed regularly in a few places, notably Switzerland and in state-level politics in the United States. But the vast majority of decisions in liberal democracies today are made by representatives.

To understand modern liberal democracies' claim to legitimacy, then, requires careful attention to how electoral representation can be equated with "rule of the common people." To say that the people rule when representatives make decisions, the electoral connection between them must be quite tight. At a minimum, voters must genuinely *choose* their representatives. Choosing implies more than just voting, as becomes clear from a glance at votes without choice. Earlier, we mentioned the 2014 vote in Syria in which President Bashar al-Assad "won" by 88.7 percent. In 2007, he "won" with 97 percent support—against no other candidates at all. Nobody could mistake such processes for meaningful choices by Syrian citizens.

For citizens' choices to be more genuine, two qualities of elections are essential: broad **participation** and real **contestation**.[11] Consider Figure 5-2. A Syrian-style, single-candidate vote, like in the upper-left corner, is not an actual choice. The case in the lower-right corner, like early nineteenth-century Britain when only rich white men could vote, features competition between candidates but few people who choose among them. Democratic choice makes sense only as we move toward the upper-right corner.

Contestation in particular is challenging to generate. It asks that all political groups agree to an open competition for office. Every group must accept that it could lose, giving its adversaries control of government. Every group must also accept that if it wins, it will tolerate opposition while in power instead of using government resources to silence rivals. When we see the level of dislike and distrust between Democrats and Republicans in the United States, it may seem surprising that they can show such restraint. When we consider attempts to hold

participation
In the context of representative democracy, the principle that the breadth of eligibility to vote must be as broad as possible.

contestation
In the context of representative democracy, the principle that more than one candidate must compete seriously in elections for government office.

Figure 5-2 Participation and Contestation in Elections

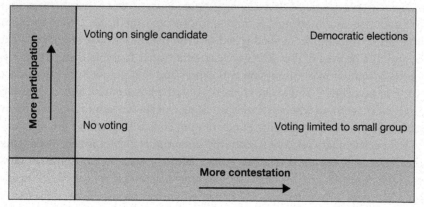

open elections in more difficult settings—in countries where groups have recently been killing each other, not just disagreeing—such a spirit of compromise can seem hard to imagine. Even if competing groups agree to a truce through one or two elections, all it takes for democratic choice to fall apart is that losers or winners of the next election decide to stop playing by the rules. As U.S. president Ronald Reagan put it in 1981, the long-term endurance of orderly contestation among political rivals is "nothing less than a miracle."[12]

To equate electoral representation with democracy, then, demands much more of a government than just holding elections. It must extend voting to as many citizens as possible. It must support contestation that provides voters with contrasting choices. And for a meaningfully representative system to endure, it must sustain contestation in the long run, across many elections. How can government possibly ensure that electoral representation maintains all these qualities? The logic of liberal democracy gives a one-word answer: rights.

How Rights Support Meaningful Representation

If the "democracy" in "liberal democracy" means electoral representation, the "liberal" refers to classical-liberal commitments that guarantee individual rights. Not only do these rights extend wide participation in voting, they support contestation by creating a space in which "the common people" can formulate views, express them, and mobilize politically without interference. In the long term, these rights must also protect contestation from democracy itself—blocking the winners of elections from later curtailing freedoms while in office. Establishing and maintaining these rights in a context of running political contestation is not easy.

suffrage
Another word for the right to vote.

The widespread right to vote, also known as universal **suffrage**, upholds the participatory quality of representation. Many elections in history have taken place without universal adult suffrage—African Americans had incomplete voting rights until 1965, and women could not vote in Switzerland until 1971!—and such restrictions clearly undercut claims to represent "the people." Beyond the opportunity to mark a ballot, real participation in selection of representatives also depends on rights that allow citizens to formulate their own views. Liberal democracies promise that citizens enjoy rights to freedom of speech, freedom to meet and associate in groups, a largely uncensored media to gather and share information, freedom from state-based discrimination for race, religion, or gender, and due process of law when accused of a crime. Together these rights safeguard a broad arena of discussion and expression that is safe from government control or favoritism. This social space beyond the government is known as **civil society**. It is an arena where citizens can think, speak, write, and interact to form their own views and participate in meaningful choice at election time.

civil society
Arenas of action in a country outside direct government influence, such as associations, churches, business affairs, media, and artistic expression.

In opening space for civil society, the same rights bolster contestation. These safeguards of guaranteed freedom not only allow citizens to formulate views about which leaders or policies they like; they also let citizens mobilize to support and *become* alternatives to their current representatives. Some citizens step forward as candidates to compete for office, defining an opposition to the winners of the last round. They develop their messages, build political parties and coalitions, and ready themselves to be credible options in the next election. Only within a secure arena of guaranteed freedoms to meet, speak, write, raise money, and create organizations can alternatives arise to generate serious contestation.

A clear commitment to these rights can further ensure that whoever wins one election does not constrict the space for competitive elections thereafter. If today's elected leaders can use their offices to harass opposing groups, tomorrow's electoral contestation may suffer. Moreover, this danger can arise not only from aggressive leaders but from voters themselves. As the classical liberal John Stuart Mill (1806–1873) noted, electoral representation runs the risk of the **tyranny of the majority**: a majority might vote for representatives who are as repressive as the most brutal tyrants.[13] Mill's point was not just theoretical: Hitler's Nazi Party won power in a free election in Germany in 1932. More recently, the winners of Egypt's post-"Arab Spring" election in 2012 were Islamist parties whose commitment to democracy was uncertain. The Egyptian military eventually gave the Islamists' erratic respect for democratic norms as the excuse to remove them from power in 2013. Only strong commitments to rights, argued Mill and other liberal thinkers, keep elections from producing unstable or repressive outcomes.

For liberal democracy to work, in other words, rights must be insulated from elections. In most democracies, rights are inscribed in constitutions, which in turn are insulated from change because they can be amended only with extremely broad support. Most liberal democracies require difficult procedures for amending their constitution; the U.S. process, which requires approval from two-thirds of Congress and three-quarters of state-level legislatures, is so onerous that the U.S. Constitution is almost immune to change. Just as important, rights must be enforced by courts that are largely independent from elected politicians. Only under these conditions are today's aggressive leaders or illiberal voters unable to erase the rights that support participation and contestation for tomorrow.

Thus rights support representation by opening space for participation and contestation, as well as by protecting that space from majority domination. This complex relationship between the "liberal" and "democracy" pillars of liberal democracy makes it a far more demanding undertaking than simply holding elections. To achieve stability over many elections requires the construction of a whole legal edifice of constitutional law and well-respected courts that can defend rights even when elected leaders are tempted to weaken them. It is unsurprising, then, that even the world's leading liberal democracies needed a long time to work out their current mix of representation and rights. It took until the mid-twentieth century for governments in the United States, Britain, France, and similar countries to eliminate major exceptions to liberal rights, taking steps to extend rights to women, to bar blatant racial discrimination, and to allow workers to form unions if they chose. They continue to debate that project today on newer terrain, like rights for transgender people. Many other countries

tyranny of the majority
The possibility that a democratic majority could vote to harm minorities or political opponents.

At the Venezuelan-Brazilian border, a man throws a rock at Venezuelan forces preventing international aid from reaching their own citizens during an economic crisis in 2019. In the preceding years, the Venezuelan regime of President Nicolás Maduro increasingly abused rights and shut down opposition.

that adopted liberal democracy even later still wrestle with the provision of core rights. In places like Mexico, Indonesia, or the Philippines, work remains to be done to consolidate constitutional rights and independent courts to protect civil society and healthy political competition.

The full liberal-democratic model is so difficult to construct and maintain, in fact, that only about thirty countries do so clearly enough to exemplify this category. Most of Europe, Canada, Australia and New Zealand, Japan, South Korea, Uruguay, Costa Rica and Chile in Latin America, and the African island of Mauritius assign authority through a stable formula of representation and rights. The United States also falls in this group, though major indexes of democracy have downgraded it toward the bottom of the group in recent years. Another fifty or sixty governments base their main authority on the same formula, and so are often labeled as liberal democracies, but their provision of rights and fair representation is less robust. On the strong end of this latter group are countries like South Africa, India, or Argentina, whereas countries like Hungary, Tunisia, or Mexico barely qualify for the liberal-democratic category. The extreme end of this spectrum overlaps with the illiberal democracies we consider in the following section.

The great strength of liberal democracy, then, is its powerful rational-legal logic wherein a long list of rights supports high-quality representation of "the common people." Its key weakness reflects the same lofty logic: it is so demanding that it can be difficult to sustain. Convincing rival groups to accept open electoral contestation requires a high level of trust. The rule of law, respected constitutions, and independent courts can buttress that trust, but these institutions take time, effort, and political support to create. If liberal-democratic governments were built on rational-legal legitimacy alone—and survived only when reason and fairness fully convinced everyone in a country to support this model—they might never have emerged at all. And yet they have, partly because they have drawn on other sources of support.

Supporting Liberal Democracy with Tradition and Effectiveness

"Ask not what your country can do for you," said President John F. Kennedy in a famous speech, "Ask what you can do for your country."[14] Taken out of context, this celebrated phrase sounds like something a king might say. The rest of Kennedy's address called on citizens to serve in the name of liberty—stressing rational-legal principles of U.S. government—but also evoked nationalism and a traditional sense of duty. And this example, it turns out, is just the tip of the iceberg. Liberal-democratic governments appeal to other bases beyond their main reliance on rational-legal principles. They invoke traditional themes and effectiveness to help sell and stabilize their demanding form of government.

Traditional emphases on history and shared identity are everywhere in democratic politics. The most obvious example is the subcategory of liberal democracies known as **constitutional monarchies**, like Britain, Japan, Denmark, or Spain. These countries assign political authority to elected leaders, but also maintain symbolic monarchs like Britain's Queen Elizabeth II or Japan's Emperor Naruhito. Such monarchs personify national tradition, ritual, and pride, which remind citizens of their shared history. Yet even democracies without monarchs employ similar pomp and circumstance, cultivating their identity with flags, anthems, parades, and national sports teams. Moreover, elected leaders themselves constantly use traditional, nationalist rhetoric. They urge us to work, fight, sacrifice—and above all, support them—in the name of national strength and bonds from the past. Such themes are so ubiquitous that almost any speech could serve as an example, like the rousing conclusion to one address by then-French president Nicolas Sarkozy in 2009: "We are an old country, on an old continent, with an old civilization. We have learned much from history... It was when France convinced herself that all is possible that she became great... Long live the Republic! Long live France!"[15] Just as nationalist rhetoric, celebration of the past, and team-building exercises (like rooting for Olympic squads) can build support for paternalistic kings, so it can for elected politicians.

Effectiveness probably plays an even greater role in support for liberal democracies. Most stable liberal democracies are rich: of the twenty-five countries that scored highest as liberal democracies in one 2018 analysis, all are high-income countries except middle-income Costa Rica and Mauritius.[16] The same high-income liberal democracies lead the world in services like education, health care, and other elements of quality of life. These benefits help maintain

constitutional monarchies
A subset of liberal democracies where a king, queen, or emperor retains a symbolic role, but without substantial political power.

democratic systems: if we compare rich democracies to countries that become democracies while still relatively poor, we find that democracy is more likely to break down in a context of poverty.[17] A more comfortable context of wealth makes it easier to persuade political rivals to accept open competition, as well as to maintain robust courts and law enforcement to support rights. In cruder terms, people tend to give some support to any government that brings them smartphones and ever-bigger televisions. To some degree, material comfort upholds these governments, irrespective of their rational-legal processes.

Just how much tradition and effectiveness contribute to the support that Americans, Japanese, or Costa Ricans give to liberal-democratic governments is hard to say. There is evidence that people find these governments' primary rational-legal justifications persuasive: across a selection of liberal democracies, roughly 90 percent of citizens agree that democracy is better than other forms of government.[18] Nonetheless, the remarkable restraint that these high-minded ideals demand is easier to maintain when bolstered by shared identity and material comfort. Liberal democracies rest on a uniquely convincing model of rational-legal authority, but also share sources of support with other regimes.

Illiberal Democracies

5.3 Identify the core features of illiberal democracy and explain how some justify this model as preferable to liberal democracy.

In a world where rational-legal process and liberal democracy enjoy special legitimacy but set hard-to-meet standards, many governments unsurprisingly imitate only part of that model. In roughly seventy countries, top leaders are selected in regular elections, but liberal rights are not strongly respected. Their leaders claim to hold authority due to electoral support, but refuse to accept that they could lose elections. Instead, they stifle rights and competition to keep control. Influential public commentator Fareed Zakaria invented the name for this model: **illiberal democracy**.[19]

illiberal democracy
A government in which leaders are selected in regular elections but liberal rights are not strongly respected.

We might see these governments as failing liberal democracies rather than a distinct "model," because they typically claim to value rights and openness while failing to do so in practice. But at the same time, leaders in countries like Singapore, Russia, or Turkey advance positive arguments about why they *should not* respect all liberal rights. In various ways, they argue that effectiveness should trump rights: too much emphasis on rights and legal process prevents government from delivering results such as economic growth or stability. Rather than trying and failing to match the liberal-democratic model, they pursue a hybrid model that lies between liberal democracy and the authoritarianisms considered later in the chapter.

Or so they claim. Not all such claims are equally plausible. Some governments abuse fair process while delivering only modest results for their people. For instance, in Russia under President Putin, the "hybrid" becomes little more than hypocrisy: he talks about democracy but acts authoritarian. Yet in a few cases, like wealthy Singapore, more obvious benefits and less egregious abuse make it harder to dismiss effectiveness-based justifications. And in some countries, especially in parts of the Muslim world, a real conundrum is difficult to deny: a majority of voters may actually prefer authoritarianism, so leaders claim that they limit voters' choices to block even worse repression. Proponents of liberal democracy may not be convinced that such limits are ever justified, but quite a few people in illiberal democracies are.

"Managing" Democracy for Effective Government

The core rationale of illiberal democracies is simple: too much insistence on fair process impedes effective results. Perhaps liberal democracies are as fair as they claim, say the leaders of these regimes, but they can also be ineffective at getting anything done. Especially for governments that face real challenges like poverty, internal conflict, or threatening neighbors, the relationship between process and results should be rebalanced. Some liberties and legitimizing process are desirable—leaders should show that they retain support in elections—but constant political competition and restrictive legal processes can prevent them from improving their citizens' lives. Leaders must "manage" democracy to tackle hard problems.

These arguments are not as foreign to liberal-democratic thinking as they may seem. Inhabitants of liberal democracies are not likely to deny that their obsession with fair process has its costs in terms of effectiveness. When confronted with truly desperate challenges, such as war or catastrophic disasters, liberal democracies often suspend parts of their normal processes to allow government to act. Rights, in particular, can be maddening in terms of results. Basic protections extend to desirable and undesirable cases alike, such as when seemingly obvious criminals are acquitted on technicalities or terrorists enjoy freedom and privacy to plot destruction. Electoral representation, too, is an odd mechanism for long-term results. In the United States, regular campaigning for elections and party strife often distract government from focusing on policy problems.

Illiberal democracies are built on these criticisms. Their leaders endorse elections and rights in the abstract, but then also assert that challenges require results-oriented leadership. In Russia, Putin was first elected in 2000 after the decade of chaos that followed the collapse of the Soviet Union. He claimed to seek a democratic Russia, but argued that economic turmoil and rebellion in the region of Chechnya made stability and national strength the first priority. Putin became popular as he crushed the Chechnyan uprising and presided over a run of economic growth, all the while centralizing power and silencing his critics. A similar process in Singapore in the early 1960s installed the rule of Prime Minister Lee Kuan Yew and his "People's Action Party" (PAP). After winning independence from British colonization, the PAP called for democracy. Yet in the face of multiple challenges—a communist rebellion, tension between its ethnic Chinese population and Malay neighbors, and modest economic resources—PAP leaders soon declared that subjugation of opposition was necessary for stability. Lee went on to run the government for thirty years, and Prime Minister Lee Hsien Loong—Lee Kuan Yew's son—continues to suppress critics today.

From these similar points of departure, illiberal democracies can evolve in different directions. Most drift from their original rationale over time: limited rights might make sense as short-term emergency measures, but become less persuasive the longer leaders stay in power. A few illiberal regimes deal with problems so effectively that their initial justifications endure.

Hypocrisy and Success across Illiberal Democracies

In its own way, illiberal democracy may be even harder to sustain than liberal democracy. While liberal democracy sets high process standards, its authority may survive in good times and bad as long as its processes are respected. Illiberal democracy's promise of effective results pressures leaders to deliver a constant stream of tangible benefits, while also maintaining some semblance of democratic processes. That is a tall order that not many governments manage to fill. Most fail to deliver strong results and gradually lose any hint of fair process, falling into a hypocritical mix of authoritarian practices and democratic talk. Yet cases exist of successful illiberal democracy, with one extreme success standing out: Singapore. This unusual case suggests that this model can be a lasting alternative to liberal democracy, but may also be hard to imitate elsewhere.

This section takes a closer look at support for illiberal democracy in both hypocritical and successful scenarios. In the next section, we will examine a third scenario in which the roots of illiberal democracy are somewhat different: the dilemma that we see in many Muslim countries, where governments claim illiberal measures are necessary to silence even more illiberal voices.

DEMOCRATIC RHETORIC, AUTHORITARIAN ACTIONS: RUSSIA. The most common path for illiberal democracies is to slide down a slippery slope into hypocrisy. After achieving meager results, they argue that they need more time and fewer constraints—which lead to still more centralization of power and repression of opposition—to get the job done. They continue to use democratic rhetoric, but act increasingly authoritarian. As they do so, they often add more reliance on traditional and charismatic themes to win support.

We find examples of this slippery slope in the recent history of countries like Pakistan, Nigeria, Haiti, or Iraq, but Putin's Russia is the most prominent case. In his early years in power after 2000, Putin appeared quite effective and won strong support. Chechnya was suppressed and annual economic growth surged to 7 percent. Many Russians praised the president for stabilizing their lives, and Putin won reelection in 2004 with over 70 percent of votes. In 2012, he won again despite an increasingly obvious turn toward corruption and repression. As one young mother, Lyudmila Guseva, told a journalist before voting for Putin in 2012, "I have a ten-year old son, a good salary, a car and a house in the country. I am happy with what I have achieved. Why should I not vote for him?"[20]

Yet like most illiberal leaders, Putin's results are actually modest, and effectiveness is a small and declining part of his story. Growth has barely made up for the deep collapse of the 1990s, and most Russians are hardly richer than a generation ago. Putin's economy has mostly benefited the super-rich, and Russia is now one of the world's most corrupt countries.[21] Especially since 2014, when the economy weakened with a fall in oil prices, he can no longer easily claim great economic success. One reason that he continues to draw support—winning the 2018 presidential election with his best score yet, 77 percent—is that he has systematically eliminated his competitors. Opposition figures have been hit with lawsuits, beaten up, and paid off. Critical media have been undercut with trumped-up court cases and even murders. Power has been centralized in the presidency and other institutions packed with Putin loyalists.[22]

Still, repression is not the only tool that illiberal leaders use when their claims to both effectiveness and partly fair process become weaker. Putin has long cultivated charismatic and traditional rhetoric as well. He grooms a charismatic tough-guy image as the hero Russia needs: besides stunts like tranquilizing a tiger or taking a submarine to the bottom of Lake Baikal (the world's deepest), he has released a judo instruction video and distributed pictures of himself shirtless on horseback.[23] Most importantly, Putin has increasingly played up nationalism. His most aggressive move was to seize the Crimean peninsula from neighboring Ukraine in 2014. Putin's aggression against Ukraine has been condemned around the world, bringing major pressure and economic sanctions from the United States and other governments, but it is hugely popular with Russian citizens.[24] Even given weak claims to effectiveness or rational-legal process, then, Putin works hard to seduce voters with nationalism and personal appeal.

As hypocritical as this pursuit of popular support while abusing rights may be, it distinguishes Russia and similar governments from authoritarianism. As we will see, authoritarians do not even claim to base their main authority in popular support. Putin and similar leaders in Pakistan, Nigeria, or Iraq, by contrast, claim to hold authority through elections and actually invest major resources in winning skewed competitions. In citizens' lives, the difference between living in a very illiberal democracy and an openly authoritarian system may be small: measures of freedom score all these countries as very close to "authoritarian."[25] Yet it may matter much more for these governments' fates

Alexei Druzhinin/RIA Novosti pool/AP Images

Russian president Vladimir Putin cultivates a tough-guy, outdoorsy image. This shot of him riding a horse was part of an officially approved collection from a Siberian summer vacation in 2009. Other photos showed him climbing trees and swimming in icy rivers.

in the long term. To claim a basis in elections, especially hypocritically, opens a door to challenges from citizens in the future.

EXCEPTIONAL ILLIBERAL SUCCESS: SINGAPORE. If all illiberal democracies were as hypocritical as Russia, Pakistan, or Nigeria, we might indeed dismiss the category as no model at all. In countries like Malaysia or especially Singapore, however, illiberal democracies have combined effective results, elements of law and fair process, and an elected government that permits little opposition.

In a competition for the most effective kind of government, Singapore is the entrant that keeps illiberal democracy in the running. In the 1960s, Lee Kuan Yew and the PAP came to preside over an island city with no resources and a level of wealth like Mexico. Today, Singapore is the financial center of Southeast Asia and its population of 5 million is the third-richest in the world. Moreover, its economic success has been accompanied by rigorous rule of law. It ranks as one of the highest-scoring countries in the world in the World Justice Project's Rule of Law Index, and as one the five least-corrupt countries overall.[26]

This government is not only the most successful but also the most explicit example of illiberal democracy. No apologetic façade hides its limits on rights. Singapore's constitution adopts British-style democratic processes and a list of rights, but allows the government to suspend them "as it considers necessary or expedient" for reasons of security, public order, or morality.[27] Among the "necessary" steps are many regulations of lifestyle—for example, it is illegal to chew gum so that the city remains clean—and the harassment of political opponents and suppression of critical media. Such steps have helped the PAP win every election for sixty years, including eighty-one of eighty-nine parliamentary seats in 2015. PAP leaders openly declare that they interpret rights as they see fit. As Prime Minister Lee Kuan Yew said during his twenty-eighth year in office, "I am often accused of interfering in the private lives of citizens. Yes . . . we would not have made economic progress if we had not intervened on very personal matters: who your neighbor is, how you live, the noise you make, how you spit, or what language you use. We decide what is right."[28] According to Lee, Singaporeans accept such leadership because "Asian values" prioritize collective goals over individual choice.[29]

Yet if this case represents the clearest, most successful instance of illiberal democracy, its exceptional nature suggests the model's limits. Not many countries can hope realistically to reproduce Singapore's results. It happened to be perfectly positioned geographically to profit from emerging globalization after the 1960s, skyrocketing to wealth as the financial and management center for trade between Asian producers and the rest of the world. More plausible is that Singapore's leaders enjoyed favorable conditions for economic success, seized these opportunities very competently, and essentially bought their citizens' support. Bigger, more diverse, or less well-placed countries will find it much harder to generate similar results.

Illiberal democracy can work, then, but governments based primarily on effectiveness may be robust only under very favorable conditions. The fact that many also slip toward authoritarianism might suggest that illiberal democracy could be a shrinking category. But not so: another large group of countries faces challenges that make this space hard to escape.

When Voters Are More Illiberal than Governments

In some illiberal democracies, leaders claim to face a deeper problem than a need for results. In perhaps thirty countries where powerful social and religious traditions tend to oppose rights and representation, a majority of voters themselves might choose to vote for authoritarian rule. Their leaders thus argue that to preserve some degree of openness, individual liberty, and positive social change, it is ironically necessary to limit voters' rights. This is still a version of the effectiveness argument, but it gives a distinct twist to the roots of illiberalism.

This phenomenon is most prevalent in Muslim countries, where Islam supports distinctive political thinking and where a history of difficult relations with the West encourages suspicion of Western ideas.[30] In the early twentieth century, "modernizing" movements arose across the Muslim world to advocate a Western model of industrialization, secularism, law, and democracy. The United States and European governments encouraged these movements, but not without ulterior motives. By supporting pro-Western governments, the United States and Europe gained access to rich oil resources in many of these countries. Not only did these developments fail to "Westernize" many citizens, they stoked widespread resentment and provoked a massive revival of Islamic fundamentalism. Thus emerged the core dynamic of regimes from northern Africa across the Middle East and into Asia: modernizing elites allied with Western governments and argued that they had to limit rights to prevent Islamists from taking over.

Egypt is a textbook case of this dynamic, and the most troubling one in recent years. For decades, the United States and other Western powers supported the illiberal regime of President Hosni Mubarak. Built around a modernizing, secular elite in the military and business class, the government held periodic elections but forcibly repressed any competitors who identified with Islamism. Resentment of the system's blatant corruption and poor economic performance finally brought down Mubarak's regime in the "Arab Spring" uprisings of 2011. Proponents of democracy everywhere welcomed this development, but then free and open elections in 2012 gave a clear majority to the best-organized alternative to the old elite: the Muslim Brotherhood. The Brotherhood is the oldest and largest Islamist-revival group in the world, and was once linked to terrorist radicals. Its views became more moderate over time and it came to profess support for liberal democracy—but once in power, the ambiguity of this commitment quickly became evident. The government of new president Mohammed Morsi was soon widely accused of stifling openness, repressing rivals and generally failing to respect rights and due process of law.[31] In July 2013, the Egyptian military intervened to end the democratic experiment. It violently repressed Morsi's supporters, killing thousands of people, and threw the Brotherhood's leadership

B.O'Kane/Alamy Stock Photo

Protesters in Cairo's Tahrir Square in 2011 take a break for prayers before returning to their calls for the resignation of President Hosni Mubarak.

in prison. In new presidential elections in 2014, with the Brotherhood banned, General Abdel Fattah el-Sisi won 96 percent of the vote. At the time, the U.S. government was frankly uncertain how to react to this series of events; it was difficult to know who were the "real democrats" in this arena.[32] Under President Trump, U.S. policy shifted toward downplaying human rights concerns and solidly supporting the increasingly repressive el-Sisi's rule.[33]

When we add secular-Islamist standoffs alongside more classic cases of effectiveness-based illiberal democracy, we must expect that this category of regime will remain large into the future. This is true even though in each separate case, illiberal democracies tend toward instability. Effective results are so hard to deliver consistently, and limited rights slide so easily into increasing abuse, that these regimes' initial justifications usually weaken. Even in cases further bolstered by fears of Islamism, poor performance of governments like in Egypt or Tunisia has pushed some of their previous supporters to take a risk on open democracy. Inevitably, many countries that endorse liberal democracy will still find it difficult to sustain, so many leaders will be tempted to prioritize effective results and some illiberal populations may voluntarily reject liberal rights. As a category, illiberal democracy may well grow rather than shrink.

Authoritarianisms

5.4 **Identify four types of authoritarianism and their core principles and describe several sources of authoritarian support using specific country examples.**

While illiberal democracies at least pretend to govern with their people's consent, regimes that subscribe to **authoritarianism** build their rule on other foundations. Their citizens do not select top leaders and cannot remove them. Leaders do not commit to be limited by individual rights or other legal processes, instead proclaiming unlimited authority to decide what is right for the country. In the most extreme cases, known as **totalitarianism**, authoritarian governments try to control every facet of citizens' lives. In Nazi Germany, Stalin's Soviet Union, or Mao's China, the government watched and controlled practically everything: not just politics but education, culture, music, clothing, sports. Only North Korea comes close to totalitarianism today, illustrating the purest assertion of unlimited government authority.

Yet governing without limits is not the same thing as governing without principles. In fact, most authoritarian regimes claim a more righteous basis than illiberal democracies, grounding authority in traditional or charismatic principles. In practice they all stray from their principles, relying on repression and other sources of compliance, but still the principles of authoritarian authority are not irrelevant. In most cases, some citizens genuinely believe them.

As with illiberal democracies, the fact that some citizens support authoritarian regimes does not mean we should endorse them as well. However, it is important to recognize *why* such governments garner support or recognition.

authoritarianism
A form of government that claims unlimited authority and is not responsible in any systematic way to citizens' input.

totalitarianism
The extreme form of authoritarianism in which government extends its control to all aspects of citizens' lives.

Otherwise, we will be surprised at how robust some authoritarian systems may be. Dismissing such regimes too lightly also deprives us of a chance to think critically about why we prefer liberal democracy to these alternatives.

Principles of Unlimited Authority

Authoritarianism is a broad label for a range of alternatives to democracy. The fact that they are *not* democracies does not mean that they share similar foundations for authority, because there are many other possible ways to justify legitimate government. Today, governments in this category feature four distinct organizational principles: monarchy, theocracy, one-party regime, and dictatorship.

monarchy
A form of authoritarianism that lodges authority in a hereditary ruler.

MONARCHY. Several centuries ago, practically all governments exhibited the same kind of authoritarianism. Governments were **monarchies** run by a hereditary ruler with a title like king, queen, emperor, sultan, or maharaja. Their authority was based in traditional notions that some group or family dynasty was intrinsically superior to other people, often with the religious note of a divine endorsement, authorizing them to rule as they wished. As Louis XIV (1638–1715), the most powerful of French kings, summarized his regime, *"L'état, c'est moi"* ("I am the state").

Today, however, monarchy is authoritarianism's least persuasive form. With the rise of modern notions of human equality, monarchical government became increasingly difficult to defend. Monarchs now claim absolute power in only six countries, and the location of such holdouts highlights this system's weak legitimacy. Besides the tiny, poorly developed African monarchy of Swaziland, all maintain considerable compliance with oil wealth: Saudi Arabia, Brunei, Kuwait, Oman, and Qatar. The era of strong traditional legitimacy has passed, and we are not likely to see new monarchies emerge.

theocracy
A form of authoritarianism that lodges authority in religious officials.

THEOCRACY. Religion often connects to the foundations of monarchies, but can also provide separate bases for regimes in which religious leaders serve as spiritual "guides" and earthly rulers. In **theocracy**, top leaders exercise authority by virtue of their special faith or expertise in religious doctrines. Rather than seeing themselves as superior to other people as monarchs might, they claim that knowledge of religious teachings allows them to make wise decisions for the common good.

Though religion often seems traditional, making religion the leading principle of government is not traditional at all. Governments that assign top authority to religious leaders are rare in history, and the one existing quasi-theocracy today, in Iran, arose by overthrowing a traditional monarchy in an Islamist revolution in 1979. Instead, theocracy rests on charismatic legitimacy, asking people to follow fundamentalist beliefs in ways that often upend traditional society. Iranian politics is full of fiery, religion-heavy speeches by charismatic preachers, creating a tone that is strikingly different from the quiet, secretive, traditional rule of a monarchy like Saudi Arabia. Iran's Supreme Leader, Ali Khamenei, has the title of Grand Ayatollah, meaning a revered source of religious wisdom. He and other religious figures do not directly run most of Iranian government—elections select many government officials, making it a quasi-theocracy—but on the basis of his religious status he claims unlimited authority to "correct" decisions by the lower officials who run Iran's daily affairs.

As a justification for unlimited authority, serving God can be powerful. On the other hand, theocrats risk undercutting their otherworldly authority by taking on messy challenges of government on Earth. The kind of life that gives leaders religious credibility also may not prepare them well for practical politics. New theocracies might someday arise, but for the moment the Iranian regime's poor performance in economic and social affairs weakens their allure.

ONE-PARTY REGIME. The most robust instances of authoritarianism today are **one-party regimes**. Such governments base unlimited authority on a charismatic ideology, championed by a party organization, that claims to be so compellingly good for citizens that nothing can be allowed to obstruct it. Other parties and movements are banned, and anyone who wishes to play a role in government— or to do well in any part of society—is encouraged to join the party. All current examples of such regimes in China, Vietnam, North Korea, Cuba, and Laos were originally built around communist ideology. They claimed, and still claim to some degree, that Marxist thinking gives their leaders unique insight into the true conditions for social progress. Fascist governments in Germany and Italy before 1945 followed the same model, though with different ideologies.

one-party regime
A form of authoritarianism that lodges authority in a political party that claims special ideological insight into good governance.

One-party regimes have broad organizational bases. Such parties typically create a hierarchy of central leaders, regional and local bosses, and heads of "cells" in settings like large workplaces, universities, and neighborhoods. At its apex this hierarchy merges with government: the general secretary who runs the Chinese Communist Party (CCP), currently Xi Jinping, is also president of the country. Further down the party is a parallel structure to government itself; most officials, judges, or military officers are not required to be party members, but since the party controls all major government decisions and promotions, success and influence pass through party membership. This vast system serves to recruit leaders, watch over society, and deliver propaganda. Generation after generation is indoctrinated as people rise through party ranks. Personal benefits for pleasing the party, like promotions and favorable treatment in everything from real estate loans to legal disputes, encourage lower-level members to report about conditions on the ground. Members of the CCP—90 million of them, or about 15 percent of the population—also spread the party's message throughout society.

Basing authority in charismatic ideology and party organization can create especially strong foundations for authoritarianism. Ideological promises to build a better society on Earth often connect better to government than theocratic themes, and parties are less vulnerable than monarchy to death of a single leader. One-party regimes often run into trouble as they drift away from their original ideology in practice, which then weakens their justification for authority, but this category is still the most likely source of challenges to the future spread of democracy.

DICTATORSHIPS. Rule by an individual dictator, lastly, is the least-principled form of authoritarian rule. Such regimes usually have some basis in charismatic legitimacy, elevating one person for his or her leadership qualities. They also typically evoke traditional themes of nationalism, portraying the leader as a benevolent defender of national security and strength. Yet these themes do not justify unlimited authority as clearly as a monarch's inherent superiority, a cleric's connection to God, or a Communist Party official's insight into the path to utopia.

dictatorship
A form of authoritarianism that lodges authority in a single person, or sometimes in the military overall, in the name of providing stability and security.

Instead, **dictatorships** build their main case on effectiveness. Dictators push forward their extreme versions of the case for illiberal democracy by arguing that their country will be overwhelmed by problems, such as ethnic conflict or external threats, unless they hold unlimited authority. In Syria, for example, the regime of Bashar al-Assad rests above all on the notion that only his leadership prevents the country from falling apart. Syria is a patchwork of identities—several tribes of Sunni Arabs, some Christians, and minorities known as Alawis and Druze—and al-Assad claims to prevent civil war between these groups. He has stuck to this notion through the bloody repression of a pro-democracy movement since 2012, insisting that the chaos without him would be worse. Most of the world sees this claim as less and less credible: could it get worse than a war that has claimed more than 400,000 lives? Still, some in Syria still seem to believe it.

As the least principled form of authoritarianism, dictatorships can be fairly easy to create but also quickly confront pressures for new justifications. They frequently arise in conditions of instability when a military leader steps forward to claim power. Sometimes they take the less personalized form of a military dictatorship, when the military as an organization, not just one individual, declares itself the guarantor of stability. In either form, dictatorships usually come to prioritize the regime's stability over real benefits for the nation, which weakens their claims. Eventually, many seek some legitimacy in electoral process and become illiberal democracies (if often of a hypocritical sort). There are few cases today that still claim unlimited power without significant rational-legal cover, such as Syria does. The longest-standing military dictatorship, in Myanmar, rapidly reformed itself after 2011. In recent years only Thailand has been clearly in this category, with the military directly running the government after taking over in 2014.[34]

In sum, authoritarian governments have principles too, at least in principle. Within certain contexts, hereditary superiority, devotion to religion, charismatic ideologies, or fear of chaos make some sense as reasons to endow government with unlimited authority. In practice, on the other hand, all such principles lend themselves to abuse. Only saintly leadership is likely to use unlimited power in a principled way, without falling into arbitrary or self-serving decisions, and no authoritarian government is run by saints. The principles of such authoritarians usually retain at least some resonance with citizens, but all such regimes drift from their initial rationales and end up depending mainly on other means of support.

Defending Unlimited Power in Practice

The old adage that "absolute power corrupts absolutely" captures much of the practice of authoritarian governments, but not all. Whether they arise in the name of tradition, God, socialist utopia, or stability, most such regimes take a steeper and faster descent into hypocrisy than illiberal democracies. As they depart from their proclaimed principles, they look to repression and other tools to shore up support. Yet effectiveness, too, remains part of the equation: few fall so fully into corruption that they fail to deliver any benefits for citizens at all. This section focuses on two very different examples that display all of these features, China and Syria.

Authoritarian leaders' hypocrisy is usually easy to see. Rather than using their unlimited authority for the welfare of their country, authoritarian leaders frequently put their own interests first, enriching themselves and doing whatever they think necessary to stay in power. In Syria, while al-Assad's military was enforcing "stability" by bombing rebels, leaked emails showed that his wife was ordering custom-made diamond jewelry and $5,000 shoes.[35] China's CCP has contradicted itself even more over time: although created to bring equality to the masses, the Party's officials are now a rich elite in an unequal country. After its early decades brought brutal equality but little prosperity, Chinese leaders performed a gradual about-face that opened the economy to private business, foreign trade, and investment. As successful as this move proved in broad terms, it undermined the CCP's original rationale. The constitution still proclaims "a socialist state under the people's democratic dictatorship led by the working class and based on the alliance of workers and peasants," but by 2010, Chinese inequality exceeded that of the United States.[36] Roughly 600 million rural citizens earn average annual incomes around $2,000, while in urban areas rich gated communities have emerged with swimming pools and a Lexus or two in the driveways.

Since the reality of their rule differs so drastically from their principles, authoritarians typically employ fallback tools to build support or at least compliance. Syria's regime was founded by the current president's father, Hafez al-Assad, who stressed not just stability but ideological appeals to the mix of Arab nationalism and socialism known as Ba'athism. He also played up charismatic politics by developing a **cult of personality**—propaganda of personal worship, later to be shifted to his son—with giant portraits everywhere and absurd boasting of his qualities as an infinitely wise, capable, and compassionate hero.[37] For those not persuaded by these appeals, the Assads created an especially brutal and omnipresent secret police. In China, the shift away from communist equality since the 1980s was mostly covered by cultivating nationalism. Propaganda now trumpets China's long history as a great nation and its rising power; external threats and insults to Chinese sovereignty receive constant attention; huge demonstrations celebrate Chinese strength. Forceful repression, too, is a constant. Considerable criticism is permitted— much more than in Syria—but the regime acts swiftly whenever critics appear to mobilize. With the bloody repression of a pro-democracy movement in Beijing's Tiananmen Square in 1989, the CCP made clear that it would tolerate no real challenge. Human rights and pro-democracy activists are regularly imprisoned, and China executes more people than all other countries combined.

Yet despite their hypocrisy, shifting messages, and forceful repression, most authoritarian regimes maintain some credible connection to benefits for their citizens. Only in a few cases, called **kleptocracies**, are leaders so absolutely

cult of personality
The use of propaganda to create a God-like charismatic image around a leader, often making absurd claims about her or his virtues and abilities.

kleptocracy
A regime that transparently plunders its country, making no attempt to benefit the population.

corrupted that they simply plunder their countries, like the thirty-year dictatorship of Mobutu Sese Seko in the Democratic Republic of the Congo. While Syria may seem to be approaching something similar—a regime that bombs its citizens is not exactly serving them—many Syrians and external observers still give some credence to Assad's claim to provide stability. At the beginning of the Syrian civil war in 2012, a study by the U.S. National Defense University concluded that given the risks of worse internal chaos, "Assad's fall may not bring improvement for the Syrian people."[38] A respectable poll at the time found that 55 percent of Syrians agreed, backing the government at the same time that its tanks rolled over rebels.[39] Widespread death and destruction since then has not endeared many people to Bashar al-Assad, but many Syrians believe that he remains the best option to restore stability.[40] No one argues that the Syrian dictatorship is close to a good government, but some question whether another regime could do better.

In China, the pervasive hypocrisy of the CCP has not prevented a striking record of economic accomplishments. In 1980, Chinese annual income per capita (in figures adjusted to reflect purchasing power, or what income could buy, as well as inflation over time) was around $300. After economic reforms launched thirty years of 10 percent annual growth, the average income per person is now around $17,000.[41] A barely developed country where hunger was common has

Yang Bo/Color China Photo/AP Images

In a picture that captures many aspects of Chinese government support today, billionaire Chen Guangbiao stands atop one of forty-three Chinese cars he bought to replace citizens' Japanese cars that were destroyed in violent nationalist protests over tensions with Japan in 2012. This is a remarkable political mix: a wealthy capitalist uses his money to make a nationalist statement and is cheered with the flags of a supposedly communist regime.

become the world's second-largest economy with towering skyscrapers and a futuristic high-speed train network. Though skyrocketing inequality contradicts the regime's communist rhetoric, the government clearly pursues an adjusted vision of progress for China overall, not just its own survival. In poll after poll, 80 or even 90 percent of Chinese citizens say they are satisfied with their government and the direction of the country. Such numbers surely reflect relatively low expectations—many are thankful for conditions that North Americans or Europeans would find abysmal—but we cannot deny that effectiveness has delivered considerable support for this government.

For people whom the Syrian or Chinese regimes have killed, tortured, or forced into silence, these benefits do not validate authoritarian rule. Nor should they for us: to recognize that some people support a regime does not mean we must do the same. In a better, simpler world—one where everyone agreed on the best kind of government—such repressive systems would not endure. But the world we inhabit is not so neat. Despite their egregious repression, many authoritarian governments attract some support with principles of monarchy, theocracy, party ideology, or stability. Effectiveness, nationalism, and charisma motivate still more acceptance. Deny these facts, and we will be perplexed at the endurance of some authoritarian regimes and puzzled at the attitudes of many citizens in places like Syria or China. Only by acknowledging these unpleasant truths can we fully understand our own preferences for a certain kind of government. As we see in the next section, critical thinking about the case for liberal democracy requires serious consideration of alternatives. Table 5-2 consolidates the core relationships we have seen so far.

Table 5-2 Types of Governments

REGIME	Defining Features	Primary Support	Weaknesses	Examples
Liberal Democracy	Electoral representation + liberal rights	Rational-legal legitimacy	Very demanding process standards	United States, Japan, Costa Rica
Illiberal Democracy	Elections with limited rights	Effectiveness + rational-legal legitimacy	Effectiveness is hard to deliver, slippery slope to abuse	Singapore, Turkey, Russia
Authoritarianism	Unlimited authority based on:			
Monarchy	Hereditary superiority	Traditional legitimacy	Obsolete notion of superiority	Saudi Arabia, Swaziland
Theocracy	Religious wisdom	Charismatic legitimacy	Hard to maintain pure religious image while exercising secular power	Iran
One-Party Regime	Ideological path to utopia	Charismatic legitimacy	Drift from ideological goals	China, Vietnam
Dictatorship	Stability and security	Effectiveness	Regime survival becomes priority	Syria, Turkmenistan

Political Ideologies and Liberal Democracy

5.5 **Evaluate the most important defenses and critiques of liberal-democratic government.**

We have now seen that there are good reasons why rational-legal legitimacy and the liberal-democratic model enjoy special influence in our era. Liberal democracies commit to a demanding logical formula for good government and make a serious attempt to stick to it. Other regimes leave leaders freer to act—and freer to abuse their power. Yet we have also seen that liberal democracy's superiority is not obvious to all. Some people argue that illiberal democracy or authoritarianism is better for the circumstances of their country. This section now sets these alternative views against each other. Such debate helps us understand both other systems and our own—sharpening our critical thinking on liberal democracy's strengths and weaknesses.

Liberal Democracy as Freedom, Voice, and Compromise

To set up a debate, consider first a brief summary of liberal democracy's appeal. If we asked any mainstream politician in the United States, Europe, Japan, or other liberal democracies to state what their model of government does for citizens, what core benefits would they mention?

Any politician within the liberal tradition, whether on its conservative or modern liberal side, would identify freedom as its most essential advantage. Other kinds of government subjugate individual freedoms to other concerns, but the bedrock of liberal democracy is a guarantee of fundamental individual rights. Its system largely leaves people alone to do as they please. It attempts to limit government actions to those necessary to protect individuals, such as policing, criminal justice, or national defense, or to support basic opportunities, like national infrastructure or schools. In principle, the whole regime aims to maximize freedom.

As a key mechanism for maximizing freedom, conservatives and modern liberals around the world would agree, liberal democracy gives citizens a voice through elections. Leaders are accountable for how well they deliver individual freedom, with others replacing them if many voters disapprove of their stewardship. The electoral process gives citizens a chance to object to how rights are being enforced, or to call for government policies they think important to support their opportunities. Citizens cannot ask for everything—constitutions and courts rule out changes to basic rights—but they have broad chances to express views and demands.

In providing a voice through elections within guaranteed rights, liberal democracy has the further major benefit of encouraging compromise. Open electoral competition means that no single group holds power for long. Since no one holds permanent authority, everyone must accept that government is shaped by a mix of different views over time. Such compromise is central to the model because disagreement always exists on what exactly "maximizing freedom" means beyond the most basic rights. For example, conservatives tend to see strong social order and defense against external threats as necessary to support meaningful freedom, and so may be willing to support police or military actions that modern liberals see as threatening certain rights to privacy or due process. Modern liberals, meanwhile, tend to see government programs to help the poor as necessary to give everyone the opportunity for meaningful freedom; to support such policies, they prefer higher levels of taxation that conservatives may see as infringing on rights to property. Both support electoral representation as a mechanism that allows them to disagree in the short run and encourages compromises in the long run.

When we hear this case for liberal democracy by itself—especially if we are citizens of liberal democracies who have grown up in a context of these ideas—it may seem hard to imagine how anyone could criticize them very strongly, let alone reject them. And that is exactly why we should consider arguments from people who do.

Liberal Democracy as Veiled Oppression

When leaders and citizens in China, Syria, Iran, or other authoritarian systems defend their regimes, they often draw on several enduring criticisms of liberal democracy. Indeed, the major ideological traditions of fascism, socialism, and Islamism were all partly constructed as attacks on the liberal-democratic model. All their critiques remain relevant in some places today.

The most complete rejection of liberal democracy is the fascist argument that individual freedoms are undesirable. People find meaning only as part of the nation, drawing sustenance from membership in a strong group identity under heroic leadership. If few people around the world call themselves fascist today— even authoritarians distance themselves from Hitler!—we hear versions of this argument from authoritarians of all sorts. Whether communists, Islamists, or simple dictators, they often suggest that people should care more about collective strength than individual freedom. In this view, liberal-democratic "freedom" is actually oppressive. It dupes people into pursuing meaningless self-interest rather than serving a great cause.

The Marxist thinking of devout socialists and communists is built around a more specific critique of liberal democracy as a form of veiled oppression. As a product of the Enlightenment, hard-core socialism shares liberalism's focus on individual rights, but argues that liberal democracy protects the wrong ones. The rights protected by liberal democracy are just a cover for the rich to control the economy. Freedoms of speech, association, or religion, and the right to vote for leaders make no difference if the rich are able to control elections and policymaking. Instead, economic rights are what matter: no real freedom exists without rights to a job, a certain standard of living, and free access to vital things such as health care, education, and support in old age. Chinese and other communist regimes still employ versions of these arguments. Such communist regimes maintain that the political rights that Western countries are always lecturing them about are less important than economic progress.

Of all the attacks on liberal democracy, though, the Islamist variant draws the most attention today. It, too, suggests that liberal-democratic "freedom" is actually oppressive, tempting weak individuals into an existence unmoored from God's guidance. Devout Muslims, like the most devout Christians or Jews, believe that religion must guide human affairs. Where the human-made, rational-legal principles of liberal democracy clash with religious authority, they must give way. For political Islamists, moreover, Muhammad's teachings depart from liberal democracy in ways that make for a better society on Earth. By following *shari'a* law to prohibit blasphemy against Islam, limiting freedom of speech, or implementing Qur'anic principles that severely restrict women's lives, political Islamists aspire to a more respectful, ordered society than the immoral hedonism of pure individualism. In their view, everyone benefits—including women—from guidance toward a more modest and spiritual lifestyle.

Do any of these arguments matter to citizens of liberal democracies? When we hear them from leaders in Iran or China, they are easy to dismiss as self-serving. Yet if we listen closely, we hear echoes of them elsewhere as well. Mainstream politicians and citizens within liberal democracies have at least some sympathy for similar views.

Mainstream Critiques of Liberal-Democratic Flaws

Even the most confident champions of liberal democracy admit that it has flaws in practice. On close inspection, their most common complaints validate some of each authoritarian critique. Modern liberals and conservatives still see liberal democracy as vastly superior even with these flaws, but their recognition of similar themes suggests that the twenty-first-century debate over governments is not entirely black-and-white.

The most widespread mainstream critique of liberal democracy is that money skews its system of representation and rights. Echoing a moderate version of socialists' concerns, many people worry that rich individuals and corporations skew the electoral process with their money, outweighing the voices of those less economically advantaged. By flooding elections with funding and buying political messages on TV and other media, richer citizens may crowd out other voices. Wealth can affect access to rights in the judicial system, too, where richer people can buy better legal counsel. This complaint is especially common on the modern-liberal side of the mainstream, which is largely defined around the notion that government must act to ensure that disadvantaged citizens are not excluded from the benefits of liberty. Unlike devout socialists, modern liberals do not see these problems as fatal flaws of liberal democracy because they believe that fixes exist within more regulated campaign finance and more equitable legal representation. In the absence of such policies, though, they share socialists' concern that liberal democracy does not deliver freedom as advertised.

On the conservative side of the mainstream we hear hints of other authoritarian critiques. In the United States, which is one of the most religious liberal democracies, religious conservatives often argue that government should draw on religious values to construct a more respectful and moral society. Also, it is common among conservatives to call for stronger common identity and patriotic duty to the nation, coupled with laments that an individualistic life of hedonism is lacking in appeal.

Similar objections to how liberal democracy may undermine social order or religious values underlie the common conservative concern about runaway expansion of rights. In the United States, the civil rights movement, feminists, and gay activists have all sought rights against the opposition of conservatives who argued for older constitutional interpretations that reflected traditional social norms. For religious conservatives, the most egregious case is the *Roe v. Wade* decision in 1973 in which the Supreme Court found that abortions are protected by rights to privacy. With a hint of the spirit of fascist or Islamist thinking, then, conservatives worry that liberal democracy can expand into freedoms of the wrong sort. They feel it provides the best kind of freedom when embedded in more traditional, older norms.

Modern liberals are not socialists, and conservatives are not fascists or Islamists, but their concerns about liberal democracy suggest that authoritarians' attacks are more overdrawn than crazy. This connection makes it less surprising that people in other systems accept extreme versions of these critiques in support of different regimes. It also gives us a clearer-eyed appreciation for our own government, warts and all. As Churchill said, liberal democracy may well be the worst kind of government except for all the others that have been tried.

Explaining a Case: Understanding the Whys of Chinese Authoritarianism

5.6 **Identify multiple plausible explanations for China's one-party regime.**

Critical thinking about democracy and its alternatives is not just about what we like or dislike about these systems. Also important is some inkling of why these systems arise and endure. Imagine, for example, if we explain liberal democracy as resulting mainly from economic development. Perhaps we would argue that people need a certain level of wealth to exercise political rights, and that the emergence of a business-oriented middle class is crucial to encourage individualism and a space for civil society. If we tell that explanatory story, we can hardly criticize very poor countries for not being democracies. It may imply that sometimes we would accept certain authoritarian regimes.

The Rational-Material Story

From a rational-material point of view, political regimes reflect the underlying distribution of material resources in a society—above all wealth. If one group can control the creation and flows of wealth, it will usually impose authoritarian rule; in states in which material power is more decentralized, democracy has more of a chance. Following this logic, the core of China's political story is that the Communists took over a poor economy with no strong business class to oppose them. When they opened the economy, the Chinese combination of repression and poverty attracted huge foreign investment, since it offered a giant pool of cheap, repressed labor. Though a business class has grown in China, creating the possibility of future political change, its members currently give the CCP credit for managing rapid growth. Both business and state leaders worry about instability in such a huge country, so at this time their material interests align with maintaining the status quo.

The Institutional Story

An institutional approach suggests that the key to political regimes is how the past history has left a legacy of organizations that support or limit central power. If earlier generations have built up organizations outside the central government—clubs, religious organizations, tribes, unions, universities, or perhaps local government—people may be able to use these tools to limit central authority and create space for rights and representation. In countries where strong organizations have not been built up beyond the central state—like China—a decentralized system like democracy is unlikely to succeed. This approach sees China's current regime as built on a very centralized institutional inheritance. China has a long history of control from the capital in Beijing, and the CCP actively smothered nonparty organization for decades. Despite reforms since the 1970s, most organizations like local governments, courts, religious institutions, and interest groups are weak and rarely able to resist the center. Until more such organizations develop a space for autonomy from the central state, the regime will likely hang on to power.

The Ideational Story

An ideational story about political regimes suggests that different cultures, identities, or ideological movements shape the governments that people support. Certain cultures and identities nudge people to demand democracy, while others make authoritarianism seem more legitimate. Chinese political culture draws most heavily on the thinking of Confucius, who put little emphasis on individual rights and more on the value of a stable, orderly community. Chinese people have no experience with democracy and often react in a nationalist way against it, interpreting it as a Western invention ill-suited to their society. China's rising power and wealth may simply strengthen their identity-based rejection of a Western model.

To get a feel for how to explain the rise and endurance of particular governments, consider the case of China. Whether or not China's one-party regime will maintain its power going forward is surely one of the most important questions for politics in the twenty-first century. As big as this question is, though, it is not too big for a critical thinker with the right tools to break down into coherent alternative arguments. The three main explanatory approaches in political science show the way. The debate among these explanations matters quite a bit: if we hope to promote democracy in China, we need to consider which argument is most convincing. Would democracy's prospects be enhanced most by continued growth of an open economy, further strengthening a business-oriented middle class that someday will object to authoritarian control? Or might the key step be the development of civil-society organizations? Maybe it is more important to foster a new narrative of Chinese political culture that includes rights?

Once again, political scientists would look for real-world evidence through quantitative research on cross-case patterns and qualitative research on within-case processes, or both.

RESEARCH ON WITHIN-CASE PROCESSES.   Like a detective tracing chains of evidence to a suspect, we can ask what detailed processes each explanation would lead us to expect on the ground in China. Table 5-3 sketches out some process expectations for our three plausible stories.

Gathering strong evidence that any of these stories best captures Chinese dynamics today would take major field research in China, but you can start the search. Find a news article on support for the Chinese government, or criticism

Table 5-3 Exploring Within-Case Evidence for Explanations of Chinese Authoritarianism

	Rational-Material Explanation	Institutional Explanation	Ideational Explanation
Who most supports authoritarian government?	Those who depend on the regime for wealth or support: party officials, state industries, the poor	Central party/government elites, plus businesses who like keeping workers repressed to minimize labor costs	Communist ideologues and nationalists
Who are key champions of democracy?	Businesspeople (especially those least connected to the state) and the middle class	Societal groups seeking autonomy from the state: local leaders, religious organizations, artists, students, environmentalists	Educated, Western-linked people who take up ideals of rights and democracy
When should pressure for democratization rise?	When economic growth produces widespread wealth independent from the state	When competing groups manage to organize effectively, ally into movements, and mobilize citizens for change	When regime is embarrassed by scandals, corruption, and hypocrisy; and prominent pro-democracy leaders arise (within or outside the CCP)
Best Evidence to Support Each Explanation	We see business leaders considering how to relate to the CCP and deciding that stability is currently best for business.	We find places where unusually well-organized local groups and organizations are exerting more autonomy.	We see that many business leaders or local groups adopt nationalist rhetoric and seem to genuinely support the regime.

of it, from a respectable newspaper, magazine, or website. Then break down the way the story is presented: who are supporters or reformers, and what appears to be empowering or limiting them?

RESEARCH ON CROSS-CASE PATTERNS. We can also look to see where China fits in cross-case patterns of support for authoritarian regimes. Is there a pattern of nondemocracy at a certain level of wealth? Is there a pattern of religious organizations, associations, subnational government, or other institutional features where we see stable liberal democracy? Do certain cultural regions of the world seem to better support democracy? Your instructor may be able to help you find data to explore some of these possible cross-case correlations.

Conclusion: Why It Matters to Understand the Many Forms of Government Authority

This chapter has simultaneously introduced forms of government authority around the world and enabled us to think critically about U.S. government. On the one hand, the advantages of liberal democracy over illiberal democracies like Russia or authoritarian regimes in China or Syria are quite clear to most people, and we can be up front about them. There is a strong case to be made that only liberal democracies should be seen as legitimate. On the other hand, liberal democracies never implement their model perfectly in practice, and draw support from appeals to effectiveness and nationalism that uphold other systems as well. And for all the beauty of liberal-democratic ideals, we must acknowledge that most other governments *are* seen as legitimate by some of their citizens. Without acknowledging the flaws of liberal democracies and the possible legitimacy of other systems, we risk a naïve exaggeration of our model's perfection, and an even more naïve expectation that all countries will soon adopt it. Multiple kinds of governments will remain on Earth for the foreseeable future.

Review of Learning Objectives

5.1 **Explain the difference between authority and power and identify five reasons why citizens may support governments and their decisions.**

Several forms of legitimate authority uphold governments: traditional legitimacy of time-honored practices, charismatic legitimacy of attractive ideas and leaders, or rational-legal legitimacy of fair process. Regimes also employ raw power by gaining support from citizens for effective delivery of benefits and exerting force to compel compliance. In the modern era, rational-legal legitimacy and its associated kind of government—democracy—are especially influential but still far from fully dominant.

5.2 Identify the two core elements of liberal-democratic government, explain their relationship, and describe how tradition and effectiveness also support such regimes.

Liberal democracy is built on a rational-legal formula of electoral representation with guaranteed rights. Rights are crucial to ensure the participation and contestation that support real choice in elections, but also limit electoral choice by barring voters from voting to erase rights. These demanding standards can be difficult for governments to maintain, and all liberal democracies also cultivate support by evoking traditional nationalism and delivering effective benefits.

5.3 Identify the core features of illiberal democracy and explain how some justify this model as preferable to liberal democracy.

Illiberal democracies select leaders in elections, but their leaders argue that liberal rights must be limited for government to provide effective results. Most attempts at this hybrid between liberal democracy and authoritarianism fall into hypocrisy, talking about democracy but acting authoritarian. An exceptional few, most notably Singapore, showcase a more successful version of this model that delivers very effective results. In a subset of such governments, mainly in Muslim countries, leaders limit rights because they fear free elections will bring a choice for authoritarian government.

5.4 Identify four types of authoritarianism and their core principles and describe several sources of authoritarian support using specific country examples.

Authoritarian governments claim unlimited authority in the name of traditional practices in inherited monarchy, charismatic religion in theocracy, charismatic ideologies in one-party regimes, or imperatives of effective stability and security in dictatorship. All such governments drift from their announced principles and rely heavily on a combination of repressive force, whipped-up nationalism, and charisma. Yet they also draw support from effectiveness, whether in Chinese economic growth or in the plausible, if distasteful, role that Syria's regime has played in smothering ethnic and religious conflict.

5.5 Evaluate the most important defenses and critiques of liberal-democratic government.

Champions of liberal democracy argue that their system is superior because it guarantees freedom, offers citizens a voice through representation, and encourages compromise among competing political groups. Authoritarian critics counter that liberal democracy is just a veiled form of oppression that forces citizens into individual alienation from the nation, economic exploitation, or separation from God. Even mainstream liberal-democratic politicians accept elements of these critiques, admitting that liberal democracy may be flawed by economic inequality or an overemphasis on individualism, but they still see it as the best option.

5.6 Identify multiple plausible explanations for China's one-party regime.

To review for this objective, try to brainstorm rational-material, institutional, and ideational explanations of Chinese authoritarianism without looking at Section 5.6:

- If we see political regimes as built on how people are positioned in the material landscape—reflecting some fairly raw distribution of material power—how might we understand China's government today?
- If, alternatively, we see political regimes as shaped strongly by a legacy of institutions—being built on an "obstacle course" inherited from earlier eras—what kind of story might we expect to lie behind the very centralized power of the Chinese CCP?
- If, lastly, we see political regimes as constructed most fundamentally around culture and ideas, what kind of a story might we tell about why authoritarianism seems strong in the Chinese context?

After brainstorming your answers to these questions, return to Section 5.6 to see if you captured the main logic of these explanatory alternatives.

Great Sources to Find Out More

Anna Politkovskya, *Putin's Russia: Life in a Failing Democracy* (New York: Holt, 2007). An account of Putin's government from a journalist who was murdered for her views.

Azar Gat, "The Return of Authoritarian Great Powers," *Foreign Affairs, 86*(4) (July–August 2007), 59–69. An analysis of why authoritarianism has enjoyed a comeback in the twenty-first century.

Barrington Moore, *The Social Origins of Dictatorship and Democracy* (Boston: Beacon, 1966). Perhaps the most famous book in comparative politics, this weighty tome traces political regimes to underlying distributions of economic power.

Daniel Bell, *Beyond Liberal Democracy: Political Thinking for an East Asian Context* (Princeton, NJ: Princeton University Press, 2006). A thoughtful argument for departures from liberal democracy in East Asia.

Donald Kagan, *Pericles of Athens and the Birth of Democracy* (New York: Free Press, 1998). A readable account of the rise of Greek direct democracy.

Fareed Zakaria, *The Future of Freedom: Illiberal Democracy at Home and Abroad* (New York: Norton, 2003). A wonderfully readable survey of illiberal democracy from the inventor of the term.

J.S. Mill, *On Liberty* (New York: Penguin, 1985[1859]). The clearest case ever made for liberal rights.

José Antonio Cheibub, Robert Dahl, and Ian Shapiro, eds., *Democracy Sourcebook* (Boston: MIT Press, 2003). A collection of writings on democracy from classic theorists to modern commentaries.

Larry Diamond, *The Spirit of Democracy* (New York: Basic Books, 2008). A lively tour of prospects for liberal democracy in countries where it is not yet established.

Lisa Wedeen, *Ambiguities of Domination: Politics, Rhetoric and Symbols in Contemporary Syria* (Chicago: University of Chicago Press, 1999). A fascinating look at how the Assad regime long kept its citizens in line.

Lucian W. Pye (with Mary W. Pye), *Asian Power and Politics: The Cultural Dimensions of Authority* (Cambridge, MA: Belknap, 1988). Though much criticized, this work by a famous political scientist suggested that culture shapes political development in Asia.

Max Weber, *From Max Weber: Essays in Sociology* (New York: Routledge, 2009). Famous essays that include Weber's breakdown of forms of authority.

Robert Dahl, *Polyarchy* (New Haven, CT: Yale University Press, 1972). A classic analysis of the minimal requirements for democracy.

Robert Dahl, *Democracy and Its Critics* (New Haven, CT: Yale University Press, 1989). A discussion of key critiques of democracy and a defense of its enduring merits.

Ruth Berins Collier and David Collier, *Shaping the Political Arena: Critical Junctures, the Labor Movement and Regime Dynamics in Latin America* (Princeton, NJ: Princeton University Press, 1991). This discussion of Latin American cases shows how institutional inheritances affect the configuration of political regimes.

Teresa Wright, *Accepting Authoritarianism: State-Society Relations in China's Reform Era* (Stanford, CA: Stanford University Press, 2010). A careful study of why Chinese citizens accept authoritarianism.

Develop Your Thinking

Use these questions as discussion or short writing exercises to think more deeply about some of the key themes of the chapter.

1. In parts of your life other than dealing with government—jobs, school, family—whose authority do you accept, and how is that authority justified?

2. How well does American representative democracy showcase "rule by the common people"?

3. Would you accept limited rights during wartime or some other major crisis?

4. If you had to choose one kind of authoritarianism for your country, which would you choose and why?

5. What do you think is the worst flaw or weakness of liberal-democratic government?

6. What do you think is the most important dynamic that keeps the Chinese Communist regime in power?

7. How much overlap do you see between the reasons why Americans accept their government and the reasons why the Chinese accept theirs?

Keywords

authoritarianism   147
civil society   136
constitution   131
constitutional monarchies   139
contestation   135
cult of personality   151
democracy   133
dictatorship   150

direct democracy   134
effectiveness   128
government   126
illiberal democracy   140
kleptocracy   151
legitimacy   126
monarchy   148
one-party regime   149

participation   135
representative democracy   134
rule of law   131
suffrage   136
theocracy   148
totalitarianism   147
tyranny of the majority   137

Chapter 6
Individual Participation and Collective Action

In one of the most famous photographs ever taken, widely known as "Tank Man," a participant in the 1989 pro-democracy protests at Tiananmen Square in Beijing, China, stands in front of tanks to block their progress toward the demonstrators.

Jeff Widener/AP Images

Learning Objectives

6.1 Identify forms of political participation from low-intensity individual expression to high-intensity actions and how they relate to the challenges of getting people to act together.

6.2 Explain the difference between economic and identity-based frames in collective action, and give examples of both from American politics on both Left and Right.

6.3 Describe salient patterns of political participation in the United States, France, and China and summarize debates about how technology has affected American participation.

6.4 Evaluate competing ideological views of the role of individual and collective concerns in political participation.

6.5 Identify multiple plausible explanations for the comparatively low turnout in American elections.

Students Take Action (or Don't): Who's Ready to Rumble?

Students are known the world over for their tendency to rebel. Young, idealistic, energetic, they rally en masse over all sorts of political issues. Or ... do they? Sometimes they do, sometimes they don't.

Recent student movements suggest powerful potential. In 2018, after a school shooting in Parkland, Florida, that left 17 dead, almost a million American high school students walked out of classes to protest gun violence. In 2019, thousands of students across several countries staged a walkout over climate change. General enthusiasm for such action is up: more American students today say they want to "do good" through civic engagement than in previous generations.[1]

On the other hand, patterns in student political action are often puzzling. For example, back in 2010, a global economic crisis was putting pressure on public budgets everywhere. Many American universities raised tuition fees hugely—some by a third!—with hardly a peep of protest. Meanwhile the French government tried to cut costs by raising the retirement age from 60 to 62. This mattered far less for students than tuition hikes, but thousands of college and high school students poured into the streets, with violence in a few places.[2]

Consider an example with higher stakes. The person in this famous picture of "Tank man" was apparently also a student, although his identity is unknown. He took part in Chinese pro-democracy demonstrations in Beijing's Tiananmen Square in 1989. The participants knew it was risky to challenge China's authoritarian government, and many paid the ultimate price. Hundreds were eventually killed. We'll never know how "Tank man" arrived at his choice to make a stand.

Why do students in one context quietly accept higher college costs while others demonstrate to defend retirees? Could any idealistic cause persuade you to stand up to a tank? To think about such questions, we must see the wide range of options and variation in political participation around the world, engage with it ideologically, and brainstorm explanations for it. This chapter does so with special attention to the political experiences of students and citizens in the United States, France, and China. ■

The Many Forms of Individual Participation and Collective Action

6.1 **Identify forms of political participation from low-intensity individual expression to high-intensity actions and how they relate to the challenges of getting people to act together.**

Political action! The phrase evokes loud rallies, students on the march, rebels on the barricades, or young interns in suits running messages around the corridors of Congress. Yet it also includes lower-intensity acts like voting, signing a petition, donating money to a cause, or writing a letter. Even nonparticipation can be meaningful political action. Many people *not* doing something together,

apathy
A state of indifference and inactivity.

Civil disobedience
The peaceful but explicit refusal to respect laws or rules.

like refusing to join in elections or joining a boycott, can hugely impact politics. Any sort of action designed to send a message about collective decision making is a political action. The most classic political actions try to send messages to decision-makers in government, though many also target other organizations like schools, universities, clubs, or businesses.

Quite a few people, however, fall into **apathy**. They take no political actions at all. For many of them, an initial obstacle is simply imagining what kind of political actions they could take, and what kind of considerations would go into such choices. We thus begin with Table 6-1's menu of possibilities.

Table 6-1 A Menu of Political Actions

INTENSITY OF COMMITMENT INCREASES	COLLECTIVE ACTION	If you engage in . . .	including actions like . . .	we call you a . . .
		Individual expression	Announce views: bumper sticker, yard sign, flag display Engage in political discussions Letter-writing to newspapers, officials Blog	Citizen
		Joining collective action	Vote Join/support party with money/time Support leader/candidate with money/time Join/support community group/organization Join public demonstrations Join strike or legal protests **Civil disobedience** like sit-ins, boycotts	Mobilized citizen
		Leading collective action	Volunteer for leadership role in community organization Volunteer for leadership role in advocacy group Help organize social movement Volunteer for substantial role in political campaign Organize demonstration or protest Persuade others to participate Approach public officials on behalf of your community, group, or movement	Activist or leader
		Professional politics	Paid work to affect public officials' choices Run for or hold paid office Paid work directly for politicians Paid work for government	Lobbyist Politician Staffer/advisor Bureaucrat
		Violent action	Riots, sabotage, insurgency Terrorism	Rebel or Revolutionary Terrorist

How Can People Act in Politics?
A Menu of Options

We find lower-intensity actions at the top of the table. Here, individuals give just a bit of their lives to politics. The degree to which the action is likely to affect one's life increases as we move down the table to higher-intensity actions. Not all actions are relevant in every context; people can only vote if they live in a democracy, for example, and violent action only arises in certain settings. The following sections touch on each kind of action from an individual's point of view, highlighting that whether someone is choosing to vote or join an armed rebellion, some aspects of those choices to participate are similar.

Individual Expression

We begin with the relatively low-intensity kinds of political actions that you, like most people, are most likely to consider. Individual expression is the simplest kind of political action. In talking with others, writing letters, or signaling views with bumper stickers, yard signs, or symbols like flags, people declare their views publicly. Usually they are not only declaring their views but also seeking to persuade others to respect and share them. In modest ways, they are trying to build or mobilize political coalitions.

Even at this simplest level, how individuals act varies a great deal. Some people are quiet about their views. Others cover their cars with bumper stickers and start political debates at the drop of a hat. Individuals can simply have different personalities, or may learn different habits of self-expression by growing up in different families. Across groups or countries, expectations in political culture also steer people to different kinds of self-expression. In the United States, many citizens fly the U.S. flag outside their homes, especially around the Fourth of July. In France, no one would think of flying the French flag at home. While Americans tend to see the flag as a symbol of the people, in France, it symbolizes the state. If a neighbor's house flew the flag, people would be puzzled. They might wonder: is Monsieur Dupont opening a government office?

Individual expression also varies tremendously due to tangible constraints and opportunities. Some constraints are brutal. In China, Iran, Syria, or other authoritarian states with large secret-police forces that monitor society, starting the wrong kind of political discussion in a public place—or making the wrong contacts on the Internet—can lead to police questioning, jail, or worse. Even societies that are generally freer sometimes constrain self-expression in targeted ways. In Turkey, where most political discussion is more open, it is illegal to criticize the founder of modern Turkey, Mustafa Kemal Atatürk, or his "legacy." Defenders of these laws extend the "legacy" clause to any criticism of the Turkish state broadly, leading to prosecutions of people for mentioning the Turkish genocide against Armenians during World War I or repression of the Kurdish minority in eastern Turkey. Similar dynamics are also known in U.S. history: the Alien and Sedition Acts of 1798 criminalized "false, scandalous, and malicious writing" about the American president or Congress. They were soon set aside, but later laws banning advocacy of revolution were used to prosecute Communist sympathizers in the 1940s and 1950s.

Today, American protections for freedom of expression are among the strongest in the world, but their limits remain contested. One example is the long-running debate on whether or not people should be free to burn the U.S. flag (as the Supreme Court has ruled they are). Another concerns "hate speech," or any sort of discourse that targets certain members of society in a threatening way. Many European countries have much stronger anti-hate speech laws than does the United States, especially targeting anything related to the symbols and ideas of the Nazis. In Germany, France, Britain, and several other countries, it is illegal to deny that the Holocaust took place, or even to engage in racist speech of any sort.

Individuals' opportunities for self-expression also vary with technology and practices of daily life. This will be obvious to the Internet generation, which has seen an explosion of options for self-expression—political or not—in blogs, Facebook interactions, and Tweets. Yet these new openings may come at the expense of others. The traditional political action of writing a letter to a local newspaper is becoming rarer today, above all because advertising spending that once supported local papers has shifted to Internet services such as Craigslist or Google. This relationship between the Internet and newspapers is part of a long history of the evolution of spaces for political self-expression. In the 1600s, the arrival of coffee in Europe from the Middle East led to the rapid spread of coffeehouses as meeting places. London's first café opened in 1650; by 1675, there were 3,000 in the city. Many historians credit this new practice of sitting and drinking coffee for opening new space for political debate and spreading ideas about individual rights and democracy across Europe.[3] The spread of "Internet cafés" in the early 2000s (where people could access the Internet in the pre-smartphone days) combined this older space with the new virtual arena—and served as key sites for the launching of revolts against undemocratic governments in Egypt and Tunisia in 2011. Technology, media, and public spaces will continue to interact in the future to shape how you and people around the world can formulate and express political views.

Collective Action: Voting and Joining

Voting may seem to belong under "individual expression." It is, after all, the most common way to register your views in a democracy. But with voting we move into the category of collective action. You may be able to form your views and mark a ballot alone, but voting is a collective choice. It only makes sense to vote if you expect others to do so.

As Table 6-1 shows, most political action is collective action. Individuals cannot vote, join a club or political party, have a march, or mount a revolution without others. That simple point raises **collective-action problems** about how individual self-interest relates to taking action as a group. A decision to vote has individual costs: it takes time out of your day. But the effects of voting are

collective-action problem
A situation in which successful action depends on the involvement of multiple people, but rational individuals would not see sufficient incentives to join in.

collective, and your single vote will almost never affect the outcome of an election. One vote hardly ever makes a difference in a university or town setting, let alone among the 200 million registered voters in the United States. This contrast creates the **Downs paradox**, named after the political scientist Anthony Downs: meaningful democracy depends on as many people voting as possible, but it seems irrational for each individual to vote!

Some countries incentivize voting to address this challenge. In about a dozen countries including Australia and Argentina, compulsory voting is enforced. The $20 fine for failing to vote in Australia is effective, with average **turnout**, or the percentage of voters who vote, among the highest in the world at about 95 percent. Across western European countries, where most voting is not compulsory, average turnout from 1945 to 1997 was 77 percent. It was 54 percent in South and Central America. Turnout in the United States is among the lowest in the world, averaging 48 percent in the same period. In so-called midterm years between attention-grabbing presidential elections, U.S. turnout falls to even lower levels. Furthermore, if we calculate turnout as a percentage of all voting-age citizens—not as a percentage of the smaller number who register to vote—the rate looks very low indeed. Eligible-voter turnout was only 32.98 percent in the 2014 midterms, though it swung back to a historic high (for midterms) of 50.4 percent in the hotly costed midterms of 2018 (see Table 6-2).

But these numbers nonetheless suggest that the Downs paradox is more of a theoretical puzzle than a real-world problem. It raises good questions about *why*

Downs paradox
The idea that the cost of voting in an individual's time usually exceeds the likely benefits, since a single vote rarely affects the outcome.

turnout
The percentage of potential voters who actually vote in an election.

Table 6-2 Political Participation in Major Countries

Country [survey date]	Political Action			Voter Turnout (eligible voters)	
	Ever signed petition (%)	Ever joined boycott (%)	Ever attended demonstration (%)		Voted in last national parliamentary election (%) (Year)
United States [2014]	66.8	37.9	21.8		50.40 (2018) 55.98 (2016) 32.98 (2014)
United Kingdom [2014]	70.4	38.9	17.8		62.88 (2017)
France [2014]	71.8	51.5	47.5		38.62 (2017)
Chile [2014]	12.0	8.4	20.9		49.55 (2017)
Germany [2014]	62.6	51.8	33.4		69.11 (2017)
South Africa [2014]	17.7	13.5	17.9		65.99 (2019)
Russia [2014]	12.7	5.2	10.9		46.04 (2016)
India [2014]	35.6	36.8	39.7		67.11 (2019)
Taiwan [2014]	23.9	28.6	11.3		65.84 (2016)
Turkey [2014]	13.4	10.2	9.5		88.95 (2018)

SOURCE: For statistics on actions, International Social Survey Programme 2014; for statistics on turnout, International Institute for Democracy and Electoral Assistance, http://www.idea.int/.

people vote, but even without incentives or fines, most people in most democracies *do* vote. U.S. voter turnout fell steadily for many decades after World War II, but then it rose back to a high of 57 percent in 2008. Those numbers remain low in comparative perspective, but 131 million Americans did choose to vote in 2008 (and 138 million voted in 2016). This suggests that most people approach voting without breaking down its rational costs and benefits for them as an individual. Studies support this: voters see their act as a duty, or vote because they think that people like them benefit from their action.[4]

Even if most people may not approach voting as an individual cost–benefit calculation, thinking about collective-action problems helps to highlight the considerations that go into more intensive political actions as well. Political actions beyond voting tend to ask more of individuals in terms of time, effort, and perhaps personal risk. Yet the benefits of actions—like volunteering for a cause, joining a group, donating money, or turning out for a protest—are often also collective: usually the participants hope to affect leaders, policies, or rules in a school, town, university, state, or country in ways that apply to many people, not just the immediate volunteers or protesters. In other words, people who stay home while others participate can get the benefit without bearing the cost. This is the broad challenge of collective action known as the **free rider problem**. Whatever cause interests you, chances are your contribution will not make it succeed or fail. Because you expect some others will volunteer their time for it, why not just stay home, let others do the work, and get the benefits anyway? Why not get a "free ride" on others' actions?

free rider problem
The category of collective-action problems in which individuals would prefer to let someone else do the work to obtain a collective benefit.

Just as compulsory voting responds to the Downs paradox, many organizations address free riding by offering **selective incentives** to participants: side benefits that are individual, not collective. For example, public radio is a collective benefit—non-contributors can tune in—but radio stations offer "swag" to those who give money or volunteer. New Sierra Club members get a backpack and magazine; Americans who join the National Rifle Association (NRA) or the American Association of Retired Persons (AARP) get discounts on many products and services; new members of the Royal Society for the Protection of Birds (one of the largest British membership groups) can choose a birding handbook or a birdhouse. Political parties give volunteers clothing, hold social events, and provide meetings with political celebrities. Demonstrations attract participants with free food or entertainment. All these enticements try to align individual incentives more with collective action.

selective incentives
Any individually targeted benefit that attempts to resolve collective-action problems.

Like with voting and the Downs paradox, though, the free rider problem is interesting partly because it does *not* correspond fully to reality. People do participate in many collective actions at high personal cost. Volunteers for public radio, churches, the NRA, or almost any other cause bear disproportionate costs for collective gain. Even in contexts where individual costs are very high, we often see collective action. Thousands joined Mahatma Gandhi in peaceful "sit-ins" to demand Indian independence from Britain in the early 1900s, or followed Martin Luther King in similar civil disobedience during the American civil rights movement in the 1950s, even though they faced possible beatings, imprisonment, and in some cases death. In China today, people do sometimes join in demonstrations that criticize the government even if most are deterred by the government's repression. Looking at collective action through the lens of the free rider problem, then, can highlight both how people make choices in action and how they do not.

Collective Action: Activists and Political Professionals

If collective action depends on participants getting past individual disincentives to act, it demands much more from leaders. People who recruit members and manage organizations and campaigns often give much of their lives to such efforts. This is true even in the most open and stable liberal democracies: collective action takes work! It is all the more true in more tumultuous contexts, where political action may carry considerable risks: Gandhi and King were assassinated, and other people around the world confront similar threats every day for political causes. In later chapters, we return to all the forms of action described in the following discussion, but first, let's examine them from the point of view of individual participation. Consider the trade-offs of collective action across different leadership roles.

ACTIVISTS.   In liberal democracies, these people volunteer for significant positions in politically involved organizations and play a key role in politics. This is less true for systems that leave less space for civil-society mobilization that is separate from government. Still, some activists exist even under most authoritarian regimes, both alongside and outside government control. Activists who criticize such regimes are often called **dissidents**, like Aung San Suu Kyi, who received the Nobel Peace Prize in 1991 for her long-running and ultimately successful efforts to reform the military dictatorship in her native Myanmar.

dissident
Someone who opposes a political system or policy, usually in an authoritarian context where such opposition is not permitted.

Activists come in many forms. In roles as *community leaders*, they volunteer to help manage neighborhoods, schools, parks, towns, and similar local public entities. Such roles are often formally apolitical, being barred from political party affiliations in most of the United States and many other countries. That does not mean that they are free from contestation: people always have a variety of views about local politics. Still, many enjoy the fray of community leadership. The main individual benefit of serving in such a role is simply that it can be interesting and prestigious. It is a way to get to know one's neighbors, and may bring interaction with officials, businesspeople, and other notable community members. Community leaders may have opportunities to advance their own views, magnifying their own voice on issues that matter to them. All governments except the most repressive regimes draw on this kind of bottom-up volunteerism. In China, for example, Homeowner Associations play a role in community management, though under surveillance.

Nongovernmental Organization (NGO)
Any legally created organization that operates independently from any government and does not operate mainly for business profit.

Advocacy-group activists volunteer for **Nongovernmental Organizations (NGOs)** that seek to influence public policy. In the United States, they might lead a chapter of the League of Women Voters, Mothers against Drunk Driving, Greenpeace, or the Society for the Prevention of Cruelty to Animals, or organize events, raise money, and make phone calls for the NRA. Such organizations often employ paid staff, but they are also membership organizations in which volunteers constitute foot soldiers and lower-level officers. In these contexts, activists gain the benefit of meeting like-minded people, and may gain access to social events, meetings with policymakers, and a variety of selective perks. Still, few volunteers fill these positions just in search of personal benefits. They tend to be willing to pay personal costs, at least in time, for a cause. Outside of the most open and stable liberal democracies, their commitments are presumably even stronger. Mexico and Turkey are largely open societies, for example, but to campaign for community security in the thick of Mexico's drug war or for gay rights in conservative Islamic Turkey is risky. Advocates of women's rights in Saudi Arabia, journalistic integrity in Russia, or free speech in China face serious risks—but some persevere despite individual consequences.

social movements
Short- or medium-term public campaigns that aim to achieve collective goals.

Advocacy-group activists are sometimes called *social movement activists*, but this label is most useful to highlight a different role. **Social movements** are short- or medium-term public campaigns around an issue of the moment. Unlike advocacy-group activists who work in an enduring organization, social movement activists are people who step forward for bursts of organizing and leadership. On September 17, 2011, for example, spurred by nothing more than a call from a Canadian counterculture magazine, organizers used Facebook and Twitter to assemble almost a thousand people in New York for a left-wing "Occupy Wall Street" protest against unemployment. Media attention soon led to related protests in Boston and other cities. On the other side of the political spectrum, the "Tea Party" conservative movement began as a similar series of protests in 2009. The 2011 uprisings in Tunisia, Egypt, and other Arabic countries also started as spontaneous social movements. Social movements sometimes

cycles of protest
When small initial protests embolden other people to join them or imitate them elsewhere.

mushroom into **cycles of protest**; small numbers are involved at first, but they embolden others, and as momentum grows huge numbers of people join in.[5] Still, such powerful dynamics cannot get going without leaders who move first to instigate and organize them. In most cases, individual benefits are unlikely to provide sufficient motivation for such a role, especially where governments try to repress movements. Leaders who do most of the early work are also likely to bear the brunt of any punishment.

Political party activists, lastly, are much like a special version of advocacy-group activists. They, too, fold fliers, staff the phones, knock on doors, and recruit people and funds, but they do so for organizations that compete directly for political office, not just to influence policy. This direct connection to power may give such individuals additional motivations for contributing to collective action, since electoral victories may bring them employment in government or other benefits. Outside of liberal democracies, though, activists who join opposition parties may also face especially sharp individual costs for their explicit work against the government.

Jacob Balzani Loov/ZUMA Press, Inc/Alamy Stock Photo

A protester sleeps on the barricades during a break in clashes with police as part of Ukraine's "Euromaidan" revolution in 2014.

POLITICAL PROFESSIONALS.   When we shift into the category of paid work, salaries provide added incentives for individuals to lead collective action. Still, it seems unlikely that many people choose careers in professional politics purely for money and other perks. Except in places where officeholders and government employees may make very large sums through corruption, careers in areas like business, medicine, or law would typically ensure financial comfort better than political jobs.

Lobbyists are the professionals who lead advocacy groups. In the United States and other liberal democracies, lobbyists advocate for many different slices of society. Many work alongside activist volunteers in NGOs that promote political causes, from the Audubon Society and the Christian Coalition to the National Association for the Advancement of Colored People (NAACP). The largest number of lobbyists in the United States and most other countries, however, work for economic entities. American **employers' organizations** include the U.S. Chamber of Commerce, the National Association of Manufacturers, and over 7,000 sectoral groups such as the American Apparel and Footwear Association or the National Association of Wheat Growers. **Unions** like the AFL-CIO or the Service Employees International Union represent workers' concerns. Any of these kinds of lobbying can be individually rewarding, combining a respectable career and interesting interactions with both private actors and policymakers. Especially at NGOs, though, most lobbyists surely share commitments that motivate them beyond individual profit.

employers' organizations
Associations that represent owners or managers of for-profit businesses.

unions
Associations that represent employees.

More authoritarian systems have fewer openings for societal input to the state, and accordingly many fewer lobbying-style associations. The main exception is employers' and workers' associations, which exist in practically every country. Yet in the most repressive systems—like Syria, North Korea or as was once the case in authoritarian systems like Nazi Germany or the Soviet Union—the role of employers' and workers' associations are at least partly reversed. Rather than serving workers or firms as channels through which they can mobilize to pursue their economic interests in politics, these associations function as top-down channels for government oversight and control of economic actors.

Politicians are people who seek paid public office as a career. It is common to see politicians as self-serving seekers of power and wealth—and there certainly are a few places where this image is borne out. To take one of the most egregious examples, not only do Kenyan members of Parliament often receive bribes, but they have voted themselves payments that sum to over 100 times the average Kenyan salary.[6] This very poor country has some of the highest-paid politicians in the world.

In contexts where corruption is less pervasive, however, politicians' individual benefits and costs do not usually look so blatantly selfish. National-level officeholders are typically paid considerably more than average salaries in their countries, it is true, and may have access to a wide variety of perks depending on their positions. U.S. senators receive about eleven times the average American salary. Top leaders everywhere are almost guaranteed to be well-off, not just during their time in office but often with pensions or special support for the rest of their lives (see Table 6-3). Of course, they also gain the power to influence collective decisions. Yet we must acknowledge the individual costs of their political careers as well. Roughly speaking, the more power they hold, the more they sacrifice their lives to their jobs. This is easiest to see in the U.S. president, often called the most powerful person in the world. "I miss being anonymous," mused Barack Obama during his presidency. "I miss Saturday morning, rolling out of bed, not shaving, getting into my car with my girls, driving to the supermarket, squeezing the fruit, getting my car washed, taking walks."[7] Powerful politicians are subject to constant demands on their time and withering media scrutiny. Even after leaving office, Obama will still be besieged by requests for his time and followed by the media for the rest of his life. Whether or not U.S. politicians are rationally self-serving, then, is hard to say. Not many people would trade places with them. In any case, the basic dilemma of collective action—that joiners and especially leaders bear disproportionate costs in pursuing collective benefits—helps us to see everyone from voters to presidents in a different light.

Looking ahead, Chapter 8 explores our last category within professional politics—staffers and bureaucrats—so for now, we move on to the most intense political actions of all: those that involve violence.

Table 6-3 Salaries and Perks for Selected Political Offices

	United States		Germany	
	President	**Legislator (House of Representatives)**	**Chancellor**	**Legislator (Bundestag)**
Salary	$400,000	$174,000	$246,000	$131,288
Perks	$50,000 annual expense account; $100,000 travel account; $19,000 for entertainment; lifetime taxable pension of $199,700; lifetime secret service protection.	Allowance for staff, office expenses, mail averaging $1,446,009; eligible for lifetime benefits after serving five years (pension, health, Social Security).	Covered contributions to pension and unemployment insurance plus benefits as legislator.	Allowances of $58,245; staffing up to $201,000; free use of public train system; chauffeur service in Berlin; survivor and death benefits; pension up to 67.5 percent of regular salary.
	India		Kenya	
	Prime Minister	**Legislator (Lok Sabha)**	**Prime Minister**	**Legislator (National Assembly)**
Salary	$11,905	$11,905	Roughly $400,000	Roughly $90,000
Perks	Annual expenses of $15,314; constituency allowance of $10,714 for staff, mail, etc.	Monthly pension of $397; daily expenses of $40 when attending parliament; constituency allowance of $10,714 for staff, mail, etc.; housing in New Delhi and 34 one-way air tickets from New Delhi to constituency.	Public funds routinely used to pay for/renovate private homes; variable retirement package up to roughly $1 million.	Various allowances total over $100,000, plus up to $190,000 for a mortgage; additional funds for personal bodyguards and state burial.

Top leaders often receive high salaries and extensive benefits, though far more in some countries than in others. All numbers from 2017 at November 2017 exchange rates except Kenya (2019).

SOURCE: International Monetary Fund, White House, U.S. Congress, German Chancellor's office, Indian Prime Minister's office; "New House Allowance Puts MPs Salary Way Above World Superpowers," *The Star* (Kenya), 11 May 2019.

Collective Action: Rebels, Revolutionaries, and Terrorists

According to the German military theorist Carl von Clausewitz (1780–1831), "War is the continuation of politics by other means." Taking up violence, in this view, is just another step in the intensity of action. This may seem harsh, and even misleading: as anyone who has been in a war zone knows, the contrast between violent and peaceful places often feels like different worlds. With respect to individual participation, though, Clausewitz's point is important. As different as they seem, some similar considerations may go into peaceful and violent strategies of collective action.

Rebels are people who take up arms against a government. This is quite a striking individual choice: if bearing individual costs for collective benefit makes *voting* irrational, how much more true is this of attacking a government? Rebels often risk jail, injury, torture, loss of property, or death. Sharp free rider problems thus seem to exist in the groups or communities in which rebellions begin: those who step forward to be the first and leading rebels are likely to bear the greatest risks, especially if the rebellion fails, but everyone may gain from a successful rebellion whether they helped or not. This is one reason why rebellions against repressive governments can be very hard to sustain.

Revolutionaries are rebels with a new kind of government in mind. Beyond rejecting control they dislike, they also seek to change the political order. This additional agenda gives revolutionaries both challenges and advantages relative to rebels. Revolution adds another difficult step to their goals: they might topple the government but fail to set up an enduring new order. The "Arab Spring" uprisings of 2011 in Egypt, Tunisia, or Libya, for example, do not yet seem to have created stable new systems (although Tunisia seems to be on its way). On the other hand, revolution can also add a powerful tool for collective action. Unlike simple rebellions, revolutionary movements recruit participants around ideological goals for a new regime. Such movements share positive aims, an ideological cause, that may help their recruits step past free rider problems. When people see themselves as "freedom fighters" with a clear mission, or in any terms that connect to a vision of a better society, they may be less likely to ask what is in it for them individually.

And what about *terrorists*? An oft-repeated line suggests they are simply revolutionaries whom the speaker dislikes: "One man's terrorist is another man's freedom fighter."[8] But terrorism is actually a very specific action that many revolutionaries avoid: the use of violence to terrorize an opponent rather than trying to defeat them militarily. It is used most often by desperate groups who have little hope of a military victory, and tends to target **noncombatants**—people other than soldiers—to pressure governments by causing fear across the population. Our image of terrorists today is dominated by a form of this strategy, which is the most intense political action of all: suicide terrorism, when people kill themselves along with victims to send a political message.

noncombatants
The legal term for civilians not taking part in an armed conflict.

With such choices we clearly reach the limits of thinking about political actions as a mix of individually rational incentives and collective benefits. A suicide terrorist has left behind any logic of individual benefits in a normal, concrete sense. Most people find it hard to relate to such a choice. Perhaps, we might speculate, people who become terrorists face entirely desperate material constraints, with little left to lose. Perhaps we must look to religion, political ideology, or personal psychology to account for something so extreme. Even then these arguments may not seem especially compelling.

Indeed, suicide terrorism is so radical that it may seem strange—and morally repugnant—to place it in a survey of political actions alongside bumper stickers, voting, and licking envelopes for the Sierra Club. It may take us beyond a menu of imaginable political actions, to something you consider unimaginable. It is useful to include it here, though, precisely for that reason. Seeing the widest possible range of political actions sets up contrasts that illuminate how you see your own options, allowing you to see new possibilities that you might consider and also, perhaps, some that you would not. We also gain a fuller sense of how to see these possibilities when we turn to explanations, since explanatory stories matter for our choices: if we explain terrorism as a response to desperate conditions, for example, we imply that we ourselves might become terrorists if placed in sufficiently desperate conditions.

Before taking that step, though, we survey a few kinds of broad patterns in collective action (and debates about them). One concerns the issues that motivate collective action: who tends to act collectively with whom? Another set of patterns concerns national contexts. Like with cuisine, people in certain countries tend to make certain selections from the menu of actions, producing nationally distinctive modes of participation.

Who's Acting with Whom? Framing and Identity Politics

6.2 **Explain the difference between economic and identity-based frames in collective action, and give examples of both from American politics on both Left and Right.**

Old political wisdom expects that concrete interests—especially economic ones—dominate collective action. People get off the couch when you raise their taxes, threaten their jobs, or propose a new garbage dump near their neighborhood. A fair amount of evidence supports that wisdom, but we also see more complex "framing" in political mobilization. People's choices to get involved or not may turn on how they identify with other people or a certain agenda. If "we" are going to do something, are "we" concerned citizens? Exploited workers? Women? Gun owners? African-Americans? Advocates of religious freedom? LGBTQAAIP? Such questions have become especially salient with the rise of so-called "identity politics" in recent years.

"It's the Economy, Stupid!": Class and Concrete Complaints as the Foundation for Collective Action

Back in 1992, the campaign staff of Democratic presidential candidate Bill Clinton famously scrawled a note on the wall of their campaign "war room": "It's the economy, stupid!" With the economy in recession, Clinton's team thought they could beat incumbent President George H.W. Bush if they hammered away about economic discontent. They were right, and their victory added to well-established political lore. Tangible, concrete benefits, typically related to people's position in the economy, have long been seen as the foundations of voting and other collective action.

There is plenty of evidence that economic conditions strongly affect who feels able or disposed to participate in politics. Voter turnout varies with income levels. Across American presidential elections since the 1990s, eligible voters with family income under $50,000 have averaged about 50 percent turnout, while those with family income above $50,000 averaged almost 70 percent.[9] Studies tend to find that socioeconomic status has even more effect on more intense political acts like giving money, joining demonstrations or boycotts, or volunteering. The better off people are, the more they have the time, resources, and inclination to get involved.[10] This pattern continues right up to the high end of wealth. The extensive political activity of the super-rich is easiest to see in their donations, which have mushroomed in tandem with rising inequality in recent decades. Between 1980 and 2012, the share of all electoral contributions coming from the 0.01 percent of donors—the 1 percent of the 1 percent, or the top ten-thousandth—increased from roughly 15 percent to over 40 percent.[11] Since the late 1990s, the conservative billionaire Koch brothers have given as much money by themselves as the entire Republican Party typically raised from all sources in earlier years.[12]

Strong patterns also suggest that when people do participate, economic conditions affect how they participate—especially in terms of voting. Study after study of voters in the United States and other democracies finds support for models built at least partly on the "**economic voter**": "Although voters do not look exclusively at economic issues, they generally weigh those more heavily than any others, regardless of the democracy they vote in."[13] Experts debate the specific mechanisms by which voters consider economic issues: do they mostly follow "**pocketbook**" voting (based on their own household's fortunes) or "**sociotropic**" voting (identifying with broader economic conditions for people like them, whatever their own ups and downs)? Do they tend to make "**retrospective**" economic evaluations—how well a president or party has managed the economy in the past—or vote on "**prospective**" expectations for how a candidate or party will handle future economic policy?[14] However we characterize these more specific relationships, the economy seems to have pervasive effects on political choices.

More broadly, this image of economics as a deep determinant of political participation is built into influential political theories and our modern political discourse. Both in the United States and elsewhere, we expect major patterns of political action to feature some version of "Left" versus "Right," and tend to assume that this divide centers on different economic positions—or classes—in society. Republicans and Democrats in the United States have always competed across many issues, but we expect that Democrats speak more for poorer citizens (the "lower" classes) and Republicans make more appeals to the better-off (or "upper" class). The same kind of expectation anchors both popular perception and classic political science about other democracies. Political contestation features a distinctive mix of concerns and cleavages in each country, but a consistent part of every democratic arena is some version of "class struggle" (as Marxists would call it) between rich and poor.[15]

economic voter
A theory of voting behavior that expects people to vote in ways that seek economic benefits.

pocketbook voting
Voting choices that focus on direct economic costs or benefits for the voter's household.

sociotropic voting
Voting choices that focus on costs or benefits for people with whom the voter identifies.

retrospective voting
Voting choices that focus on evaluating the past record of political candidates or parties.

prospective voting
Voting choices that focus on projecting the likely future actions and policies of political candidates or parties.

The same can be said for classic understandings of rebellion, revolution, and even (in somewhat different terms) terrorism. Substantial rebellions or revolutions usually draw some of their power and appeal from complaints about economic challenges or inequality. From age-old flare-ups of peasant rebellions to the French Revolution to the Arab Spring of 2010–2011 to the protests that brought down Sudanese dictator Omar al-Bashir in 2019, accusations of economic oppression or mismanagement are a common theme. The most famous theorists of revolution, like Theda Skocpol of Harvard University, ground their explanations in concrete economic resentments.[16] Terrorists often focus their complaints more on issues of political authority, not directly on economic terrain, but many experts also see terrorism as ultimately motivated by concrete complaints about getting the short end of the stick. In the background to many terrorist actions around the world today are objections to the Western countries' economic dominance. In the foreground, argue political scientists like the University of Chicago's Robert Pape, are concrete strategic calculations about how to strike effective blows against powerful adversaries.[17]

Still, the observation that concrete considerations like economic costs and benefits frequently influence people's choices in collective action does not mean that these considerations fully drive these choices. Far from it. Human beings are complex creatures, and their political choices are rarely simple. Poorer Americans may tend to vote for Democrats, but millions still vote for Republicans. Protestors against a dictatorship may point to oppression as their motivation, but many equally oppressed people may not rebel. Though the presence or absence of concrete complaints surely makes collective action more or less likely, such action also varies powerfully with political "framing." Whether and how people overcome "free-riding" and the obstacles to collective action depends on how they connect their identities to a political agenda.

Identity Politics of the Left: Race, Gender, and Sexual Identity

The importance of framing in political participation is especially easy to see on the American Left today. Many leading voices in and around the Democratic Party seek to mobilize people against economic inequality, casting themselves as champions of the poor. Others argue that an economic frame glosses over injustices affecting particular groups like African Americans, women, or transgendered people, advancing what has become known as **identity politics**. Collective action has always been shaped by identity frames, but rarely has their competition been so explicit.

Most progressive rhetoric in the United States long prioritized a liberal call to unite around political rights and economic opportunity for all. Even as Democrats incorporated themes of women's suffrage, feminism, civil rights for African Americans and other racial minorities, and gay rights

identity politics
Politics in which people emphasize membership in a group as the basis for political action, rather than policies, ideologies, or status that could be shared with other groups.

through the twentieth century, the dominant frame remained one of ironing out differences in treatment.

In the famous speeches of Reverend Dr. Martin Luther King, for example, a constant theme was the extension of the promises and rights in the Declaration of Independence and the U.S. Constitution to everyone, black or white.[18]

The same kind of universalistic discourse was stressed by Barack Obama during his two terms as President. As he put it in the Democratic Party convention speech in 2004 that made him a star, "There's not a black America and white America and Latino America and Asian America; there's the United States of America." Similar phrasing comes from leaders who most want to emphasize economic inequality, like Vermont Senator Bernie Sanders. In one not-so-subtle swipe at both identity politics and Hillary Clinton, his rival for the 2016 Democratic presidential nomination, Sanders said, "It's not good enough for someone to say, 'I'm a woman! Vote for me!' No, that's not good enough. What we need is a woman who has the guts to stand up to Wall Street...."[19]

But many passionate leaders, activists, and citizens today do want to take "I'm a woman" more seriously (as well as membership in other categories). They argue that an equal-treatment-for-all framing has downsides. Their simplest point is that more focused frames may be necessary to draw attention to the sharpest social problems. For example, in 2013, three young African American women launched a movement with the hashtag *#BlackLivesMatter*. They drew criticism for not choosing a more universalistic frame—some suggested "All Lives Matter"—but responded that the whole point was to raise awareness that Black lives are endangered at especially high rates.[20] More deeply, proponents of action around identity groups fear that the older language of equal treatment understates the challenges of discrimination. That language can seem to suggest that achieving straightforward legal equality will resolve these problems—and that the goal is to someday finally stop thinking about people's differences. For these advocates, many forms of discrimination are so deep that equal legal treatment only touches the tip of the iceberg. To achieve real equality, we must *celebrate* difference. Ongoing consciousness of differences in race, gender, or sexuality is necessary to counteract our implicit biases. In its strongest form, identity politics suggests that even these efforts may have limited success. People from one group may never really understand others' experiences. That just makes explicit celebration of difference all the more important.

Collective action on the Left today features running debates about these identity frames. On the one hand, recognition of distinct identities has energized members of many groups into political action. Black Lives Matter has emboldened a generation of African American activists to highlight their unique status as the only minority ever enslaved in American society. Many now argue for some form of **reparations**: money spent to benefit Black citizens

reparations
Actions or payment to make amends for past harm.

that could make amends for this past. Female solidarity has been galvanized by the explosion of another hashtag-led movement, *#MeToo*. By encouraging women to share stories of harassment and discrimination, it pushed gender-based action from its broader political focus on rights into direct accusations that have brought down many powerful men. Transgendered people and other diverse sexualities have received distinct recognition as the notion of "gay rights" has expanded to acknowledge LGBTQQIAAP (Lesbian, Gay, Bisexual, Transgendered, Queer, Questioning, Intersex, Asexual, Allies, and Pansexual).

On the other hand, distinct identity claims can compete and complicate collective action. One striking example is the feud between two leading African American figures, Ta-Nehisi Coates and Cornel West. Coates is a writer for *The Atlantic* and author of best-selling books about race in America, including one on the Obama presidency titled *We Were Eight Years in Power*. He concentrates on issues of race and has made a prominent case for reparations.[21] West is a Harvard philosophy professor who accuses Coates of white-washing economic inequality by focusing exclusively on race. He was scathing about *We Were Eight Years in Power*, asking, "Who's the 'we'? When's the last time he's been through the ghetto, in the hoods, to the schools and indecent housing and mass unemployment? We were in power for eight years? My God. Maybe he and some of his friends might have been in power, but not poor working people."[22] Parallel tensions bedevil the Women's March, which emerged to generate the largest one-day protest in American history the day after President Trump's inauguration. Black women complained that white women in the organization refused to acknowledge their own racial privileges as white people. Some white women responded by bowing out. "This is a women's march," said one white woman who stayed home. "We're supposed to be allies in equal pay, marriage, adoption. Why is it now about, 'White women don't understand black women'?"[23]

Some of the biggest questions in American politics concern which frames ultimately define who acts collectively with whom. They confront everyone at the individual level: do you connect most easily to politics in terms of your economic status? Race? Gender? Sexuality? Something else? They also pose major dilemmas of political strategy at the highest level of political parties and presidential candidates. And this is not just true of the Left, even if identity politics are best known on their side of the spectrum. Identity frames are powerful on the Right as well.

Identity Politics of the Right: Race, Social Conservatism, and the Urban/Rural Divide

Many political figures on the American Right delight at the Left's struggles with competing frames of identity politics. This has been especially true of leading figures in Donald Trump's circle of advisors, who often portrayed their victory in 2016 as based on economic appeals to middle-class Americans threatened by globalization and job-stealing immigrants. As Steve Bannon, Trump's Chief Strategist, said in 2017, "...the longer they talk about identity politics, I got 'em. I want them to talk about racism every day. If the Left is focused on race and identity, and we go with economic nationalism, we can crush the Democrats."[24]

The odd thing about Bannon's remark is that he does not represent a priority on economics over race. To the contrary, he and Trump made identity politics more central to Republican Party strategy than ever before. Trump's campaign certainly altered Republican economic priorities—shifting a historically free-trade, pro-globalization party to a protectionist "America First" stance—but placed even more emphasis on racialized anti-immigration appeals to white voters. After repeatedly characterizing Latin American immigrants as "rapists and murderers," Trump went on to make more obviously racist remarks than any other major figure in recent U.S. politics.[25] The strategy that Bannon helped define was not one that prioritized economic concerns as an alternative to Democrats' focus on identity. It connected the two, linking white voters' worries about their socioeconomic status to threats from people with other identities: Latino immigrants, Muslim terrorists, and a rising China. According to research by Ashley Jardina, a political science professor at Duke University, this identity emphasis best explains the key voter shifts that won Trump the Electoral College in 2016: "Trump drew in certain white voters who were especially concerned about protecting their racial group and its interests."[26]

Just as the Left wrestles with economic and identity frames, then, so does the Right. Historically economics came first in defining the Republican Party. It saw itself as the party of business. Under Abraham Lincoln it also became the party that fought the Civil War in the name of African American emancipation, though economic ties encouraged that connection: back then it was the party of northern-state industrialists, whose economic interests diverged from those of southern slave owners. In the mid-twentieth century, however, these links between economics and racial identity reversed. The Democratic Party that had historically dominated the South began to focus more on mobilizing workers and the poor, including African Americans. Republicans saw an opportunity to move into the South. Their "Southern strategy" allied pro-business policies with a socially conservative, religious Right agenda that appealed mainly to white voters.[27] It consolidated powerfully around the presidency of Ronald Reagan in the 1980s, by which time the parties had partly swapped their audiences. Democrats had become the party of big cities, especially on the East and West coasts. They targeted an urban coalition of educated social liberals, lower-class voters, and minorities. Republicans had become a coalition of business elites plus social conservatives in rural areas, especially white Southerners.

In principle, then, the American Right today confronts competing frames for collective action just as much as the Left. Do they foreground a pro-business frame? That has traditionally meant being pro-globalization and openness (including pro-immigration). Or do they lead with identity politics? That means pitches to mostly rural white voters whose identity contrasts to non-white immigrants, African Americans, and urban liberal cosmopolitans. Key mobilizing themes for this audience include gun ownership, religious values, and opposition to immigration. In practice, Trump's election and dominance of the Republican Party swung the Right squarely toward these latter themes. Still, debates over political frames will remain fundamental elements of collective action going forward. We can expect this sort of contestation on both Right and Left to continue.

In sum, when we look at individual choices or competing groups within the American national political arena, we see a complex mix of concrete considerations and less tangible political framing. Political participation is clearly responsive to economic conditions in particular, but framing debates also matter for how people mobilize collectively. Next we turn to national-level variations. When we compare participation across countries, we see that different political arenas have also developed their own distinctive patterns of collective action.

National Patterns in Individual Participation and Collective Action

6.3   Describe salient patterns of political participation in the United States, France, and China and summarize debates about how technology has affected American participation.

Political participation varies at all levels: across different individuals in the same household, across schools and towns, regions and ethnic groups, and so on. In a world where politics is framed first and foremost in states and nations, though, different patterns stand out especially strongly at the country level. For example, this chapter's opening hinted at differences between how (and how much) students protest in the United States and France. Though these countries' liberal democracies offer a similar menu of options for action to their citizens, their populations make quite different choices in voting, membership, activism, and protest. Such differences then grow if we shift to an authoritarian setting like China, where both the available menu and the typical pattern of choices take other shapes.

United States: Bowling Alone or Bowling . . . Differently?

"The political activity that pervades the United States," wrote Alexis de Tocqueville after his visit in the 1830s, "must be seen in order to be understood. No sooner do you set foot upon American ground than you are stunned by a kind of tumult."[28] Everywhere Tocqueville looked, he saw Americans forming clubs and associations, talking politics, and volunteering and running for offices at many levels.

About a century and a half later, observers increasingly made the opposite point about American political participation: the country was beginning to stand out for political apathy. Though participation of most sorts had been high in the years after World War II—led by the "Greatest Generation" of people who lived through the Great Depression and the war—it seemed to be dropping off rapidly. Turnout in American elections was consistently close to the lowest among all industrialized democracies. Participation in many kinds of social and political organizations seemed to be falling as well. This trend was documented most famously in a book published in 2000 by Harvard political scientist Robert Putnam, titled *Bowling Alone.* He pointed out that more Americans were going bowling than ever, but fewer did so in bowling leagues—and most membership in other clubs, religious organizations, and attendance at public meetings had dropped steeply after the 1960s. Putnam worried that America had drifted ever further from Tocqueville's vibrant image, losing what he called the **social capital** of a connected, participatory citizenry. Another book by Professor Mark Bauerlein at Emory University made similar points more provocatively. Under the title *The Dumbest Generation*, he cited studies that described young people as ever less knowledgeable, less trusting, less publicly minded, and more apathetic than their forebears.

social capital
A resource gained from making social connections to other people in society.

Putnam and Bauerlein share a view about the main cause for declining participation and collective action in the United States: technology. As of the 1950s, television gradually replaced many kinds of entertainment outside the home. Rather than going out to collective social events, people increasingly sat down separately in their living rooms. Even those interested in politics watched political speeches and events at home rather than going to them. This technological "individualizing," as Putnam calls it, took another big step with the Internet in the 1990s. Especially with social media, he suggests, a whole range of human relationships that once took place face-to-face began to migrate online. Most recently, smart phones took this "individualizing" trend outside the home, pulling people into the online world even when they are out in public. Completely new kinds of noninteraction became possible. In October 2013, for example, a disturbed man openly brandished a gun for several minutes on the San Francisco Bay Area's BART metro. Security cameras show that literally all the passengers were absorbed in their phones. They only looked up when the gunman shot and killed a college student.[29] Bauerlein spelled out his overall diagnosis of the problem behind such incidents in his subtitle for *The Dumbest Generation: How the Digital Age Stupefies Young Americans and Jeopardizes Our Future (Or, Don't Trust Anyone Under 30).*

On the other hand, other experts see a more mixed story based in data on American social capital and on the impact of technology, and perhaps even one that maintains Tocqueville's optimism. Putnam's critics argue that social capital has just moved into new forums: we may have fewer bowling leagues, Elks Clubs and Boy Scouts, but we see higher membership in places like broad advocacy groups, health clubs and soccer leagues, and support groups. Today, more than 30 percent of Americans belong to an advocacy group of some sort, which is three times the level in France, Britain, or Germany.[30] As we saw in Table 6-1, Americans sign petitions, participate in boycotts, and join demonstrations at respectable rates. Except in comparison to the extremely participatory peoples of Scandinavia, more Americans than Europeans say they have recently worked with others in their community and have been in contact with a political campaign or volunteered for one. The Internet, too, is not obviously a net loss for political participation. In many ways, technology makes engagement in politics easier. Email and social media are now the most common way to contact members of Congress. We have seen the emergence of political organizations that are primarily Internet-based, like *Moveon.org* (on the political Left) or *Townhall.com* (on the political Right). According to research by the well-respected Pew Research Center, political participation online mainly just parallels and extends political action offline. "It's not the case," says project director Lee Rainie, "that [Internet users] are withdrawing to the artificial worlds of virtual life at the expense of engagement with their neighbors."[31]

Many experts also contest the notions that young Americans today are notably apathetic or that technology is eroding their political connections. Although a somewhat smaller part of the overall population engages in political action or discussion online than offline (see the bottom line of Table 6-4), this is not true for young people. Their online political engagement rates greatly exceed their offline participation (see Table 6-5). Nor do their levels of offline political participation look that different from their elders'. Some surveys of the "millennial generation"—born between 1982 and 2003—even suggest that they are more inclined than earlier generations to be civic-minded, tolerant, and to have a "can-do" attitude. Rates of volunteerism by young people have risen in recent years. For the most optimistic observers, the millennials may be "the next great generation."[32]

Ross D. Franklin/AP Images

Student volunteers for "Promise Arizona," a group focused on empowerment of Latinos and immigrants, prepare to canvass a neighborhood in Phoenix before an election. Although many people worry about political participation in the age of the Internet, levels of youth volunteering in the United States are higher than ever.

Table 6-4 Comparing U.S. Political Participation Offline and Online

In the past 12 months, have you . . .

Offline Options	%	Online Options	%
Worked with fellow citizens to solve a problem in your community	35	"Liked" or promoted material related to political/social issues that others have posted	23
Attended a political meeting on local, town, or school affairs	22	Encouraged other people to vote	21
Been an active member of a group that tries to influence public policy or government, not including a political party	13	Posted your own thoughts/comments on political or social issues	20
Attended a political rally or speech	10	Reposted content related to political/social issues	19
Worked or volunteered for a political party or candidate	7	Encouraged other to take action on political/social issues that are important to you	19
Attended an organized protest	6	Posted links to political stories or articles for others to read	17
		Belonged to a group that is involved in political/social issues, or working to advance a cause	12
		Followed elected officials, candidates for office, or other public figures	12
Total (have done at least one of these)	**48%**	**Total (have done at least one of these)**	**39%**

SOURCE: Pew Research Center report, *Civil Engagement in the Digital Age*, April 25, 2013.

Table 6-5 U.S. Political Participation Offline and Online by Age Group

In the past 12 months, have you participated in any . . .

Age	Offline Civil Event, Activity, or Group (%)	Online Political Activity on Social Networking Site (%)
18–24	48	67
25–34	42	54
35–44	50	45
45–54	53	37
55–64	51	24
65+	42	13

SOURCE: Pew Research Center report, *Civil Engagement in the Digital Age*, April 25, 2013.

There is, however, one way in which Americans—young and old—clearly stand out for less political action than many other people. They do not get out in the street for demonstrations and protests as much as people in many European democracies (see Table 6-1). With partial exceptions in a few locations famous for radicalism—like Berkeley, California—Americans are less likely to engage in actions like occupying buildings, politically themed workplace strikes, or riot-ing. Even when protest movements develop in the United States they tend to attract fewer people than in France, Italy, or Germany. In 2011, for example, the U.S. press gave huge attention to the "Occupy Wall Street" protest, which drew as many as 5,000 people to march over several weeks in New York. An imitation protest was soon organized in Rome, Italy: it drew 300,000 people and left 70 injured in fighting with police. Events like the huge Women's March of 2017 or student-led protests against gun violence may hint at a growing American dis-position to get out in the streets, but in this category Americans still stand out for relative restraint.

Now we can see that our chapter-opening anecdote about American students quietly accepting tuition hikes fits with the overall pattern of political participation in the United States. Protest and voter turnout have long been modest in compar-ative perspective. In other forms of participation, though, there are at least some signs that Tocqueville's image of vibrant activism has survived and is adapting to changing technologies.

France: The Rebellious Republic

To Tocqueville's eyes, the kinds of vibrant associational life and political "tumult" he saw throughout the young United States were rare in his own country in the mid-nineteenth century. The French kings had created such a powerful central gov-ernment, he argued, that they had smothered the development of a separate sphere of civil society. Even after the French Revolution of 1789, when the monarchy was weakened and eventually abolished, Tocqueville feared that France continued to have an overly strong government that largely stifled individual expression and political participation. Along with a muffled civil society, he hinted, came bursts of radical revolution. Because people's concerns and grievances were less actively expressed in everyday life, they would sometimes erupt into the streets.

Like with the United States, there are signs that things have changed in France since Tocqueville. French government remains one of the more centralized liberal democracies, but associational life expanded very rapidly in the late twentieth century to reach levels close to those of the United States and northern European countries. Today, this country of 67 million has roughly 1.3 million NGOs, with close to two million employees and over 13 million volunteers.[33] Membership in politically engaged advocacy groups remains lower than U.S. levels, and rates of petition-signing or interaction with political parties and campaigns are slightly lower than in most European countries. Organizations and social movements re-lating to environmentalism, women's rights, and gay rights are also somewhat less developed than elsewhere, and union membership is very low—lower even than in the United States, where unions are weak—at about 9 percent of the workforce. Still, participation in the French arena of associations, political groups, and parties measures as fairly average for industrialized liberal democracies overall. And in electoral turnout, France has always done fairly well. In recent presidential elec-tions, close to 80 percent of the eligible population has voted. Turnout in legislative elections has recently fallen closer to American levels—even dipping under 40 percent in 2017—but for an obvious reason. In 2002, these elections were shifted to take place several weeks after presidential elections. Each French election has two rounds of voting separated by two weeks. Even some highly participatory citizens may not turn out for *four* votes in the space of two months.

On the other hand, Tocqueville's logic also still captures some distinctive patterns in French political action today. Its conventional political participation may be close to average for liberal democracies, but France still stands out for bursts of radical protest. As Table 6-1 shows, French people are more than twice as likely as Americans to have joined a demonstration. Even more striking to American visitors to France, though, would be ... strikes: work stoppages to pressure employers or governments to respect workers' demands. France is periodically gripped by intense combinations of union-led strikes, demonstrations and sometimes more radical actions. The 2010 student demonstrations against retirement reforms mentioned at the beginning of this chapter, for example, were just a small part of a wave of protest that disrupted train and airport services and blocked refineries and ports, leaving many gas stations empty of fuel. Just as notable as the intensity of these actions was the broad sympathy for them: though many people were inconvenienced by the disruption, at its height 70 percent of the population supported it.[34]

Even more striking was the "Yellow Vests" protests of 2018–2019. To the surprise of everyone, a new tax on diesel fuel in November 2018 provoked a spontaneous protest movement where mostly rural citizens poured into Paris every weekend for months. Some of the early marches turned violent, with burned cars, smashed store windows, and fights with police. Then it calmed down a bit, but displayed remarkable staying power. For more than six months, marches attracted over 20,000 people each weekend. Polls consistently showed support from about half of the public.

Political participation in France today still reflects the identity of a "revolutionary" nation with traditions of protest and revolt, fitting some of Tocqueville's observations almost 200 years later. Alongside modest everyday political activity we see flare-ups of major mobilization. A small but intense slice of society in unions and radical advocacy organizations protests frequently and aggressively, and much of wider society tends to support them when they do. Most French people expect regular protests, especially with radical students at the forefront, and feel that they send useful messages to French leaders.

China: Petitioning and Participation within Constraints

In many ways, political participation in the single-party dictatorship of the People's Republic of China looks like a different planet from American or French liberal democracies. Voting is only allowed in local elections. Even at that level, the ruling Communist Party routinely steps in arbitrarily to bar candidates it dislikes. Clubs and associations must receive government approval and are subject to monitoring, both explicit and secret. The same is true in virtual space:

the Chinese government attempts to limit Internet activities behind "the Great Firewall," sorting out what it sees as threatening content and constantly monitoring all electronic interaction. During the pro-democracy uprisings in Egypt in January 2011, for example, the government blocked searches with words like "Egypt" or "Cairo" to keep the uprising from inspiring anything similar from its citizens.[35] Today China's government runs far and away "the largest and most sophisticated online censorship operation in the world."[36]

Yet Chinese people do have some opportunities for political participation. Since the 1980s, when Communist leaders decided to allow the gradual emergence of a capitalist market economy alongside their political control, the government has increasingly allowed more space for individual action. This opening is clearest in business, where entrepreneurialism has exploded as China's economy has grown very rapidly in the past few decades. Business associations have proliferated to lobby the government for helpful regulations and other support. They resemble lobby groups in the United States or France at a basic level. In a context with little respect for the rule of law and practically no public accountability or transparency, however, business wealth often influences public decision making in blatantly corrupt ways.

Openings exist for the expression of normal citizens' concerns, too, even if they are constrained and subject to arbitrary government responses. With 1.4 billion people and a rapidly changing society, China's leaders realize that they need bottom-up help and input to manage the country. Homeowners Associations are allowed to run most of their own affairs and can play significant roles in the developments and housing blocs of China's huge, dense cities.[37] NGOs have been allowed to proliferate in areas like charity for the poor, public health, or environmentalism, though they must be careful in their activities. Town and county-level governments usually have public opinion forums on the Internet, and in recent years have increasingly solicited public input on certain issues. Starting in 2011 the national government raced to embrace Sina Weibo, a microblogging site that combines features of Twitter and Facebook. In 2012, Chinese President Xi Jinping happily embraced a Weibo group called "Fan Group to Learn from Xi," which the government claimed (rather implausibly) had been started by citizens. As of March 2013, government agencies and officials had opened more than 175,000 Sina Weibo accounts to communicate with the public.[38]

These forms of online participation connect to an ancient Chinese practice known as **petitioning** (*xinfang*) that survived through the Communist era. Thousands of Chinese citizens travel every year to provincial capital cities or the national capital, Beijing, to deliver petitions with complaints about problems like corruption, environmental damage, or unfair treatment. Since 2013 they can also use a vast online petitioning system. The government is not terribly responsive; many petitions go unanswered, and petitioners can be thrown in jail, leading one Chinese law professor to describe the *xinfang* system as "drinking poison to quench a thirst."[39] Still, the notion that government should receive such complaints, and might respond to some of them, is well established. The legitimacy of petitioning also creates some openings for public protest. The government has

petitioning
In China, an ancient practice in which citizens bring complaints or demands to the attention of central authorities.

Zhang Duo/Xinhua/Alamy Stock Photo

Chinese government officials pose after winning recognition as "the most beautiful staff members in dealing with petition letters and calls" in 2017.

not published any data about the frequency of protest since 2006, but one official source in 2010 suggested that there were over 150,000 "disturbances to public order" that year. According to experts who attempt to study this surveilled space, protests have probably become even more numerous since then.[40]

And what of rebellion, or at least dissidence, against this dictatorial regime? In response to a journalist's question about Liu Xiaobo, the jailed Chinese pro-democracy activist who won the Nobel Peace Prize in 2010, a government spokesman said, "There are no dissidents in China."[41] This was an absurd claim for a government that continues official prosecutions and jailing of thousands of people for political reasons. It is difficult to know their numbers, however, since many are cowed into silence by threats, torture, and disappearances. Dissidence still operates in the shadow of the massacre of pro-democracy demonstrators at Tiananmen Square in June 1989. That spring, student-led groups had met in Beijing's Tiananmen Square to mourn the death of a Communist Party official, Hu Yaobang, who had been supportive of more political freedoms. Seven weeks of growing demonstrations followed, sometimes involving over 100,000 students and including the erection of a Statue-of-Liberty-like "Goddess of Democracy" statue in the square. On June 4, 1989, though, a military crackdown killed somewhere between several hundred and a thousand people. No comparable mobilization has developed since, from students or otherwise, and under Xi Jingping's increasingly centralized leadership dissidents have been pursued relentlessly.[42] Still, an uncounted number of them continue to test the regime's limits.

When we set the American and French cases alongside the Chinese one, it seems clear that nothing matters more for political participation than the type of government. That is hardly surprising: liberal democratic governments are premised on popular input and guarantee rights within which people can express themselves and organize largely as they wish, opening up space for individual and collective action in ways that are formally or informally off-limits under other regimes. On the other hand, some mobilize in China despite the risks and costs of action, and the fact that U.S. or French citizens are *allowed* to mobilize does not mean that everyone (or even a majority of the population) actually *does*. To the contrary, in most liberal democracies we hear constant and well-justified anxiety about the failure of most citizens to participate energetically in politics. Furthermore, when people do act politically, they often choose different ways to express themselves or act collectively for reasons that seem a good deal more complex than just following from their broad kind of government. Their differences may reflect contrasting ideological views about how people should participate in politics, or a variety of conditions that might cause people to act out or not. We explore these views and conditions in the last two sections of the chapter.

Political Ideologies and Participation

6.4 **Evaluate competing ideological views of the role of individual and collective concerns in political participation.**

Almost everyone can agree in principle that participation is generally better than apathy. From all sorts of perspectives, a life well lived is one that touches other peoples' lives and tangles with important questions or problems in the human experience. Some such questions may be considered private and apolitical, like aspects of religious faith, but most connect in some way to political arenas of collective decision making. Beyond thinking that being a couch potato is not a good and meaningful life, though, people begin to disagree. The major ideological traditions take quite different views of why and how people should get off the couch and participate politically.

Participation in the Liberal Tradition: Pursuing "Our Own Good in Our Own Way"

In the classical liberal tradition of which today's conservatives and modern liberals are both descendants, the motivation for political participation can be summarized by an old Burger King advertising campaign: "Have It Your Own Way!" For classical liberals, individuals should be seen as autonomous persons who each have a particular mix of interests and concerns that well up inside them. From religion, to political causes, to how to dress a burger, each person should be free to follow their bliss as long as they do not hurt others in doing so. As the great liberal theorist J.S. Mill wrote in his book *On Liberty*, "The only freedom which deserves the name is that of pursuing our own good in our own way, so long as we do not attempt to deprive others of theirs, or impede their efforts to obtain it."[43] In this conception, self-interest—pursuit of whatever it is you personally want—is the normal basis for political action. Liberals expect people to do so in social ways, however, connecting with each other in all sorts of clubs, associations, and interest groups to create a flourishing civil society. All individuals also share interests in establishing or protecting liberties, so they should participate when necessary to create, support, and defend a liberal system of government.[44]

Conservatives and modern liberals today maintain this core philosophy, though people on both sides are usually slightly uneasy with a vision of participation based purely in self-serving individualism. Among conservatives, the social-conservative themes of Edmund Burke or religiously based traditionalism generally suggest that pursuing "our own good in our own way" should be tempered by concerns about social order, tradition, and faith. Individual liberty remains a central goal, but they worry about leaving individuals to form their own preferences and define their "own good" without guidance from tried-and-true traditions and religious wisdom. Many will make poor choices, they fear, leading to social chaos. Therefore, there should be some bounds on people's choices or at least collective support for certain choices and discouragement of others. A healthy society is one in which responsible people mobilize to build and preserve a certain kind of enriching civil society that reinforces traditional families, religious institutions, and other pillars of a stable lifestyle. Such people should also press government to set some hard limits on choices like abortion or drug use that undercut what they see as a stable atmosphere for healthy liberty.

Modern liberals tend to be closer to classical liberals on issues of social choices, arguing that people do not need traditional society or government to tell them how to construct healthy lifestyles. Indeed, they think it especially important to encourage those who prefer less traditional lifestyles to mobilize strongly in politics to overcome any social obstacles that government or traditional norms leave in their way. Their concerns with pure individualism, by contrast, lie in worries about unlimited economic liberties. Once some people accumulate wealth, their riches may allow them an unfair level of participation and influence in society and politics. Poor people, on the other hand, may find themselves unable to pursue their own good in their own way even if they have the legal freedom to do so. Poverty may prevent them from pursuing their interests and concerns, or doing anything more than to scramble for food and shelter every day. A healthy society is one in which all people have sufficient resources and support to participate and mobilize in pursuit of the widest possible range of lifestyles. Responsible people should press government to lessen economic inequalities and the restrictive social pressures of tradition.

If conservatives and modern liberals tend to accept the classical-liberal view that the deepest point of political participation is to allow autonomous individuals to "have it their own way," then, they add that individual participation should be partly bounded or channeled by other social considerations. Social order should be reinforced, or economic inequality combated, for the right kinds of individual participation to prevail. A good individual does not just participate by doing whatever he or she wants, but also strives to respect and support these collective goals.

Communitarians and More Critical Challenges

For political thinkers who draw more heavily on challenges to the liberal tradition, and for the devotees of ideologies outside its lines, we should not build our views of political participation on the individual having it his or her own way. In these views, people rarely get off the couch just out of selfish interest, nor should they. Motivations for political participation come more from our attachments to community, collective norms, and identity than from separate individual concerns.

A moderate and influential version of this "communitarian" view overlaps with both modern liberalism and conservatism, giving a more direct voice to their uneasiness with pure individualism. For political theorists like Michael Sandel, classical liberalism is wrong to see politics simply as an arena in which autonomous individuals pursue self-interest.[45] Our political inclinations derive from our communities to begin with, says Sandel: we are born into certain families, nations, and cultures that give us certain interests and duties. This means that the idea of "unencumbered" individuals with their own autonomous views is an undesirable fiction. We do not and should not participate through a shapeless, morality-free freedom to do whatever suits us. Instead we should focus on developing and strengthening our communities, norms, and identities. Although Sandel stands on the left wing of modern liberalism, similar views also resonate strongly on the traditional Right. William Bennett, for example, a conservative American politician, author, and spokesman for traditional values, is often described as a communitarian. Where Sandel and other Left communitarians think we must downplay individualism and upgrade community solidarity to fight inequality and other social ills, Bennett and other Right communitarians think we must do so to reinforce traditional values, religion, and social order.[46]

Both Sandel and Bennett fuse communitarianism with support for modern inheritors of liberalism, but ideological positions outside the liberal tradition assert communitarian views more forcefully. A strong version of environmentalism, for example, builds on deeply communitarian notions. From this point of view, people's lives are so intertwined with the natural environment that individuals' welfare cannot be understood as separate from each other or from the surrounding natural systems. If you consume or pollute too much, that affects me and everyone else; if we all fail to attend to the Earth, environmental problems will eventually swamp any other individual concerns. Thus our political participation must be defined and orchestrated collectively. We must pursue collective goods in pro-environmental ways, not our own good in our own ways.

A strong version of socialism has similar communitarian foundations. For devout socialists, people's lives are so intertwined in economies that political participation must be motivated and shaped by community-level thinking. People are deeply "encumbered," to use Sandel's term, by their place in the economy; as Marx suggested, my attempts to become rich profoundly affect your attempts to become rich. The same goes for our political participation: the notion that we can just be free to pursue "our own good in our own way" ignores the powerful ways in which your actions may alter my opportunities, intentionally or unintentionally. For convinced socialists, then, meaningful political participation must target the whole system of economy and government. Therefore, a just society can be achieved only by collectively refashioning the system to deliver enough resources and opportunities for all.

Islamism, too, sees the community defining the individual and his or her political motivations and concerns. Upholding a political system defined around the religious rules of *shari'a* is a collective project in which all believers must participate. Indeed, it is the duty of a devout Muslim to push back against laws, leaders, or governments that contradict *shari'a*.

Fascism, finally, is the most communitarian ideology. Though it may seem surprising, it is also centered on intense political participation. Indeed, for fascists, individuals only have meaning and value to the extent that they participate in the politics of the nation. People should be not only encouraged but forced, if necessary, to celebrate and contribute to national strength and glory. In Hitler's system, people were compelled to constantly rehearse their political loyalty, from children in Youth Leagues to obligatory Nazi unions at the workplace, constant parades, and vast political rallies. Such a view of participation, with the community fully dictating the worth and actions of the individual, is the opposite of a liberal civil society in which you "Have It Your Own Way!"

Fascists, radical Islamists, and hard-core socialists attract few sympathizers in the United States today, of course, or in other societies that commit strongly to liberal rights. The notion that strong individual autonomy is the desirable basis for political thinking and action is powerfully anchored in such systems. Even within the more mainstream politics of liberal democracies, however, it is far from clear that everyone feels comfortable with a pure liberal conception of politics as the pursuit of individual happiness. Within a system of liberal freedoms, many people clearly derive much of the meaning in their lives from national identity, ethnic connections, religious communities and other collective causes that they would willingly rank as more important than their own individual comfort and happiness. In many ways, the same American political culture that prioritizes individual autonomy also celebrates shared beliefs, charity, volunteerism, and selfless commitment to doing the right thing. Just what kind of political participation we should hold up as the ideal model is very much an open question.

Explaining a Case: Understanding the Whys of Low Voter Turnout in the United States

6.5 **Identify multiple plausible explanations for the comparatively low turnout in American elections.**

We have seen that voter turnout is a weak point of American political participation. Since World War II, the highest level of turnout in an American presidential election (63 percent of eligible voters in 1960) is about 5 points lower than the *lowest* level of turnout in a French presidential election (67.9 percent in 1969). In legislative elections since 1945, France has averaged an eligible-voter turnout of 62.4 percent, or 15 percent higher than the U.S. average of 47.4 percent.[47] Why would the country where Tocqueville saw an unparalleled "tumult" of democratic spirit have so many citizens who ignore their main process of representation?

The Rational-Material Story

A fairly straightforward feature of the material landscape underlying American politics may tell much of the story of low turnout. The U.S. economy has relatively high levels of inequality, with a larger percentage of poor people than any other industrialized democracy, and the likelihood of voting in the United States is highly correlated with wealth. Poorer people may not be able to afford time off from work or may have difficulty getting to polling places. This is perfectly rational: for poorer people the relative costs of taking time out to vote seem especially high, so they are more likely to abstain.

The Institutional Story

An institutional approach suggests a different but equally plausible story about low turnout. In many democracies, all eligible citizens are automatically enrolled to vote and sent materials at election time. In some, nonvoters are fined. Americans, by contrast, must make the effort to register themselves. The multilevel American political system also asks voters to make more distinct electoral choices than in any other country—for presidents, senators, representatives, governors, state legislators, local officials, and so on—which contributes to voter fatigue. And while some democracies hold elections on weekends, most U.S. citizens' votes are on Tuesdays, when work and school make voting more difficult. In all these ways, U.S. institutional rules are not set up to encourage high turnout.

The Ideational Story

Ideational thinking suggests still other reasons why many Americans do not vote. Broad antigovernment political sentiment is better developed in the United States than it is in other democracies, encouraging many citizens to see government as inherently bad. This distrust of government and emphasis on individualism in American political culture undercuts civic participation. Relatively high diversity of racial and ethnic identities may also lower turnout, as some citizens may feel less connected to candidates from other social groups. Even if inequality or institutional rules did not get impede many Americans' choices to vote, we still would expect more Americans to choose not to participate.

All these conditions probably contribute to low turnout in the United States, but it seems likely that some might be more powerful than others. If money were set aside to pay poor Americans to vote, would U.S. rates converge on other nations' turnout? If we changed the institutional rules to make voting easier, might we see considerably more voting even in highly unequal communities? Could we design surveys that would show that nonvoting is associated with strong antigovernment views? If we want to engage more citizens in American democracy, our sense of the most promising paths depends on which of these alternatives carries the most explanatory force. Just as we do for other subjects, we can seek evidence for these alternative explanations in within-case processes and cross-case patterns.

RESEARCH ON WITHIN-CASE PROCESSES. Voter turnout is inherently about a pattern across many people, but still we might learn something about it by tracing the processes behind particular cases of voting or nonvoting. We might choose a few towns during an election and selectively interview people who voted or not to see what motivated their decisions. To capture other dynamics in the population, we might identify various types of citizens—by location, income, race, gender, age, and so on—and interview people in each category to see if they approached the choice to vote differently. Table 6-6 lays out the process expectations of our theoretical explanations in more detail.

To begin to gather evidence for or against these views, find a news article that addresses voter turnout somewhere in the United States—including not just overall patterns, but a story on some individual's or group's choice to vote or

Table 6-6 Exploring Within-Case Evidence for Explanations of U.S. Voter Turnout

	Rational-Material Explanation	Institutional Explanation	Ideational Explanation
Who votes most?	Richer people, who have the time and resources to vote and the education to formulate their views	People who are mobilized by organized groups (registration drives, churches that bus people to the polls, parties who knock on doors, etc.)	People who see U.S. government in broadly positive terms
Who votes least?	Poor people, who find the time and effort of voting more costly and who are less informed	People who face institutional obstacles, like inflexible jobs on election days, or who are not mobilized by political organizations	Those with the strongest antigovernment views and/or minorities in strongly ethnically divided communities
Where and when is turnout likely to rise?	As more people get wealthier in a community	When voting is made easier (like "voting by mail" in some U.S. states) or when political organizations mobilize more widely or aggressively	When overall trust in government rises
Best evidence to support each explanation	We find that most people talk about choice to vote in terms of individual costs in time and effort.	We find otherwise-similar people who vote or do not depending on membership or connection to organizations.	We find that most people talk about choice to vote in terms of duty, connection to U.S. government.

not—from a respectable newspaper, magazine, or website. Then look for hints in the article that support or contradict these explanatory alternatives.

RESEARCH ON CROSS-CASE PATTERNS.   Our other main source of empirical leverage on this question is to see where the United States fits in cross-case patterns of voter turnout. Does voter turnout across countries correlate to inequality? Does it instead vary generally with registration rules, the number of elections held each year, or the timing of elections? Does it seem to reflect broader cultural or ideological attitudes about government? Your instructor may be able to help you find data to explore some of these possible cross-case correlations.

Conclusion: Why Understanding Political Participation Matters to You

Whether we dream of changing the world or just securing a comfortable niche within it, we need to know our options for participating in collective decision-making processes. For many people around the world, including a distressingly large number of disengaged American citizens, unfamiliarity with these options is the most immediate reason for feeling disconnected and resentful about politics. They simply cannot quite imagine how to take political action, or how to consider the costs and benefits of actions they dimly perceive. Given a political menu and tools to help read it—such as a sense of collective-action problems, ideological views of participation, and explanatory alternatives— these first obstacles to political participation fall away.

Will that awareness alone turn quiet students into French-style protestors, send new waves of young people off to the halls of Congress, or embolden more people to stand up to tanks in the name of a beautiful cause? Certainly not. Intense political action takes further commitment and usually some self-sacrifice. But awareness lets us consider consciously and critically whether we want to make such commitments and sacrifices, and that is no small thing.

Review of Learning Objectives

6.1   Identify forms of political participation from low-intensity individual expression to high-intensity actions and how they relate to the challenges of getting people to act together.

Individuals express their political views in many ways, from bumper stickers to bar fights. Most participation, however, is collective action, when one person's choice to act depends on what others do. Even voting is a collective action, since voting only makes sense if others vote too. Mobilized citizens in liberal democracies may also sign petitions; march in demonstrations; volunteer for causes; and join boycotts, organizations, or political parties. Some become activists, volunteering to help support or lead collective action. The most intensely engaged citizens become professionals, with paid careers as lobbyists or politicians. When a government loses legitimacy, citizens may make even more intense choices to rebel or launch a revolution in pursuit of a different system. Considering collective-action problems helps display the logic of such choices. For example, the more intensely I act in politics, the more I bear individual costs for benefits that others will share. The logic of collective-action problems both illuminates the rationality of some political action and suggests that people often act collectively despite such trade-offs.

6.2   Explain the difference between economic and identity-based frames in collective action, and give examples of both from American politics on both Left and Right.

Classic political wisdom holds that people's decisions to participate in politics vary above all with concrete costs and benefits for their lives, especially with economic conditions. There are good reasons to emphasize economic positioning as an important foundation for collective action. Political debates between groups representing poorer and richer citizens contribute to "Left-Right" contestation all democratic systems; better-off citizens tend to engage in most political activities more frequently than poorer ones; and support for current leaders typically tracks ups and downs in the economy. At the same time, people can frame their political identities in multiple ways to foreground class, race, gender, or other priorities. "Identity politics" have become prominent both on the American Left (like in Black Lives Matter or the #MeToo movement) and the American Right (like with religious Christians or various pitches to white rural voters).

6.3   Describe salient patterns of political participation in the United States, France, and China and summarize debates about how technology has affected American participation.

National patterns in political participation can be very different, even within broadly similar liberal democracies like the United States and France. The United States stands out for low electoral turnout and little propensity to conflictual strategies like protests and strikes, but on most other measures of participation—volunteerism, connections to parties, and petitioning—its people are comparatively involved. France has stronger electoral turnout and average levels of conventional political participation. It stands out mainly for the intense involvement of a small segment of the population in strikes and protest, and for the sympathy they receive from other citizens. Participation under China's dictatorship is much more severely constrained. Nonetheless it draws on ancient practices of "petitioning," and has proliferated as the Chinese economy has opened up.

6.4   Evaluate competing ideological views of the role of individual and collective concerns in political participation.

From the classical liberal point of view, people are autonomous individuals who participate in politics (or do not) in whatever ways their individual interests suggest. Classic liberals' descendants in modern liberalism and conservatism maintain this emphasis on individualism, but often add that community-level considerations should set boundaries on certain kinds of participation or guide it in certain ways. In "communitarian" views on the left, individual participation should acknowledge concerns for economic and ethnic solidarity. Parallel views on the right incorporate concerns about traditional norms, order, and religious faith. Ideologies outside the liberal tradition take stronger communitarian stances, setting individualism below goals like environmentalists' collective respect for nature, socialists' emphasis on economic solidarity, or Islamists' duty to religious community. Fascists are the greatest advocates of political participation in their own way: they call for individuals to give themselves utterly to the state.

6.5 Identify multiple plausible explanations for the comparatively low turnout in American elections.

To review for this objective, try to brainstorm rational-material, institutional, and ideational explanations of U.S. turnout without looking at Section 6.4. Start by asking yourself the following questions:

- If we see a person's decision to vote or not as based mainly on his or her material resources and the costs of taking the time to vote, how might material conditions in the United States impede voting for some parts of the population?
- If, instead, we see a person's decision to vote or not as shaped more by institutions and rules, how might the timing, frequency, or process of U.S. elections discourage turnout?
- If, alternatively, we see a person's decision to vote or not as defined mostly by their beliefs or cultural norms, what elements of American political culture might possibly steer some people away from voting?

After brainstorming your answers to these questions, return to Section 6.4 to see if you captured the main logic of these explanatory alternatives.

Great Sources to Find Out More

Alexis de Tocqueville, *Democracy in America* (New York: Vintage Press, 1945 [1838]). Still commonly ranked as one of the greatest books on politics ever written—and still as engaging and readable as ever.

Andrew Gelman, *Red State, Blue State, Rich State, Poor State: Why Americans Vote the Way They Do* (Princeton, NJ: Princeton University Press, 2009). Still a fascinating dissection of data on American voting.

Ben Berger, *Attention Deficit Democracy: The Paradox of Civic Engagement* (Princeton, NJ: Princeton University Press, 2011). A thoughtful application of political theory to civic-engagement debates today, as well as an argument that not all engagement is good engagement.

David Vance, *Hillbilly Elegy: A Memoir of a Family and Culture in Crisis* (New York: Harper, 2016). A memoir of growing up poor in Appalachian Ohio that is often read as an explanation of votes for Donald Trump.

Donald Green, Bradly Palmquist, and Eric Schickler, *Partisan Hearts and Minds: Political Parties and the Social Identities of Voters* (New Haven, CT: Yale University Press, 2004). A powerful demonstration that voters' choices are guided by political parties as much as the reverse.

John Zaller, *The Nature and Origins of Mass Opinion* (New York: Cambridge University Press, 1992). This famous book argues that most people hold many incoherent views, but that events and flows of information lead particular views to dominate at any given moment.

Mark Lilla, *The Once and Future Liberal: After Identity Politics* (New York: Harper, 2017). A provocative criticism of identity politics from a political theorist who sees himself as a committed liberal.

Mancur Olson, *The Logic of Collective Action: Public Goods and the Theory of Groups* (Cambridge, MA: Harvard University Press, 1965). The original statement of collective-action problems.

Michael Sandel, *Liberalism and the Limits of Justice* (New York: Cambridge University Press, 1998). A critique of liberal individualism that calls for more attention to the community.

Robert Nozick, *Anarchy, State and Utopia* (New York: Basic Books, 1974). One of the clearest and most provocative libertarian book on political thought and action.

Robert Putnam, *Bowling Alone: The Collapse and Revival of American Community* (New York: Simon & Schuster, 2000). A famous portrayal of declining civic associations in the United States and suggestions for their renewal.

Sidney Tarrow, *Power in Movement: Social Movements and Contentious Politics*, 3rd ed. (New York: Cambridge University Press, 2011). This book from one of the leading scholars of social movements explains why people do and do not pursue collective action in certain ways.

Xi Chen, *Social Protest and Contentious Authoritarianism in China* (Cambridge, MA: Harvard University Press, 2014). An exploration of the rise of social protest in China.

Develop Your Thinking

Use these questions as discussion or short writing exercises to think more deeply about some of the key themes of the chapter.

1. If you have voted (or plan to), what motivates you? If you haven't (or won't), why not?

2. Are people your age more or less involved in politics than earlier generations—or involved differently?

3. Which is better: a society in which each person focuses on his or her own self-interest, or one in which people think of themselves as members of groups or communities?

4. What do you suspect is the most important reason why relatively few Americans vote?

5. Should democratic governments incentivize or even require voting or volunteering?

Keywords

apathy 166
civil disobedience 166
collective-action problem 168
cycles of protest 172
dissident 171
Downs paradox 169
economic voter 178
employers' organizations 173

free rider problem 170
identity politics 179
noncombatants 176
Nongovernmental Organization 171
petitioning 189
pocketbook voting 178
prospective voting 178

reparations 180
retrospective voting 178
selective incentives 170
social capital 184
social movements 172
sociotropic voting 178
turnout 169
unions 173

Chapter 7
Inside Liberal Democracy I: Representation

A young woman in Iowa indicates her support for Democratic presidential candidate Bernie Sanders. Does good representation mean that voters choose representatives for their policies, political skills and electability? Should it also—or alternatively—mean that voters get representatives who look like them and share their experiences?

Learning Objectives

7.1 Explain and contrast the logic of majoritarian, proportional, and descriptive representation.

7.2 Identify the most common systems of voting rules and how they relate to different principles of representation.

7.3 Describe the roles parties play in representation and explain variation in their number and strength across countries.

7.4 Describe the core features of presidential government and evaluate its advantages and disadvantages.

7.5 Describe the core features of parliamentary government and evaluate its advantages and disadvantages.

7.6 Evaluate contrasting institutions of representation from conservative and modern-liberal points of view.

7.7 Identify multiple plausible explanations for Iraqi Sunnis' preference for proportional representation.

Does Democratic Representation Mean Majority Choice or Something Else?

Representation stands at the core of liberal democracy: within a framework of liberal rights, the people choose representatives to govern. For Americans, choice by "the people" is usually understood to mean that in any election—for a mayor, a senator, a president—the candidate with the most votes wins. Representing a population means letting its majority choose the leaders.

Or does it? Some might argue that representation is not just about majority choice. Would the 12 percent minority of U.S. citizens who are African Americans feel represented, for example, if majority choices produced no African American political leaders at all? Similar questions are hugely important in countries with major internal divisions, such as Iraq. As Iraqis attempted to create a liberal democracy in the early 2000s, the toughest skeptics came from their minority of Sunni Muslims. From their point of view, if the majority of Shi'ite Muslims comes to dominate Iraqi democracy, Sunnis will not be meaningfully represented. These questions apply not just to racial or religious minorities but also to political views. For example, Democratic voters have little impact in Republican-dominated Oklahoma. Republicans are marginalized in Democrat-heavy Vermont. If such voters can hardly affect the choice of "their" representatives, how can we say that they are "represented"?

To think critically about how you are represented—or not—you must come to see alternative ways to understand representation and how these principles work in practice. How might elections work besides choosing the candidate with the most votes? Is it good for representation to have just two political parties competing for votes, like our Republicans and Democrats, or would more parties be better? Are Americans represented well by a president, or are citizens' views better transmitted through the differently elected office of a prime minister? Grasp the different arrangements of representation in voting rules, political parties, and elected offices, and you can reclaim your own critical voice in liberal democracy. ■

Alternative Principles of Representation

7.1 **Explain and contrast the logic of majoritarian, proportional, and descriptive representation.**

Modern liberal-democratic governments are representative democracies, not Greek-style direct democracies. Rather than making policy decisions directly, the large mass of citizens votes in elections for a smaller number of representatives who make decisions about public policy. The legitimacy of this process, then, depends on the quality of representation. If many citizens are not well represented, liberal democracy is not clearly much better than other kinds of government.

Just what it means for selected people to "represent" the population, though, is not obvious. Three contrasting principles of representation are especially notable in our world today:

- **Majoritarian representation** is the most familiar idea to Americans: representatives are chosen simply by receiving the most votes in a competition. Strictly speaking, this principle does not demand a majority, which means *more than half* of the votes overall, but just a **plurality**, which means *the most* votes. Under what we typically call "majoritarian" rules, someone who receives 43 percent of votes is a legitimate representative as long as no competitor receives more.

- **Proportional representation** suggests that any group includes diverse views that cannot be transmitted through a single winner, so multiple representatives should represent these different views in proportion to their weight in the population. If 30 percent of the population supports a certain political platform, representatives who champion that platform should receive roughly 30 percent of positions in government.

- **Descriptive representation** suggests that citizens should be represented by people who are like them, not just by representatives they like. If half the population is female, an all-male set of representatives is inappropriate even if many women support male candidates. A racially or ethnically diverse population calls for similarly diverse representatives. This amounts to a special kind of proportionality, with representatives who mirror citizens as types of people, not just as advocates of their political views.

These are all powerful ideas. It is hard to argue that representation should reject the most widely supported views, that it should ignore diversity in the population, or that people should be content with representatives who are not like them. Better than taking majoritarianism for granted, then, would be a careful balance of these principles—right?

majoritarian representation
The principle that a group's representatives should be those who receive the broadest support among the group.

plurality
The largest number of votes cast, whether or not it is a majority.

proportional representation
The principle that a group's representatives should proportionally speak for diverse views within the group.

descriptive representation
The principle that a group's representatives should proportionally reflect racial, ethnic, gender, and other kinds of diversity within the group.

But again we must say: not so fast. Democracies can and do mix majoritarianism, proportionalism, and descriptive representation to some degree, but these principles cannot be fully combined because they point to different practices on the ground. Debates about representation are thus more often about which principle to prioritize than about the ideal mix. Like in much of politics, we confront trade-offs: building institutions around the advantages of one principle means living with its disadvantages as well.

Not only do contrasting principles and trade-offs complicate the pursuit of meaningful representation, but representative institutions also always have several moving parts. Indeed, the rules that shape representation are as complex as those for sports like baseball—and anyone who has tried to explain baseball to the uninitiated knows how complex it is! Fortunately, the main rules and conditions organizing the "game" of representation come in three fairly discrete segments that we can discover step-by-step. *Voting rules* define how citizens join in the game, determining how they vote to select representatives. The configuration of *political parties* organizes the "teams" of representatives that compete for citizens' support and coordinate the game among representatives once they are elected. The shape of *elected offices*, like whether citizens elect a president or a prime minister, defines the "leagues" within which the teams compete (shaping who exactly competes for what) as well as the winnings (the powers that winners receive as selected representatives). To understand how representation works in our world, we must see how each aspect of the game can take different shapes that prioritize certain principles of representation.

Voting Rules: How Citizens Choose

7.2 Identify the most common systems of voting rules and how they relate to different principles of representation.

For most people, voting rules are the part of the game of representation that they encounter most directly. Such rules define the experience of choosing representatives: what a voting ballot looks like and how the choices of many voters are aggregated into an overall selection of political leaders. Despite this direct impact in the experiences of average citizens, though, the powerful way in which these rules shape representation usually draws little notice. In the same way that Americans can watch baseball without thinking much about its rules, and soccer may seem natural to Germans or Argentinians, so voters typically go to the polls without realizing that they are choosing their representatives under very particular, nonobvious rules.

Once we set alternative voting rules alongside each other, it becomes clear that they represent citizens' views in profoundly different ways and that they connect to contrasting principles of representation. The two most common kinds of rules—which directly apply majoritarian and proportional principles—are known as "single-member plurality" (SMP) and proportional representation (PR) systems. Several other variations modify or combine these two main systems, but let's first examine the SMP and PR options.

The Majoritarian Option: "SMP"

The fancy phrase **single-member plurality (SMP)** is the official term for the simple voting rules used in the United States, Britain, Canada, India, and more than forty other countries. A single seat is designated to represent a district of voters, like the inhabitants of a town in a mayor's election or the inhabitants of a state for a U.S. senator. Individual candidates compete to be named the single representative of the district. The candidate with the most votes wins. SMP is sometimes known as "first past the post," since it is much like a footrace. In this race, though, there is no silver medal for second place. One candidate wins and the others simply lose. For this reason, it is also often called a "winner take all" system.

> **single-member plurality (SMP)**
> Majoritarian voting rules in which individual candidates compete to win the most votes for a single seat representing a district.

Such rules apply most simply to elections for a single representative, like the governor of a U.S. state. These are "winner take all" contests by definition: there is one seat to win, and only one person can sit in it. The implications of SMP rules become more important, though, when voters are choosing many representatives at the same time, as we typically do in voting for an assembly. In American elections that take place every two years for the 435 members of the House of Representatives, for example, the results are massively shaped by the format of SMP contests in 435 districts. The main effect is straightforward: "first past the post" rules systematically benefit the most common views in society and hinder less common positions. The biggest political movement wins big. Others lose out.

Why? These effects are easiest to grasp in an imaginary scenario. Suppose Republicans and Democrats were close to an even split everywhere in the United States, each drawing support from 50 percent of each House district's population. Now imagine that a scandal hit Democratic leaders, and opinions in every district across the country tipped to 51 percent for Republicans. If elections were held the next day, the Republican candidate would win in every district with 51 percent of votes. Republicans would win *all* of the seats and hold 100 percent of the House of Representatives. The rest of the nation—the 49 percent of citizens who did not vote for Republicans—would not have the representatives they preferred.

Of course, nothing so extreme ever comes to pass. Party support often clusters geographically, so all U.S. districts are never evenly split. Democrats still win in Vermont even when Republicans are popular overall, and Republicans win in Oklahoma during a Democratic wave. Still, the real world can come surprisingly close to our example: in the 2001 SMP elections to the assembly of the Canadian province of British Columbia, the Liberal Party won 58 percent of the vote and

Figure 7-1 Votes and Seats under Britain's SMP Rules since 1945

The big Conservative and Labour parties are overrepresented, with seat shares (dotted lines) usually above their voting shares (solid lines). The smaller Liberal Democrats are under-represented.

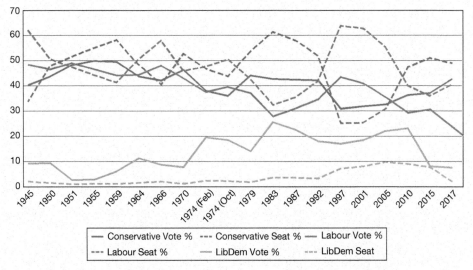

Source: Political Science Resources website, http://www.politicsresources.net/area/uk/uktable.htm.

overrepresentation
A situation when a group receives more offices than its population share suggests, sometimes called disproportionality.

97 percent of the seats! In general, a "first past the post" system magnifies the gains of front-runners and penalizes everyone else. It rewards the loudest voices with **overrepresentation**, favoring the biggest parties and political movements over smaller ones.

Consider elections to Britain's House of Commons from 1945 to 2017 in Figure 7-1. Britain uses SMP rules like the United States. Much like in the United States, power has long swung back and forth between two dominant parties: the Conservative Party on the right and the Labour Party on the left. But unlike in the United States, British voters also have usually had a third significant option, the Liberal Democratic Party, which, ideologically, falls between the big two. Figure 7-1 shows two striking effects of SMP rules. First, note the Conservative and Labour vote percentages relative to the seats they win (the distance between the blue solid and dotted lies and between the red solid and dotted lines). Both swing back and forth over time, but in years where one party has a modest lead in votes they win a landslide in seats, like the Conservatives in 1983 or Labour in 1997. Second, consider the plight of the poor "Lib Dems." As a small party, their yellow dotted line (seats) is far below their solid line (votes). They come in second in many districts but first in very few.

Are such rules fairly representative? Supporters of the Liberal Democrats think not, and tried to change British voting rules in 2010. They ran into opposition from Conservative and Labour supporters, however, most of whom thought majoritarian principles were just fine. Leaders and many voters of the two big parties, like committed supporters of Democrats and Republicans in the United States, tend to see virtue in the way SMP rules can manufacture a clear governing majority out of a mere plurality of voters. Such swings, they say, make government more accountable and allow for strong shifts when voter sentiment changes. As British Conservative leader David Cameron said in opposing the Liberal Democrats' call for new rules, "You want to know the best thing about First Past the Post? It is often decisive—and sometimes ruthlessly so."[1]

The Proportional Option: "PR"

SMP rules may seem as natural as baseball to Americans, but just as soccer is far more popular around the world, so **proportional representation (PR) voting rules** are more common than SMP. Operating in roughly 70 countries, they too have a simple mechanism: a party receives the same percentage of seats that it gets in votes. If a country with PR rules had an assembly like the House of Representatives—but with 100 seats, for example—a party that got 41 percent of the vote would get 41 seats. A party that got 6 percent of the vote would get six seats, and so on. As its name says, PR makes representation proportional to the vote.

proportional representation (PR) voting rules
Voting rules in which parties are assigned the same share of offices that they win in votes.

Behind this simple principle, though, lie some complexities. Since PR allots seats by percentage of votes for a *party*, not an individual candidate, voters do not vote for individual politicians. For example, on a ballot in Israel's PR system, voters put a mark next to names not of people but of parties like Likud, the Labor Party, or Yesh Atid (see Table 7-1). Prior to the election, each party creates a *party list* of individuals in rank order, usually with the main leaders and most popular figures in the top positions. If the party gets twenty seats, the top twenty people on the list fill them; the more seats it wins, the more names from the list are elected. In the 2019 elections, the Likud list received 26.46 percent of votes, which as a proportion of 120 seats in the main Israeli assembly (the Knesset) translated into about 32 seats. (We see below why it actually received 35.)

Which is better, baseball or soccer? They have different strengths and weaknesses, as does proportional representation relative to single-member plurality. PR is unambiguously superior in matching voters to representatives. In SMP, votes for second-place and other finishers are "lost votes" with no effect, whereas under PR these voters get representatives too. For this reason, it has special appeal for minorities. In the design of voting rules in Iraq, for example, it was clear that Sunnis and other minorities opposed anything other than a PR-based system. Some among the Shi'a majority would have liked SMP rules, but they agreed to PR rules so that minorities would not reject the new government.

PR's more faithful representation of diversity is not, however, without downsides. While SMP simplifies disagreements within the population by crowning one winning position, PR passes on the diversity of opinions to representatives. If people have many different opinions—and they often do!—PR

Table 7-1 Party-List Voting under Israel's PR Voting Rules

In the 2019 elections within Israel's PR system, parties got close to the same share of seats and votes.

Party Name	Total Votes	Vote Share	Seats	Seat Share
Likud	1,140,370	26.46%	35	29.16%
Blue & White	1,125,881	26.13%	35	29.16%
Shas	258,275	5.99%	8	6.66%
United Torah Judaism	249,049	5.78%	8	6.66%
Hadash-Ta'al	193,442	4.49%	6	5%
Labor	190,870	4.43%	6	5%
Yisrael Beiteinu	173,004	4.01%	5	4.16%
United Right	159,468	3.70%	5	4.16%
Meretz	156,473	3.63%	4	3.33%
Kulanu	152,756	3.54%	4	3.33%
United Arab List	143,666	3.34%	4	3.33%
New Right	138,598	3.22%	0	0%
29 other smaller lists	227,418	5.24%	—	—

SOURCE: Central Election Committee of the Knesset.

can fragment assemblies chaotically into many small parties. Israel's Knesset is currently a bewildering landscape of over a dozen parties (since some of the lists in Table 7-1 are actually alliances of smaller parties). Likewise, Iraq's Council of Representatives includes more than ten parties.

Besides favoring diverse voices, PR carries with it another profound difference in representation from SMP rules that influences politics at the national level. SMP voters select a single person to represent their district. Every person in the United States connects to one congressperson who speaks for the district; members of the House or Senate see themselves as speaking for their territorial **constituency**. Under PR rules, there are no districts and no one ends up with "their" representative. Everyone votes for national-level parties in one big combined contest. Elected representatives speak for a percentage of the overall national vote, whether their supporters are clustered in one place or scattered across the country.

This feature of proportional representation has pluses and minuses relative to SMP's districts. Many citizens in the United States and other SMP systems appreciate having "their" representative to contact, criticize, or champion. District constituencies also encourage representatives to pay attention to local problems and voices. PR representatives have no such connection. On the other hand, SMP legislators can be susceptible to **pork-barrel politics** in which they focus on delivering government spending in their district over other goals at the expense of coherent national debates. Representatives who must win districts

constituency
The voters whom an elected official represents.

pork-barrel politics
The practice of securing government spending for an official's constituency without considering goals of desirable policy.

have incentives to bring in national-level spending to their districts, like building bridges and roads or subsidizing local companies, whether or not they make sense in terms of broader national-level policy. PR representatives, by contrast, are selected for their positions in national-level debates. They have incentives to develop appealing national-level policies.

Overall, PR rules have considerable appeal, especially if we consider representation in a very basic way. It is simply true that more people get the representatives they want under PR than under SMP rules. Whether it delivers better representation in politics overall, however, is a tougher question. It calls for thinking about issues like fragmentation or representatives' connection to a local constituency. Small groups might get their own representatives under PR rules, but they might also get a fragmented assembly that prevents their representatives from delivering on policy goals.

When we add in these trade-offs alongside those of SMP rules, we may find ourselves wondering: Are there other alternatives to SMP and PR? Do we always have to play the same old games? And indeed there are other, more complicated options.

Modified Majoritarian and Proportional Rules

Whatever their downsides, both SMP and PR rules have the advantage of simplicity. The average citizen can understand how they work. Since these models tend toward overrepresentation or fragmentation, though, many democracies modify them into more complex options. These systems may well have more balanced and subtler effects on representation, but also make representation harder for citizens to understand.

Two examples tweak an SMP model to temper its winner-take-all qualities. In a **two-round system** (also known as a "runoff system"), if no candidate receives an outright majority of 50 percent in an SMP vote, the top two finishers compete in a second vote. The runoff forces the top two to reach out to supporters of losing candidates, whose shifting votes determine the victor. Used in France, in twenty-one other countries, and in three U.S. states (Louisiana, California, and Washington[2]), this system tends to give minority voices more influence while still ensuring that big movements win overall.

In an **alternative vote (AV)** system, rather than choosing one candidate, voters rank them in order of preference: first, second, and so on. If no one wins 50 percent of first preferences outright, the candidate with the fewest first-preference votes is eliminated and their voters' ballots are reallocated by second preferences. This continues until someone has 50 percent overall. Used in Australia, Papua New Guinea, and since 2018 for federal elections in the U.S. state of Maine, AV also encourages leading candidates to pay attention to smaller groups.

PR rules can also be modified to diminish risks of fragmentation. The most common adjustment is a **threshold rule**. In Israel, parties that receive less than 3.25 percent of votes get no seats. No fewer than thirty party lists fell below this threshold in 2019. Their small percentages are reallocated to parties as a

two-round system
A modified version of SMP voting rules, also known as a "runoff system."

alternative vote (AV)
A modification of an SMP system where voters rank candidates in order of preference.

threshold rule
Under PR voting systems, a rule that parties receive a share of seats only if they receive more than a certain percentage of votes, typically from 2 to 10 percent.

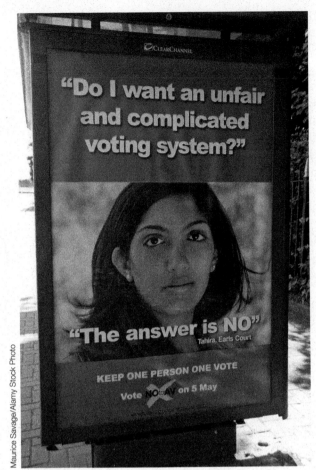

Maurice Savage/Alamy Stock Photo

In 2011, Britain held a referendum on shifting its electoral laws from SMP rules to the alternative vote (AV) system. The two biggest parties, the Conservative Party and the Labour Party, led the "No" campaign with the arguments we see on this bus stop poster: AV is too complex and breaks the sacred principle of "one person one vote." The smaller Liberal Democrats led the "Yes" campaign, arguing that AV is a fairer system that encourages pragmatic cooperation—but they lost resoundingly, with almost 68 percent rejecting the shift to AV.

function of their size, and this is why the two biggest lists party received a somewhat higher percentage of seats than votes. Other countries have thresholds of 4, 5, or even 10 percent (in Turkey). Another common way to limit fragmentation is to combine PR and SMP rules. About thirty countries have such **mixed-member systems**, including Germany, Japan, and New Zealand. In the main Japanese assembly (the Diet), for example, 300 seats are elected by SMP rules in single-member districts, and 180 are elected by PR voting. They try to balance some SMP encouragement of decisive mandates for large political movements with some PR openings for greater diversity of voices.

These modifications to basic SMP or PR rules nicely illustrate that we may reach the most meaningful representation by combining principles of representation—but also that the search for the perfect voting formula itself entails some costs. Each of these tweaks lessens the downsides of SMP or PR models, and mixed-member systems may deliver some of the benefits of both. In moving away from elegant SMP or PR systems, though, more sophisticated rules often become so complex than only computers can project how voting translates into representation. It may be worth living with the downsides of SMP or PR rules to offer citizens voting rules they can easily understand.

mixed-member systems
Voting rules in which some seats are won under SMP rules and some seats are won under PR rules.

gender quotas
Rules that incentivize or require that a certain portion of candidates or elected officials be women.

Descriptive Possibilities in Voting

Across SMP, PR, and other systems, voting rules often mix in descriptive representation as well. The most common examples are **gender quotas**. In about thirty countries, mostly in Europe and Latin America, parties are legally required (or incentivized with funding) to run female candidates. In Brazil, for example, 25 percent of each party's candidates must be women. In about forty other countries, parties voluntarily set proportional targets for female candidates. Importantly, both rules ensure only women candidates, not that women get elected. Today, women comprise about 15 percent of national-level Brazilian representatives. In the United States, without specific quotas, close to 25 percent of congressional representatives are women. Iraq by contrast, is one of a few countries with "hard" gender quotas that require that women be elected, not just that they be candidates. Parties must include enough women on their PR party lists to ensure that they fill 25 percent of seats.

Race and ethnicity can also motivate voting rules. Seven countries guarantee some seats by race or ethnicity, like for New Zealand's Maori minority, or by religion, like for Muslims and Christians in Lebanon. Iraq reserves eight of 325 seats for Christians and other tiny minorities. Much more common, though, is to factor descriptive goals into choices for voting rules that do not seem to be descriptive. Depending on where minorities live in a country, SMP, PR, or other rules can have predictable effects on minority representation. A minority that is scattered across the country—therefore, not being the majority anywhere—may insist on PR rules, since SMP would give it little chance of winning seats. A minority that is concentrated in one region might want SMP rules, since its members may win first-past-the-post contests within their region.

Within SMP rules it is also possible to engineer descriptive racial or ethnic representation by the technique known as **gerrymandering**: drawing oddly shaped districts to accomplish political goals. People often live in racial or ethnic clusters, and descriptive majorities can be constructed or diluted by drawing districts that map onto them. North Carolina's 12th district, for example, was drawn in 1992 to construct an African American majority (see Map 7-1). This might be perceived as

gerrymandering
Within SMP systems, this term means the redrawing of electoral districts to capture certain kinds of voters.

Map 7-1 Gerrymandering in North Carolina

North Carolina's 12th district, designated in this map by the blue-shaded area, snakes around the state to concentrate African American voting.

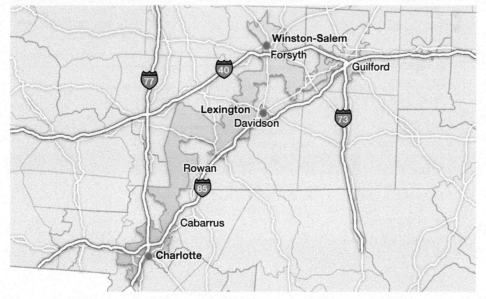

Source: U.S. News and World Report Congress Tracker, http://www.usnews.com/congress/watt-melvin-l (consulted February 16, 2012). Used with permission

good: if a minority is scattered across districts, with little influence anywhere, an odd-shaped district may give them decisive influence over one seat. New districts drawn in the 1980s increased African Americans in the House of Representatives from eighteen in 1980 to twenty-eight in 1991. There are more than fifty today.

But gerrymandering attracts serious criticism as well. For example, a Pulitzer Prize–winning African American journalist from Atlanta, Cynthia Tucker, has argued prominently that she cannot support racially drawn districts. In her view, they encourage polarization between very liberal black representatives in African American districts and very conservative white representatives in neighboring districts, worsening representation overall. She quotes a sharp comment from a South Carolina politician, Richard Harpootlian: "When the only issue is race, idiots win, black and white."[3]

When we set these complex possibilities for descriptive representation next to SMP, PR, and their many variations, we can no longer head to a voting booth and take for granted that we are being represented in a simple and obvious sense. Awareness of these alternatives need not turn Americans against SMP rules, of course; watching a good World Cup soccer match may not convince baseball fans to drop their allegiance. It does make us aware, though, of the peculiar features—good and bad—of the game we have chosen. Understanding the many possible rules compels us to think about how we interpret meaningful representation. Table 7-2 sums up the options and their key features.

Table 7-2 Principles, Strengths, and Weaknesses of Electoral Laws

	Principle of Representation		
	Majoritarian	**Proportional**	**Descriptive**
Kind of Electoral Law	Single-member plurality (SMP)	Proportional representation (PR)	There are no electoral laws based solely on descriptive principles, but they can be added with gerrymandering or seats reserved for certain groups
Likely Effects	Largest political forces are overrepresented	Many different voices are represented	Representatives look more like mirror image of society
Strengths	Gives clear mandate to largest group to lead	Largest number of citizens get the representatives they want	All groups see themselves reflected in their government
Weaknesses	Tends to stifle small voices and overall diversity of views	Tends toward creating fragmentation, instability	May encourage social and political polarization
Modifications			
	Two-round system (gives smaller groups the chance to affect which big one wins the second round)	Thresholds (eliminates smallest groups and so decreases fragmentation)	
	Alternative vote (encourages candidates to reach out to voters who are not their core supporters)		
	Mixed-member system (combines SMP and PR voting with mixed effects)		

Voting rules just define part of the representative game, however. They profoundly shape representation but do not fully dictate how citizens connect to government. Just as important are the nature and number of the "teams" that arise to compete within voting rules: the political parties. Parties respond carefully to voting rules, just as any team responds to the rules of its game, but the way they "play" is not simply dictated by the rules. These teams carry their own features that shape representative relationships.

Political Parties: Intermediaries of Representation

7.3 **Describe the roles parties play in representation and explain variation in their number and strength across countries.**

Political parties serve as the key intermediaries for representation in a liberal democracy, organizing citizens' choices and coordinating the action of their representatives. It follows that representation is powerfully defined by how many parties participate in the competition, and how each works as a team. To some degree, this second element of the game of representation is intertwined with the first, since a country's voting rules strongly affect the number and quality of its parties. Yet the nature of parties' intermediary role also reflects the society they represent, which adds other components to how representation works. In some countries, the various characteristics that can divide citizens tend to overlap—such as with ethnicity, race, religion, geography, or economic inequality—and so encourage the formation of a small number of large parties. In other countries, such lines diverge and fragment a representative arena into a large number of small party teams. Depending on these dynamics, parties can collectively reinforce majoritarian, proportional, or descriptive-style representation for their citizens.

Parties as Organizers of Debate and Action

In the United States today, political parties are often seen as self-serving elites who play up disagreements with others to win power. Far from new, this view extends back to the birth of the first parties in the early United States. As early as 1796, President George Washington distained the back-stabbing partisan competition he saw emerging in early U.S. elections, and warned against the "baneful" effects of parties that prioritized their own desire for power over the real problems confronting the nation.[4] Washington was a bit hasty, though, in overlooking the positive ways in which the emerging parties were contributing to representation. Today, experts agree with a famous line by political scientist E.E. Schattschneider: "Modern democracy is unthinkable save in terms of parties."[5]

Schattschneider and other defenders of parties tend to note four major services these organizations render to democratic representation:

- **Aggregating interests:** Parties seek out what voters want in politics. This is difficult for governing officials to do in a direct sense, since they are often busy making or managing policy. Parties play a middleman role of trying to discern what is most important to significant chunks of society and providing representatives to appeal to them.

- **Packaging and branding voter's options:** Parties create specific "brands" of core commitments, discourse and symbols, and key policy goals out of the near-infinite range of possible political choices. This is the top-down complement to bottom-up interest aggregation: voters do not always know what they want, and party brands help voters decide by focusing electoral competition into manageable debates.

- **Mobilizing citizens and recruiting leaders:** To do well in electoral competition, parties prod citizens to vote, develop political views, and get off the couch in general. Just as important, they serve as the major pathway for recruiting and training successive generations of leaders for political office.

- **Giving direction and coherence to government:** Once in power, parties hold groups of representatives together around common agendas. They tie leaders into group platforms, keeping government on a course and solving collective action problems between the many different people who hold authority in any modern state.

Parties, in other words, give shape to electoral debate and government action. The smallest-scale, simplest elections can operate without them, as we often see in local politics, but on the large scale of modern governments, with millions of diverse voters, an enormous range of issues to debate, and many elected officials who must coordinate their actions for policies to work, parties are essential to organize the scene.

On the other hand, to say that parties are essential does not mean they are perfect. George Washington's criticisms were insightful. As organizations created to compete for power, they often exaggerate differences with their opponents—just as competing business brands play up superficial differences between dishwasher detergents. More worrisome still, parties that become large and successful may shout down or crowd out other political voices, acting like abusive business cartels or monopolies. In the United States, Democrats and Republicans may not agree on much, but they have consistently allied to block other political formations. Both have supported laws that make it difficult for "third parties" to be listed on voting ballots or to share the millions of dollars available in public campaign financing. Both usually refuse to debate third-party candidates, since doing so would give media attention to upstart challengers. Similar dynamics arise in many democratic arenas around the world. In many ways, parties both play with the bounds of fair competition and may cross them to stay ahead.

President Donald Trump hosts a meeting with leading Congresspeople from his Republican Party to discuss their agenda in early 2017. Party ties help leaders advance a collective agenda once they're elected.

Not only may successful parties stifle competitors, but they may not always represent their own supporters very well. They may become stuck in their ways and unresponsive to voters' changing views. The longer a party manages to have some electoral success, say some experts on parties, the more its top leaders control their "brand" in a top-down way, play to their core supporters, and tell voters what to think rather than representing them. Robert Michels, a famous German expert on parties, called this the "iron law of oligarchy," since he saw each party becoming a little oligarchy: a top-down organization ruled by a few elites.

Parties may also become less responsive because they are "captured" by certain segments of the population. Among U.S. parties, a common complaint about "capture" concerns the use of **closed party primaries**. In this system, which operates for all parties in nine U.S. states and for some parties in seven others, only registered members of a party may vote in "primary" elections to select the party's candidates. The **party base**—the most dedicated and often most extreme core of voters—typically turns out in the greatest numbers to vote in such primaries, so these processes tend to favor more extreme candidates. The result is that parties often select candidates who are further to the right or left than most of their own voters. In a two-party system, this can mean that more moderate voters are offered a choice only between extremes in the main election, contributing to overall political polarization.

"Can't live with 'em, can't live without 'em," sums up parties' role in representation. Their very nature as the organizers of competition for power makes

closed party primaries
Elections to select candidates for a party in which only registered party members can vote.

party base
Voters who are most strongly committed to a party.

them divisive and sometimes unpleasant: this kind of team sport can make football look gentle and sweet. Yet they nonetheless form an unavoidable part of the citizen-government connection. Voters cannot make informed choices without packaged options; potential leaders cannot jump into the complex world of politics without organizations to recruit, train, and support them; and elected officials depend on party connections to help coordinate their work. For better and for worse, the competition for representation at the heart of liberal democracy needs intermediaries to shape the game.

But which shape do parties give to representation? That depends on how many parties emerge in a democratic arena and how they are organized internally. The next two sections consider how the quantity and quality of party organizations can steer democracy toward different principles of representation.

Party Systems, Voting Rules, and Social Divisions

Duverger's Law

The observation that SMP rules encourage two-party systems, since they favor large parties, and that PR rules encourage multiparty systems.

Different systems of parties, with different numbers and types of teams, arise partly as a consequence of voting rules. **Duverger's Law**, named for French political scientist Maurice Duverger, observes that single-member plurality rules encourage two-party systems while proportional representation rules encourage multiparty systems. The logic is easy to grasp. Only the largest competitors win representation under SMP, so these rules encourage political players to ally into large parties. PR rules, by contrast, allow multiple groups to succeed electorally on their own, even if they are relatively small. A glance across liberal democracies reveals three major configurations of party systems:

- *Dominant-party systems.* In a few countries, one party manages to stay in government in election after election. The best example today is the African National Congress (ANC) in South Africa, which regularly wins roughly 70 percent of votes and seats. This configuration is very rare in open and free liberal democracies, though, because eventually voters tend to look for alternatives.

- *Two-party systems.* The United States is the clearest example in the world of a party system with only two large contenders. One is seen as representing the Left, the other the Right. This configuration is also rare, occurring enduringly in only a few countries.

- *Multiparty systems.* In the vast majority of liberal democracies, at least five or six parties play significant roles in representation. Such systems, as in Germany, usually feature an ideological right-left divide, like in two-party systems, but also have multiple parties on either side of that divide, and sometimes in the middle (known as centrist parties). In Germany, the Christian Democrats form the Right, the Free Democrats are perceived as center-right, the Social Democrats represent the mainstream Left, "The Left" (*Die Linke*) party speaks for the far Left, the "Alternative for Germany" (*Alternative für Deutschland*) represent the far Right, and the Greens emphasize environmentalism and left-leaning views.

As Duverger's law suggests, behind these different party systems often stand voting rules that encourage these outcomes. All the countries that have had something like two-party systems at some point—the United States, Britain, Canada, Australia—use SMP rules (though Australia now uses the AV tweak on SMP). In contrast, Israel, Iraq, and other systems with a high number of parties typically use PR rules. Countries with fewer parties but still more than two, like Germany, often use mixed-member rules.

On the other hand, party systems are more than simple reflections of voting rules, and there are many exceptions to Duverger's Law. Voting rules may encourage a few large parties or many small ones, but they do not require them. Parties are created, split, and succeed or fail for reasons that may ignore incentives in electoral rules. In SMP systems, ideological fights or rivalries between leaders may sustain multiple smallish parties. Britain's Liberal Democrats have soldiered on as a small party, for example, because they have distinct views from both Conservatives and Labour.

The most diverse societies often produce many parties no matter what the rules, since parties arise to cater to their ethnic, religious, or other divisions. India has straightforward SMP rules, but the extraordinary diversity across the world's largest democracy—with 900 million eligible voters and over 100 different languages—still produces almost forty parties in its main assembly. On the other hand, dominant parties sometimes emerge even under PR rules. South African elections operate by PR, but because much of the black population still perceives the ANC as the party that overturned racist white rule in the 1990s, it wins recurring majorities.

Only when SMP rules combine with other conditions—usually a low number of fragmenting ideological or ethnic divisions in society—does a two-party system arise. In such a case, like in the United States, the two-party system powerfully reinforces majoritarian politics. The lack of third-party options pushes voters and politicians alike into a loudest-voice logic: if a citizen wants his vote to matter, or a politician wants her efforts to have influence, both face incentives to align with one of the two major parties. To help their big party win a majority, candidates and voters are generally encouraged to downplay any minority views they hold.

Where multiparty systems arise—usually but not always within PR rules—less pressure exists for people to rally around the loudest voices. The availability of many parties reinforces proportional-style logic in which citizens and politicians may reasonably focus on carving out a distinctive message rather than coming in first overall. Multiparty systems frequently create space for descriptive representation as well, allowing for racial or ethnic parties that cater to certain groups. Iraq's new parties, for example, have settled out mainly along ethnic and religious lines.

Criticisms of different party systems, unsurprisingly, echo criticisms of the representative principles to which they connect. Leaders of small parties or minorities who complain about majoritarianism tend to dislike two-party systems. For Theresa Amato, who managed third-party candidate Ralph Nader's U.S. presidential campaigns back in 2000 and 2004, a two-party system has the flaw of majoritarianism: it squelches all but the loudest, best-funded voices. The United States suffers, she writes, from "the myth of voter choice in a two-party tyranny."[6] In Britain, advocates of a distinct identity for the Scottish minority similarly object to the dominance of the Conservative and Labour parties, and have championed the rise of the Scottish National Party with increasing success.

People who worry about the fragmentation of proportionality, on the other hand, tend to emphasize the downside of multiparty systems. For Zev Chafets, an American political commentator who spent part of his life among Israel's many parties, multiparty systems get bogged down in representing too many different views. Parties *should* cater to the loudest voices, he says: "If you had a party that fit the tastes of every group, you'd have hundreds of parties that would make it impossible to govern."[7] As the saying goes, "the grass is always greener on the other side of the fence." People in two-party systems often wish for more choices, and people in multi-party systems often wish for more simplicity and stability.

Variations in Party Strength

Just as sports teams are run in different ways, so political parties vary not just in quantity but also in internal qualities. Some are centralized, tightly run organizations whose leaders demand that their candidates stick to the party platform and that all their elected officials pursue common policy goals. Those who speak or vote against the party's priorities may be denied jobs in the party or in government, deprived of campaign funds for their next election, or even excluded from the party. Some are much looser alliances between politicians who cooperate on some things but often act independently.

Party strength generally serves as an amplifier for the varying effects parties can have on representation (see Figure 7-2). The stronger and more centralized a party is, the more it tends to have both the benefits Schattschneider expected and the drawbacks emphasized by critics like Michels. Strong, tightly controlled parties usually present the most coherent positions to voters and best deliver coordinated action in government, but also may be less flexible and responsive to voters' demands. Furthermore, not only do strong parties amplify the general costs and benefits of parties, but they tend to magnify the specific effects of different party systems. Strong parties in a two-party system further reinforce a powerful logic of majoritarianism, as two large parties whip their troops into line to win overall control. Strong parties in multiparty systems tend to reinforce a logic of proportionalism, empowering each party to advance a distinct message and to bargain with other parties to push its agenda.

Figure 7-2 Party Systems and Principles of Representation

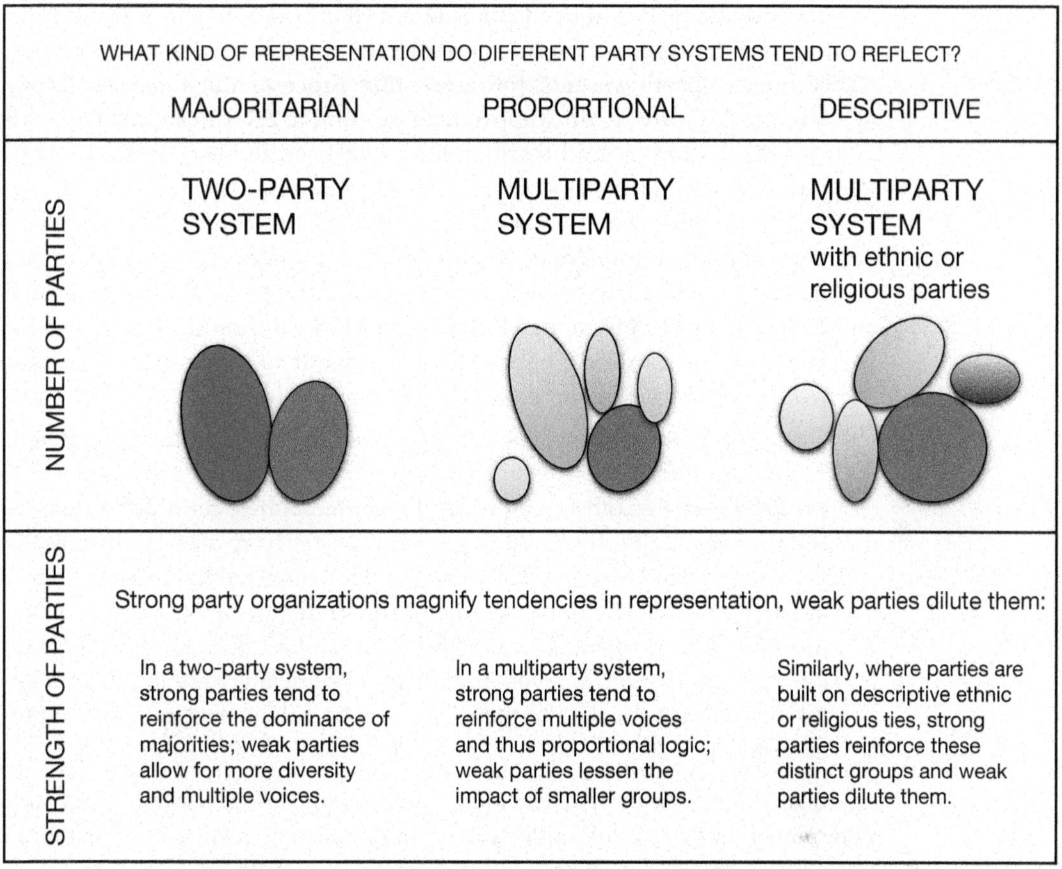

WHAT KIND OF REPRESENTATION DO DIFFERENT PARTY SYSTEMS TEND TO REFLECT?

MAJORITARIAN	PROPORTIONAL	DESCRIPTIVE
TWO-PARTY SYSTEM	MULTIPARTY SYSTEM	MULTIPARTY SYSTEM with ethnic or religious parties

NUMBER OF PARTIES

STRENGTH OF PARTIES

Strong party organizations magnify tendencies in representation, weak parties dilute them:

| In a two-party system, strong parties tend to reinforce the dominance of majorities; weak parties allow for more diversity and multiple voices. | In a multiparty system, strong parties tend to reinforce multiple voices and thus proportional logic; weak parties lessen the impact of smaller groups. | Similarly, where parties are built on descriptive ethnic or religious ties, strong parties reinforce these distinct groups and weak parties dilute them. |

Given how many Americans complain, like Theresa Amato, about a "two-party tyranny," it may surprise them to know that American parties are fairly weak in organizational terms. Republicans or Democrats act more as individual politicians—voting in Congress more independently from other members of their party, campaigning on their own themes, and mobilizing their own support and money—than politicians in most other democracies. Several interlocking reasons help explain why:

- *Voting rules.* Voting rules can make elected representatives answer to different masters. Under SMP rules, representatives must win a plurality in a district. Their bottom-line incentives are thus to please voters in their district—or run the risk of being voted out of office. Under PR rules, officeholders have no districts and their political future depends on the overall votes for their party. Representatives in SMP systems face pressures to prioritize local constituencies over party coherence, whereas their counterparts in PR systems are more likely to prioritize the interests of their party over local issues.

- *Candidate selection.* In the United States, candidates in most elections run in primaries in which party supporters select who will run as the Democratic or Republican candidate in their district. Party leaders can endorse individuals but do not dictate candidate selection. In most countries, party leaders influence this process much more directly. Voting rules are again important here: under PR rules, parties create lists of candidates, and the higher a name is on the list, the more likely they are to be elected. Since party leaders often influence the rankings on the list, they have leverage over who gets to run. Politicians in the party must listen to party leaders to ensure a good spot on the list for the next election. Even many parties in countries with SMP voting rules have similar levels of party influence over candidate selection, however; leaders of strong parties do not leave it to voters to choose who will play on their team.

- *Campaign finance.* Electoral campaigns cost money. Candidates use television, the Internet, billboards, mailings, and armies of paid workers to get their message out to voters. In the United States, candidates do most fund-raising individually (though recent years have seen an increase in more centralized funding[8]). This makes politicians relatively independent of party control once in office. In most other democracies, more money is raised by party organizations than by individual candidates. Party leaders thus hold powerful levers to influence politicians once in office: a representative who bucks the party line can find their next campaign short on funds.

Like the number of parties, then, party strength is affected, but not fully determined, by voting rules. PR rules encourage strong parties more than SMP, but parties also become strong or weak for their own reasons, and amplify or muffle the representational principles of their arenas. Thus in Britain, despite SMP rules, parties have tended to exert fairly strong control of their candidates and elected officials. Strong control by two parties for much of British history has reinforced the majoritarian logic of its politics. In the United States, weak parties lessen the majoritarianism of SMP rules and a two-party system. The relative independence of members of Congress creates the opportunity for more diverse positions representing the varying concerns of their districts. Yet it also leaves the two parties less able to present coherent overall platforms to voters or to coordinate action once in office. Indeed, foreigners are often surprised at how much American politics is dominated by wrangling between individual congresspersons' concerns.

Strong or weak, numerous or not, parties are simultaneously essential to representation and widely reviled by citizens. Parties are often held in low esteem, partly due to their failings, certainly, because they sometimes block or skew representation rather than facilitating it. Yet parties' poor reputation also simply reflects the inherently difficult role that democracy assigns to them. As

Members of the Bundestag (the German lower house) raise their hands in a vote in 2019. Parties in European countries are generally stronger organizations than those in the United States: party leaders set more of the collective agenda, members vote together more consistently, and finance and party decision making are typically more centralized.

intermediaries between citizens and government, they mobilize and structure the competition for power that is necessary to meaningful electoral choice. Sometimes in unpleasant ways, they struggle to win voters' confidence and end up producing both different party systems and levels of party strength, depending on voting rules, social divisions, and other conditions like the sources of campaign finance. Divisive though parties can seem, liberal democracy depends on a competition to represent citizens, and parties are essential to organizing that contest.

Elected Offices: Executives and Legislators in the Presidential Model

7.4 Describe the core features of presidential government and evaluate its advantages and disadvantages.

If voting rules shape the "bottom-up" input of citizens into representation, and party intermediaries organize the competition among citizens' choices, the arrangement of elected offices shapes representation in a "top-down" way. Elected offices are the positions representatives hold once elected, defining which kinds of jobs they fill and with which kinds of powers they can act. The configuration of these jobs influences how representation works just as much as the channeling of citizens' choices through votes and parties. The form of these offices shapes the game at the highest level, structuring the overall leagues within which it is played and what winners get for winning.

In all democracies, candidates for representation compete to win two kinds of elected offices: executive and legislative. **Executives** are government's chief officers, with responsibility for setting forth a policy agenda, making the most immediate policy decisions, and implementing policies. **Legislators** are representatives in an assembly, or legislature, who propose, debate, amend, and approve laws. The main distinction between different models of elected offices concerns the relationship between winning legislative offices and winning the top executive office. In some countries, they are two separate competitions that form two separate channels of representation, with an executive leader selected in one vote and legislators selected in another. In other countries, they are chosen as part of a single fused process.

The separate-channels model, which was pioneered by the United States, is known as presidentialism. The single-channel model is known as parliamentarism. In this section and the next, we discuss their core rules, their relationship to the principles of representation, and the most commonly perceived advantages and disadvantages.

The Presidential Model and the Separation of Powers

In the United States, Latin American countries, and a few other democracies, citizens' most visible representative is a president. Behind the executive office of the presidency stands a distinctive concept about organizing representation known as the **separation of powers**. Reaching back to Greek and Roman roots and especially the political thinking of the French Enlightenment philosopher Montesquieu (1689–1755),[9] this concept holds that the best government has multiple, separate branches that draw on their own sources of authority. By creating several poles of power, each with a legitimate claim to authority, abusive government becomes less likely. Across these separate poles, the presidential system assigns a variety of **checks and balances**, or specific powers for the branches to watch and limit each other.

For the drafters of the U.S. Constitution, who drew on these philosophical ideas to create the first presidential system, this meant that representation should flow through at least two separate channels. In one channel, voters connect to the chief executive office, choosing their president. The chosen individual is simultaneously the head of government, running government affairs and setting the policy agenda, and the ceremonial head of state, symbolizing national unity.

In most presidential systems, the direct election of the president connects this top leadership post strongly to citizens. The U.S. founders, however, added a wrinkle that requires a little aside: selection of the president by the Electoral College.

executives
A government's leading officers, with responsibility for setting a policy agenda, making immediate decisions, and implementing policies.

legislators
Representatives in an assembly, or legislature, who propose, debate, amend, and approve laws.

separation of powers
The principle that branches of government hold separate authority, keeping each other from abusing their powers.

checks and balances
More specific powers assigned to separate branches of government to allow them to prevent each other's abuses.

The fifty U.S. states each receive one electoral college vote for every seat they hold in Congress (in the House of Representatives and in the Senate). Because House seats are allocated by population, populous states have more representatives and thus more electoral college votes: huge California has fifty-five, little Vermont only three. Whichever presidential candidate wins the most citizens' votes in each state obtains its electoral college votes,[10] and the candidate who reaches 270 electoral college votes becomes president.[11] Usually, the electoral college winner also wins the most citizens' votes overall, but in four elections since 1789, the electoral college winner lost the overall popular vote—most recently Donald Trump in 2016, and before him George W. Bush in 2000. Thus the U.S. system typically works out like an SMP election, but sometimes the electoral college wrinkle alters the outcome. A long-shot effort to sideline the Electoral College called the "National Popular Vote" got underway in 2006, asking U.S. state legislatures to award their Electoral College delegates to the winner of the national popular vote in all cases. If it were to pass in states that hold 270 electoral votes—and withstand likely legal challenges—U.S. presidential elections would operate like direct elections in other presidential systems.[12]

Looking past this complication, the U.S. president holds the same basic constitutional role as directly elected presidents in other presidential systems. The president chooses a cabinet of secretaries, or ministers as they are known in most countries, to cover executive responsibilities in various policy areas: the secretary (or minister) of Defense, of Commerce, of Agriculture, and so on. Each member of the cabinet typically oversees a government department (or ministry) in which nonelected bureaucrats work on their policy area. The president, cabinet, and departments form the executive branch of government.

The other channel of representation connects voters to the legislature. In most presidential systems, voters elect representatives to two legislatures that must both approve laws on equal terms. In the United States, the 435 members of the House of Representatives represent districts with roughly equal population. The Senate, by contrast, represents territory, with two senators for each of the fifty states. Most other presidential governments have imitated this two-house or **bicameral** legislative model, though some, like Peru and Venezuela, have **unicameral** (one-house) legislatures.

At the heart of representation in a presidential separation-of-powers model is the notion that the executive and legislature hold distinct, yet equally valid claims to represent the people. They must work together to make major policy decisions: the legislature must turn the president's proposals into laws and approve them, and the president must sign the laws the legislature passes. They work together as separate partners, watching and limiting each other. They have nonoverlapping personnel—secretaries or ministers in the cabinet cannot be members of the legislature—and neither branch can unseat the other. The legislature has oversight committees to supervise the executive, watching what the president and other officials are doing, but it can get rid of a president only by convicting him or her of criminal actions in a process known as impeachment. Presidents, for their part, can legally do little to pressure legislators other than

bicameral/ unicameral

These terms refer respectively to legislatures consisting of two "houses" (bi-) or one (uni-).

to bargain with them. All are stuck with each other, quite deliberately, to create a watchful tension among multiple channels of representation.

Presidentialism and Principles of Representation

How do the presidential model's multiple channels relate to principles of representation? On the one hand, the channel of a directly elected president takes an inherently majoritarian format. Presidential elections assign executive power to one winner, with no proportional-style way to split up influence over the executive across various groups. France and some other countries with directly elected presidents use a two-round modification of SMP rules to encourage presidential candidates to attend to smaller voices, but it still remains a majoritarian kind of choice.

On the other hand, the broader logic of the separation of powers overlaps somewhat with proportional-style thinking. The idea that president and legislature balance each other also presumes some diversity in citizens' choices, implying that the separate channels of elections often end up giving power to different groups. In the United States, this expectation is borne out: it is uncommon that either Democrats or Republicans control the presidency and both houses of Congress at the same time, occurring only about a quarter of the time since 1945. The American norm is **divided government**, when opposing parties each control major institutions.

divided government
A situation in a separation-of-powers system in which representative branches of government are controlled by different parties.

Yet divided government in a separation of powers addresses the population's diversity in a different way from the proportional representation of social groups. The logic of the American founders was one of multiple majorities, not of proportional empowerment of multiple voices. Different communities across the American states, they envisioned, would have different majorities and send different representatives to Congress. Minorities in each district would still be out of luck, but would have a voice as long as they were the majority somewhere in the country. Congress overall would be a diverse body that would "check" the national majority represented by the president, keeping the executive in a modest role.

Overall, then, presidential government reflects a special version of majoritarian thinking. It tempers simple rule by the greatest number with a clash between the winners of multiple competitions that may mobilize different points of view. Presidentialism itself does not directly incorporate proportional or descriptive representation, though these principles can be introduced into presidential systems through other features of representation, especially voting rules. The U.S. House includes descriptive representation of African Americans through gerrymandering. Other countries use PR voting rules for legislatures in presidential systems, such as Brazil, Ecuador, and several other Latin American systems. In these countries, majoritarian presidents are forced to work with proportional politics in multiparty legislatures.

The Case for Presidential Representation

American leaders have never been shy about praising their presidential model of representative government. "The happy Union of these States is a wonder," said James Madison, one of the lead drafters of the U.S. Constitution. "Their Constitution [is] a miracle; their example [is] the hope of Liberty throughout the world."[13] This model has been imitated in many other countries and remains appealing today: dozens of countries in Latin America, Asia, and Eastern Europe who have adopted new democratic constitutions since the 1980s have chosen presidentialism. Its proponents emphasize several advantages:

- *Only broadly represented policies get past the checks and balances.* For Madison and other founders, the system's key advantage lay in its separation and balance between legislature and executive. By organizing representation through multiple majorities—the presidency, a lower house, and an upper house, too, in most presidential systems—presidentialism makes it especially difficult for any single viewpoint to push its agenda through the government. On major issues, only policies with very broad support across the executive and legislatures are likely to succeed.

- *Representation has a unifying national face.* A chief executive elected by the citizens (or almost, in the U.S. case) plays a powerful symbolic role, giving a face to the choice of the nation overall. It offers citizens the sense that they have a personal connection to their leadership, especially with popular presidents like John F. Kennedy, Ronald Reagan, or Luiz Inacio Lula da Silva, Brazil's president from 2003 to 2010. The need to win a nationwide majority typically encourages presidential candidates to construct broad appeal and emphasize unity, potentially bringing a diverse country together.

- *Clear leadership on a predictable timetable provides stability.* The relative predictability of presidential elections, untroubled by some of the complexities of parliamentary government that we will see in the next section, may foster stability. After each term, every four or five years depending on the country, citizens know that one person will receive a mandate to exercise executive authority. They know that barring death or criminal impeachment, that person will be the leader until the end of his or her term. Within the executive office, at least, presidentialism avoids potentially ambiguous power-sharing arrangements.

- *Voters are consulted frequently and in varied ways.* Presidentialism's multiple channels to citizens offer frequent opportunities for representation. Presidential and legislative elections offer voters several differently packaged choices. A voter may even choose representatives from opposing parties, if she or he wishes, in what is known as **split-ticket voting**. An American voter might choose a Democratic senator and a House Republican, or legislators from one party and a president from the other—and some voters do. Whether or not voters spread their support around, though, presidential systems gauge the public mood frequently and in multiple ways.

split-ticket voting
Giving votes to members of different parties in the same election.

All of these benefits flow from the separation of powers at the core of presidentialism. Its two channels of representation make decisive government action dependent on broad support across multiple majorities, demand consultation of voters in multiple elections, and create a majoritarian executive who may foster symbolic unity and stable leadership. The separation of powers also leads to the major downside of presidentialism, which even its supporters will admit: the risk of impasse, or stalemate between the separate branches. Both president and legislative majority can claim to represent the people, and if they disagree without budging, nothing gets done. On ten occasions since 1980 the U.S. president and Congress have failed to agree on basic spending bills, shutting down the government—a phenomenon that is uniquely American.[14] Moreover, since neither side can overturn the other, opponents may remain locked in impasse for whole terms of office. For Madison and other proponents of this system, though, this is part of the design. Government action should be possible only with broad support, and so a checked-and-balanced structure best connects the people to government.

Elected Offices: Executives and Legislators in the Parliamentary Model

7.5 **Describe the core features of parliamentary government and evaluate its advantages and disadvantages.**

Many Americans may feel that the preceding section makes an open-and-shut case for their familiar presidential model. Yet we cannot reach that conclusion without first acknowledging that a widespread alternative model exists. Just as the appeal of baseball must not be obvious, since fairly few countries play it, so we know that presidentialism is not obviously ideal because a majority of liberal democracies around the world employ the very different parliamentary model. Consider now its logic, principles of representation, and strengths.

The Parliamentary Model of Fusion of Powers

fusion of powers

The organizing principle of parliamentary government, in which the executive depends directly on the support of a legislative majority.

The parliamentary configuration of elected offices is based on the principle of **fusion of powers**. It grew historically out of attempts to limit monarchs' power by forcing executive authority to submit to the will of a representative legislature. In Britain and several other European countries, the first or "prime" minister was originally the top official who managed government affairs on behalf of the monarch. Opponents of monarchical power eventually demanded that kings and queens cede major decisions to the majority of an elected legislature, including choice of the prime minister. This created a model that fused legislative and elective powers: citizens elected the legislature, and their legislative representatives chose the executive. Rather than having a separate election for the executive, it stood or fell depending on its support in the legislature.

In a parliamentary system, then, citizens vote only for their legislators. In some parliamentary systems, citizens vote for representatives in two houses, called an "upper house" and a "lower house," which have these labels because they descend from chambers that once represented the "upper" class of aristocracy and the "lower" class of everyone else. However, in almost all parliamentary systems, the upper house has limited powers, and the main political action is in a single "lower house" like the British House of Commons, the Dutch House of Representatives, or the Iraqi Council of Representatives. A prime minister can take office only given the assent of a lower-house majority. After a legislative election, each leader of the parties that won substantial numbers of seats in the lower house attempts to attract a majority of the newly elected legislators to vote for him or her to become prime minister. Thus the person who becomes the head of government—the British Prime Minister, Germany's Chancellor (which is their version of the prime minister title), and most other democratic executives around the globe—is not directly chosen by voters to be leader. A prime minister holds executive authority because his or her party did well in *legislative* elections and the legislators then chose him or her to lead.

Unlike presidential models in which the "head of state" and "head of government" are one person, parliamentary systems maintain a separate head of state office, distinct from the prime minister as head of government. This person has little to no political power, instead typically playing a symbolic role of presiding over national rituals and events like major funerals. In constitutional monarchies like Britain, the king or queen is head of state. In parliamentary republics like Germany or Iraq, this largely ceremonial role is known—a bit confusingly—as the president. Chosen by parliament, not directly elected, presidents in parliamentary systems are typically well-respected senior politicians at the end of their careers. They rarely receive much attention and in no way resemble the powerful presidents of presidential systems. The real authority of elected offices in parliamentary models lies with the prime minister.

The key politics of parliamentarism, therefore, focuses on how a prime minister forms a lower-house majority. Sometimes this process is quite straightforward, but sometimes it becomes very complex. When a single party wins an outright majority in the lower house, the party's top leader becomes prime minister and forms a cabinet of ministers chosen from her or his political party. Like in a presidential system, ministers each typically take control of one ministry—Defense, Agriculture, and so on—and begin formulating and implementing policy. Because two-party systems are actually quite rare, though, most parliamentary governments do not form from a one-party majority. Instead they must stitch together a **coalition government** that draws on multiple parties' seats in the lower house to form a majority. Most often, the leader of the party with the most seats in the lower house becomes prime minister, and leaders of other parties in the majority coalition are assigned ministerial roles in the cabinet. Thereafter, policymaking

coalition government
A government in a parliamentary system in which the prime minister and cabinet depend on the support of more than one party in the legislature to form a majority.

and passage of laws require constant negotiations among the coalition partners, because members of the coalition parties must be able to agree to form a legislative majority that can pass legislation.

The parliamentary executive's "fusion" with a legislative majority creates dynamics that are unknown to citizens of presidential separation-of-powers systems. Four are especially notable:

vote of no confidence

A vote by a legislative majority to withdraw its support from the executive in a parliamentary system.

- *The vote of no confidence:* Since the executive gains power by legislative vote, so a legislative vote can unseat the executive. If a lower-house majority approves a **"vote of no confidence"** in the government, the prime minister typically resigns. This usually requires that legislative elections be held to designate a new majority and government.

- *Changing executives without an election:* If a party or coalition of parties holds a majority but wishes to change its prime minister, it can do so, revote support for a new prime minister, and continue without an election. British prime minister Tony Blair handed off power to his successor, Gordon Brown, in this way in 2007.

dissolution

The act of the head of a parliamentary system to resign and call a new election.

- *Snap elections:* Not only can the legislature get rid of the executive with a vote of no confidence, but in most parliamentary systems, the executive can **dissolve** the legislature by calling "snap" elections in which all must resign: the prime minister, government, and the legislators. New elections must then be held within a certain amount of time. Prime ministers sometimes use this tool to call elections at a time that suits their party or coalition and disadvantages their opponents. British Prime Minister Theresa May called a snap election in 2017, when polls showed her party in the lead. But this strategy is risky: in May's case, opinion turned against her and her party lost seats, barely holding on to power.

- *An irregular electoral calendar:* Since either a legislative "vote of no confidence" or dissolution by the executive can bring sudden elections, elections in parliamentary systems often are not held with perfect regularity. In presidential systems in which neither executive nor legislature can unseat the other, elections operate on a strict calendar that can be predicted into the future; we know that a U.S. presidential election will occur in 2076 or, with luck, 2204. Parliamentary governments are constitutionally required to hold elections after some period— usually four or five years from the last election—but often end up holding them earlier. The future timing of elections can be unpredictable.

All these possibilities follow from the fused roots of the executive and legislature into a single main channel of representation. If the executive's existence depends on a majority in the legislature, then the legislature can unseat the executive or the executive can resign and call for election of a new legislature, and these moves can happen at any time and shift the electoral calendar. Because parliamentarism has a simpler core than presidentialism's multiple branches, the relations between the former's fused executive and legislature are more fluid than the distinct executive and legislative roles and the strict calendar of the presidential model.

Parliamentarism and Principles of Representation

In parliamentarism, the fact that representation flows solely through the legislature means that it can relate to principles of representation in different ways, depending on the nature of the legislative majority. Its representative logic can be powerfully majoritarian or thoroughly proportional, depending on whether or not a single-party majority exists in the legislature.

When parliamentary institutions operate with a two-party system, the result tends to be a winner-take-all, majoritarian kind of politics. At any given time, one party or the other usually wins an outright majority in the lower house. The winning party's leader becomes prime minister and selects party members for the cabinet. Unlike in a presidential system, this executive faces no other strong pole of power (except in the few parliamentary systems with powerful upper houses, like Italy). This is a truly winner-take-all situation, since such a prime minister needs only to persuade her or his own party to pass laws. British prime ministers under these conditions have often launched massive programs of change, like Conservative leader Margaret Thatcher after winning in 1979 or Labour leader Tony Blair after winning in 1997. Given the fusion of powers, no one stood in their way.

When parliamentary institutions operate with a multiparty system, by contrast, they tend to display proportional politics that amplify small voices. When no single party wins a majority, the largest parties look for partners to build lower-house coalitions. This process often exaggerates the power of small parties, who become "kingmakers" because their few legislative seats are needed to approve the government. In Germany in 1998, for example, the Social Democrats won 45 percent of seats in the lower house (the Bundestag). They needed the Green Party's 7 percent to form a majority, and in return the Greens successfully demanded control of the Ministries of Environmental Policy, Agriculture, Health, and the powerful Foreign Ministry. In Iraq after the 2010 elections, Prime Minister Nouri Al-Maliki needed no less than nine months to persuade enough parties to give him a majority. Demands from many different minor voices had to be satisfied for the coalition to work.

In countries with severe ethnic or religious divides like Iraq, this proportional coalition building often emphasizes descriptive representation. To build his coalition, Al-Maliki faced descriptive demands to include a certain number of cabinet ministers from Sunnis and other groups. Displaying carefully negotiated numbers of ministers from minority groups is a simple way for a coalitional government to signal to minorities that they have a voice in governance.

Parliamentary systems can thus work in radically different ways (see Figure 7-3). With a solidly two-party system and single-party government, they can display the most majoritarian kind of democratic government that exists: a single majority runs the legislature and the executive. The same institutions in a multiparty system produce a kind of forced partnership and proportional power sharing among rivals that requires constant negotiation, can make small players into kingmakers, and often empowers descriptive demands.

Figure 7-3 Elected Offices and Principles of Representation

The most majoritarian political system is a parliamentary system with a single-party majority: the same big party holds both the legislature and the executive, so that party controls the agenda. Presidential systems are also basically majoritarian—by definition, only the top vote getter wins the presidency—but because voters elect the legislature separately, there is the possibility of a more proportional sharing of power if one party wins the presidency and another party wins the legislative majority (the situation of "divided government" shown here). When parliamentary systems have no single-party majority, they operate in much more proportional ways: multiple parties must form a coalition government, and the coalition parties typically divide up the government minister positions among them.

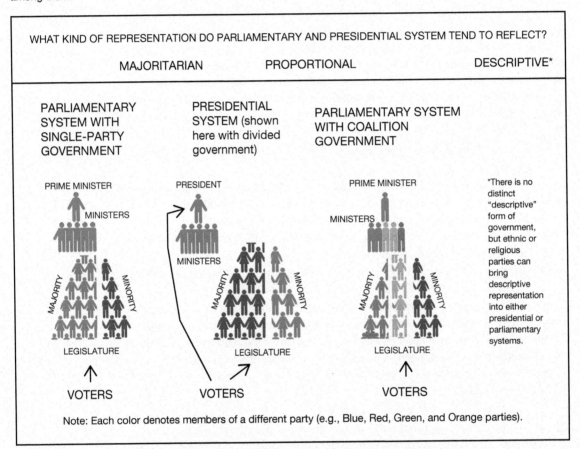

WHAT KIND OF REPRESENTATION DO PARLIAMENTARY AND PRESIDENTIAL SYSTEM TEND TO REFLECT?

MAJORITARIAN   PROPORTIONAL   DESCRIPTIVE*

PARLIAMENTARY SYSTEM WITH SINGLE-PARTY GOVERNMENT

PRESIDENTIAL SYSTEM (shown here with divided government)

PARLIAMENTARY SYSTEM WITH COALITION GOVERNMENT

PRIME MINISTER
MINISTERS
MAJORITY
MINORITY
LEGISLATURE
VOTERS

PRESIDENT
MINISTERS
MAJORITY
MINORITY
LEGISLATURE
VOTERS

PRIME MINISTER
MINISTERS
MAJORITY
MINORITY
LEGISLATURE
VOTERS

*There is no distinct "descriptive" form of government, but ethnic or religious parties can bring descriptive representation into either presidential or parliamentary systems.

Note: Each color denotes members of a different party (e.g., Blue, Red, Green, and Orange parties).

The Case for Parliamentary Representation

Why might people prefer their representatives to compete in parliamentary-style leagues rather than presidential ones? As we might expect from the wider use of the parliamentary model, many see it as superior. Indeed, for all the admiration the U.S. Constitution still attracts, almost all of the countries that score highest on broad measures of human development and good governance have parliamentary governments.[15] Even some influential Americans lean in this direction. For Woodrow Wilson, U.S. president from 1913 to 1921 and also a professor who helped found modern political science, the separation of powers in the U.S. Constitution was a "grievous mistake."[16] The fusion of powers, say proponents of parliamentarism, delivers better representation for several reasons:

- *The connection to voters is simple and clear.* With only one major channel of representation through the legislature, citizens know where to focus their attention. Every few years voters know that a national legislative election is the decisive moment. Presidential systems may offer too much of a good thing—too many different elections—and create voter fatigue that leaves citizens less engaged.

- *Representatives can deliver on their promises.* A single channel of authority also means that when citizens vote, they can be fairly confident that representatives will act on their campaign promises. By definition, a winning party or coalition controls both the legislature and the executive and can usually deliver policies once in office. When citizens vote for a president under the separation of powers, by contrast, they must expect that the new leader will get only some—or none—of her or his priorities past the separate legislature. From this point of view, parliamentarism delivers "more" representation in giving voters what they want, even if presidentialism offers more elections.

- *Disagreements lead to bargaining, not impasses.* Especially when coalition governments form in parliamentary systems, they enter difficult negotiations. Yet participants know that they must bargain out a workable coalition in order to form a government and remain in control of the executive. If they fail to work out a deal to form a government, or if a governing coalition later finds itself unable to agree, it typically falls into a vote of no confidence and the stalemate is broken by new elections. Presidential systems, by contrast, can be locked in impasse throughout an entire fixed term of office.

- *Parliamentarism adapts to changing societies.* In societies with few dividing lines (like ethnicity and religion) and in which large or majority parties may be most likely to arise, parliamentarism enters a majoritarian mode. A single party that can form a government gains a largely unchecked ability to pursue its agenda. In more fragmented societies, the system encourages power sharing. Many players must negotiate over the choice of a prime minister and other ministers, resulting in coalition governments in which powerful ministers come from multiple parties. Sometimes a country shifts from one mode to the other. Britain, for example, has usually had a very majoritarian two-party system. Falling support for its Conservative and Labour parties, however, produced no majority party in its 2010 election. To become prime minister, Conservative leader David Cameron had to bargain with the Liberal Democrats to form Britain's first coalition government since World War II, including making Liberal Democratic leader Nicholas Clegg the powerful deputy prime minister. Their cooperation over the next five-year term was awkward, but at least parliamentarism allows for a coalitional executive when no single-party majority emerges. The same thing happened again in 2017, when Theresa May's bungled snap election forced her into a coalition with the small Democratic Unionist Party of Northern Ireland. Presidentialism, by contrast, always assigns executive authority to one person. This can lead to resentment in more fragmented conditions in which no single individual winner actually represents a majority.

- *Adaptability has special appeal for divided societies.* Parliamentarism's coalitional possibilities make it especially suitable for divided societies. Given conflictual groups, no candidate might be able to win a presidency without causing resentment (or even rebellion) from rival groups. Multiparty parliamentarism may then be best to lure them into a negotiated, proportional politics. After the U.S.-led invasion of Iraq in 2003, for example, almost all experts recommended this format for a new government. With ethnically Arab Shi'a as 55 percent of the population, ethnically Arab Sunnis as 20 percent, ethnic Kurds around 15 percent, and other tiny minorities, many felt that only proportional-style institutions could endure. Multiple parties were sure to emerge, and a parliamentary executive would depend on the support of a diverse legislative coalition. This could lead to messy coalitional politics—and it certainly has in Iraq—but a prime minister would have no choice but to work through them. A presidency, though, would likely be won by a Shi'a who might be tempted to claim that he represented the majority and could ignore the other groups. Sunnis and other groups might have rejected such a system and taken up arms, or such a president might have become frustrated with minorities and slipped toward dictatorship.

Dominic Lipinski/PA Images/Alamy Stock Photo

British Prime Minister Theresa May greets the head of the small Democratic Unionist Party (DUP), Arlene Foster, after the 2017 election when May's Conservative Party fell short of winning a majority by itself. May had to accept several DUP demands to gain their support.

All of these benefits flow from a fusion of powers in which the executive reflects the composition of the legislative majority. Rather than presidentialism's stark executive-legislative separation with distinct mandates and fixed terms, it creates a single fused flow of representation into a government that can flexibly adapt to the presence or absence of a cohesive majority in the legislature. In fragmented places like Iraq, where people may rebel if they do not see their own group included in office, this flexibility may be crucial to win over skeptics to democracy.

On the other hand, the fusion of powers also carries the main cost of parliamentarism, as even its proponents will admit: the executive's interdependence with the legislature can bring instability. If there are too many parties, or if parties cannot maintain agreement on a coalition, votes of no confidence or dissolutions can become frequent. This has been the case in Iraq and seems likely to continue in its future—if it is lucky enough not to fall into civil war. Iraqi Prime Ministers in the past fifteen years have generally held onto power by alternating between negotiating fractious coalitions across rival parties and increasingly authoritarian moves to weaken their competitors. The selection of a pragmatic economist, Adil Abdul-Mahdi, as Prime Minister in October 2018 raised hopes for new attempts to work together. But similar hopes had arisen around Abdul-Mahdi's predecessor, Haider Al-Abadi, who had largely failed to overcome divisiveness—and by December 2019, Abdul-Mahdi's resignation opened a new period of even greater instability. The flexibility and proportionality of parliamentary institutions still offer the best chance to draw Iraqis into the game of democratic representation, but it cannot guarantee that they will achieve stable representative government.

When we set the arguments for parliamentarism and presidentialism next to each other, one thing becomes clear: neither model is the perfect way to organize representation. Neither one offers a simple, unambiguous way to allow the winners of elections to do what voters elected them to do. Instead, these models arose from complex historical debates—not just over representation itself, but also over concerns like stability, limits on government intervention, effective leadership, and so on—that produced complicated institutional arrangements, each with its own distinct strengths and weaknesses.

There may yet be significant improvements to be made to these models, and other options exist. The most widespread is the French **semipresidential** model with both a president *and* a prime minister. After years of parliamentary government that many French people perceived as fragmented and unstable, they created a directly elected president in 1962. Since they wanted the president to be a unifying and stabilizing leader "above the fray" of politics, they kept a prime minister to run daily government affairs. Thus the prime minister has two masters, being nominated by the president but requiring approval from a majority in the lower house. The resulting politics are complicated: usually the president dominates, with the prime minister as first lieutenant, but in cases of divided government—when the president and lower-house majority

semipresidentialism
A democratic institutional model with both a directly elected president and a prime minister who is responsible to a legislative majority.

come from different parties—the prime minister tends to take the lead. Almost thirty countries have imitated the semipresidential model, but interestingly, few are solidly democratic. In fact, among countries that score as full-fledged liberal democracies in all indexes, France remains the only semipresidential regime. That hints that this alternative may not be much of an improvement on the classic options.

Because the vast majority of democracies reflect one of the two classic models, the first step toward grasping representation today is to consolidate your understanding of the logics and trade-offs of each model. Like with voting rules or party systems, no arrangement of elected offices can escape having both advantages and disadvantages. The pursuit of meaningful representation is not about perfection, but about choosing your priorities (and your poison too). Figure 7-4 summarizes how different institutions in liberal democracies relate to contrasting majoritarian, proportional, and descriptive principles of representation.

Figure 7-4 Summarizing Different Forms of Democratic Representation

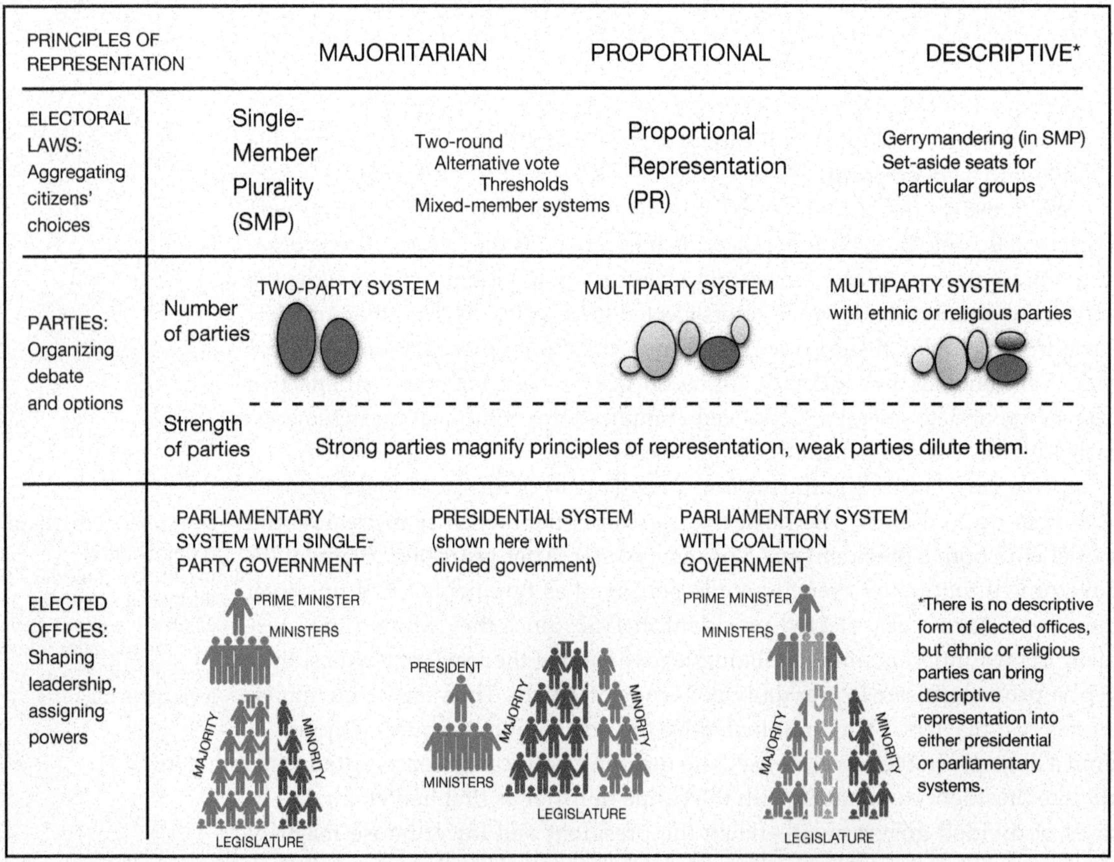
PRINCIPLES OF REPRESENTATION
MAJORITARIAN
PROPORTIONAL
DESCRIPTIVE*
ELECTORAL LAWS: Aggregating citizens' choices
Single-Member Plurality (SMP)
Two-round
Alternative vote
Thresholds
Mixed-member systems
Proportional Representation (PR)
Gerrymandering (in SMP)
Set-aside seats for particular groups
PARTIES: Organizing debate and options
Number of parties
TWO-PARTY SYSTEM
MULTIPARTY SYSTEM
MULTIPARTY SYSTEM with ethnic or religious parties
Strength of parties
Strong parties magnify principles of representation, weak parties dilute them.
ELECTED OFFICES: Shaping leadership, assigning powers
PARLIAMENTARY SYSTEM WITH SINGLE-PARTY GOVERNMENT
PRIME MINISTER
MINISTERS
MAJORITY
MINORITY
LEGISLATURE
PRESIDENTIAL SYSTEM (shown here with divided government)
PRESIDENT
MINISTERS
MAJORITY
MINORITY
LEGISLATURE
PARLIAMENTARY SYSTEM WITH COALITION GOVERNMENT
PRIME MINISTER
MINISTERS
MAJORITY
MINORITY
LEGISLATURE
*There is no descriptive form of elected offices, but ethnic or religious parties can bring descriptive representation into either presidential or parliamentary systems.

Political Ideologies and the Design of Representation

7.6 **Evaluate contrasting institutions of representation from conservative and modern-liberal points of view.**

We have now considered costs and benefits of many different designs of representation, but with a rather neutral emphasis on trade-offs. Political ideologies may provide us with a more aggressive takes on these important subjects. Can we say, for instance, that there is a *conservative* take on how best to design voting rules, party systems, and elected offices? Is there a *modern-liberal* recipe for representation? Does the Right or the Left prefer one way of setting up the competition for power in liberal democracy?

Since these questions concern the specific design of liberal democracy, it only makes sense to put these questions to the two ideologies within the liberal tradition: conservatives and modern liberals. Only the two camps within the tradition that created liberal democracy are strongly interested in the precise design of electoral representation within it. Fascists, devout socialists, and Islamists are skeptical about electoral representation overall. Environmentalism is sympathetic, but does not carry a distinctive message about how representation should be shaped.

Many conservatives and modern liberals will answer with a qualified "yes" to the preceding questions: they do have broad leanings about designing representation. Conservatives have a broad affinity with majoritarianism, in both voting rules and two-party systems, as well as with presidentialism. They place priorities on social stability and unified national strength, so they tend to appreciate the way SMP voting rules and a two-party system assign a clear mandate to representatives, even if it comes at some cost in the diversity of voices. Conservatives also tend to be skeptical of active efforts to boost minorities of whatever sort, fearing that maneuvers to render representation more proportional or descriptive will just aggravate divides in society.

With respect to elected offices, today's conservatives are the most direct inheritors to classical liberalism, and the American founders who invented presidentialism were classical liberals. It is no accident that presidentialism makes decisive government action difficult and tends toward impasse; these classical liberals saw limiting abusive government as their main goal, and created the separation of powers as a tool to that end. As Thomas Jefferson put it, "The government governs best that governs least." The twenty-first-century politicians who are most likely to see checked-and-balanced channels of representation as desirable are conservatives who have stuck most closely to Jefferson's philosophy of limited government.

Modern liberals, meanwhile, are at least somewhat more likely to admire PR voting rules, multiparty systems, provisions for descriptive representation, and parliamentarism. They tend to believe that government must be designed to encourage, not just permit, the participation of historically disadvantaged groups and minorities. Indeed, some of the key social, economic, and political problems they perceive concern the exclusion of women, minorities, or other sorts of disempowered voices. PR rules and multiparty systems tend to facilitate the mobilization of such groups. Steps in descriptive representation—like gender quotas or "majority-minority" districting—have usually been instigated by the Left. Their ideal for elected offices is to bring diverse voices together in support of an active government that confronts society's problems. Thus modern liberals tend to prefer a parliamentary system in which representative government is not hamstrung by checks and balances. Woodrow Wilson saw the separation of powers as a "mistake" for precisely this reason: as an architect of modern liberalism, Wilson thought the U.S. model impeded the kind of active government he thought could improve the lives of most citizens.

The answers to our questions are only a qualified "yes," though, because conservatives and liberals in different countries often disagree about which representative institutions best fit their political ideology. One reason is that people tend to favor the models of representation that they have known over the long term. People become familiar with ways of organizing representation in their country—like whether they grow up with baseball or soccer—and politicians of both right and left tend to favor whatever institutions they know best. Americans of either political party are thus much more likely to favor majoritarianism than Swedish or Dutch people who are used to a game along proportional lines. Another reason is that politicians often support whatever arrangement of representation might advantage their cause in the short term. Smaller parties, whether liberal or conservative, are more likely to favor PR rules that help small parties. Big parties do the reverse: modern liberals in the Democratic Party, for example, enjoy their strongly represented position in American democracy, and often defend the U.S. two-party system and SMP voting rules just as much as Republicans. Over time and across countries, due to long-term national traditions and complex calculations of short-term political advantage, we can find politicians on right and left criticizing and praising many different institutions of representation.

Explaining Cases: Understanding the Whys of Iraqi Sunnis and Representation

7.7   Identify multiple plausible explanations for Iraqi Sunnis' preference for proportional representation.

We now have some key tools for critical thinking about representation: a sense of different games of representation that democracies play, and of various arguments for and against the options. To grasp what these alternatives mean to us, though, we must also be able to imagine *why* people are represented in certain ways. Explanations make a difference in which options we consider relevant. If we argue that majoritarian-style representation arises and endures only under certain conditions, for example, it may be pointless to endorse it where and when conditions are different.

To think about why people might call for certain kinds of representation, consider one piece of the game of representation in Iraq. Why has the Sunni Muslim minority been so opposed to majoritarian representation in their new democracy, calling instead for PR voting rules, multiple parties, and coalitional parliamentarism? African Americans or other minorities in the United States rarely seem to reject majoritarianism so strongly. What explains the Sunnis' different demands? Our three classic explanatory approaches suggest different answers.

The Rational-Material Story

If we see the politics of representation flowing from people's rational reactions to the material landscape around them, we will explain Sunni attitudes as a response to raw threats and competition for material resources. Their history of conflict with the Shi'a majority makes it rational to perceive a threat of domination. Given an economy centered on oil, and oil reserves mostly in Shi'a regions, Sunnis have additional reasons to fear that a majority-run Iraq might cut them out of sharing oil proceeds. For both reasons, Sunnis insist more on proportional representation and other nonmajoritarian rules than minorities in less threatened positions elsewhere.

The Institutional Story

In an institutional approach, the politics of representation mainly reflect the ways in which existing institutions protect and present people's interests. The deepest problem for Sunnis lies in the weak infrastructure within the Iraqi institutions established to protect rights and the rule of law. If Iraqi police, courts, and the political process were better developed, Sunnis would not feel so threatened. Although they might still lean toward proportional representation to express their distinct minority identity, having better-protected rights might help Sunnis see the advantage of having strong leadership to confront Iraq's challenges and might make them willing to take more steps toward majoritarianism.

The Ideational Story

From an ideational point of view, representation is most profoundly about identity and beliefs. People who identify as a group tend to be comfortable with majoritarianism. However, the more diversity that exists in a society—and the more that these diverse identities have been defined in antagonistic ways through conflict among groups—the more minority groups will reject majoritarianism. Whether or not Shi'a genuinely threaten the Sunni, their beliefs clash and the Sunnis feel separate. Even if Sunnis received generous assurances on security, oil, and the protection of rights, they might still insist on proportional representation because they see themselves as fundamentally distinct from other Iraqis.

Once we can imagine alternative explanations, we begin to wonder which best fits this case. And then we can look for evidence with the two main research strategies of political scientists per the following discussion.

RESEARCH ON WITHIN-CASE PROCESSES.   The most direct strategy to assess the plausibility of these explanations is to look carefully at how Iraqi Sunnis have acted and talked about representation. Table 7-3 lays out the process expectations of our theoretical explanations in more detail.

To begin to gather evidence for or against these views, find a news article about Sunni-Iraqi views on Iraqi institutions from a respectable newspaper, magazine, or website. Then look for hints in the article that support or contradict these explanatory alternatives.

Table 7-3 Exploring Within-Case Evidence for Explanations of Iraqi Conflicts over Representation

	Rational-Material Explanation	Institutional Explanation	Ideational Explanation
How strongly and consistently have Iraqi Sunnis felt threatened by the Shi'a majority?	A strong perception of threat for a long time. A widely perceived zero-sum game between Sunni and Shi'a meant that majoritarianism was not an option.	A moderate sense of threat, at least when efforts at democracy began. If stronger rule of law and security could have been established, majoritarianism might have been an option.	The issue is not so much threat as perception of difference. Even if Shi'a are not terribly threatening, Sunni want descriptive representation in the Iraqi government.
Who has been most opposed to majoritarianism and insistent on proportionality?	Most Sunnis as a block.	Sunnis in areas with worst problems of crime and corruption, or nearest Shi'a-dominated areas; otherwise not so concerned.	Most Sunnis, and especially those in their own communities far away from Shi'a areas.
What has most Sunni criticism of the Shi'a majority looked like?	Complaints mainly about Shi'a control of resources and fear of domination.	Complaints mainly about poor governance, corruption, and insufficient protections for a diverse population.	Rejection of collective identity and insistence that Iraq is populated by distinct groups.
Best evidence to support each explanation	We see that most Shi'a and Sunni see each other as threatening, even if they are not devoutly religious themselves.	We find places where relatively good local governance and security have created good Shi'a/Sunni relations.	We find that even in spots where local governance is better and threats appear modest, the groups remain starkly separate.

RESEARCH ON CROSS-CASE PATTERNS. We can also look for comparable cases to see how much each explanation is supported by patterns in the politics of representation. We might look for other societies that have tried majoritarian voting rules, for example. Did those who did so successfully, without major conflict have less threatening internal strife and resource competition than Iraq? Did they quickly fashion protective institutions (or fall into chaos if they failed to do so)? Were their competing ideologies or identities less divisive? Your instructor may be able to provide you data to explore these possible relationships.

Conclusion: Why It Matters for You to Understand Alternatives in Representation

Although this chapter compared the competitive selection of representation in liberal democracies to sports, representation is not really a game. To the contrary, it is one of the most serious political processes imaginable. Elections constitute our key mechanism for assigning political power. Only if citizens are meaningfully represented through those processes can liberal democracy claim superiority over other kinds of government.

The metaphor of sports like baseball or soccer helps to emphasize, though, that different liberal democracies have designed representative institutions whose rules and dynamics are just as varied as the different games people play around the world. Awareness that other countries organize representation differently may be especially important for Americans, too, because our polity features the less common option in every feature of its game. The U.S. choices of SMP rules, a two-party system, weak parties, and presidentialism are all somewhat unusual among liberal democracies. Their combination is unique: no other country has this configuration of representation. It is important to understand our special format for representation both to engage with our own system and to grasp politics elsewhere. When we see Congress and the president locked in impasses that seem rare in other countries, we must recognize this as a consequence of a presidential system. When we complain of "two-party tyranny" and covet wider choices in other polities, we must acknowledge that our situation reflects the trade-offs around SMP rules that encourage the two-party system. When we see Sunnis in Iraq rejecting majoritarian rules like those that we use, we must allow that they are not necessarily expressing hostility to democratic values in general. Rather, the Sunnis may be arguing that in their context, democratic representation has a different meaning that calls for different institutions.

Review of Learning Objectives

7.1 Explain and contrast the logic of majoritarian, proportional, and descriptive representation.

Several different views debate the essence of electoral representation. Majoritarian principles connect representation to the most widely held views in a population. Proportional principles recognize multiple voices according to their share of the population. Descriptive principles connect representation to types of people according to their share of the population, suggesting that government should be a mirror image of social diversity.

7.2 Identify the most common systems of voting rules and how they relate to different principles of representation.

Voting rules define how average citizens participate most directly in the "game" of representation and shape how their views are expressed. Single-member plurality (SMP) rules assign seats to the first-place candidate in a district. They are very majoritarian in spirit and favor large political parties. Proportional representation (PR) rules assign seats to parties according to their share of votes. They produce proportional and sometimes descriptive representation. Other rules, such as a two-round system, alternative vote, or mixed-member systems, modify or mix these models and principles.

7.3 Describe the roles parties play in representation and explain variation in their number and strength across countries.

Political parties play several essential roles as intermediaries in representation: aggregating interests, packaging voters' options, mobilizing citizens and recruiting leadership candidates, and coordinating politicians' action once elected. The number of parties in a country varies due both to its voting rules and also to the issues and identities that unify or fragment social groups. Party strength is also affected by voting rules (with stronger parties favored by PR rules), as well as by practices of candidate selection and campaign finance.

7.4 Describe the core features of presidential government and evaluate its advantages and disadvantages.

The configuration of elected offices in presidentialism is based around a separation of powers between a directly elected president and a legislature. This model aims for limited, stable, predictable government, but is susceptible to impasses among its separate branches.

7.5 Describe the core features of parliamentary government and evaluate its advantages and disadvantages.

The configuration of elected offices in parliamentarism is based around a fusion of powers in which a legislative majority selects a prime minister to form the executive. This model makes the government responsive to the distribution of seats in the legislature. It operates in a majoritarian mode if one party holds a legislative majority but a proportional mode if many parties form a coalitional majority. It is simple and flexible, but can suffer from fragmentation and instability.

7.6 Evaluate contrasting institutions of representation from conservative and modern-liberal points of view.

From a conservative point of view, majoritarian voting rules and fewer parties are usually desirable because they favor stability, the construction of unity, and are likely to uphold traditionally dominant social views. Presidentialism, too, tends to appeal to conservatives because it is designed to limit government action with checks and balances. Modern liberals tend to prefer proportional voting rules and more parties for favoring greater diversity and more openings for minority voices. They also tend to admire the more adaptable and less constrained model of parliamentarism, which can allow strong government action when a majority favors it and can respect diversity and compromise in a more fragmented polity.

7.7 Identify multiple plausible explanations for Iraqi Sunnis' preference for proportional representation.

To review for this objective, brainstorm rational-material, institutional, and ideational explanations of Sunnis' views on Iraqi representation without looking at Section 7.7. Start by asking yourself the following questions:

- In what kind of material conditions—such as a certain distribution of resources, or a context of threats—would we expect members of a minority group to be rationally concerned about majoritarian rules?
- How might the presence or lack of certain institutions in a country make majoritarian rules more or less threatening? For example, are there institutions (other than electoral laws themselves) that might help protect a minority if they were robust (and the absence of which might leave the minority feeling vulnerable)?
- Which aspects of cultural identity or beliefs might encourage a sense of difference and danger for Iraqi Sunnis in their relationship to the majority?

After brainstorming your answers to these questions, return to Section 7.7 to see how well you have imagined plausible alternatives to explain this case.

Great Sources to Find Out More

Anne Philips, *The Politics of Presence* (New York: Oxford University Press, 1995). A powerful argument that descriptive representation should be taken seriously.

Arend Lijphart, ed., *Parliamentary Versus Presidential Government* (New York: Oxford University Press, 1992). A marvelous collection of key documents and points of view on the merits of these systems.

Arend Lijphart, *Patterns of Democracy* (New Haven, CT: Yale University Press, 1999). A survey of democracies and an argument for proportional, parliamentary "consensus democracy" over majoritarian principles.

Ben Reilly, "Electoral Systems for Divided Societies," *Journal of Democracy*, 13(2) (April 2002), 156–170. A look at how conflict-ridden societies have tried innovative voting rules to create more unity.

Bruce Ackerman, *The Failure of the Founding Fathers: Jefferson, Marshall, and Rise of Presidential Democracy* (Cambridge, MA: Harvard University Press, 2005). A critique of certain features of presidentialism in the U.S. context.

David Farrell, *Electoral Systems: A Comparative Introduction* (Basingstoke, UK: Palgrave, 2001). A comprehensive discussion of voting rules around the world.

David Mayhew, *Partisan Balance: Why Political Parties Don't Kill the U.S. Constitutional System* (Princeton, NJ: Princeton University Press, 2011). One of the most prominent scholars of U.S. politics argues that parties help the divided institutions of government to work.

Giovanni Sartori, *Parties and Party Systems* (New York: Cambridge University Press, 1976). A clear presentation of variations in parties and party systems across countries.

Hannah Pitkin, *The Concept of Representation* (Berkeley: University of California, 1972). The single most famous discussion of different basic views of representation.

Jane Mansbridge, "Rethinking Representation," *American Political Science Review*, 97(4) (2003), 515–528. A wide-ranging discussion of new ways to conceive of representation and how to evaluate them in the real world.

Juan Linz and Arturo Valenzuela, eds., *The Failure of Presidential Democracy*, 2 vols. (Baltimore: Johns Hopkins University Press, 1994). A collection of essays arguing for parliamentarism, especially with reference to Latin America.

Kenneth Benoit, "Electoral Laws as Political Consequences: Explaining the Origins and Change of Electoral Institutions," *Annual Review of Political Science*, 10 (2007), 363–390. A condensed overview of how political scientists have explained countries' choices for different electoral laws.

Mickey Edwards, *Reclaiming Conservatism: How a Great American Political Movement Got Lost—and How It Can Find Its Way Back* (New York: Oxford University Press, 2008). A thoughtful defense of the original ideas of the U.S. presidential system as the core of modern conservatism.

Robert Dahl, *How Democratic Is the U.S. Constitution?* 2nd ed. (New Haven, CT: Yale University Press, 2003). A penetrating discussion of the good and bad aspects of the rules of American democracy.

Robert Michels, *Political Parties* (Piscataway, NJ: Transaction, 1999 [1915]). A classic discussion of the reasons why political parties arise, but fail to represent adequately.

Sanford Levinson, *Our Undemocratic Constitution: Where the Constitution Goes Wrong (And How We the People Can Correct It)* (New York: Oxford University Press, 2008). This book by a liberal law professor focuses on arguments to lessen the separation of powers in U.S. institutions—making them somewhat more like parliamentary ones.

Seymour Martin Lipset and Stein Rokkan, *Party Systems and Voter Alignments: Cross-National Perspectives* (Toronto: Free Press, 1967). This famous discussion of how countries develop different party systems traces back to their historical patterns and the timing of major conflicts in each society.

Simon Hix, Ron Johnston, and Iain McClean, *Choosing an Electoral System* (London: British Academy Policy Center, 2010). Available at http://www.britac.ac.uk/policy/choosing-electoral-system.cfm. A user-friendly guide to different voting rules.

Steven Calabresi, "The Virtues of Presidential Government: Why Professor Ackerman Is Wrong to Prefer the German to the U.S. Constitution," *Constitutional Commentary*, 51 (Spring 2001), 51–104. A wide-ranging and readable reply to Bruce Ackerman.

Develop Your Thinking

Use these questions as discussion or short writing exercises to think more deeply about some of the key themes of the chapter.

1. Which seems more meaningfully "democratic" to you: majoritarian or proportional representation?

2. Is gerrymandering districts along racial lines a good thing or a bad thing?

3. Would you like to have more viable political parties in American politics?

4. Are the "separation of powers" and "checks and balances" fundamentally good ideas or fundamentally bad ones?

5. Is the simplicity of parliamentary representation—one main election to choose the legislative majority and the executive—a good thing or a bad thing?

6. Do you think it is more important to prevent government from doing bad things or to empower government to achieve collective goals?

7. Is your gut feeling that Iraqi democracy was never going to win over its Sunni minority—so it was bound to fail—or that more proportional and inclusive government could have succeeded?

8. Do you feel well represented in American politics? Explain why or why not.

Keywords

alternative vote (AV)   209
bicameral/unicameral   223
checks and balances   222
closed party primaries   215
coalition government   227
constituency   208
descriptive representation   203
dissolution   228
divided government   224
Duverger's law   216
executives   222

fusion of powers   226
gender quotas   210
gerrymandering   211
legislators   222
majoritarian representation   203
mixed-member systems   210
overrepresentation   206
party base   215
plurality   203
pork-barrel politics   208
proportional representation   203

proportional representation (PR) voting rules   207
semipresidentialism   233
separation of powers   222
single-member plurality (SMP)   205
split-ticket voting   225
threshold rule   209
two-round system   209
vote of no confidence   228

Chapter 8
Inside Liberal Democracy II: Power and Policymaking

Michael Reynolds/Pool/CNP/Dpa picture alliance/Alamy Stock Photo

A frustrated-looking President Donald Trump meets with House Speaker Nancy Pelosi and her Democratic Party colleague, Senate Minority leader Chuck Schumer. Though the U.S. president is often described as "the most powerful person in the world," his or her position is not actually as powerful as the executive in many other democracies. The president's ability to make policy is hemmed in by one of the world's most powerful legislatures (the U.S. Congress), and also by one of the world's most powerful courts (the U.S. Supreme Court).

 Learning Objectives

8.1 Identify the typical place of executives and legislators in policymaking processes and describe factors that enhance or decrease legislators' influence.

8.2 Identify the principles of bureaucratic organization and describe several reasons why bureaucrats' policymaking influence varies across liberal democracies.

8.3 Identify the principles of common- and code-law legal systems, American and European models of judicial review, and how they relate to judicial influence.

8.4   Evaluate competing American arguments for and against bureaucratic and judicial authority.

8.5   Identify multiple explanations for the weakness of the U.S. federal bureaucracy in policymaking.

Who Holds Policymaking Power?

Once the dust settles after elections and representatives take office, the business of liberal-democratic government begins. But who then calls the shots? Is it presidents and prime ministers? Or might these executives be more like figureheads, with real power held by the legislators who haggle out laws? Perhaps there is a balance of power between executives and legislators?

Or maybe most power lies elsewhere. In Japan, considerable influence is held by unelected administrators, or "bureaucrats," who work in the executive ministries. Though in principle they are just support staff for politicians, in practice they strongly influence policy choices. Likewise, in the United States, it is difficult to overlook another kind of unelected official. Federal judges are appointed for life and regularly alter policies by interpreting or striking down laws. At the highest level, the nine justices of the U.S. Supreme Court arguably shape policy as much as any politician.

Tracing policymaking power in any liberal democracy raises thorny questions about the allocation of authority among politicians, bureaucrats, and judges. In a simple sense, bureaucratic or judicial power is flatly undemocratic. Yet liberal-democratic government is not only about representation. It prioritizes rights and rule of law, creating the basis for judges' influence. At the same time it depends on bureaucratic policy experts too. To make and implement effective policies, politicians need staff with technical expertise: professional soldiers to advise and enact defense policy, economists at the Treasury, transport experts to manage public infrastructure, and so on. No democratic government can work without unelected officials.

Liberal democracies have chosen many different ways to distribute power in policymaking, and by understanding these alternatives we empower ourselves to think critically about the machinery of government. This chapter surveys executive, legislative, bureaucratic, and judicial power, with special attention to the *unelected* officials whose influence seems—at first glance—to conflict with the democratic principles of representation. ■

Executives and Legislators in Policymaking

8.1   Identify the typical place of executives and legislators in policymaking processes and describe factors that enhance or decrease legislators' influence.

Policymaking is the flip side of representation. Citizens make demands to protect the country from external threats, maintain internal order, build infrastructure, provide schools, verify the safety of water and food supplies, and so on, and governments make **policies** to respond. Policies are the series of

policies
Series of decisions that establish goals and patterns of government action in an issue area.

decisions that establish goals and patterns of government action in a certain issue area. They may include passage of new laws, adoption of finer-grained regulations within the framework of laws, and direct government actions. For example, in 2019, the leader of the Spanish Socialist party, Pedro Sanchez, won another term as Prime Minister partly with promises of a new environmental policy. It included new laws limiting the production of greenhouse gases, regulatory changes on renewable energies, and negotiations to shut down coal production while funding worker-retraining programs in coal-producing regions.

Our look at policymaking begins with the elected officials who hold the main authority in liberal democracies. At a broad level, "executive" and "legislator" are the same kinds of categories across presidential and parliamentary systems, creating basic patterns in how these kinds of politicians influence policy. Within these similarities, the two systems structure their executive-legislative relations differently, though not in the way one might expect: parliamentary regimes tend to have weaker parliaments and stronger executives. Furthermore, a closer look brings more surprises. Some of the most important factors affecting the executive-legislative balance of power arise in lower-level rules of agenda setting, procedure, and resources inside legislatures themselves.

The Classic Executive-Legislative Division of Labor

Specific powers vary hugely across such executives as the Brazilian president, the Japanese prime minister, or the German chancellor. These powers vary even more across members of legislatures, like the French National Assembly, the Italian Chamber of Deputies, or the U.S. Senate. Yet we still recognize the former as "executives" and the latter as "legislators" because these offices exhibit similar formal roles in policymaking.

Executive presidents or prime ministers, together with the secretaries or ministers appointed to their cabinets, typically play a leading part at the beginning and the end of policymaking (see Figure 8-1). Policymaking begins with a formulation stage, in which officials identify goals or problems and propose new laws, regulations, or action. This is a classic function of executive leadership: presidents, prime ministers, and their cabinets attempt to set the broad agenda with policy proposals. Policymaking ends with the implementation stage, in which officials put the policy into practice. This is the other classic executive function, "executing" adopted policies by directing staff and resources to implement them.

The classic role of legislators arises in the middle stage. Not all policymaking passes through this stage: there are many direct actions and specific regulations for which executives do not need legislative approval. But for anything that changes laws or requires a new budget—and all major policies have these components—executives must typically submit proposals to the legislature. Before budgets and

Figure 8-1 Classic Policymaking Roles of Elected Representatives

In principle, policy processes begin when executives formulate proposals. Legislators then amend, reject, or approve them, and return them to the executive for implementation.

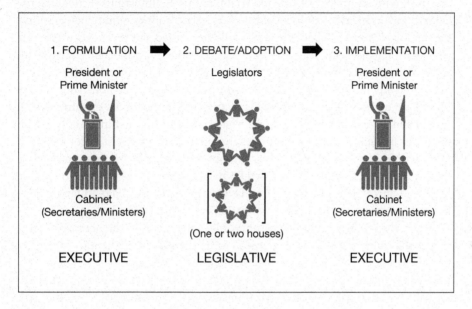

proposals for laws (known as bills) come before the legislature, they must pass through scrutiny and debate, and are amended, adopted, or rejected. Those bills that are approved then are passed back to the executive for implementation.

At this broad level, we might expect executives and legislators to have fairly even influence over policy. The classic executive role creates and manages policy in a more direct way than do legislators, but the need for legislators' approval presumably forces executives to respect their wishes. When we move from these abstract roles to concrete examples, though, we rarely find equal partnerships. In most liberal democracies, the executive dominates policymaking. Only in a few democratic systems is the legislature a major site of policymaking action.

Why Parliamentarism Doesn't Mean Policymaking Parliaments

In which countries would we expect legislatures, or parliaments, to play an active role in policymaking? Parliamentary systems, we might suspect, will have powerful parliaments. Unlike presidents, prime ministers depend directly on support in the legislature. It seems like prime ministers have little choice but to keep legislators happy, and that should give the average legislator influence over policy. Yet this turns out to be mostly wrong. Most parliaments in parliamentary regimes have little policymaking power. Some notably powerful legislatures—like the U.S. Congress—operate in presidential systems.

How might the threat of a "vote of no confidence"—when a legislative majority withdraws support and forces a prime minister to resign—fail to empower legislators? The reason is simple: it is very hard to use. It is like "going nuclear" in a war, with so many risks for its wielders that it almost never makes sense. When a government loses a confidence vote, most regimes require new elections for the lower house. Rebel legislators who just voted out their executive must also run for reelection. That is a huge disincentive: no politician wants to run again for reelection unnecessarily. Moreover, the rebels must seek reelection after having greatly annoyed the leader of their own party or coalition. They may be kicked out of their party or deprived of campaign funds for the ensuing vote. In proportional representation electoral systems, party leadership usually shapes the party list, and can often simply exclude rebels from a shot at reelection. In other words, a no-confidence vote may not only force legislators into an election, it may cost them their careers. Ultimately, such moves are extremely rare. In Britain, three no-confidence votes have succeeded since 1900. In Japan, it has happened four times since democratization after World War II.

With the nuclear option often unusable, leverage in parliamentarism tends to run the other way—from executives to legislators. Parliamentary majorities and their executive leaders are elected as a team in a single election, and the leaders dominate the team. This is especially true in countries with single-party majorities and strong party organizations, where prime ministers use the party to whip the majority into line. Average members of the legislature without a leadership position, known as **backbenchers**, are enticed to cooperate with promises of future party leadership roles or help in the next election; threats of marginalization from party jobs and funds serve the same purpose. A prime minister with a single-party majority thus often controls the legislature tightly, securing passage of most proposals with little amendment. In Britain, where such majorities have been the norm until recently, little policymaking takes place in the House of Commons. It is largely a debating club that focuses on political theater for the media, not policy details. Japan's House of Representatives has long suffered from similarly severe executive dominance. A single party, the Liberal Democratic Party (LDP), won majorities for over fifty years after 1955. Policymaking moved almost entirely out of the formal legislature, to the point that it was often ridiculed as irrelevant. Less complete LDP dominance more recently has led to more significant bargaining over policies in the House, but it remains a fairly weak body.

Parliamentary legislatures take on more importance when prime ministers face small majorities, difficult coalitions, or weak parties. If the majority has only a few seats more than its opponents, rebels can more easily threaten to block votes or even win a no-confidence vote, and can thus make demands. For example, in May 2015, the Conservative Party of British prime minister David Cameron won a slim single-party majority of 331 out of 650 seats. A majority requires 326 votes, creating a situation of running challenges because only five defections could unseat his government. On the other hand, this was an improvement over the situation

backbenchers

"Normal" legislators who hold no leadership position in their government or party.

Cameron faced as prime minister from 2010 to 2015, when he had no single-party majority and had to operate in coalition with the Liberal Democrats. Leaders of multiparty coalitions face a constant need for support from legislators outside their own party, and this dependence typically shifts some policymaking from the executive into bargaining in and around the legislature. Weak party organizations, too, can limit the executive's ability to advance a policy agenda. An extreme case was Italy before 1988, when parliamentary votes were by secret ballot. Since party leaders could not know how legislators voted, they could not exert discipline. This is one reason why the Italian Chamber of Deputies became one of the most powerful parliamentary system legislatures. It constantly blocked prime ministers' agendas and forced their resignations, toppling governments year after year.

Yet even Italy's legislature has never been as central a site for policymaking as legislatures in some presidential systems, especially the U.S. Congress. At first glance, this is surprising: presidential regimes offer legislatures no option to unseat the executive, and also subject legislation to executive **veto** (when the president refuses to sign a bill the legislature has passed). But despite these constraints, presidentialism gives legislators something that lets them resist executives better than their parliamentary peers: autonomy. Presidential system legislators have their own separate electoral bases, encouraging them to act as a check on the executive, not a team that it leads. In the United States, even representatives and senators from the same party as the president tend to defend congressional autonomy and bargaining power. For example, though Republicans controlled the presidency, House, and Senate from 2016 to 2018, and Republicans in Congress mostly supported President Donald Trump's desires to change health-care laws and cut taxes, both priorities ran into major challenges from Republican congresspeople. The tax cuts barely passed, and health care legislation failed entirely. The president could not take the support of his own party's legislators for granted.

At a broad level, then, the separation of powers in presidentialism better supports legislators' influence than does parliamentarism. Usually, prime ministers can easily discipline party members in the fusion of powers into a docile team. Within this broad generalization, however, some parliamentary legislatures still hold more power, like Italy's. Some presidential legislatures are largely dominated by the executive, like Brazil's. Reasons for these exceptions, plus additional factors for the weakness of many parliamentary legislatures and the strength of the U.S. Congress, are partly hidden in the internal rules of legislatures themselves.

veto
The ability to block a law or decision, like a president's refusal to sign a bill passed by the legislature in a presidential system.

The Impact of Legislative Rules and Resources

A legislator's ability to stand up to the executive, altering the executive's proposals or advancing his or her own initiatives, turns heavily on three aspects of procedure inside legislatures. If legislative leaders control the legislature's agenda, if the legislature has strong internal committees, and if individual legislators hold substantial resources in staff and budgets, then legislators can make policy. Legislatures without one of these features—and especially, as in Britain or France, those with none of them—tend to become "talk shops" for speech making. In such cases, policymaking shifts toward executive dominance.

agenda control
In legislatures, the power to schedule what will be debated or voted on and when.

The most obvious internal condition for legislative influence is **agenda control**, or rules for scheduling the legislature's work. In some countries, leaders in the legislature determine what bills the legislature will debate or vote on and when. In others, the executive sets the legislative agenda. In countries in the latter category, including Britain or France, the executive effectively convenes legislators to pass its priorities. Backbenchers' ideas have little chance of receiving attention: in Britain they receive ten-minute slots on ten Fridays a year to present their own bills, which rarely go anywhere. The power relationship shifts in countries where legislative leaders control their agenda, which includes most presidential regimes like the United States, plus some parliamentary ones like the Netherlands or Italy. The president or prime minister may want to push a proposal, but if legislative leaders do not, it goes nowhere. In these systems, backbenchers may also gain openings to initiate substantial legislation. Germany, Spain, Sweden, and a few other parliamentary regimes fall between these extremes, with the agenda negotiated between executive and legislative leaders. A presidential system that is in the middle is Brazil: its Congress has agenda control in theory, but in practice specific rules allow the president to force congressional votes. It is difficult to exaggerate the effects of agenda control: control of *when* things are decided hugely influences *what* is decided. Those with agenda control can simply avoid issues or decisions they dislike, or they can choose timing to address their priorities and pressure others to comply.[1]

plenary
A full meeting of an assembly.

Just as important for legislative influence is committee structure. All modern legislatures have committees on specific issues, like Agriculture, Foreign Affairs, and so on. If these committees are weak and most business takes place in the **plenary**, or meetings of the whole assembly, the legislature weakens overall. If these committees hold strong powers, like the ability to amend or reject bills before they ever reach the plenary, legislative influence increases. Why? In plenary voting, all legislators are interchangeable: if one member rejects an executive's proposal, any other legislator's vote can replace it. This gives executives many options to rally support. The more that committees make decisions, however, the more their members become policy gatekeepers. Small groups of legislators and even individual chairpersons gain vetoes over policy areas. Thus weak legislatures like the House of Commons almost invariably have weak committees: Britain's cannot amend or reject bills and so have very little influence. Strong legislatures like the two U.S. houses generally have powerful committees. Famous committee chairmen in U.S. congressional history have ruled policy areas as if they were fiefs, defying presidents and everyone else. Republican Jesse Helms of North Carolina (1921–2008), for example, became known as "Senator No" during his thirty years in office. He used chairmanships of the Senate's Agriculture and Foreign Relations committees to single-handedly extract all sorts of concessions, like blocking payment of U.S. dues to the United Nations to demand changes he wanted in American foreign policy.

In a simple way, lastly, concrete resources inside legislatures affect the executive-legislative balance. Making policy requires staff, offices, and budgets to gather and analyze information. Without such resources, a single legislator cannot develop an informed opinion on one piece of complex legislation, let alone make specific recommendations across the many bills that pass through a typical legislature. Legislators have little ability to question what the executive proposes without aides to help study issues and to dialogue with constituents, interest groups, and other politicians. Likewise, legislators require a budget to fund fact-finding trips, commission surveys, or consult with independent experts so they can make informed decisions. A glance at staff support for a member of the Japanese House of Representatives, French National Assembly, or British House of Commons shows just this sort of situation (see Table 8-1). Typical members have a small office with a few helpers.

U.S. legislators' resources put them in another category. A typical U.S. representative has *ten times* as much support as members of these other legislatures. U.S. senators have even larger entourages. In addition to their own budgets, U.S. congresspeople also draw even more resources from committees that can have dozens of staff and annual budgets that run as high as $20 million. Committees in Britain or France, by contrast, often have a single staff member. When the U.S. president attempts to push legislation through Congress, he thus faces hundreds of richly staffed policy analysis teams with their own well-developed, detailed policy positions. When the British prime minister or French president does the same, they face literally no one with significant resources.

Despite similar formal roles of executives and legislators across democracies, then, their actual jobs differ in radical ways. Executives formulate and implement policy, and legislators approve it, but the latter influence policy only where autonomy, agenda control, committees, and resources let them develop

Table 8-1 Staff Support in Selected Legislatures

Country	Legislature	Budget for Staff in U.S. Dollars*	Number of Staff per Typical Member of Legislature
Japan	House of Representatives	$136,625	2–3
France	National Assembly	$92,783	2–4
Britain	House of Commons	$168,107	1–2
United States	House of Representatives	$1.5 million	14
	Senate	$3.46 million	34

*Approximate average budget; exchange rate controlled for purchasing power parity (PPP).

SOURCES: Philip Brasor, "Spare a Thought for the Secretaries," *Japan Times*, July 29, 2017; "Combien gagnent les agents de l'Assemblée nationale?" *Europe1.fr*, June 7, 2018; "Annual Report and Accounts, 2017–18," House of Commons document HC 1381, July 23, 2018; Ida Brudnick, "Congressional Salaries and Allowances," Congressional Research Service brief, April 11, 2018. PPP calculations based on OECD data.

distinct policy views. It may be tempting to conclude that such influence is obviously good. After all, "executive dominance" sounds ominous in a democratic context. Before we celebrate the powerful U.S. Congress and deplore the weak British Commons or French Assembly, though, we should note that citizens often have very low opinions of politicians in legislatures. In a December 2018 poll, Americans ranked members of Congress as the least trustworthy profession. (To be fair, they were tied with car salesmen.)[2] A 2016 survey that asked people in thirty-two European countries to rate their "trust in politicians" on a ten-point scale found twenty-two countries with average scores below four.[3] Those kinds of numbers make it reasonable to ask whether it is such a bad idea to shift policymaking away from legislatures full of elected politicians.

There is, after all, an alternative. In democracies where legislatures are weak, policy is made mainly in the executive departments or ministries. Besides empowering elected executives, this option shifts policymaking power to another kind of player entirely: bureaucrats.

Unelected Policy Experts: The Power of Bureaucrats

8.2   Identify the principles of bureaucratic organization and describe several reasons why bureaucrats' policymaking influence varies across liberal democracies.

"Darn bureaucracy!" is something we might say after filling out forms and standing in lines at the Department of Motor Vehicles. Such grumbling captures the negative everyday meaning of "bureaucracy": excessive rules that make it hard to get anything done.

bureaucracy
A hierarchical organization of salaried professionals who apply systematic rules to accomplish tasks.

For political scientists, though, it means something different. **Bureaucracy** is a certain kind of organization—roughly speaking, a nonpolitical body of professional experts—that executives employ to help formulate and implement policies. All democratic governments assign authority to such organizations because they need technical expertise to make and implement policy effectively. On occasion, democracies also turn policymaking over to bureaucracies to shield it from too much meddling by politicians.

Yet if all liberal democracies use bureaucracies for these reasons, some assign them more policymaking power than others. In Japan or France, bureaucrats often play a leading role. The United States falls near the other end of the spectrum. Its career bureaucrats typically have much less influence.

We have already seen part of the reason why this is so. The United States has an unusually powerful, resource-rich legislature in which policy is made. In other words, the United States assigns less power to bureaucrats than many other democracies because it assigns more power to another little-loved group: darn politicians! So while Japanese or French people often gripe about powerful bureaucrats, Americans often complain that their system is too deeply gripped by partisan politics. These alternative ways of relating elected representatives and bureaucratic experts give rise to some important trade-offs.

The Bureaucratic Model

To understand bureaucrats, we must start with the principles of bureaucracy. It is a very specific kind of organization, but also extremely widespread. Indeed, bureaucracy is such a pervasive aspect of modern life—not just in governments, but in business and elsewhere too—that we often take it for granted. As the saying goes, fish are the last to discover water.

Bureaucracy's features stand out best in a bit of historical perspective. For much of history, most jobs in governments around the world were either hereditary or for sale. Officials like military officers or tax collectors passed on their posts to their children, or bought a position from the monarch to gain the prestige and salary that came with it. Unsurprisingly, such practices tended to be terrible for getting anything done. Officials who inherited or bought their jobs were often incompetent and corrupt as well. Eventually, leaders who wanted things done well—especially seeking disciplined militaries and better tax collection—experimented with other ways to organize the people who worked for them. Starting first in ancient China and other empires, and later in early European states, leaders designed organizations to separate technical, professional work from political favoritism, corruption, or profit making. They eventually developed the four key elements that define bureaucracy today:

1. *Knowledge-based recruitment:* officials gain positions through examinations or special schools to show they have proper expertise.

2. *Salaried professionals:* workers are paid a fixed salary to perform specific tasks, without other opportunities for personal enrichment. Promotions reflect seniority and merit.

3. *Systematic procedures:* all decisions operate by impersonal application of explicit and general rules to discourage uncertainty and corruption.

4. *Hierarchy:* lower-level units with distinct responsibilities report up a chain of command.[4]

The bureaucratic model thus tries to forge a body of experts into an impartial, predictable tool. Militaries are still some of the best examples. The U.S. Army has all the elements of a classic bureaucracy: officers trained at the special school at West Point, strict salaries at each grade, endlessly systematized rules, and extreme hierarchy. It assembles a large number of people into a focused technical machine.

To make a long story short, this organizational innovation proved enormously powerful and spread far and wide. In fact, though the bureaucratic model originated in states and is still often identified with government, it eventually shaped almost all large organizations. Inside big corporations like Microsoft, Toyota, or Bank of America, middle managers come to work each day to enforce systematic rules, tackle technical tasks sent down a chain of command, and receive a salary. The Sierra Club, the NRA, large churches, or other big nonprofits typically work on a similar model. The sociologist Max Weber thought bureaucracy was a central and inevitable element of modernity: bureaucracy defines the modern, rational way in which human beings control their environment and get things done.[5]

Within some modern governments, though, the bureaucratic model came to be combined with the very different organizational principles of liberal democracy. These governments still wanted to get things done, and so set up militaries, post offices, and other bureaucracies, but they made their top leaders accountable to citizens through competitive elections. From this mix arose one of the basic issues within liberal democracy: what kind of relationship exists between elected representatives and the bureaucrats who work for them?

The Bureaucrat–Politician Relationship in Principle and Practice

In principle, bureaucratic experts and elected politicians in liberal democracies have a simple relationship: politicians call the shots and bureaucrats provide technical support. In practice, things can be very different. Bureaucrats can use their expertise to shape how politicians perceive policy options. They can affect how politicians' choices are implemented as well. In some policy areas, moreover, such active bureaucratic influence is quite deliberate; politicians willingly shift major policymaking power to bureaucrats. Bureaucrats are thus often more than just technical support staff. They are substantial political players in their own right.

Democracy decides and bureaucracy implements: that is the relationship in theory. Elected executives and legislatures devise laws to deliver policies citizens want. Then they assign bureaucracies with policy implementation, employing elected executives to oversee them. Under the leadership of secretaries or ministers in the cabinet, the bureaucracy gathers together experts—generals in the army, economists for the central bank, logistics experts for the national post office, and so on—to translate laws into effective rules and procedures. These top bureaucratic officials often have many levels of lower officials working for them, creating a chain of command down to the employees who perform concrete tasks like soldiers, mail carriers, teachers, police officers, firefighters, social workers, or restaurant safety inspectors. The whole hierarchy exists to implement the decisions made by the people's representatives—in principle.

Figure 8-2 Bureaucracy Plays a Similar Basic Role in Presidential and Parliamentary Regimes

In presidential systems, voters elect both president and legislature (usually two houses, except in Venezuela); in parliamentary systems, voters elect a lower house that chooses the executive. In some parliamentary systems, voters also elect an upper house, but it cannot affect the choice of the executive (except in Italy, where both houses choose the executive). Despite these complex differences in representation, the basic place of bureaucracy is the same in all these systems: it comprises the staff of executive departments led by ministers.

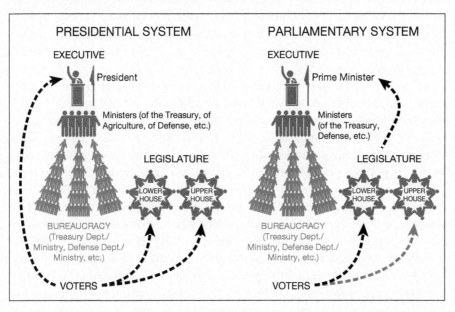

We might also expect that in principle, these basic relationships would be roughly similar across liberal democracies. The same need for expertise and implementing staff arises in both presidential and parliamentary systems, and the bureaucracy fits into their overall organization of government in similar ways (see Figure 8-2). Bureaucrats staff the executive branch, filling posts in what Americans call departments and most of the rest of the world call ministries.

In real life, these relationships are more complex, especially between higher-level bureaucrats and the executive politicians who are their formal superiors. The main reason is that expert knowledge is a source of power. Politicians turn to bureaucracies for expertise—they need professional soldiers to fight wars, trained police to handle criminals, engineers to craft building codes—but they can rarely evaluate the knowledge these experts provide. Few politicians have backgrounds in technical fields. Even those that do are so busy with elections, party politics, and decision making that they have little time to consider technical issues carefully. Politicians may also spend a short time in office, and even a shorter time dealing with any policy issue, while bureaucrats can develop knowledge of a policy area across an entire career. The British television comedy *Yes, Minister* was built around this point: in every episode bureaucrats ran circles around their ill-informed political "bosses."

Before passage of a law or policy decision, experts can structure choices by presenting options as technically unworkable or superior. In the 1980s, for example, bureaucrats at the U.S. Environmental Protection Agency (EPA) created strong pressure to ban a category of coolants called chlorofluorocarbons (CFCs)—a $100 billion industry—by pointing to scientific work suggesting CFCs were eroding the Earth's atmosphere. Many politicians close to President Ronald Reagan resisted the bureaucrats' arguments for a CFC ban, arguing that the science was unclear or that a ban would be too costly for American businesses. But ultimately, they accepted it.[6]

After politicians make decisions, bureaucratic experts can influence how laws are implemented. To take another American example, the "War on Poverty" agenda launched by President Lyndon Johnson in the late 1960s ran into a wide variety of obstacles when it was launched. A book on this experience, titled *Implementation*, emphasizes that many decisions by "street-level bureaucrats" affected how the laws were put into practice. Its subtitle—*How Great Expectations in Washington Are Dashed in Oakland*—referred to an opening anecdote about a $23 million "emergency" program that Congress awarded to Oakland, California, in 1968 to boost minority employment and calm racial tensions. Although politicians trumpeted the program as a model initiative for other cities, this study three years later found that it had gotten bogged down in local disagreements and bureaucratic procedures. Only $3 million had been spent, with no clear results on the ground in Oakland.[7]

That is not to say that well-designed bureaucracies cannot act efficiently, or that it is necessarily bad that bureaucrats affect politicians' decisions. We would not want politicians to ignore the advice of generals about options in wartime. Nor would we want politicians to micromanage how the military implements war strategies. The same applies to expertise in policing, education, environmental policies, and other areas in which governments act. Few would dispute that experts should help structure policy options and choices in implementation. The challenge of bureaucrats' role in democratic policymaking is not that their input is illegitimate in general, but that it can be difficult to strike a desirable balance of expertise and representation. Too much reliance on bureaucratic expertise smothers representation; too little expertise and politicians may choose ineffective policies.

Another complication in this balancing act is that politicians sometimes willingly shift the burden of decision making to bureaucrats. They do so to protect certain policies from political manipulation, like economic policies at election time. To increase their chances for reelection, politicians may be tempted to pump government money into the economy to boost growth—even if such moves make for poor economic policy in the longer term. To "tie their hands," politicians may thus agree to turn some decisions over to more neutral bureaucrats. For instance, most liberal democracies discourage electoral manipulation of the economy by guaranteeing the independence of the national central bank. Politicians still appoint top officials at banks like the U.S. Federal Reserve, the Bank of Japan, or the European Central Bank, but in daily policymaking these government banks are quite autonomous from politicians. Many similar **independent regulatory agencies** exist in the United States, such as the Federal Trade Commission or the Securities and Exchange Commission. This model has proliferated around the world as a conscious movement "to strengthen the autonomy of professionals and experts in the public policy process."[8] Thus even elected politicians sometimes agree that expertise should trump representation.

In sum, a simple view of bureaucrats as tools for elected politicians is rarely realistic. Politicians need experts to help them conceive and enact policies, and that dependence gives bureaucrats political influence. Just how much influence these bureaucrats gain, however, varies a great deal. In the presence of a strong legislature, the executive bureaucracy is much less likely to dominate policymaking. In the next two sections, we consider how several other factors also place bureaucrats at the heart of policymaking in some democracies or distance them from it in others.

Civil Service and Bureaucratic Prestige

Imagine asking a group of high school students, "Who wants to be a government bureaucrat?" Not many hands would go up in a U.S. classroom. Most ambitious Americans dream of careers in business, law, medicine, academia, or possibly running for political office—not working for the Department of the Treasury. Yet many would choose the bureaucratic track in Japan or France, where working for the Ministry of Finance (their Treasury) may be the most prestigious career a student can follow. In both contexts, prestige follows power: U.S. career bureaucrats are relatively weak, while those in Japan or France craft their nation's policies. Behind these contrasts lie profound differences in views of government service and the structure of higher education.

Japan, France, and most liberal democracies have a tradition of **civil service** that is more established than in the American context. Civil service is the formal term for government work outside the military; civil servants are unelected government employees who are not soldiers. In most developed countries, this kind of national service has a long history. Military service was the earliest form of government work, since early states did little besides fight wars. But in the eighteenth and nineteenth centuries, many states developed civil services for tasks like tax collection or engineering of roads, bridges, and canals. Working in these roles for central government was typically a respected profession, and one of the few early ways for bright people to move up in society through education and merit. As modern governments expanded their activities, some created highly competitive schools to train their personnel. The French state created the *École des Ponts et Chaussées* (School of Roads and Bridges) in 1747, and in 1794 added

independent regulatory agencies
Government bureaucracies that regulate a certain issue area and are deliberately given some independence from politicians' oversight.

civil service
Nonmilitary career professionals employed by government, classically with guarantees of neutrality from party politics.

the *École Polytechnique* for engineers and the *École Normale* for teachers. Over time, roughly eighty specialized schools emerged for the training of civil servants.[9] Japan imitated these programs after it shifted toward a Western model of modernization in 1868, founding the University of Tokyo in 1877 to train many kinds of experts for government administration. Ambitious young Japanese and French people came to see an elite public school and a civil service career as one of their most appealing opportunities.

In countries that created this nexus of selective schools and respected national service, government bureaucracy took on great prestige. By the time French democracy consolidated in the late 1800s, and even more so by the time Japan democratized after World War II, top civil servants tended to receive more respect than politicians. In the French or Japanese Ministries of Finance—for which the educational track and hiring procedures were most selective of all—it was taken for granted that the bureaucrats were far more competent in economic policy than the politicians who were supposedly their bosses. When Japanese politician Kakuei Tanaka took the office of finance minister in the 1960s, he reportedly said to "his" new staff, "You are the true elite of the elite. Studying at the topmost university in this country, your brains are the highest quality in Japan. I will, therefore, leave the business of thinking to you, and I will, with your permission, take responsibility for the results."[10] While Japanese and French people also grumble about this extreme elitism, it still attracts powerful respect. As a

White House Photo/Alamy Stock Photo

Are these military cadets? No, they are France's top engineering and science students from the elite public *École Polytechnique*, marching in the traditional Bastille Day parade (and wearing the revolutionary-era hats they have worn for 200 years). The uniforms and parade symbolize that *Polytechnique* and other elite French schools are still seen as prestigious public educational pathways into an expert civil service.

French businessman once remarked (with sexist phrasing, but a sentiment that still holds true), "Ninety percent of the population wants to abolish the *École Polytechnique*, but they also want their sons to go there."[11]

Though all developed countries have created civil services over time, not all connected it to a prestigious image of bureaucrats as the best and brightest. As government departments grew to take on more responsibilities in countries like Italy, Greece, and most of Latin America, they were treated as the spoils of war for electoral winners. When new politicians took power, they would fire or demote many occupants of government posts and dole out jobs to their own supporters. Known as **patronage**, these practices often worked well to build political support, and in some places they still do today. In Mexico, for example, up to 30,000 positions have typically changed hands with a new president.[12] Yet patronage deeply impairs the emergence of merit-based bureaucracy. Where such practices are widespread, bureaucratic careers have much less prestige and career civil servants have little influence overall. Patronage has nonetheless been difficult to reform in many poorer democracies in which supporters often expect politicians to deliver very tangible payoffs.

patronage
The allocation of government jobs as rewards for political support.

In the United States, an early emphasis on patronage and late development of the central government produced a civil service with modest prestige and influence. In the tiny federal government of the early 1800s, the first several presidents gave the few available jobs to their supporters. In the 1830s, President Andrew Jackson loudly proclaimed that patronage was appropriate in democracy: "to the victor go the spoils" was the saying of the day. But as federal responsibilities increased after the Civil War—such as supporting war veterans, administering Western territories, regulating an expanding economy—complaints of corruption and incompetence spread and eventually produced the **Pendleton Act of 1883**. Modeled on British rules, it established a merit-based federal civil service accessed by competitive exams. These steps away from patronage were late relative to Europe, though, and the newly professional civil service attracted little prestige because federal government remained a weak entity. U.S. government was so decentralized that in 1900, spending by towns and counties alone—without even counting state-level governments—still exceeded the federal budget! In such a context, few ambitious Americans saw federal civil service as a pathway to societal influence. Meanwhile, higher education also developed in decentralized ways. With no large government to staff, universities arose in many locations and focused on business, law, medicine, and other nongovernment careers. By the time the federal government expanded to approach the size of other rich-country governments, during the Great Depression and World War II, the best and brightest in American society tended to move in other directions. Today, roughly 2 million civilians work for the federal government, but the notion of civil service as a career aspiration is still not part of the "American dream."[13]

Pendleton Act of 1883
The U.S. law that created the federal civil service.

Thus the political role of bureaucrats has deep historical roots. In states where educational pathways and strong central government made bureaucracy prestigious, both politicians and the public have tended to perceive it as holding legitimate authority. Where illustrious educational programs did not connect to civil service and where patronage persists, bureaucracy has a lower status. As we see in the next section, this intangible prestige of civil service also influences concrete organizational features inside governments today. Prestigious bureaucracies have substantial autonomy from politicians, but lower-status bureaucracies are penetrated by party politics.

Politicization and Appointees in the Bureaucracy

From the preceding section, we might imagine that bureaucratic departments across countries look similar but have different levels of influence. That is, we might think that all are hierarchical organizations staffed with professional civil servants, and some simply play a bigger policymaking role than others. Yet varying power also affects these departments internally: not all look like a classic hierarchy of professional civil servants. Countries with weak civil services, like the United States, replace professional civil servants at the top of the hierarchy with political appointees.

In democracies with strong civil services like Japan, Britain, and France, career bureaucrats occupy the highest positions in departments. They extend up the hierarchy to a single top official, known as an "administrative vice minister" in a Japanese ministry, a "permanent secretary" in Britain, or a "secretary general" in France. This person is the direct interface between the civil servant hierarchy and the politician serving as minister (see Figure 8-3). When elections change the executive and bring in a new cabinet of ministers, a new politician occupies each minister's office but most of the same civil servants stay in place. In Japan, there are usually few or no changes at all. In Britain, a new minister may shuffle top officials around from post to post because some are seen as most supportive of her or his political priorities. In France, top civil servants are moved around for political reasons even more frequently, plus each minister brings in a dozen or so political advisers. Overall, though, the basic rule in all three countries is that the bureaucratic hierarchy remains largely intact. Top civil servants stay in high posts and work with whichever elected politicians come along.[14]

In some other democracies, by contrast, politicians' influence is much more important. Arrival of a new minister means replacement of most of the top of the bureaucracy with political allies of the new boss, either chosen from the ranks of the department or brought in from outside. These practices are related to patronage—these government posts are selected on political ties rather than technical merit or civil service seniority—but at the top end of the bureaucracy they are often better described as **politicization**: installing political allies to push a certain policy agenda, not just as a payoff for electoral support. A minister of

politicization
The selection or promotion in civil service to bureaucratic posts due to political views rather than merit or seniority.

finance might select a certain person with ties to his or her political party to run an office on banking regulations to make sure the office works toward the minister's party's goals, not to reward that individual. In Mexico, Argentina, Brazil, most Eastern European countries, and the United States, the upper bureaucracy is largely based on a mix of politicization and patronage. At lower levels, these countries have varying levels of patronage. In the United States, less important jobs generally reflect merit-based selection of career civil servants in the Pendleton spirit.

Figure 8-3 suggests what these contrasts look like inside bureaucracies. In the Japanese case, career civil servants fill the hierarchy below the minister. In the United States, career civil servants rarely hold any top posts and, besides the secretary, political appointees usually fill the next three levels down. These jobs add up across the government: when a new U.S. president is elected, she or he appoints about 4,000 new people to the top layers of federal departments and agencies. In the United States, then, career bureaucrats do not even run the bureaucracy itself.

Most U.S. presidents' choices reflect politicization more than patronage. A Republican president might select top Justice Department officials with conservative records for being tough on crime and EPA officials who prefer looser environmental regulations; a Democratic president might chose Justice Department

---

Figure 8-3 The Politician–Civil Servant Interface

In Japan and most other democracies, career civil servants comprise the entire staff of executive departments to the level just below the minister. In the United States, political appointees fill the top-level positions under the secretary, while career civil servants serve at the lower levels.

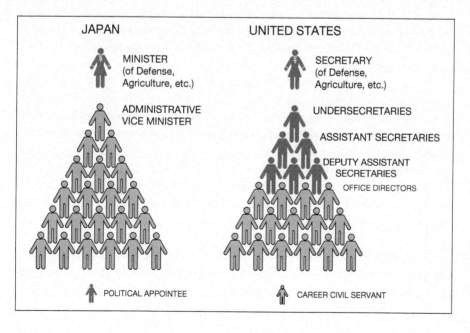

officials with liberal records favoring generous civil rights and EPA officials committed to fighting climate change. Sometimes these choices draw from the ranks of career civil servants, promoting them up the ladder, but usually they come in from other careers in business, academia, law, or politics. Patronage also still plays a role. One famous example was Michael Brown, a college roommate of President George W. Bush's election-campaign director, who became director of the Federal Emergency Management Agency (FEMA) despite weak qualifications. When the Hurricane Katrina disaster hit New Orleans in 2005, Brown was quickly fired as criticism mounted of FEMA's incompetent response. President Obama, too, imitated his predecessors in giving supporters ambassadorships, especially on tropical islands. Major Obama donors became ambassadors to the Bahamas, Belize, and other cushy locales.[15] President Trump has been even more willing to appoint people without relevant expertise. In one widely criticized move, his son's wedding planner took charge of billion-dollar federal housing programs in New York and New Jersey.[16]

With these last points about politicization and patronage, we now have a broad enough view of the role of bureaucracies to connect them to our earlier survey of legislative power. Liberal democracies allocate policymaking power across elected executives, legislators, and unelected bureaucrats in many different mixes, but two clear options highlight some common patterns. In democracies like Britain, France, or Japan, the growth of a strong central state and professional civil service centralized policymaking power in the executive. As both cause and consequence of that result, their legislatures developed into arenas for showy debates but not for significant decisions. The French Assembly is a talk shop partly because the French bureaucracy is so strong and prestigious, and vice versa. In the United States, unusual weakness of the central state and professional civil service was both cause and consequence of major policymaking power in the legislature. The U.S. Congress is rich in policymaking resources and influence because the federal bureaucracy never became very powerful, and vice versa.

Which of these options is preferable? At first glance the choice may seem obvious for most Americans, for whom the very thought of powerful elite bureaucrats provokes a shudder. Most would expect strong bureaucracies to produce elitist, unresponsive policymaking—and Japanese and French citizens indeed complain about these characteristics in their governments. Yet as we saw earlier, most Americans also have abysmal views of a Congress that they see as distastefully partisan and frankly corrupt. That implies some desire for the neutral, professional policymaking that a strong civil service might provide. Furthermore, Americans already tend to accept the allocation of major power to a special kind of elite expert: judges. In fact, as we see in the next section, the United States assigns judges very unusual levels of policymaking influence. Once we survey the power of these other unelected experts across liberal democracies, we will hold all the elements for critical thinking about how policymaking is configured.

Unelected Legal Experts: The Power of Judges

8.3　**Identify the principles of common- and code-law legal systems, American and European models of judicial review, and how they relate to judicial influence.**

"The law" plays a profound role in liberal democracies, and the experts who interpret it hold a special kind of power. In these countries where politics is framed in deeply respected legal constitutions, "it's the law" carries a force of its own: just making a rule into part of the legal order generally means that people obey it. Yet at the same time, law is profoundly ambiguous. No law can anticipate all circumstances, and overlapping laws often contradict each other. Thus legal experts—judges—are called upon to interpret the law, directing its power in certain directions.

Though judges play this role in all liberal democracies, countries have worked out different roles for them in managing legal ambiguity. Some legal systems give judges more freedom to interpret the law, and some countries' political institutions have bigger built-in ambiguities that judges may be asked to resolve. In relatively simple, centralized polities, where the predominance of one pole of power left little ambiguity as to where authority lay, judges have traditionally had little influence over policymaking. In more complex federal polities with many players—like the United States—judges have had to arbitrate fights among these players, ultimately giving the judiciary enormous power over policies and politics.

The Power and Ambiguity of Law

Human societies are full of social rules about how and how not to behave in various situations. We have rules of etiquette, like shaking hands or using the right fork, and rules of ethics like the Golden Rule. Our parents, schools, religious institutions, and peers both teach us that it is morally right to follow these rules, and enforce them with disapproval and punishments when we transgress. Then there is a special subset of social rules that are presented as so important that they must be written down and enforced by state power: laws.

In the rational-legal thinking that led to the creation of liberal-democratic government, the rule of law comes before democracy itself. Since we are all equal and rational human beings, laws should apply equally and similarly to all of us, and the one-person-one-vote process of electoral democracy attempts to apply this legal equality to the selection of leaders. In a phrase from a nineteenth-century British law professor that nicely emphasizes the priority of law over democracy, the deepest logic of good government is to replace a "government of men" with a "government of laws."[17] Thus liberal democracies do not begin with elections, but with the drafting of constitutions—the frameworks of basic laws that define rights and political institutions, including how elections are to work. We may not be very conscious of it, but citizens in liberal democracies are taught from an early age that laws deserve even deeper respect than democracy itself. You may scorn your leaders, parties, and the democratic process, but you may not ignore the law. Whether or not you vote is up to you . . . except in countries like Australia or Brazil where compulsory voting is the law!

In countries where rule of law is well established, then, "it's the law" is a powerful statement that is typically taken as reason enough to affect our behavior. Whether or not we think a law is a good one, and whether or not it benefits us personally to follow it, we tend to obey laws out of respect for the state's legitimate authority and for its capacity to enforce these laws. There are exceptions, of course. Some people steal or murder, and almost everyone breaks the speed limit, parks illegally, or crosses some legal line now and then. To make a political point we may engage in civil disobedience, explicitly refusing to respect certain rules in a nonviolent way. In everyday life, we also constantly test the limits of laws, working the system to pay less tax or otherwise gain an advantage. Yet the care that most people take in getting away with speeding or taxpaying is itself evidence of the power of law. If we did not accept its power, we would not expend so much energy testing the legal limits.

As powerful as it is, "it's the law" is also always ambiguous: *what* exactly is the law in any specific case? Even very simple laws, such as "you must wear a seat belt in a moving car," do not apply simply to all scenarios: if a child is choking in the back seat on a highway with no shoulder for pulling over, is it really *illegal* for a mother in the passenger seat to unbuckle herself? These ambiguities become profound at the abstract level of basic rights and principles in constitutions. All liberal democracies stipulate a right to free speech as fundamental, for example, but not without limits. All criminalize shouting "fire" in a crowded theater, and that exception raises questions about what other speech is so dangerous that it might legitimately be prohibited. Not only do ambiguities become deeper in more fundamental laws, they become more common as laws proliferate in number. When multiple laws with different goals overlap, they often create contradictions, or at least confusion. For example, do laws that seek to limit the role of money in electoral campaigns contradict constitutional guarantees of free speech? If yes, does the possibility that money might skew elections become one of the dangerous exceptions that can legitimately limit free speech or not? There are always judgment calls on what the law means in practice.

Judgment calls demand judges—and, as most of the world agrees, unelected ones. (The fact that many judges are elected in the United States is almost unique in the world, as we discuss below.) The rule of law implies that the law has a logic that applies whether we like it or not, so it is awkward to assign the interpretation of law to elected politicians whose authority depends on getting people to like them. Politicians will always face incentives to do what is popular, but if interpretations of laws are too easily affected by shifting popular opinion, the rule of law has little integrity. It calls for legal experts who know the law and how it has been applied to date, and who can be trusted to focus on how the logic of the law relates most reasonably to a new scenario.

Thus the power and ambiguity of law create the need for assigning authority to the unelected officials we call judges. These conditions also make it imaginable that such officials could play a major role in how liberal democracy works—if deep ambiguities on rights and other big questions are perceived as legal matters for them to arbitrate. Imaginable, but not necessary: democracies might prefer to classify such big questions as political matters to be resolved by elections and elected representatives, asking judges only to clean up smaller bits of ambiguity in the legal landscape. As the next two sections show, liberal democracies exhibit huge variation across these options. In some countries, judges have almost no impact on significant policymaking. In others, they hold the ultimate political power in the land.

Who is the most powerful figure in U.S. politics? We tend to think more of presidents, but another candidate is John Roberts, chief justice of the U.S. Supreme Court (shown here after swearing in President Trump in January 2017). As the head of an institution that delivers final judgments on some of the biggest issues in U.S. politics, he has presided over earth-shaking decisions on campaign finance, health care, abortion, and same-sex marriage. He will rule on many more during a lifetime appointment that lasts through many presidential terms to come.

Judicial Power and Everyday Justice

As many of us glean from watching courtroom dramas, judges form an independent branch of government called the judiciary. They sit as impartial arbiters, refereeing an even-handed process of justice and respecting the fundamental principle that all accused are innocent until proven guilty. They make their rulings, above all, by looking at **precedent**: the record of other cases in which other judges have decided similar issues.

Or do they? None of these sentences applies to judges in all liberal democracies. The notions of judges as a separate branch of government, of "innocent until proven guilty," and of ruling on the basis of precedent are all part of the tradition known as **common law**. Despite its name, it is less common across liberal democracies than the tradition known as **code law**, or sometimes "civil law" (see Map 8-1). These different legal arrangements reflect contrasting ways of resolving the everyday ambiguity of law, with profound implications overall for procedures of justice and for the role of judges in policymaking. This section considers the foundations of these systems, and the next shows how common and code law interact with other political institutions to give some judges, in some democracies, the final word on government policies.

precedent
A court ruling that suggests how laws should be applied to subsequent cases.

common law
The legal system that casts judges as impartial interpreters of unsystematic laws, ruling substantially by precedent.

code law
The legal system that attempts to create more systematic laws and regulations and leaves less interpretation to judges.

Map 8-1 Legal Systems around the World

Common law is used in Great Britain and its former territories (except Malta). Code law prevails elsewhere except in mixed systems, or nondemocracies that employ Islamic *shari'a* law.

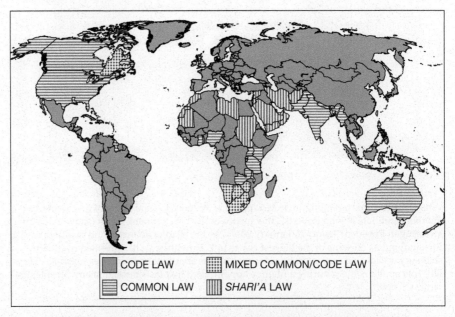

CODE LAW   MIXED COMMON/CODE LAW

COMMON LAW   *SHARI'A* LAW

Source: World Legal Systems Research Group, University of Ottawa, http://www.juriglobe.ca/eng/.

JUDGES IN COMMON LAW.   To understand the role of common-law judges, we must return to the origins of this legal system in England roughly a thousand years ago. Long before the modern state, there were no written constitutions, no standing parliaments to make laws, and no government agencies to make regulations. Feudal judges—usually just the local lord—adopted a principle of judging local crimes and conflicts on the basis of "common" practices. If one peasant's dog killed another's sheep, the judge looked to informal tradition in such cases to indicate a ruling. Perhaps the dog owner might have to pay for the sheep. Over time, such cases were increasingly written down and shared across jurisdictions, so judges could point to precedents in each other's rulings to support their own. This created a body of "common law."

In time, the growth of the modern English state produced a growing volume of explicit laws passed through parliaments, which became known as **statute law**. Later additions to the legal system were **constitutional law**, which designated a set of especially fundamental legal principles, and **administrative law**, or regulations that fill in the details of statutes to define how government agencies enact and enforce their tasks (see Table 8-2). In cases where these other kinds of laws were perceived as clear, they were understood to take priority over common-law rules. For example, if parliament passed a law saying that restitution for a killed sheep was twice its value, that statute superseded previous judges' decisions. In other words, the constitution, statutes, and administrative regulations gradually built a more explicit legal system around common-law practices. Yet even these formal laws also contained ambiguities and contradictions, and judges did not break with their older common-law mode. Now they just had to figure out how constitutional principles, statutes, administrative regulations, common social practices, *and* other judges' precedents fit together to decide a case. Since judicial precedents retained an important role, this whole legal architecture became known as a "common law" system.

In Britain, the United States, Canada, India, and other places where British colonialism carried its influence, judges today operate in this same mode of common law. It has the following key features:

- *Case-based rulings:* All laws are understood as fundamentally incomplete. Judges must look first to constitutions, statutes, and regulations, but because they are not seen as comprehensive, judges are guided most directly and concretely by looking at judicial rulings in comparable cases.

statute law
Formal laws passed through legislatures.

constitutional law
Formal laws included in constitutions.

administrative law
Regulations within a statutory framework that specify how government agencies act and implement policies.

Table 8-2 Sources of Common Law

Judges in common-law systems decide cases by working out how constitutional, statute, and/or administrative law apply to a case in light of precedents from other related cases.

Form of Law	Definition
Constitutional Law	Fundamental laws that trump all others (usually in a special constitutional document)
Statute Law	Normal laws passed through the legislature
Administrative Law	Regulations that guide actions of government agencies
Precedent	Previous court rulings on relevant cases

- *An emphasis on precedent:* Because past cases guide today's decisions, the law evolves as situations in individual cases set new precedents. Judges can re-interpret or modify previous rulings in light of new circumstances, shaping the legal terrain for later cases.

- *Judges as arbiters in an adversarial system:* Judges are understood to be im-partial referees. In criminal cases, when the state accuses a person of break-ing a law, the judge referees a clash between lawyers for the accused and the prosecutors (lawyers) for the state. In civil cases that pit private parties against each other or a private individual's complaints against the state, the judge referees a clash between their legal representatives. In most cases, the actual decision of guilt for a crime (or fault in civil cases) is left to a jury. Judges arbitrate the process and decide criminal sentences or other conse-quences. This role as impartial referee is related to the notion of "innocent until proven guilty"; the state's prosecutors argue for guilt, but the impartial judge ensures that this remains just an accusation until a jury accepts it "be-yond a reasonable doubt."

- *Judges as deeply independent from the state:* Since judges arbitrate between the state and individuals, judges are understood as constituting a distinct branch of government, not as normal state employees. Unlike civil servants, who tend to work their way up a bureaucratic hierarchy, judges are often ap-pointed to their judgeships late in their careers after having worked in other roles in society like private law practice. Higher-level judges, like federal judges in the United States, are then appointed for life on the logic that this makes them largely immune from political pressure.

A common-law system thus asks judges directly to sort out the challenges of legal ambiguity. It conceives their role as independent interpreters of a funda-mentally fragmented legal order. Most of the time judges stick closely to concrete cases; as the English jurist Lord Wright said in 1938, they tend to "proceed from case to case, like the ancient Mediterranean mariners, hugging the coast from point to point, and avoiding the dangers of the open sea."[18] Yet common law is also called "judge-made law" for this reason: their case decisions can affect policy quite broadly. To take a famous U.S. example, the 1966 decision in *Miranda v. Arizona* ruled that unless police inform people of their right to silence before taking them into custody, the suspects' statements cannot be used as evidence against them. The "Miranda rights," as they are known, deeply shaped police procedure.

One important exception sits awkwardly alongside this image of indepen-dent common-law judges. In the United States, while federal judges have strong independence from electoral politics, roughly 90 percent of state- and lower-level judges have no independence from electoral politics at all. They are elected by voters—a practice that exists nowhere else except in a few cantons (prov-inces) of Switzerland. It has many critics: as retired U.S. Supreme Court Justice Sandra Day O'Connor once remarked flatly, "No other country in the world does that because they realize that you're not going to get fair and impartial judges that way."[19] This unusual feature dates from the 1830s, when President Andrew Jackson argued that all government positions should be controlled by the people through elections (and through patronage in the bureaucracy). For the broad lines of our survey, note simply that the practice of electing judges contradicts the place of higher-level judges in the United States and is not part of the common-law tradition.[20]

JUDGES IN CODE LAW.   The main alternative to common law takes almost the opposite approach to legal ambiguity. Rather than empowering independent judges to resolve ambiguities, code-law systems craft more systematic, comprehensive laws that leave less to interpretation. From the Code of Hammurabi in ancient Babylonia and Rome's Justinian Code to the Tang Code in China, many leaders attempted to systematize rules into logical wholes. The biggest wave of such codifications took place not long after the rise of modern European states. These states were building up bureaucracies to better systematize their policies, and moves to rationalize laws were part of that movement. In the most famous example, the regime of French emperor Napoleon Bonaparte replaced an inherited patchwork of feudal laws with a comprehensive, coherent code that would be easier and fairer to administer. The Napoleonic Code of 1804 has since been imitated all around the world, making it one of the most influential written works of all time.

Ann E Parry/Alamy Stock Photo

Should the logic of representation in democracies extend to judges, or does making them elected undercut the impartial logic of law and rights? The practice of electing judges exists only in the United States (for most state- and local-level judges, but not federal ones) and in parts of Switzerland. This truck carries campaign signs for a candidate running for a seat on the New York State Supreme Court.

Code laws can never fully resolve legal ambiguity, which is inescapable, but they can create a different role for judges. They shift influence to bureaucrats or politicians who draft comprehensive statutes and detailed regulations that leave judges less room for interpretation, as reflected in the following key features:

- *Comprehensive lawmaking:* Drafters of statutes and regulations make them as comprehensive and detailed as reasonably possible.

- *Judges apply the code more than precedent:* Since the body of law is regarded as a comprehensive code that should be directly applicable to cases, the role of judges is to know the details of the law and apply them. The Napoleonic Code specifically barred judges from using precedents from other cases, requiring that they reason only from the Code itself to rule solely on the specific case before them.

- *Judges in an inquisitorial role for the state:* Judges are seen as state officials charged with finding the truth. Low-level judges work directly with police to investigate crimes and even make a preliminary finding on guilt *prior* to a trial. Once in court, the judge—not lawyers representing the parties—directly questions witnesses. The lawyers play a much smaller role than in a common-law court, intervening when they can to highlight facts that help their side. Juries are often used, but after the trial the juries deliberate *with* the judge, not separately—with the judge typically taking a leading role. In tasking the judge to find the truth, such systems traditionally have no presumption of innocence that must be disproved "beyond a reasonable doubt." The jury just decides whether the evidence adds up to guilt or innocence.

- *Judges as semi-bureaucrats:* Unlike judges in common-law systems, who tend not to work for government for their whole careers, most code-law judges follow a track like civil servants. They are typically recruited soon after their studies through special exams and gradually work their way up in a hierarchical judicial corps. In most countries, they are guaranteed strong independence when they reach higher-level jobs—effectively gaining lifetime appointments—but their status more closely resembles bureaucrats.

The key implication of these differences between code-law judges and their common-law peers is a smaller impact on policymaking. In terms of daily justice, judges in code-law democracies like France, Sweden, or the Netherlands generally enjoy as much independence in their rulings as common-law judges, even if the procedures are different. In terms of policies, however, code-law judges have much less opportunity to alter anything through their decisions. They typically enforce policy with as much autonomy as common-law judges, but they rarely shape it.

These differences have admittedly become less sharp since Napoleon's days, as common- and code-law systems have borrowed features from each other over time. Common-law statutes have sometimes been more specifically codified to constrain judges, like the "Three Strikes" laws that spread across U.S. states in the 1990s to require specific sentences for repeat criminals.[21] Most code-law democracies have strengthened judicial independence in various ways, and have also increasingly permitted some appeals to precedent—cracking the door open to "judge-made law." Still, the daily practices of common-law systems set much stronger bases for judicial influence in policymaking. Especially when complex, ambiguous political authority is built on common-law foundations, judicial power can reach very far.

Judicial Review and Judges as Policymakers

The ambiguity of law becomes especially important when it arises over the allocation of political authority itself. Judges' ultimate influence over policymaking largely reflects the varying degrees to which peoples across liberal democracies have perceived their internal distribution of power as complicated and ambiguous. In the face of such political uncertainties, judges have often been called upon to resolve them through **judicial review**: the power to review whether statutes, regulations, or government actions fall within the bounds set by the constitution. In countries with strong judicial review, judges can strike down or change rules or actions they deem unconstitutional. They have the final, supreme word on major issues of policy and politics.

judicial review
The ability of judges to question the constitutionality of statutes or regulations and to void them in the event of contradictions.

What conditions, then, make for political ambiguity? To some degree it arises in all liberal democracies out of tension between their "liberal" and "democratic" elements. Liberal democracy depends on enforcing many rights to deliver its promise of meaningful representation. If elected officials are free to interpret or alter rights according to the shifting winds of public opinion, what prevents a popular elected leader from weakening such rights—or erasing them entirely, as Hitler did? There is thus a strong case to be made that judges must hold the power to evaluate the policies and actions of elected officials against constitutional limits.

Such political ambiguity tends to be especially strong in democracies where authority is shared between multiple players. The more unitary and centralized a government, the simpler its allocation of authority. Parliamentary systems also tend to reduce ambiguity, because the authority of all their elected representatives flows from the single source of parliament. In countries that distribute authority more widely—like large, decentralized, federal countries, and presidential systems with a separation of power—more opportunities arise for contestation of authority. Federal and state governments may dispute their relative responsibilities; so may separately elected presidents and legislatures. Looking to judges to arbitrate such disagreements is one obvious solution.

Neither kind of ambiguity appears to have troubled democracies like Britain, Finland, the Netherlands, or New Zealand, as these countries traditionally had no substantial judicial review at all. They all have fairly simple and centralized parliamentary systems, and have stuck with the doctrine of **parliamentary sovereignty**: all authority ultimately flows from parliament, and it has the final say over the law. To date, at least, their elected politicians have generally respected liberal rights even without strong judicial guardians. Part of the explanation may be that these peoples all have strong political cultures of liberal tolerance, encouraging politicians and citizens to respect rights directly. In Britain, this cultural commitment to rights is especially hard to deny: it is the only liberal democracy that has never even written up its constitution in a single document, relying instead on an informal consensus on constitutional-level rules. After long practice in liberal politics, British people seem to be comfortable allowing elected politicians to wrangle out major political questions rather than turning to judges.

Other liberal democracies have developed two major models of judicial review: the very strong American model, which first invented judicial review, and the more constrained but more widely adopted European model.

parliamentary sovereignty
The principle that all fundamental authority flows from parliament, implying that judges cannot overturn parliamentary statutes.

SUPREME COURTS IN THE U.S. MODEL. Judicial review was born in the United States as political actors fought over ambiguous authority. The U.S. Constitution of 1789 separated powers both between federal and state authorities and between the president, Congress, and an independent judiciary capped by a Supreme Court. It left plenty of uncertainty about their relative roles, however, and made no direct mention of judicial review. Not until fifteen years later was that idea affirmed when the Court stepped into a bitter fight between early political parties and struck down statutes that had attempted to alter certain constitutional provisions. In the *Marbury v. Madison* decision of 1803, Chief Justice John Marshall argued that the whole point of constitutions was to create limits that elected politicians could not change by statute: "To what purpose are powers limited, and to what purpose is that limitation committed to writing, if these limits may, at any time, be passed by those intended to be restrained? . . . This doctrine would subvert the very foundation of all written constitutions."[22] This logic assigned the Court the final word on what was allowed under the constitution.

Over the next 150 years, the decentralized, multiplayer context of U.S. politics provided many opportunities for judges to build the *Marbury* principle into active judicial influence. Disputes over federalism and the separation of powers kept calling for judicial resolutions. Through the Civil War and the growth of a national economy in the late 1800s, fights over the distribution of powers between federal and state government and the appropriate balance between the president and Congress repeatedly handed judges the final word on major issues. By the twentieth century, judges had become key players in even the most sensitive questions in policy and electoral politics. In the 1954 case of *Brown v. Topeka Board of Education*, the Supreme Court struck down segregated schools, contributing to the huge political changes of the civil rights movement. In the 1973 *Roe v. Wade* decision, the Court held that the Constitution implied a right to privacy that limited antiabortion laws. In *Bush v. Gore*, the Court literally decided the presidential election of 2000 in a hotly contested ruling on the constitutionality of vote-counting procedures.

The end result was a model of strong judicial influence that has been reproduced fully or partly in federal countries like Canada or Australia and in some presidential systems in Latin America. Its key features include:

- *A process of concrete review:* Judicial review arises through concrete court cases in which an individual pleads certain rights. For example, someone might defend him or herself by arguing that their rights were violated by a police search, or when a partner failed to respect a contract. This invites the judge to consider what rights must be respected in the case, which can often mean considering how relevant statutes or regulations compare to constitutional rights. The judge's task is to rule on the concrete case, but along the way she or he may find that statutes or regulations must be struck down or changed to resolve contradictions with constitutional rights in this case.

- *Review within all courts:* In the United States and similar systems, judges at any level of the legal system—not just the Supreme Court—can perform judicial review within a case ruling. Their rulings may be appealed to a higher court, if necessary continuing up to a final decision by the Supreme Court, but judges throughout the legal system are empowered to review the constitutionality of statutes or regulations.

- *Supreme judges set their own agenda:* Lower-level courts deal with whatever cases come into the system as people are accused of crimes and civil suits are filed, but the Supreme Court chooses which cases it will hear. This gives top judges some ability to pick and choose the issues they address, increasing their discretion and power.

Overall, the U.S. model can be seen as an extension of the common-law tradition of "judge-made law" into the highest levels of politics. When the underlying English tradition of judges as independent arbiters was placed in an American context with a much more complex distribution of political authority, judges evolved into the arbiters of the deepest questions about what government policies can do. The U.S. combination of common law, federalism, and presidentialism was rare, however, and so the United States still stands out for unusual judicial power. The more common and less "supreme" model of judicial review today grew out of political ambiguities in the tighter context of code law.

CONSTITUTIONAL COURTS IN THE EUROPEAN MODEL. Only after World War II did judicial review become well established outside of the United States and the similar common-law, federal-state contexts of Canada and Australia. In three countries that were recovering from the ashes of defeated fascism—Germany, Austria, and Italy—new democratic governments turned to judicial review as part of a new commitment to rights and decentralized power. They sought stronger judicial anchors for liberal rights, hoping to prevent another Hitler, and also foresaw challenges of political ambiguity as they adopted more complex federal or (in Italy's case) semifederal rules that divided power between the center and regions. Yet these were code-law countries with little previous tradition of judicial influence. They worked out a more limited format for judicial review with the following features:

- *A process of abstract review:* Rather than allow courts to review already-established statutes and regulations within their decisions on concrete cases, the European model created a process in which statutes can be reviewed before their enactment. After a statute has been passed but before it enters into force, political players may request that judges review its constitutionality. The review is "abstract" because it takes place before the law has attracted any concrete objections in a real case.

- *Review in a specialized constitutional court:* Instead of empowering all courts to initiate review, these countries created a special, separate court to do so. Whereas the U.S. Supreme Court is just the highest instance of ordinary courts, ruling like all U.S. courts on both concrete cases and issues of constitutionality, Constitutional Courts are set apart as special bodies to decide on the constitutionality of laws.

- *An agenda set by politicians:* Abstract review is initiated at the request of the executive, leaders or substantial groups in the legislature, or in some countries by subnational (that is, regional) governments. If one of these groups wishes to challenge the constitutionality of a law, they request a review by the Constitutional Court before it has entered into force. Thus the Court's agenda is set by other political players, not the court itself.

The European model of constitutional courts amounts to a more fenced-in version of judicial review, with politicians usually better able to manage which issues come before the court. This system makes sense as an invention of federal countries within the code-law tradition of more restrained judges. It has since spread across most of Europe, much of Latin America, and other countries like South Africa and Taiwan. Often countries without a tradition of judicial review adopt constitutional courts at moments when the complexity—and so ambiguity—of their political institutions increases. For example, France did so when it moved from parliamentarism to the "semipresidential" mix of parliamentarism and presidentialism in 1958. Some countries have mixed the European model with elements of the U.S. system to produce quite powerful constitutional courts, like Germany and Italy, which ended up allowing both abstract *and* concrete review processes. For the most part, though, the political influence of judges in constitutional-court countries falls somewhere between the powerful U.S. model and the negligible political role of judges under parliamentary sovereignty.

With these distinctions about legal systems and judicial review in mind, we conclude by stepping back and considering how judicial power relates to that of executives, legislatures, and bureaucrats. Figure 8-4 maps out this section's points, emphasizing that the combination of common law and complex political institutions tends to produce the most powerful judges. At least to some degree, there seems to be a relationship between where countries fall on Figure 8-4 and other

Figure 8-4 How Much Power Do Judges Wield?

The most powerful judges arise where the everyday ambiguity of common law combines with complex, ambiguous political authority. Some countries have shifted toward more complexity over time, as in 1958 when France adopted more complex institutions and, as a result, increased judicial power.

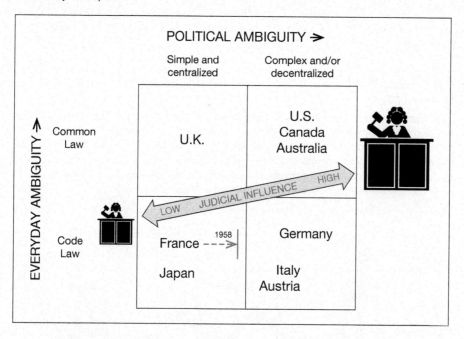

aspects of their policymaking: Japan, France, and the United Kingdom, which were our leading examples of weak legislatures and (especially for Japan and France) powerful bureaucrats, all have judiciaries with weak to modest political influence.

This relationship is no accident. As we saw previously, the early growth of centralized states and strong civil services in France and the United Kingdom is one reason why their legislatures never became major sites of policymaking power. Their choice for parliamentary systems further tended to create executives that dominate legislatures. These same features left little political ambiguity that could serve as openings for judicial influence: early centralization created simple unitary states with clear political authority, as did the fusion of executive-legislative powers in a single set of parliamentary elections. Constitutional changes that complicated French political institutions in 1958, however, shifted this equation somewhat, which upgraded the judicial role. Japan, too, displays these relationships. After World War II, U.S. influence led to creation of an American-style Supreme Court system in Japan. Yet in this very centralized country, where a strong bureaucracy writes tightly defined code law and regulations, the Supreme Court has not been asked to resolve any substantial ambiguity at all. It may be the tamest Supreme Court in the world.[23]

In the United States, meanwhile, we see the reverse: for some of the same reasons that we give little power to unelected bureaucrats, we give major power to unelected judges. A decentralized federal government impeded the development of a federal civil service, and the presidential separation of powers helped consolidate policymaking resources in a highly autonomous Congress. These same features invited judges into a major political role as arbitrators of fights between the federal government and the states, as well as between presidents and the legislature. Judges have further used the "supreme" position they acquired to impact policy around contested liberal rights, from the civil rights movement to abortion and health care. Figure 8-5 contrasts this American configuration of policymaking to the British one.

Figure 8-5 Distribution of Policymaking Power in the United States and the United Kingdom

This illustration depicts political players in the United States and the United Kingdom, with their size roughly indicating their degree of influence. The U.S. president faces a strong legislature and strong courts, and the bureaucracy that works for the executive branch has little prestige of its own. The British prime minister sits at the head of a civil service bureaucracy with a stronger policymaking role and faces a legislature and judiciary with less influence. Overall, the British prime minister has more control over policymaking than the U.S. president.

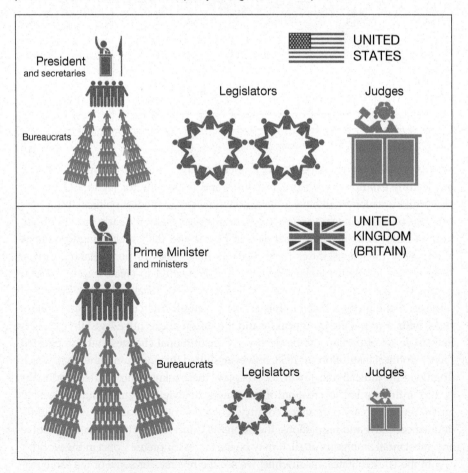

Yet significant legislatures, strong bureaucracies and strong judiciaries still can coexist. Some liberal democracies have worked out mixes between U.S. and Japanese extremes: Germany, for example, has a robust civil service, a stronger legislature than Britain or France, and quite powerful practices of judicial review. The clearest and most important takeaway point is simply that the choices that democracies make about executive-legislative relationships, bureaucrats, and judges can powerfully affect each other. Because power is a zero-sum relationship—if one part of government has more, another part of government has less—the roles we assign to these different political players are not à la carte items on a political menu that we can order without thinking about trade-offs. The next section engages critically with these issues of trade-offs, drawing on the main ideologies within American politics to construct alternative views.

American Political Ideologies and Unelected Authority

8.4   Evaluate competing American arguments for and against bureaucratic and judicial authority.

Some of the deepest questions about liberal democracy arise when we set bureaucrats and judges alongside elected politicians and ask how they should interrelate. Is unelected authority in a democratic framework a necessary evil to be minimized, or a positive force whose role alongside elected representatives should be celebrated?

Given the radically different places of bureaucrats and judges across liberal democracies, alternative answers to these questions are heavily framed in national terms. For example, most Japanese people are more likely to see bureaucratic power as legitimate when compared with most Americans. Contrasting configurations of government also connect differently to ideologies of right and left: in Japan, the elitist bureaucracy is generally seen as a conservative bastion to be opposed by the Left, while the U.S. bureaucracy tends to be reviled by conservatives and defended by the Left. To make this discussion manageable, we focus here on mainstream debates over unelected authority in the American context. We will see that other countries, nonetheless, sneak back in because Americans' thinking on these issues relates to their views of other democracies as well.

Unelected Expertise as Modern Tyranny

For Andrew Jackson, the popular but controversial U.S. president from 1829 to 1837, unelected authority was unaccountable, elitist, and dangerous. Today, few fully share Jackson's views that all judges should be elected and all bureaucracy should become "spoils" for politicians—but fear of unelected tyranny still resonates across the American political spectrum. Bureaucratic power is mainly opposed by the Right, which sees it as threatening the liberty upon which the United States was founded. Judicial power raises objections from both sides: the Right complains that judges have forced unwanted social change, and the Left argues that they have blocked social progress.

The danger of bureaucracy is a key theme of American conservatism. At its core, conservatism is skeptical of technical expertise in policymaking in general. In the tradition of Edmund Burke, conservatives tend to doubt that government can successfully identify and implement expert solutions to engineer progress. Their key concern is not so much that bureaucrats will be evil tyrants, tossing people in jail or cutting off heads, but just that bureaucrats' input in policymaking will be ineffective and may abuse rights. Unlike elected politicians who lose their posts if they are unresponsive to voters, career civil servants are rarely fired and so have insufficient incentives to produce effective policies. Even if they mean well, they tend toward policies that are poorly informed by conditions on the ground, hard to implement, and prone to unintended consequences. Thus we must rein in the ability of government agencies to make rules, shifting power from the federal bureaucracy back into

David Goldman/AP Images

A conservative Atlanta man wears a shirt criticizing the Environmental Protection Agency (EPA) during a rally against new EPA pollution restrictions. Note that his message focuses first on opposing a bureaucratic "power grab" and "more red tape"—challenging the legitimacy of bureaucratic rules themselves—rather than on the issue of pollution.

the rightful hands of elected legislators. As one devoutly conservative blogger complains, the Founding Fathers

> vested all legislative powers of our republic in Congress . . . [and] provid-
> ed that each Congressman voting for or against the laws was directly sub-
> ject to the ballot box. We no longer live in that world . . . Our nation now
> most clearly resembles the socialist regulatory bureaucracy of the European
> Union, where mountains of regulations with the full force and effect of law
> are passed by unelected bureaucrats.[24]

As this quote shows, such conservative American complaints often also target the liberal democracies with more powerful bureaucracies, and Europe in particular. In this view, the United States must reject a European model, reducing bureaucratic authority to a minimum to safeguard liberty.

Powerful U.S. judges attract similar complaints from a wider range of political views. Conservatives often object that "judicial tyranny" has forced social change by stretching rights far beyond the text of the Constitution.[25] Such steps were most notable in the Supreme Court under Chief Justice Earl Warren from 1953 to 1969, whose expansive interpretations of rights ended racial segregation, banned prayer in schools, strengthened the rights of accused criminals, and established a right to privacy that later led to the *Roe v. Wade* decision defending abortion. Similar recent steps include federal-court rulings supporting homosexual rights by striking down laws against same-sex marriage.[26] Yet equally loud today are complaints from the Left that the current Court, now under conservative Chief Justice John Roberts, keeps the United States stuck in the past. For modern liberals, the Roberts court has kept the United States mired in age-old inequality by ruling that its 220-year-old Constitution blocks the federal government from requiring states to expand Medicare coverage in the "Obamacare" health insurance law, or by allowing unlimited corporate spending in elections in the 2010 *Citizens United* decision. Liberals often compare U.S. inequality unfavorably to other democracies and call for reasserting elected legislators' authority against the judges. For example, consider this entry from a liberal blogger, who suggests that conservative judges are making the United States into a "banana republic"—evoking the phrase for a country run like a plantation for the benefit of big business—and who recommends reducing the power of the Supreme Court:

> As the most unequal of industrial democracies, [the United States] is joining
> the ranks of banana republics. . . . Both political and economic inequality can
> be addressed by restoring the traditional boundary demarcating the separa-
> tion of legislative and judicial powers, thereby excluding the Supreme Court
> from regulating and judging [how congressional and presidential] elections
> [are held and their results processed]. . . . [Congress must] defend its legisla-
> tive power from unconstitutional encroachment by a politicized majority [the
> judges] on the Court.[27]

Thus Jacksonian ideals still echo across twenty-first-century America. For conservatives, bureaucratic authority and expansive judicial interpretations risk making the liberty-loving Americans as downtrodden as they imagine Europeans to be. For liberals, conservative judges anchor the United States to the world's oldest written constitution and prevent it from addressing today's social problems. Both sides often argue that to avoid a modern sort of tyranny, elected politicians must beat back the authority of unelected officials.

Unelected Expertise as Source of Wisdom and Stability

Despite Jackson's enduring resonance, robust ideological positions also defend bureaucratic expertise and judicial influence in American policymaking today. These defenses connect implicitly to criticisms of elected politicians. Few would disagree that elections motivate politicians to think in the short term, to prioritize show over substance, and to adopt policies erratically in response to the latest fad or crisis. In various ways, most Americans on the right and left accept that unelected officials help make policymaking more stable and far-sighted.

Because the leading criticisms of bureaucrats come from the Right, their chief defenses are formulated on the Left. Representation is just as fundamental to modern liberalism as to modern conservatism, but liberals are optimistic that representation and expertise support each other. Their ideology is built on the Enlightenment idea of social progress through rational thinking, and they see government actively pursuing a better society with two kinds of consultations: with citizens to define the goals and major features of policies, and with knowledgeable experts to make policies work. Civil service experts also bring a welcome neutrality to policymaking, decreasing the infighting of party politics. For these reasons, liberals championed the construction of a federal civil service in the late 1800s and have supported its role ever since. Perhaps the clearest illustration today is in environmental policy debates over climate change. Liberals call for basing policy on preponderant views among scientific experts that pollution is warming the planet. They would insist that environmental legislation receive democratic approval, of course, but then these liberals would gladly hand implementation of tough antipollution rules to the EPA. Liberals regret that a politicized bureaucracy and skepticism of expertise and science have made the United States a laggard on climate change, well behind other democracies.

Even most conservatives accept some need for bureaucratic expertise, but usually only in the few areas where they see a need for government action. Chief among these are defense, policing, and money. Conservatives tend to see a threatening world in which democracies need professional protectors. Thus they lead the call for funding the bureaucracy with the biggest budget in the world—the U.S. Department of Defense—and often defer to military officials' counsels on defense policy. In policing and internal security, the vast Department of Homeland Security (DHS) is also a conservative creation. With respect to money, the independent authority of the Federal Reserve grew out of conservative thinking that government should seek background economic stability and not actively cater to citizens' demands. To prevent interest rates and other "Fed" tools from becoming playthings of active government, bank officials were isolated from politicians' influence. Even these positions are admittedly challenged by the most antigovernment conservatives; libertarian icon Ron Paul (father of current senator Rand Paul) called for cutting defense spending and abolishing the Fed and the "monstrous bureaucracy" of DHS. Yet the dominant conservative view is that more-than-minimal bureaucratic expertise is important for accomplishing a few fundamental government tasks. They favor influence for military experts, police and central bankers, but not for environmental regulators or experts in public health or social policy.

Much deeper support for judicial power is evident on the American Left and Right, despite gripes from both sides about what they see as its misuse. If we reverse their respective complaints about judicial tyranny, we see that judges are important to conservative and liberal goals—and to restraining what each side sees as the misguided agenda of its rivals. For liberals, judges compel Americans to live up to the progressive rights to which their founders aspired. Elected politicians often are afraid to challenge what liberals see as antiquated social rules that hypocritically limit rights, like racial segregation or discrimination against homosexuals; judges are more likely to act on what liberals see as the logic of rights to resolve these exceptions. Some conservative judges may slow this process, but in the long run judges play an important role in making American society better. For conservatives, judges compel Americans to retain the fundamental liberties enshrined by the founders. Elected politicians may be tempted to abuse liberties in the faddish name of progress, but judges limit them, thanks to the far-sighted Constitution. Some liberal judges may misread its principles, but at least on several key issues—the ability to spend money as one pleases, or the Second Amendment's right to bear arms—judges play an important role in ensuring that Americans conserve their original vision of a good society.

Judges are thus more than a necessary evil for almost all American thinkers, while the role of bureaucrats is more contested. As we have seen, these positions reflect the shape of American government. Against the backdrop of a decentralized state in which judges became key arbiters of politics, Americans sharply debate constitutional interpretations but rarely question the American-invented notion that judicial review is fundamental to liberal democracy. In a decentralized state that constructed only a modest role for an expert civil service, however, the power of bureaucrats is less widely accepted. Conservatives who most celebrate the original American model see bureaucratic experts as valuable only to defend and stabilize it. Liberals who see America more as a work in progress tend to admire the stronger role of expertise in other democracies, welcoming expert input into further improving society.

Explaining Cases: Uncovering the Whys of the Weak American Bureaucracy

8.5   Identify multiple explanations for the weakness of the U.S. federal bureaucracy in policymaking.

How we ultimately judge arrangements of policymaking authority around the world depends heavily on how we explain them. If France or Japan empowers bureaucrats due to certain cultural views of authority, and if the United States has weaker bureaucrats and judicial arbitration due to different cultural beliefs, national differences in the configuration of policymaking become harder to criticize. Like sushi versus hamburgers, it is a matter of taste. If we explain their arrangements as responses to material or institutional conditions, we have more scope to argue that certain options are better or best. Especially in an increasingly connected world, we might expect countries to learn from each other over time.

To explore some explanations, consider the focused question of why the United States assigns only modest power to career civil servants. Earlier sections have suggested that this weak role for bureaucrats is related to America's decentralized origins, but we can still imagine several different bottom-line explanations for how the United States got on this distinctive track.

The Rational-Material Story

From a material point of view, strong bureaucracies arise where populations face strong pressures for coordinated central action against major threats or policy challenges. The United States began with plentiful resources, low population, and no strong local competitors, and flourished with little need for central expertise and control. The same material conditions eventually favored the emergence of a very large economy that produced powerful big businesses. These powerful players are generally hostile to bureaucratic regulation and prefer to deal with legislators whom they can influence more easily. Thus early material conditions created little need for a strong central bureaucracy and later material conditions set limits on its later emergence.

The Institutional Story

An institutional explanation sees today's relatively weak central bureaucracy as a direct legacy of the early American institutions. The federal bureaucracy was originally tiny and dominated by patronage. By the time federal government expanded to take on new tasks in the twentieth century, policymaking resources and expertise had consolidated in the legislature. Higher education had also been configured in ways that channeled talented people away from bureaucratic jobs. Even if Americans had wanted to build a more expertise-based civil service with policymaking power, it would have been difficult to reorient these institutional rules and channels that they had already built.

The Ideational Story

An ideational explanation of the American balance of power in policymaking centers on the distinctive ideas of government around which the United States were built. America's founders believed in limiting central government. Even once the federal government expanded, continued distrust of its authority left the bureaucracy subject to dominance by elected politicians. Efforts to create or strengthen federal agencies to tackle policy problems have generally faced stronger opposition than they might have confronted in other countries with similar policy problems but different dominant ideas about government. Americans accept judicial authority, on the other hand, because it focuses mainly on arbitrating political battles that have developed among citizens or elected officials, not on asking government officials what to do to begin with.

As in preceding chapters, we can seek evidence for these competing explanations in two broad ways:

RESEARCH ON WITHIN-CASE PROCESSES. We can look at sources on U.S. history and survey or interview people today to gather evidence about why the federal bureaucracy developed as it did. Historically, we could look at moments when the bureaucracy expanded—around the Pendleton Act, in the 1930s, and after World War II—to see what people said and wrote about it. For the current era, we could survey citizens and interview legislators, businesspeople, and bureaucrats to get at what sustains these arrangements. Table 8-3 lays out the process expectations of our theoretical explanations in more detail.

On close inspection, does the development of the U.S. bureaucracy look most like a story in which few concrete problems ever called for a strong bureaucracy? Or one in which many people over time might have wanted a stronger bureaucracy but found U.S. institutions too difficult to reform? Or one in which most Americans saw strong bureaucracy as illegitimate no matter what their problems were? Find a news article about the power of an American department or agency—like the EPA, or the Food and Drug Administration—from a respectable newspaper, magazine, or website. Look for hints in the article that support or contradict these explanatory alternatives.

RESEARCH ON CROSS-CASE PATTERNS. In principle, we could also look at other countries to compare with the United States to see which conditions have

Table 8-3 Exploring Within-Case Evidence for Explanations of the Weak American Bureaucracy

	Rational-Material Explanation	Institutional Explanation	Ideational Explanation
Who has championed more bureaucratic power?	Policymakers and citizens wrestling with real challenges that called for effective central policies	Policymakers and citizens wrestling with real challenges that called for effective central policies	Ideological advocates of central government action, mostly on the Left (except relating to defense, where advocates are mostly on the Right)
What or who has limited bureaucratic power?	Real challenges that required government expertise have been rare in the resource-rich setting of the United States	Very decentralized original U.S. institutions have been hard to reorganize to build up more central power and prestige	Widespread American predisposition to mistrust central government, especially unelected officials
When or where has bureaucratic power increased?	Only when clear challenges called for government experts to act (for defense, food or workplace safety, air traffic control, etc.)	Only when truly major policy challenges pushed people to overcome the difficulty of rebuilding institutions (for example, when the poverty caused by the Great Depression created pressure to introduce central welfare-state policies)	At moments of major ideological shifts: the Progressive era around 1900, the anti-Communist Cold War era, environmentalism in the 1970s
Best Evidence to Support Each Explanation	We see that wherever policy problems clearly called for government expertise, the United States did create robust bureaucracy.	We find that only the biggest policy problems that required central solutions led to effective federal bureaucracy; other attempts to build federal bureaucracy failed due to a lack of money and "know-how" at the center.	We find that even when policy problems seemed to call for government expertise, stronger bureaucracy was widely rejected as illegitimate.

tended to go along with strong or weak bureaucrats. Do countries with the most prestigious bureaucracies share features in terms of geography, resources, or other institutional arrangements? In practice, however, this topic offers a lesson in the challenges of quantitative methods. No good quantitative data exits on bureaucratic power across many countries, so the concept is difficult to relate to correlations.

Conclusion: Why Understanding Policymaking Matters to You

Government policymaking massively affects our lives, from taxes, roads, and wars to health care, schools, and more. While liberal democracies largely attempt to make policymaking representative of their citizens' wishes, policies are never just a simple reflection of elections. Executive and legislative representatives can relate in many different ways, often for reasons of internal rules that the public hardly perceives. All liberal democracies depend on the policy expertise of bureaucrats and the legal expertise of judges, but in hugely different roles from country to country. Only if we understand who calls the shots in our own government can we begin to think critically about how we want it to look and act on our behalf. Getting a broad view of alternative policymaking arrangements in other democracies is especially important for critical thinking about policymaking in the United States because the United States, yet again, stands out for a rare configuration: unusually active legislators, unusually weak bureaucrats, and unusually powerful judges. Whether knowledge of these alternatives make us question our own model or value our country's choices all the more, it helps us to reclaim politics for ourselves.

Review of Learning Objectives

8.1 Identify the typical place of executives and legislators in policymaking processes and describe factors that enhance or decrease legislators' influence.

In all liberal democracies, elected executives formulate and implement policy and elected legislators debate and approve it. Only in some liberal democracies does this middle debate and approval stage in the legislature significantly affect policymaking. Parliamentary-regime legislatures tend to be fairly weak, since the fusion of the legislative majority with the executive frequently allows the prime minister to use control of his or her shared political party to discipline legislators. Presidential-regime legislators often have more autonomy. Most important for legislative power, however, are internal rules of agenda control, committee structure, and legislators' resources for staff support.

8.2 Identify the principles of bureaucratic organization and describe several reasons why bureaucrats' policymaking influence varies across liberal democracies.

For political scientists, "bureaucracy" refers to a hierarchy of salaried professional experts. Government bureaucrats outside of the armed forces are also known as civil servants. All liberal democracies include substantial bureaucracies that serve as staff for the executive and help to formulate and implement policy. In principle, they exist just to support elected executives, but in practice their policy expertise often gives them substantial influence over policymaking in their own right. In some countries, like France, early centralization of government and competitive training programs for civil servants produced prestigious, elite bureaucracies with major influence in policymaking. The United States lies at the other extreme among democracies: a decentralized polity and educational system, and a bureaucracy deeply penetrated by party politics, which left its career civil servants with only modest policy influence.

8.3 Identify the principles of common- and code-law legal systems, American and European models of judicial review, and how they relate to judicial influence.

Law has a special power in liberal democracies, yet ambiguity always arises in how laws apply to real situations. Judges' authority is based on their role in resolving legal ambiguities and so orienting the power of law in certain ways. In countries following the English common-law tradition, including the United States, the interpretive role of judges is very explicit. Judges make legal rulings on the basis of precedent from concrete cases. New rulings can alter precedents and reinterpret how laws apply in the future—giving judges real impact on policy. In countries in the code-law tradition, laws and regulations are written more comprehensively and judges have less room for interpretation and influence. In common-law countries that have a complex distribution of political authority—especially federal states, but also presidential regimes—judges have often been called upon to resolve major political ambiguities as well. Judges thereby gain tremendous influence through judicial review of laws and the actions of government. A more restrained version of judicial review later emerged in some code-law countries, particularly federal ones like Germany. Only in a few democracies today is there no substantial judicial review at all. In Britain or the Netherlands, political authority follows the simple rule of parliamentary sovereignty—all authority lies in parliament—and so judges play a much smaller role in resolving major political questions.

8.4 Evaluate competing American arguments for and against bureaucratic and judicial authority.

Arguments against unelected authority in the tradition of Andrew Jackson are common in American politics today. Conservatives frequently object to the influence or very existence of many government agencies, arguing that unaccountable civil servants tend systematically to abuse rights and make inefficient policies. Both the Right and Left sometimes object to judicial influence when judges rule against their priorities: conservatives criticize rulings that expand conceptions of rights in new directions, and liberals dislike those that they see as defending inequality or outdated social traditions. On the other hand, both sides of the political spectrum generally accept at least some legitimate role for both judges and bureaucrats. Liberals defend bureaucratic expertise as important to well-informed policies to improve lives, and even conservatives accept expertise in policy areas they see as important, like defense or policing. Both liberals and conservatives tend to endorse judicial authority as an instrument to protect their political agenda from the other side.

8.5 Identify multiple explanations for the weakness of the U.S. federal bureaucracy in policymaking.

To review for this objective, try to imagine rational-material, institutional, and ideational explanations of why the United States ended up with a weak bureaucracy without looking at Section 8.5. Start by asking yourself the following questions:

- In what sort of material landscape might we most expect a society to develop strong central administrative capabilities (like military experts, tax collectors, and other expert groups to perform central tasks)? Under what kind of material conditions might people perceive less need for creating a well-developed expert bureaucracy for their government?

- If we focus instead on possible institutional explanations for bureaucratic strength or weakness, what sort of past institutional arrangements might make it difficult to develop a centralized civil service as a country develops?
- From an ideational point of view, are there elements of common American beliefs or culture that might have gotten in the way of the construction of a strong expert civil service at the federal level?

After brainstorming your answers to these questions, return to Section 8.5 to see how well you have imagined plausible alternatives to explain this case.

Great Sources to Find Out More

Charles Goodsell, *The Case for Bureaucracy: A Public Administration Polemic* (Washington, DC: CQ Press, 2004). A defense of the positive role of bureaucrats in the U.S. government.

Eric J. Segall, *Supreme Myths: Why the Supreme Court Is Not a Court and Its Justices Are Not Justices* (Santa Barbara, CA: Praeger, 2012). An argument that the Supreme Court is a political actor, not a body that upholds the rule of law.

Ezra Suleiman, *Politics, Power and Bureaucracy in France: The Administrative Elite* (Princeton, NJ: Princeton University Press, 1974). An equally classic account about how institutions and political culture gave French civil servants a powerful role in policymaking.

Gerhard Loewenberg, Peverill Squire, and D. Roderick Kiewiet, eds., *Legislatures: Comparative Perspectives on Representative Assemblies* (Ann Arbor: University of Michigan Press, 2002). A collection of essays on legislatures by experts from ten countries.

James Q. Wilson, *Bureaucracy: What Government Agencies Do and Why They Do It* (New York: Basic Books, 1991). A very readable classic about bureaucracy in the United States.

Jeffrey Toobin, *The Nine: Inside the Secret World of the Supreme Court* (New York: Doubleday, 2007). An engaging look inside this Court.

Mark C. Miller, ed., *Exploring Judicial Politics* (New York: Oxford University Press, 2008).

Martin Shapiro, *Courts: A Comparative and Political Analysis* (Chicago: University of Chicago Press, 1986). Perhaps the clearest discussion ever of how and why courts become powerful.

Neal Tate and Torbjorn Vallinder, eds., *The Global Expansion of Judicial Power* (New York: NYU Press, 1995). A survey of the spread of judicial review around the world.

Peter Hartcher, *The Ministry: The Inside Story of Japan's Ministry of Finance* (London: Harper-Collins, 1998). An engaging account of the heights of the Japanese bureaucracy.

Peter Irons, *A People's History of the Supreme Court* (New York: Penguin, 2000). A lively and readable history by a constitutional scholar.

Robert Caro, *Master of the Senate: The Years of Lyndon Johnson* (New York: Vintage, 2003[1982]). One of the greatest political biographies and a dissection of Senate politics.

Robert Rogers and Rhodri Havard Walters, *How Parliament Works*, 8th ed. (Harlow, UK: Pearson, 2018). An excellent introduction to the British parliament.

Roger Davidson et al., *Congress and Its Members* (Washington, DC: CQ Press, 2007). An accessible introduction to Congress.

Stephen Skowronek, *Building A New American State: The Expansion of National Administrative Capacities, 1877–1920* (New York: Cambridge University Press, 1983). A classic institutionalist argument about how the decentralized nature of the early U.S. government made it difficult to construct an effective central bureaucracy on these foundations later on.

Woodrow Wilson, *Congressional Government: A Study in American Politics* (New Brunswick, NJ: Transaction, 2002 [1900]). A critique of U.S. government by a professor who later became U.S. president.

Develop Your Thinking

Use these questions as discussion or short writing exercises to think more deeply about some of the key themes of the chapter.

1. How much do you trust congresspeople to make good public policy?
2. How important is expert knowledge in making good public policy? Give an example.
3. How comfortable are you with the influence of the Supreme Court in American politics?
4. How much should military officers influence the policy choices of a democracy? How about environmental scientists?
5. Given unlimited power, would you redesign American policymaking to give more influence to bureaucratic experts?
6. Are you more comfortable with policymaking influence for bureaucratic experts or for judges? Comfortable or uncomfortable with both? Explain.

Keywords

administrative law   267
agenda control   250
backbenchers   248
bureaucracy   252
civil service   257
code law   266
common law   266

constitutional law   267
judicial review   271
independent regulatory
  agencies   257
parliamentary
  sovereignty   272
patronage   259

Pendleton Act of 1883   259
plenary   250
policies   245
politicization   260
precedent   266
statute law   267
veto   249

Chapter 9
Political Economies

Ulrich Baumgarten/Getty Images

How would you like to be guaranteed a paid apprenticeship that led to a skilled job? A majority of German teenagers pass through vocational training programs (like the metal working training seen in this photo) and into paid apprenticeships. This vast partnership among business, government, and labor unions requires a level of coordination that is hard to imagine in the American economy. As a measure of its success, Germany maintains the highest rate of employed youth in Europe—and its youth unemployment is usually well below that of the United States.

 ## Learning Objectives

9.1 Describe three concrete ways in which national economies vary, the abstract economic models of market and command economies, and how mixed economies today relate to those models.

9.2 Describe key features of the U.S., German, and Malaysian economies in terms of labor, finance, and government interventions and explain how they represent contrasting political choices.

9.3 Explain the classical-liberal case for markets as good, the Marxist case for markets as bad, and how modern liberals and social democrats stand between these options.

9.4 Identify three plausible explanations for Germany's generous redistributive policies.

Good Times, Bad Times: Are Economies Like the Weather?

The economy often seems as uncontrollable as the weather. In sunny times, like the late 2010s or late 1990s in the United States, we bask in prosperity. Jobs are plentiful. Incomes rise. In darker periods, like the "Great Recession" of 2009 and the slow recovery afterward, jobs are scarce. We get by as we can. Over the years, good times come and go in ways that even the most powerful people seem unable to direct or foresee.

On the other hand, economies are not natural systems like weather. Human beings built them. At their cores, they are collective decision-making arrangements for the production and allocation of wealth. Even if economies are so complex that they escape tight control or prediction, they represent a series of choices—extremely *political* choices—about how to set up human interactions.

Cross-country comparisons often make these choices very visible. Germany, for example, managed to maintain plentiful jobs and highly competitive industries even in the years coming out of the 2009 recession—all while offering far more public benefits than Americans receive. While U.S. B.A. graduates now average well over $25,000 in debt, German students pay no college tuition.[1] All also receive monthly payments to live on. Over 60 percent of German students pass through a huge public/private apprenticeship system that connects them to jobs. Other public benefits, like free health care and other welfare support, are much more generous than U.S. programs.

Would young Americans thus be better off in Germany? Not necessarily. Americans remain richer than Germans on average. Germans pay higher taxes. U.S. universities rank as the best in the world. Judging which economic system is best overall is a complex and deeply political question. And that is the point of the comparison: people's economic experiences are radically different in Germany for *political* reasons. Reclaiming politics for yourself means seeing how politics pervades the economy as well. ∎

Nuts and Bolts of Economies

9.1   **Describe three concrete ways in which national economies vary, the abstract economic models of market and command economies, and how mixed economies today relate to those models.**

An economy is the sum total of all exchange in an area, or all the buying and selling that goes on. If you mow your own lawn, that is not an economic activity; if you pay someone to do it, it is part of the economy. Buying and selling can involve goods, which are exchangeable things that you can drop on your foot (like shoes, soccer balls, or computers), or services, which are exchangeable things that you cannot drop on your foot (like mowing your lawn, surgery, or accounting work). Buying or selling these products and services typically involves using money—a value-carrying medium of exchange, classically bills or coins—but can also operate through barter, in which people exchange one good or service for another. Barter is rare in most modern economies, though, because it makes exchange much less fluid. A doctor would generally rather be paid in money than in eggs or car-washing services. Barter helps that doctor only when she or he wants those specific items; money can be used now or later to buy eggs, a car wash, or anything else.

All economies today are built around goods, services, and money (perhaps with a bit of barter). Beyond that, they can be radically different. Most concretely, they can vary in how wealthy their inhabitants are, how wealth is distributed within each economy, and the technology by which wealth is produced. Just as important is their political organization: how they assign rights to own, produce, and exchange goods and services. This first section gives you an overview of these variations before the later sections delve more deeply into examples of different national economies.

Concrete Features of Economies: Wealth, Industrialization, Inequality

Almost all American households own a car, with over 800 cars for every 1,000 people in the United States. In Afghanistan—one of the poorest countries in the world—car ownership is far rarer, with roughly 40 cars per thousand people.[2] A similarly vast gulf exists on any other measure of material wealth. Where wealth comes from, too, is strikingly different in the two countries. Almost 45 percent of Afghans work in agriculture. A little over 18 percent work in industry—manufacturing goods—and the other 37 percent of employed people make their money providing services. In the United States, over 80 percent of jobs are in services. Another 12 percent work in manufacturing and construction. Less than 1.5 percent work in agriculture, forestry, and fishing combined.[3]

These are the most concrete features of national economies: how much material wealth do citizens hold on average, and how is that wealth produced? Overall wealth of countries is measured by **gross domestic product (GDP)**: the total value of goods and services produced in the country. To get at wealth on average, though, we must divide GDP by population to calculate **GDP per capita**. Figure 9-1 displays the overall GDP and GDP per capita for selected countries around the world (calculated to allow for the actual "purchasing power" of a U.S. dollar in each economy). In total GDP, China recently surpassed the United States as the largest economy in the world. China is much poorer on average, falling much lower on the vertical axis of GDP per capita, but its overall economy comes first because its population is so huge. In GDP per capita, only a few small countries are richer on average than the United States. Some European countries, Canada, and some Asian countries are not far from U.S. levels.

Variation in the main sources of wealth is commonly described in terms of **industrialization**. Industrialization is the shift to large-scale production

gross domestic product (GDP)
The total value of goods and services produced in a country.

GDP per capita
The most common measure of average wealth, calculated by dividing GDP by population.

industrialization
The adoption of modes of production that include mechanized technology and the separation of jobs into specific roles for each step in a production process.

Figure 9-1 Overall GDP and GDP per Capita for Selected Countries

This chart shows the size of national economies (GDP) in two ways, by the size of bubbles and by placement along the horizontal axis.* The height of the bubbles on the vertical axis shows each country's wealth per person (GDP per capita). The Chinese and American economies are the world's largest and are currently close in overall size, but U.S. GDP per capita is far higher. The bubbles are colored by region, showing that most of the richest economies per capita (toward the top of the figure) are in Europe, Asia, and the United States and Canada.

*Note that the horizontal axis is "logarithmic": each step goes up by a factor of 10, to capture the huge range in size of economies.

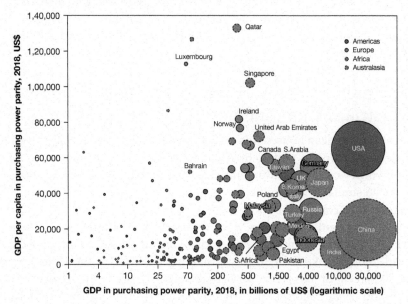

Source: International Monetary Fund, World Economies Outlook Database, October 2018 figures.

division of labor

The specialization of roles in an economy.

post-industrial society

A society in which advanced industrialization, mechanization, and trade shift most jobs into service sectors.

that involves advanced technology and a **division of labor**, when people do more specialized jobs and buy most of what they need from others. In nonindustrialized societies, most people work in agriculture. They produce most of their own food, housing, and other goods. In more industrialized societies, people move into manufacturing jobs. They develop a higher division of labor, buying their food and other essentials from other people. Technology and the division of labor bring a gigantic expansion in overall productivity, as the first Industrial Revolution did in eighteenth- and nineteenth-century Europe. Since the 1960s or so, North America, Europe, Japan, and a few other places have taken a further step to become **post-industrial societies**. Such societies have very low employment in agriculture because they have either mechanized most food production or buy food from other countries. These societies also usually have fairly low employment in industry, with machines replacing many jobs in manufacturing and with many manufactured products bought from elsewhere. Most jobs—again, about 80 percent in the United States—are in services like retail, food service, health care or finance.

One other feature is important to grasping the most basic concrete contrasts between economies: inequality. Neither GDP nor GDP per capita tells us how equally wealth is distributed within a country. Mathematically speaking, a country with 1 million citizens and a GDP per capita of $50,000 could have 1 million people who each make $50,000 a year or one person who makes $50 billion a year and 999,999 who make nothing at all. Those scenarios would obviously be rather different in economic and political terms. The most common measure of inequality is the **Gini coefficient**, which is a complex calculation that measures the distribution of wealth and assigns a country a number between one (which would mean that one person owns everything) and zero (everyone in society is equally wealthy). As Figure 9-2 shows, the United States stands out for higher inequality than other post-industrial nations. Its distribution of wealth is more similar to certain countries in the process of industrialization, like China, Venezuela, or Malaysia.

Gini coefficient
The most widely used measure of inequality.

We can describe any economy in terms of its overall wealth, industrialization, and inequality. These are very important things to know about an economy, but they are also very broad and crude; they only highlight some of the most basic features of the economic landscape. They tell us nothing about the rules and processes by which each economy works. Fundamentally, economies are collective

Figure 9-2 Inequality: Gini Coefficient Scores of Selected Countries

The Gini Coefficient of inequality is a complex calculation, but the basic idea is that the higher the bar, the more wealth is distributed unequally in that country. Inequality is usually higher in poorer countries than in richer ones, but the United States has the highest inequality score among developed nations. Gini studies across countries do not happen very frequently. These figures were compiled in 2016–2017 from various sources by the CIA World Factbook.

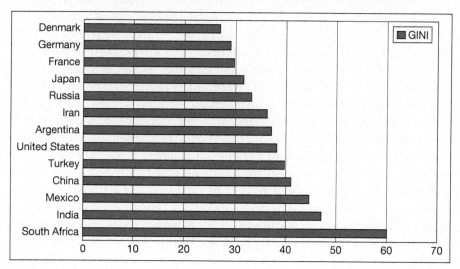

Source: CIA World Factbook.

decision-making arrangements for the production and distribution of wealth—not just unorganized piles of resources and technology—so to understand what these concrete measures really mean, we have to understand the political-economic systems in which these economies are framed.

Abstract Political-Economic Systems: Market versus Command Economies

The most classic distinction in political-economic systems is between market and command economies. In the pure version of a **market economy**, private individuals own all property and do what they want with it. In truly "free markets," that is, people can sell and buy goods and services at whatever prices others offer or accept. If everyone in the market has good information—that is, there is no cheating or ignorance—then fluctuating prices lead to efficient allocation of resources and effort. Plentiful materials, like potatoes or rice (given a good harvest), will be cheap. Producers of cheap things might shift to another product to make more money for less labor; for instance, farmers might switch to strawberries if they bring a higher price. But if too many farmers stop growing potatoes and spuds become harder to find, potato lovers will offer a higher price, drawing some producers back to producing that crop. In this way, prices naturally adjust within a transparent, competitive free market, fluctuating to match supply with demand. Everyone is drawn to make and sell goods or services that they can produce more efficiently than others, or what the economist David Ricardo (1772–1823) called their **comparative advantage**. Individuals become as efficient as they can be, and even without anyone overseeing the whole market, it produces and allocates things efficiently—operating, as the economist Adam Smith (1723–1790) said, as if by an "invisible hand."

A market system is often also called a **capitalist** system, though strictly speaking "capitalism" is just one process inside a market system. Capitalism is when people who own money (known as "capital") make more money without directly doing the labor to produce goods or services. They make their money by owning businesses that make a profit, investing their money in someone else's business and getting a return on that investment, or charging interest on loans to others. Capitalists make profits on their capital.

In a pure version of a **command economy**, private individuals do not own property, so they cannot buy or sell things. Such systems are also known as "planned economies" because government planning determines what such economies produce: government organizations study what people need and command that these goods and services be produced and distributed accordingly. This kind of system has no price signaling or "invisible hand" working to make it efficient. If the central planners get things wrong, people end up with too little, too much, or the wrong kind of products. Yet in principle, a command economy saves people from the uncertainty and potential for inequality in a market. Properly functioning free markets might be good for overall efficiency, but they

market economy
An economic system based on private property where people can freely exchange goods and services.

comparative advantage
Whatever a person can produce relatively more efficiently than other people.

capitalism
The making of money (or "capital") through ownership or investment in a profit-making enterprise.

command economy
A system in which government authorities dictate the production and distribution of goods and services.

have winners and losers: some people do very well while others lose the economic competition (at least partly, making less money). If command-economy planners get it right and produce things that people need in roughly the right quantity and quality, the economy is not divided between winners and losers.

We also often hear a command economy described as a **socialist** system. As we saw in earlier chapters, there are many strands of socialist ideology, so we should be careful with the term. This common use of "socialist" reflects the logic of state socialism that inspired the Soviet and Chinese Communist regimes. That version of socialism defined a command economy as the necessary response to the problems of private property, open markets, and capitalism. Allocating wealth in competitive markets is inherently unfair to those who start out with disadvantages, argued leaders like Lenin or Mao, and capitalism is as an immoral process in which the rich make more money just for being rich while others do the work. Thus, government should step in, claim ownership of economic resources and production processes, and allocate things more fairly. As the leaders of state socialism saw it, a government that does so is "socializing" the economy: owning resources in the name of all of society, and reorganizing exchange for the collective social good.

socialism
A system where government owns most or all economic activities, with little private property.

Political-Economic Systems in the Real World

These abstract principles of market-capitalist and command-socialist systems are very important in how people talk and think about economies today, but not quite in a directly relevant way. They are conceptually pure models of imagined economies, not concretely real descriptions of economic arrangements on the ground. In fact, no economy in the world today comes very close to either model.

Something close to command economies *did* once exist on a large scale. The Union of Soviet Socialist Republics (USSR) and the countries it dominated in Eastern Europe from the 1940s to 1989 were mostly command economies. Yet, far too often, the central planners of the Soviet economy got it wrong by producing too many things their people did not want and not enough of things they did. Store shelves often featured unused items while soap and toilet paper were in short supply. Overall quality and variety in the goods and services available were terrible. After a long period of economic stagnation, the USSR collapsed in 1992, shattering into the Russian Federation and fourteen other new countries. To varying degrees, these countries moved toward more market-capitalist economies.

The People's Republic of China (PRC) was the other major command economy in the world from the 1950s to the 1980s. Though China never suffered a collapse like the USSR, it began a series of reforms in the 1980s that incorporated market economy characteristics alongside its command economy. Today, China and the similar regime in Vietnam feature complex mixes of private-property-based market economies with remnants of socialist command economies. As intricate as these systems are, they seem to work. China averaged about 10 percent growth for twenty-five years, and more recently is averaging roughly 7.5 percent growth.

Vietnam has consistently averaged around 6 percent—close to the fastest growth among more market-capitalist countries. Cuba, the main ex-Soviet ally near the United States, has followed a less strongly reformed mix with less success, averaging about 3 percent growth a year since the mid-1990s. North Korea, which held onto a pure command model the longest and has reformed the least in recent years, has sometimes struggled on the edge of collapse, with tens of thousands of deaths from famine. Even there, though, the government has increasingly allowed farmers to sell some of their crops, shopkeepers to set up stores, and permitted some banking and foreign investment.[4]

The market model, meanwhile, never came as close to real implementation as the command model did in the USSR. In a pure market economy, government would protect property ownership and take an otherwise "**laissez-faire**" stance—a French phrase meaning roughly "let them do what they want." The industrializing economy of the nineteenth-century United States probably came closest to this model of any real society in history. Yet even during that time, the U.S. government did much more than just protect property ownership. The young U.S. government imposed **tariffs** on imports, taxes on land and items like alcohol and sugar, and created the First Bank of the United States (1791) to issue money. Tariffs added to imported goods made them more expensive, thus giving domestic producers a price advantage over imports and protecting U.S. businesses as they caught up with European competitors. The early United States also regulated many things, like limits on how much interest banks could charge. The government intervened

laissez-faire

A French phrase meaning "let them do what they want" that is often used as a synonym for unregulated markets.

tariffs

Taxes levied on goods brought into a country from outside (imports).

David Guttenfelder/AP Images

A girl looks at shoes in a shopping center in Pyongyang, North Korea. The North Korean government has encouraged the opening of shops for consumers in recent years, but the economy remains troubled by shortages, including basic food items.

heavily with targeted grants of public land, which powerfully shaped the rise of industries like railroads and mining. Also, to the extent that the mid-1800s marked a high point for markets in the United States, it was a short period. The perception spread that an unregulated industrializing economy led to many social ills, from unsafe factories to abusive monopolies that stifled competition. The late 1800s brought a burst of new regulation in the "Progressive Era" around the turn of the nineteenth to twentieth centuries. The Sherman Antitrust Law of 1890 outlawed monopolies, the 1893 Safety Appliance Act targeted workplace safety, and many other kinds of economy-shaping intervention followed.[5]

However close the nineteenth-century United States may have come to a pure market economy model, no society is anywhere near such a model today. We live in a world of **mixed economies**, where a combination of market mechanisms and government policies allocate resources. The vast majority of governments today would say that they adhere to the principles of market capitalism, and they do in important ways, but most also intervene substantially to shape their markets. Governments everywhere regulate workplace conditions, product safety, financial transactions, monopolies and competition, pollution, and many other things. As

mixed economy
An economy that combines market capitalism with various kinds of government policies that shape the market.

Figure 9-3 Government Spending's Share of GDP in Selected Countries

Though all rich countries today have economic systems based on markets and capitalism, some have government spending that accounts for over 50 percent of the economy.

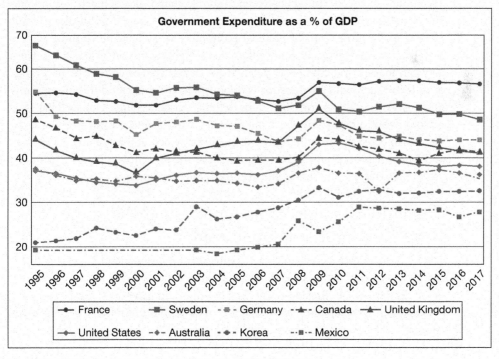

Source: Organization for Economic Cooperation and Development (OECD).

Figure 9-3 shows, governments generally spend more money than any other organization in their respective countries, accounting for at least 15 percent of the economy. For example, U.S. government spending overall—including federal, state, and local governments—rose above 40 percent of GDP in 2009 (though this was an unusual year in a deep recession) and this percentile stands in the high 30s today.[6] Even this remained below average across industrialized countries. Governments with the lowest levels of spending and regulation tend to be in poor countries or "failed states" where government is simply not able to do much at all.

The fact that we live in a world of mixed economies, not one of pure free markets or pure command models, does not mean that all political economies are similar, or just middle-ground mixtures of markets and government action. As the next section shows, a variety of different political choices have led national economies around the world to develop a wide range of different mixes.

The Varying Political Shape of Mixed Economies

9.2 **Describe key features of the U.S., German, and Malaysian economies in terms of labor, finance, and government interventions and explain how they represent contrasting political choices.**

Though the historical conflict between capitalist champions of market economies and socialist champions of command economies has shaped political-economic debates for centuries, mixed political economies today vary much more widely than this contrast suggests. Rather than just spreading out on a simple spectrum between market and command poles, these mixed economies represent a range of different national strategies for economic success that can differ along many dimensions. Some countries take steps to limit market dynamics for socialist-style reasons, while others step away from pure laissez-faire and use government intervention to boost the growth of private business. A look at the American, German, and Malaysian economies gives a glimpse of the enormous diversity of mixed economies and the different political choices they represent.

The United States: "The Chief Business of the American People Is Business"

The United States is commonly seen as the most market-friendly country in the world. The perception is that "the chief business of the American people is business," as Republican president Calvin Coolidge said in 1925. The U.S. economy is mixed and government plays a major economic role, but relative to most other countries, the American system relies more on market-style interactions and less on explicit government action.

One important area where the U.S. economy stands out for its flexible, market-style relationships is in **labor markets**, where employers pay employees for their labor. "Hire and fire" processes in American labor markets are very open. Either the employee or the employer can end employment at any point, usually without even giving a reason, except for rules barring discrimination on the basis of race, religion, sex, or national origin. Other government constraints on labor markets include federal and state regulations on working conditions with minimum wage laws and safety regulations, and the requirement that U.S. employers allow workers to form unions that bargain for more pay and better conditions. Yet if **collective bargaining** between unions and firms takes place in some sectors of the U.S. economy, it is far less common than in most other developed countries. Union membership in the United States is comparatively low at about 10 percent of workers. Large unions like the Service Employees International Union (SEIU) or the American Federation of Labor-Congress of Industrial Organizations (AFL-CIO) can still be powerful in certain sectors, but most jobs are not affected by union bargaining. A key consequence of easy hiring, easy firing, and the modest role of unions shows up in how Americans firms tend to adjust to economic shifts. When the economy slows down, firms fire people and unemployment rises quickly. Hiring has historically picked up quickly in recoveries (though this was less true in the years after 2009). Overall, American employers buy and sell labor very freely to fit their market needs.

Another slice of the economy that is notably flexible in the United States is **financial markets**, where businesses borrow money for investment. Stock markets are very flexible ways for firms to raise money, and American firms have long raised an unusually large share of their investment funds through them. A firm sells a small share of ownership in the company (a stock share) to a buyer. The firm is effectively borrowing money from the buyer, raising capital for investment, and promising future payments to the buyer of the share. The buyer may then turn around and sell that share to someone else in the stock market if she or he so chooses. Large investors can accumulate large stakes of ownership in firms by buying up many shares of their stock, which means that whole companies can be bought and sold quite fluidly. Stocks shift hands frequently, with daily volume on the New York Stock Exchange—the largest stock market in the world—often reaching above 5 billion shares and values over $50 billion. Just as U.S. employers flexibly hire and fire workers to suit their economic needs, so firms and investors flexibly sell and buy stocks to raise money and to invest.

In addition to organizing its economy in comparatively fluid open markets for labor and finance, the United States also counteracts the market less with **redistribution**—taxing the rich to give money to the poor—than most rich countries. This is not immediately obvious in terms of the taxes the U.S. government takes in, which actually fall more on the rich than in many other countries. As Figure 9-4 shows, U.S. taxes are quite progressive overall, meaning that the richest people (in the highest income "decile," or the top 10 percent) pay a higher share of taxes than poorer groups. But the U.S. government then spends less of

labor markets
Parts of the economy in which employers hire (and perhaps fire) employees.

collective bargaining
The process of determining pay or other conditions of work in negotiations between representatives of workers and representatives of employers.

financial markets
Parts of the economy in which businesses raise money for investment.

redistribution
The transfer of income from richer people to poorer people, classically through government programs.

Figure 9-4 What Share of Taxes Do the Richest 10 Percent of the Population Pay?

The richest 10 percent of Americans have a larger share of national income than in most other countries (the blue bars) but pay a higher share of taxes (the reddish bars). So, the wealthiest 10 percent of Americans receive about a third of America's income and pay a little less than half of America's taxes.

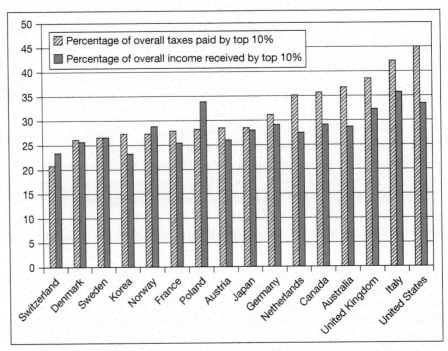

Source: Organization for Economic Cooperation and Development (OECD), *Growing Unequal: Income Distribution and Poverty in OECD Countries* (Paris: OECD, 2008).

welfare state

The set of policies that redistribute wealth from rich to poor in market-capitalist systems.

its revenue on programs for the poor than most other rich-country governments. The redistributive programs that are commonly referred to collectively as the **welfare state**—including old-age pensions and insurance for health care, unemployment, and accidents—shift relatively modest benefits to poor American citizens, which makes less difference in their incomes than the larger welfare-state programs in almost all other rich countries (see Figure 9-5).

For most Americans, their economy's strong reliance on open, flexible markets and relatively small redistribution may seem very natural. Whether we like these arrangements or not, it can be hard to imagine how things could be different. A look inside economies in Germany or Malaysia hints at alternatives and also highlights the political choices Americans have made.

Germany: Redistribution, Codetermination, and Bank Finance in the Social Market Economy

social market economy

A mix of market capitalism with policies and institutions that help disadvantaged people in the market.

Germans often refer to their "**social market economy**": a model that mixes market capitalism with government programs intended to help poorer

Figure 9-5 How Much Do Government Programs Reduce Inequality?

This chart displays the percentage difference between the Gini coefficient of inequality in market income (measuring inequality in how much people are paid directly from jobs and other sources) and the Gini coefficient of inequality in actual disposable income (how much people actually have to spend) after transfers from government programs that benefit poorer people in each country. While initial market-income inequality is not very different between the United States and Germany, German government programs lessen inequality by roughly twice as much as the United States. As we can see from the other lines for France, the United Kingdom, Canada, and the average of the Organization for Economic Cooperation and Development (OECD, an association of thirty-four rich countries), the United States stands out for redistributing less.

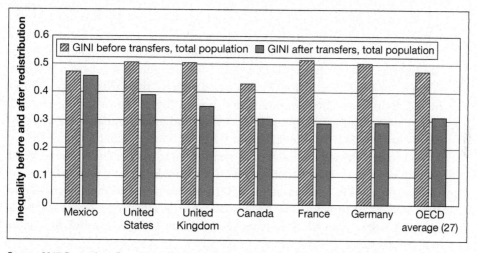

Source: 2017 figures from Organization for Economic Cooperation and Development (OECD).

citizens and to encourage cooperation between the state, firms, and workers. The word "social" does not mean "socialist" like the Union of Soviet Socialist Republics (USSR), however. Public ownership of economic assets, which is the core of state socialism, is only a little more widespread in Germany than in the United States. "Social" in the German economic model is much more in the spirit of social democracy—the most reformist, moderate strand of socialist ideology. It generally translates into two concrete features of everyday economic life. First, redistribution of wealth provides strong protection to the average citizen within a market-capitalist economy. Second, long-term partnerships between various economic players—unions and businesses, businesses and banks—set economic decision making in a social, cooperative context.

The German welfare state operates on a different scale from the American one. As a share of its overall wealth, Germany spends almost three times as much as the United States on direct welfare-state redistribution.[7] Other policies—like free university education and widely available public transport— effectively shift money from rich to poor in more indirect ways. Yet more redistribution means higher taxes to pay for it: taxes in Germany add up to about 37.5 percent of GDP, versus about 27 percent of the GDP in the United

progressive/ regressive taxes

Taxes are progressive when richer people pay a higher proportion of their income, and regressive when poorer people pay a higher proportion of their income.

States. Taxes overall are slightly more **regressive** (meaning the rich do not pay a larger share, the opposite of **progressive**) than in the United States, largely because Germany's taxes are relatively more focused on consumer goods and services that people purchase, rather than on income. Since richer people spend a smaller share of their income on buying things—instead usually saving some of their surplus income—taxes that fall on purchases, like sales taxes, fall disproportionately on poorer citizens. Yet because German government spends such a large share of its revenue on redistributive programs, it ends up transferring a great deal more money to its poorer citizens than the U.S. government does.

Probably more striking to an American eye than the scale of German redistribution, though, are differences in the organization of German labor markets. German employers and employees interact in a system known as "**codetermination**" that is built around less flexible, longer-term relationships with bigger roles for workers and unions than exist in the United States. Employees and employers are bound together in running negotiations about training, pay, hiring and firing, and even company strategy. The core reason is that it is legally much harder to fire someone in Germany. Laws require firms with over five employees to recognize worker-elected "works councils." The councils must be consulted on many management decisions, and in big companies (of 2,000 workers or more) they elect half the firm's board of directors. To fire anyone, a firm effectively needs approval from its works council. Thus management has little choice but to consult with workers.

codetermination

A system in which workers have a say in company management.

Beyond consultation within each firm, collective bargaining is also strong across firms. Unions (such as the German Chemical Workers Union) and employers' federations (like the German Chemical Industry Association) often hold talks about pay and other issues across the sector. Though union membership is not dramatically higher than in the United States, at 17 percent of workers, even most companies with nonunionized workers usually follow the deals reached in union negotiations. Thus, collective bargaining ends up covering almost 60 percent of the workforce. As Figure 9-6 shows, this extension of collective bargaining beyond unions themselves is quite common across rich countries, though it is practically unknown in the United States.

Codetermination between employers and employees is tied to other facets of the German economy. Since employers cannot easily fire one worker and hire a replacement, they face strong incentives to train employees well. Codetermination thus ties into a huge system of education and apprenticeships. In addition to academically focused schools, well-developed vocational schools educate roughly two-thirds of German workers. Upon graduating from vocational school, most students enter a publicly supported, two- to three-year apprenticeship in one of over 300 legally recognized trades, which connects them to employers and jobs.[8] In an economic downturn, German firms are more likely to negotiate with workers to shorten hours or

Figure 9-6 Union Density and the Reach of Collective Bargaining

The United States ranks very low in both the percentage of unionized workers (red bars) and the percentage of jobs covered by collective bargaining agreements (blue bars). In Germany, unions include somewhat more workers, but the big difference is that union-negotiated deals are extended to a majority of workers through collective-bargaining agreements.

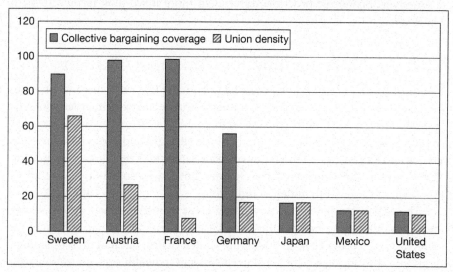

Source: Organization for Economic Cooperation and Development (OECD) Employment Outlook 2017.

implement retraining programs rather than to resort to outright firing. On the downside, German employers are slower than their U.S. counterparts to hire when the economy turns up, since hires are costly, long-term commitments.

In finance, too, the German economy contrasts sharply to that of the United States. Rather than relying mainly on stock markets, modern German firms grew mostly by getting long-term loans from big banks. This tied the banks' fates tightly to the businesses to which they loaned—if the business failed, the bank lost its money—and so banks insisted on close relationships in which they consulted over business strategies and held seats on the businesses' corporate boards. In the long run, these relationships produced almost the opposite situation from U.S. stock market finance: rather than a fluid market where money shifts hands rapidly and companies are bought and sold, German firms and banks build long-term partnerships in which they work together for decades. In the United States, "corporate takeovers"— when outsiders buy up a firm's shares and take it over—are common. But in Germany, it is almost impossible to aggressively take over a company because such ownership is not widely for sale, and the banks guard their investments carefully. Like in the United States, then, the shape of the financial system parallels other economic arrangements. German employees and employers engage in long-term partnerships through codetermination and apprenticeships; German businesses and banks engage in long-term partnerships, too.

Redistribution, codetermination, and bank financing collectively make up the "social" in Germans' "social market economy." In all these ways, Germans coordinate their economic interactions in long-term relationships, making economic life a deeply different experience from life in the United States. And if these features seem rather odd to American eyes, they are just a taste of global alternatives. Economic practices differ even more if we look farther away, to Malaysia.

Malaysia: Intervention for Capitalist Growth

Malaysia provides a fascinating contrast to both the United States and Germany because its government undertakes command-market forms of intervention—like planning, regulation, and public ownership—with a mix of intensively market-capitalist policies. Germany may redistribute strongly and promote a variety of long-term relationships, but its government rarely tells businesses what to do. The Malaysian government effectively does, but it does so mainly to strengthen the private sector, not to undercut or limit it.

The Malaysian landscape is very different from the American or German one, with purchasing-power-adjusted GDP per capita about half the American level. Its Gini score is close to that of the United States, but it addresses inequality mostly by offering free or subsidized services in health care, education, utilities, and some transport, while doing very little in terms of transfers of income.[9] In labor markets, unions cover about 10 percent of workers—just under the U.S. percentage—but play an even weaker role than in the United States. Hiring and firing are very flexible. The main exception to flexible labor markets is similar to that of the United States: Malaysia has strong programs to favor the hiring of certain ethnic groups, like U.S. "affirmative action" programs. They are designed to boost ethnic Malays, who make up about 60 percent of the population, in an economy where business has been historically dominated by an ethnic Chinese minority.[10]

Since the 1970s, though, the Malaysian government has steered its economy in ways that contrast sharply to economic policies in the United States or Germany. Unlike in the Soviet Union, which steered its economy as a replacement of private business and markets, the goal of Malaysian planning is to grow the private sector economy more rapidly. An Economic Planning Unit that reports directly to Malaysia's prime minister creates multiyear goals and plans for the whole economy and for every sector. The Eleventh Economic Plan, covering 2015 to 2020, aimed for 6 percent annual growth, huge infrastructure investments, and development of more knowledge-based industries like information technology.

While the Malaysian government does not require private sector business to adhere to the plans, it has many tools to encourage their cooperation. The state channels favorable loans, tax incentives, and infrastructural support to the activities it endorses. It runs huge "sovereign wealth funds"—government-owned funds that invest in private companies—that push tens of billions of dollars toward its priorities. Its large state-owned corporations mix profit making and public policy goals. Finally, the government intervenes in a few command-style ways too. It fixes artificially low prices for essential products like flour, bread, rice, gas, and cooking oil. Also, since a financial crisis in 1997 when many foreign investors tried to pull their money out of the country, the state has closely managed international trading of its currency, the ringit. The government tries to maintain the ringit's value relative to the dollar (currently, roughly 4 ringit to U.S.$1), and people need central-bank permission to take more than 10,000 ringit out of Malaysia.

In sum, setting Germany and Malaysia next to the United States gives us a glimpse of the alternative choices that arise in political economies today. Still, this short introduction may leave us wondering if these are truly viable alternatives. After all, the United States is somewhat richer than Germany and a great deal richer than Malaysia. Whatever their intentions, don't these alternatives just amount to impairments of free markets that lessen economic productivity? The next section gives a few more reasons to take these alternatives seriously. Critical thinkers may legitimately reach different conclusions about their political merits, but their economic success cannot easily be denied.

Different Economies, Different Political Choices

In a simple sense, Germany and Malaysia step away from a free market model and toward socialist-style intervention. Germany stands out for redistribution, which is one element of socialist thinking, and Malaysia for economic planning, which is another. Neither country can be portrayed as leaning far toward the command-economy pole—as U.S. businesspeople working in either country might tell you—because both remain far closer to the market-capitalist pole than to anything like the old Soviet Union. However, both countries are "more socialist" than the United States and they pay a cost in less wealth. Right?

Actually, it is not obvious that these countries' systems impede the growth of their private wealth. For one thing, the U.S. wealth advantage today might not mainly reflect the brilliance of its economic model. The United States industrialized earlier than Germany and long before Malaysia. In addition to this head start, it developed on a continent with few organized competitors and vast resources. It never suffered major destruction in war, as did Germany in World War II. Poor Malaysia was a British colony until 1957. At least part of the story of U.S. wealth, then, might be about advantages it enjoyed rather than about the greater productivity of its economic model.

Nor do statistics on recent decades easily display Germany or Malaysia paying a price in growth for their not-so-free-market arrangements. Since 1960—roughly the period when the welfare state has existed on a large scale—German GDP per capita has grown just slightly less quickly than American GDP per capita. Germany exports almost as much as the United States, though it has a fourth of the U.S. population. Though the World Economic Forum ranked the United States as the most competitive economy in the world in 2018, Germany was third (after Singapore).[11] Overall, if a foreigner told German businesspeople that Germany is a "socialist country" that does not focus on generating wealth, they would be puzzled. They might ask the foreigner if she had ever heard of Deutsche Bank (one of the largest banks in the world), Daimler (maker of Mercedes and the second-largest global manufacturer of trucks), Siemens (Europe's largest engineering company), or Deutsche Telekom (Europe's biggest telecommunications firm, which owns T-Mobile in the United States).

In Malaysia, private markets seem to have been helped, not harmed, by interventionist planning. Over the past fifty years, the country has grown roughly 6 percent a year. The World Economic Forum ranked it as the world's 25th most competitive economy in 2018—but it was the top-ranked middle-income country on the list. Its growth has made a material difference to average Malaysians: the percentage living below the nationally defined poverty line has gone from almost 50 percent in 1960 to under 4 percent today.[12] But it has also generated many millionaires and more than a handful of billionaires. "Socialist" is not exactly how a visitor might describe the view from the Petronas Towers in the capital of Kuala Lumpur. The tallest twin towers in the world, they house the government-owned oil corporation (Petronas), which has long been among the most profitable nonfinancial companies in Asia.[13]

This is not to say that private business always loves German redistribution or Malaysian planning. Wealthy Germans grumble about high taxes and the cost of redistribution, and German bosses sometimes have fights with their works council and union "partners." Malaysian firms and foreign investors do not always enjoy being "guided" by government. In both countries, like in the rest of the world, there are major debates about which kinds of public policies encourage the most economic growth. At a broad level, though, we cannot say that these economies have rejected an American-style goal of private market economic growth in favor of something else. They pursue that same goal but mix it with different political choices.

Lai Seng Sin/AP Images

Children play at a waterpark in front of the Petronas Twin Towers in Kuala Lumpur, Malaysia—headquarters of the state-owned oil company and the tallest twin towers in the world. Substantial planning and investments by the Malaysian government seem to have worked to deliver rapid economic growth.

Table 9-1 The American, German, and Malaysian Economic Models

	Main Economic Goal	Additional Goals	Core Strategy to Reach Goals	Key Features
The United States	To increase private wealth	Liberty to use wealth freely	Flexible economic ties that permit rapid adaptation and innovation	Largely flexible hiring and firing, stock market finance, modest redistribution
Germany	To increase private wealth	Mitigating inequality, encouraging cooperation	Long-term partnerships among economic players and government	Codetermination, collective bargaining, bank finance, strong redistribution
Malaysia	To increase private wealth	Catching up to the West, empowering Malay majority	Long-range government planning to guide investment	Largely flexible hiring and firing (but ethnic preferences), modest redistribution, government interventions to encourage investments

In other words, the U.S. economy is not distinctive in pursuing growth in private wealth, but in the *way* it pursues it (see Table 9-1). Within a widely shared basic preference for market capitalism, the U.S. economy endorses a stronger focus on individualistic economic liberty than Germany or Malaysia. It stands out for its relative rejection of high taxes or government guidance, and an acceptance of more inequality. In both Germany and Malaysia, the government is an active participant in the quest for economic success. In Germany, the partnership is geared toward mitigating inequality and generating cooperation between employers and workers. In Malaysia, it is focused on catching up to wealthier countries through targeted investment and on shifting benefits to the ethnic Malay part of the population.

So what? Whether or not you ever dream of moving to Germany or Malaysia, understanding the connection between their economies and their political choices helps you understand your own place in the U.S. economy. And once you begin to see your own place in a certain political economy, you can intelligently engage in an ideological debate about it.

Political Ideologies and Political Economies

9.3 **Explain the classical-liberal case for markets as good, the Marxist case for markets as bad, and how modern liberals and social democrats stand between these options.**

We have considered what it means to recognize the role of politics in economies: people face certain economic opportunities and challenges due to the political shape of the American economy, and would live very different economic lives if they lived in Germany, Malaysia, or almost anywhere else. Engaging thoughtfully and critically with political economies takes us to a deeper level: *Should* we try to create very fluid "free" markets? Should government redistribute money from rich to poor, or intervene in other ways in the economy? Any answer combines analytic views of how and why economies are set up and function with normative views of what ought to be. Unlike our views on the weather, our answers matter. Our preferences for sunny days have no effects, but our views of human-made economies may well shape our lives.

In previous chapters, we have seen some of the historical bases of the main debates on economies in the traditions of classical liberalism on the one hand and Marxism and socialism on the other. In future chapters on development and growth (Chapter 10) and globalization (Chapter 13), we will engage directly with today's ideological debates about the economy. This section builds a bridge between the two, clarifying the philosophical roots of today's political-economic debates.

Markets as Naturally Good

When people promote markets and capitalism in our world today, they usually draw on arguments that trace back to classical liberalism. We have seen that this school of thought originated in Europe in the 1600s as a philosophy that placed individual liberty, or freedom, above all else. If liberty was the fundamental good, reasoned early liberal theorists, a person's right to act as he or she pleases should be limited only for very compelling reasons. During this time, Europe was dominated by kings, queens, and aristocrats, as well as by many obstacles to open trade, so liberalism mainly took the form of a normative call for a more equal and freer society. Only later, in the 1800s and 1900s, did liberalism take a more analytical direction. By that time, classical-liberal notions of individual rights and free markets had spread and were well established in much of Europe and the United States. Liberals came to see their ideas not just as a desirable blueprint for society but as an accurate analysis of how the world around them worked.

Especially central to early classical-liberal thinking were rights to private property, which liberal thinkers emphasized in reaction to kings or aristocrats who arbitrarily fined, taxed, or simply took away subjects' belongings. From the great liberal theorist John Locke (1632–1704) came the leading account of where property rights come from. While all things on Earth initially belong equally to everyone, he wrote, if someone puts "Work of his Hands" into improving something—cutting a tree into boards, building a house, fencing and plowing a field—it becomes his property.[14] Thereafter, the improved product is his, as is anything he might get by exchanging it for something else. No one else should be able to tell him what to do with it. In practice, classical liberals who followed Locke increasingly allowed any nonviolent way of acquiring property to meet this criterion: if a factory owner invests money in the production process, even if she does not actually do "Work of [her] Hands" in building or running the factory, she has contributed to improvement and can legitimately dispose of the proceeds as she pleases.

An endorsement of markets followed strongly from these foundations in property rights. Your property is really yours only if you can exchange it openly with others. Adam Smith's analytic notion of the "invisible hand" greatly strengthened this connection by arguing that there is no contradiction between the individual pursuit of private property and overall collective good. If we all focus on individual gain, he argued, competition in markets will guide us to the most efficient, most productive, richest society possible. This combined call for private property and unconstrained markets, bolstered by Smith's analysis of market efficiencies and coupled with some political liberties beyond the economy (such as freedoms of religion, speech, association, and so on), became the core of the classical-liberal agenda. Markets are the naturally rational, efficient, and liberty-enhancing way to organize societies.

Arguments for markets today thus powerfully combine normative arguments about rights and justice with more analytical claims about how human societies work. Among the modern conservatives who are the most direct descendants of classical liberals—and especially in the United States where market-centered thinking is unusually influential—wide-open markets are seen as the most natural and desirable basic framework for the realization of human happiness.

Markets as Naturally Bad

Not everyone thought it obvious in Smith's time that markets were always good for most of society—nor do they today. When people criticize markets and capitalism in the twenty-first-century world, they usually draw on (or at least overlap with) some of the most famous critiques of classical liberalism, and especially the thinking of Karl Marx (1818–1883). Marx criticized liberal thinking on both explanatory and normative grounds: he judged capitalism as morally wrong and explained that it was spreading in nineteenth-century Europe precisely because it so efficiently exploited most of the population. At the core of Marx's thinking was a "surplus value" theory of profit in capitalism. Like Locke, he saw labor as the key to the creation of value: when someone works to make or improve something, they add value to it. Yet Marx disagreed with the broad interpretation that classical liberals in the Lockean tradition had given to "Work of [the] Hands." According to Marx, owning or investing in production cannot count as true labor. Simply funding or owning a factory does not entitle you to profits if other people do all the real work.

Such profits are, however, the essence of capitalism: owners or investors make a profit by selling the products for more than they pay the workers. In other words, Marx wrote, capitalists short-change the workers and skim off "surplus value" without laboring themselves. For Marx, this was morally equivalent to stealing, and was also how capitalists were increasingly dominating society. As long as some people owned what Marx called "the means of production"—factories and other businesses—they would skew the terms of exchange and skim this exploitative surplus off the top. Marx argued that the solution was socialism, where society as a whole, or government on its behalf, owns the means of production. He saw markets as a profoundly exploitative, oppressive way of organizing societies. Sooner or later, Marx thought, people would rise up in revolution against the capitalist system.

Convinced socialists in the Marxist tradition are rare in the United States today, but their themes and related rhetoric have seen a rebirth. The "Occupy Wall Street" movement that began in New York in September 2011 introduced the slogan, "We are the 99 percent"—evoking a society of workers creating value and a top 1 percent of exploitative capitalists whose "greed and corruption" must be stopped.[15] Left-wing politicians like Bernie Sanders and New York Congresswoman Alexandria Ocasio-Cortez have consolidated a "democratic socialist" wing of the Democratic Party. Their discourse has considerable resonance, especially with young people: a 2018 Gallup poll found that 51 percent of 18- to 29-year-olds viewed socialism positively. Only 45 percent said the same for capitalism.[16]

Markets as Crafted Political Institutions

Classical liberals see markets as naturally good, Marxists see markets as naturally bad, but on one thing they agree: markets are roughly the same everywhere. Other ideologies reject this notion of economic universals in one of two ways. Noneconomic traditions—such as environmentalists, fascists, and Islamists—suggest that economies should simply not be our first priority, implying that economies can and should be shaped around other goals. Falling between classical liberals and devout Marxists, both modern liberals and social democrats suggest that markets can be modified to work in very different ways—perhaps achieving some of the benefits classical liberals see in markets without some of the problems that Marxists expect.

For most environmentalists, a focus on or against markets simply misses the most important point in human existence: we must replace (or at least temper) our fixation with economic wealth to focus more on our broader environment. Market capitalism is partly to blame for this fixation, encouraging an obsession with rising incomes and economic growth that can lead to environmental devastation. But the solution is not a Marxist-style one of shifting to a different economic system. It is to reframe our economic system by focusing on larger environmental priorities.

From their different points of view, fascists or Islamists similarly downgrade the importance of markets and interpret them, at best, as potentially useful tools. Mussolini, Hitler, and other fascists had no major problem with private property and capitalism as long as economic activities contributed to national strength.

With their main focus on government authority and military power, however, they gradually took over private businesses to direct their war efforts. Islamists subscribe to certain limits on capitalism—the Qur'an forbids the charging of interest on loans, for example—but otherwise they tend to see business and markets as acceptable, as long as they respect the primacy of religious tenets.

Far more influential in our world today, though, is economic thinking that stands between liberal and Marxist influences. The British philosopher T.H. Green (1836–1882) was an early thinker along these lines who argued for a mixed-economy model. Looking out on nineteenth-century England during the Industrial Revolution, he saw that inequality and misery persisted even though classical-liberal principles were increasingly dominant. What classical liberalism needed, he argued, was a more expansive definition of liberty: liberty was an individual's freedom to realize his or her human potential. Individuals need more than to be free from interference (as classical liberals stressed); they need decent levels of welfare, education, and social support. To achieve real liberty, he concluded, government had to intervene in markets to build institutions and policies for redistribution and social services.

One hundred years later, the American philosopher John Rawls (1921–2001) took an abstract route to a similar conclusion. He sought to identify standards for a free, just society without appealing to religious or other external spiritual guidance. To do so, he invented the device of the "veil of ignorance": if rational individuals

Kay Nietfeld/picture-alliance/dpa/AP Images

Can societies have both significant economic liberty and substantial equality? Sweden is the country that has been most consistently governed by Social Democrats who think so. Swedish business often grumbles about high taxes and generous redistribution, but their country is one of the richest in Europe and also among the most equal. (This photo shows shopping crowds and Christmas lights in the capital, Stockholm.) Whether and how a similar mix of liberty and equality can be achieved elsewhere is debatable.

were asked to draw up rules for society before knowing their place within it—not knowing if they would start out rich or poor, powerful or not—he argued that they would agree on certain standards. He thought that they would endorse basic liberal rights, including for private property, but would also design institutions and policies with some redistribution and other programs to benefit the least-advantaged citizens. If people thought they might be placed in disadvantaged positions in society, they would support policies to ensure some economic equality.

Thinkers like Green and Rawls contributed to the foundations of modern liberalism and social democracy, the ideologies that inspire most of the political Left today in the United States and other democracies. They begin from a classical-liberal focus on liberty but end up shifting that focus because of some concern for equality. If classical liberals argue that liberty must trump equality in order for markets to deliver their benefits, and devout socialists argue that equality must trump liberty to end exploitation and misery, modern liberals and social democrats argue that liberty and equality can be mutually supportive given the right institutions and policies. Table 9-2 summarizes the core ideological positions on markets.

Table 9-2 Ideologies and Markets

Core View of Markets	Ideology (from positive to negative views of markets)	The broader and less regulated our markets, the more we will see . . .	How can we organize a morally good economy?
Markets are naturally good	Classical liberalism	Liberty, productivity, and self-improvement for all	Liberalize markets and minimize active government discretion
	Modern conservatism	Ditto (includes classical-liberal views alongside other noneconomic themes like defending social traditions or religious values)	Liberalize markets and minimize government except for security and order (and possibly to defend some social values)
Markets take various shapes depending on political institutions	Modern liberalism (and social democracy)	Liberty and productivity but also inequality	Encourage largely liberalized markets but mitigate inequality and other social ills with redistribution and other government action
	Political Islamism	Productivity, but also distraction from more important religious principles	Allow markets as long as they are consistent with religious and social values as set out in the Qur'an
	Fascism	Productivity, but sometimes distraction from more important strength of the nation	Allow markets as long as they are consistent with pursuing national strength and cultural purity
	Environmentalism	Overconsumption, waste, and environmental destruction	Allow markets as long as they can be regulated to respect environmental concerns
Markets are naturally bad	Socialism	Exploitation and class conflict	Replace markets with a system of distribution that guarantees equality for all

Explaining a Case: Uncovering the Whys of German Redistribution

9.4   **Identify three plausible explanations for Germany's generous redistributive policies.**

The United States and Germany are both rich, powerful, industrialized countries with market-based capitalist economies, but Germany shifts considerably more of its money to its poorer citizens. Why? This question is not just an academic one. Admirers of Germany in the United States, or people who like the United States in Germany, might want to know why this difference developed to help them think about whether they could push their own country toward the other's model. As always, our main explanatory stories in political stories help us brainstorm plausible answers.

The Rational-Material Story

The material context for German industrialization and its post–World War II growth offer some plausible reasons for its policies today. Germany industrialized late, well after nearby Britain, and felt huge competitive pressure from its neighbors to catch up. It was also playing catch-up in military strength relative to Britain and long-powerful France. Faced with sharp needs for maintaining internal order while fostering rapid change, German leaders created the world's first welfare-state programs in the 1880s to pay off workers and prevent rebellion. Similar incentives arose after World War II, when Germany was divided in the Cold War between a capitalist West Germany and a communist East Germany dominated by the USSR. Competing with communist appeals that promised equality, capitalist West German leaders again saw especially powerful reasons to buy the population's support with redistributive benefits.

The Institutional Story

From an institutional point of view, German redistribution followed from the ways in which Germans organized their polity and economy over time. As a federal state that came together late in history, Germany has generally lacked a strong top-down central government like in France or Britain (except briefly under the Nazis), and thus leaned toward more negotiated, compromise-based politics. German employers and German workers are both unusually well organized, favoring long-term deals that are more difficult to work out in other countries. Germany's educational system produced strong vocational schools and apprenticeships, leading Germany business to invest heavily in training and keeping their workers, including providing generous benefits. Due to a combination of political decentralization and strong societal organization, Germany developed a model of long-term employer-employee, government-citizen partnerships and compromise of which redistribution was one element.

The Ideational Story

An ideational explanation sees the main cause of German redistribution in a political culture that has long emphasized stability, social order, and national solidarity. In many ways, the Germans defined their modern identity against both the British penchant for individualistic rights and commerce and the French tradition of revolutionary utopian change. Germans, by contrast, identified as the people who put their first priority on a stable, orderly national community. This identity inclines German conservatives and business toward a paternalistic support for redistribution—the welfare state is their duty to the community—and has long encouraged German workers and the political Left toward reformist positions on economic policies that also favor compromise and solidarity.

Consider what these explanations imply about the relevance of German redistribution for American political debates. Do the greatest differences between the German and U.S. economies flow from their material setting? Perhaps, then, the United States might adopt more German-style solidarity if it is ever faced with very strong outside pressures—or Germany might weaken its redistribution given a long period without major external challenges. Are institutions the main cause? Then some elements of German rules and organizations could be imported and incorporated into the U.S. context, or vice versa, as long as their champions could manage to overcome resistance from those who would defend existing institutional configurations. Is the story ultimately about culture? Then these economies might remain very different—though rising immigration and diversity in Germany society might weaken the sense of community and undercut its commitment to redistribution in the long run.

In research on these questions, political scientists would pursue two strategies:

RESEARCH ON WITHIN-CASE PROCESSES. The "detective-style" option is to look both today and historically at why Germans have supported redistribution. Who exactly supports or supported it, and how did the German welfare state arise? Table 9-3 elaborates a bit more of what we might look for in such research.

Table 9-3 Exploring Within-Case Evidence for Alternative Explanations of German Redistribution

	Rational-Material Explanation	Institutional Explanation	Ideational Explanation
Who have been the key champions of redistribution?	National political and business leaders who felt that they needed to buy lower-class support because Germany faced such strong economic and military competition	National leaders who felt that—in a relatively decentralized Germany, with strongly organized workers and business associations—the government had to focus on brokering compromises	Moderate social-democratic workers/leaders and moderate paternalistic businesspeople who preached the value of compromise
Who or what questioned or opposed it?	Businesspeople in sectors that faced less international competition and viewed such concessions as unnecessary	Businesspeople or workers in sectors that were/are less tied into vocational education and other institutions of the social market economy (like, say, manufacturers seeking to move factories abroad)	Critics of compromise on either side (more radical workers, less generous businesspeople), but these arguments generally had weak legitimacy in German culture
When did redistribution arise or increase?	At moments of intense international competition, either economically or militarily (or both)	In times of prosperity when generous compromises were easier to work out on both sides	When moderate leaders acquired political power (and when less compromising leaders lost legitimacy by losing wars)
Best Evidence to Support Each Explanation	We find records of influential businesspeople arguing that redistribution is helpful to hold the country together or compete with communism.	We find records of both businesspeople and labor leaders arguing that given long-term business-labor partnerships, redistribution is reasonable and appropriate.	Even before today's institutions were fully built, or at moments of less international pressure, we find many people arguing that German-ness is defined by compromise and partnerships.

Doing the detective work to assess German motivations to redistribution would be a major research project, but you can begin it in a small way. Find a news article about the German welfare state from a respectable newspaper, magazine, or website. Then break down the way it presents the history or current support for redistribution: where do you see mentions of the economy, institutions, or culture and ideas?

RESEARCH ON CROSS-CASE PATTERNS.   We can also look at other countries to compare with Germany to see what conditions appear to form cross-case patterns that vary with redistribution. Is there a pattern of generous welfare states among states that faced strong external threats as they developed? Your instructor may be able to help you find data to explore some of these possible cross-case correlations.

Conclusion: Why Understanding the Politics of Economies Matters to You

Political science and economics are organized as separate disciplines, encouraging us to draw a line between politics and government on the one hand and economies and markets on the other. The mere existence of this separation seems to hint that the economy should, ideally, be free of politics. Consider, though, the opening lines of a book by one of the most famous economists of the twentieth century, Nobel Prize winner Milton Friedman: "It is widely believed that politics and economics are separate and largely unconnected," he began, but "such a view is a delusion . . . there is an intimate connection between economics and politics."[17] The reason is simple: an economy is a giant, complex set of collective decision-making processes. It is, in other words, a special kind of political arena—one that focuses on producing and allocating wealth.

Just as countries around the world construct different spaces for politics in terms of governing institutions and many policies, then, so their economies also reflect a wide range of different political choices. The notion of "free" markets versus interventionist government is one spectrum we can use to contrast these choices and economic models, but the old fight between markets and socialism obscures how many governments today see themselves as intervening economically to support markets and business, not to limit or undercut them. We have many options in the politics of economies, and perceiving those alternatives is crucial to arguing critically for or against any one of them.

Review of Learning Objectives

9.1 **Describe three concrete ways in which national economies vary, the abstract economic models of market and command economies, and how mixed economies today relate to those models.**

National economies can be concretely characterized by how much wealth they produce, how they produce it (or their level of industrialization), and how they distribute it (or their pattern of inequality). More abstractly but just as important, they can be organized on different principles. One classic model is the market (or capitalist) economy, in which individuals own almost all property and freely buy and sell as they please. Its opposite is a command (or socialist) economy, in which the state owns almost all property and dictates production and distribution. Though these models often frame debates about economies, no real-world economies fully fit them because no pure market economy ever existed. To at least some degree, governments always play a variety of roles in organizing and intervening in exchange. Some communist countries once came close to a command model, but all such economies ultimately have disintegrated or reformed. In today's world, we have only mixed economies that combine some market mechanisms with some government action.

9.2 **Describe key features of the U.S., German, and Malaysian economies in terms of labor, finance, and government interventions and explain how they represent contrasting political choices.**

To understand any political economy today, we must see how its mix of markets and various kinds of government action reflects certain political choices. The United States tends to favor market relationships within modest government regulation, as we see in its flexible hiring and firing, stock-market-based finance, and comparatively low levels of redistribution. Germany has opted for a "social market economy," which sets capitalist production within long-term "codetermination" partnerships between employers and employees, long-term business-bank partnerships in finance, and generous welfare state redistribution. Malaysia displays fairly open market relationships in some ways—flexible hiring and firing and not very extensive redistribution—but has sought to catch up to richer countries rapidly by orienting private sector economic growth under the guidance of strong-handed intervention by government planners. All three countries are perceived as among the most competitive in the world, but the American model places its political emphasis on economic liberty, the German model places its political emphasis on coordination and solidarity, and the Malaysian model prioritizes rapid industrialization and growth above all.

9.3 **Explain the classical-liberal case for markets as good, the Marxist case for markets as bad, and how modern liberals and social democrats stand between these options.**

For classical liberals, markets are naturally and universally good for all. Not only do individuals have basic rights to private property, but freedom to exchange in unfettered markets is part of that right, and also delivers the most efficient, productive, healthy society overall. For Marxists, markets are naturally and universally bad for most of the population. We cannot allow private property without generating high inequality, since those who acquire more property use their wealth and power to exploit others. Private property and market exchange should be replaced by public ownership and a planned economy. Nonliberal ideological traditions—such as environmentalism, fascism, and Islamism—seek to reorient the liberal-Marxist debate toward other priorities, whereas modern liberals and social democrats develop their views in its middle ground. Inspired by thinkers like T.H. Green and John Rawls, they see private property and market exchange as good, but argue for government action on behalf of disadvantaged citizens to generate what they portray as genuine equality of opportunity.

9.4 **Identify three plausible explanations for Germany's generous redistributive policies.**

To review for this objective, try to brainstorm rational-material, institutional, and ideational explanations of why Germany could have decided to adopt generous redistributive policies without looking at Section 9.4. Start by asking yourself the following questions:

- What sort of material challenges might make a country (and especially the wealthier people in a country) decide to shift some of their wealth to poorer citizens?

- If we think instead of possible institutional explanations for choosing redistribution, what sort of organizational features in a country might make poorer people more able to demand redistribution, or richer people more inclined to compromise with them?
- From an ideational point of view, might there be features of German identity and culture that would make richer people more likely to accept to share their wealth with poorer citizens?

After imagining your answers to these questions, return to Section 9.4 to see how well you have brainstormed plausible alternatives to explain this case.

Great Sources to Find Out More

Alberto Alesina and Edward Glaeser, *Fighting Poverty in the U.S. and Europe: A World of Difference* (New York: Oxford University Press, 2008). A brief and readable comparison and explanation of inequality and redistribution in the United States and Europe.

Alexander Gerschenkron, *Economic Backwardness in Historical Perspective* (Cambridge, MA: Harvard University Press, 1962). This series of essays by a famous economic historian argues that Germany developed its "coordinated" economy as a way to catch up to the first industrialized country, Great Britain.

Barbara Ehrenreich, *Nickel and Dimed: On (Not) Getting By in America* (New York: Holt, 2001). This social critic chronicles the year she spent deliberately working minimum-wage jobs to investigate problems of inequality in the United States.

Barry Eichengreen, *The European Economy since 1945: Coordinated Capitalism and Beyond* (Princeton, NJ: Princeton University Press, 2007). Both an accessible account and a powerful analysis of European economic growth and challenges.

Charles Wheelan, *Naked Economics: Undressing the Dismal Science* (New York: Norton, 2002). An easy-to-read and short introduction to key ideas in modern economics.

Jacob Hacker and Paul Pierson, *Winner-Take-All Politics: How Washington Made the Rich Richer—and Turned Its Back on the Middle Class* (New York: Simon & Schuster, 2010). An accessible explanation of rising American inequality by two famous political scientists.

John Rawls, *A Theory of Justice* (Cambridge, MA: Harvard University Press, 1971). This famous text in political theory imagines how people would construct a just society if they did not know what position they would occupy within it.

Karl Polanyi, *The Great Transformation* (Boston: Beacon Books, 1944). A classic account of the "rise of market society" during the Industrial Revolution that portrays markets as powerfully productive but ultimately destructive of human happiness.

Peter Hall and David Soskice, eds., *Varieties of Capitalism: The Institutional Foundations of Comparative Advantage* (New York: Oxford University Press, 2001). The most famous presentation of different organization of capitalist markets around the world.

Richard Heilbroner, *The Worldly Philosophers: The Life, Times, and Ideas of the Great Economic Thinkers* (New York: Simon & Schuster, 1953). This summary of great economic thinkers like Adam Smith and Karl Marx lays the conceptual basis for most fundamental economic debates.

Sheri Berman, *The Social Democratic Moment: Ideas and Politics in the Making of Interwar Europe* (Cambridge, MA: Harvard University Press, 1998). This book compares the ideas of the German and Swedish Social Democrats and traces how they shaped German and Swedish politics and welfare states.

Thomas Piketty, *Capital in the Twenty-First Century* (Cambridge, MA: Belknap, 2014). In one of the most widely read economics books in recent history, this French economist offers an argument about why capitalism has tended to produce worsening inequality.

Tim Harford, *The Undercover Economist* (London: Little, Brown, 2006). A lively and accessible version of an economics textbook.

Develop Your Thinking

Use these questions as discussion or short writing exercises to think more deeply about some of the key themes of the chapter.

1. Would you be happier as a relatively poor person in a rich society, or as someone who is even poorer but is relatively well off in a poorer society?

2. In economic terms, would you rather be a university student in the United States or Germany?

3. For your own economic prospects, should the American government take a more or a less active role in the economy?

4. What do you think is the biggest reason why the United States redistributes wealth less than most other democracies?

5. How much does the current American economy provide equality of opportunity to its citizens?

Keywords

capitalism   294
codetermination   302
collective bargaining   299
command economy   294
comparative advantage   294
division of labor   292
financial markets   299
GDP per capita   291

Gini coefficient   293
gross domestic product
   (GDP)   291
industrialization   291
labor markets   299
laissez-faire   296
market economy   294
mixed economy   297

post-industrial society   292
progressive/regressive
   taxes   302
redistribution   299
social market economy   300
socialism   295
tariffs   296
welfare state   300

Chapter 10
Economic Development and Growth

Marco Cristofori/Alamy Stock Photo

What policies should governments choose to make their people wealthier? Does the production of wealth necessarily bring greater inequality, or are there ways to lift most or all citizens out of poverty? From "developing" countries like India—where this slum stands a stone's throw away from gleaming tech-sector offices—to "developed" countries like the United States, political life is frequently dominated by debates over economic growth.

 ## Learning Objectives

10.1 Identify common supporting conditions and challenges for growth in market economies and explain how they encourage or hamper growth.

10.2 Describe the main alternative recipes for growth in developing countries and evaluate their records in achieving development.

10.3 Describe the main alternative positions on fostering growth in developed countries and evaluate their records in recent decades.

10.4 Evaluate arguments for and against a reliance on liberalized markets to generate economic growth.

10.5 Identify three plausible explanations for Taiwan's rapid economic growth.

Freer Markets, More Growth?

Most Americans are wealthier than most people elsewhere in the world. But do we find such comfort satisfying? Hardly. Beyond wealth, we expect economic *growth*. Past experience created this expectation: U.S. income per capita rose 70 percent from 1950 to 1975 and another 75 percent by 2000. When growth slows or reverses, as it did in the United States in 1990–1991 or in the "Great Recession" from 2007 to 2009, Americans complain—and often vote out their leaders.

So what delivers growth? People around the world today broadly agree on the key instrument: markets. Competitive buying and selling in markets can unleash remarkable dynamics of productivity and innovation. Huge global patterns support this point. The richest big country, the United States, is the leading exemplar of open markets. The clearest attempt to reject markets, as seen in the USSR's socialist planned economy, eventually crumbled. The greatest rising power, China, "marketized" its planned economy and multiplied per capita income almost *fifty times* since 1975.

Yet global patterns complicate a simple conclusion that freer markets are always better. Fast-growing China remains far from laissez-faire: though China now is second only to the United States in its number of companies on the "Fortune Global 500" list of biggest firms, almost all are government owned. The other fastest-growing countries in recent history, such as Taiwan, Japan, or South Korea, also used active government intervention. Even one of the titans of American industry, Intel cofounder Andy Grove, once wrote in *BusinessWeek* that free marketeers might learn from Asia. "While free markets beat planned economies," he said, "there may be room for a modification that is even better."[1]

Calling for the United States to imitate interventionist Asian economic practices is a highly charged political statement—and on close inspection, all economic debates about growth are deeply political. They raise basic questions of political authority and who gets what. To empower you to think critically about them, this chapter considers alternative views of growth and development, as well as the ideological and explanatory debates they evoke. ■

Basics of Market-Based Growth

10.1 Identify common supporting conditions and challenges for growth in market economies and explain how they encourage or hamper growth.

Economic growth is a complex process with a simple definition: expansion in the volume of goods and services exchanged in an economy. One of the more remarkable features of human societies is that they can expand

economic growth
Expansion in the volume of goods and services exchanged in an economy.

exchange almost indefinitely, transforming poor societies into much wealthier ones. Such a process follows partly from using more resources—cutting down more trees, mining more metals, growing more crops—but is driven more profoundly by reorganizing how people interact. Even a small island country with few resources, like Taiwan, can massively increase its wealth by inventing or importing new technologies, developing citizens' knowledge and skills to be more productive, and exchanging goods and services with the outside world.

Why would people want economic growth? People generally like to have snazzy clothes, ever-bigger TVs, and other trappings of materialism—and rising wealth carries deeper effects. Wealth brings power. Countries that grow may better control their own destinies and become more influential in the world. Their people also seem to become more satisfied with their lives (see Figure 10-1), and typically see huge increases in life expectancy, health, and even how tall they are. That is not to say that all growth brings benefits to everyone in society; some economies grow overall but distribute the benefits unevenly. Patterns of height around the world nicely display the deep effects of growth and the distribution of benefits. Rich societies in general are much taller than poor ones. Americans were the tallest people in the world into the 1950s. But because the U.S. economy has relatively high inequality—with more poor people who tend to be short—they have been outstripped by European societies that have somewhat lower levels of wealth but

Figure 10-1 Rising Satisfaction with Wealth

Generally speaking, the richer we are, the more we say we are satisfied with our lives, as seen in the increase along this ten-point "life satisfaction" scale. Countries such as Denmark and Luxembourg clearly show more satisfaction than Hungary, or Portugal.

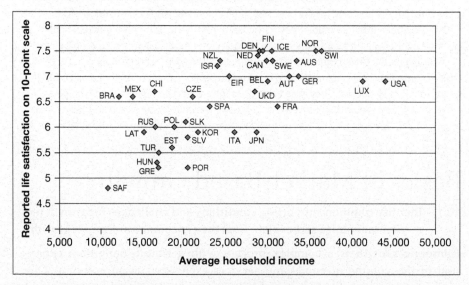

Source: World Bank for GDP per capita (2017); Organization for Economic Cooperation and Development (OECD), www.oecdbetterlifeindex.org, 2017 survey.

distribute the gains from growth more evenly. Today's height champions are the Dutch. They overshadow Americans by more than two inches on average.

Economic development is a broader process in the historical background to growth. It refers to the creation of the conditions that allow for sustained economic growth. It is thus a process of ongoing reorganization that occurs in poorer societies, also often called **developing countries**. In wealthier **developed countries**—mainly in North America, Europe, and East Asia (see Map 10-1)—we typically understand the development phase to be over, though other kinds of economic change continue within them. By definition, these countries already put in place the conditions for sustained growth—that is how they became wealthy—and they typically see their economic challenge as maintaining growth.

That is not to say that economic growth and development should clearly be every country's leading goal. A pure focus on growth can have downsides like pollution and sprawling cities. It can devalue other aspects of life, prioritizing crude materialism over truly healthy societies. Many people today argue for focusing on broader measures of **human development**, such as the United Nations' Human Development Index, which tracks health and education alongside material wealth.[2] Still, this perspective does not deny that economic development remains an important part of human development. Voices that dismiss material goals of ending poverty and generating more wealth are rare. Economic growth is thus *an* important goal practically everywhere.

economic development
Processes of reorganization in poorer societies that create the conditions for sustained economic growth.

developing/ developed countries
Labels commonly attached to poor or middle-income countries on the one hand and rich countries on the other.

human development
A concept that sets wealth as one criterion alongside others like health and education as measures of social progress.

Map 10-1 Developed and Developing Countries around the World

This map shows countries' wealth per person—the overall size of the economy divided by the population—grouped by color into the categories the World Bank designates as high, medium, and low income. The dark-green "high" category is often called the "developed countries," which includes the United States, Europe, Japan, South Korea, Taiwan, Australia, and New Zealand, plus a few oil-rich states.

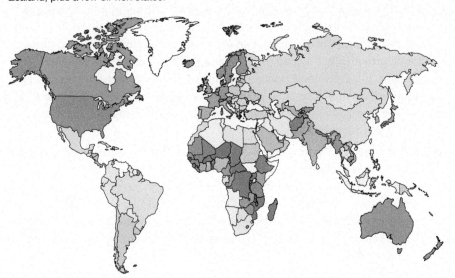

Source: World Bank, 2017 figures.

That point justifies this chapter's main theme: that policies for economic development and growth are hotly debated around the world, forming some of the core conflicts in political life. To set the scene for those fights, we start with some underlying nuts and bolts of economies that are less contested. First, we consider the minimal features of a market-based economy, without which expanding market exchange is hard to imagine. Next, we survey some common problems that economies confront and the classic policy responses to them. People from a wide range of perspectives can agree that countries must assemble certain conditions for development, must maintain them for subsequent growth, and must handle certain problems successfully. We will then see that their disagreements, which animate huge political battles from Toledo to Timbuktu, concern both how to put the conditions in place and how to best avoid the problems.

Minimal Elements of Market-Based Development and Growth

Even Americans who have never thought about the core elements of market-based economies know something about them from experience. We have lived in such an economy and interacted with many people in businesses who are trying to become wealthier—trying, in other words, to make economic growth happen. If we picture someone near us trying to grow a business, and consider what kind of context would be important for her success, we can imagine the basic conditions for economic growth. Just as individuals tend to do best within a supportive household, any business draws support from the following features in the surrounding economy:

- *Political and legal stability:* People invest time and resources to build a business only if they are reasonably sure to sell their wares without too much chaos. War is generally bad for business, even if it might help specific vendors like arms manufacturers. Other uncertainty over political leadership and institutions, such as fear of an imminent revolution, can also deter economic growth. Just as bad is to be stuck with a stable but arbitrary government. If government policies are unconstrained by any predictable rule of law—if an unaccountable ruler can change the rules on a whim and advantage or disadvantage businesses without due process—citizens tend to avoid taking economic risks.

- *Clear property rights:* Property rights are legal guarantees of ownership that make market exchange possible in a fundamental way. In markets, we can exchange only things that we own, so we must first have clear rules of ownership to have market exchange. Consider, for example, how blurry land ownership sets limits on growth in many developing countries.[3] If a poor farmer has an official deed to his land, the land becomes tradable wealth: he might sell off a plot to obtain cash for a new business, or use the land as collateral to get a loan from a bank. But in many poor countries, it can be difficult to get an official deed, and records of land ownership are sketchy or nonexistent. Without an official system for recognized ownership, the farmer's land has only its direct use—farming—and cannot be traded against other things. Similar issues arise for all sorts of property, even ideas: musicians or authors have difficulty profiting from their ideas unless **intellectual property rights** protect their work from being copied by others. Without documented property rights enforced by government, people are uncertain to profit from any business venture. They may not even try, leaving their skills and resources untapped.

intellectual property rights
Ownership rules for creative products such as books, music, or inventions.

- *Some government-provided infrastructure and basic services:* Businesses need roads, bridges, railroads, and ports to move goods around; water, energy, and sewage systems to keep factories or offices going; and wires or satellites for communication. They may see public schools as important to supply future employees who can read and write—let alone use a computer—and some sort of health policies so their employees are not sickly. Businesses vary in which infrastructure and services they see as crucial, but all depend on such supports. Sometimes other businesses arise to sell services related to infrastructure, such as private toll roads or for-profit hospitals, but often only government is big enough and inclined to provide them.

- *Sound money:* A small business might begin by bartering with others, swapping its products for eggs or doctors' advice, but this becomes burdensome as it expands. Businesses need a flexible medium of exchange across many transactions, and one that can also be stored (whether under a mattress or in a bank) to hold profits. Crucially, people need money to keep its value over time: if someone pays them $1 today, they want that dollar to buy something equivalent next week or next year. In other words, they need the general level of prices to be fairly stable, which is known as a low level of **inflation**.

inflation
A general rise in prices, which means a drop in the value of money.

- *Investment:* Especially if a business's products are selling well, its owners may see opportunities to expand further by opening new locations, buying new equipment, or moving into bigger offices. The up-front expenses of expansion may exceed current profits, though, so they will need an infusion of money to make more money. They could get money from a bank loan, or perhaps by selling bits of the business as "shares" on a stock market. Either way, their prospects depend on access to **capital**—another word for money—from investors. If investment capital is scarce, expansion is hard to sustain.

capital
Another word for money, often used with respect to investment.

- *Some openness to the world:* Very few countries come close to self-sufficiency for foodstuffs, energy, and other obvious inputs to economic growth. Even in those that do, most businesses can benefit from foreign imports to help their production—whether of raw materials, technology, or expertise—and from opportunities to export their products to markets elsewhere. We will see that the degree of desirable openness is one of the most contested points

autarky
Extreme self-reliance and isolation.

in economic debates, but no one today argues that complete separation from the outside world (known as **autarky**) is promising for development and growth. The most autarkic countries, like North Korea, are universally seen as miserable failures.

It is hard to deny that without the conditions summarized in Table 10-1, few businesses will prosper, therefore limiting growth overall. Practically everyone today can agree that poorer countries must create these conditions to develop, and that developed countries must maintain them to grow. To go further, they can agree on a bit more: besides getting these elements of their economic houses in order, all countries must surmount some common problems that arise within them.

Common Problems in Economic Policy

Trying to develop or grow a market-based economy is no picnic. Sometimes economies enter periods of slow or no growth that bring rising unemployment (a lack of jobs). Periods of fast growth can bring problems, too, notably inflation (rising prices). Governments often feel trapped between the two, hoping for enough growth to uphold employment without runaway inflation. Another linked pair of problems arises between the generation and distribution of growth. If governments allow low levels of competition—coddling businesses with state support—they may foster inefficient businesses that depend more on handouts than competitiveness. Rather than growth, they get stagnation. If, on the other hand, governments fully open their economy to the broadest competition in global markets, the growth they generate may not be distributed as they would like—with most benefits flowing outside of their country or, at least, leaving certain regions behind. People of all political stripes recognize these common

Table 10-1 Minimal Elements of Market-Based Growth

Element	Why Important for Market-Based Growth?
Political and legal stability	People will not invest time and money in growing a business if they are uncertain about enjoying the profits later on.
Clear property rights	Clear ownership encourages people to invest time and money in developing their land, other resources, or ideas and inventions by giving them confidence that they will be able to sell them and reap the profits.
Some government-provided infrastructure and services	Businesses depend on many conditions that other businesses may not provide: education, health care, bridges, ports, roads, and so on.
Sound money	Money allows for much more fluid exchange than barter, but only if it holds most of its value over time.
Investment	Even businesses that have great products and ideas typically need to borrow money to expand their capacities as they grow.
Some openness to foreign trade	Even in the largest economies, businesses may need imports from abroad, and foreign trade may give them opportunities for more customers.

economic problems and some of the typical policy responses to them. As we will see in later sections, though, they disagree on which problems deserve the most attention, and, therefore, on which policies are the best for growth.

UNEMPLOYMENT. Probably the most obvious common economic problem to people in market-based economies is when economic activity slows and jobs become scarce. This brings a rise in the **unemployment rate**: the percentage of people seeking a job who cannot find one. Economic slowdowns can begin for many reasons, including a natural disaster like the tsunami (and accompanying meltdown at the Fukushima nuclear plant) that rocked the Japanese economy in 2011. No matter what initiates a slowdown, economies can then fall into vicious cycles: people become less certain about their economic future, so they pull back on spending and investing, so businesses make less money, are forced to shorten employees' hours or fire them, so more people have less money to spend . . . and so on. When shocks are severe, like in the massive collapse of global financial markets in 2008, the cycle can move very fast. In January 2008, U.S. unemployment was under 5 percent. By late 2009, it reached 10 percent and 6 million jobs had disappeared.

When unemployment rises, governments' most common policy response is to make more money available to people, hoping to jump start a virtuous cycle in which consumers spend more, economic activity expands, and businesses hire more. These steps are known as **economic stimulus**, or "Keynesian" policies, after the British economist John Maynard Keynes (1883–1946) who first argued for them. Keynesian stimulus can take two forms. One is through **fiscal policy**, or the use of taxes or government spending to influence the economy. Lower taxes leave more money in people's pockets; higher spending can put more money in people's pockets, especially by boosting programs that employ people (such as road construction) or that encourage consumption (such as benefits for poorer people). The other is through **monetary policy**, or steps to influence the supply of money. The key monetary tool for stimulus is **interest rates**, which set how much a borrower must pay a lender for a loan. Governments' central banks constantly lend money to private banks, and central-bank officials can set interest rates for the whole economy by changing the rates they charge these private banks, which then pass on similar rate changes to their clients. When unemployment rises, the central bank can stimulate the economy by lowering interest rates. This makes it cheaper for businesses to obtain investment and for individuals to get mortgages for houses or car loans, effectively pumping more money into people's hands to nudge economic activity along. All these Keynesian policies "prime the pump" of the economy, putting more money in the hands of private consumers and businesses to get growth going.

INFLATION. Given how important stable money is for business, rising prices can be just as threatening as unemployment. Some inflation is normal in any economy, but if it exceeds 5 or 6 percent a year, odd incentives arise. Because

---

unemployment rate
The percentage of the population seeking a job but unable to find one.

economic stimulus
Government action to inject money into a weak economy.

fiscal policy
Policies of government budgets, including revenue (taxes) and government spending.

monetary policy
Policies that affect the availability of money, like when the central bank raises or lowers the interest rates it charges to private banks.

interest rate
The additional amount of money a borrower must pay back in addition to the borrowed sum. Interest rates set the price of borrowing money.

money will buy less tomorrow, people save and invest less. Since goods will command higher prices tomorrow, people may hoard goods rather than exchange them. In the worst cases, known as **hyperinflation**, money becomes unusable and the economy collapses. In Germany in 1923, for example, their currency (the Reichsmark) lost value so quickly that prices doubled every two days. People made purchases with wheelbarrows full of 100-trillion-mark bills. The economy melted down.

hyperinflation
Extreme drops in the value of money, which are devastating for an economy.

What causes inflation? Very high inflation can result when governments print too much money, as happened in Germany. Government central banks literally create money, and leaders can be tempted to pay their bills just by printing more. As they issue more money, however, people see each bill as worth less, so prices rise. In extreme cases, bills become worthless. A less dramatic version of this problem can arise when governments run large **deficits**, spending more than they receive in taxes over long periods. This, too, means that government is pumping more money into the economy, possibly decreasing the value of each bill and so pushing up prices.

deficits
The shortfall in a budget when an organization spends more than it takes in.

The most common source of inflation, though, is when growth itself causes the economy to "overheat." If activity is expanding faster than businesses can increase production—so they are selling everything off their shelves—firms happily raise their prices. What business does not raise prices if customers will pay more? Workers in fast-growing economies also frequently demand pay raises, driving up businesses' costs and encouraging them to raise prices. In some of China's boom years in the early 2000s, for example, policymakers were very worried as rapid growth pushed inflation over 5 percent, and they sought ways to slow down growth a bit.[4]

The common policy response to inflation reverses the cure for unemployment: to take money out of the economy. The less money circulates, the more each bit of it has value, and prices stop rising. Monetary policy is the most common tool to "cool down" inflation. If the central bank raises interest rates, it becomes more expensive for businesses and households to borrow money. Higher interest rates also encourage saving, since banks then pay higher rates of return to people who park their money in savings accounts. Money is pulled out of the economy as businesses expand less, people buy fewer big-ticket items like houses and cars, and more money is set aside for savings. Fiscal policy is also sometimes used to fight inflation, since higher taxes or cuts in government spending pull money out of the economy as well. Very high interest rates and/or substantial cuts in government spending are known as **austerity** policies, since they may impose painful cutbacks on consumers and businesses. By making it very costly for people to borrow, or by spending less on any of the many things governments fund—road and bridge construction, social programs, research at universities, and so on—governments make money more scarce and thus more valuable.

austerity
Policies that cut government spending and/or raise interest rates severely.

The contrasting common responses to unemployment and inflation tend to force governments into a balancing act between them. Fight inflation too aggressively with high interest rates, higher taxes, or spending cuts, and activity can slow so much that unemployment worsens. Stimulate the economy too much with lower interest rates, tax cuts, or spending, and inflation can run wild. This trade-off is known as the Phillips Curve: unemployment often goes down as inflation goes up, and vice versa. Some unfortunate conditions bring both unemployment and inflation at the same time, creating so-called **stagflation**, but usually governments feel caught between these two challenges.

"RENT-SEEKING" AND STAGNATION. At a deeper level than the trade-offs between unemployment and inflation, market-based economies can fall into stagnation due to insufficient competition. Nobody actually *enjoys* market competition—businesspeople will happily take guaranteed contracts for their products, and workers will gladly accept good guaranteed jobs—and people tend to seek whatever anticompetitive advantages their governments allow. Governments often succumb to these pressures, coddling people in the economy in ways that lessen competitive pressures for efficiency and innovation. The generation of wealth slows down.

Such pursuit of anticompetitive advantages, also known as **rent-seeking**, is pervasive in all economies. This is a special meaning economists assign to the word "rent": it means any payment not related to productive processes. Alongside the pursuit of market profits, businesses often work hard to secure rents: subsidies, tax breaks, special contracts, or regulations that boost their competitive position. Businesses may also seek rents through anticompetitive business practices, such as colluding with competitors or trying to set up monopolies that capture whole markets. When workers mobilize through unions, they, too, can be seen as pursuing both market remuneration and rents: some benefits they win reflect their contributions to production and some may just reflect additional payoffs. Government spending, similarly, often combines necessary spending for widely desired productive outcomes—running schools, building bridges—with rents for "special interests" involved in these activities. Rents are always somewhat in the eye of the beholder, since people will disagree about how high profits, salaries, or government budgets should be to support productive processes, but everyone can agree that rent-seeking is a problem in market-based economies. The more businesses obtain special advantages, employees are remunerated separately from their productivity, or governments spend in unproductive ways, the less the competitive mechanism at the heart of a market-based economy functions. People feel less competitive pressure to be efficient and contribute less to growth.

The classic government response to the problem of rent-seeking is to encourage more competition. The main tool to this end is **liberalization**: opening exchange to a wider range of competitors and decreasing government involvement in their successes and failures. For example, airlines in the United States and Europe were once cozily supported by policies that prevented new airlines from forming. In the 1970s, liberalization began to introduce more competition, allowing for the rise of low-cost airlines such as Southwest, Ryanair, or EasyJet. Often accompanying liberalization is **privatization**, when governments sell publicly

stagflation
A condition of simultaneous slow growth (and so unemployment) and inflation.

rent-seeking
In economist lingo, any "excess" payment beyond a reasonable compensation for contributions to production.

liberalization
Policies that encourage market competition in an economy.

privatization
Selling of government assets or activities to private owners.

owned entities to private buyers. Between 1980 and 2000, for example, many countries around the world privatized national telephone monopolies, turning them into private companies. Another tool is **competition policy**, which deters business from collusion and monopoly. Agencies like the U.S. Federal Trade Commission (FTC) or the European Union's Directorate for Competition fine or even break up firms that engage in anticompetitive rent-seeking. In high-profile cases, the FTC fined Google millions of dollars for abusing its dominance in the Internet search market, and Europe's regulators fined Microsoft billions for monopolistic practices.

competition policy
Policies that prevent businesses from avoiding competition, such as the breaking up of monopolies.

DISTRIBUTIONAL PROBLEMS.   Much like fighting unemployment can create inflation, and vice versa, so responses to rent-seeking can bring other problems. If governments try to deter rent-seeking by encouraging competition internally and in global markets, they often encounter challenges in the distribution of wealth. The core argument for liberalization, dating back to Adam Smith, is that open markets increase wealth *overall*: the more goods, capital, and labor flow freely, the more people compete to put these resources to more efficient uses, generating wealth overall. But Smith paid less attention to how these gains would be distributed—and the fact is that overall wealth is not what people usually care most about. They typically seek wealth *for themselves*. In towns, regions, or countries that attract less growth than elsewhere—or less desirable kinds of growth, such as unpleasant jobs or polluting industries—people commonly urge government to intervene and channel growth in other directions.

Problems in the distribution of growth take many forms. For richer countries and expensive urban areas, a common problem is that large employers shift activities to poorer countries or regions where wages are lower and production is cheaper—a practice known as **offshoring**. For poor countries or out-of-the-way regions inside richer countries, a lack of the technology, infrastructure, and lifestyle that skilled people seek makes it difficult to sustain high-paying jobs. This can bring **brain drain**, when the most skilled and innovative people leave for more cosmopolitan locales. Also common in poorer regions or countries are **infant industry problems**. Infant industries are young businesses that try to grow in a new location while facing better-established competitors elsewhere. In the 1700s, for example, American colonialists sought to create a textile industry against more advanced competitors in Britain. The scale of British production brought advantages in lower costs, plus it had leading technologies, deep sources of investment, and more experience. A contemporary example might be a Peruvian firm trying to sell soft drinks against competition from Coca-Cola and Pepsi. Even if an entrepreneur had a good product, much larger competitors could drown out his advertising, entice his best workers to their companies, influence his distributors, or just buy him out. These big companies might simply be competing fiercely, not acting monopolistically, but their huge head start can stifle growth elsewhere. Although it may not matter much for global growth whether the profits end up with American or Peruvian firms, it matters for the

offshoring
Relocation of a business practice from one country to another.

brain drain
The departure of talented people from a location to places with better opportunities.

infant industry problems
Challenges relating to creating new firms under pressure from more experienced competition elsewhere.

people in Peru. Inside the United States, we might hear similar concerns from poorer areas that suffer even when the overall economy booms.

How do governments respond to distributional problems? In principle, they may do nothing, since Smithian theory suggests that such problems resolve themselves in the long run. People in disadvantaged locales eventually discover activities in which they are competitive, or just move to better locations. In practice, even the governments most committed to open markets have difficulty waiting for the long run. If good jobs seem to be moving elsewhere or skilled workers are leaving, citizens do not happily shift to entirely new careers or gladly move away. They usually demand action. Thus, governments turn to responses that are effectively the opposite of those that address rent-seeking—offering targeted benefits to business to affect the location or form of growth. The simplest options are **protectionism**, or defensive policies that lessen competitive pressures. It may take the form of subsidies, tariffs that raise the price of imported competitors' products, or quotas that restrict imports to certain amounts. High tariffs protected U.S. textiles from British competition, for example, for a hundred years. Some governments mount more proactive **industrial policy**, seeking not just to protect existing firms but to promote certain growth priorities in the longer run. Industrial policy may include protectionism, but also employs tools such as tax breaks, special loans, or exemption from regulations to incentivize growth in desired locations and market sectors. Recent U.S.-China relations have seen a contest between these policy tools. The Trump administration raised tariffs on Chinese imports in an attempt to force China to back off from industrial policies that support its businesses.

protectionism
Any policy that provides advantages to local business over outside competitors.

industrial policy
Policies that actively seek to strengthen particular local or national industries or firms.

Just as unemployment and inflation form horns of an economic policy dilemma, so do rent-seeking and distributional problems (see Table 10-2). Open up economic activity to competition across large areas, especially into vast global markets, and it is possible that desirable jobs, skilled people, and profits may tend to flow to other locations. But intervene to support desirable economic activity at home, and business may relax to enjoy these rents and become uncompetitive.

Now you have a rough overview of collective wisdom on market-based economies today. Few policymakers or economic experts around the world would dispute that development and growth call for political stability, property rights, stable money, investment, infrastructure, and some openness. Few would disagree that all economies must avoid problems of unemployment, inflation, rent-seeking, or losing out in the distribution of gains. Yet if policymakers everywhere would recognize these basic nuts and bolts, the consensus goes no further. As we will see in the following sections, in both developing and developed countries, we find bitter debates about how to achieve growth. Alternative strategies disagree about which policy problems are most pressing and the best responses to them. The stakes could not be higher: these strategies affect not only our immediate wealth but our future opportunities and the global distribution of power. It is hardly surprising that these debates form much of the content of twenty-first-century politics.

Table 10-2 Common Problems and Apparent Trade-Offs in Economic Growth

Challenge	Classic Sources	Common Policy Remedies	Possible Trade-Offs
Unemployment (not enough jobs)	Slow growth reduces available jobs.	**Stimulus policies**: increase government spending or lower interest rates to put more money in people's pockets and encourage economic activity.	High government spending or low interest rates may eventually cause **inflation**.
Inflation (prices rise, money loses value)	Too much money in the economy; fast growth; or jumps in the prices of important goods (i.e., when oil prices rise).	**Austerity policies**: cut government spending or raise interest rates to make money more scarce and thus more valuable.	Government spending cuts and high interest rates force cutbacks on businesses and consumers and may cause **unemployment**.
Rent-Seeking (profits unjustified by contributions to the economy)	Either low competition or special political influence allows economic players to demand high prices or extract subsidies.	**Liberalization policies**: open up markets widely and stimulate competition to prevent rent-seekers from abusing their positions.	More competition and free flow of money and people may worsen **distributional problems**.
Distributional Problems (undesired distribution of economic gain or pain)	Movements of money and people concentrate economic activity in certain locations, draining other areas of money and talented people.	**Protectionist policies:** impose costs on economic flows with tariffs or other obstacles. **Industrial policies:** make government investments in certain places and sectors to attract economic activity where desired.	Protectionism or government support through industrial policies may lessen competition and facilitate **rent-seeking**.

Development: Alternative Pathways from Poverty

10.2 **Describe the main alternative recipes for growth in developing countries and evaluate their records in achieving development.**

In 1960, Taiwan's GDP per capita was a bit above Madagascar's—an island nation off the eastern cost of Africa with roughly the same population. Today Madagascar's inhabitants are slightly poorer than they were in 1960. Most live on less than $1 per day. Taiwan's citizens are as rich as Germans. Their high-tech capital, Taipei, is home to world-beating technology companies like computer maker Acer, smart phone maker HTC, or Foxconn—maker of the iPhone and the world's largest electronics-manufacturing firm.

How can poorer countries best ensure that their economic fate will be more like Taiwan's than Madagascar's? Few (if any) are likely to match Taiwan's rise—it is the most successful case of economic development in history—but all governments feel intense pressure from their citizens to do what they can to become wealthier. This is unquestionably a challenge mainly for societies and their governments, not for individuals, because even poor people in wealthy countries tend to be relatively well off: the poorest 5 percent of Americans are richer than two-thirds of the world's people.[5] Some individuals in poor countries may

Wally Santana/AP Images

The country we live in hugely affects our individual opportunities for wealth. The poorer people in developed countries typically have more material comforts than all but the richest people in the least developed countries. Here, we see thousands of morning commuters on scooters in Taipei, Taiwan—a country that leapt from poverty into the ranks of rich countries in less than two generations.

make it on their own, but the life chances of most people are heavily tied to broad development of their national economy.

Yet the way forward is hardly obvious. The next three sections introduce three views that have shaped debates over development for the past half century. One powerful strand of development advice recommends an open-market recipe known as the "Washington Consensus." These views largely supplanted an alternative strategy called "import-substitution industrialization" to which many Latin American countries subscribed from the 1950s into the 1980s. In the 1990s, though, it became clear that Taiwan and other Asian countries were growing rapidly by using another, more interventionist kind of model. Asia's rise posed new questions about how best to develop a market-based economy, leaving us with a wide-open debate today.

Open Markets and the "Washington Consensus"

The notion of a "**Washington Consensus**" on development reflects the fact that Washington, D.C., is home to powerful organizations that give development advice to poorer countries: the World Bank, the International Monetary Fund (IMF), and the U.S. government itself. Through loans and foreign aid, these three organizations attempt to boost economic development around the world—and also pressure governments that receive their support to take their economic advice. These organizations tend to advise poor countries that the best route to

Washington Consensus

The open-market package of advice for developing countries formulated in the 1980s by the International Monetary Fund, the World Bank, and the U.S. government.

development is to construct the most open market economy possible: creating the minimal conditions for market growth, cutting back on other government interventions, and opening themselves widely to global trade and investment. Proponents of this recipe can point to successes, but critics also see failures and a mixed record overall.

At its core, the Washington Consensus posits three reasons why poor countries are poor. One is true by definition: they tend to lack capital for investment (since they are poor), as well as technology and top-notch business expertise. Second is that in their rush to grow their economies, their governments tend to intervene too heavily in markets, stifling competition and fostering rampant rent-seeking. Third is that in their haste to stimulate growth, they also tend to spend too much, run large deficits, or even print money to cover their bills—all making inflation one of their most common problems. The leading priority for developing-country policies, then, must be liberalization. Freeing internal markets and foreign trade will allow much-needed investment, technology, and expertise to flow in from richer places. The competition it brings will sweep away the cobwebs of rents and will stimulate local productivity. Also crucial is that governments focus on modest spending and low deficits to keep inflation in check.

In more concrete terms, the Washington Consensus advises the following policies:[6]

- *Openness:* Cut back protectionism to encourage foreign trade and investment, stimulating competition and reducing rent-seeking.

- *Domestic liberalization:* Relax domestic regulations to stimulate internal competition. Wherever possible, decrease government ownership in the economy through privatization.

- *Clarification of property rights to attract investment:* Establish clear records and rules of ownership of land and other resources so that they become tradable. Leave businesses free to manage their property and profits, provide a reliable legal system, and minimize corruption. Make clear that when domestic and foreign investors bring their money into the economy, they will later be able to get it out by selling their stakes and taking the profits. Investors will not inject their money into a business unless guaranteed that they can withdraw their profits in the future.

- *Sound money:* Aim for low inflation both to bring internal stability and to make the currency convertible to support foreign trade and investment.

- *Infrastructure only:* Fight inflation and cut back on rents by adopting a low-spending, low-taxes fiscal policy that is limited to infrastructure, education, and public health.

As you can see, the Washington Consensus suggests just a few changes to our earlier list of minimal conditions for market-based growth: openness becomes the first priority, domestic liberalization and low spending receive added emphasis, and political stability is assumed in the background. It is a "back to basics" open market policy that is also referred to as **neoliberalism**—meaning a rebirth of the classical-liberal commitment to open markets.

To what extent has this advice helped poor countries? It has been hugely influential since the 1980s, sometimes because poor-country leaders chose it and sometimes because the Washington organizations pressured them to do so. Its greatest success came in Chile, where far-reaching liberalization since the late 1980s produced the steadiest growth in Latin America. In Eastern Europe after the fall of communism, too, Poland and several other countries made a sudden shift to these policies—known as **shock therapy**—and after a rough transition achieved respectable growth. The champions of this approach also argue that fast-growing Asian countries have at least used many elements of their recipe: Taiwan, for example, sought international trade and investment, focused government spending on key infrastructure, kept inflation low, and strongly respected property rights. Still, broader patterns leave the payoff unclear. The Consensus agenda was enacted most deeply and widely in Latin America in the 1980s, but since then that region has grown slower than it had before 1980, and much slower than Asia (see Figure 10-2).[7] Broad studies find that IMF programs, which have tended to give poorer countries loans in return for Washington Consensus reforms, actually correlate with somewhat slower growth and worse inequality.[8]

neoliberalism
A political movement since the 1970s to decrease active government intervention in market economies.

shock therapy
In the context of post-communist or very poor economies, government action to suddenly deregulate, liberalize, and privatize to open up markets.

Figure 10-2 GDP Growth by Country Groups from 1960 to 2017

If we smooth out growth rates into regional averages by five-year period,[9] we see that Latin America has grown far slower than most of Asia since 1980.

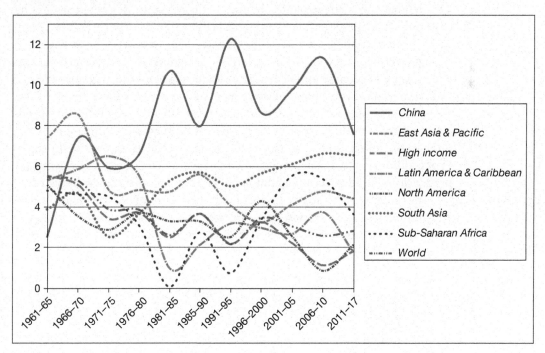

Source: World Bank data compiled by Alberto Lioy.

Dependency and "Import Substitution Industrialization"

For many people in poorer countries, Washington Consensus–style advice always sounded like a suspiciously good deal for rich countries. Liberalization would open up access for big corporations to poor countries' resources and workforces, locking poor countries in roles of "**dependency**" that limited them to providing raw materials and labor to support rich-world firms. In other words, people in poorer countries suspected that the Washington Consensus was wrong to see rent-seeking as their main problem; their real challenge was their losing position in the distribution of growth. This criticism pointed to the opposite of Washington's advice. Rather opening up with liberalization, poor countries should *lessen* their exposure to global markets. Adopted mainly by Latin American countries from the 1930s until the 1980s, as well as by some in the Middle East and Africa, the strategy had some success. Then, however, it succumbed to its great weakness—poor countries' need for foreign investment—and so this policy has been largely abandoned.

From the perspective of dependency theorists, poor countries are poor mainly because rich countries skew the distribution of growth away from them. In the colonial era, rich countries plundered poor-country resources and flooded their markets with rich-world products. Though rich countries surrendered political control in the post-colonial era after 1950, they continued to extract resources and dominate markets through trade and investment. Some versions of the dependency view were socialist, seeing poor countries as the global "proletariat" that was being exploited by the "bourgeoisie" of rich countries. Yet its most influential advocates were economists trained in the free market tradition, such as the Argentinian Raúl Prebisch (1901–1986), who came to believe that strong government action was necessary for development. Prebisch argued that poor countries become trapped in a subordinate role of producing raw materials, agriculture, and cheap labor while buying manufactured goods, technology, and services from richer countries. Other economists stressed infant-industry problems and brain drain: if poor countries liberalize, then big multinationals buy up their key assets, dominate their markets, and recruit away their best people. Poor countries could develop only if they sheltered their economies from foreign pressures and used government industrial policy to jump-start new industries.

The concrete policy advice that resulted from this thinking was called **import substitution industrialization (ISI)**. Instead of importing industrial products and technology from rich countries, poor countries should build up their own industries to substitute for these imports. Their recipe had these elements:

- *Protection:* Set tariffs or quotas on industrial imports to encourage domestic consumers and businesses to buy them at home.

- *Large investments in infrastructure:* Create a context for more advanced industry with government spending on transport, energy, education, and other supportive policies.

dependency
The notion that developing economies are trapped in disadvantaged positions in world markets.

import substitution industrialization (ISI)
An economic strategy to end dependency by limiting imports from rich countries and building up domestic industries for the home market.

- *Promotion of large public corporations:* Create large government-owned firms to promote domestic production, especially in heavy industry.

- *Steering of investment to certain sectors:* Use government influence over interest rates and regulations to encourage banks to lend money to preferred industries.

- *Deals with foreign firms to support domestic growth:* Use government power to bargain with foreign multinationals, requiring foreign firms to share technology and expertise with local firms in return for access to the domestic market. For example, General Motors, Ford, and Volkswagen were allowed to sell cars in Brazil only after agreeing to form joint ventures to build up a Brazilian car industry.

For several decades, ISI was fairly successful. From 1950 to 1980, Latin America GDP overall grew at an average rate of 5.5 percent. The largest Latin American country, Brazil, grew especially fast and managed to reduce imports from almost 20 percent of economy in 1949 to less than 5 percent in 1964.[10] But then the strategy ran into problems. One was the limited ability of these countries' internal markets to buy more products. This kind of growth depended on domestic consumers to buy the "substituted" industrial goods, but especially given high inequality in all Latin American countries, small upper and middle

Paulo Fridman/Corbis Historical/Getty Images

The Brazilian government worked for decades to license technologies from developed-country aerospace producers to launch a domestic aircraft industry, eventually producing the state-owned corporation Embraer in the late 1960s. One of their assembly plants is pictured above. Embraer now competes with the Canadian company Bombardier for the title of third-ranked aerospace manufacturer in the world after Boeing and Airbus. The firm was privatized in 1994, but the government retains a large share of its stock.

classes could buy only so much. Another problem was pervasive rent-seeking. Protectionism and government subsidies sheltered domestic firms from competition, allowing many inefficient, low-quality producers to survive.

The key weakness of ISI, though, was dependence on foreign investment. To get funds for infrastructure spending and industrial policy, governments borrowed vast sums from rich-country banks. By the 1970s, slowing economies made the debt harder and harder to pay off. The final blow came when the U.S. Federal Reserve raised its interest rates sky-high in 1980–1981. Though this was a domestically oriented decision—the U.S. central bank was focused on controlling runaway inflation inside the United States—it had a huge side effect elsewhere: much of debt to the United States was in dollar loans from U.S. banks that were now forced to raise their rates, so the interest rates that Latin American governments had to pay for their debt suddenly jumped. Thus an inward-looking policy change in the powerful United States caused huge hardship elsewhere: the result was the so-called Latin American debt crisis, in which countries from Mexico to Argentina defaulted on their debts and fell into a deep recession. In the 1980s, the IMF, the World Bank, and other lenders offered them new loans for rebuilding their economy—on condition that they accept the advice of the Washington Consensus. Even though ISI had enjoyed some success, its champions were largely forced to abandon it in the 1980s due to their need for rich-country capital.

Asian Models of Export-Led Development

By the early 1990s, the Washington Consensus reigned as the dominant advice for developing countries. Latin America was moving to implement this agenda; in Eastern Europe and Russia communism had fallen and "shock therapy" liberalization was the order of the day. But the era of any consensus on development was not to last. Already, some economists were drawing attention to the remarkably rapid growth of East Asia, and especially to the surprisingly interventionist policies that accompanied it. By the late 1990s, even the World Bank—a bastion of free market economists—accepted the idea that "state-led growth" could be possible, suggesting that a "reinvigoration of the state's capacity" might be crucial to development.[11] Today, in the shadow of a rising and very interventionist China, the appropriate balance between state intervention and liberalization in development is again a topic of fierce debate.

The thinking behind "Asian models" of development combined elements of free market economics, with its emphasis on fighting rent-seeking by encouraging competition, and dependency theory–style ideas about government action to affect the distribution of growth. In the three countries that best represent this strategy—Japan, Taiwan, and South Korea—governments after World War II faced a complex mix of economic incentives. They were allied with the United States against communist China and Russia, and so fell clearly on the pro-capitalism, pro-market side of the Cold War. Yet they were poor—even Japan was poorer than Mexico in 1955—and felt pressure to grow very rapidly because of both security threats of communist neighbors and economic threats of dominant American industry. These three Asian governments also had economic bureaucrats with major policymaking power, especially in Taiwan and South Korea, which had authoritarian regimes at the time. Insulated from domestic political demands, their economic policymakers worked out long-term strategies built around "export-led development." These policies focused on building industries to export products to the vast markets of the United States and other rich countries. This priority on economic engagement with rich countries implied a Washington Consensus–style view that their key challenge was a lack of capital, technology, expertise, and access to larger markets. In the ways they pursued this goal, though, they also accepted dependency-style advice that they must carefully manage their exposure to richer economies and foreign competitors to boost infant industries, avoid brain drain, and incentivize the location of advanced industry on their soil.

In the words of Harvard economist Dani Rodrik, economic policies in these countries "effectively combined *incentives* with *discipline*" to encourage growth of advanced industry.[12] In several ways that looked similar to aspects of ISI, these Asian governments created support and incentives for private firms to develop new industries on their soil:

- *Targeted protectionism:* Protect prioritized sectors with tariffs and quotas so they are not swamped by bigger foreign competitors.

- *Steering of investment to certain sectors:* Either through government-owned banks or government incentives for private banks, channel favorable loans to priority areas.

- *Deals with foreign firms to support domestic growth:* Use government agencies to help firms find foreign partners and negotiate with them, exchange access to domestic markets for investments, and create technology-sharing opportunities that build domestic industry.

Unlike most Latin American countries, though, these Asian countries forced considerable market discipline on their domestic firms as well. They targeted interventions in what economists call "market-conforming" ways—looking for promising investments much like a capitalist investor would, rather than trying to build up industries irrespective of whether or not they looked like good economic bets. They also kept broader government action closer to the minimal conditions for growth, more like in the Washington Consensus strategy, by initiating:

- *A focus on exports and technology:* Prioritize firms that show promise in exports and technology. Support their exports with such tools as tax breaks on expenses related to selling abroad, or creating special "export zone" areas where firms enjoyed lower taxes, less regulation, and special infrastructure. Import key technologies directly through the government and make them available to domestic firms.

- *Promotion of internal competition:* Support promising sectors overall but let firms within them fight it out. Allow weak firms to die.
- *Strong property rights:* Intervene by offering incentives (not by dictating businesses strategies) and respecting ownership of profits and assets.
- *Fiscal restraint:* Keep overall taxes and government spending low, relying more on incentives for private sector growth than on large direct government expenditures.
- *Sound money:* Prioritize low inflation and a stable currency that is convertible into other currencies to facilitate international economic engagement.

Overall, then, the rapid economic ascent of Japan, Taiwan, South Korea, and later developers like Malaysia undercut the expectations of both the Washington Consensus and dependency theory. On the one hand, these countries intervened in markets much more than neoliberal thinking suggests is ideal. On the other, they rejected the inward focus of ISI, instead building their strategies around encouraging trade with rich countries.

Additionally, China's more recent inclusion to the list of fast-developing Asian countries further complicates development debates. Earlier members of this club all grew as clearly capitalist, market-based economies, even if their governments intervened fairly systematically. China's starting point was a state-run planned economy. While the Communist Party regime began to gradually liberalize the economy in 1979, allowing more property rights and private business, its extraordinary run of growth has mixed expanding market exchange with far more government intervention than in any of its noncommunist neighbors.

China's odd market/government mix is evident both in broad government policies and in the enduring role for publicly owned firms in its economy. While attempting to strengthen property rights, to manage "overheating" inflation amid rapid growth, and generally to offer a stable background platform for market-based growth, the government continues to implement long-term plans to channel investment to certain sectors, protect many infant (and not-so-infant) industries, and force foreign firms to share both technology and profits in return for market access. On the ground, millions of private businesses have sprung up since 1979, but much growth has also taken the form of **state-owned enterprises (SOEs)**. Rather than privatizing most old industries of the planned economy, government officials turned them into money-making businesses that remained under state control. SOEs still account for close to half the entire economy. Their ties to government typically give them privileged access to government loans, favorable treatment with taxes and regulations, and sometimes subsidies.[13] Whether these pervasive interventions help or hurt Chinese growth overall is hard to say: many SOEs and some politically connected private businesses are flabby, bloated organizations that live off protection and subsidies, but many private firms and some SOEs are extremely competitive as well. What is clear, though, is that China has achieved rapid market-based growth while employing major government intervention.

state-owned enterprises (SOEs)
Commercial businesses owned by government organizations.

Should we conclude, along with Intel founder Andy Grove, that Asia's economic success displays something that is "even better" at wealth creation than free markets? No consensus exists today. Some experts on development agree with Grove that by intervening to affect the distribution of growth in "market-conforming" ways, many Asian governments have brought their countries faster growth than freer markets could have delivered.[14] Drawing on such thinking, websites and bookstores are full of predictions that Asia—and especially China—will dominate the twenty-first century.[15] Yet others argue that most of Asia's rise reflects a peculiar historical transition to, and respect for, largely free market policies—suggesting that even if Asian governments have intervened in their economies, these interventions do not deserve much credit for their growth. In a famous essay, Nobel Prize–winning economist Paul Krugman insists that no special model has driven Asian growth.[16] He suggests that these countries had many underused resources, which they mobilized in recent decades by constructing fairly stable, predictable societies, managing broad economic policies well, and encouraging international openness and especially exports. He suspects most of their interventions were a wash—sometimes helping growth, sometimes hurting it—and that these countries' growth will soon slow as they exhaust the early, easy gains in mobilizing resources. In his view, their future may follow Japan, where decades of rapid growth slowed into stagnation as of the mid-1990s. For similar reasons, many China watchers have been waiting for its growth to fall prey to the inefficiencies of bloated SOEs and to the country's overall context of opaque, often-corrupt government favoritism.[17]

Thus the debate over development remains open. Experts can agree on basic elements that developing countries should assemble: political stability, property rights, sound money, decent infrastructure, and international engagement to attract trade and investment. As a simple fact, too, no one can deny that the fastest-growing countries in history have intervened economically in many ways beyond these basic elements. There is room for interpretation and disagreement, though, about whether these countries have grown *because* or *in spite of* intervention. And so in Washington, D.C., and political arenas around the world, we continue to argue over the best advice for raising developing countries out of poverty.

Growth: Alternative Strategies in Developed Countries

10.3 **Describe the main alternative positions on fostering growth in developed countries and evaluate their records in recent decades.**

Though the politics of wealth creation may seem most urgent in poorer countries, it is just as central to rich-country politics. In every American election, like in practically every election across developed countries, contending candidates debate why growth has happened in the past and who deserves credit for booms or blame for busts. They claim that they can deliver growth—or the right kind of growth, benefiting the right people—in ways that their rivals cannot. These debates constitute much of the enduring core of democratic politics.

Like with advice for developing countries, however, these debates evolve over time. As the Washington Consensus reached its height in the early 1990s, neoliberal thinking achieved a period of near-supremacy within rich countries as well. Then the neoliberal quasi-consensus came crashing down around 2009, when a financial crisis in the United States spread into the deepest global recession since the 1930s. These divisions were heightened by a context of rising economic inequality, and even more so by the election of an American president, Donald Trump, who scrambled the long-established lines of economic debates. Political fights over growth became sharper—but also more confusing—than ever.

The Age of Neoliberalism

"Neoliberalism" was first coined to refer to a revival of classical-liberal-style emphasis on liberalized markets in Europe and the United States in the 1970s. Economic growth had slowed from the boom years following World War II. New or "neo" liberals saw rent-seeking and creeping government intervention as the cause and new steps in liberalization as the remedy. Since the most direct inheritors of classical liberalism stood on the conservative Right, its flag bearers were strong conservative leaders like British prime minister Margaret Thatcher and U.S. president Ronald Reagan. So forceful was their message that by the 1990s, even the Left had become pro-liberalization in most rich countries. A relative right-left consensus emerged on policies for economic growth.

To restore growth, argued neoliberals, the rich countries must take aggressive steps to create a new era of "small government":

- *Cut back regulation:* Governments had increasingly regulated what individuals could do in the name of goals like public health, safety, or environmental protection. Neoliberals argued that even if such rules are well intentioned, deregulated markets would better solve social problems. For example, if environmental pollution is really a problem, people will eventually pay more for "green" products and businesses will arise to sell them.

- *Privatize:* For neoliberals, government ownership of economic activities ruins the profit motive that generates efficiency and growth. Only entrepreneurs competing to become rich have strong incentives to develop more efficient and effective ways to deliver the goods and services that people want. In particular, European governments that had previously nationalized major businesses—such as airlines, banks, coal mines, and telecommunications—now came to believe that privatization would reenergize these sectors.

- *Trim welfare states:* Overly generous welfare states also blunted the potential for growth. Sheltering poorer people from the market only encourages them to become dependent on government, removing their drive to improve their condition. Benefits should be lowered and offered only to those who made clear efforts to find work.

- *Lower taxes:* Taxes take a cut of everyone's income and thus weaken motivation to work and innovate. Also, because taxes pay for welfare and other interventions, cutting taxes has the additional benefit of limiting such programs—thereby "starving the beast" of government.

- *Minimize government debt:* When governments spend more than they take in (that is, run a deficit), they must borrow money from others. The main way in which governments borrow money is by selling bonds, which are pieces of paper with a certain value payable at a certain future time (such as, say, $10,000 in thirty years). When people give the government money today for a bond, they are effectively loaning money to the government and getting paid back when the bond "matures" (that is, when it is payable). For neoliberals, the problem with governments that borrow too much—issuing too many bonds—is that when people park their money in government bonds, they may invest less in productive private activities. Neoliberals fear that government debt "crowds out" private investment and slows growth.

This recipe for growth resonated especially strongly in the countries that already had the least interventionist policies: Britain and its ex-colonies of the United States, Canada, Australia, and New Zealand. Thatcher and Reagan became symbols of the movement to deregulate, privatize, and cut government spending and taxes. Yet even the more interventionist and redistributive countries of Europe took steps in similar directions. France, once the most interventionist of Western countries, lessened its intervention and privatized many corporations. Europeans also agreed to the "Single Market 1992" program in the European Union, locking the continent into a far-reaching agenda for liberalization. Most strikingly of all, neoliberal enthusiasm spread not just across countries but across political divides into the Left. Modern liberals and social democrats who had once advocated regulation, nationalizations, generous welfare, and high taxes largely dropped these themes. In the United States, President Bill Clinton led the Democratic Party in a shift to more centrist views that accepted much of neoliberalism. In Britain, Labour Party leader Tony Blair similarly endorsed elements of Thatcher's legacy. Social Democrats and Socialists in continental Europe buried their old rhetoric and endorsed more market-friendly government. By the late 1990s, people across the developed countries complained that voters no longer had meaningful economic choices at election time. The Right and Left shared a neoliberal consensus.[18]

Did the age of neoliberalism deliver on its promise of restored growth? In the United States, Britain, and other Anglo-American countries that embraced neoliberalism most strongly, growth was relatively strong in the late 1990s and early 2000s (see Figure 10-3). For the United States, this was especially notable in the late 1990s, when Clinton presided over a run of sustained growth, low unemployment, low inflation, and a government surplus. Neoliberal reforms were more modest on the European continent, and so was growth. Japan was the rich country that liberalized the least, and its growth fell almost to zero in this period. From this pattern, many concluded that neoliberalism had indeed put rich countries on a higher-growth track: with government interfering less, economies could be more efficient and dynamic than ever. Also widespread was the view that rich-world economies had become more stable. In 2004, the future head of the Federal Reserve Ben Bernanke said that smoother and more efficient markets meant that economic recessions had become "less frequent and less severe."[19]

Yet those who perceived a broad era of neoliberal success also confronted a major complaint: that the benefits of restored growth went disproportionately (and, by some measures, almost entirely) to the wealthy. Inequality crept upwards in most developed countries (see Figure 10-4). Still, champions of neoliberalism argued that even if the rich were making disproportionate gains, aggregate growth was a rising tide that would eventually lift all boats. Storms were gathering on the horizon, though, that would reintroduce major debates about pathways to growth.

Figure 10-3 GDP Growth in Selected Developed Countries 1980–2017

The United States [dark blue], United Kingdom [green], and Australia ([light blue]) grew at middling rates into the 1990s, but these most neoliberal countries tended to grow faster than other rich countries thereafter.

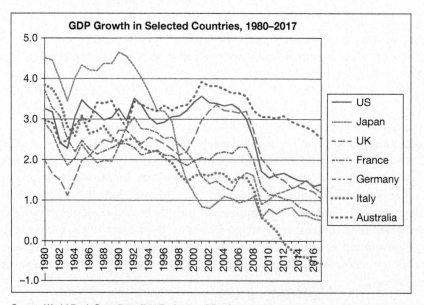

Source: World Bank Open Data (2017), data.worldbank.org.

Figure 10-4 Rising Inequality in Developed Countries

When we track studies of the Gini index in developed countries (the most common measure of inequality), we can see that inequality rose in most developed countries in the aftermath of the widespread adoption of more neoliberal policies in the 1980s and 1990s.

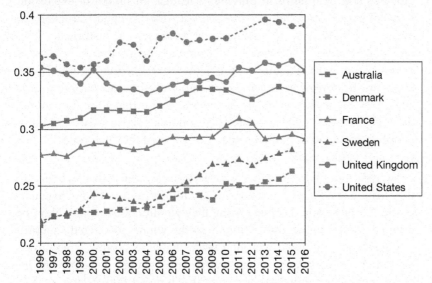

Source: Organization for Economic Cooperation and Development (OECD), 2017.

The Great Recession Reopens Debates

If debates over rich-country growth narrowed into a neoliberal consensus by the early 2000s, they soon reopened with a vengeance. With the "Great Recession" that began in 2008, the neoliberal era of deregulation and globalization suddenly collapsed into the worst economic crisis in living memory. The July 2009 cover of *The Economist* magazine showed a book titled *Modern Economic Theory* melting into a puddle. Stock markets and housing values plummeted, eliminating $16 trillion from the net worth of American households—more than the entire annual GDP of the U.S. economy. Unemployment doubled to over 10 percent. Political fights over the causes and solutions for the recession took center stage.

To understand those debates, consider the widely agreed circumstances behind the Great Recession:

- *Housing bubbles:* The run-up to the recession was a **financial bubble** in the American housing market. European housing bubbles contributed too. A bubble is when people pay higher and higher prices for something, far beyond normal views of its worth. As prices rise rapidly, more buyers try to get in on the action, hoping to make money as prices go still higher—until the bubble bursts, prices collapse, and those left holding the devalued asset lose a great deal. More and more people invested more and more money in real estate in the United States and Europe in the early 2000s, making them vulnerable to big losses when the bubble burst and prices fell after 2006.

financial bubble
When prices for something rise very rapidly to implausible levels, typically leading to a sudden collapse.

- *Easily available loans:* Housing bubbles are common, but this one became huge because borrowing money became easier than ever. After a mild recession in 2001, central banks in the United States and Europe kept interest rates low to stimulate their economies. Also important was the globalization of finance in previous decades: an immense expansion in flows of money, especially from Asia, left American and European banks awash in funds. They could thus offer mortgages at historically low interest rates, making it cheaper for people to borrow to buy houses. With prices rising and mortgages cheaper than ever, people figured: we'd be crazy not to borrow as much as we can and buy a house! From 2002 to 2007, U.S. banks loaned at three times the rate that they had in earlier decades.[20] Once prices started to fall, economies slowed, incomes fell, and people began to lose their jobs, many discovered they had borrowed more than they could repay.

- *Newly risky lending:* Not only were banks loaning more than ever before 2008, they loaned in riskier ways than ever. Traditionally, they did not loan to people without a steady income, fearing they would not be repaid. Now, however, banks seemed to throw caution to the wind and offered "subprime" mortgages to those who had long been unable to borrow. They invented new kinds of loans to win these customers, such as adjustable-rate mortgages with a low initial "teaser" rate that jumped higher later, or NINJA loans ("no income, no job, no assets") that required no documentation.

- *A tightly interconnected financial system:* In recent decades, financial firms became much more tightly interdependent. Mortgages had been increasingly **securitized**: lenders bundled together many loans and resold them to banks and investors, turning them into securities (a generic word for something you can invest in). Mortgages were seen as fairly safe investments, especially as housing prices soared, and even financial firms snatched up subprime securities. This increased the potential for collapse: if many loans went sour at the same time, big losses would hit the financial sector very widely.

securitization
The practice of taking something that cannot usually be bought or sold, such as a home mortgage, and turning it into a financial product that can be bought and sold.

These conditions compounded in dangerous ways in the late 2000s. U.S. housing prices topped out and began to fall. Over-leveraged homeowners increasingly defaulted on their mortgages. Banks holding vast volumes of securitized mortgages saw their investments wiped out. Yet information about financial firms' holdings was private, so no one knew the extent of the emerging losses. When the giant Wall Street firm Lehman Brothers suddenly went bankrupt in September 2009, financial markets froze up around the world. Everyone suspected that other banks were close to bankruptcy—and many were—so no one would lend to anyone else. Normal daily business loans and transactions came to a standstill. The financial crisis quickly became a broader economic free-fall, with economies shrinking everywhere (see Figure 10-3). Trillions of dollars of wealth and millions of jobs simply disappeared.

Who was to blame? Two big interpretations of the crisis emerged that reinforced competing views of growth in rich countries. The most widely held view in both the United States and Europe traced the collapse to unregulated financial markets: liberalization of financial markets in the 1990s had allowed wealthy financiers to run amok with other people's money. These financiers invented such complicated new investments that neither government regulators nor even the financiers themselves could track the risks involved, and the banking sector also seduced homeowners into borrowing mortgage loans beyond their means. As a bipartisan U.S. Senate report concluded in April 2011, "The crisis was not a natural disaster, but the result of high risk, complex financial products; undisclosed conflicts of interest; and the failure of regulators, the credit rating agencies, and the market itself to rein in the excesses of Wall Street."[21] This was a striking change in tone from the neoliberal era a decade before: Democratic and Republican senators agreed that "the market itself" was partly to blame for economic collapse. The solution, then, was better government oversight and regulation of markets.

Yet neoliberalism was far from gone. Defenders of market liberalization pointed the finger in other directions. Banks had not forced people to borrow more than they could afford. Were not the individuals who took out subprime mortgages responsible for their financial decisions? Government, too, could be accused of having intervened in unhelpful ways. The Republican-appointed members of another congressional inquiry, the Financial Crisis Inquiry Commission, wrote their own report that placed more emphasis on the "loose money" policy of the Federal Reserve: government itself had pushed interest rates too low, which fueled borrowing and the bubble.[22] Government also attracted blame for encouraging subprime lending. The federal government had aggressively promoted home ownership, especially for poorer and minority groups. Politicians explicitly asked banks to lend to previously excluded categories. In this view, the ultimate fault for the cataclysm lay with too much government intervention in markets. Government had pushed banks to lend, lowered interest rates inappropriately, and so lured both financial firms and borrowers into decisions that they would never have made themselves.

In other words, people saw two opposite lessons in the Great Recession. For most people on the Left, the crisis showed that the neoliberal era had gone too far in reducing government control of markets. For many people on the Right, it showed that neoliberalism had not gone far enough. And as this debate played out in the wake of the recession, a deeper background context raised its stakes. Left and Right had different views about how the crisis related to longer-term concerns about inequality and the economic role of government.

Complaints about Inequality and Government Action

The policy responses to the Great Recession highlighted two deep and controversial themes in the political economy of the United States and other rich countries. One was inequality. To salvage a financial system on the brink of collapse, the U.S. and European governments bailed out financial firms with hundreds of billions of dollars in public money. Much less was done for the average citizens who lost their homes or jobs (or both) and suffered very concrete consequences in the crash. For many people on the Left, this was a final confirmation that the interests of "the 1 percent" of wealthy capitalists were prioritized over "the 99 percent" of everyone else. The other theme was concern about government intervention in the economy. Governments bailed out banks and also borrowed and spent more to handle the crisis—and in the United States, the federal government simultaneously legislated major new programs in health care. Much of the Right responded with its own outrage about a "government takeover" of the economy.

At an elite level in Washington, D.C., and across many other rich capitals, the immediate responses to the Great Recession initially attracted relatively broad support. Governments everywhere felt compelled to rescue big banks that were teetering on the edge of failure. Many people had misgivings about public help for these pillars of wealth, but key policymakers on both Right and Left—first in the George W. Bush administration, then in the Obama administration—concluded that some banks were "too big to fail": if they collapsed, they would take the whole world down with them. Besides these bailouts, the other major response to the crisis was Keynesian stimulus. Though the bank rescues staved off total financial collapse, the U.S. and European economies plunged into recession, and governments pumped money into their economies to encourage growth. First under Bush and then under Obama, the U.S. government lowered interest rates (a monetary stimulus, making it cheaper to borrow money) and increased spending (a fiscal stimulus, using government-funded activities to kickstart the private economy).

But the relative consensus on crisis response was thin and short-lived. For most of the Left, it was outrageous that a neoliberal era of rising inequality had culminated in a massive public bailout for some of the world's richest organizations. A new surge of research on inequality produced charts like Figure 10-5, suggesting that the richest Americans had captured a hugely disproportionate share of economic gains since the 1980s. Another widely noted complaint was pay for Chief Executive Officers (CEOs) in large American companies: in the 1950s they typically earned about 20 times the average salary of their employees, but by the 2010s they averaged over 300 times a worker's salary.[23] The combination of these apparent trends with the Wall Street bailouts sparked a wave of new mobilization on the left of the Democratic Party. A protest movement in New York in 2011, "Occupy Wall Street," grabbed attention with its slogan, "We are the 99 percent." The wave later sparked the presidential candidacy of Vermont Senator Bernie Sanders in 2015, whose "Democratic Socialist" campaign for the Democratic Party nomination mounted a powerful (if unsuccessful) challenge to the more centrist

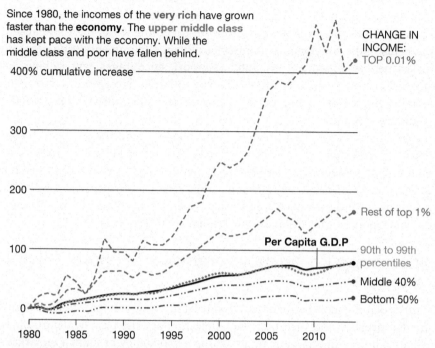

Figure 10-5 Income Inequality

Since 1980, the incomes of the **very rich** have grown faster than the **economy**. The **upper middle class** has kept pace with the economy. While the middle class and poor have fallen behind.

400% cumulative increase

CHANGE IN INCOME: TOP 0.01%

300

200

Rest of top 1%

Per Capita G.D.P

100

90th to 99th percentiles

Middle 40%

Bottom 50%

0

1980   1985   1990   1995   2000   2005   2010

Source: A new study says much of the rise in inequality is an illusion. Should you believe it?, Vox Media, LLC, 2018. Retrieved from https://www.vox.com/policy-and-politics/2018/1/10/16850050/inequality-tax-return-data-saez-piketty
Did Thomas Piketty Get His Math Wrong?, The New York Times Company, 2014. Retrieved from https://www.nytimes.com/2014/05/24/upshot/did-piketty-get-his-math-wrong.html.

candidacy of New York Senator Hillary Clinton. These voices insisted that American economic growth was not benefitting most Americans. Correcting these imbalances required higher taxes on the rich, more regulation of big corporations, and redistributive spending for health care and education. Sanders and other similar figures also challenged the openness of international markets, criticizing free-trade deals and calling for government to protect American workers and standards.

But outrage was not limited to the Left. Many conservatives were already inclined to blame the crisis on what they saw as government meddling in the economy, and the bailouts and stimulus looked to them like more of the same. Worse, in their eyes, was the agenda of the Democratic president who was elected as the crisis hit. President Obama's leading priority was government support to extend health insurance to the 50 million Americans who lacked it at the time. Perception of a "government takeover" of the economy in bailouts, stimulus, and "Obamacare" became the rallying cry for the "Tea Party" movement, which mobilized opposition to taxes, spending, and regulation on the right wing of the Republican Party. In parallel, a Wisconsin Congressman and devout free-marketeer, Paul Ryan, emerged as the new intellectual leader of the more mainstream Republican establishment. He diagnosed "an un-relenting and wide-ranging expansion of government" as the root cause of problems in the American economy.[24] For Ryan, government action generally makes people dependent on public support, encourages rent-seeking and stagnation, and tends to result in runaway inflation. The solution is dramatic cuts to government spending, lower taxes, and liberalization of regulation wherever possible.

In sum, an increasingly mobilized Left called for action to turn back the neo-liberal era of Reagan and Thatcher, while an assertive Right argued for pushing the pro-market agenda further. Sharp growth debates once again took center stage in the United States and in some other developed countries as well. And then came a wild-card development: the American election of 2016 rearranged economic-policy fights in complex ways that are still playing out.

The Trump Presidency Scrambles Economic Debates

In 2016, defying most predictions, Donald Trump won first the Republican pres-idential primary and then the general election against Democratic candidate Hillary Clinton. In economic terms Trump's presidency brought a remarkable mashup. A flamboyant billionaire championed protectionism and government spending to help American workers. At the same time he pleased big busi-ness with deregulation and tax cuts for the rich. Outcomes on the ground were mixed as well. The American economy boomed, reaching new lows of unem-ployment. Benefits still went disproportionately to the better-off, however, to the point that life expectancy for the poor displayed an unprecedented decline.

Trump's victory over Clinton in 2016 was related to big changes to the Republican economic pitch. Long seen as the party of business, Republicans had generally championed limited government spending, low taxes, lightened regula-tion, and open international markets since World War II. Trump reversed his party's positions on two of these major issues. On spending, he proposed a trillion-dollar initiative to upgrade American infrastructure—more than doubling similar propos-als from his Democratic rival Clinton. On international markets, he called for im-posing tariffs on both rivals like China and allies like the European Union to force them to renegotiate the terms of trade. Both ideas drew criticisms from more classic Republicans like Paul Ryan.[25] Despite these intra-party tensions, though, Trump's plans for muscular government action to build roads and bridges and strong-arm other countries for "better deals" were popular with some voters. They appealed in particular to less educated white Americans in the midwestern states, where Trump made key electoral gains over Clinton.

At the same time, however, Trump catered to big business and the wealthiest Americans on taxes and deregulation. It was in these areas where he delivered the

President Donald Trump poses in the Oval Office with his Vice President Michael Pence (to his right) and then-House Speaker Paul Ryan and Senate Majority Leader MItchell McConnell (to his left). Trump shifted economic priorities of more traditional Republicans like Ryan or McConnell by endorsing economic protectionism and running huge budget deficits.

most results once in office. The main legislative achievement of his first several years in office was a major tax cut. Its biggest element lowered taxes on corporations, and most other benefits were weighted toward wealthy individuals. In many more specific ways, too, the Trump White House worked to loosen or eliminate regulation in areas like energy production, labor rules, and financial markets.[26] Perhaps most importantly for these constituencies, President Trump successfully nominated two very conservative judges to fill openings on the Supreme Court. According to ratings of judges' positions, his appointees Neil Gorsuch and Brett Kavanaugh are close to the court's previous "arch-conservative," Clarence Thomas.[27] Both have strongly pro-business legal records, and their appointments should favor business interests far into the future.[28]

On the ground, the American economic recovery that began under Obama continued under Trump. Ongoing growth delivered the longest period of steady job creation in U.S. history and carried unemployment to historic lows. The distribution of these gains remained uneven, however. Stock markets and housing values soared again, especially boosting the wealthy. But average wage increases did not begin to outpace inflation until very late in the recovery, in 2018.[29] More dramatically, in 2015, the United States began a multi-year run of declines in life expectancy—a drop never seen in any rich country outside of wartime or pandemics. Leading contributors to this drop, which is concentrated among the poor, were what experts called "deaths of despair": opioid overdoses, suicide, and liver disease (from alcoholism).[30]

Overall, President Trump's reshaping of the Republican Party steered American economic debates into uncharted terrain. Prior to 2016, the sharp economic fights in the wake of the Great Recession had looked quite familiar. The Left called for more government action to redress inequality and regulate markets; the Right called for less government action and more open markets. Trump's shift to a more nationalist version of conservatism blurred the lines of political competition, combining stances on taxes and deregulation that would have pleased Reagan with views on trade, spending and borrowing that would have horrified him (since they overlapped heavily with views from far-Left figures like Sanders). It is hard to predict where these debates will go, but it seems clear that voters will be offered new political choices about growth strategies in coming years.

Political Ideologies and Economic Growth

10.4   **Evaluate arguments for and against a reliance on liberalized markets to generate economic growth.**

Alternative ideas about development and growth are so fundamental to modern politics that this chapter, more than others, began engaging with political ideologies in its earlier sections. Thatcher's and Reagan's plan for growth represents the core of modern conservatism, especially in the United States and other Anglophone countries. Modern liberalism has been substantially defined around the goal of achieving equitably distributed economic growth. This section delves a bit deeper into the relationship between economic analysis and normative political philosophy within these stances. Also, by considering other ideologies—such as socialists who reject market-based growth, and environmentalists who question the goal of economic growth in general—this section underscores where conservatives and liberals agree.

Why the Freest Markets Deliver the Most—and Most Just—Growth

When politicians champion liberalized markets and small government as the path to economic growth, they typically believe that this growth strategy is good in both analytic and normative terms. Deregulated markets generate more wealth *and* make people and society morally good.

We have seen the roots of this ideological position in classical liberalism and its legacy in modern conservatism. Locke and others argued normatively for individual liberty and private property; Adam Smith and later economists added analytic logic that when people enjoy these rights in open markets, wealth grows. Lured forward by the possibility of wealth and threatened by fears of poverty, individuals are forced by competition in markets to identify and develop their own strengths. Each person becomes as productive as he or she can be, and overall wealth rises as society together becomes more efficient and innovative. Furthermore, because human creativity is nearly boundless, growth and moral self-improvement can go on indefinitely—as long as competition in open markets upholds this mechanism.

Modern conservatives, led by Thatcher and Reagan to embrace the "neo" version of classical liberalism, follow this legacy closely in stressing the dangers of straying from the freest possible markets. Theirs is not an easy path, they suggest, since it faces analytic and normative challenges that are seductive but wrong. Well-meaning critics will see inequality in markets and make Robin Hood–like calls for higher taxes on the rich to support the poor. Analytically, however, this slows growth—by weakening motivations for rich and poor alike to work hard and innovate—and decreases the consequences of failure and the rewards of success. Morally speaking, such efforts to make the poor comfortable also overlook how important self-reliance is to moral character. As one of Congressman Ryan's reports argued, government intervention "fosters a culture in which self-reliance is a vice and dependency a virtue—and as a result, the entire country weakens from within."

Other seductions, such as the temptation for stimulus policies in a recession to ease suffering among the unemployed, are similarly morally soft and analytically shortsighted. Stimulus mutes incentives for people to become still more productive when times are tough, leads to government debts that crowd out productive investments, and floods markets with easy money that eventually causes inflation. Even more misguided are longer-term government programs in such areas as scientific research or health care that purport to support growth. Politicians and bureaucrats are too far from market incentives to make good economic choices—they do not get rich if growth succeeds or poor if it fails—and so their interventions are bound to be negative on balance. Even if they could "help" businesses grow, they would weaken private actors' self-reliance and moral fiber in so doing. Thus governments *cannot* and *should not* push growth themselves. They must be limited to background policies for security, legal order, protection of private property, and stable money.

Why Targeted Intervention in Markets Delivers More Justice and More Growth

The "public–private partnership" growth strategies typical of modern liberals are also built on a mix of analytic and normative arguments. Their champions see both practical and moral reasons for governments to shape and channel market-based growth to better distribute its gains, and believe that smart policies lead to faster growth and more just societies.

We encountered the foundations of this ideological view in the transition from classical to modern liberalism. Once governments had been limited by individual rights and democracy in the United States and some of Europe, some classical liberals concluded that new government policies were necessary to further pursue liberty and equality. Their key analytic point was that some people lose or win in market competition for reasons unrelated to their own merits or efforts. Sickness, discrimination, a lack of access to education or other opportunities for self-improvement, and sheer bad luck can leave hardworking individuals poor; if dealt a good hand, some unimpressive individuals end up rich. Worse, challenges in market competition compound over time for those who fell behind and become too easy for those who get ahead. Even a brilliant and industrious poor kid might not make it, while even a lackluster rich kid rarely ends up on the street. It is a short step from this analytic view to the moral judgment that government should act to help the disadvantaged realize their potential. As Barack Obama once summarized when he was president, "Preserving our individual freedoms ultimately requires collective action."[31]

Modern-liberal thinking led to further analytic arguments that government action can increase the production of private wealth, not just redistribute it. Even redistribution itself can increase rather than decrease overall growth, according to liberal (and Nobel Prize–winning) economist Paul Krugman: "Extreme inequality means a waste of human resources," because the poorest people are unable to develop their talents, and welfare programs can boost long-term growth by expanding the number of citizens who can be productive.[32] Deregulated markets don't tend to provide conditions that support sustained growth, because businesses do not offer services unless they can make money on them; educating poor people promises few direct profits, for example, but all economists agree that an educated populace enhances growth. Similarly, growth-supporting tasks of government may include not only national defense, firefighters, or police (which even conservatives would see as important supports for the economy), but also provision of large-scale infrastructure, basic scientific research, health care, and environmental standards. Such government regulations and spending must be targeted—the liberal argument is not that *any* government program would boost growth—but there is a wide range of ways in which government action is helpful to the productivity and competitiveness of private business.

As we saw in the U.S. government's Keynesian response to the Great Recession, modern liberals also see moral and practical reasons for government to steer the economy at the broadest level. For Keynes, governments should spend money in recessions both to mitigate the suffering of the unemployed and to reach a higher growth trajectory overall. If government stimulus can pull the economy out of recession faster—or head off a recession as growth slows—it may maintain higher growth than a less interventionist government that waits for markets to restore themselves. Keynes did not reject more conservative economists' arguments that markets might naturally recover in the long run, but in one of his famous phrases, he suggested that good economic policy does not just sit by and wait: "In the long run," he said, "we are all dead."[33]

Is modern liberals' emphasis on government action, then, the opposite of conservatives' agenda for cutting it back? It can seem that way in American, British, and other countries' politics, which often sound like fights between "less government" and "more government." Yet that perception misses what both these mainstream ideologies share. Modern liberals, like conservatives, seek to promote individual liberty and the wealth of private actors. They disagree over the means to those ends in terms of government policy. This common foundation stands out more clearly when we consider ideological alternatives outside the legacy of classical liberalism.

Just Say No: Rejecting Markets or Rejecting Growth?

Conservatives and liberals may seem to agree little when it comes to growth, but in a broader perspective they remain part of the same liberal philosophical tradition. Both seek market-based growth that empowers and enriches individuals, even if they have radically different views of how that process can and should work. Other philosophical traditions place no priority on market-based growth at all. Fascists and Islamists are concerned with national power or Muslim faith and pay little direct attention to economics. Socialism and environmentalism have much more developed thoughts on market-based growth but reject it for different reasons. Socialists reject markets; environmentalists question growth.

During the Obama presidency, opponents often called Obama a socialist. But real socialists—rare though they are in America—hasten to correct this use of the label. Frank Llewellyn, national director of the Democratic Socialists of America, argues that politicians like Obama, Hillary Clinton, or other mainstream Democrats are ultimately friends of big business. Obamacare effectively saved the private insurance industry with government support; the government response to the Great Recession bailed out Wall Street bankers and General Motors more than the average Joe. These interventions are not socialist, explains Llewellyn: "The mere fact that the government owns something or has a stake in it doesn't make it socialist. If that was true, you would say we have a socialist army. The government owns the army." As for mainstream Democrats, they're "trying to save capitalism from itself rather than trying to change it into a new system."[34]

Committed socialists see economic growth as a fundamental goal, but not *market*-based growth. In their view, a good society is one that delivers a rising standard of living to *all* of its citizens, especially those who are least able to fend for themselves. Market competition sets up a constant race between wealthy and poor people with predictable results: those who already have advantages do well, and those who are disadvantaged in some way suffer. Though Marx himself recognized that capitalist competition can be very productive, he thought it socially perverse: not only does it incentivize businesspeople to be creative and innovative, it incentivizes them to pay employees as little as possible. Thus market-based growth tends to benefit only a tiny minority. Liberals or social democrats are fooling themselves by thinking that market-based growth can be shaped to serve broader interests. The only solution is to reject private property and market competition entirely, replacing them with a command economy that guarantees results for all.

Strong environmentalists break even more fundamentally with the liberal tradition, rejecting not just market-based growth but the goal of economic growth itself. Arguably the core theme of environmentalism—expressed in its founding statements, such as Rachel Carson's 1962 book *Silent Spring*—is that economic growth eventually destroys the natural world. Some environmentalists argue that growth is thus simply shortsighted: a focus on narrow economic

Table 10-3 Political Ideologies and Economic Growth

Ideology	What is the best path to growth?	Analysis at "macro" (economy) level	Analysis at "micro" (individual) level	Moral arguments
Classical Liberalism/Modern Conservatism	Minimize government spending and regulation; resist the urge to try to use government to accelerate growth	Markets tend to allocate resources and investment efficiently, except in occasional slowdowns—which soon self-correct if left alone.	Individuals and businesses can identify their strengths and respond to incentives efficiently only if market signals are not blurred by intervention.	Interventions to "help" disadvantaged people make them dependent on support and *less* able to reach their full potential, not more able.
Modern Liberalism/Social Democracy	Support the participation of disadvantaged people in markets; support business activity broadly by investing in infrastructure, education, etc.	Markets tend toward inequality and are subject to crises that self-correct only very slowly; government can stimulate the economy to faster recoveries from crises and higher growth overall.	Even rich individuals and businesses depend on many government investments to make markets work well (such as in education of future workers); poor individuals need direct support to become productive.	Only with government action to support the disadvantaged, including some redistribution of wealth, does a market-based economy offer morally fair equality of opportunity.
Socialism	Replace markets with command mechanisms that guarantee equality	Markets always produce growing inequality and thus tend to fall into class conflict.	Rich people tend to "succeed" in markets without much effort; poor people tend not to succeed no matter what their effort.	Markets are inherently unfair mechanisms for allocating wealth; a moral society must be built on a different economic system.
Environmentalism	Growth should be a secondary goal at most.	No distinctive economic analysis; environmentalists tend to share modern liberal/social democratic views.		A moral life balances (or replaces) economic goals with the pursuit of environmental sustainability.
Political Islamism	Growth is a secondary goal.	No distinctive economic analysis		A moral life focuses first on religious righteousness.
Fascism	Growth is a secondary goal.	No distinctive economic analysis		A moral life focuses first on the glory of the nation.

criteria will lead us all into misery as we destroy the broader conditions for a healthy and pleasant existence. Money-based measures of personal and societal "success" must be complemented—or replaced—by more balanced visions that include our environment. Environmentalist economists and activists have launched "no-growth" or "degrowth" movements that try to elaborate this vision.[35] More radical, less human-centric environmentalists oppose even taking human happiness as the main goal. In their "deep ecology" view, the ethical path considers human needs alongside those of other creatures and of the planet itself.[36]

Devout socialists or deep ecologists certainly make mainstream Democrats and Republicans look more aligned, as Table 10-3 summarizes. Liberals share some of socialists' concern for inequality and have taken on important elements of environmentalism, but still tend to argue that government action in these areas is compatible with, and even supportive of, a focus on economic growth. Like almost everyone in the American political mainstream, and similarly in most other countries around the world, they still see the lure of economic growth as enormously powerful. The voices that genuinely call for rejecting markets or rejecting growth are more marginal, but suggest valuable alternatives even for the most mainstream thinkers. At the very least, these alternatives help us sharpen our beliefs and values. For some, they may be persuasive in their own right.

Explaining a Case: Uncovering the Whys of the Taiwanese Miracle

10.5 Identify three plausible explanations for Taiwan's rapid economic growth.

Rarely is the connection between political action, ideology, and explanation more obvious than with development and growth. The policies we recommend to develop poor countries or grow rich countries depend heavily on how we explain the generation of wealth in the past. For advocates of spending cuts and liberalization today, for example, it is important to argue that the freest markets have delivered growth in the past; for advocates of government action, it is equally important to point to cases of successful interventions. A critical thinker must consider, at least in a rough way, how alternative explanations support or challenge their ideological commitments and positions in today's economic debates.

Rarely does a case of growth cry out for explanation as much as Taiwan's. It is the clearest economic success story in history, leaping from poverty to wealth in two generations. Much less clear, though, is how to best explain what happened on this Asian island. Several different explanations drawn from the main explanatory approaches in political science seem plausible at first glance and connect to different ideological and policy views today.

The Rational-Material Story

From a rational-material point of view, Taiwan's remarkable growth mainly reflects its material position relative to market opportunities and security threats. The Taiwanese occupied a special place in global security competition: as communist China's closest enemy, they attracted the United States as an ally and gained excellent access for their exports to the huge American market. Beyond these geopolitical conditions, a rational-material view suggests that openness to global competition was the key to Taiwan's success. In this view the government's economic interventions made little difference, and ultimately Taiwanese businesses stood or fell by how competitively they exported. Those who support the rational-material view hold that the Taiwanese government effectively got out of the way and allowed its businesses to confront strong, clear structural incentives—access to rich-world markets and pressures from global competition—and thus became steadily more productive.

The Institutional Story

Probably more common today as an explanation of Taiwanese growth is a story that centers on the institutions of Taiwanese government. After World War II, this island nation hit on an institutional arrangement of its political economy that combined both free market incentives and effective government support for growth. A powerful economic bureaucracy set long-term strategies and boosted Taiwanese business in dealings with larger foreign firms. Sharp internal competition and the goal of exporting to highly competitive foreign markets also kept Taiwanese firms from turning into protected rent-seekers. Thus, Taiwan achieved an advantageous institutional balance for growth, with just the right amount and kind of government action to foster the rapid creation of private wealth.

The Ideational Story

Given that the fastest-growing countries in history are all East Asian, another explanation of Taiwanese growth zeroes in on culture. In this view, the cultural values of Taiwan's Chinese population fit unusually well with market-based growth. They stress hard work, striving for education and self-improvement, saving money for investment, and a balance between fierce competition and respect for the community. At another level, the dominant political ideology of Taiwan after World War II also helped: their hostility toward communist mainland China made them very pro-capitalist and eager to outpace their mainland rivals, and threats from mainland China encouraged the Taiwanese to see economic growth as a route to security.

Which explanation of Taiwanese growth is most convincing? Our initial answers are likely to be entangled with our ideology. The rational-material story connects best to conservative ideology, arguing that fast growth results when business competes in wide open markets with minimal interference from governing institutions. The institutional story fits best with a modern-liberal ideology, suggesting that the fastest growth in history resulted from public–private partnership. We should make some effort, though, to question our ideological points of departure by looking for some evidence. As always, two strategies organize research options:

RESEARCH ON WITHIN-CASE PROCESSES. To study how Taiwan grew, the most straightforward research strategy is to gather historical evidence of what actually happened. How open were their markets to competition? What did the government do, and how did those actions seem to impact business action? Table 10-4 spells out what each of our alternative explanations would expect to find.

Find a news article about Taiwan's economic success from a credible newspaper, magazine, or website, and look for signs that seem to fit best with one version of the story.

Table 10-4 Exploring Within-Case Evidence for Alternative Explanations of Taiwanese Growth

	Rational-Material Explanation	Institutional Explanation	Ideational Explanation
What did government officials do to generate growth?	Generated background stability and promoted openness; other interventions were modest and erratic.	Systematically incentivized long-term investment in export industries with economic promise, while keeping up competitive pressure	Emphasized community-based values, nationalism, and the threat of mainland China; stressed a sense of duty to build up economic strength
Which parts of the economy grew most?	Those in which broad market conditions were most favorable (strong demand, available investment, new technologies) grew most.	Those that economic bureaucrats chose to feature for government support and incentives grew most.	Growth was broadly based; hardworking, frugal Taiwanese businesses generally succeeded across the board.
Which parts of the economy grew least?	Those in which government officials intervened too much grew least.	Those in which government officials did not intervene grew least.	See above.
When did growth surge in certain parts of the economy?	Growth surged in any given sector whenever broader market conditions were favorable to growth.	Growth surged in each sector not long after government policies created new support and targeted incentives for it.	High growth surged fairly consistently, perhaps most when threats from mainland China increased.
Best Evidence to Support Each Explanation	We find that Taiwanese businesses simply grew in sectors that had openness to markets and available resources and investment; government interventions in particular sectors made little difference or were harmful.	We find that even when Taiwanese businesses faced difficult challenges and were starting from scratch, government policies helped some businesses grow very quickly.	We find Taiwanese businesses and government players saying that they were able to work together to pull off long-term growth strategies due to their distinct values and shared identity.

RESEARCH ON CROSS-CASE PATTERNS.   We also gain leverage on Taiwanese economic performance by looking at how its case fits into patterns of growth. Is there a pattern that links fast growth to the degree of openness to foreign competition? Do states with strong economic development bureaucracies tend to grow faster? How strong is the pattern that societies with Asian cultures have tended to grow especially fast? Your instructor may be able to help you find data to explore some of these possible cross-case correlations.

Conclusion: Why Understanding the Politics of Growth Matters to You

What are economic development and growth doing in an introduction to politics? Generating wealth is so important to people around the world, and so much contestation surrounds strategies to achieve it, that these issues form much of the core of political life. We debate whether market-based growth comes when government gets out of the way or when government acts to encourage it. We disagree whether market-based growth naturally tends to help everyone or naturally tends to exclude certain populations. In certain places and times, particular views dominate these debates and create a tenuous consensus on growth strategies—but never for long. Today, and for the foreseeable future, these debates are especially fierce. In the developing world, the rise of Asia gave champions of active government new arguments to fragment the neoliberal consensus. The Great Recession did the same among the richer countries. When national growth strategies are so contested, at least one imperative is clear for individual citizens: we must grasp the main alternatives so we can understand and claim a part in the politics swirling around us.

Review of Learning Objectives

10.1   **Identify common supporting conditions and challenges for growth in market economies and explain how they encourage or hamper growth.**

Developing countries around the world want to become rich, and the rich developed countries want to become richer. Behind today's debates over how to foster market-based growth there is some agreement on basic conditions: political and legal stability, property rights, infrastructure, sound money, sources of investment, and some openness to broader markets. There is also agreement that countries must avoid common problems of unemployment, inflation, rent-seeking, and unequal distribution of the locations of growth. Debate rages, though, about which of these challenges are most pressing and how to best surmount them.

10.2   Describe the main alternative recipes for growth in developing countries and evaluate their records in achieving development.

The main advice that developing countries receive from powerful organizations like the IMF, the World Bank, or the U.S. government is a recipe of market liberalization known as the "Washington Consensus." As of the 1980s, these views largely vanquished an alternative strategy called "import-substitution industrialization," which called for protecting developing economies from rich-world imports. Since the 1990s, though, strong free market views have confronted another challenge from the seemingly successful interventionist strategies of Taiwan and other Asian countries. Asia's rise posed new questions about how best to develop a market-based economy, leaving us with a wide-open debate today.

10.3   Describe the main alternative positions on fostering growth in developed countries and evaluate their records in recent decades.

As of the 1980s, neoliberal thinking inspired a fairly powerful consensus within rich countries. Not only the conservative Right but much of the Left agreed that growth would come by lessening government intervention and allowing markets to operate more freely. This neoliberal quasi-consensus came crashing down in 2009, though, when a financial crisis in the United States spread into the deepest global recession since the 1930s. Some argued that unregulated markets caused the crisis; others maintained that the crisis showed a need for still more deregulation and liberalization. Government responses to the crisis sparked new mobilization on the Right against a perceived "government takeover," and new mobilization on the Left to protest increasing inequality. Then these sharp Left-Right economic debates were blurred under Donald Trump. He altered Republican positions to combine traditionally conservative priorities on lower taxes and deregulation with traditionally liberal positions on international trade and government spending.

10.4   Evaluate arguments for and against a reliance on liberalized markets to generate economic growth.

For the most coherent modern conservatives—those who avoid the mixed positions of Donald Trump—the key to growth remains the classical liberal wisdom of competitive markets. These "neoliberals" see the widest possible operation of market competition as most likely to generate more wealth and as the most moral way to distribute it. For modern liberals, on the other hand, market-based growth depends on targeted government action to reach its productive potential and to distribute wealth fairly. Government and business can work together to increase productivity, and government must support the disadvantaged to deliver true equality of opportunity. These two views generate sharp debates, but their shared goal of market-based growth to generate private wealth stands out sharply when contrasted to ideological views outside the liberal tradition. For devout socialists, the competitive mode of market-based growth is immoral and destabilizing because it systematically advantages the strong over the weak. For convinced environmentalists, economic growth of any sort can threaten both the destruction of natural beauty and disregard for other living things.

10.5 **Identify three plausible explanations for Taiwan's rapid economic growth.**

To review for this objective, try to imagine rational-material, institutional, and ideational explanations of how Taiwan could have achieved such a rapid economic ascent without looking at Section 10.5. Begin by asking yourself the following questions:

- Taiwan had few resources and a peripheral location, but still some material conditions could have connected its populations to wide market opportunities and incentivized them to seize them. What geopolitical or economic ties or pressures could have helped?

- What sort of story could we construct about how the institutions of Taiwanese government gave its leaders special capacities and inclinations to deliver rapid economic growth? In what sort of institutions might leaders have the most leverage over the economy?

- From an ideational point of view, might there be features of Taiwanese identity and culture, or the dominant ideologies of Taiwanese society, that could have oriented its people toward hard work and a priority on economic goals?

After brainstorming your answers to these questions, return to Section 10.5 to see how well you have constructed plausible alternatives to explain this case.

Great Sources to Find Out More

Aaron Ross Sorkin, *Too Big to Fail: The Inside Story of How Wall Street and Washington Fought to Save the Financial System—And Themselves* (New York: Penguin, 2010). One of the most readable accounts of the financial crisis that brought on the Great Recession.

Amartya Sen, *Development as Freedom* (New York: Knopf, 2000). A Nobel Prize–winning economist proposes how to think about development.

Bill Devall and George Sessions, *Deep Ecology: Living as If Nature Mattered* (Layton, UT: Gibbs Smith, 1985). A classic statement of environmental values.

Carmet Reinhart and Kenneth Rogoff, *This Time Is Different: Eight Centuries of Financial Folly* (Princeton, NJ: Princeton University Press, 2009). A famous (and hotly contested) overview of economic crises.

Fernando H. Cardoso and Enzo Faletto, *Dependency and Development in Latin America* (Berkeley: University of California Press, 1979). A classic statement of dependency thinking.

Friedrich Hayek, *The Road to Serfdom* (Chicago: University of Chicago Press, 1944). A classic statement of conservative (neoliberal) thinking.

Hernando de Soto, *The Mystery of Capital: Why Capitalism Triumphs in the West and Fails Everywhere Else* (New York: Basic Books, 2000). An argument that property rights are the key to development.

Lawrence White, *The Clash of Economic Ideas: The Great Policy Debates and Experiments of the Last Hundred Years* (New York: Cambridge University Press, 2012). A remarkable overview of fights over economic policy.

Mark Blyth, *Austerity: History of a Dangerous Idea* (New York: Oxford University Press, 2013). A critique of arguments for cutting government spending to generate growth.

Paul Krugman, *End This Depression Now!* (New York: Norton, 2012). Growth advice for the United States from a leading liberal economist.

Robert Wade, *Governing the Market: Economic Theory and the Role of Government in East Asian Industrialization* (Princeton, NJ: Princeton University Press, 1990). An influential study of how Taiwan's government fostered growth.

Stephan Haggard, *Pathways from the Periphery: The Politics of Growth in Newly Industrializing Countries* (Ithaca, NY: Cornell University Press, 1990). A wide-ranging argument that traces developmental success to both geopolitical and institutional conditions.

William Easterly, *The Elusive Question for Growth: Economists' Adventures and Misadventures in the Tropics* (Cambridge, MA: MIT Press, 2002). A readable survey of economic thinking on development.

(See also the books on basic economics cited in Chapter 9.)

Develop Your Thinking

Use these questions as discussion or short writing exercises to think more deeply about some of the key themes of the chapter.

1. Which is a bigger problem in the American economy: rent-seeking (some people get undeserved benefits) or liberalization (too much harsh competition)?

2. How well would "Washington Consensus"–style policies work to bring wealth to a poor town or neighborhood near where you live?

3. Do your personal economic prospects depend on some supportive government policies, or more on being left alone to pursue market opportunities?

4. Are markets with minimal government action a morally good way to create and allocate wealth?

5. Do you think that the success of Asian economies mostly reflects a favorable material situation, good institutions, or something cultural?

6. How confident are you that you will be better off than your parents? Should the American government do something different to increase those chances?

Keywords

austerity 328
autarky 326
brain drain 330
capital 325
competition policy 330
deficits 328
dependency 336
developing/developed countries 323
economic development 323
economic growth 321
economic stimulus 327
financial bubble 345

fiscal policy 327
human development 323
hyperinflation 328
import substitution industrialization (ISI) 336
industrial policy 331
infant industry problems 330
inflation 325
intellectual property rights 325
interest rate 327
liberalization 329
monetary policy 327

neoliberalism 335
offshoring 330
privatization 329
protectionism 331
rent-seeking 329
securitization 346
shock therapy 335
stagflation 329
state-owned enterprises (SOEs) 340
unemployment rate 327
Washington Consensus 333

Chapter 11
Political Change: Authoritarianism and Democratization

During the 2011 "Arab Spring" uprising, Egyptians gathered in Cairo's Tahrir Square to demand the end of President Hosni Mubarak's corrupt regime. Mubarak's fall brought high hopes for democracy, but soon Egypt fell back under the dictatorial rule of General Abdel Fattah al-Sisi.

Learning Objectives

11.1 Identify multiple organizational strategies by which authoritarian regimes maintain political control, and give country examples.

11.2 Identify conditions that weaken authoritarian regimes and the organizational vulnerabilities of different types of authoritarianism.

11.3 Specify key conditions that help or harm a country's chances for successful democratization.

11.4 Evaluate competing arguments for and against the notion that democracies like the United States should actively promote democracy elsewhere.

11.5 Identify multiple explanations for the fall of authoritarian regimes in the Arab Spring.

Toppling Dictators Is Easier than Building Democracy

"I'm 21 years old and this is the first time in my life I feel free," exulted Abdul-Rahman Ayyash, celebrating the resignation of dictatorial Egyptian president Hosni Mubarak in February 2011.[1] Egyptians were thrilled to end a thirty-year dictatorship that violently repressed opposition, silenced the media, and prioritized its own control over benefits for society. But the celebration did not last long. Elections in 2012 installed a government of the Islamist Muslim Brotherhood. Critics soon accused it of reproducing some of Mubarak's practices: using government resources to favor supporters, disadvantage rivals, and stifle openness in society and the media. Protests mounted, and in 2013 the Egyptian military intervened to oust the elected government. Though it claimed to act in the name of peace and stability, the new military regime killed hundreds of people, arrested thousands, further restricted the media, and eventually held a skewed election that anointed General Abdel Fattah al-Sisi as president. Today, Egyptians are hardly freer than they were under Mubarak, and prospects for change are murkier than ever.

There is no bigger political issue for humanity's future than the prospects for change in countries that held out against earlier waves of democratization. Beyond the post-Arab Spring regimes in Egypt, Tunisia, and Libya, the fate of many nondemocracies will deeply shape the twenty-first century: countries like rising China, unstable (and nuclear) Pakistan, fundamentalist Iran, resentful Russia, chaotic Syria, isolated North Korea, and conflicted Nigeria. Will the citizens of these countries someday mix freely and easily with Americans for study, tourism, business, and international cooperation? Or will we see continued barriers, political tensions, or even violent conflict? These two scenarios suggest radically different futures for young people everywhere.

Despite the Arab Spring, the overall trend is worrisome: Freedom House's index of "freedom in the world," which is one of the most widely used measures of democracy, has fallen every year since 2006.[2] As Egypt suggests, ending a tyrannical regime is one thing, but crafting a stable democracy is another. This chapter begins by looking inside authoritarian regimes and seeking to understand how and why they come under pressure to change (or not). Then it surveys the challenging process of democratization itself. The chapter concludes by considering alternative answers to the question that these potential scenarios pose: what, if anything, can and should the United States do to promote democratization? ■

Inside Authoritarianisms

11.1 Identify multiple organizational strategies by which authoritarian regimes maintain political control, and give country examples.

"Happy families are all alike," wrote Leo Tolstoy to open his novel *Anna Karenina*, "Every unhappy family is unhappy in its own way." With a bit of poetic license, Tolstoy's point can extend to governments. The happy families of our age, we can say, are liberal democracies. Their citizens are not always cheerful—they grumble quite a bit—but they are fairly confident in their shared family model. Good government, they agree, requires a certain mechanism for controlling the state, such that citizens choose legislative and executive representatives who direct the government.

When we look inside countries that deviate from our era's normatively dominant democratic model—that is, look inside the "unhappy families"—we see a wider range of strategies for control. Dictatorships and monarchies build networks of loyalty around one leader. Military variants of dictatorship use the armed forces to govern. One-party regimes create a vast political apparatus that penetrates and oversees the state. In quasi-theocratic Iran, the clergy similarly looms over the political system. These variations become even more complicated because most authoritarian regimes include some partial concessions to normative pressures for rights and democracy. Most allow some participation within carefully watched limits.

To understand twenty-first-century authoritarianisms, then, we must see the varying ways in which they control the state, as well as the complex ways in which they are not simply authoritarian. In the next section, we see how these alternative arrangements foreshadow their future prospects. While some unhappy families may well endure, others seem more likely to fall apart.

Organizational Bases of Concentrated Control

Authoritarian governments face major challenges of organization. They attempt to place tight control of the state—always a vast, sprawling entity—in the hands of a small number of people. To have such concentrated control, they need especially robust ways to bend the far-flung personnel and powers of the state to their will. Strong chains of command must give top leaders leverage over distant officials; channels of recruitment must draw in new people to support the authoritarians' cause over time. In rough parallel to the kinds of authoritarian legitimacy we encountered in Chapter 5, authoritarians have developed four broad ways of meeting this organizational challenge (see Table 11-1). They build their power on personal networks, militaries, dominant parties, or religious hierarchies.

PERSONAL NETWORKS. The least systematically organized foundations for authoritarianism are the **personal networks** that undergird governments that are built around an individual leader or a ruling family. In classic dictatorships, top leaders operate much like heads of Mafia families. They cultivate chains of loyalty that extend through many links to control the state apparatus. The ruler may deal directly with only a few handpicked supporters, but members of this

personal networks
Ties of personal loyalty that can allow leaders to control large groups.

Table 11-1 Political Foundations of Authoritarian Regimes

Type of Regime	Basis for Authority	Organizational Strategy
Dictatorship	Effectiveness + charismatic leader	Personal networks
Military regime	Effectiveness + charismatic leaders	Military organization
One-party state	Charismatic ideology	Party hierarchy (cadres)
Theocracy	Traditional legitimacy	Religious hierarchy

inner circle develop their own circles of loyalists further down in government. They have their own henchmen, and so on. Often these chains are built on shared backgrounds, such as origins in the same region, education at a certain school, or ethnicity. In Syria, for example, President Bashar al-Assad's inner circle consists almost entirely of Alawites from the northwestern coastal mountains. They also hold the majority of positions in the upper ranks of the military and the security forces, and key posts in the rest of the state.[3]

Monarchies are a bit different, usually building networks of loyalty that are both personal and connect more broadly to the family dynasty. In the Kingdom of Saudi Arabia, King Salman has assigned most active government leadership to his son, Crown Prince Mohammed bin Salman. Carefully chosen allies command the key security forces, which are largely recruited from regions and tribes the king sees as especially loyal.[4] Yet some of these loyalties are to the royal family as a traditional form of rule, not just to King Salman. That gives the regime additional foundations that are lacking in typical dictatorships. If personal loyalty to King Salman were to wane, internal pressure might lead to crowning a new member of the House of Saud (the current royal family), but the regime would likely remain. But if Syria's Bashar al-Assad leaves office, no organized group or process exists to replace him with a family member or another Alawite. Although ethnicity helped him build personal networks, Bashar al-Assad ultimately rules through personal networks alone.

MILITARIES.   Rather than relying on personal or dynastic networks to dominate security forces and the state, some authoritarian governments take direct organizational control: they *are* the security forces. Military dictatorships simply merge a military command hierarchy with broader governance responsibilities. At a basic organizational level, this solves the challenge of governance. Militaries are typically tight organizations with clear chains of command and processes for recruitment and promotion. Their top commander can take a title such as president, like General Augusto Pinochet did in Chile from 1974 to 1990; or a group of commanders can govern as a military council, like the generals of the "State Law and Order Restoration Council" who ruled Myanmar from 1989 to 2006. (They were later renamed the "State Peace and Development Council" to sound friendlier.) Senior officers take on the responsibilities of government ministers, with lower ranks of officers filling subordinate policymaking roles and overseeing civilian staff further down. Maintaining this kind of military takeover of civilian affairs can be difficult, as we will see shortly. But given that almost all countries have this "off the shelf" option for control—to take an existing large security organization and put it in charge—it is no surprise that authoritarians sometimes use it to take over a government.

DOMINANT PARTIES. The most sophisticated authoritarian regimes, however, turn more to political professionals than to loyalist networks or military men. One-party regimes create massive organizations of political operatives, often called **cadres**, to supervise and direct the state. In places like China or Vietnam today, or historically in Nazi Germany or Soviet Russia, single parties direct the state but do not fully merge with it. Incorporating all state officials into the party is too unwieldy, especially in large countries in which regimes need a more organizationally focused means for controlling the state. By reserving party membership for a special subset of policymakers, leaders can recognize and indoctrinate the most committed individuals and employ them as overseers of the state. The party structure also helps to recruit future leaders, such as through China's Communist Youth League, which has over 100 million members.[5]

China is the clearest and most important example of such a system today (see Figure 11-1). Every substantial job in the state has a parallel party representative to watch over it. For example, central-government ministries—such as

cadres
Groups of party officials that supervise and manage a one-party state.

Figure 11-1 Organizational Strategies of Authoritarian Regimes

Each type of authoritarian regime uses a different organizational strategy to control the state.

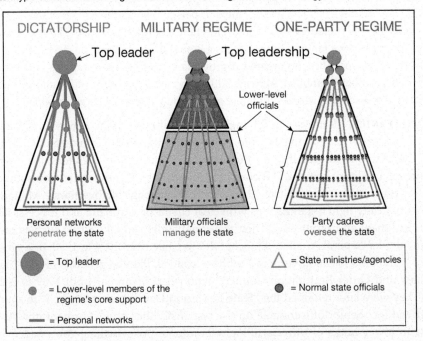

Agriculture or Energy—are shadowed by party units that address these policies. While a governor formally heads each of the twenty-seven Chinese provinces, the provincial party secretary holds the real power in each province. The same follows down to the lowest level of government, where each of the roughly 1 million village mayors has a party overseer. At higher levels, the parallel state and party hierarchies overlap, since higher-level officials are more likely to be party members themselves. At the very top they merge, and key party and state positions are held by the same person; for example, the president, who is head of state, is also the chairman of the Central Military Commission (which oversees the military) and the general secretary of the Chinese Community Party (CCP). Since March 2013, these combined offices are held by Xi Jinping, China's paramount leader. Below him are seven or eight people who are simultaneously top state officials (the prime minister and other leading ministers) and top party leaders (forming the party's ultimate decision-making body, the Central Politburo Standing Committee of the CCP).

RELIGIOUS LEADERSHIP.   The world's only partial theocracy, Iran, displays some organizational similarities to single-party regimes. Rather than a formal party organization that parallels and oversees the state, however, Iran's government is watched by a loose religious order. The Shi'a **clerics** who led the Iranian revolution in 1979 gradually expanded the clergy from roughly 20,000 members to some 350,000 today. Top religious leaders centralized control over religious seminaries; bureaucratized programs for religious credentials, housing, health care, and other benefits; and generally developed Iranian Islam "from a traditional, oral-based order to a modern, digitized system."[6] Most clerics are not political professionals like CCP members; in fact, the large majority is not even politically active. Somewhat like CCP members, however, clerics comprise a group of people with special status from whom the overseers of the state are selected.

clerics
Members of religious orders, or the clergy.

The leaders of this clergy form a religious elite that supervises all levels of government. At the top, the religious hierarchy merges with the state. Iran's current Supreme Leader, Ayatollah Ali Khamenei, is commander of the armed forces and appoints many key figures, including the main military leaders, the chief justice (who largely controls all other judicial appointments), and half of the members of the Guardian Council that must approve laws and candidates for national office. Though Iran has a president who is not necessarily part of the clergy—the current president, Hassan Rouhani, is a cleric, but his predecessor Mahmoud Ahmadinejad was an engineer—the Supreme Leader's influence on the Guardian Council gives him strong control over who can run for president or any other office, as well as over the passage of all laws. At lower levels, the Supreme Leader and higher clergy have representatives throughout the military, police, and other government agencies. An "Office of the Supreme Leader in Universities," for example, oversees higher-education curriculum and practices.[7] The clergy even runs its own military corps—the Revolutionary Guard, separate from the normal army—and a volunteer paramilitary enforcement network, the Basij, which recruits youth and operates as a vigilante "morality police."[8]

In each kind of authoritarianism, then, concentrated groups control the state through a particular organizational solution. Each organizational strategy manifests the principles of legitimacy that these regimes use to justify themselves. These different strategies allow authoritarian groups to either penetrate or parallel the state, but never to fully merge with it. This incomplete overlap of authoritarian organization and the state is important because it highlights a "space" that many authoritarian regimes have entered in recent years to attract more supporters in innovative ways. While maintaining authoritarian supervision, they have partly opened their state institutions to a variety of participatory practices.

Not Grandpa's Authoritarianism: Managed Accountability and "Hybrid Regimes"

There was a time, a couple of generations ago, when authoritarianism was unapologetic. The Nazis, Soviets, or China's early Communists saw nothing to admire in democracy; they created totalitarian regimes that sought to stamp out any space not controlled by the ruling party. Some of their contemporaries in monarchies and dictatorships similarly dismissed democracy. Today, though, only a few dinosaurs continue in that same mode, such as North Korea or the central Asian dictatorship of Turkmenistan. Other authoritarians still employ the basic organizational strategies developed earlier, but have followed a "learning curve" to sell their regimes in more sophisticated ways.[9] In Iran, China, and many other places, authoritarian leaders carve out space within the state to invite some citizen participation. They thus converge with the most illiberal democracies, like Russia, in a zone of slickly modified authoritarianism that some call **hybrid regimes**.[10]

hybrid regimes
Governments that incorporate features of both authoritarian and democratic government.

Iran is the most striking example of an authoritarian government that includes substantial elections with universal adult suffrage and some real contestation. Religious hard-liners do not always like the electoral results. In 1997, 2001, 2013, and 2017, a relatively reformist presidential candidate beat out the candidate backed by Supreme Leader Khamenei. Even in 2005 and 2009, when the hard-liners favored the winner, Mahmoud Ahmadinejad, the elections were still hard-fought campaigns whose results were considered unpredictable.[11] Iran also has regular elections for its parliament, the Majlis. Even the Assembly of Experts, the eighty-eight-member body that chooses the Supreme Leader, is elected, though its members must be chosen from the ranks of the clergy. The twelve-member Guardian Council vets candidates and bars most reformists from running for any of these national offices—but not all. Reformists are frequently permitted to run in lower-level elections to provincial, city, and village councils. Once approved, candidates are even given roughly equal radio and TV time. While it remains clear that the religious hierarchy would block any candidate, election, or legislation that truly threatens the regime, Iranians do have some choices, and elections have some effect on the regime's public face and policies.

China remains a purer authoritarian system, but it, too, experiments in hybrid ways. It has no parallels to Iranian presidential elections, but does permit votes at the lowest level of village councils. Even these selections are rarely very open; many party-favored councilors remain in power for long periods of time. In some cases, however, the CCP allows more competition. In one famous case, the southeastern village of Wukan rose up in protest against a corrupt council that illegally sold villagers' land to developers. Rather than suppressing the protests—a common government response—the regional governor called new elections that were won by the protesters' leaders.[12] Similar victories can be found across the broader pattern of tens of thousands of protests that occur in China every year. While protests in China often are met with crackdowns, the government does allow a large number of protest actions to take place and sometimes tries to respond to their demands. These victories are usually partial at best: Wukan's new council made little headway in recovering the village land, and the watchful party monitored them closely.[13] Still, these villagers were allowed to elect leaders that were not selected by the CCP.

In more important ways, the CCP has invited some discussion of rights and accountability at the national level. Back in 2006, an article called "Democracy Is a Good Thing" appeared in all major Chinese newspapers. Written by Yu Keping, a university professor and CCP insider, its core theme was, "Democracy is a good thing, but that does not mean everything about democracy is good."[14] In his widely read writings, Keping endorses democracy and rights quite strongly, but also argues that China should move slowly and carefully in these directions. The final goal, moreover, should be democracy with "Chinese characteristics," not a Western model. An institute he directs offers prizes for innovations in "local democracy," recently awarding localities that broadcast public hearings on the Internet, use public polling to measure government performance, or boost responsiveness in health care.[15] A bit paradoxically, perhaps, CCP leaders do not hide that their intention is to strengthen support for the regime. As *Slate* magazine's foreign policy editor William Dobson writes, "The aim is to make the government more responsive, improve the delivery of social services, and win the public's trust to enhance the durability of the Chinese Communist Party's rule. . . . It is democratic innovation in the service of Chinese authoritarianism."[16]

With these innovations, Iran and China enter a zone of partly participatory authoritarianism that overlaps with the category of illiberal democracy. The most abusive illiberal democracies share this space with authoritarianism, but reach it from the reverse direction, starting with regimes supposedly premised on public participation but then restricting rights until leaders can ignore most public input. Russia, for example, is a liberal-democratic regime on paper— its constitution is much more like a Western model than Iran's or China's, and the top leader is directly elected—but President Putin has so illiberally

Chinese schoolchildren and police officers swear an oath around a giant copy of China's Constitution to mark the country's first "Constitution Day" in 2014. The celebration was part of President Xi Jinping's drive to suggest that China embraces the rule of law.

abused rights that he is hardly more accountable than Ayatollah Khamenei or Xi Jinping. Many regimes move around in this "hybrid" zone as they evolve over time, sometimes looking clearly authoritarian, sometimes better fitting the label of illiberal democracy, but never developing anything beyond very partial forms of **managed accountability**. Prior to the Arab Spring, Egypt and Tunisia fit this description, as do Pakistan, Nigeria, and many other countries in Africa, the Middle East, or Central Asia. Overall, it is fair to say that managed accountability has become a pervasive feature of authoritarian systems in the twenty-first century.[17]

Whether regimes enter this murky zone by updating authoritarianism or by "backsliding" from democracy,[18] their mixed elements make any attempt to predict the future spread of democracy more complicated than ever. Does Iranian electoral competition or China's small steps toward accountability open the door to further steps in a more democratic direction? Or are these steps just shoring up authoritarian rule? Both dynamics are probably operating. Some authoritarians, given the right conditions and strategies, may succeed in harnessing managed accountability to strengthen their control. Others may find that small openings to democracy create fissures in their regime that widen into a collapse. Just which scenario is likeliest for each country is very hard to predict. We can glean some hints, though, by considering how countries have transitioned from their authoritarian rule in the past.

managed accountability
When citizens have opportunities to vote or criticize government within parameters managed by leaders whom citizens cannot choose.

How Authoritarians Fall

11.2 Identify conditions that weaken authoritarian regimes and the organizational vulnerabilities of different types of authoritarianism.

There are a variety of organizational fixes and claims to legitimacy that hold "unhappy families" together. But what matters most for a more democratic future is asking the opposite question: what makes them fall apart?

Especially in a world dominated by powerful democracies, we might expect repressive regimes to collapse due to war and diplomatic pressure. Yet the more common challenges to these regimes come from the economy. Economic crises frequently contribute to their downfall. Under any regime, economic failure breeds resentment. Economic success can also cause problems for authoritarians. When citizens gain more resources, they may become more inclined and empowered to demand rights. So both economic failure and economic success can threaten the concentrated power of an authoritarian regime.

However, not all authoritarians are equally vulnerable to such challenges because their different organizational strategies carry different strengths and weaknesses. Further complications that fuel an authoritarian demise are waves of protest that can suddenly well up within countries and ripple across national borders. The sudden collapse of the USSR in the early 1990s or the regional earthquake of the Arab Spring in 2011 suggest that "contagion" may shake even rulers who seem firmly in control. While it is not often possible to predict the end of a regime, usually a mix of economic challenges, regime vulnerabilities, and waves of protest come before the fall.

War and International Pressure

In a world where democracies in North America and Europe hold the majority of military and economic power, authoritarians' main worries might seem to come from abroad. After all, the Nazis and imperial Japan were crushed in war. The Soviet Union collapsed after a long military standoff with the West. More recently, the United States and its allies have intervened against authoritarians in such places as the former Yugoslavia, Somalia, Afghanistan, and Iraq. The United States arms and protects communist China's rival Taiwan and maintains almost 25,000 troops on North Korea's southern border. U.S. leaders refuse to rule out a military strike on Iran. The list goes on.

Rich and powerful democracies exert nonmilitary pressure on authoritarians as well:

- *Comprehensive economic sanctions* block trade and financial interactions with a country in hopes that economic distress will force compliance. In the 1990s, the United Nations imposed broad **sanctions** that barred any economic dealings with the repressive regimes—and businesses—in Iraq, Haiti, and Yugoslavia. More recently, to deter the development of nuclear weapons and

sanctions
In international relations, penalties imposed by some countries on others to force changes in behavior.

to encourage opposition to Iran's regime, sanctions have blocked the sale of Iranian oil in most of the world.

- *Targeted economic sanctions,* which have become increasingly common, direct specific pressure on political leadership.[19] To discourage North Korea's nuclear program and weaken its regime, for example, the Americans and Europeans pressured North Korean leaders by freezing their personal financial assets and blocking trade in luxury goods. Similar pressures often single out key individuals, families, or businesses close to authoritarian regimes to make their lives difficult.

conditionality

Offering support such as foreign aid, trade access, or diplomatic recognition on condition that a country adopts specific behaviors.

- **Conditionality** is the diplomatic name for "dangling a carrot at the end of a stick": offering benefits on condition of changed behavior. Since the 1990s, it has become common for the United States, the EU, and Japan to offer foreign aid or loans to countries on condition that they take steps to fight corruption, encourage openness, or hold elections.

civil society programs

Policies usually funded by Western countries to promote the development of pro-democracy groups in authoritarian countries or illiberal democracies.

- **Civil society programs** are longer-term tools aimed at building up pro-democracy groups in authoritarian or illiberal countries. American and European democracies fund a wide range of such programs to promote uncensored journalism and media, human rights, or political debate through governmental or quasi-governmental foreign policy organizations such as the U.S. National Endowment for Democracy (founded in 1983), the Millennium Challenge Corporation (created by U.S. legislation in 2004), and various arms of the European Union.

Even though the military might and diplomacy of democratic regimes make life less comfortable for many authoritarians, most transitions from authoritarianism to democracy do not result directly from the forms of pressure just described (see Figure 11-2). Instead, the most common death for authoritarian regimes is to be overthrown by internal rivals staging a **coup d'état**. The next most common cause is for leaders to be ousted in popular uprisings, and then comes the voluntary resignation of leadership to make way for democracy. External pressure can contribute to these internal developments by weakening current leaders and boosting challengers, but the overall effects of international pressure are mixed.

coup d'état

An unconstitutional and sudden removal of a government, usually by small groups of insiders including the military.

In a broad view, pressure from democracies on authoritarian regimes has often been ambiguous. At the same time that the National Endowment for Democracy promoted civil society in Egypt and other Middle Eastern countries, for example, the United States gave massive military aid to the Mubarak regime in Egypt because American leaders thought Mubarak helped stabilize the region. Even in settings where U.S. policy seems more systematically pro-democracy, like Iraq since the 2003 invasion, it is hard to miss that the United States is also strongly allied with nearby authoritarians like the Saudi Arabian monarchy. European democracies, too, send ambiguous signals, such as using targeted trade sanctions to punish Putin's conflicts with Ukraine while continuing to purchase huge amounts of Russian oil and gas.

Figure 11-2 Causes of Death for Authoritarian Regimes

Whether they are only briefly in control or survive at least a year, the most common death of authoritarian regimes is through a coup d'état.

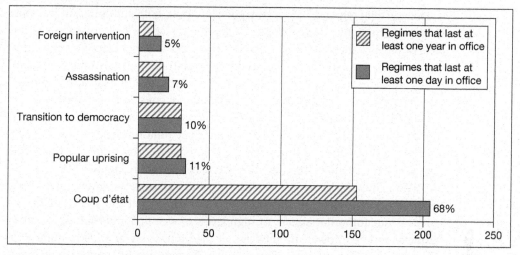

Source: Milan Svolik, *The Politics of Authoritarian Rule* (New York: Cambridge University Press, 2012), p. 7. Used with permission.

International pressure for democracy can even sometimes be counterproductive, provoking reactions that reinforce authoritarian regimes.[20] Repressive rulers label threats of military intervention from the outside as illegitimate infractions of sovereignty and encourage their citizens to reject such patronizing interference in their national affairs. In North Korea, for example, the regime constantly plays up supposed military threats from the United States to rally the population around the party and leader Kim Jong-Un. Sanctions, too, often paradoxically build support for authoritarians and stir up resentment against outsiders.[21] In Iran, though citizens assign some blame for a weak economy to their own leaders, they also blame the United States for imposing sanctions.[22] In Russia, Putin made a show of expelling the U.S. Agency for International Development and all other American pro–civil society agencies in 2012, casting them as treacherous and disrespectful of Russian sovereignty.[23]

Should the United States and other democracies not even try, then, to undermine authoritarians and promote democracy? Might such efforts be ineffective? We will debate these questions later in the chapter. For the moment, such points simply emphasize that to understand how authoritarians can fall, we must look beyond international pressure and consider the dynamics of economies, regime organization, and public protest.

Economic Crises and Authoritarian Transitions

Economic crisis and authoritarian transitions have a long relationship. Ever since economic troubles set the scene for the French Revolution of 1789, which brought down Europe's most powerful monarchy, many authoritarian collapses have begun in similar ways. Economic crises can rock democracies too, but there are reasons why authoritarian regimes may be especially vulnerable to short-term economic failure.

To understand this vulnerability, first consider how poverty and wealth relate to how long regimes last. In very poor countries, both authoritarian and democratic governments often collapse.[24] Extreme poverty offers governments few tools to stabilize their authority, with few resources to either help their citizens or repress them. The opposite is true in very rich countries. Both rich democracies and the wealthiest authoritarian regimes—largely oil-rich Middle Eastern regimes—are very stable. With plenty of money to go around, governments have numerous ways to deliver services or deal out repression and payoffs. For middle-income countries, democracy tends to "stick" better than authoritarianism. The relationship between wealth and enduring transitions away from authoritarianism to democracy thus follows the bell-shaped curve we see in Figure 11-3—low, rising, then falling again. At low levels of wealth, authoritarian governments may be instable, but attempts at democracy rarely "stick" well and countries usually fall back into authoritarianism. At high levels of wealth, authoritarians use their resources to keep power. In between, at medium levels of wealth, authoritarian governments that become instable may be replaced by democratic regimes

---

Figure 11-3 How Wealth Relates to Authoritarian Stability

This bell-shaped curve shows that the likelihood of a shift from authoritarianism to enduring democracy is most likely to occur in regimes with a middle level of income.

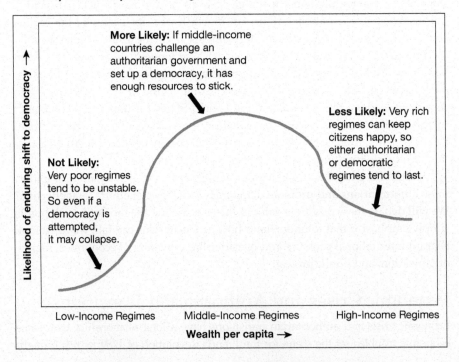

that "stick" and shift the country enduringly into the democratic column.[25] That isn't a guarantee: in Argentina in 1975, or recently in Venezuela or Hungary, middle-income democracies have sometimes slipped toward dictatorship when popular politicians gradually shut down liberal rights and electoral competition. Still, there are many more cases that run the other way—when middle-income authoritarian regimes shift enduringly to democracy.

Several examples hint that the relative instability of middle-income authoritarian regimes relates to economic crisis. In the 1980s, a global recession and the Latin American debt crisis contributed to the fall or reform of dictatorships in middle-income countries such as Argentina, Brazil, Chile, and Uruguay.[26] Around 1989, when the USSR and its "satellite" communist regimes collapsed, they confronted a crisis of slow growth rather than poverty. Most of those regimes already had achieved middle levels of wealth, but seemed unable to deliver increasingly comfortable lives for their citizens.[27] The Libyan and Tunisian regimes that fell in the 2011 Arab Spring had presided over solidly middle-income economies—but economies that shared a sense of crisis with poorer neighbors like Egypt. All these regimes had rising inequality, high unemployment, and the widespread perception that for most citizens, life was not going to get any better.[28]

So why would middle-income authoritarian regimes be especially vulnerable to crisis? Even democratic leaders lose support as the economy weakens—as we saw in the U.S. electoral wisdom from Bill Clinton's 1992 campaign: "It's the economy, stupid!" But one resilient aspect of the democratic system is that its citizens can kick out leaders without changing the form of government. Authoritarians, on the other hand, have less credible mechanisms for blaming crises on old leaders and bringing in new ones. Also, democracy rests its legitimacy on process—electoral representation and legal rights—that stands separately from results. Despite failing economic policies, duly elected leaders in democracy get to serve out their term in office. But because authoritarians' legitimacy rests less on transparent and legitimate selection processes, the life span of their regimes depends more on delivering benefits for citizens. This contrast makes little difference in very poor countries, where any regime has trouble "sticking," or in very rich ones, where any regime can buy support. For the middle-income cases where most recent authoritarian collapses have taken place, though, it matters that these regimes have difficulty surviving crises.

Should advocates of democracy thus welcome—or even instigate—economic crises in middle-income authoritarian countries like China or Iran? Before accepting that conclusion, we should consider another common generalization: authoritarians may be most vulnerable when their economies flourish.

Economic Success and Challenges to Authoritarianism

If the link between economic failure and authoritarian breakdown has a long history, the link between economic success and authoritarian demise is even older. The most common cause given for the French Revolution and the eventual fall of monarchies across Europe focuses on growth. At a time when the European continent was dominated by kings and aristocrats, expanding markets created increasingly rich towns and businesspeople, who eventually used their new resources to reject repressive government. The long-term Achilles' heel of authoritarianism, then, may be prosperity rather than crisis.

In the short term, certainly, economic growth tends to stabilize any regime. Growth keeps citizens happier and gives the regime resources to distribute. In the long term, though, market-based development can erode the concentrated control on which authoritarianism is founded. In societies where decentralized markets and business are less developed—due either to poverty, state-socialist-style government ownership, or perhaps the dominance of highly concentrated industries like oil or mining—there are few people outside the state with strong resources of their own. As a market economy grows more diverse and decentralized, more economic power tends to emerge beyond direct state control. Also, a growing commercial sector tends to spread education and information, as well as incentives and opportunities to connect to the world beyond a country's borders. In principle, people who make their own money in business also value individual rights to spend their money as they please and to exercise political rights. Thus, in European history, the business-based "bourgeois"—the people of the "burg" or town—provided the main impetus to the centuries-long process that erased European authoritarianism.[29] In recent history, the examples that best support this view are two of communist China's neighbors, Taiwan and South Korea. Both countries had authoritarian regimes into the 1980s. Both were pro-capitalist regimes opposed to communist China, the Soviet Union, and North Korea, and the United States overlooked their repressiveness and supported them as allies. In addition, Taiwan and South Korea received major military aid and favorable access to the giant U.S. market for their exports. Under this American umbrella, they became two of the greatest economic successes of all time, reaching high-middle-income levels by the 1980s. In the late 1980s, long-running protests against both abusive governments snowballed into huge movements for democratization. After internal struggles between hard-liners and reformers within the regimes, both countries took gradual steps toward more openness. By the mid-1990s, the two countries were settling into full liberal democracy. The most common interpretation for this transition is that both repeated the path of several European countries: their market-based economic development spread wealth, education, information, and concern for rights across Taiwanese and South Korean citizens. Their rising power and demand for freedom forced the authoritarians to reform.

How do we square this notion with the economic failures that often precede authoritarian collapse? Contradictory though they may seem, the two observations reflect the same principle. To summarize, authoritarianism depends on concentrated control of state and society. Economic crisis can upset that control quickly by fueling broad resentment against the regime. Market-based economic growth can upset it more gradually by fostering social power outside the state.

These two generalizations suggest patterns, but cannot predict whether either economic crisis or long-term economic success will undo any particular authoritarian regime. Given how different "unhappy families" can be, we can understand their vulnerabilities more concretely only by looking again at their internal organization.

Organization and Authoritarian Vulnerability

Economic crises or a growing business class generally threaten concentrated power, but not all authoritarians are equally susceptible to such threats. We see a hint of these differences in their durability over time. According to one study of authoritarian breakdown between 1945 and 2000, for example, military regimes had an average life span of eight and a half years. Personal dictatorships averaged fifteen years. Single-party regimes typically lasted almost twenty-four years.[30] Some "unhappy families" are organized more durably than others.

RETURNING THE MILITARY TO THE BARRACKS.   Military regimes may be vulnerable to change because they are the simplest and most explicitly force-based form of authoritarianism. As an "off the shelf" form of concentrated authority—taking the existing security system and giving it broader responsibility for governance—military regimes are easy to dismantle. The military can be put back "on the shelf" in a nongoverning security role.

As a model of authoritarianism, putting the military directly in charge has one clear advantage: there is little doubt about top leaders' capacity for violent repression if necessary. However, its main weakness reflects the same fact: militaries are designed to be security forces, not governing bodies. Once they seize the state, they soon face pressure to return to a "normal" military role that leaves broader governance to political leadership. Such pressure typically comes from domestic opposition and democratic governments elsewhere, who call for the military to hand power over to civilians, but it also often comes from inside the regime. Many military officers find broader governance uncomfortable. Untrained to handle issues like economic or social policy, they may be painfully conscious that they are better suited to implementing clear orders than to arbitrating complex political and policy issues. It can also be fairly easy to convince officers to give up political power because a respectable position may await them in post-dictatorship arrangements. Unlike some other authoritarian rulers, military officers can survive the end of authoritarianism if they step back into the role of professional security forces.

Thus military regimes frequently suffer from internal splits when some officers call for resuming the role of a "normal military." In Argentina and Chile in the 1980s, or more recently in Pakistan or Myanmar, transitions from military rule to democracy began when reformist officers reached out to opposition figures to negotiate a path of reform. Many key officers eventually agreed to return to their barracks if they could retain military posts under a new government. Similar processes can happen in personal dictatorships that rely heavily on support from a well-organized military, like the Mubarak regime. The Egyptian military has a long and proud self-identity as a professional force that defends stability and the constitution. Crucial to Mubarak's fall was that top officers began to see the corrupt regime as bad for the military itself. They signaled that they would rather negotiate a military role in a new regime than crack down on protesters.[31] Egypt's current strongman, Abdel Fattah al-Sisi, learned something from Mubarak's mistakes. He has launched a very public **anticorruption campaign**, relied more on military officers than on shady businessmen to run the state, and generally tried to keep the military behind him with a focus on strict and repressive order.[32]

anticorruption campaigns
Showy government action to convince citizens that corruption is not tolerated.

PERSONAL NETWORKS AND CORRUPTION. As the Mubarak case hints, perceptions of corruption are the key weakness of personal dictatorships. Corruption is a major problem in all authoritarian systems, admittedly, since all refuse the ultimate rule of law. Yet the champions of corruption tend to be regimes headed by a single leader and built on networks of personal loyalty.

Though dictatorships sometimes arise with somewhat-plausible motivations like stabilizing their countries, with time they typically turn toward personal enrichment. Lacking military discipline or a well-developed party ideology and organization, they tend to reward and recruit loyalist supporters in a direct and personal way. It quickly becomes irresistible to use state budgets and power over business dealings for these ends. In the impoverished Caribbean country of Haiti, for example, François "Papa Doc" Duvalier established a government in the 1950s that promised to improve public health and promote Haiti's black

Megapress/Alamy Stock Photo

A poster in Cairo in 2011 objects to widespread corruption. It reads, "No to bribes!"

majority. These goals were gradually replaced by self-enrichment, however, reaching a height with the plundering of hundreds of millions of dollars under the subsequent rule of Jean-Claude "Baby Doc" Duvalier. Syria followed a similar trajectory. Though Hafez al-Assad originally built his dictatorship around calls for stability and Ba'athist ideology, it evolved into a pyramid of corruption, "with a range of politicians close to Assad and security officials who ran their own mafias, spreading corruption throughout the country."[33] In 2000, Assad's son Bashar inherited a regime in which one cousin, Rami Makhlouf, was rumored to control almost half of the whole economy. There are even worse cases of pure kleptocracy, where leaders build regimes purely by stealing public money for their cronies. In one of the few countries that is poorer than Haiti, President Mobutu Sese Seko of the Democratic Republic of Congo (then called Zaire) stole as much as $5 billion from 1965 to 1997.

The logic of loyalty and corruption in personal dictatorships also carries advantages that can make them durable—if in perverse ways. The more that authoritarian rule depends on networks of corrupt benefits, the more we can expect the regime to employ violence to remain in power. Unlike officers in some military dictatorships, personal cronies of Assad will not serve in any accepted role in their countries if the regime falls or reforms. The same was true in Libya before 2011, where Colonel Muammar Gaddafi built control on a bizarre personality cult and tribal alliances. The fact that the Libyan and Syrian governments were held together by personal loyalty and payoffs—and ran even their militaries more like a Mafia family than a professional security force—helps explain why these two countries engaged in bloody civil wars during the Arab Spring. Everyone with influence in Libya or Syria was so personally identified with the regime that it was hard for them to imagine a future if the dictatorship fell.[34] With so few options for a negotiated future, Gaddafi and Assad loyalists clung to power with all the violence they could command.

PROFESSIONAL AUTHORITARIANS AND INTERNAL REFORMERS. Single-party regimes tend to be the longest-lived authoritarian regimes because they are the political professionals of authoritarianism. Rather than turning to the generals or to Mafia-style networks, they construct large organizations and ideological movements that are designed to take on the broad tasks of governance. These more sophisticated organizations can better manage perceptions of corruption too.

Consider how China's CCP handles corruption. By all accounts—including those from the CCP itself—the country is rife with it. State officials at all levels tend to profit personally from their positions, both through dealings with the massive public sector State Owned Enterprises (SOEs) and in complex interactions between political power holders and private business. As a hint of this nexus of capitalism and "communist" power, consider one startling fact: in 2018, the 150-odd members of the Standing Committee of the National People's Congress—the main body that rubber-stamps Chinese legislation—had a net worth of about $650 billion, almost *two hundred times* the combined net personal worth of all 535 members of the U.S. Congress, the president and cabinet, and the whole Supreme Court![35] To date, however, the CCP has managed to create the perception that its leaders are committed to rooting out corruption that largely occurs at lower levels.[36] They have rolled out repeated anticorruption campaigns and dealt severely with a rising number of lower- and middle-level officials, including by execution. The organization of power through the vast party bureaucracy has also helped distance top leadership from such accusations: rather than identifying power with the face of a Mubarak or Duvalier in a presidential palace, Chinese citizens have generally seen bland bureaucrats operating in collective councils. So far, at least, many Chinese citizens see individually corrupt officials as the problem and the CCP hierarchy as an ally against them.

The broad, impersonal organization of single-party regimes often helps them survive leadership successions and policy changes better than dictatorships. Many personal dictators eventually hand off power to their children, like Duvalier or Assad, but the absence of any logic for such inheritance invites criticism and usually weakens second-generation dictators. Military regimes have processes for promoting lower officers, but typically lack mechanisms for changing the very top of the hierarchy. Single-party regimes, by contrast, can use the party to manage careful consultation processes in which leadership contenders and factions gradually agree on a transfer of power. In the 1980s, the CCP adopted the practice of top leaders serving for two consecutive five-year Party Congresses, and that top leaders cannot begin a new term past the age of sixty-eight (or so). In principle, as each ten-year transition approaches, a regular cycle of party meetings and Congresses allows the leadership to encourage managed discussions and symbolic acceptance of successions. The same mechanisms of gaining support for candidates, through several descending circles of regular party meetings that range from the Politburo down to much wider assemblies, allow the CCP leadership to test the waters and build support for policy changes.

In reality, the authoritarian CCP regime is much less bound by institutional rules and due process than it likes to suggest. Top leaders have generally exerted major influence over the choice of their successors, using party deliberations more as cover for political maneuvering than for real input. The current leader, Xi Jinping, has centralized more power in his own hands than any leader since party founder Mao Zedong, to the point that he broke with convention and ignored the expected designation of his successor in 2017.[37] Even given Xi's extraordinary consolidation of power, however, Chinese single-party authoritarianism presents a more professional face to the world than many other repressive regimes. Its broad organizational basis cultivates support and continuity on the basis of party loyalty, and hides personal control and power struggles behind a veil of party business.

Though the CCP shows few signs of vulnerability today, the strengths of single-party regimes are also their weaknesses. Their professional political organization may be especially effective in smothering external challenges to their control, but the huge size of the party itself can become a vehicle for internal reformists to gain power. This is roughly what happened to the Soviet Union.

A growing number of Communists became convinced that both economic and political reforms were necessary. When reformist Mikhail Gorbachev became party secretary in 1985, an accelerating process of reforms brought out rising calls for change from the party itself and eventually undid the Soviet system. This is the most likely source of future challenge for the CCP: its anticorruption campaigns and processes of managed accountability may cultivate a new generation of party members who eventually reject tightly concentrated control from the inside.

RETURNING THE CLERICS TO THE SEMINARIES? Iran's unique regime, lastly, features an intriguing mix of resources and weaknesses. This decades-old quasi-theocracy enjoys some of the organizational strengths of a single-party regime. It may be vulnerable, however, to calls to "return to the seminaries," much like the pressure for military regimes to return to their barracks.

Iran's religious hierarchy possesses some organizational advantages that even Chinese Communists might admire. Their Supreme Leader claims a kind of authority no earthly party head can assert: under the Iranian Revolution's version of Shi'a doctrine, he is the steward of the Prophet Mohammed's authority on Earth until the coming of a future messiah (the "Twelfth Imam"). Most of the clergy's power is also extremely concentrated, with roughly eighty or so top clerics forming Ayatollah Khamenei's inner circle. They have a formal mechanism for leadership succession: the elected clerics in the Assembly of Experts will chose the next Supreme Leader after Khamenei's death. They have built strong mechanisms to recruit new leaders and supporters, using seminaries to teach clerics not only traditional religious doctrine but direct justifications of Iran's version of theocracy. Mosques then spread these ideas throughout society. With God-given authority, a tight circle of power, succession processes, and pervasive channels for regular ideological reinforcement of the regime, Khamenei and his allies have strong tools to maintain their control.

In some ways, the regime also looks relatively resistant to charges of corruption or economic failure. As a group, the clergy is easier to present as pure, wise, and deserving of special respect than a typical party elite. Many Chinese join the CCP for access to influence and possible wealth, irrespective of real commitments, but that accusation is harder to make of people who take the larger step of entering a religious seminary and life as a career cleric. Furthermore, Islam promises mainly to lead people to a moral life—not, like communism, to make everyone better off economically—so failure to deliver material benefits is less likely to erode the cleric's status. However, these defenses are far from bulletproof. In fact, Khamenei and other top clerics have faced rising complaints of corruption that include mutual accusations of large-scale embezzlement of oil money between members of the political elite. Iranian business complains bitterly about a weak economy and the international sanctions that the regime's nuclear program has provoked. But if reformists like President Rouhani have tried to capitalize on these complaints, they have not yet won a major victory. Their biggest success to date was a 2015 deal with Western countries to drop some sanctions in return for international inspections of Iranian nuclear facilities—until the Trump administration pulled out of the deal in 2018 and strengthened sanctions again. This episode ended up strengthening Iranian hardliners' view that there is no point negotiating with the West. So did a new leap in tensions in January 2020, when U.S. forces assassinated Iran's top general, Qasem Soleimani, and Iran retaliated with missiles strikes on U.S. bases in Iraq.

For the longer term, the religious foundations of Iranian authoritarianism nonetheless carry an obvious vulnerability. Like military officers, religious figures are not trained to be professional politicians and, likewise, can hold respected nonpolitical roles in nonauthoritarian societies. Therefore a common call from external critics and reformists in Iran is for clerics to return to the seminaries. They suggest that less clerical power would make for more effective governance, and would free the clergy from the compromises of politics to focus on religion and morality. Importantly, it is not only secular people who hold these views. In fact, a long history in devout Muslim thinking has tended to view clergy as jurists who interpret Qur'anic law, not as active political leaders.

Whether Iranian reformers will eventually take steps forward without provoking violent reactions from religious conservatives is hard to foresee. The same is true of the probability that CCP reformers will push for substantial change, or of the likelihood of further uprisings against corrupt personal regimes. We can identify reasons for opposition to authoritarianism, and we can analyze regimes' vulnerabilities and resources—but the moments that actually produce change often emerge in unforeseeable waves of revolt.

Collective Action and "Contagion"

On December 17, 2010, a Tunisian street vendor named Mohamed Bouazizi set himself on fire. He was not any sort of leader—his gripe was police harassment over permits for his vending cart—but his suicide sparked protests that toppled several governments. Ripples reached as far as Beijing, where the CCP authorities blocked Internet searches for words like "Tunisia" or "Egypt."[38] Was this paranoid? Maybe not. Chinese leaders knew that history has seen many international waves of protest. As far back as the mid-1800s, long before Facebook and Twitter spread rebellious ideas, there was the "Springtime of the Peoples." A French revolt in 1848 ignited antimonarchy protests in over fifty countries across Europe and Latin America.

The unpredictability and scope of waves of protest complicate a simple view of authoritarian collapse as a balance of power between a country's citizens and its regime. Clearly, the potential for regime change depends on the balance between citizens' resentments and resources on one side and the regime's vulnerabilities and resources on the other. Yet if these conditions told the whole story, we would be much better at predicting change than we actually are. Before December 2010, the Egyptian, Libyan, and Syrian governments were widely viewed as firmly in control. Despite their problems of corruption, not a single expert predicted their fall in the near term.[39] The same was true prior to the rapid collapse in 1989 of communist governments—single-party regimes across Eastern Europe—that had been in place for forty years. Their citizens' economic dissatisfaction was obvious, but no one thought they were likely to simply fall over. It seems clear that citizen/ regime balances can change very rapidly. Perhaps even more surprising, changes in one country seem to massively affect others.

Yet waves of international **contagion** do not mean that revolt is random. These waves build as a result of the dynamics of collective action under repressive governments—first internally, then across borders.[40] Many people may resent a government, but until it is clear that others are ready to revolt, few will step forward to bear the first brunt of possible repression. They may not even be honest with themselves about how much they want change: people who think successful rebellion is almost impossible have psychological reasons to tell themselves that the regime is not so bad. In such situations, a small symbolic shock like Bouazizi's act may get people talking about their resentments. As they realize that they are unhappy and that others are too, they may come to think revolt is not so impossible after all. Initial protests may embolden others, creating a swelling movement. In Eastern Europe in 1989 and in the Arab world in 2011, these waves built until even previous supporters of the regimes "bandwagoned" as well—since once the regime's fall looks likely, the incentives and psychology reverse to encourage participation. Contagion of protest effectively crosses borders using the same mechanisms, despite differences in citizens' resentments and regimes' strengths. Uprisings in one country spark similar cycles in others.

Where does that leave our understanding of the fall of authoritarian regimes? When we see how sudden waves of protest interact with complex internal balances of power, we realize that specific, confident predictions are hard to come by. Still, we know to look for regimes that are losing economic control, or that seem to be playing into their own vulnerabilities, and to watch for snowballing processes of protest. In the next section, The Challenges of Democratization, there is another important lesson to be gleaned from past transitions from authoritarianism. When we see the convergence of events that typically foreshadow the demise of authoritarian rule, we should now expect celebrations to be tentative and short. As Russians found out two decades ago, and Egyptians are finding out today, the fall of an authoritarian system does not guarantee the rise of a democratic one.

contagion
In a political context, when rising opposition to a government encourages opposition to other governments as well.

The Challenges of Democratization

11.3 **Specify key conditions that help or harm a country's chances for successful democratization.**

Members of an unhappy family may be relieved when domineering figures pass on, but they face new challenges in attempting to construct a healthier household. Family members must forge new roles and develop skills of compromise that their previous experience gave them little opportunity to practice. So it is with governments too. Liberal democracy is not a default arrangement that springs into place when repression is removed. Rather, liberal democracy is the opposite: an elaborate set of rules and practices that emerges only given considerable care.

Several kinds of conditions make democratization more or less likely. Like with the fall of authoritarians, economic success and failure play a major role. Also important is the organization of the previous regime, which affects whether or not its supporters can find a place in the new democratic system. As with authoritarian breakdown, international pressure and domestic policies of powerful democracies matter greatly, but often in mixed ways.

Economic Growth and Democracy's Foundations

When processes of market-based economic growth challenge authoritarian control, it is logical to expect that they simultaneously lay the groundwork for democratization. The growth that enables citizens to challenge repressive rulers *also* provides foundations for a newly competitive political arena. While history does show that market-based growth at times can undercut authoritarians and empower democratization, it does not always do so automatically. The more general pattern is that market-based growth *supports* but does not necessarily *cause* democratization.

This might seem like hairsplitting, but this distinction connects deeply to how we understand the prospects of a democracy emerging. To see why, first consider the older view that market-based growth automatically challenges authoritarianisms and causes democratization. As the great political economist Joseph Schumpeter summarized in 1942, "History clearly confirms . . . modern democracy is a product of the capitalist process." To extend some concepts we saw earlier, capitalist development creates both the kind of individuals and the kind of society that challenge authoritarians and produce democracy. Successful market development depends on literacy and information, and so it tends to produce a relatively educated class of businesspeople. These "self-made" individuals, unlike more traditional aristocratic or religious elites, tend to favor freedom to act as they please. Market development also tends to create a variety of competing poles of power across the social landscape. In open markets, many different businesspeople or business communities gain substantial resources. They each have their own agendas and sufficient power and information to mobilize around them. Thus a healthy market-based economy directly creates the foundations for a competitive political "market" for leadership—or democracy. This theory that economic development and democracy naturally go together is known as **modernization theory**, since it suggests (in its strong form) that all modern countries will gradually develop similar features.

More recent thinking, however, generally steps back from the strong modernization-theory view that market-based growth necessarily topples authoritarians and boosts democratic competition. If we look at all modern cases in which authoritarian regimes have fallen and been replaced by democracy, we

modernization theory

A rational-material theory in the liberal tradition that sees history as a march toward liberal democracy and capitalism.

see attempts at such transitions across the spectrum of economic development. Some countries have tried democracy when quite poor, while others attempted it only after becoming quite rich. The early United States, for example, though rich for its time, was a preindustrial society that would rank among the poorest countries given today's standards.[41] Countries like Germany or Japan reached far higher levels of wealth before they ever took steps toward democracy. All this makes it hard to accept Schumpeter's claim that "Democracy is a product of the capitalist process." It seems, therefore, that countries initiate moves from authoritarianism to democracy for a variety of reasons that do not simply reflect certain levels of capitalist development.

There is still an important relationship between market-based growth and democracy, however, as we see from the data points in Figure 11-4. Richer countries do tend to be democratic. But rather than showing simply that wealth brings democracy, it shows that democracy "sticks" better at higher levels of development. That is, if a country takes steps toward democratization, for whatever reason, then the better developed its economy, the more likely that democracy will endure.[42] Countries that established democracy at some point and have surpassed middle levels of income rarely return to authoritarianism. This seems true for the reasons highlighted in Schumpeter-style thinking: if many people in a society have decided they want to attempt democracy, a better-developed market economy gives them more resources for upholding and defending that

Figure 11-4 The Relationship between Wealth and Democracy

If we score 145 countries on an index of democracy, from –10 (fully authoritarian) to 10 (fully democratic) and plot those points against their levels of wealth (GDP per capita), we see that the wealthier the country, the more likely it is democratic.

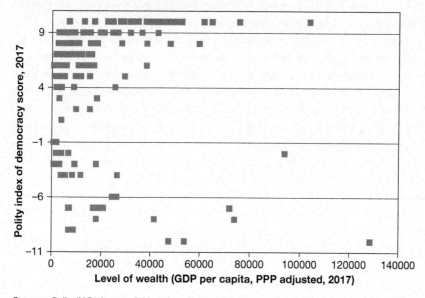

Sources: Polity IV Project, available at http://www.systemicpeace.org/polityproject.html; World Bank.

consolidation

The process between establishing democracy and making it an unchallenged system of governance.

system. Market-based economic growth does not necessarily create convinced democrats, but it helps convinced democrats **consolidate** democracy.

The distinction is critical for anticipating what might happen in developing authoritarian countries like China. Until fairly recently, some observers expected that the explosion of Chinese capitalism would create inevitable pressure for democratization.[43] Others suggested that China's business class might not demand rights and democracy as some other rising capitalists have done.[44] Similar to other countries that long retained authoritarianism despite rising wealth—such as Germany, Japan, and Russia—the Chinese "bourgeois" might continue supporting authoritarianism for a variety of reasons. They might fear that democratic competition would make such a big country unstable. They might reject Western models of government out of Chinese nationalist pride. They might feel that individual rights are less important in a Chinese culture that strongly emphasizes the good of the broader community. For the moment, some version of these dynamics seems to be dominant: under Xi Jinping, the CCP regime has moved toward more centralization and repression, not less, without much public challenge. The meteoric rise of Chinese capitalism could still provide foundations for future moves toward democracy, but there is no guarantee that Chinese citizens will build on them.

The Challenge of Double Transitions

Authoritarianism may fall due to either economic growth or economic crisis, but only the former scenario is helpful for democratization. When new democracies take over economies in crisis, citizens have typically turned to democracy not only to gain political rights but to solve economic problems. New democratic leaders face a dicey **double transition**: trying to establish a new, complex kind of political regime *and* to launch major economic reforms.

double transition

When a country simultaneously attempts democratization and major economic reforms.

Especially in cases where economic crisis reflects deep problems in the economic system—rather than a passing recession—economic and political transitions can contradict each other. When Eastern Europeans threw off their communist governments in 1989, they confronted economic reforms that were arguably more profound than the political move from authoritarianism to democracy. Most of their countries were not terribly poor, but it was widely agreed that their route to future growth lay in tearing up their command economies and building capitalism almost from scratch. The most challenging aspect of this task was that it was sure to cause economic pain in its early phases. Before market-based growth could be imagined, the entire organization of jobs and benefits in the command economy had to be unraveled. Consequently, leaders feared two possibilities. One was that citizens might use their new voting rights to end painful economic reforms, so the political transition would undercut the economic one. The other was that voters might react to painful economic reform by turning to authoritarian leaders, ending the political transition. To some degree, both fears were realized. The dismantlement of command economies brought an economic collapse that erased as much as 60 or even 70 percent of the economy in some countries.[45] In some countries such as Poland, the Czech Republic, or Estonia, both transitions proceeded mostly successfully. In other places in Eastern Europe and the former Soviet Union, voters limited economic reform (like in Bulgaria and Ukraine) or soon gave considerable support to illiberal leaders who shifted back toward authoritarianism (like in Russia and Belarus).

Similar double-transition dilemmas arise in poorer countries where the economic crisis reflects challenges in economic development rather than overcoming the legacies of the former command economies. Across Latin America, for example, a wave of new democracies replaced authoritarian or illiberal regimes that had been weakened by the Latin American debt crisis in the early 1980s. Though the new democratic regimes did not need to tear down communist systems, they did face strong internal and external pressures to adopt the "Washington Consensus" over the next decade—opening their economies to foreign trade and investment, cutting back state spending and regulations, and pushing through a variety of other complex economic reforms. Such reforms were painful in the short term, so leaders who advocated both democracy and more liberalized markets faced double-transition problems much like those in Eastern Europe. Here, too, the results were mixed. In a few countries, the consolidation of democracy and economic openness worked fairly well together, most notably Chile and (to a lesser extent) Brazil. In others, popular opposition to neoliberal economic reform has sometimes contributed to the rise of authoritarian-leaning leaders, such as dictatorial president Alberto Fujimori in Peru from 1990 to 2000 or socialist president Hugo Chavez in Venezuela from 1999 to 2013.

Thus double transitions complicate many attempts at democratization. Citizens' grand hopes for newfound freedom and demands for greater prosperity can easily become contradictory, forcing young democratic governments into tough spots. In Egypt or Myanmar today, or in a future post-authoritarian Syria or North Korea, new democratic leaders who take over crisis-ridden economies must carefully navigate both economic and political reform.

Deals with the Devil? Opposition, Pacts, and Democratic Consolidation

Even if we set aside the economic problems of young democracies, their political challenge alone is daunting. The core of liberal democracy is meaningful electoral competition—representation supported and bounded by rights—so early leaders must create space for opposition, even as they build their own authority. Welcoming opposition requires considerable restraint, especially vis-à-vis the remnants of the authoritarian regime. Democratization has the best chances if ex-authoritarians are enticed to compete in lawful opposition. Given that repressive regimes always leave a legacy of bitterness, this is easier said than done.

Consider, for example, the profound dilemmas that arose after World War II regarding treatment of Nazi supporters or of the Japanese military dictatorship.

On the one hand, the oppressive groups that had dominated these countries had to be broken up and prevented from returning to power. On the other hand, a new government could hardly operate without relying on many people associated with the old system. These odious rulers had killed off, imprisoned, or banished all opposition, so leaders without authoritarian ties were hard to find. In both Germany and Japan, the victorious United States and its allies reluctantly decided to rehabilitate all but the highest-ranked leaders of the defeated regimes. This strategy was fraught with moral and political issues: it meant overlooking the pasts of many people and asking their victims to forgive or forget. In hindsight, it looks like a good choice in both cases. Supporters of the old regimes were absorbed into democratic politics.

Other cases show how the exclusion of ex-authoritarian supporters, though seemingly the more moral route, can put democratization in question. After the fall of Iraqi dictator Saddam Hussein in 2003, the U.S.-led occupation dismissed from government anyone who had held a significant position in Hussein's Ba'ath Party. It also disbanded the entire Iraqi Army that had upheld his regime. This marked a clean break with the dictatorship, but also cut off hundreds of thousands of people from incentives to support the democratic transition. Worse, since Hussein's regime was largely built on Sunni Muslim tribes who had long feared dominance by the Shi'ite majority, these steps fed into ethnic and religious polarization. Iraqi democratization would have been difficult in any scenario, but all observers agree now that the exclusion of regime supporters from post-transition politics made it harder.[46]

pacts

Attempts to persuade antidemocratic leaders to accept democratization by allowing them to retain certain privileges or immunity from prosecution.

Successful democratization, then, often includes **pacts** that offer members or supporters of the old regime a less threatening path to participate in the emerging democracy. These arrangements are justified in terms of effectiveness rather than morality: cutting them a deal decreases the chances of instability and violence. In other words, pacts "move the polity toward democracy by undemocratic means," advancing democracy "on the installment plan" as more actors buy into the new regime.[47] Such deals became especially prominent in transitions in southern Europe in the 1970s, when dictatorships fell in Spain, Portugal, and Greece, and in Latin America in the 1980s. They are now seen as a standard part of the democratization toolkit.

Just like politicians in established democracies often compromise with rivals they detest, making "deals with the devil" are frequently part of creating a democratic arena. Democracy is built on tolerance and compromise, and becomes stable only once everyone joins in, making it "the only game in town."[48] All groups must compete electorally and renounce the seizure of power by other means. Certainly, there is a limit to who can be invited into the game—no one could have welcomed Hitler back after the Holocaust—but successful democratization often stretches the limit. In Iraq, Egypt, or Afghanistan today, it is hard to see how democracy can consolidate without persuading Islamist fundamentalists to join the democratic game.[49] Whether that persuasive effort can succeed is anybody's guess, but no other route seems available.

Benefits and Costs of International Support

And now for some good news—or mostly good news. Daunting though the challenges for young democracies may be, they do not face them alone. Just as today's authoritarians face pressure from rich and powerful democracies in North America and Europe, so young democracies tend to receive international support. Like putting pressure on authoritarians, however, that support ultimately has mixed effects on democratization. It can boost steps toward democracy, but may also keep local advocates of democracy from learning to stand on their own feet.

Promoting democracy became an increasingly important priority for the United States, Canada, and Europe after the end of the Cold War. Their earlier aid and activities abroad prioritized a fight against communism rather than support for democracy, but when rivalry with the Soviet Union disappeared, more money and effort were channeled into supporting democratizing regimes. These efforts included aid and support for democratizing governments, such as $5 billion in support and $15 billion in forgiven debt that Russia received in 1993, as well as a rising flow of money to nongovernmental organizations (NGOs) in hopes that they would build thriving civil societies.[50] Both American and European efforts concentrated mainly on post-communist Europe from 1990 to the early 2000s, but then turned more toward Iraq and Afghanistan.[51] For the United States, the lead organization in this process has been the Agency for International Development (USAID), an arm of the State Department, but many other agencies participate as well. This work continued under the Trump administration, though new questions were raised about American support for democracy. President Trump repeatedly went out of his way to state his support for dictatorial or illiberal rulers like Egypt's al-Sisi, Russia's Putin, Hungarian Prime Minister Viktor Orban, or President Rodrigo Duterte of the Philippines.

American pro-democracy policies attracted some contestation even before Trump began challenging them. Even pro-democracy activists have sometimes worried that they may overwhelm and skew local progress toward democratization. Today in Afghanistan, like in post-communist Europe two decades ago, almost all activities broadly relating to governance, the media, education, and civil society are swarmed with international agencies and NGOs. At a simple level, it is hard to deny that the intentions and some effects of this activity are good: outside experts and funds have helped democratizing countries draw up new constitutions, frame laws, build administrative capacity, develop free media, and enhance schooling and public information. The downside is that this volume of international support can reorient domestic action in unintended ways. Local leaders and activities can be seduced into focusing on what pleases resource-rich outsiders rather than on what matters on the ground. As one study of international NGOs in Russia found, "The result is a creation of patron-client ties between the international donor and the Russian recipient rather than horizontal networks of civic engagement among Russian NGOs and their domestic audience."[52] Also worrisome is that highly visible international support can make pro-democracy groups appear to their compatriots like tools of foreigners. Especially in democratizing counties where independent media are not strongly established, critics can easily malign internationally supported NGOs as untrustworthy fronts for foreign intervention.[53]

In the final analysis, international support for democratization surely helps would-be democratizers more than it hurts them. Still, it struggles with the same problems that bedevil anyone's attempt to help an unhappy family reform itself. Friends or government programs may offer support and guidance, and their material aid can make a difference in difficult times of transition. Stable and happy families ultimately arise and endure, though, only when their members themselves commit to change.

Political Ideologies and the Promotion of Democracy

11.4 **Evaluate competing arguments for and against the notion that democracies like the United States should actively promote democracy elsewhere.**

Our survey of authoritarians' prospects and the challenges of democratization sums to a sense that the further spread of democracy is uncertain. Some authoritarians today are tenacious, politically sophisticated, and draw on strong resources. Though a few may succumb to inherent vulnerabilities, we cannot assume that stable democracy will emerge to replace them. International pressure against authoritarians and for democratization is rarely as effective as we would like.

Should democracies refrain from expending resources for such uncertain prospects? Or should champions of democracy act precisely because its chances are uncertain? These questions do not interest antidemocratic socialists, fascists, or Islamists, but they are increasingly salient within liberal-democratic countries. In the early 2000s, new lines of conflict around the U.S.-led invasions of Afghanistan and Iraq shook up American politics and echoed across other democracies as well. Liberal endorsements of democracy promotion were echoed more aggressively by so-called "neoconservatives." More traditional conservatives joined voices from the far Left in criticizing that agenda. Their debates showcase evolving ideological traditions and the alternatives from which we can choose on this important issue.

Democracy Promotion as the Key to a Just and Safe World

When we hear that the family next door is acting badly, perhaps in ways that harm vulnerable people, we may feel compelled to act. It may seem morally wrong to turn a deaf ear, or we may hope to make our own lives more pleasant by cultivating better neighbors. Many democratic leaders give these basic reasons for promoting democracy. Duty and self-interest, they say, call us to clean up the neighborhood.

The most famous of these calls was when U.S. president Woodrow Wilson appealed to "make the world safe for democracy" by defeating imperial Germany in World War I.[54] The logic of "Wilsonian interventionism," as it has come to be known, is straightforward. Built on universal human rights and truths, liberal democracy offers the best chances for human happiness everywhere. Morally, then, all who inhabit democracies should advocate that other political families be governed in this way. This moral position creates natural conflict with nondemocratic governments who reject our values and who often will seek to weaken or overpower us. So it is in our self-interest to adopt the model of beating them back to "make the world safe."

How, though, should we try to influence unpleasant neighbors? Though Wilson was a Democrat and an architect of modern liberalism, most of his brethren on the mainstream Left hesitate to promote democracy through war. In general, modern liberals prefer to engineer change through support for disadvantaged people and the construction of persuasive incentives, not through harsh consequences and force. With an unruly family next door, modern liberal solutions focus on advice or help for the most sympathetic members of the household, or perhaps rallying the neighborhood to support them. With democracy promotion, liberals favor similar tools. Pro-democratic forces can be boosted with aid and advice, they hope, and authoritarians can be pressured with nonmilitary sanctions. Only in grave humanitarian crises—when authoritarians are harming their own people—do liberals turn to military options. We see these leanings in President Obama's justification for offering military air support to Libyan rebels during the Arab Spring in 2011:

> In this particular country, Libya, and this particular moment, we were faced with the prospect of violence on a horrific scale. We had a unique ability to stop that violence, an international mandate for action, a broad coalition prepared to join us, the support of Arab countries, and a plea for help from the Libyan people themselves. . . . To brush aside America's responsibilities as a leader and—more profoundly—our responsibilities to our fellow human beings under such circumstances would have been a betrayal of who we are.[55]

For Obama, force was briefly necessary in Libya to protect the innocent. But for the longer-term promotion of democracy in Libya and elsewhere, softer diplomatic action works more effectively. Just as targeted government programs can craft a better society at home, so does steady nonmilitary support for democratization abroad.

In the early 2000s, Wilson's strong democracy-promotion rhetoric also echoed on the conservative side of the American political spectrum. Though the Right traditionally has questioned the effectiveness of democracy promotion—thinking it wiser to leave neighbors to their own problems—the presidency of Republican George W. Bush (2000–2008) was "unmistakably Wilsonian" in "the idea that it is the destiny of the United States to use its great power to spread American ideals of democracy."[56] His administration empowered a group of "neoconservatives" who advocated the unapologetic assertion of democratic values through strength and force in places like Afghanistan and Iraq. "Neocons," such as Donald Rumsfeld (Bush's secretary of defense) or Paul Wolfowitz (a deputy secretary of defense), were conservative in their championing of established American values and their sense that only harsh consequences—not liberal-style support and softer incentives—could alter undesirable behavior. They were "neo" in their unconservative ambition to use government power to pursue idealistic goals abroad.

Despite differences over appropriate tools, the old mainstream Left and the brief heyday of the "neoconservative" Right under George W. Bush agreed that Americans and Europeans should promote democracy for both moral and self-interested reasons. At the same time, though, both these views confronted critics within their liberal-democratic families. Confident though we may be in our family model, say the skeptics, we should not try to impose it on others.

Democracy Promotion as Risky, Arrogant, or Disingenuous

Our other possible response to bad behavior next door is to mind our own business. It may be morally painful not to act, but we should not exaggerate our ability to engineer change in other countries. We must also be wary of preaching to others when our own household is far from perfect. Political thinkers on both right and left echo these arguments that question the wisdom of active democracy promotion.

The foolishness of trying to solve other people's problems is an old tenet of conservatism. Whatever moral concerns we have about the family next door or the authoritarians across the border, meddling in their affairs risks making things worse. Authoritarians denounce outside pressure as infractions of national sovereignty, which often bolsters their nationalist support at home. Even if our support for pro-democracy forces helps them initially, reliance on external support may weaken them in the long run. Robust democracies, like healthy families, result only when homegrown forces develop the capacity and desire to make democracy work. In the words of Daniel Larison, an editor at the conservative journal *The National Interest*, democracy promotion since the Cold War has been an "enduring failure."[57] Where democracy was already on its way, such as in the wealthier countries of Eastern Europe, democracy promotion made little difference. Its ineffectiveness is all the more obvious in places where domestic conditions have been less supportive. From Russia to Afghanistan and Iraq, we have little to show for the billions of dollars spent and thousands of lives lost.

Many conservatives defend these old views, often called "realist," against neoconservatives' aspirations to change the world with overwhelming power.[58] "Realism" here means the line of thinking through Machiavelli and Hobbes that portrayed a dangerous world populated by highly imperfect human beings. Crusading for utopian change in this type of world is risky at best and usually pointless; instead, it usually generates chaos and resentment rather than progress. Happy families should focus on defending themselves and keeping their own houses in order. For these reasons, the invasion of Iraq in 2003 was opposed by most older Republican experts on foreign policy, such as Henry Kissinger or James Baker III (respectively secretaries of state to Presidents Nixon and George H.W. Bush). Republicans on the more libertarian side of conservatism, such as Senator Rand Paul, hold similar foreign policy views. In one high-profile speech (testing the waters for his failed presidential run in 2016), Paul called for a more "restrained" foreign policy and suggested that meddling in other countries just increases global hostility to America.[59] Under the Trump administration, even the conservatives who have advocated interventions abroad—like John Bolton, Trump's third National Security Advisor—do so with realist arguments about defending American security and maximizing American power, not idealistic calls to spread democratic ideals.[60]

Political figures on the Left in the United States and Europe, especially the fairly far Left, agree that the United States should not try to impose its values abroad—but for different reasons. Rather than questioning the effectiveness of democracy promotion, they see it as arrogantly immoral and often misleading, cloaking the pursuit of power and economic gain. Progressive author and critic David Rieff describes American democracy promotion as a version of religious proselytizing, "marked by a mystical sense of mission, a belief in the redemptive role of the United States in global affairs, a missionary zeal in which remaking the world in America's image seems not an act of hubris but the fulfillment of a moral duty."[61] Though he supports democracy, Rieff sees its promotion as reflecting more righteousness and pride than genuine concern for improving lives. Powerful democracies have often paid little attention to meaningful liberty, equality, or prosperity. Instead, they have focused more on symbolic elections and thin aspects of civil society. Worse, say far-left figures, the missionary rhetoric of democracy promotion has just hidden American dominance and economic imperialism. Consider, for example, what a far-left Democratic Congressman from Ohio, Dennis Kucinich, said in asserting that the Iraq war was motivated by oil interests:

> The United States does not have a history of bringing democracy to nations out of pure altruism. Rather there is usually something we have to gain by overthrowing a nation and the promotion of democracy is the excuse we use to do it . . . when it is in our interest to leave undemocratic governments alone, we do.[62]

Thus voices from the far Left, the libertarian Right, and moderate conservatives in the old realist mold all caution against major attempts to change the neighbors' behavior. All of them may value democracy just as much as their opponents in the debate, but they argue that the leading democracies cannot or should not try directly to engineer political change elsewhere (see Table 11-2). Which side is more persuasive about how the happy families of the political world should treat their less happy neighbors? That is for you to decide.

Table 11-2 American Ideologies and Democracy Promotion

Liberals favor democracy promotion with support and soft incentives. So-called "neoconservatives"—once powerful in Republican circles, though much less so today—call for imposing democracy abroad with force. Liberals favor using softer approaches. Classic conservatives fear such policies will do more harm than good, and the Far Left sees such steps as arrogant or hypocritical.

Can we make a difference?	Should we impose our values?	
	Yes	No
Yes	Liberals (with support and advice) "Neoconservatives" (by strength and force)	Radical Left
No	Conservative realists	(No common view combines these critiques)

Explaining Cases: Uncovering the Whys of the Arab Spring

11.5   Identify multiple explanations for the fall of authoritarian regimes in the Arab Spring.

The stance we take on democracy promotion relies heavily on how we explain why countries have authoritarian or democratic regimes. If political regimes derive fairly directly from economic development, for example, it may be pointless to press democratic reforms on impoverished Afghanistan or sub-Saharan Africa. If democracy is more the product of institutions, we may have more hope that well-crafted constitutions and new political and civil society organizations can spread democracy regardless of economic conditions. If we explain authoritarianism or democracy as rooted in ideas, then we might lean either way—concluding that certain cultural traditions might block the spread of democracy *or* that ideas can be exported like institutions.

The explanation of democracy has received more attention than any other topic in political science. Most modern political scientists have lived in democracies, after all, and cared about why such governments may or may not arise. This section connects their core ideas to the cases of political change that have most excited the world in the second decade of the twenty-first century: the Arab Spring transitions in Egypt, Tunisia, and Libya. Why did authoritarians fall in these countries? If they are to achieve successful democratization—which seems close in Tunisia today, but very far off in Egypt or Libya—what would be the key cause of that outcome?

Most likely the real tale of the Arab Spring combines these stories. Material, institutional, and ideational dynamics all probably affect prospects for

The Rational-Material Story

It is not difficult to interpret the Arab Spring through the lens of material explanations that trace political regimes to underlying material conditions in economy and society. Authoritarian regimes in the Arab world came under rising pressure in recent decades from a huge demographic wave of young people, coupled with relatively weak economies and a long-term absence of jobs. The region also depends heavily on wheat imports—Egypt imports more than any other country—and soaring world wheat prices sparked bread riots around 2011. Technological change further strengthened political opposition, with Facebook and Twitter empowering the new expression and coordination of opposition. Democratization will succeed only if the economy can be stabilized and grow in an open, competitive, market-friendly and decentralized way.

The Institutional Story

From an institutional point of view, the Arab Spring is more about the organizational vulnerability of certain government institutions than an unstoppable materially empowered wave of dissatisfaction. Material conditions were challenging, certainly, but the reason why regimes in Egypt, Tunisia, and Libya fell when others did not is that these were the most personalized dictatorships in the Arab world. Without well-developed dominant parties, full support from a disciplined military, or the traditional authority of monarchical or religious regimes, top leaders were increasingly perceived as simply corrupt. Successful democratization will depend mostly on the design of democratic institutions that incentivize participation by all major political forces, including Islamic fundamentalists.

The Ideational Story

An ideational explanation interprets the Arab Spring as a set of ideas that converged in these countries in 2011. Democracy is itself an idea; Egyptians, Tunisians, and Libyans faced challenging material conditions for thousands of years, but it was their twenty-first-century ideational context that made democratization their priority. These countries' political cultures also help explain why revolts against authoritarianism initially succeeded here and not elsewhere. Egyptians, in particular, see themselves as the old cultural and intellectual leaders of the Arab world, and northern Africans have more secular national identities than those closer to the center of Islam in Saudi Arabia. The waves of protest in 2011, too, mainly reflected changes in people's ideas and perceptions, not sudden shifts in material conditions or institutions. For democratization to succeed, leaders must recast national identities to represent democracy as compatible with Islam and Arabic nationalisms.

democratization. Qualitative and quantitative research can help us look more sharply at how much evidence supports each view.

RESEARCH ON WITHIN-CASE PROCESSES. If we want to know how to explain the Arab Spring, the most direct thing to do is to gather all the information we can about the processes that led to the uprisings. Exactly who mobilized, with which complaints or demands, and from where did they draw their strength? Table 11-3 begins to flesh out what these processes could look like.

As we have seen in other chapters, the expected processes for some of these explanations run parallel to each other: institutional and ideational explanations, for example, could expect the same kinds of people to constitute the main body of protesters, even if their reasons differ. But in other ways, these theoretical views still suggest different stories that we could trace. See for yourself: find a news article about the Arab Spring events from a respectable newspaper, magazine, or website and look for signs that fit best with each version of the story.

RESEARCH ON CROSS-CASE PATTERNS. We can also look at a wide range of governments to see what conditions correlate with the fall of authoritarian regimes. We could highlight patterns in how certain levels of wealth, rates of growth, or economic crises to challenges to authoritarian regimes. Perhaps we could somehow measure international pressure for democracy and relate

Table 11-3 Exploring Within-Case Evidence for Explanations of the Arab Spring

	Rational-Material Explanation	Institutional Explanation	Ideational Explanation
What was the major complaint about the old regimes?	Poverty, lack of economic growth, poor services	Corruption of regimes and their disconnection from society; little support from all groups outside of the regimes' own elite	For liberal thinkers, repression and lack of democracy; for Islamists, corruption and secularism
Who constituted the main body of the uprisings?	Middle class and poor who suffered most from the weak economy and ineffective services	The best organized nonstate groups: Islamists of the Muslim Brotherhood and university students	Those most ideologically opposed to the regime—liberal elites and university students, plus Islamists
When did the turning point come for the regimes' fall?	When bread prices jumped—the last straw after years of stagnation	When militaries—the sole major organization tied to these regimes—wavered in their support of authoritarian rule	When the self-immolation of Mohammed Bouazizi led many Arab citizens to join in verbally expressing their own dissatisfaction
Best Evidence to Support Each Explanation	We find that even highly ideological groups—Islamists and university students—mostly complained about economic issues and mainly reacted to them.	We find that some military units or social organizations could have supported these regimes, but due to lack of more organized support, the militaries and other groups leaned toward revolution.	We find that many people whose conditions of life did not change dramatically around late 2010 still shifted from tolerating (or even supporting) their government to later calling for its fall.

it to instances of authoritarian collapse over time. Your instructor may be able to help you find data to explore some of these possible cross-case correlations.

Conclusion: Why the Future of Democratization Matters to You

Whether or not liberal democratic governments choose to actively pressure authoritarians and support democratizers, their citizens' future prospects are tied to the fates of political regimes elsewhere. If China's Communists eventually allow political competition, if Iran's ayatollahs return to their seminaries, and if generals in Myanmar, Egypt, and Pakistan fully leave government to civilians— just to mention a few big but imaginable changes—today's young democratic citizens could enjoy a future with less political tension, more openness, and greater mobility. Such a world would not be free of conflict, and even might be more chaotic in some ways. Unhappy families are sometimes more predictable than happy ones. It would evoke a new sense that the vast majority of humankind shares some similar values, however, and that would be a huge thing.

If, on the other hand, China's regime retains a confidently different model, Iran's clerics continue to build support by defying the West, and countries like Pakistan and Egypt fail to establish meaningful electoral competition, our perception of rising waves of democracy may shift to look like a receding tide. After all, it is already thirty years ago that the "third wave" washed across Latin America, Eastern Europe, and the Soviet Union. If no forceful "fourth wave" follows, we may begin to interpret these earlier steps in democratization as an unusual historical shift, rather than as a continuing global trend. Future generations might see the division of the world into such tensely competing models of government as being normal, like returning to the conflicts between democracy, communism, and fascism in the early twentieth century.

Which scenario will prevail? Can and should we do anything to encourage political change? We cannot predict grand political change very well, but we can think critically about a changing world with empirical, ideological, and explanatory alternatives.

Review of Learning Objectives

11.1   **Identify multiple organizational strategies by which authoritarian regimes maintain political control, and give country examples.**

To consider democracy's future prospects, we must first understand how nondemocracies maintain power. They use a variety of organizational strategies:

- Dictatorships and monarchies build networks of personal loyalty.
- Military regimes use the armed forces to manage the state.

- One-party regimes create huge party organizations that oversee the state.
- In theocratic Iran, a religious hierarchy plays a similar role.

Across all these variants, twenty-first-century authoritarians have also increasingly experimented with carefully controlled mechanisms of accountability, such as limited elections in Iran or administrative responsiveness in China. These fairly sophisticated "hybrid" mechanisms may strengthen authoritarian regimes, or may create inroads for reform or revolt.

11.2 Identify conditions that weaken authoritarian regimes and the organizational vulnerabilities of different types of authoritarianism.

Authoritarian regimes occasionally succumb to invasion or diplomatic pressure, but their most common threats lie in the economy. Economic crises often encourage critics to challenge these regimes. Economic success, too, may lead to pressures for change as the growth of a strong business class empowers people who are not directly controlled by the state.

Each kind of authoritarian regime tends to be vulnerable to certain kinds of challenges. The personal power of dictators often encourages corruption that citizens ultimately reject. Reliance on professional militaries in military regimes tends to invite calls for the military to return to its professional security role and leave politics to civilians. Theocracies attract similar criticisms that call for clerics to concentrate on the religious sphere rather than worldly government. Single-party regimes create professional political managers who may begin to prioritize their management tasks over loyalty to the regime, therefore becoming internal reformers. However, it is very hard to predict just when regimes might succumb to any of these vulnerabilities. Sudden waves of "contagion" can quickly shift public opinion against a regime that seemed solidly in control.

11.3 Specify key conditions that help or harm a country's chances for successful democratization.

Like with the fall of authoritarians, economic success and failure play a major role in the chances for successful establishment of a new democratic government. Economic crises that topple authoritarians also make democratization harder; democratization is more likely to succeed in an environment of economic success, coupled with a rising business class. Especially problematic are situations of "double transition," when countries simultaneously confront major political changes and attempts to reconfigure economies for market-based growth. Citizens who feel pain from the economic transition may disrupt the political transition. Also important is the degree to which the organization of the previous regime enables its supporters to find a place in the new democratic system. Integration of dictators' supporters is often extremely difficult, but in principle other authoritarians have better chances: militaries can return to the barracks, clerics can return to the religious sphere, and dominant parties can become one party among many. International pressure from powerful democracies can often support the establishment of democracy, but it also often provokes counterproductive reactions against external meddling.

11.4   Evaluate competing arguments for and against the notion that democracies like the United States should actively promote democracy elsewhere.

Antidemocratic ideologies like fascism, Islamism, or devout socialism are not interested in promoting liberal democracy, and environmentalists tend to see it as a secondary issue. Even within the liberal tradition on which liberal democracy is built, there is substantial disagreement about whether established democracies should actively spread their model. The common modern-liberal position is that promotion of democracy abroad is a moral imperative for the same reasons we value it at home, and thus targeted support and pressure for democratization should be a core aspect of all democracies' foreign policy. Diverse voices speak up against these democracy promoters, like when traditional conservatives argue that meddling in other countries' affairs rarely achieves positive results. Far-right libertarians are even more skeptical that government action can promote democracy successfully, as part of their general skepticism of active government. Far-left radical liberals tend to see democracy promotion as a cover for rich countries to exploit and control poorer ones.

11.5   Identify multiple explanations for the fall of authoritarian regimes in the Arab Spring.

To review for this objective, try to imagine rational-material, institutional, and ideational explanations of the fall of authoritarian regimes in the Arab Spring without looking at Section 11.5. Begin by asking yourself the following questions:

- What long-term or shorter-term shifts in the material resources of these regimes or the material resources of their citizens might have led to revolutions?

- How could the institutional structure of these regimes have made them vulnerable to challenges? What institutional features might we suspect that they have lacked?

- If neither material nor institutional conditions shifted decisively before the Arab Spring, how might the spread of certain ideas have led to the Arab Spring?

After brainstorming your answers to these questions, return to Section 11.5 to see how well you have constructed plausible alternatives to explain this case.

Great Sources to Find Out More

Andrew Reynolds, *Designing Democracy in a Dangerous World* (New York: Oxford University Press, 2010). An experienced observer and policy-maker analyzes how to craft democracy in divided states.

Elizabeth Economy, *The Third Revolution: Xi Jinping and the New Chinese State* (New York: Oxford University Press, 2018). A balanced look at ongoing processes of change in authoritarian China.

Guillermo O'Donnell and Philippe Schmitter, *Transitions from Authoritarian Rule: Tentative Conclusions about Uncertain Democracies* (Baltimore: Johns Hopkins University Press, 1991).

A brief summary of a famous study on the fall of authoritarian regimes.

Jeff Bridoux and Milja Kurki, *Democracy Promotion: A Critical Introduction* (New York: Routledge, 2014). A provocative critical discussion of the assumptions and actors behind the promotion of democracy.

Joshua Kurlantzick, *Democracy in Retreat: The Revolt of the Middle Class and the Worldwide Decline of Representative Government* (New Haven, CT: Yale University Press, 2014). A provocative attack on the expectation that democracy will continue to spread.

Larry Diamond, "What Went Wrong in Iraq," *Foreign Affairs*, 83(5) (September–October 2004), 34–56. Insights from a political scientist who served as a democracy-building expert in Iraq.

Marc Lynch, *The Arab Uprising: The Unfinished Revolutions of the New Middle East* (New York: Public Affairs, 2012). One of the most engaging and well-informed analyses of the Arab Spring.

Michael Axworthy, *Revolutionary Iran* (New York: Penguin, 2013). The story of Iran's regime since 1979 told by an ex-British diplomat.

Michael McFaul, *Advancing Democracy Abroad: Why We Should and How We Can* (Lanham, MD: Rowman & Littlefield, 2010). The case for democracy promotion from a political scientist who became U.S. ambassador to Russia.

Nader Hashemi and Danny Postel, eds., *The Syria Dilemma* (Cambridge, MA: MIT Press, 2013). A series of essays on the Syrian civil war and its possible solutions.

Peter Burnell, *Promoting Democracy Abroad: Policy and Performance* (New Brunswick, NJ: Transaction, 2011). A balanced middle-ground assessment of the record of democracy promotion.

Steven Levitsky and Daniel Ziblatt, *How Democracies Die* (New York: Crown, 2018). Two political scientists highlight the signs of impending democratic collapse.

William Dobson, *The Dictator's Learning Curve* (New York: Doubleday, 2012). A very readable analysis of how dictators have become better at staying in power in recent decades.

Develop Your Thinking

Use these questions as discussion or short writing exercises to think more deeply about some of the key themes of the chapter.

1. If you wanted to establish authoritarian control over the United States, which authoritarian model would you choose?
2. Speculate: will China's Communist Party lose power during your lifetime? Why or why not?
3. How optimistic are you for the further global spread of democracy? Why?
4. Can the American government make a difference in democratization around the world?
5. Has the United States remained a stable democracy for so long mainly for material, institutional, or ideational reasons?
6. Do Egypt's troubles since the Arab Spring suggest that sometimes we should not encourage attempts at democratization?

Keywords

anticorruption campaigns 380
cadres 368
civil society programs 374
clerics 369
conditionality 374

consolidation 388
contagion 385
coup d'état 374
double transition 388
hybrid regimes 370

managed accountability 372
modernization theory 386
pacts 390
personal networks 366
sanctions 373

Chapter 12
Political Violence: War and Terrorism

David Pollack/Corbis Historical/Getty Images

Beginning in the 1950s (when the U.S. Federal Civil Defense Administration distributed this poster) through the mid-1980s, many Americans thought it likely that they and the entire world would soon be destroyed in a nuclear war. Today, fears of major war have been largely replaced by fears of a very different kind of threat—terrorism. Which period would you rather live in?

∨ Learning Objectives

12.1 Explain how wars today, and the prospect of war, differ from patterns of political violence in the past.

12.2 Identify the distinctive features of terrorism and explain why it is so salient in our era.

12.3 Identify four theoretical views of why people fight wars and assess the plausibility of each.

12.4 Evaluate competing arguments about the just use of political violence.

12.5 Identify multiple plausible explanations for the Iraq War of 2003.

Has the Threat of Major War Disappeared?

On November 20, 1983, 100 million Americans watched *The Day After*, a TV movie about nuclear war with the USSR. It was not just entertainment. The U.S. military's Joint Chiefs of Staff had a private screening. President Ronald Reagan's viewing left him "greatly depressed."[1] The network offered call-in counseling for viewers. They needed it: at the time, most Americans rated chances of an unsurvivable nuclear war above 50 percent. In other words, *most* Americans in 1983 told pollsters they *expected* to die in war.[2]

A few decades later, the world has changed. Prospects of major war look fairly remote. The United States certainly confronts tensions with a rising China, and some experts see chances of a U.S.-China war as "not negligible and growing."[3] Still, much would have to change for the chances to go from "not negligible" to "likely." Prospects of a U.S. war with Iran are stronger, but fighting such an overmatched adversary would probably not affect the American "home front" much. Wars are also more imaginable in some regional-level conflicts, like between Pakistan and India, but such scenarios would not directly involve the world's major powers. And in terms of *active* wars today, almost all are inside countries, not between them, like in the power struggles in Afghanistan, Yemen, Syria, Iraq, or Somalia. While American and European soldiers are still present in some of these arenas, back home, few civilians can imagine dying in war. American polls no longer mention the possibility.

Instead what Americans and Europeans fear is terrorism. Ever since September 11, 2001, people worry about being in the wrong place at the wrong time when terrorists strike. Tensions with Iran scare the average citizen not because they fear an Iranian invasion but because we can imagine Iran-supported terror attacks and around the globe. Does that mean we inhabit a new era where major war has been replaced by more fragmented threats of regional infighting and the uncertainties of terrorism? Or are we just in a transitional period before the threat of global war returns? This chapter traces the changing configurations of violence and security in politics over time, considers the main alternative views of the roots of security threats, and concludes with a normative debate about the notion of "just war." ■

The Rise (and Fall?) of Major War

12.1 **Explain how wars today, and the prospect of war, differ from patterns of political violence in the past.**

Ever since early human beings formed primitive bands, no historical period has been free of sustained, organized violence between groups—the definition of war. Warfare has undergone striking changes over time, though, especially with the rise of states since the 1500s. Fairly constant clashes between smallish groups gave way to episodic, state-framed, larger-scale wars. This evolution of bigger, more intense, better-organized wars culminated in the two world wars that killed almost 100 million people.[4]

Then the trends seemed to change. The potential scale of war got even bigger: after World War II the American and Soviet "superpowers" faced off with nuclear weapons that threatened the entire planet. The superpower standoff remained "cold," however, and actual "hot" wars shifted back to smaller and somewhat more frequent conflicts. When even the threat of major war evaporated with the fall of the Soviet Union in 1991, it left behind a world where only smaller wars linger within poor, unstable countries. Surprising though it may seem, by many measures we now inhabit "the most peaceable era in our species' existence."[5]

The Expansion of War into the Twentieth Century

At the core of the history of modern warfare is a political tale of how nation-states organized and focused violence into highly concentrated form. Ever-bigger political organizations used ever-more-destructive technology and ever-broader mobilization of societies to fight ever-more-intensive wars. Deaths per war in major battles doubled from the 1300s to the early 1800s and then multiplied another ten times by the 1900s.[6] In generating more intensive violence, though, states also corralled it overall. War became somewhat rarer and far more destructive.

Consider first a picture of pervasive, modestly destructive, elite-dominated warfare in medieval Europe—since it is Europe that mainly invented the later "total wars" of modern times. Around 1300, most Europeans perceived war as an affair of aristocrats. Kings and nobles fought constantly for territory and prestige, but little changed for the population no matter who won. Horsed aristocratic knights in armor dominated actual fighting, with supporting roles for poor men compelled to serve as untrained infantry. Forces were small, with 5,000 men considered a large army.[7] Ill-developed organization and supplies kept forces from remaining long in the field, so most conflicts centered on the siege of fortresses. Attackers supported themselves by plundering local populations.

Technological changes over the next four centuries encouraged the rise of much larger armies that drew more on lower-class troops. Tight formations of infantry using pikes, or long spears, scored victories over mounted knights. The spread of powerful longbows that could pierce armor weakened knights' dominance as well. Then the arrival of gunpowder in Europe from China further leveled the battlefield—literally. Sieges became known less for heroic charges than for castle-demolishing artillery. Development of effective muskets by the 1600s made commoner-based forces still more dangerous, since they required far less training than longbows. Ranks of musketeers and rows of cannon gradually displaced nobles on chargers, and military power depended increasingly on recruiting large forces. By 1600, several European sovereigns could call up over 50,000 soldiers.

Organizational changes interacted with technology to hasten these transformations. States became more centralized to provide the framework for larger armies. Where leaders had once just thrown together whatever knights and commoners their vassals could provide, or hired paid troops of fighters known as **mercenaries**, now they increasingly built up official state regiments. In this way, the first European bureaucracies arose to organize military ranks and promotion,

mercenaries
Soldiers who fight for whomever pays them.

provide standardized equipment and materiel for military campaigns, and—just as important—collect taxes to fund wars. Though nobles remained dominant, bureaucratization brought new emphases on competence and professionalism that cracked open the door for nonaristocrats to gain status through military careers. Military competition spread all these innovations rapidly around the continent. The French kings in the 1600s played an especially key role, developing the most powerful centralized state in Europe and forcing neighboring powers to copy their innovations or be overwhelmed. By 1700, France's "Sun King" Louis XIV fielded 400,000 soldiers.[8]

It was also in France that other political changes magnified these technological and organizational evolutions into much deeper social mobilization. In 1789, the radical Enlightenment ideas of the French Revolution overpowered the continent's leading monarchy. Frenchmen were not subjects that served the king, argued the revolutionaries; they were citizens of a nation that government should serve. Therefore, in military affairs, it followed that all citizens should fight to defend the nation. As other European monarchies moved to suppress the revolution, its leaders called for the entire citizenry to rise up. In 1793, they launched a mass **conscription**, or requirement of military service, in ringing terms:

conscription
A requirement that all young men serve in the military, sometimes called "the draft."

> From this moment until such time as its enemies shall have been driven from the soil of the Republic, all Frenchmen are in permanent requisition for the services of the armies. The young men shall fight; the married men shall forge arms and transport provisions; the women shall make tents and clothes and shall serve in the hospitals; the children shall turn old lint into linen; the old men shall betake themselves to the public squares in order to arouse the courage of the warriors and preach hatred of kings and the unity of the Republic.[9]

In imagining a society that served all citizens, revolutionary France introduced a future in which war involved all citizens. The new French citizen army quickly became far larger than any other in Europe, reaching 800,000 men. Ironically, this mobilization soon served another monarch: career officer Napoleon Bonaparte declared himself emperor in 1803 and used the massive new armies to briefly take over the entire continent. Yet even though the Republic fell, it left behind the innovation of citizen armies. The Napoleonic invasions soon pushed other countries to mobilize similar conscript forces, and also awakened a new nationalist spirit as entire populations collided. As the great theorist of war Karl von Clausewitz wrote, "Nothing now impeded the vigor with which war could be waged."[10]

The remaining step from Napoleon's citizen army to "total war" was industrialization. The technologies and massive productive capacity of the Industrial Revolution radically altered the battlefield, giving the American Civil War of 1860–1865 the label of the first modern war. Railroads carried soldiers and supplies rapidly from place to place. Telegraphs allowed commanders to communicate at distance. Tin cans permitted armies to travel further with unspoiled food.

These industrial technologies put more men on the front and gave them new weapons as well: sophisticated mortars, grenades, and early machine guns. More carnage was the result, claiming 750,000 American soldiers. It took another fifty years, though, for the combination of tightly organized nation-states, vast citizen armies, and industrialization to develop into full-fledged modern warfare. In what its survivors called "The War to End All Wars"—World War I from 1914 to 1918—deep social mobilization and massive weaponry brought industrialized death to 10 million soldiers and 27 million civilians.

But even World War I was not quite the high point of major war. Despite the rise of a huge **pacifist** (or antiwar) movement after 1918, Europeans found themselves launching an even more intense conflict barely a generation later. World War I had been a largely defensive war: troops huddled in trenches on the battlefront and pounded each other with gigantic artillery and machine guns. By the time Hitler's Germany initiated World War II by invading Poland in 1939, technology had shifted to favor a more offensive war that brought still wider destruction. Tanks smashed through trenches and other defenses to rapidly penetrate opposing territory. Airplanes bombed not just soldiers but entire cities into rubble. Not only were societies entirely mobilized to put forces in the battlefield, then, but mid-twentieth-century technology decreased the separation between battlefield and the home front. More than 20 million soldiers and 40 to 50 million civilians were killed. This was worldwide industrial-scale total war.

pacifism
Opposition to the deliberate use of violence.

There was at least some positive side, however, to the nation-state's amplification of violence. The same processes that allowed states to organize warfare of unprecedented intensity brought stronger control of their territories and internal violence. From a world in which poorly organized groups engaged in fairly constant, low-intensity warfare, states gradually constructed one with longer periods of peace punctuated by horrific clashes. The sheer ferocity of modern wars, which soon left little standing, also made it more difficult for wars to linger on like in the days of the Hundred Years' War (1337–1453) or the Thirty Years' War (1618–1648). As Figure 12-1 shows, major war became less common over time.

Up until World War II, the rising intensity of major war clearly mattered more for people's lives than its decreasing frequency. Even if major wars became rarer, they reached far more deeply and destructively into society and marked more lives more profoundly. After World War II, though, the infrequency of war seems to have become more important than its intensity. War between great powers literally stopped happening. Had war become so intense that it was unthinkable? Was this period of peace just a lucky accident? Or, perhaps, is the absence of major war since 1945 a lull before a worse storm still to come?

War in the Bipolar Era: Globally Cold, Locally Hot

People living through the first four decades after World War II did not have the impression that they had begun a golden era of global peace. Quickly, the postwar world came to be dominated by a standoff between the United States and the

Figure 12-1 The Declining Frequency of Great-Power War

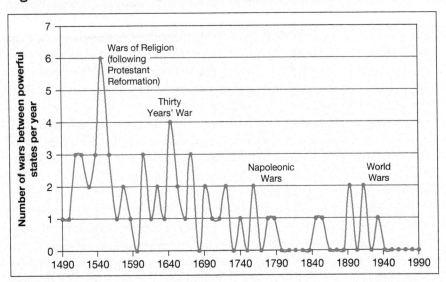

Source: Jack Levy and William Thompson, William, *The Arc of War: Origins, Escalation, and Transformation* (Chicago: University of Chicago Press, 2011).

multipolar
The term for an international system with multiple major centers of power.

bipolar
The term for an international system with two centers of power that surpass all others.

Warsaw Pact
The alliance between the USSR and its satellite states in Eastern Europe from 1955 to 1991.

North Atlantic Treaty Organization (NATO)
The alliance between the United States, Canada, and their European allies established in 1949 against the USSR. It still exists today.

Soviet Union. Their nuclear weapons threatened far more destruction than anything mankind had ever seen. This period gave rise to the kinds of expectations most Americans held around the film *The Day After*: death in war was probably a matter of time. In the end, however, no major war took place. The U.S.–USSR impasse only produced a series of local wars that the superpowers encouraged between their smaller allies.

That the potential intensity of war again increased after World War II was unmistakable. The scale of competing political organizations took a new leap as the United States and the USSR rose to "superpower" status. By 1945, these two countries dwarfed the long-dominant European nation-states, thanks to their large populations, rich resources, and huge territories. At the end of the war, the United States accounted for a third of the whole world's economy. Its communist (or state-socialist) rival, the USSR, was far less rich, with only about 10 percent of world GDP, but it still overshadowed all powers besides the United States in military terms.[11] It was widely perceived that the global distribution of power had shifted from a **multipolar** arena with several great powers to a **bipolar** situation dominated by two giants. Furthermore, the two giants rapidly fell into mutual hostility. After their uneasy alliance to defeat Nazi Germany, the capitalist democratic Americans and socialist-authoritarian Soviets both feared that the other sought to restrain, weaken, or overthrow their political system—and both were right. Hardly had they demobilized from World War II before they geared up against each other. The USSR claimed control over Eastern Europe, including East Germany, and gathered communist governments into a military alliance known as the **Warsaw Pact**. The United States grouped Western Europe into an alliance called the **North Atlantic Treaty Organization (NATO)** and created similar ties with Japan in Asia. The two sides settled into a standoff that became known as the **Cold War**.

The potential intensity of war took an even larger step up due to the new technology of nuclear weapons. The very largest non-nuclear (or **conventional**) bombs used in World War II carried the explosive force of roughly 10 tons of dynamite. In 1945, the United States forced Imperial Japan to surrender by dropping one nuclear bomb on the city of Hiroshima and one on Nagasaki, each equaling about 12.5 kilotons (12,500 tons) of dynamite.[12] Over 200,000 people died. By 1949, the Soviets tested their own nuclear bomb, which led to a superpower race to build the largest nuclear arsenal (see Figure 12-2). When Soviet nuclear stockpiles caught up with American ones around 1970, the two countries' weapons together were equal to 24,000 megatons (24 million tons) of TNT—roughly 8,000 times the total energy of all explosives used in World War II (including the Hiroshima and Nagasaki bombs). To put this in human perspective, consider this: a single 1-megaton bomb can destroy *80 square miles* of territory.[13]

Did the United States and USSR's hostility remain "cold," then, because war had become so big it was unthinkable? On the one hand, the context of nuclear-armed superpowers gave all leaders pause. While many politicians had advocated war in the lead-up to World War I, and the Nazis had eagerly launched World War II, it had become hard to argue that anyone could "win" a U.S.–Soviet nuclear exchange. The two sides had reached a point where powerful weapons served the purpose of **deterrence**—creating major disincentives to fight—and entered a state known as **mutually assured destruction (MAD)**: any attacker was unlikely to survive the other side's response. Furthermore, as nuclear arsenals grew, scientists pointed out

Cold War

A hostile stand-off in the late 1940s through the late 1980s between the communist USSR and its allies versus the capitalist-democratic United States and its allies.

conventional weapons

Classic projectiles and explosives—guns and bombs—that are perceived as "normal" military tools, in contrast to nuclear, chemical, or biological weapons.

deterrence

The use of threats to deter another party from attacking.

mutually assured destruction (MAD)

A situation of successful deterrence in which adversaries cannot strike without being destroyed in return.

Figure 12-2 U.S. and Soviet Nuclear Arsenals in Megatons of TNT Equivalent

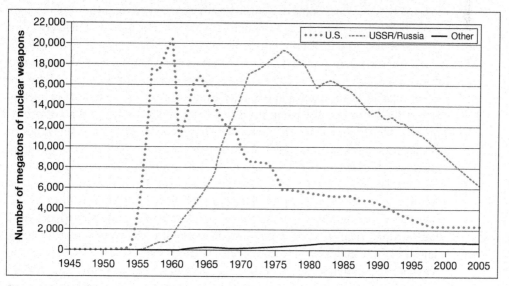

Source: U.S. Department of Energy, compiled by William Robert Johnson, Johnston Archives, http://www.johnstonarchive.net/.

nuclear winter
The possibility that nuclear war could cloud the atmosphere with enough dust to block all sunlight and kill all life on Earth.

that a full-scale nuclear war might ruin the entire planet. It could throw up enough dust to block the sun, causing a "**nuclear winter**" that would kill all life.

On the other hand, Cold War leaders in the United States and the USSR did not publicly treat nuclear war as unthinkable. To the contrary, both sides often argued that they had little choice but to present nuclear war as possible for strategic reasons. If either side admitted that they would never launch a full-scale nuclear attack, then the other side could undertake either conventional or small-scale nuclear attacks without fear of massive retaliation. Ironically, leaders thought they had to plan for nuclear war in order to deter the other side from starting it. Far from stepping back from serious consideration of war as their nuclear weapons piled up, then, both Americans and Soviets made increasingly specific and concrete preparations for war. Until the 1990s, huge waves of nuclear missiles stood ready for launch at a moment's notice. Elaborate plans existed about how exactly a nuclear war would be fought.

Moreover, the Cold War came dangerously close to going hot at points. In June 1961, war almost erupted over the status of Berlin, the German capital that had become a Western-defended island in the middle of Soviet-controlled East Germany. In September 1983, Soviet warning systems wrongly detected a U.S. attack and instructed their personnel to launch, but a cool-headed lieutenant-colonel refused. Yet probably "the most dangerous moment in human history," according to historian Arthur Schlesinger, was the Cuban Missile Crisis of October 1962.[14] Schlesinger knew what he was talking about: he was a close adviser to President John F. Kennedy at the time. On October 14, U.S. spy planes found evidence that the Soviets were preparing to install nuclear weapons in Cuba, their communist ally off the coast of Florida. The Soviets insisted that they sought only to defend Cuba, which had been the object of repeated American attacks, but U.S. leaders reasoned that such close Soviet missiles were unacceptable—allowing the USSR, possibly, to knock out U.S. nuclear forces before they could retaliate (and thus possibly making the Soviets able to actually win a war). Some of Kennedy's advisers argued for invading Cuba right away, but the president opted to mount a naval blockade to prevent delivery of the Soviet missiles to the island. During the next several days, as we now know, the world almost fell into cataclysm. One Soviet officer acted against orders and shot down a U.S. spy plane over Cuba. A Soviet submarine commander ordered the launch of a nuclear torpedo and retracted it at the last second. Hundreds of nuclear-armed American planes were in the air with ambiguous orders and no devices to prevent pilots from making their own decisions. When a deal was finally struck on October 28—no Soviet missiles in Cuba versus removal of U.S. missiles in Turkey and Italy—top leaders on both sides felt they had dodged a very, very large bullet.

Even if some luck kept the Cold War cold between the superpowers, it nonetheless produced "hot" effects by exacerbating lower-level conflicts around the world. Both Americans and Soviets sought allies on all continents and tried to block overtures by their rival. The result was a proliferation of **proxy wars** in which the two sides of local conflicts received arms and aid from the superpowers. Some proxy wars pitted communists against capitalists, such as in Greece in 1947, Cuba in 1953, or Nicaragua in 1979, so superpower involvement made at least some sense in ideological terms. So intent were the superpowers on winning supporters and frustrating

proxy wars
Wars fought through representatives, or "proxies," rather than between the main antagonists.

each other's designs, though, that they also armed combatants fighting for entirely different reasons, such as in multiple Arab–Israeli wars or the Iran–Iraq War from 1980 to 1988. In many of these conflicts, the recipients of U.S. or Soviet aid manipulated the superpowers as much or more than they served as proxies for the two giants. In religious, ethnic, or post-colonial conflicts within many of the poorer, less stable parts of the world, clever leaders realized that they could gain access to superpower arms and support just by mouthing a few communist or capitalist slogans.

Some of the biggest wars of the period arose when one superpower fought directly against the other's proxies—but usually, to their surprise, with little success. The United States fought to beat back a communist takeover in Korea from 1950 to 1953, losing 36,000 men and gaining only a draw that divided Korea into a communist North and a capitalist South. Then the United States gradually entered Vietnam in the late 1950s to fight a communist movement led by nationalist Ho Chi Minh. Though the United States eventually sent half a million soldiers to Vietnam and dropped five times more bombs there than in all of World War II,[15] they and their local allies were driven out in 1973. The Soviets had little more luck with direct interventions abroad, especially in their full-scale invasion into neighboring Afghanistan in 1979. Afghanistan became their Vietnam: an embarrassing, drawn-out, expensive fight in which heavy weaponry proved unable to suppress local resistance. In all these contexts, local populations showed that great-power forces that had been developed to destroy an opposing military in total war were not well suited to the more targeted goals of controlling and pacifying foreign territories. With ambushes, sabotage, and raids by mobile combatants who melted in and out of the civilian population—known as **guerrilla warfare**—even poorly armed locals could keep up the fight.

guerrilla warfare
Irregular warfare that uses highly mobile, surprise-based tactics like ambushes and sabotage.

By the time the Cold War and bipolar era ended with the collapse of the USSR in 1991, the pre–World War II trends of warfare seemed to have shifted in two ways. Among the most powerful countries the potential intensity of war had grown past an important threshold, reaching such a terrifying level that total great-power war had become harder to conceive. Some luck had still been necessary to avoid destruction of the planet, but nonetheless it was harder than ever before in history to find leaders who thought that major war could serve their interests. Among smaller and poorer countries, by contrast, warfare had been encouraged to proliferate. Not only had a whole host of new conflicts emerged as the developing world tackled decolonization, state building, nationalism, and growth, but the superpowers had actively handed out advanced weapons and played up ideological divides. The experiences of Vietnam and Afghanistan also suggested that the awesome destructive force now held by the great powers was fairly useless to control or pacify poorer regions. The stage was set for the post–Cold War world.

After the Cold War: War Gets Smaller—So Far

After 1991, the role of warfare in global politics further differentiated in two directions. Among major powers, the menace of war practically disappeared. On the peripheries of world power, smaller wars continued and even increased.

Though Cold War rivalries no longer stirred up proxy wars, fights over ethnic identity, religion, and resources motivated a steady stream of civil wars. Overall, then, the overarching trends that preceded World War II were reversed. Violence shifted away from bursts of major, high-intensity, state-organized wars toward smaller, long-running conflicts among less formally organized groups within weaker countries. Attempts to use great-power force to control local conflicts, most notably by the United States, had little success.

A GREAT POWER PEACE.   In the global distribution of power, the shift from an aggressive, heavily armed Soviet Union to a pro-capitalist Russia with diminished military spending ended any sense of a worldwide bipolar standoff. Some describe the post–Cold War era as a **unipolar** world dominated by the United States, while others portray it as more multipolar; but experts tend to agree that war between great powers is unlikely under current conditions.[16] Consider the top countries in the world by population, economic size, wealth per capita, and military expenditure (as in Table 12-1) and the current tensions between them. The only three large concentrations of very rich people in the world (with high GDP per capita) are all close allies: the United States, Europe, and Japan. The United States is clearly in a category of its own, whether or not it qualifies as a "unipolar" power. If we group the United States with its

unipolar
This term describes an international system with one state that is so dominant that no other state or combination of states can truly threaten it.

Table 12-1 Indicators of National Power Today

China may be biggest in population and overall GDP (when calculated at Purchasing Power Parity), but the United States is in its own category in military spending.

Ranking by Population (2019)	Share World Pop.	Ranking by Overall GDP	Share World GDP (2018, PPP)	Ranking by GDP per Capita (2018, PPP)	Ranking by Military Expenditure	Share World Mil. Expend. (2018)	States with Nuclear Weapons
1. China	18.10%	China	18.70%	Singapore	United States	35.08%	United States
2. India	17.50%	United States	15.12%	Norway	China	13.11%	Russia
3. United States	4.27%	India	8.86%	United Arab Emirates	Saudi Arabia	3.99%	United Kingdom
4. Indonesia	3.48%	Japan	4.16%	Switzerland	Russia	3.81%	France
5. Brazil	2.72%	Germany	3.24%	United States	India	3.67%	China
6. Pakistan	2.65%	Russia	3.09%	Netherlands	France	3.32%	India
7. Nigeria	2.51%	Indonesia	2.59%	Saudi Arabia	United Kingdom	2.71%	Pakistan
8. Bangladesh	2.16%	Brazil	2.51%	Taiwan	Japan	2.61%	Israel
9. Russia	1.91%	United Kingdom	2.24%	Sweden	Germany	2.55%	North Korea
10. Mexico	1.64%	France	2.19%	Germany	South Korea	2.25%	

SOURCES: International Monetary Fund; Stockholm International Peace Research Institute Military Expenditure Database.

close allies in Europe and Japan—among whom war is unimaginable—they comprise more than 40 percent of the world economy and over 50 percent of military spending.

The simple existence of this massive preponderance of allied power is one reason why anything like World War III seems unlikely. China is the most plausible challenger, and its authoritarian government, huge population, meteoric economic rise, and escalating military spending make it the main source of great-power-level tensions today. Before assessing its role, though, consider the general absence of major threats from other leading states:

- *Russia* under Putin has difficult dealings with the Western powers, especially over Ukraine since 2014, where direct Russian support for an insurgency brought active war back to the European arena for the first time since the breakup of Yugoslavia in the 1990s. While war involving Russia is one of the scenarios for which American and European militaries prepare today, it seems difficult to imagine either side seriously risking direct war. Nuclear weapons still make any such war a catastrophic prospect, helping to keep the peace—and both sides have dismantled most of their nuclear arsenals since the 1990s. Even most proponents of a large U.S. military no longer argue for large nuclear forces. As President George W. Bush reportedly said at his first briefing on nuclear forces in 2001, "I had no idea we had so many weapons. What do we need them for?"[17]

Sergei Grits/AP Images

Have Russian troops fought in the separatist war in Ukraine that broke out in 2014? Russia denies it, but all external observers agree that they have supplied major weapons and men to the fight. Here, we see an armored vehicle and troops without insignia passing through a pro-Russian rebel checkpoint in the town of Slovyansk. As troubling as Russian actions in Ukraine may be, however, few observers think a broader conflict is likely.

- *Brazil* is a democracy with modest military spending (1.4 percent of GDP), no nuclear weapons, and good relations with the rich democracies. Since an agreement in 2010, the United States and Brazil have developed new levels of military cooperation.

- *India* is a democracy with somewhat higher military spending (2.5 percent of GDP), nuclear weapons, and cordial but careful relationships with the United States, Europe, and Japan. India and China fought a small border war in the 1960s, but these two giant countries signed peace agreements in the 1990s and their improving ties have gone as far as joint military exercises. India's tense relationship with its smaller but nuclear-armed neighbor, Pakistan, is one of the most plausible sites for substantial cross-border warfare in the world today, but any such conflict would likely remain between them.

What, then, of China? We cannot lightly dismiss the friction it generates with other powers. In addition to longstanding critiques of China's human rights record from all Western countries, and newer clashes in a the "trade war" President Trump launched with tariffs on Chinese goods in 2019, many security-related challenges also bedevil their interactions:

- The tensest issue is Taiwan, the U.S.-allied island country that China portrays as a rebel regime on its own territory. Large numbers of Chinese missiles target Taiwan, the Chinese military often conducts operations that mimic war with it, and the Chinese object loudly to U.S. sales of advanced arms to the island.

- Other tensions have arisen over China's claims to uninhabited islands in nearby seas, bringing testy exchanges with Japan, the Philippines, Taiwan, and Vietnam.

- The large U.S. military presence in Korea, Japan, and the Philippines also has an uneasy relationship with Chinese forces. In the most dramatic incident so far, a Chinese fighter jet accidentally collided with a U.S. EP-3 spy plane in 2001, killing the Chinese pilot and forcing the U.S. plane to land on Chinese territory.

- In February 2013, an American report accused a unit of Chinese military hackers—People's Liberation Army unit 61398—of being the source of cyberattacks and industrial espionage against 141 U.S. companies.[18] Since then Western countries have experienced a steady stream of similar Chinese cyberattacks.[19]

Some security experts have begun to think that these problems suggest real possibilities of war on the distant horizon. Harvard political science professor Graham Allison argued in a 2017 book that the United States and China were "destined for war," and in 2018, recently retired U.S. General Ben Hodges predicted it would come within fifteen years.[20] Yet many other experts criticize these predictions as alarmist, and even those who take them fairly seriously tend to admit that they depend on speculation about possible future changes, given that threats of war are currently "remote."[21] Despite talk of a new Cold War, the underlying dynamics of U.S.–Chinese relations are quite different from the old U.S.–USSR standoff.

The most critical differences lie in the economy. The United States and the USSR had almost no economic ties during the Cold War. Today, massive trade and financial exchanges link China and the United States. Americans depend on China to manufacture a vast assortment of consumer products and China depends on the United States as its largest market, with $660 billion in trade between the two countries in 2018.[22] Because Americans buy far more from China than they sell—$419 billion more in 2018—China has accumulated huge amounts of dollars. Its government holds reserves of more than $3 trillion, plus over $1 trillion in U.S. bonds.[23] In other words, the Chinese government has huge and direct interests in the strength of the U.S. economy.

Also reassuring is the role of ideology in China's foreign relations—or the lack thereof. CCP leaders display little of the USSR's communist hostility to Western regimes. Rather than propping up many neighboring regimes and acting to spread its ideology elsewhere, as the Soviet Union did, China does almost nothing to promote its version of communism globally. It has poor relations with state-socialist Vietnam, with which it both fought a border war in 1979 and has clashed recently over the South China Sea. China's leaders support state-socialist North Korea with economic aid, but they have agreed to U.S.-led sanctions against its nuclear weapons program and have gradually lost patience with its bizarre and threatening behavior.[24]

In sum, while significant tensions exist between the rich democracies and China, almost no one thinks they make great-power war likely in the near term. Things can change, of course, and below we consider arguments like Allison's about whether a continued rise in Chinese power will increase risks of major war in the future. Yet the world will indeed have to change for major war to return as an active fear. As one renowned scholar of international security put it at the turn of the millennium—in an observation that still holds true two decades in—the absence of great-power tensions is "a breathtaking change in world politics" relative to earlier history.[25]

INSTABILITY AND WAR ON THE PERIPHERY.   All active wars in our world today—roughly two dozen—are civil conflicts in developing countries. Some stretch across several neighboring countries, but none is a classic interstate war. Three countries have seen tens of thousands of battlefield deaths in recent years—Afghanistan, Syria, and Yemen—and five other places saw over 1,000 in 2018 (Iraq, Somalia, Nigeria, Niger/Chad, South Sudan, and Mali).[26] Interstate wars remain imaginable between several pairings of middle-level powers, like between Israel and Iran, Pakistan and India, or somehow involving North Korea, but all these stand-offs remain cold for the moment.

As Figure 12-3 shows, these internal struggles largely extend the upsurge in local conflicts from the Cold War period. There is one important difference: while the superpowers often incited conflict in weaker states during the Cold War, now the rich and powerful states are more likely just to ignore violence in many corners of the world. Without Cold War rivalries, great-power leaders generally prefer not to be involved in the kinds of ethnic or religious disputes that motivate most ongoing wars. Such wars—primarily concentrated in Africa, the Middle East, and Asia—often reflect conflict within the disparate populations upon which state borders were imposed from the colonial era. Over time, groups with ethnic or religious differences (or both) have taken up arms to contest the allocation of power in their state. Fights over resources often intensify such clashes, such as the lure of oil wealth in Nigeria or Iraq or mining in the Central African Republic.

Three kinds of connections have nonetheless drawn great powers into post–Cold War conflicts in the developing world. First, **humanitarian crises** can press the leading states to intervene. Television and the Internet make it difficult to turn a blind eye when civil wars become especially violent. When the state-socialist federation of Yugoslavia broke into six countries in the early 1990s, conflict among its populations of Serb, Croats, and Bosnians culminated in **ethnic cleansing**, or eliminating a group from a territory through killing and displacement. Only after heinous atrocities did a U.S.-led aerial bombing campaign force a negotiated peace. In the east African state of Rwanda in 1994, ethnic Hutus

humanitarian crises
Situations in which the safety or health of large populations are threatened.

ethnic cleansing
The systematic killing or expulsion of an ethnic group from a territory.

Figure 12-3 State-Based Armed Conflicts, 1946–2017

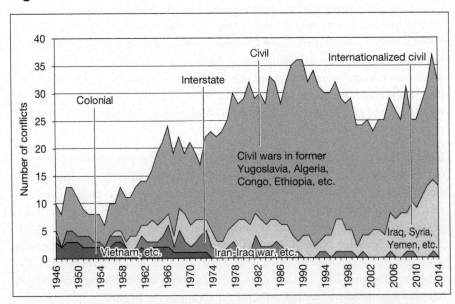

Source: Uppsala Conflict Data Program (UCDP)/Peace Research Institute Oslo (PRIO) Armed Conflict Dataset. Examples of wars added by author.

launched a full-scale **genocide**—mass slaughter of a people—that killed at least half a million ethnic Tutsis. A belated French intervention did little to prevent the violence. After other notable failures to prevent humanitarian disasters, like in the Sudanese region of Darfur after 2003, the United States and European allies acted more decisively in Libya in 2011. When its Arab Spring uprising dissolved into a bloody civil war, a NATO bombing campaign weakened the Gaddafi regime's ability to kill its own citizens. In 2018, the United States and its allies launched missiles strikes to punish Syria for using chemical weapons on its own citizens, but this did not stop the brutal Syrian regime from consolidating control at home. Overall, humanitarian motivations in great-power intervention remain limited and erratic.

genocide
The systematic destruction of an ethnic, religious, or national group.

Second, local conflicts over resources, religion, or ethnicity can threaten what great powers perceive as their interests in either economic or security terms. The key post–Cold War example is Iraq. In August 1990, the dictatorial Iraqi regime of Saddam Hussein took over its tiny, oil-rich neighbor Kuwait. The United States and other leading states objected in principle to this unprovoked attack, but what truly grabbed their attention was the prospect of Hussein controlling the largest share of the region's strategically important oil. Judging U.S. interests and regional stability to be threatened, American leaders rallied a coalition of thirty-four nations to fight the **First Gulf War** in early 1991. The U.S. military was confident that it could easily push outdated Iraqi forces out of Kuwait, thanks to its continued technological advances, especially newly precise guided bombs and missiles. And they were right. After massive aerial bombing that earned the label "the video-game war," the ground campaign smashed Iraqi forces in only 100 hours of fighting.

First Gulf War
The U.S.-led invasion in 1991 to expel Iraq from its small neighbor Kuwait.

The danger of such interventions is that they rarely end cleanly. Conceived as a limited mission, the 1991 war began a continuing U.S. involvement that brought another invasion in the **Second Gulf War** of 2003. In the interim, the United States and its allies had tried to weaken Hussein's regime with international sanctions, but he continued to defy and threaten his neighbors and U.S. forces. In 2002, President George W. Bush's advisers also accused Hussein of developing new **weapons of mass destruction (WMD)**—chemical, biological, and possibly nuclear—and argued that the Iraqi threat must be ended once and for all. Most U.S. allies were skeptical of the evidence of Iraqi WMD (and later attempts to find them turned up nothing at all), but U.S. forces invaded with support from three allies (Britain, Australia, and Poland). In an upgraded repeat of the 1991 performance, high-tech U.S. weaponry scored a rapid victory. Widely watched videos that showed guided missiles hunting targets through Iraqi streets—while their operators sat safely on bases or ships far away—made clear that computers were producing a new revolution in military technology.

Second Gulf War
The U.S.-led invasion of Iraq that toppled the dictatorship of Saddam Hussein in March 2003.

weapons of mass destruction (WMD)
Another name for nonconventional weapons: nuclear, chemical and biological.

Unfortunately, the ease with which the leading great power destroyed enemy forces did not extend to stabilizing Iraq after the invasion. U.S. efforts to rebuild Iraq painfully recalled its experience in Vietnam. Attempts to foster a stable, democratic, U.S.-friendly government were stymied by the complex tensions between Shi'ite and Sunni Muslims and among ethnic tribal groups. A running insurgency brought a steady stream of American deaths. Billions of U.S. dollars disappeared into corruption among the Iraqi groups competing to influence the post-war government. When U.S. forces finally formally withdrew in December 2011, they had suffered over 4,000 dead, more than 30,000 wounded, and spent over $1 trillion. And what did they have to show for it? Iraq had a not-very-democratic regime that was somewhat friendlier, but also divided and corrupt. Worse, it soon faced a new challenge from Islamist ultra-radicals called the Islamic State in Iraq and Syria (ISIS). Their campaign of terror from 2014 to 2018 ended only with more U.S. involvement in the region. In early 2020, in response to the U.S. killing of Iran's leading general on Iraqi soil, Iraq's government requested that all U.S. forces leave the country. Overall, Iraq today is less stable and more menacing than when the United States first invaded.

Iraq's sobering results may well further deter the United States and other powerful states from future major interventions—except, that is, when they are drawn in by a third sort of connection to peripheral conflict. In the late twentieth century, the instability of some developing countries emerged in a new way that threatened the great powers. Partly out of resentment of the power and wealth of the leading states, and above all of the United States, certain groups in the developing world turned increasingly to international terrorism. With a series of dramatic attacks around the turn of the millennium, terrorism largely replaced major war as the most salient security concern of our time.

ZUMA Press, Inc/Alamy Stock Photo

An American soldier fires a Javelin handheld missile at a structure in Afghanistan. This self-guided, heat-targeting missile has a range of three miles—far shorter than larger missile systems based on trailers, ships, planes, or drones—but still illustrates the role that advanced guided weaponry has come to play in recent American military actions.

The Age of Terrorism

12.2 **Identify the distinctive features of terrorism and explain why it is so salient in our era.**

It is often said that we now live in an age of terror. When terrorist-guided planes toppled New York's World Trade Center on September 11, 2001, many people in the United States and other rich and powerful societies suddenly realized that the end of the Cold War had not guaranteed their security. Major terrorist attacks followed in Russia, Spain, the United Kingdom, Nigeria, and across the Middle East in the early 2000s. A bomb at the 2013 Boston Marathon claimed three lives and wounded 170. A spate of attacks in France in 2015–2016 included the murder of eleven people in the Paris offices of *Charlie Hebdo,* a French satirical magazine that had published cartoons that offended Islamists; an assault on a Paris nightclub that left 137 dead; and a rampage by a cargo truck along a seaside boulevard in the city of Nice that killed 86 and wounded 458.

Still, horrific as these events were, older generations might question whether our age is all that terrifying in longer perspective. We face no giant battles like in World War II, no threat of nuclear annihilation like in the Cold War. Even the worst imaginable terrorist attack—a nuclear bomb in a city, perhaps—would be a localized event compared to threats of total war. In recent years, rare hazards like accidental electrocution or brain-eating parasites have killed far more Americans than terrorism.[27]

Yet it is precisely the erratic nature of terrorism that makes it frightening. It introduces sudden violence into nonwar contexts. Even if it is unlikely to kill us, we care that terrorism has become a larger part of the global scene. Originally invented in the late 1800s, it gradually spread to groups around the world. Terrorism's key step to global prominence came in the late twentieth century when one especially large international movement—radical Islamism—came to portray it as a heroic tactic. This intersection is only partial: most radical Islamists are not terrorists, and many other extreme groups still use terrorism. But Islamic fundamentalism is the most potent agenda in the world today that often connects to terrorism, as symbolized by 9/11. When the United States responded to that event with a "war on terror," global violence took on a new shape for the twenty-first century.

The Invention of Terrorism

Terrorism is politically motivated violence that aims to terrorize an opponent rather than trying to defeat their military forces. Just what qualifies under this definition can be blurry. The U.S. nuclear attacks on Japan in 1945, for example, targeted cities rather than the Japanese military itself. Is that terrorism? Usually we see such wartime acts by organized militaries just as part of total war, picturing terrorism mainly as violence between civilians rather than uniformed soldiers. Our clearest image of terrorism is of political violence against noncombatants outside a context of war, like on 9/11.

Terrorism
Politically motivated violence that aims to terrorize an opponent rather than trying to defeat them militarily.

Masatomo Kuriya/Corbis Premium Historical/Getty Images

In the event that created the notion of a new "age of terrorism," the second of two hijacked planes prepares to strike the World Trade Center on September 11, 2001. Both towers soon collapsed. Together with casualties from two other planes that were crashed in Washington, D.C., and Pennsylvania as part of the same plot, more than 3,000 people died.

What are the origins of that image? Bloody attacks against civilians are strewn across history, but terrorism as a distinctive tactic can be traced specifically to Russia in the 1870s. In that era, the heavy-handed imperial Russian government of Czar (or Emperor) Alexander II attracted a rising wave of criticism. Though Alexander II was a reformer who liberalized a rigid monarchy, his strongest critics argued that a better society required the destruction of the entire system. Most radical of all were **anarchists**, who wanted to eliminate government entirely ("anarchy" means a lack of government) in favor of self-governing small communities. Calling for assassinations of political leaders to create chaos and incite revolution, they turned to a new technology invented in the 1860s: dynamite. Dynamite appealed to these revolutionaries precisely because it often killed both target and bearer—making clear that they were idealists, not criminals. A wave of terrorism claimed many public officials over the next several decades, including Alexander II himself in 1881. Other radicals elsewhere were inspired to join the "Golden Age of Assassination" around the turn of the century, when bombs and guns killed monarchs, prime ministers, and presidents including U.S. president William McKinley.

From its initial focus on assassinating top leaders, terrorism morphed over time into its contemporary emphasis on other targets. In the early twentieth century, a variety of anticolonial movements took up terrorism to drive

anarchism
A political philosophy that calls for erasing government or reducing it to a very small scale.

out colonial occupiers. Focusing less on leaders and more on sudden bombings of police forces, military installations, and public buildings, the Irish drove out the English, Israelis forced the British out of Palestine, and other independence movements created new states in Cyprus and Algeria. Around the middle of the twentieth century, various radical-revolutionary groups in Western societies also used the new technology of airplanes to take terrorism in new directions, introducing the tactic of hijacking. In shifting from directly political targets to planes full of random passengers, terrorists generated new levels of fear and outrage. Political assassinations and bombings of police had at least targeted parts of the government the terrorists opposed; such steps could be portrayed, in principle, as a radical version of normal political conflict. Once targets shifted to innocents with no government-related role at all, the full extremism of terrorism became clear. It went in the opposite direction from any direct attempt to persuade or force political actors to change their ways. Sheer unfocused terror, ran the logic, could compel change. If no one felt safe anywhere, citizens would insist that governments give in to terrorists' demands.

Terrorism nonetheless remained a fringe issue for most of the twentieth century. Except in a few contexts where it occurred frequently—the territory of the Irish Republican Army in northern Ireland, for example—it could be seen as a rare aberration in political life, the tactic of a few of the most desperate (or crazy) radicals. The perception of an "Age of Terror" would arise only when terrorism connected to a large international movement.

The Partial Intersection of Radical Islamism and Terrorism

Radical Islamism motivates the most notable terrorists groups today. We must keep in mind that they are far from alone in the terrorist category: seven of the ten worst terrorist attacks on U.S. soil have not involved Islamists, including the second-worst event, which killed 168 people in Oklahoma City in 1995 (see Table 12-2). Still, Islamist extremists claim the most deadly terrorist act ever, on 9/11, and have carried out a majority of terrorist attacks around the world in recent years.[28] The radical-Islamism/terror connection is especially important for our age.

Terrorism was initially a minor strand in the religious revival of Islamic fundamentalism in the early twentieth century. Thinkers like Hassan al-Banna (1902–1949) and Sayyid Qutb (1906–1966) called for purifying Muslim societies that had been corrupted by the Western powers. Al-Banna's Muslim Brotherhood focused its main attention on peaceful social programs in Egypt and other countries—and still does today—but its leaders also organized violent attacks against "impure" targets. In parallel, some Palestinians adopted terrorist tactics of assassination and hijacking in their conflict with the Jewish state of Israel in the 1960s and 1970s. The main Palestinian leaders were secular Arab nationalists,

Table 12-2 Ten Worst Terrorist Attacks on U.S. Soil (by Number of Deaths)

Deaths	Event	Date	Perpetrator
3,021	Hijackers crash planes into the World Trade Center in New York City and two other locations	September 11, 2001	Radical Islamist network Al Qaeda
169	Truck bomb destroys a federal building in Oklahoma City	April 19, 1995	Timothy McVeigh and Terry Nichols, anti–federal government radicals
50	Shooting at Pulse nightclub in Orlando, FL	June 12, 2016	U.S. citizen Omar Mateen, with Islamist ties
38	Bombing outside Morgan Bank in New York City	September 16, 1920	Unsolved; Italian anarchists suspected
21	Bombing at the Los Angeles Times building	October 1, 1910	Radical labor activists
17	Cubana Airlines hijacked from Miami and crashed	November 1, 1958	Cuban communists
16	Shooting at governments offices in San Bernadino, CA	December 2, 2015	U.S. citizens Syed Rizwan Farook and Tashfeen Malik, with Islamist ties
13	Shootings at Fort Hood military base in Texas	November 5, 2009	U.S. citizen and Army Major Nidal Malik Hasan, with some Islamist ties
12	Bomb thrown at police at labor rally in Haymarket Square in Chicago, and subsequent police shooting	May 4, 1886	Anarchists
11	Bomb explodes in locker at La Guardia Airport, New York	December 29, 1975	Unsolved; Croatian nationalists suspected

SOURCE: Compiled by William Robert Johnson, http://www.johnstonsarchive.net/.

not fundamentalists, but their clash with Israelis resonated powerfully with religious Muslims all the same.

Three key events cemented the ties between radical Islamism and terror:

mujahedeen

An Arabic word meaning "those who struggle for Islam." The term can simply designate very devout Muslims, but has come to be identified with radical Islamists who make that struggle violent.

- *The Soviet invasion of Afghanistan* in 1979 opened a long war that eventually became a training ground for Islamist terror groups. Ironically, the United States' Cold War rivalry with the USSR led it to arm Afghan groups known as the **mujahedeen** ("those who struggle for Islam") and effectively encouraged Islamists from around the world to join the fight in Afghanistan.

- *The Iranian Revolution*, also in 1979, gave Islamists control of one of the Middle East's most powerful states. Iran soon funded an organization known as Hezbollah in Israel's neighbor Lebanon that launched anti-Israeli terrorism—bringing the next key event.

- *The terrorist attacks of October 1983* marked the first great success of Islamist terrorism. In 1982, Israel's invasion of Lebanon prompted the United Nations (UN) to send an international peacekeeping force to calm the violence. Hezbollah's leaders perceived the U.S., French, and Italian troops as Israel's allies, however, and acted to drive them out. In October 1983, suicide bombers drove two trucks laden with explosives into U.S. and French barracks, killing 299 soldiers. These attacks achieved their goal: the U.S. and other international forces left Lebanon.

By the mid-1980s, the elements of a broader wave of Islamist-related terrorism were coming together. Israel, Soviet forces in Afghanistan, and American influence all represented what radical Islamists saw as unacceptable incursions into their region. The Lebanon bombings gave them newfound confidence that terrorist strikes could indeed drive Westerners out. Iran offered support to a variety of terrorist groups, as did the Syrian regime and some private individuals with massive oil wealth. Afghanistan amounted to a vast training camp. Once the Soviets withdrew in 1989, these emerging terrorist networks increasingly looked to other arenas where attacks might bring them notoriety and political pressure on their perceived enemies. Major bombs struck Israeli buildings in Argentina in the early 1990s, an underground parking ground at New York's World Trade Center in 1993, a U.S. barracks in Saudi Arabia in 1996, U.S. embassies in Tanzania and Kenya in 1998, and the destroyer USS *Cole* in a harbor in Yemen in 2000.

Then these elements converged in the event that symbolically opened the "Age of Terror." In Afghanistan the disgruntled son of a rich Saudi Arabian family, Osama bin Laden, formed an Islamist network called Al Qaeda ("The Base"). Betting that terror could drive Western influence out of Muslim societies, they enacted a plan to crash hijacked planes into the World Trade Center and other sites on September 11, 2001. At first glance, the Al Qaeda terrorists succeeded beyond their wildest dreams; they had not expected the towers to collapse, killing almost 3,000 people.[29] On a larger level, their strategy backfired. Rather than scaring the West into withdrawal, American pursuit of Islamist terrorists became the dominant theme in global security.

A War on Terror?

Nine days after 9/11, President George W. Bush declared to the U.S. Congress the opening of a "war on terror." It included elements of standard warfare, since it began with a U.S.-led invasion of Afghanistan. Yet it also suggested a kind of conflict that bore little resemblance to classic wars of the past, to the point that "war" seemed an awkward label. Rather than battlefield clashes between organized, uniformed militaries, it took the form of intelligence and police action against secretive opponents both abroad and at home.

The Afghan invasion itself began as a rather classic war and reiterated lessons from earlier wars. Afghanistan had been the direct source of the 9/11 attack, since Al Qaeda drew support from its Islamist government (known as the **Taliban**). Thus the U.S. response fell there first and foremost. The U.S.-led coalition quickly smashed the Taliban and took control of the country. As previous generations had seen in Vietnam and Americans would soon again encounter in Iraq, however, crafting a stable and friendly society was

Taliban
A radical Islamist group that ruled Afghanistan from 1996 to 2001 and now leads an insurgency against the current government.

another challenge entirely. Though the U.S. military budget swelled hugely (see Figure 12-4), stabilization of Afghan security and governance remained frustratingly difficult. Around 2007, the Taliban began to regain strength and fighting became fiercer. Despite the addition of more U.S. troops, peaking at over 100,000 in 2011, areas of the country increasingly fell under Taliban control. Much as the mujahedeen had once expelled the Soviets from their territory, so they resisted even the vast technological superiority of American forces. In the long run, exerting American military power seemed to provoke opposition as much as suppressing it.

On the other hand, the clash in Afghanistan departed in important ways from classic warfare. Only in its early phases did the invasion pit organized militaries against each other. Much of the conflict was a U.S.-led hunt for "hostiles" who melted in and out of the civilian population. New technology, too, shifted the scene away from battlefield engagement. Unmanned aerial drones emerged as the key American tool to seek and hit targets, creating scenarios more like robot policing than clashing battalions. In a territorial sense, the conflict soon lost any resemblance to war between sovereign states. Since Al Qaeda was Islamist, not actually Afghan, and also because the Taliban was based on ethnic Pashtun tribes that extend into neighboring Pakistan, the role of borders and sovereignty in the fight blurred. U.S. forces pursued their targets into Pakistan, sometimes with approval from Pakistan's government and sometimes not. One unapproved intervention was the raid that killed Osama bin Laden in a Pakistani town in May 2011.

Figure 12-4 The U.S. Defense Budget since World War II

After a post–Cold War decline, the U.S. defense budget grew rapidly in response to 9/11 even if we set aside the direct cost of the wars in Afghanistan and Iraq.

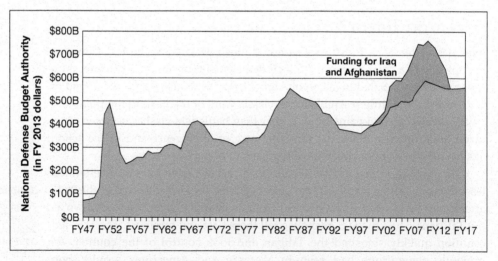

Source: Brad Plumer, "America's Staggering Defense Budget, in Charts," *Washington Post*, January 7, 2013 (data updated by *Washington Post* in 2018). Used with permission.

Even blurrier was the status of Al Qaeda and Taliban members captured by the U.S.-led coalition. They were not members of a formal military fighting an interstate war, so they did not clearly hold the rights of prisoners of war that states had negotiated in treaties like the **Geneva Conventions**. The United States largely lacked evidence that could convict them of crimes in normal courts. Unwilling to let them go or to allow them legal processes as either prisoners of war or normal criminals, the U.S. government kept them in legal no-man's-land at its naval base in Guantanamo Bay, Cuba. About 40 remain imprisoned as of June 2019.[30]

Geneva Conventions
Treaties that set rules for warfare and ban the use of chemical and biological weapons.

Just as the pursuit of terrorists blurred the lines of interstate war, so it reached into domestic life as well. The U.S. Patriot Act of 2001, like similar legislation in Great Britain following the London bombings of 2005, strengthened law enforcement agencies' ability to gather information, regulate financial transactions, and detain suspects. Intelligence and counterterrorism forces were beefed up around the world, most notably in the combination of twenty-two U.S. federal departments and agencies into the massive Department of Homeland Security. Airport security tightened, including shoe removal at checkpoints, thanks to an Afghanistan-trained terrorist who tried to detonate explosives-packed shoes on a plane in December 2001. The U.S. National Security Agency (NSA) launched a program to listen in on most of the world's telecommunications, until leaks about the secret surveillance prompted an outcry that led to new limits. Many government officials on both right and left across democratic countries have nonetheless generally defended these steps as necessary to head off threats. Critics on both right and left, meanwhile, argue that limiting rights at home means "the terrorists win"—prioritizing fear of violence over individual freedoms.[31] Of special concern to many skeptics is that governments' powers to confront terrorism may eventually be misused against their citizens.

The overall change that Islamic terrorism brought to global security was captured well by George W. Bush even before 9/11. As a presidential candidate in 2000, Bush contrasted the clear "us" versus "them" of the Cold War to the uncertainties of terrorism: "When I was [growing] up, it was a dangerous world, and you knew exactly who 'they' were," he said. "It was us versus them, and it was clear who 'them' was. Today, we are not so sure who they are, but we know they're there."[32] Not a very elegant statement, perhaps, but it sums up the landscape of security in the new millennium. Until the late twentieth century, governments' security policies had prepared for interstate war on an ever-growing scale. Terrorism had occasionally emerged as an additional challenge but never as the leading fear. With the decline of great-power tensions and the forging of a strong link between radical Islamism and terrorist tactics, the main security problem for the United States and many of its allies shifted in profound ways. We entered an era that may be far safer on average than previous periods of history, but in some ways may be more terrifying.

What remains to be seen is whether these shifts are enduring changes or passing transitions. Might prospects of large-scale war rise again? Will terrorism continue—or even grow—as an international challenge? To answer such questions, we must step beyond simple historical stories to some deeper analysis. Explanatory alternatives in political science point to different sources of violence and hint at different future scenarios.

The Roots of International Violence

12.3 **Identify four theoretical views of why people fight wars and assess the plausibility of each.**

We have seen that violence in international politics varies hugely across time and space. In earlier chapters, our surveys of varying political configurations in the world led directly into ideological debates about what is good about them—but not in this one. It is easy to debate what is good or bad about alternatives such as presidential versus parliamentary systems or different strategies for economic growth. That question is harder to answer with war or terrorism: almost no one sees them as good! Rather than arguing that violence is good, people who employ it tend to argue that it is necessary. We had compelling reasons, they say, to turn to force.

Such arguments push us quickly into debates about *why* people choose violence. Our normative judgments depend heavily on how we explain such choices. If we see human nature itself as inclining us toward violence, for example, can we blame people for acting human? Alternatively, we might trace violence to bad institutions of governance or to truly desperate material conditions, or perhaps to ideas and culture. If we argue that German culture encouraged the Nazis to launch World War II, we will judge their violence differently than if we explain them as reasonable reactions to unfortunate material challenges or bad institutions. So central are these explanatory debates to how we think about war and terrorism that this chapter features a major section on these potential roots of violence—the psychology of human nature, political institutions, ideas and culture, and the shape of the material landscape—in addition to discussion of a particular explanatory case like in other chapters (explaining the U.S. invasion of Iraq in 2003 in Section 12.5).

Human Nature and Violent Conflict

"The root of all evil is man," summarizes a famous essay on views of political violence since antiquity, "and thus he is himself the root of the specific evil, war."[33] We are, after all, "political animals," said Aristotle, and animals often resort to violence. To Mark Twain, we are even the worst of animals. Our bigger brains elevate natural inclinations into systematic slaughter: "Man is the only animal that deals in that atrocity of atrocities, war. He is the only one that gathers his brethren about him and goes forth in cold blood and calm pulse to exterminate his own kind."[34]

These old views echo powerfully in modern-day thinking about political psychology. Modern humans evolved on the African savannah, and many experts argue that the hardwired psychology we developed there shapes our actions today. Just as chimpanzee bands launch brutal raids to wipe out rival tribes (to lightly contradict Mark Twain), so humans are programmed to cluster into groups that fall into violent conflict. Psychological experiments demonstrate that we suffer in general from what psychologists call "herding" behaviors, "intergroup biases" (favoring those close to us), and "attribution bias" (seeing other people's behavior as driven by their inherent nature, but our own behavior as driven reasonably by surrounding circumstances). As a result of this irrational human hardwiring, we tend to judge people close to us as more trustworthy than others. Since we lean toward interpreting outsiders as threatening, we often feel compelled to become threatening ourselves. During the Cold War, for example, both Americans and Russians interpreted their own military buildups as defensive and the other's as designed for offensive attacks (a common dynamic known as the **security dilemma**). Radical Islamist terrorists, too, usually see their cause as centered defensively on expelling foreign influences, not on taking over the world. Americans see terrorists as bent on eradicating their freedoms and feel compelled to eradicate terrorism to defend themselves. To complete the circle, much of the world sees the "war on terror" as aggressively offensive. As the journalist and author Robert Wright summarized his view of global security problems in 2013,

> The world's biggest single problem is the failure of people or groups to look at things from the point of view of other people or groups . . . . So, for Americans, that might mean grasping that if you lived in a country occupied by American troops, or visited by American drone strikes, you might not share the assumption of many Americans that these deployments of force are well-intentioned and for the general good. You might even get bitterly resentful. You might even start hating America.[35]

So if this common failure to comprehend others' points of view is hardwired into human psychology, we may be stuck in cycles of violence. Human nature is not something we can change. We may see brief periods of peace, but conflict will return. Chances are that the United States and China will eventually become confrontational, since each will perceive the other's defensive moves as threatening. American pursuit of terrorists is similarly likely to provoke more terrorism.

Still, this view has a major weakness. Human nature offers little explanation of variations in violence across time and space. Why do wars break out here and not there? Why is major war so hard to imagine at our current moment in history? Why does terrorism arise in certain places? These questions push us toward other explanations.

security dilemma
The common problem that one group's defensive moves are seen by others as preparation for an attack.

Does basic human psychology make it difficult for us to escape violence between groups? Some of the more intractable conflicts in the world can make it seem so. Here, Israeli soldiers fire tear gas canisters at Palestinian protesters during a clash over Jewish settlements near Palestinian communities.

Governments, War, and the Democratic Peace

Might the activation or suppression of our violent tendencies depend on the institutions around us? Another tradition in the explanation of political violence also sees repressive governments as the main cause of war and terrorism. When U.S. president Woodrow Wilson called for entering World War I against Imperial Germany, he famously argued that a defensive fight was necessary to "make the world safe for democracy." Authoritarians are inherently warlike while democracies are peaceful, as he explained in a famous speech:

> Self-governed nations do not fill their neighbor states with spies or set the course of intrigue to bring about some critical posture of affairs that will give them an opportunity to strike and make conquest. Such designs can be successfully worked out only under cover and where no one has the right to ask questions . . . . They are happily impossible where public opinion commands and insists upon full information concerning all the nation's affairs.[36]

For Wilson, it was the institutional setting that permitted or prevented war. Just as authoritarian leaders seek repressive domination at home, so they tend toward aggressiveness and conquest abroad. In democracies, even bad leaders cannot get away with aggressive war plans due to open political competition and transparent information.

Several generations after Wilson's presidency, political scientists noticed an interesting pattern that gave greater weight to his views. It is known as the **democratic peace**. No full-fledged democracy has *ever* fought a war with another full-fledged democracy.[37] All wars erupted between nondemocracies or pitted nondemocracies against democracies. This observation points toward a broad explanation of why major war intensified until the mid-twentieth century and then fell off. Until World War II very few countries were democracies. The "third wave" of democratization from the 1970s through the end of the Cold War spread democratic institutions much further, creating fewer opportunities for conflict.

democratic peace
The observation that no two democracies have ever fought a war with each other.

We might also expect that authoritarianism encourages terrorism and that democracy might temper it. If people are strongly repressed and have no political voice, they may turn to desperate tactics that they would not consider in more open political organizations. So President George W. Bush suggested in 2003. He referred to democracy as "the alternative to instability and to hatred and terror," and went on: "If the greater Middle East joins the democratic revolution that has reached much of the world, the lives of millions in that region will be bettered, and a trend of conflict and fear will be ended at its source."[38] The recently launched Iraq War, he hoped, would lessen terrorism by sparking a shift from dictatorship to democracy across the region.

Unfortunately, the democracy-terrorism pattern so far does not parallel its record on interstate war. Some studies even find that democratization tends to *increase* terrorism.[39] The logic of this argument is that authoritarian governments rarely suffer from much terrorism because they stamp it out brutally. Democracies, by contrast, find their hands tied by the rule of law. Democratic political competition may also sometimes encourage terrorism, especially if radical groups fear that they may not win out in electoral contests. This has been part of the logic of Sunni terrorists in Iraq. Fearing that the Shi'a majority will always win a peaceful competition, they see violent attacks as giving them better odds.

An institutional explanation of political violence offers a mix of optimism and pessimism for future scenarios. It suggests that a world without war is at least imaginable if democracy continues to spread. Robust democratic governments may even tame risks of terrorism in the long run if they can draw all their citizens into participating peacefully. At the same time, the fact that democracy's spread is uncertain today hints at pessimism. Authoritarian China may well come into more serious conflict with the democratic United States, just as Soviet Russia did. Repressive or shaky governance in developing countries may foment terrorism for decades to come.

Culture, International Society, and Violence

Equally plausible is the notion that patterns of violence are rooted in cultural beliefs. Many societies have celebrated war. Monarchs and aristocrats across all continents long cultivated the notion that war was the most glorious pursuit. Modern nationalism raised these themes to new heights, making "dying for one's country" the highest honor. Authoritarian regimes may have trumpeted these ideas most loudly, but democratic polities joined the chorus. Around World War I, British schoolchildren still learned the Latin line "Dulce et decorum est pro patria mori" ("It is sweet and right to die for your country") and French citizens sang similar songs:

> *By the voice of the cannon France calls its children*
> *Come says the soldier, to arms!*
> *She is my mother, I defend her*
> *To die for the fatherland*
> *Is the most beautiful, most enviable fate!*[40]

Cultural beliefs also often legitimate violence by portraying certain groups as subhumans. From the Spanish extermination of Aztecs and U.S. wars against Native Americans to the Nazi genocide against Jews, racist ideas rationalized horrific violence. Such views still echo today: many observers argue that the West would not have ignored the Rwandan genocide of 1994, for example, if its victims had been white rather than black.[41] Religion has sometimes provided similar rationales. Just as Christians in the Crusades of the Middle Ages assigned no value to the life of non-Christian "infidels," so radical Islamists today often hold what are known in Islam as *takfiri* views: that they are entitled to kill non-Muslims as well as Muslims whom they see as betraying the true faith. For both the Crusaders and many radical Islamists, religious beliefs also set the reward of eternal salvation for dying in the fight against unbelief.

If certain beliefs encourage war or terrorism, others may account for peace. The idea that peaceful liberal ideas dominate our age may contribute to an alternative interpretation of the pattern of "democratic peace" and the current lack of great-power tensions. First the defeat of fascism in 1945, and later the self-destruction of communism in 1989, left the liberal tradition as the last powerful global ideology—a victory that political scientist and public commentator Francis Fukuyama provocatively (and, with hindsight, rather hastily) called "the end of history."[42] Believers in classic liberal rights, democracy, and capitalism tend to seek peaceful resolutions to conflicts, and the strength of liberal states in North America, Europe, and Japan restrains even the nondemocratic holdouts. These ideas have also encouraged the emergence of a dense "international society" that has gradually and subtly constrained how states can act. The UN, other international organizations like the International Criminal Court, and a dense complex of nongovernmental organizations (NGOs)—such as Amnesty International, Human Rights Watch, or Freedom House—pressure and shame those who launch aggressive wars, endorse terrorism, or otherwise employ violence outside of legal processes of law and order.

If international violence is rooted in ideas and culture, what should we expect in the future? That depends on whether liberal ideas continue to prevail. Democratic values, human rights, and cooperation in international institutions may have cultivated a growing space of peace and law, but China's rise, newly confident illiberalism in places like Russia, and the challenge of radical Islamism hint that we have not simply reached the "end of history." This perspective suggests that if China in particular were to move toward democratizing change in coming years, liberal principles might remain dominant and the great-power peace could endure. If not, new cold (and perhaps hot) wars may return.

Even in a world in which democratic identities and liberal principles become steadily stronger, marginalized groups will sometimes challenge the dominant ideas. Islamist radicalism and Putin's repressive rule, and to some extent the continued strength of China's Communists, are built directly on aggressive reactions to liberal-democratic power and success. These non-Western players resent what they see as the preachy, righteously liberal West with its claims to universal values, and cultivate this resentment among their supporters. A future organized around liberal ideals would likely still confront violent challengers on its cultural and geographic fringes.

Anarchy and the International Balance of Power

A final view traces the roots of international violence to the basic structure of international relations itself. From this perspective, In the absence of a world government, human groups inevitably come into conflict no matter what their psychology, institutions, or ideas are like. The core reason lies in the simple material lay of the land. In an anarchical international system—without any overarching authority or global police force—the only way for people to guarantee their own security is to assume the worst about everyone else. Not only must they be prepared to defend themselves, they must aggressively maximize their own power to make sure they stay ahead of threatening rivals. Any group that does not do so will fall prey to those who do. Like a business that must grow or be outcompeted in a tough market, states have little choice but to focus coldly on international threats and opportunities.

Known as **realism**, this structural view of international violence has cropped up across many different cultures, institutions, and historical periods. The ancient Greek historian Thucydides, the ancient Indian philosopher Kautilya, and later the Italian courtier Machiavelli all argued that power drove the wars of their day: the powerful do what they want and the weak must adapt. The English theorist Thomas Hobbes took up the same theme, arguing that politics between states, unlike politics inside states, naturally forms a violent "war of all against all." Inside states, government authority creates order, but the lack of international authority forces states into an anarchical scrabble for power to preserve their security. We are thus trapped in what political scientist John Mearsheimer calls "the tragedy of great power politics."[43] International relations have been, and always will be, a threatening game where states jockey for power and come into violent conflict.

realism
The theory that international relations is always dominated by an anarchical conflict between states.

balance of power
The distribution of military capability around the world, which realists see as shaping how states act in any given era.

Within its overarching view that international violence is inevitable, realism also offers an explanation of variations in war over time. The global **balance of power** can take a variety of shapes, some of which may bring temporary peace. In a multipolar international system, when multiple states hold enough power to threaten each other, major war tends to come fairly quickly. Each state is threatened from several directions, often leading to rapidly shifting alliances, uncertainty, and pressure on leaders to strike aggressively before the balance shifts against them. Realists see these kinds of conditions as the main causes of both world wars. In a bipolar international system, when two states occupy very dominant positions—like the United States and the USSR during the Cold War—an uncomfortable peace is more likely.[44] Both great powers can focus carefully on the sole rival capable of threatening them; shifting alliances or changes in smaller countries' capabilities are not significant enough to destabilize the balance. Peace can also arise in a unipolar system dominated by one superpower that acts as a **hegemon**: a dominant power who polices the weaker players.[45] For realists, then, neither institutions nor ideas account for the great-power peace since World War II. Bipolarity led to a tense peace in the Cold War. Ever since the USSR fell, American-dominated unipolarity has kept major war off the scene. The salience of international terrorism is largely a consequence of unipolar dominance: America's far weaker challengers can do little other than employ such desperate tactics.

hegemon
A state that becomes so powerful that it dominates the world (or at least its region).

This rather grim perspective implies pessimism for the future. If an international "war of all against all" is inevitable, we are indeed only in an odd phase of history before great-power conflict returns. Unipolar systems, say realists, tend not to be durable.[46] The hegemonic power tends to expend huge resources in policing the world, and rising states will seek to challenge its leadership. The United States' political in-fighting and failed interventions, together with China's rapid growth, lend some credence to this scenario. Realists predict that the United States and China will fall into the "Thucydides trap," replaying the power struggles of Athens and Sparta in ways that make them "destined for war."[47] The prospect of major war, or at least another global Cold War, will return. Such global tension will eclipse the importance of terrorism, even if it remains an annoyance.

Table 12-3 sums up these alternative explanatory views of the roots of political violence. In the next section, we consider war and terrorism from the viewpoint of alternative ideologies. As we have seen, these different explanatory views of war and terrorism may be even more heavily entangled with normative judgments than the analytic-normative overlaps we see on other political subjects. Our gut leanings on these contrasting analytic theories tend to reinforce certain normative judgments of how and when war or terrorism are legitimate—and our normative leanings about "good guys" and "bad guys" steer us toward certain analytic theories. Political ideological debates on war and terrorism thus combine these two modes of normative and analytic explanations very deeply.

Table 12-3 Summing Up Alternative Explanations of Political Violence

Category of Explanation	Arguments in These Categories That Explain Political Violence	Why violence?	Historical Examples That Could Support Each Argument	Possible Challenges
Rational-Materialist	The most influential example in this category is the international relations theory known as realism.	When the distribution of power is not balanced between two sides (which is usually the case in a multipolar system), some players will think they can get away with aggression.	The landscape of many powerful states before World War I and World War II made it unclear who would respond (and how) to aggression, encouraging some states' risky choices to launch these two wars; the bipolar world after World War II brought a balanced stability.	Do all states and leaders really perceive and respond to the distribution of power similarly, regardless of their institutions and ideologies?
Institutional	The most prominent example is the "democratic peace" argument.	Without open and transparent institutions, leaders can make selfish or irrational decisions. In democracies, where more people have a voice, more common preferences for peace tend to prevail.	The Nazis' attacks that started World War II, the Argentinian dictatorship's aggression in the Falklands War of 1984, or Iraq's invasion of Kuwait in 1990 all display authoritarians launching wars for their own purposes.	Are democracies really so peaceful? Can't leaders in democracies whip up enthusiasm for war?
Ideational	This category includes a wide range of arguments about nationalism or aggressive ideologies.	Some cultures or ideologies prioritize conflict and portray violence as legitimate.	Major wars in modern history tend to include strong nationalism or clashes of ideologies (fascism, communism, etc.). With the global dominance of liberal thinking since the end of the Cold War, prospects of major war seem to have evaporated.	Don't even the most extreme nationalists or ideologues pay some attention to the international distribution of power?
Psychological	This includes arguments about "herding," "intergroup bias," "attribution error," and other irrational patterns in perception.	Human beings are hardwired to get into group conflict.	In the Cold War, the Middle East today, and across history, people have fallen easily into "security dilemmas" where their concern with defending themselves threatens other groups (and vice versa).	Basic human psychology doesn't vary across history, but political violence varies a great deal across time and places.

Political Ideologies and International Violence

12.4 Evaluate competing arguments about the just use of political violence.

Can war be just? Probably. Few would dispute the morality of fighting against an evil tyrant like Hitler. How about terrorism? Targeting noncombatants seems like quite a moral stretch. Perhaps, though, we could see terrorism as legitimate for truly desperate people under assault by enemies as bad as the Nazis.

Still, most decisions to employ violence lack the moral clarity of self-defense against a genocidal war machine bent on world domination. Consider, for example, the U.S.-led war in Afghanistan. Most of the world endorsed the invasion after 9/11. As the conflict dragged on, moral criticisms escalated, especially over drone attacks that look much like assassinations. To take an even tougher example, most of the world interpreted the U.S. attack on Iraq in 2003 as illegitimate aggression. Our own moral compass need not follow world opinion, certainly, but these conflicts and the "war on terror" raise thorny questions. To work out our principles about them, we can draw on some established ideological positions about violence and security.

All Is Fair in Love and War

In the contexts of love and war—contexts where we may be vulnerable to devastating psychological or physical pain—the old saying suggests that we do whatever we must to protect ourselves. To do otherwise is naïve. Stricter moral codes may seem nice, but the loser of a war may not be around to enforce strong morals. Severe threats may call for hitting first and asking questions later. At an extreme, ruthless tactics like torture may be necessary to defeat the advocates of *worse* torture.

The more we see the world as a threatening place, the more these views seem persuasive. Two ways of explaining international violence tend to encourage such positions. One is to see at least some people as culturally bent on violence. If we think our main threats come from ideological Nazis or suicidal religious fanatics, we may conclude that drastic measures are unavoidable to defend ourselves. The other route is to interpret threats of violence simply as inevitable parts of our world. If violence is deeply rooted in either human nature or the anarchical landscape of international politics, as realists theorize, we may have little choice but to prioritize a strong defense. No matter what morals we hold dear, other groups will eventually threaten us. On some occasions the best defense may even be offense—striking preemptively before a devastating attack.

Fascist thinking combines these points to portray a stark choice between dominating and being dominated. In the paranoid world of Hitler or Mussolini, many groups were ideologically out to get them: rich Jews, communists, big business, liberals. Beyond any particular ideological threat, they also saw politics as fundamentally about a violent contest for power. Given this analysis, it became both prudent and moral to launch aggressive attacks on threatening neighbors. At the other political extreme, the most revolutionary socialists like Lenin or Stalin argued that the material landscape of economic exploitation made violence inevitable. The capitalist system would continue to oppress workers everywhere until it was smashed in revolutionary war.

We cannot let extremists tar all such thinking as illegitimate, however, because moderate versions arise in the liberal tradition itself. Especially from modern conservatives we often hear that defending a good society requires strong security policies. For some conservatives, especially among the religious Right, the main reason is cultural: they see a fairly black-and-white world where evil beliefs threaten good ones. For others, the key logic is more realist: international politics is a raw game of power in which we must play hardball. Either way, most conservatives see a powerful military as a high priority.

In fact, most conservatives see the military, together with internal security forces like police and prisons, as the *only* government policies that should be large and well funded. Their calls for strong steps to confront a threatening world are linked to their views that other government action should be minimized. Both rest on the conservative notion that people tend to be fairly weak and sometimes wicked. Weak or wicked people will corrupt most policy interventions into waste, so government should not attempt to remake society in economic and social affairs. Weak or wicked people at home and abroad will also threaten others, so government must defend actively against external threats and enforce internal order.

In their strongest formulations, these views come close to a broad statement that the ends justify the means. Defending our values and safety in a threatening world may require aggressive tactics. U.S. use of nuclear bombs in 1945 followed this logic: by forcing Japan to surrender without a long, drawn-out invasion, a horrible evil served the greater good. A similar logic became known as the "Bush Doctrine" in the early "war on terror," when a U.S. National Security Strategy document argued for "preventive wars" before opponents become active threats:

> We must be prepared to stop rogue states and their terrorist clients before they are able to threaten or use weapons of massive destruction against the United States and our allies and friends … Given the goals of rogue states and terrorists, the United States can no longer solely rely on a reactive posture as we have in the past.[48]

Around the same time, internal debates arose in the Bush administration over arguments for legalizing certain forms of torture in interrogations of terrorists.[49] For its proponents, harsh steps were regrettably unavoidable to defend against a secretive and implacable enemy. Precisely because we treasure our liberal-democratic rights, they suggested, we must sometimes do whatever it takes to defeat their opponents.

Fighting Only the Good Fight: Just Wars

On the other hand, we might try to stick to the moral high ground. Peace activists around the world make the case that we cannot give in to violence, echoing Jesus's advice to "turn the other cheek." Though few politicians in modern democracies subscribe to full-blown pacifism, many agree that we should place strong moral bounds on the use of force. International violence should be framed as much as possible, they argue, within moral and legal limits.

Ever since Roman times, political thinkers have tried to define morally acceptable limits on "just war." Even Jesus was not advocating suicide, after all; if we expect that the other cheek will just get punched—or worse—we may need to defend ourselves. We may also feel responsible for someone else's cheek: violent threats against the innocent or weak may require responses in kind. Arguments about "just war" typically build on these ideas of self-defense and protection of innocents. One influential formulation is in the Catechism of the Catholic Church adopted in 1992:

- Use of force can be legitimate only in self-defense or to protect the innocent.
- The damage inflicted by the aggressor . . . must be lasting, grave, and certain.
- All other means . . . must have been shown to be impractical or ineffective.
- There must be serious prospects of success.
- The use of arms must not produce evils and disorders graver than the evil to be eliminated.[50]

Support for standards of just war tend to be built on beliefs about the potential for progress in human societies. The more plausible it is that we can construct a better future, the more it makes sense for us to restrain our own behavior in hopes of achieving that progress. For the pope, as for a variety of other religious leaders, such progress may come about through the spread of religious beliefs.

More widespread in contemporary politics, though, is the Enlightenment version of this thinking displayed in modern liberalism and social democracy. These traditions parted ways with the thinking that gave rise to modern conservatism in taking a more positive view of human nature. Human nature is generally good, they suggested, and bad behavior and violence are mainly the result of poorly designed institutions in government and society. Enlightened change to better government can bring peace—perhaps even to the whole world if good institutions spread far enough. Repressive authoritarian governance can turn people toward violence, leading them to extreme ideas—such as fascism or destructive strands of radical Islamism—against which, on occasion, progressive societies may need to defend themselves. If they operate within clear moral standards of just war, however, they will eventually demonstrate the advantages of better governance to the holdouts and skeptics.

In concrete terms, this hope for progress leads modern liberals and social democrats to advocate for government action that is roughly the opposite of what conservatives tend to suggest. Some funding for the military and internal security are certainly necessary, but ideally security policies should take a back seat to an emphasis on education, the fight against poverty, combating environmental problems, and other government action to build a better society. The more clearly we can signal a defensive posture and an emphasis on international cooperation, the more likely it is that other countries or hostile groups will come around to accepting peaceful relationships. From this viewpoint, the conservative priority on defense risks feeding violence rather than lessening it, especially if coupled with aggressive tactics like preventive war or torture.

To draw a contrast to the "Bush doctrine," these themes were central to a major speech by the next U.S. president, Barack Obama, when he called for an end to the "war on terror." In responding to 9/11, he said, the United States went too far:

> In some cases, I believe we compromised our basic values—by using torture to interrogate our enemies, and detaining individuals in a way that ran counter to the rule of law. . . . From our use of drones to the detention of terrorist suspects, the decisions we are making will define the type of nation—and world—that we leave to our children.[51]

Conservatives responded that Obama's liberal sentiment, while nice, was naïve and dangerous in a threatening world. "It is a nice thought, the end of war," wrote conservative columnist Kathleen Parker, but ". . . the war on terror is not over and saying so won't make it so."[52] Another pundit, Ben Stein, used stronger words: "Peace, while the other side is still attacking, is not peace. It is surrender."[53] The debate neatly displays how analyses of threats and normative ideologies combine to inform debates about war and terrorism today.

Is One Man's Terrorist Another Man's Freedom Fighter?

Most people around the world agree that terrorism is morally repugnant. They may disagree, however, about what counts as terrorism. The more we sympathize with a political cause, and the more we perceive its fight as a desperate one against powerful and evil enemies, the more we may think terrorist-style tactics may sometimes be legitimate. Might it be plausible, as an Irish terrorist says in a 1975 thriller, that "one man's terrorist is another man's freedom fighter"?[54]

We have seen that defining terrorism is difficult. Consider an exchange back in 1989 between U.S. congressman Lee Hamilton and Ned Walker, deputy assistant secretary of state in Middle East affairs about the Palestinian Liberation Organization (PLO):

HAMILTON: Well, how do you define terrorism? Do you define it in terms of non-combatance?

WALKER: The State Department definition which is included in the terrorism report annually defines it in terms of politically motivated attacks on non-combatant targets.

HAMILTON: So an attack on a military unit in Israel will not be terrorism?

WALKER: It does not necessarily mean that it would not have a very major impact on whatever we were proposing to do with the PLO.

HAMILTON: I understand that, but it would not be terrorism.

WALKER: An attack on a military target. Not according to the definition. Now wait a minute; that is not quite correct. You know, attacks can be made on military targets which clearly are terrorism. It depends on the individual circumstances.

HAMILTON:	Now wait a minute. I thought that you just gave me the State Department definition.
WALKER:	"Non-combatant" is the terminology, not "military" or "civilian."
HAMILTON:	All right. So any attack on a non-combatant could be terrorism?
WALKER:	That is right.
HAMILTON:	And a non-combatant could include military?
WALKER:	Of course.
HAMILTON:	It certainly would include civilian, right?
WALKER:	Right.
HAMILTON:	But an attack on a military unit would not be terrorism?
WALKER:	It depends on the circumstances.
HAMILTON:	And what are those circumstances?
WALKER:	I do not think it will be productive to get into a description of the various terms and conditions under which we are going to define an act by the PLO as terrorism.[55]

When we set such ambiguity alongside wartime massacres of noncombatants it may seem even harder to denounce terrorism as especially immoral. The total wars of the twentieth century included massive attacks on civilians, pounding cities into dust. Often these attacks were clearly intended not just to destroy military-related capabilities but to terrorize the population. Would-be suicide bombers today may make such parallels to claim that they are just as morally righteous as a World War II bomber pilot.

Is there a way out of such dilemmas? The simple position is to hold that any violence that targets noncombatants is immoral. For a more nuanced view, thinking about "just wars" may provide some moral guidance through this confusion. Like with formal wars, we could argue that the morality of terrorizing violence off the battlefield depends on its purpose, the nature of the threat, and reasonable expectations that the violence will succeed. To imagine a limiting case of "just terrorism," picture an attack on Earth by aliens with vastly superior technology and a total disregard for human life. Our militaries are defeated. The only hope for survivors lies in driving the aliens away through terrorist-style attacks—even suicidal ones—on their settlements. This sounds like a movie where many people would cheer for terrorists.

Some radical Islamists today probably picture themselves in this script with Westerners and Israelis in the alien role—but if so, they are not applying just-wars thinking very plausibly. In their situation, each step in the moral calculation is debatable (to say the least). They may perceive their purpose as self-defense against foreign invaders, but in a case like bin Laden's, objections to U.S. influence in his native Saudi Arabia are not about self-defense in any normal meaning. Other options are generally available to negotiate with their opponents. And as we have seen since 9/11, they have little chance of success. Their terrorism is more likely to increase Western involvement in their societies than to drive it out. Even if we find it difficult to draw abstract moral lines around terrorism in general, we can make clear judgments that real cases of terrorism are morally indefensible.

Explaining a Case: Understanding the Whys of the 2003 Invasion of Iraq

12.5   Identify multiple plausible explanations for the Iraq War of 2003.

We have seen that the explanatory stories we tell about international violence massively influence our political judgments about it. To make that point more concretely, consider alternative ways to explain one prominent case of launching a war. On March 20, 2003, the United States and a coalition of allies invaded Iraq and quickly toppled the government of dictator Saddam Hussein. At the time, the U.S. government under President George W. Bush justified the invasion in terms of structural threats to U.S. security. Intelligence sources ostensibly suggested that Iraqi programs to produce chemical, biological, or even nuclear WMD could soon threaten the United States or its allies. But this claim was contested at the time—earlier inspections by personnel of the UN had not found any WMD—and after the invasion, it was clear that there were no substantial WMD in Iraq. This sparked a huge debate, which continues today: why did U.S. leaders launch a war that cost over 4,000 American lives, over 100,000 others, and more than $1 trillion of the U.S. budget?

The Rational-Material Story

The most widely believed story about the invasion, probably, is that it reflected the importance of oil in the international balance of power. Iraqi weapons were actually not much of a threat to the United States or its allies, but maintaining U.S. access to oil in and around Iraq was crucial. Iraq ranks fifth on the list of largest oil reserves by country. More than half of the world's oil reserves are found in the Middle East region around Iraq. The United States is a major importer of oil, and the smooth running of the American economy depends on that flow. The Iraqi government of Saddam Hussein was uncooperative and made access to important oil reserves uncertain, so the United States eventually invaded Iraq to secure its own dominant global position.

The Institutional Story

An institutional approach traces the invasion to the organization of American government. Besides broad tension between American democracy and authoritarian Iraq, a closer look suggests that U.S. electoral institutions encouraged the invasion. When President Bush beat his Democratic rival Al Gore in the 2000 election, Gore actually received more votes. Bush won because the Electoral College that elects presidents somewhat overrepresents rural areas that tend to be conservative. Bush's chief electoral strategist, Karl Rove, argued that Republicans could win future elections mainly by better mobilizing their conservative "base." Those voters—who live more in rural areas and especially the South and Midwest—tend to favor a strong military and tough foreign policy. In emphasizing the possible Iraqi WMD threat and then invading, says this view, U.S. leaders were thinking mostly about winning more votes in the institutional game at home. Had different electoral institutions existed, these incentives could have run in other directions.

The Ideational Story

Another very common story about the invasion reflects the distinctive ideology of certain American leaders. "So why did we invade Iraq?" writes Senator Chuck Hagel (a Republican who was usually allied with President Bush). "I believe it was the triumph of the so-called neo-conservative ideology."[56] Hagel suggests that key members of the Bush team, such as Vice President Dick Cheney and Secretary of Defense Donald Rumsfeld, shared the neoconservative view that the United States should invade and rebuild Iraq in the U.S. image. The core of Hagel's story—which many have echoed—is that these beliefs were distinctly *not* shared by many other people in the U.S. government at the time (including other Republicans like Hagel). This explanatory story suggests that the United States invaded Iraq only because we happened to have a set of leaders who held a certain very specific interpretation of the world around them.

The Psychological Story

When explaining choices made by a small number of individuals—President Bush and his close advisers—psychological explanation can often provide a plausible fourth story. In this case, observers have often remarked on the fact that President George W. Bush and his most loyal advisers were personally eager to attack Saddam Hussein because he had defied, insulted, and even tried to assassinate the previous Bush family president, George H.W. Bush. If we reason that human beings often have strong psychological reactions when members of their family are threatened, we can argue that the invasion happened partly because the younger Bush followed his father as president. A different president, even from the same party, would not have had the same psychological baggage and might not have pushed for the invasion.

When we consider these explanatory options in light of debates between the American political parties, it becomes clear how heavily explanatory analysis can be entangled with political ideology. Conservatives who are sympathetic to President Bush will lean toward a rational-material explanation, perhaps, that casts the invasion as necessary given the lay of the land. They might accept that electoral rules mattered, since politicians have little choice but to play that game. Liberals who tend to criticize President Bush may lean toward an ideational explanation, portraying the war as an ideological crusade, or as a psychological story of family loyalty.

Table 12-4 Exploring Within-Case Evidence for Alternative Explanations of the Invasion of Iraq

	Rational-Material Explanation	Institutional Explanation	Ideational Explanation	Psychological Explanation
What were the main arguments policymakers made privately for the invasion?	The American economy, and especially the well-being of oil-related sectors, were gravely threatened by Iraqi influence over Middle Eastern oil supplies.	Conservative voters expect a tough foreign policy from their president; the administration would suffer politically if it allowed a dictatorial, Middle Eastern regime to defy it in the wake of 9/11.	Especially in the context of the "War on Terror" since 9/11, the United States can and should use its military power to defeat its enemies and to build new governments on American principles.	Saddam Hussein had defied, insulted, and threatened President George H.W. Bush; his son had to finish the job his father had begun in the first Gulf War of 1990.
Who pushed hardest for the invasion?	Interest groups linked to oil, and economic policymakers concerned about overall stability and economic growth	Political party strategists who saw a quick, forceful war as a way to help mobilize the most conservative Republican base	Politicians and policy experts who had previously made clear their distinctive "neoconservative" views of foreign policy	Bush family loyalists, and especially figures who played earlier roles in the George H.W. Bush administration
Who in the United States opposed the invasion (besides pacifist types who would always oppose invasions)?	Critics of the oil industry, and possibly military officials or security experts who argued that Iraq presented no immediate security threats	Military officials or security experts who argued that there were no immediate security threats; also economic officials or experts who argued that Saddam Hussein was not likely to greatly affect access to oil supplies, or that other policies could contain him	More traditional conservatives who tended to be wary of foreign intervention except when absolutely necessary; also military and economic officials who doubted the military or economic rationale for invasion	Other people in the administration who had weaker personal ties to the Bush family: Republican party officials, military officials and experts, or economic party officials who were skeptical of the electoral, military, or economic benefits of invasion
Best Evidence to Support Each Explanation	The more closely people in and outside government were tied to oil interests, the more they supported the invasion.	The more directly people were responsible for Republican domestic political strategy, the more they supported the invasion.	The more people in or outside government were previously identified with neoconservative views, the more they supported the invasion.	The more tightly people in and outside government were personal friends and loyalists of the Bush family, the more they supported the invasion.

Political scientists would organize research on the Iraq War with the same two broad empirical research strategies they use on other subjects:

RESEARCH ON WITHIN-CASE PROCESSES. If we want to know why the Bush administration launched the Iraq War, one strategy is to find out as much as we can about their pressures, incentives, intentions, and decision-making process. We would read all possible sources in published work, seek out government documents if they are available, and interview relevant people who were willing to talk about it. Table 12-4 sketches within-case evidence that could support each explanation.

Find a new article about the Iraq War from a credible newspaper, magazine, or website and look for facts that seem to fit best with one version of the story.

RESEARCH ON CROSS-CASE PATTERNS.   Alternatively or additionally, we can look at the outbreak of other wars (or choices not to go to war) and whether they suggest a pattern around the 2003 invasion. If we look at all U.S. military interventions since World War II, for example (and perhaps interventions by other countries), where have they been and how did they relate to concrete military threats or economic incentives? How were they timed relative to national elections, and did the top leader's party appear to gain electorally from military action? Can we see a pattern in which interventions take place under top leaders with certain kinds of ideological views? Data on all these possibilities can be difficult to gather, but your instructor may be able to help you find data to explore some of these possible cross-case correlations.

Conclusion: Why Understanding Political Violence Matters to You

Violence sets some deep limits on politics. When threatened with pain or death we care less about other things. Politics is powerfully shaped by the evolution of patterns of violence across history and our interpretations of them today.

In every era, people tend to think that the violence they confront is especially horrible. There is no shortage of nastiness on our contemporary scene. The threat of international terrorism reaches into our lives in ways that more ordered interstate war rarely did. No day goes by without news of atrocities in the chaotic civil wars that bedevil many fragmented societies. Overall, the potential destructiveness of humankind continues to increase. We still hold gigantic stockpiles of nuclear bombs. The increasing sophistication of drones and other computer-guided armaments lends itself to all sorts of futuristic nightmares.

In the long view, though, we may have reasons for hope. Great-power tensions remain at a historic low. If many local wars persist around the world, few threaten to expand to broader conflicts, and the number of wars has fallen since its 1991 peak. One of the reasons we can give so much attention to relatively low casualties from rare terrorist attacks, frankly, is because we face no threats of broader war. The lack of broader organized conflict brings no comfort to the victims of those attacks, of course, nor to those who bear the brunt of today's localized wars. But it certainly matters for how we understand our lives and our future overall.

Review of Learning Objectives

12.1   **Explain how wars today, and the prospect of war, differ from patterns of political violence in the past.**

Over the centuries, wars became rarer but more intense. As political organization and technology advanced, constant clashes between smallish groups gave way to less frequent but larger wars between states. This process culminated in the two world wars of the twentieth century. Then the invention of nuclear weapons appeared to make warfare as big as it could be—threatening the whole planet—and also as rare: no war has been fought between major powers since 1945. Within a

"Cold War" nuclear standoff between the United States and the USSR, however, a number of smaller conflicts became fairly common, often as proxy wars among the superpowers. Next, even the "cold" threat of major war seemed to evaporate with the USSR's disintegration in 1991, but a new wave of small wars burst out within poor, unstable countries. Today the threat of major war seems remote, despite tensions around a rising China, but many "hot" civil wars rage in poorer countries.

12.2 Identify the distinctive features of terrorism and explain why it is so salient in our era.

The notion of pursuing political goals by terrorizing adversaries with sudden, almost random destruction—terrorism—was fittingly invented by nineteenth-century anarchists who opposed all large-scale government and social organization. It became a pervasive global issue only at the end of the twentieth century. The rising movement of fundamentalist Islam came to see terrorist strategies as promising, and declining fears of major-power war made it possible to see terrorism as the dominant security concern of the new millennium—especially once Al Qaeda launched its strike on the United States on September 11, 2001. Today most of the world's citizens do not face strong prospects of major war, but many fear sudden terrorist strikes at unlikely places and times.

12.3 Identify four theoretical views of why people fight wars and assess the plausibility of each.

Some of the oldest debates about politics focus on the roots of violence. For some, its source is human nature. Evolution has left us hardwired to identify with people around us and fear outsiders, and we easily fall into conflict. Yet this psychological view cannot tell us why the frequency of violence varies so much across history. Another argument traces violence to institutions. Hierarchical, authoritarian, oppressively organized groups tend toward conflict; open, transparent, democratic groups tend toward peace. This notion is supported by the historical observation that democracies have almost never fought with each other. A third view sees violence as a cultural phenomenon. People who are taught to glorify violence and the superiority of their own people—as most have been across history!—tend to be warlike. The rise of human rights and a more law-governed, cosmopolitan world in the past half century explains why major war has left the scene. Lastly, the most dominant view in studies of war sees international violence as a rational reaction to the structure of the global landscape. In an international arena with no central authority, all rational people must safeguard their security first and foremost. War breaks out when people's positions in the balance of power make it look like their best option.

12.4 Evaluate competing arguments about the just use of political violence.

To what extent can political violence be moral, and under what circumstances? In broad terms, conservatives tend to be more ready to use military means than liberals for two reasons. First is that conservatives tend to see the world as somewhat more threatening. Most conservatives view human nature in rather pessimistic terms: at least some people are inherently bad and dangerous. Second is that conservatives are more skeptical of the possibilities for progress in human societies. Just as police and prisons will always be necessary for domestic security, so a strong military and occasional wars will always be necessary internationally. For liberals, a more positive view of human nature and greater optimism for progress tends to place a priority on diplomacy and international cooperation over military action. From this viewpoint, we should fight the most "just wars" only out of self-defense or protection of innocents. Neither conservatives nor liberals ever consciously endorse terrorism—deliberately taking civilian lives is the terrain of radical Islamists, and possibly fascists or extreme environmentalists—though under extraordinarily dire circumstances such mainstream thinkers might support terrorist acts.

12.5   Identify multiple plausible explanations for the Iraq War of 2003.

To review for this objective, brainstorm rational-material, institutional, ideational, and psychological explanations of the Iraq invasion without looking at Section 12.5. Begin by asking yourself the following questions:

- What basic material interests might the United States have in the Middle East, and why might it appear rationally necessary to intervene militarily in that region?
- From an institutional point of view, are there ways in which the political "rules of the game" in American politics might have given the Republican administration of George W. Bush incentives to favor an invasion?
- To take an ideational approach, what distinctive ideological beliefs in and around the Bush administration might have made an invasion seem desirable?
- From a psychological standpoint, what unusual psychological stakes might President George W. Bush and his close allies have perceived in the long-running U.S. conflict with Iraqi dictator Saddam Hussein?

After imagining your answers to these questions, return to Section 12.5 to see how well you have constructed plausible alternatives to explain this case.

Great Sources to Find Out More

Bruce Russett, *Grasping the Democratic Peace: Principles for a Post–Cold War World* (Princeton, NJ: Princeton University Press, 1994). An argument that democracies have built-in conflict-resolving mechanisms that promote international peace.

Fred Kaplan, *Daydream Believers: How a Few Grand Ideas Wrecked American Power* (Hoboken, NJ: Wiley, 2008). This very critical but well-researched account of the Bush administration's foreign policy comes from a Pulitzer Prize–winning journalist at *Slate* magazine.

Graham Allison, *Destined for War: America, China, and the Thucydides' Trap* (New York: Houghton Mifflin, 2017). A provocative realist analysis that predicts war between the U.S. and China in the medium term.

John Lewis Gaddis, *The Cold War: A New History* (New York: Penguin, 2005). An overarching account by one of the best-known historians of the Cold War.

John Mearsheimer, *The Tragedy of Great Power Politics* (New York: Norton, 2003). A pure statement of realist thinking about war and power.

Marc Sageman, *Leaderless Jihad: Terror Networks in the Twenty-First Century* (Philadelphia: University of Pennsylvania Press, 2008). A close study of data and some surprising conclusions about Islamic terrorist groups.

Martha Finnemore, *The Purpose of Intervention: Changing Beliefs about the Use of Force* (Ithaca, NY: Cornell University Press, 2004). A fascinating look at how norms and patterns of military intervention have changed over time.

Michael Burleigh, *Blood & Rage: A Cultural History of Terrorism* (New York: HarperCollins, 2009). A sweeping and well-written account of terrorism since the nineteenth century.

Michael Howard, *War in European History* (New York: Oxford University Press, 1976). A brief and readable classic history of European warfare.

Philip Bobbitt, *Terror and Consent: The Wars for the Twenty-First Century* (New York: Knopf, 2008). A sophisticated call for a robust but legally framed response to terrorism.

Richard McGregor, *Asia's Reckoning: China, Japan, and the Fate of U.S. Power in the Pacific Century* (New York: Penguin, 2017). A breakdown of Asian geopolitics by a longtime political journalist.

Robert F. Kennedy, *Thirteen Days: A Memoir of the Cuban Missile Crisis* (New York: Norton, 1999 [1969]). A gripping account written by President John F. Kennedy's brother and attorney general.

Rory Stewart and Gerald Knaus, *Can Intervention Work?* (New York: Norton, 2011). A careful dissection of the ethics and effectiveness of military intervention.

Stephen Rosen, *War and Human Nature* (Princeton, NJ: Princeton University Press, 2005). An analysis of how human psychology disposes us to war in certain ways.

Develop Your Thinking

Use these questions as discussion or short writing exercises to think more deeply about some of the key themes of the chapter.

1. How likely is major war in your lifetime? If it is imaginable, where might it happen?
2. What do you think is the most common and fundamental cause of wars in history?
3. Would you rather live with a threat of terrorism or a threat of major war?
4. Is there really such thing as a "just war"? If so, do few or many wars qualify?
5. What do you suspect is the main reason why the United States invaded Iraq in 2003?
6. In the year 2100, will life be more peaceful or more violent than today? Why?

Keywords

anarchism   420
balance of power   432
bipolar   408
Cold War   409
conscription   406
conventional weapons   409
democratic peace   429
deterrence   409
ethnic cleansing   416
First Gulf War   417
Geneva Conventions   425
genocide   417

guerrilla warfare   411
hegemon   432
humanitarian crisis   416
mercenaries   405
mujahedeen   422
multipolar   408
mutually assured destruction (MAD)   409
North Atlantic Treaty Organization (NATO)   408
nuclear winter   410
pacifism   407

proxy wars   410
realism   431
Second Gulf War   417
security dilemma   427
Taliban   423
Terrorism   419
unipolar   412
Warsaw pact   408
weapons of mass destruction (WMD)   417

Chapter 13
Globalization and Governance

Lu Bo'an/Xinhua/Alamy Stock Photo

What has changed as a result of "globalization"? We see hints of its impact in this Chinese coat hanger factory—one of over 100 such factories in the same part of southwest China, just for coat hangers—where workers do the kind of semiskilled manufacturing jobs that are hard to find in the United States today. Is globalization good for these Chinese workers? Is it good for the Americans who buy the coat hangers, but no longer make them? Overall, should we see these economic shifts as a political triumph for openness, exchange, cheaper goods, and a cooperative world—or as something more worrisome?

 Learning Objectives

13.1 Identify the main ways in which globalization has changed economic patterns in the past fifty years.

13.2 Identify several reasons for the growth of international law and international organizations, and cite influential examples in both areas.

13.3   Assess who has gained or lost economically from globalization and evaluate how this has affected democracy at the national level.

13.4   Evaluate competing arguments about the costs and benefits of globalization.

13.5   Identify multiple plausible explanations for the American shift away from supporting open trade.

Is a "Flatter" World Better?

New York Times columnist Thomas Friedman tells a story about meeting Nandan Nilekani, the Indian software billionaire, back in the early 2000s.[1] First, they toured the ultramodern facilities of Infosys, the company Nilekani cofounded that sells brainpower to Western firms online: software design, medical evaluations, accounting, you name it. Then Nilekani summed up what he was seeing: "Tom," he said, "the playing field is being leveled."

He meant that technology and economic flows—globalization, in a word—were eroding old hierarchies. North America and Europe were once rich enclaves whose businesses faced little global competition. They bought (or took) raw resources from other countries and sold higher-value products and services everywhere. Today, firms in China, India, Brazil, and other developing countries compete with them across the board. Western firms also increasingly "outsource" or "offshore" work to them. Big differences remain between rich and poor countries, but they share more of a single playing field. In Friedman's pithy phrase, "The world is flat."

With a flatter world economy come some flatter politics too. Powerful states that once decided their own fates now consult about many decisions within international institutions. Big countries still dominate the scene—the United States above all—but their decision making increasingly operates within a web of international rules. In the remarkable case of the European Union (EU), a powerful regional organization integrates twenty-eight states and half a billion citizens.

Is a globalized world a better one? Dominant views in most places portray it as bringing wider opportunities, greater innovation, and more cooperation. Yet even Friedman worries that global competition may not be good for everyone. In particular, it may harm the most disadvantaged citizens—those least able to compete. Worsening inequality in most countries poses questions about which playing fields are really being leveled. Western democracies could also lose the competition more broadly, surrendering their leading global position. Democracy could weaken as decision making withdraws into distant international institutions. For some, then, globalization is more threatening than promising. Donald Trump's election as U.S. president gave new voice to these concerns, shifting the United States government from its traditional role on globalization from champion to critic.

This book's recipe for critical thinking on these questions is now familiar: we must begin from a sense of political alternatives. We must see how globalization has changed politics over time and confront contrasting ideological and explanatory views of these evolutions. ∎

The Changing International Political Economy

13.1 **Identify the main ways in which globalization has changed economic patterns in the past fifty years.**

globalization
Rising flows of goods, services, money, people, and ideas across borders.

Globalization is a phenomenon of rising flows of goods, services, money, people, and ideas across national borders. Critical thinking about it must begin from a concrete picture of the economic changes at its core. Flows of trade, investment, and money across borders have been growing for a long time. They reached a previous peak before World War I—often called the "first era of globalization"—but then ebbed as national economies became more separate through the world wars (see Figure 13-1). We pick up the story after World War II, when today's bigger wave of globalization began to build. If we contrast "before" and "after" pictures of this wave—contrasting economic patterns before it began to crest, around 1960, with those of today—globalization's effects stand out sharply.[2]

Three main contrasts before the first era of globalization and after the second era of globalization tell the fuller economic story:

- *Trade:* The most visible change is the growth of international trade. As more goods traveled internationally, economic opportunities shifted around the world.

Figure 13-1 The First and Second Eras of Globalization

World trade rose into the early twentieth century. It started falling in Europe in World War I (1913) and fell worldwide as of the Great Depression (1929). After 1950, global trade recovered rapidly and began a steady rise into the era we know as globalization.

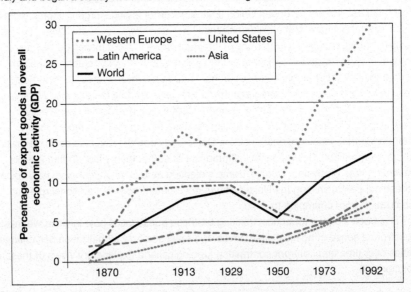

Source: Jean-Yves Huwart and Loïc Verdier, *Economic Globalisation: Origins and Consequences* (Paris: OECD, 2013), p. 46.

- *Foreign direct investment:* A bit harder to see, but even more important, is globalized investment. Expansion in direct investments across borders—such as owning factories—has enabled much deeper economic changes.

- *Globalized money:* The third shift is the globalization of financial markets. Global flows of money have reached a gargantuan scale, bringing new opportunities and new risks.

We examine each of these shifts—in trade, foreign direct investment, and globalized money—in the sections that follow.

Trade

International trade is nothing new. It has shaped economies and polities for centuries. Several decades ago, though, trade began to expand more rapidly than ever before. At the beginnings of this process, around 1960 or so, the global web of exchange was thin and full of holes. Today, the web is much thicker and has few gaps. Foreign trade directly affects everyone's life.

Especially in big countries, most citizens around 1960 perceived a nationally framed economy in which trade seemed fairly marginal. Americans traded mostly with themselves, with a **trade-to-GDP ratio** (exports plus imports as a share of the whole U.S. economy) of less than 8 percent.[3] There were a few exceptional early pockets of globalization in small, rich countries: in Norway or the Netherlands, trade in 1960 already made up over 70 percent of the economy. Yet most countries were far closer to the U.S. pole in 1960, with trade under 10 percent of the world economy (see Figure 13-1).

The content of international trade in 1960 was also starkly uneven. It bore the imprint of the colonial period that was just ending. Latin America, Africa, and Asia sold mostly mining resources and agricultural products to North America and Europe, much as they had done under colonial empires. These northern economies, far ahead in industrialization, sold them manufactured goods in return. The latter were higher **value-added** products—production processes had added value to the raw materials of these developing countries—and these manufactured goods generally commanded higher profits. This was one reason why European and North American countries typically enjoyed **trade surpluses**, selling abroad more than they bought. Overall, developed-country economies enjoyed a privileged position with little competition from poorer neighbors.

In North America and the larger European countries, this era of nationally framed, industrially dominant economies encouraged an inward focus and a sense of national control. People perceived that they were mobilizing their national resources, modernizing their own societies, and working out national policies that defined their economic fates. More citizens were acquiring the elements of modern consumerism—cars, televisions, household appliances—and domestic production was geared to meet these internal demands. American or European producers made the full gamut of products for their citizens; not just high-end goods like automobiles or planes, but everything from textiles and shoes to toys

trade-to-GDP ratio
The sum of exports and imports as a proportion of a whole economy.

value-added
The worth that a production process adds to its materials; steel has more "value-added" than iron ore and thus sells for a higher price.

trade surplus
When a country exports more than it imports, the trade surplus is the difference.

and electronics. National workforces were largely separate pools of labor that did not compete directly. In politics, competing parties on the right and left shared the impression that their national debates mattered a great deal, because the shape of their economy was determined at the national level. In the developing world, too, many countries turned inward at this time, attempting import substitution industrialization in hopes of crafting stronger national economies of their own.

Yet in 1960, two trends already were visible that would pry open national frameworks to international trade. One was technological. International telephone lines, modern ships, jet planes, and expanding oil production to power it all rapidly cut the cost of doing business abroad (see the left-hand scale in Figure 13-2). In addition, a humble invention in 1956—**containerization**—became a key step in the history of transport. By packing all goods in standardized containers that could be stacked easily on ships and transferred to trains or trucks, miscellaneous cargo

containerization

Packing goods in trailer boxes that can be easily transported and stacked.

Figure 13-2 Falling Costs of International Business and Tariff Reductions Boost Globalization

This chart shows two important trends that contributed to globalization. The black, green, and blue lines, which are measured against the left-hand axis, take the prices of shipping, air travel, and phone calls in 1930 as a baseline—calling those values "100" and showing the relative drop in prices across the twentieth century. The red line shows average tariffs on goods around the world, which are measured against the right-hand scale. Average tariffs rose above 20 percent in the 1930s but were below 5 percent by 2000.

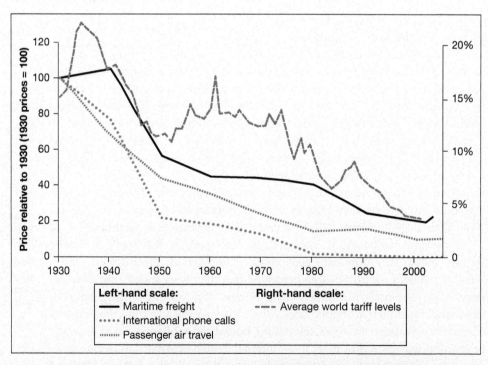

Sources: Jean-Yves Huwart and Loïc Verdier, *Economic Globalisation: Origins and Consequences* (Paris: OECD, 2013), p. 36; Silvia Nenci, "Tariff Liberalization and the Growth of World Trade: A Comparative Historical Analysis of the Multilateral Trading System," *The World Economy*, 34(10) (October 2011), pp. 1809–1835.

became far cheaper to move. Brokers emerged to fill containers in both directions of a trip and to connect shipping and land transport.

Just as important was a steady rollback of political barriers to international exchange (see the right-hand scale in Figure 13-2). After World War II, the United States led an effort to eliminate trade barriers, hoping to prevent any return to the rampant protectionism that had shut off national economies during the Great Depression. In 1947, twenty-three countries signed the General Agreement on Tariffs and Trade (GATT), which led to several rounds of negotiations on reducing tariffs and quotas. Huge cuts were agreed in the so-called Kennedy Round of talks in the 1960s, the Tokyo Round in the 1970s, and the Uruguay Round in the 1980s. GATT membership steadily expanded to more than 100 countries in the 1970s. In 1995, the GATT became the World Trade Organization (WTO). Its 164 members continue to negotiate further tariff cuts, in principle, but without much recent progress.

With transport costs and trade barriers plummeting, international trade soared. While global GDP multiplied by 22 from 1970 to 2010 (and population by 1.8), world exports grew by a factor of 48. Trade thus steadily claimed a larger share of national economies. Today in the United States the trade-to-GDP ratio is close to 30 percent, and the world overall has almost reached this level. In the EU, it averages over 40 percent. In a few small countries that serve as hubs through which global trade passes, such as Singapore or Ireland, trade is well *over* 100 percent of their GDP.

With the increased volume of international trade came major changes in its character. Especially in Asia and Latin America, rapidly industrializing countries increasingly exported manufactured goods to North America and Europe. First in low-tech sectors like textiles or toys, then later in higher value-added sectors like steel or electronics, these developing countries used a powerful advantage to take on developed-world competitors: lower costs. People in poorer countries flocked to factories to work for a small fraction of what workers earned in North America or Europe. In 1975, for example, the average Taiwanese factory worker cost about three times less per hour than their American counterparts.[4] In Mexico, it was less than one-fourth.[5] Developing-country businesses also often faced less stringent regulation (or none at all) of safety, workers' rights, or environmental effects, making production cheaper. Gradually poorer countries came to supply more and more of the world's manufacturing (see the blue line in Figure 13-3). The developed economies retained the lead in some higher-end manufacturing—aerospace and computers, for example—but increasingly shifted their economies toward services and "white collar" jobs.

The effects of these changes are huge and still playing out today. As consumers, no matter where we are, most of our clothing, household goods, appliances, tools, or toys come from developing countries. China stands out as the origin of everything from socks to iPhones, and for the rapidity of its transformation into a factory for the world: from negligible exports in 1980, it is now the world's leading exporter with over 12 percent of world markets.[6] In our roles as producers, the growth of developing-world manufacturing has altered job

Figure 13-3 Developing Country Manufacturing and the U.S. Trade Deficit

This chart shows another two trends during the era of globalization. The blue line, measured on the left-hand scale, shows that developing countries that had once exported mainly agriculture and raw materials shifted into exporting manufactured goods to the world in the 1970s and 1980s. The red line, measured on the right-hand scale, shows the balance of U.S. trade with the world. Until the 1970s, the United States had a trade surplus; then its balance of trade crossed the dotted line (when exports and imports were balanced) and tipped into a trade deficit that increased thereafter.

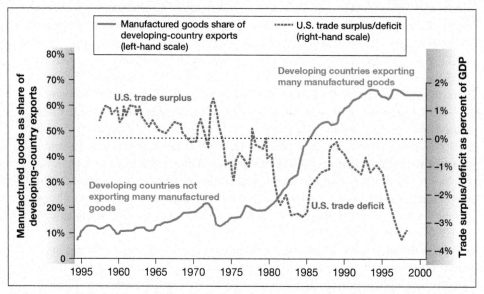

Sources: United Nations Conference on Trade and Development (UNCTAD) Statistics Data Center, consulted May 2013; U.S. Department of Commerce, Bureau of Economic Analysis, U.S. Economic Accounts Database, consulted May 2013.

opportunities everywhere. Classic assembly line jobs became rare in Europe and the United States, replaced largely by service industry occupations ranging from retail sales, cashiering, and food preparation to office work and nursing (the five largest U.S. occupations in 2018).[7] At the same time, hundreds of millions of people in developing nations left farms and villages to work in factories. At the higher level of national trade balances, too, patterns shifted massively. Most international exchange is trade in goods, since many services are inherently local: restaurant meals, nursing, or haircutting are what economists call **nontradables**, or things that cannot be sold abroad. The shift of developed countries away from manufacturing and toward services thus helped shift many rich countries from traditional trade surpluses to significant **trade deficits**. A few richer countries maintained strong manufacturing, such as Germany, but the U.S. trade deficit in particular steadily widened. (See the red line in Figure 13-3. You can also refresh your knowledge of the distribution of developed and developing nations around the world by looking back at Map 10-1 in Chapter 10.)

Thus growing international trade brought us an astonishing array of affordable products—all those shelves of Chinese-made goods at Target or Walmart,

nontradables

Things that cannot be sold abroad, such as a haircut.

trade deficit

When a country imports more than it exports, the trade deficit is the difference.

not to mention polo shirts from Pakistan, shoes from Brazil, and flat-screen TVs from Taiwan—while altering individual and national positions in broad patterns of wealth and power. There is more to this story, though, than this massive flood of goods. If trade alone defined globalization, national economies might still be quite national: Americans would exchange more with the Germans or Chinese, but they would still make American products to trade against German-made or Chinese-made products. Yet that is not the world we live in. Globalization goes far deeper.

Foreign Direct Investment and Outsourcing

Companies like Ford, John Deere, or Levi Strauss are American icons. Or are they? Each now sells many products that are mostly made elsewhere. The Ford Fusion, for example, draws most of its parts from outside the United States. And that symbol of American ingenuity, Apple's iPhone? Entirely built by the Taiwanese company Foxconn in China. The cross-border mixing of firms and goods runs in the other direction too: of the ten "most American" cars in 2018, four had Japanese brands.[8] The Honda Odyssey ranked second for "American" content (after the Jeep Cherokee). Clearly something more is at work than trade between separate national economies.

The source of this ambiguity—and of the deeper ways in which globalization has penetrated our lives—relates to the rapid growth of certain types of **foreign direct investment (FDI)**, or ownership of productive assets in other countries. To grasp how a certain type of FDI defines globalization today, it is helpful to return to a "before" picture around 1960.

foreign direct investment (FDI)
When foreigners own or fund businesses inside a country.

Like international trade, owning assets in foreign countries was already an old practice in 1960. Under the protection of colonialism, European and American **multinational corporations (MNCs)** acquired huge assets abroad. For example, the Boston-based United Fruit Company (known now as Chiquita Brands) owned vast plantations and was the largest employer in Central America for decades. Mining and oil companies similarly came close to ruling large parts of poorer regions. As of 1960, though, most of these MNC activities had an economic profile much like normal trade. They pumped oil, dug up copper, or boxed bananas in poorer countries and shipped them to their home markets. In the other direction, manufacturing firms like Ford, General Electric, or the German industrial giant Siemens owned foreign affiliates for international sales. Sometimes they did final assembly of complex products in a few sites abroad. The parts and products themselves, though, were made in their home country.

multinational corporation (MNCs)
A business with significant operations in more than one country.

So a good deal of trade flowed through MNCs around 1960, but it still basically took goods made in one place and sold them in another. And for good reason: many obstacles prevented companies from attempting to internationalize more complex production processes. Transport and tariff costs were high. Long-distance communication was difficult and expensive. Even if an American or European firm wanted to contract out for certain parts or tasks to foreigners,

global supply chain
A chain of operations across multiple countries to produce a good.

preferential trade agreements (PTAs)
Treaties that set trade barriers at especially low levels between certain countries, lower than their trade barriers for others.

they could not be confident that contracts across borders would be respected. What if a foreign government decided to confiscate foreign investments on its territory? Much had to change before many firms could build the elaborate **global supply chains** that we see in the Ford Fusion today.

By the 1980s, those changes were increasingly in place. As we have seen, transport and communication costs fell and tariffs were bargained down. In parallel, international investment agreements (IIAs) emerged to protect foreign investors. In bilateral investment treaties (BITs), two countries mutually guarantee property rights for foreign investors, as well as the ability to remove their money and recourse to international arbitration if need be. First invented in 1959, BITs proliferated increasingly rapidly. Groups of countries also signed **preferential trade agreements (PTAs)** that lowered trade barriers between them and typically included investment guarantees as well. Examples of the latter include the EU, the North American Free Trade Association (NAFTA), the Association of Southeast Asian Nations (ASEAN), or Mercosur in South America. By the early 1990s, BITs, PTAs, and these other acronyms were spreading legal protections for investors across the entire globe (see Figure 13-4). Today, every country in the world has signed at least one IIA.[9]

As these conditions consolidated, global FDI skyrocketed. Its average pace of growth from 1985 to 2000 was almost four times global GDP growth and twice as fast as trade growth.[10] The curve was less smooth in the new millennium, as economic crises in Asia, Argentina, and Russia scared investors off around 2000 and then investment pulled back sharply with the 2008 crisis, but the upward trend quickly resumed (see Figure 13-4).

Behind the FDI curve was a revolution in the global organization of production. With low transport costs and more standardized international rules, companies began to de-localize their operations. The most common motivation was cutting costs, classically by moving labor-intensive steps of production to poorer countries with cheaper labor. At first, firms often stayed close to their own neighborhoods, with American firms producing in Mexico or Central America, Japanese industry looking to Korea or southeast Asia, and European firms to Turkey or northern Africa. In the late 1980s and 1990s, these investments diversified around the world in response to what is known as the "great doubling" of the global labor force.[11] Liberalization in China and India—and the fall of communism in Eastern Europe—collectively made 3 billion people available as potential workers. More cheap labor was suddenly more available than ever before.

Yet if cost cutting is a major impetus to FDI growth, it also reflects other motivations. FDI flows between rich countries are even larger than those to the developing world. Companies in Europe, North America, and Japan have increasingly developed elaborate operations in each other's markets. For Honda, producing the Odyssey and other models in the United States lowers transport costs and carries the political and marketing benefit of a "Made in America" claim. With the increasing ease of electronic communications, large firms have greater flexibility to locate various pieces of their production and sales in multiple places.

Figure 13-4 As International Investment Agreements Spread, Foreign Direct Investment Soars

The red line, measured on the right-hand scale, shows the rising number of international investment agreements over time. The blue area, measured against the left-hand scale, shows that foreign direct investment (FDI) accelerated in the late 1980s and reached an annual flow of $2 trillion in 2007. Financial crises in 1999 and 2008 led to dramatic drops, but the upward trend soon returned.

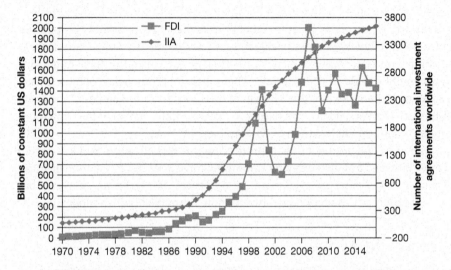

Source: United Nations Conference on Trade and Development (UNCTAD) statistics, at https://unctad.org/en/Pages/statistics.aspx.

In the developing world, too, cost is not the only consideration. For Apple executives, low cost is not even the main appeal of Foxconn's Chinese factories. More important is scale, speed, and flexibility. "The scale is unimaginable," remarked one Apple executive during a visit to Foxconn's 230,000-worker facility in Chengdu, China, where workers not only work but also live and relax. "You need a thousand rubber gaskets? That's the factory next door. You need a million screws? That factory is a block away. You need that screw made a little bit different? It will take three hours." Another ex-Apple employee stressed Foxconn's ability to scale up instantly for a new contract: "They could hire 3,000 people overnight. What U.S. plant could find 3,000 people overnight and convince them to live in dorms?"[12] Similar dynamics arise in India, which has dominated the global outsourcing of services—programming, bookkeeping, and so on—much as China leads in manufacturing. Huge outsourcing firms like Tata Consultancy Services, Infosys, HCL, and Wipro can throw tens of thousands of well-educated Indians at computing and paperwork tasks. They win contracts not just on cost, but because they can address big-business challenges rapidly with immense human resources.

If rising trade launched our era of globalization, then, investment captures more of its core dynamics. The changes we have seen since 1960 are not simply—or even mainly—about how low-cost foreign competition in poor countries wrestled manufacturing work away from developed-world firms. More commonly, it was rich-world businesses themselves who sought out opportunities in other countries for cost cutting and efficiency. As costs and barriers to FDI fell, business reorganized production to stretch across borders. Investing in foreign factories, creating joint ventures, or contracting out processes to foreign partners generated far deeper international relationships that those that existed in 1960. For business managers, it became common to scrutinize every task to ask: can we do this more cheaply or better elsewhere? For workers, competition with foreign labor became very direct. Not only might their jobs shift away if a foreign firm outcompeted their home-country employer, but their home employer might decide to shift jobs elsewhere. For governments, economic policy became more complex. If "our" firms are not clearly producing "our" products with "our" workers, it becomes harder to decide what "we" want for regulation, standards, and the distribution of economic gains.

And even FDI does not fully capture economic globalization. Still less visible to most citizens, but also carrying important consequences, is the globalization of finance. Goods and production processes traverse borders more than ever before, but nothing flows more quickly and more dramatically than money itself.

Globalized Money

As international trade and investment expanded, global flows of money grew as well—and even faster. People doing business abroad had to make payments in other moneys, so huge markets emerged to exchange currencies like U.S. dollars, Japanese yen, Russian rubles, or Mexican pesos. Businesses and governments found it increasingly easy to borrow money from foreigners, creating an enormous international web of debt. Though international financial markets arose to facilitate trade and investment, they also became important in their own right.

Foreign exchange markets—where people can trade dollars, British pounds, Brazilian reals, and other currencies—are the largest and most fluid markets in the world. At points $5 trillion in currencies are traded in one day—100 times as much as a heavy day of trading on the New York Stock Exchange. "Forex" markets are centuries old, since international trade always required trade in currencies, but these immense volumes have developed largely since the 1960s. They reflect the growth of global trade and investment, which has led more businesses to need more foreign currencies, as well as technological change that allows money to zip electronically across borders at the push of a button.

Also important is the increased **volatility** (or rapid fluctuation) of currencies. Volatility was low for a few decades after World War II, because governments set the **exchange rate** between each pair of currencies: a U.S. dollar was officially valued at a certain number of British pounds, Indian rupees, or French francs, as were other pairs of currencies. Then in 1970, exchange rates began to "float": just as the price of a product like oil fluctuates depending on what people will pay for it, so the

volatility
The rate and degree of fluctuation in a market.

exchange rate
The cost of one currency in terms of another, such as the number of Japanese yen it takes to buy a U.S. dollar.

number of yen equal to a dollar (or any other exchange rate) is now just whatever people offer on Forex markets. Floating rates made currency markets much more volatile—and much more important. Businesses and governments had to worry about shifts in the value of their home currency, which could change the cost of imports or the competitiveness of their exports. Moreover, floating rates made currency trading a moneymaking business in itself. If a trader bets correctly that the yen will rise against the U.S. dollar, for example, they sell dollars to buy yen; once the yen rises, they exchange those yen back into dollars, and end up with more dollars than they started with. Some currency speculators make billions on such bets.

International debt is another key piece of financial globalization. Banks have increasingly made loans across borders, and the even bigger development since the 1960s is the growth of international bond markets. A bond is just another form of a loan: the U.S. Treasury, for example, borrows money by selling bonds that are worth $10,000 ten years after the sale (when the bond "matures"). If someone buys the bond for $8,000 today, they are lending the U.S. government $8,000 now to be paid back with $2,000 interest in ten years. Governments and large businesses have issued bonds since the 1700s, but our era stands out for the scale, global scope, and, above all, the geographical directions of borrowing. Until the 1980s or so, most lending and borrowing went on within developed countries or from the developed world to poorer countries. In other words, North American and European countries were **creditors** to the world, lending more than they borrowed. Since the 1980s, many rich countries have become net **debtors**, most notably the United States. Part of the reason was the shift of manufacturing to poorer countries and the rise of developed-country trade deficits: in 2018, for example, Americans bought $419 billion more from China than they sold there, and had to borrow money to do so. Also contributing was a rise in government debt in the richer countries. Since the 1970s, most developed-country governments have regularly spent more than they received in taxes, issuing bonds to cover the difference. Their own citizens have bought most such bonds, but foreigners have increasingly purchased them as well. Probably the most striking international financial relationship that has resulted is that the Chinese government now holds over $1 trillion in U.S. Treasury bonds. China's state-socialist regime is one of the biggest financiers of the American government.

creditors/debtors
Creditors are people who are owed money; debtors are people who owe money.

Is the rise of a vast sea of free-flowing money a good thing? Economic growth requires investment, and globalized finance increases access to investment around the world. We might expect that this tide of capital has opened up new economic possibilities around the world, lifting all boats. On the other hand, the swell of global finance is now so huge and fluid that it may sometimes swamp national economies in destabilizing ways. Foreigners may suddenly decide to take their money out—sometimes for foreign reasons not related to the receiving country—and businesses or even governments that depend on foreign funds may suffer. Later, we explore these costs and benefits of globalized finance, as well as those of trade and investment. First, though, consider some political changes that have accompanied economic globalization.

International Law and Organizations

13.2 **Identify several reasons for the growth of international law and international organizations, and cite influential examples in both areas.**

Globalization is much more than an economic phenomenon. A time traveler from 1960 would be struck not only by today's flows of trade, investment, and money but by the power of international governance. International law emerged well before 1960, but only since then has it gained major influence. Equally striking is the growth of international organizations, many centered on the United Nations, which have multiplied massively in number and power. The most extreme case is the EU—an international organization that has become something like a federal government that extends over twenty-seven member-states.

The Rise of International Law and Human Rights

Law and rights are awkward notions in international relations. The international arena is traditionally seen as an ungoverned arena of anarchy. The basic principle of state sovereignty seems to deny that international law can ever supersede national authority. Even if states agree to respect certain rules, no overarching global power exists to enforce them against rule breakers (especially powerful ones). Despite all these hindrances, however, international law has come a long way in the past several decades. It has developed an increasingly dense network of rules that invoke certain universal human rights. Even the most powerful states pay attention to most of these rules most of the time.

International law has its origins in the mutual self-interest of competing groups to set some limits on their rivalries. Already in ancient Indian epics before 2000 BC, we find mention of **diplomatic immunity**, or the custom that messengers and diplomats should not be mistreated. The pillaging Mongol leader Genghis Khan scrupulously respected foreign diplomats (and razed whole cities if his diplomats were harmed). More explicit **bilateral treaties** (or two-party agreements) also arose very early, such as in boundary-line arrangements between city-states in ancient Mesopotamia. As polities grew and governance became more sophisticated, treaties developed as well. An especially dense network of bilateral deals emerged with the first modern states in Europe in the 1500s and 1600s, with elaborate agreements on boundaries, alliances, and trade. To break such agreements made it harder to strike credible deals in the future, so even powerful leaders were hesitant to breach treaties openly.

As dense as the web of treaties became, though, it was only loosely constraining. These were voluntary deals between leaders who could drop them if they wished—and they regularly did. Cardinal Richelieu, the powerful minister of French king Louis XIII, summarized this reality to an early advocate of international law, Hugo Grotius, in 1626: "The weakest," he said, "are always wrong in matters of state."[13] The powerful ultimately did as they pleased. Additionally,

diplomatic immunity
A status that protects diplomats from mistreatment or prosecution in other countries.

bilateral treaty
A legal agreement between two (and only two) countries.

the one principle of international law that became consolidated in the 1600s—sovereignty—added another obstacle to the creation of other international rules. It formalized the idea that each state held supreme authority over its territory and leaders could do whatever they wished at home.

Only several centuries later did international law begin to become more robust. Mutual self-interest among states still drove its development, but the web of rules became broader, deeper, and less flexible. Most notably it became more **multilateral**, with many treaties between multiple states. Some treaties came to include almost every state in the world. This was an important shift: much more than with bilateral deals, it can be awkward and costly for one country—even a powerful one—to draw back from rules that the whole world condones.

multilateral treaty
A legal agreement between more than two countries.

The first impetus to broader international law came from the horrors of industrialized war. In 1864, after the Crimean War in Europe, European states agreed in the First Geneva Convention on rules for medical treatment of combatants. They also founded an international organization, the International Committee of the Red Cross, to care for victims of war. Over time other countries signed the Convention. Further negotiations produced other Conventions on issues like treatment of prisoners of war and a ban on use of chemical and biological weapons. After World War II more talks strengthened the Geneva Conventions and made them truly global, attracting signatures even from the Soviet Union and Maoist China. Today, the Conventions apply almost everywhere, with 194 signatories. Violations cause states serious problems even though no body exists to enforce them. In the Syrian civil war, for example, the United States was reluctant to become involved, but felt compelled to support the rebels after the Assad regime broke the Geneva ban on use of chemical weapons. The United States too has come under pressure from these rules. Many saw violations in American use of "waterboarding," a form of torture, under the George W. Bush administration, and in the refusal to accord prisoner-of-war rights to terrorism suspects at the U.S. naval base in Guantanamo Bay, Cuba. States that question the Geneva Conventions suffer widespread criticism and diplomatic costs. These rules of war set some of the most tangible bases for human rights today.

specific reciprocity
The practice of specifying exactly what each signatory to a treaty offers to others (such as specific tariff reductions).

The second major impetus to broader international law came in the realm of trade after World War II. Bilateral trade treaties had become common in the 1700s and 1800s, but the GATT agreement of 1947 was the first wide multilateral framework. Seeking to anchor themselves to broad free trade, the United States and its European allies introduced a new principle. Rather than the **specific reciprocity** of classic bilateral deals—with two countries bargaining down specific tariffs—they agreed on somewhat more **diffuse reciprocity**. All parties would reduce overall tariff levels by certain percentages, without haggling over each specific tariff, and would accord each other "most favored nation" status: any trade privileges offered to one member would extend to all. They added a ban on unfair trade practices like **dumping**, or selling at prices below production cost, and a dispute resolution mechanism where arbitrators judge accusations of rule violations. In 1995, the GATT transformed into the WTO, grafting an international

diffuse reciprocity
The practice of agreeing to broad, general cooperation over time, placing less importance on highly detailed commitments.

dumping
Selling a product at prices below its cost of production to wipe out the competition.

organization onto the multilateral treaty to give it powers for monitoring and enforcement. The dispute mechanism became stronger, leading to a steady stream of cases that compel states to alter protectionist practices. Even the United States has lost multiple cases and changed its policies as a result. Today, the 164-member WTO serves as the main global framework for international trade law.

International law and human rights have even begun to include criminal cases, trying individuals for crimes their governments are unwilling or unable to prosecute. The first concrete steps toward this idea also came after World War II. In the **Nuremberg Tribunal**, the Allied powers tried Nazis for war crimes that violated the Geneva Conventions, as well as for larger "crimes against humanity." A similar court indicted Japanese leaders. Yet if Nazi and Imperial Japanese leaders were surely as guilty of such charges as anyone in history, these courts still seemed more political than legal: the wars' victors judged the losers. Not until the 1990s did more legalistic and broadly multilateral courts emerge, prompted by the savage ethnic war in Yugoslavia and the Rwandan genocide. The United Nations (of which more is said in the following sections) opened special International Criminal Tribunals for each conflict. Then in 1998, 120 countries agreed to create a general International Criminal Court (ICC) for war crimes and genocide. Today, 122 states have ratified its treaty. Huge exceptions limit the ICC's reach, however: China and Russia, as well as Israel and the United States, currently do not participate. Each fears that ICC cases could expose their soldiers to politically motivated indictments.

Nuremberg Tribunal
The special court that tried the leadership of Nazi Germany in 1945–1946.

Xinhua/Alamy Stock Photo

Convention-goers observe a sophisticated Chinese-made robot in Chongqing, China. Through many different mechanisms, including foreign direct investment and joint ventures, Chinese industry has caught up to American and European competitors in many sectors.

Still, even the United States' absence at the ICC underscores the power of international law and human rights today. If international law had no authority, why would a powerful state worry about signing such a treaty? American leaders know full well that they are constrained by other international rules. In general, the degree to which states take international law seriously marks a huge change from international relations just a few generations ago. Leaders in Washington, D.C., and other power centers spend much time and resources working out how national policies fit with international rules on war, human rights, or trade. They also spend time thinking about or meeting with the people who manage international rules: the leaders of international organizations.

Global International Organizations and the United Nations System

Followers of international news are familiar with national leaders whose photos they often see together, like the presidents of the United States, China, Russia or France, the German chancellor, or the prime minister of Britain, India, or Australia. Yet many such photos include people who do not represent major countries, such as the secretary general of the United Nations (UN); the managing director of the International Monetary Fund (IMF); the director general of the WTO; or the president of the World Bank. Their presence hints at the power of international organizations.

Like international law, organizations without a national base fit awkwardly in a world of sovereignty. And like international law, international organizations entered the state-dominated scene when state leaders perceived a need for some coordination. Especially as states took on more active governance internally—building infrastructure and developing economies—cross-border challenges in economic management arose that called not only for international rules but for coordinating organizations. The first instance was a five-country treaty in 1815 to create the Central Commission for Navigation on the Rhine, which coordinated management of one of Europe's key waterways. Other early examples were the International Telegraph Union (ITU) in 1865 and the Universal Postal Union (UPU) in 1874. All three technical bodies still exist to address logistical problems that no country can solve alone.

As with international law, World War II marked a key shift toward a world where international organizations could become powerful. After World War I, a failed attempt had been made to broker global peace in an organization called the League of Nations, and after a second horribly destructive war many countries professed a desire for a stronger body. Thus was born the United Nations (UN) in 1945. Aspiring to balance the principle of state sovereignty with some capacity to enforce peace, the UN included a **General Assembly (UNGA)** where every country receives a vote and a **Security Council (UNSC)** where five leading states hold permanent seats: the United States, Russia, China, Britain, and France. Though the UN has no military forces of its own, the Security Council can authorize national military forces to act as they see fit for peace or humanitarian aid.

UN General Assembly
The main assembly of the United Nations. It lacks major powers.

UN Security Council
The UN's center of power, with ten rotating members and five permanent members (the United States, Russia, China, Britain, and France).

It took many years after World War II, however, for the UN to develop anything like the authority its founders intended. During the Cold War, from 1950 to 1990, the United States and USSR blocked the UNSC from action by vetoing each other's proposals. Once this impasse evaporated, the number of interventions authorized by the Security Council skyrocketed. Tensions nonetheless remain in the UNSC, with the United States, Russia, and China often disagreeing over issues like the Syrian civil war. Nor have all countries always respected UNSC decisions since 1990: the U.S. invasion of Iraq in 2003, for example, went forward without UNSC approval. Even in the breach, though, we can see that the UN has acquired some authority over the legitimate use of international force.[14] Before U.S. leaders launched the invasion, they spent much time and resources trying to secure UNSC approval. Failing to win support, they shifted to arguing that earlier UNSC resolutions effectively authorized a new invasion. It remained important to the world's most powerful country to present its actions as consistent with UN procedures.

Today, the UN also acts as the umbrella over a vast network of international organizations that coordinate national policies and take action with their own resources. With roughly 10,000 employees of its own and a budget over $5 billion, the UN directly runs a huge array of programs in areas like development, refugees, women's rights, environmental issues, or drug control. It has additionally become the central coordination site for other international agencies, from old bodies like the ITU and UPU to postwar creations like the International Monetary Fund, the World Bank, the World Health Organization, or the International Labor Organization. The UN is now the heart of a complex and dense web of multilateral governance. The power of nodes in this web varies tremendously, from technical bodies that just help states coordinate on certain issues (such as the World Meteorological Organization) to weighty bodies that control huge resources (such as the World Bank or the IMF). Even the latter organizations remain responsible to national governments, with steering committees consisting of states' representatives. Still, their staff have autonomy from any given national government. In the years after the Great Recession, for example, then-IMF director Christine Lagarde loudly criticized U.S. government budget cuts that she and her staff saw as bad for the U.S. and global economies.[15]

Within the global arena organized by these bodies created by international treaties, another kind of international organization has also come to be important. The UN and other treaty-made agencies are international governmental organizations—created by states to help govern international space—and **international nongovernmental organizations (INGOs)** have grown up around them. Like NGOs in domestic politics, INGOs are private, nonprofit lobbying organizations and service providers. From human rights organizations like Amnesty International to environmental groups like Greenpeace to antipoverty organizations like CARE International to medical providers like Doctors Without Borders, they campaign for governments to tackle international problems and

international nongovernmental organization (INGO)
Private, nonprofit organizations with operations across multiple countries.

often confront them with their own resources and personnel. When natural disasters or violent conflicts strike in developing countries with limited resources, CARE, the Red Cross, or Oxfam are often the first responders. Developed-country governments channel much of their foreign aid through INGOs, contracting with them to work on health, development, and other priorities in poorer countries. They generate a swarm of private activity around international governmental organizations, filling in the global arena with societal actors.

Regional Organizations and the Remarkable European Union

If global international organizations provide the broad architecture of worldwide governance, the densest nodes of international authority are regional. Multilateral organizations for regional cooperation preceded the emergence of global bodies in several places. In a few regions, they have advanced well beyond global governance overall, most dramatically in Europe.

That regional organizations are often stronger than global ones is hardly surprising. Problems of international coordination often arise first among regional neighbors, and multilateral cooperation is often easier between neighbors than with the entire world. The first instance came when the United States and its neighbors formed the Pan American Union in 1890. Now known as the Organization of American States (OAS), this forum for dispute settlement and cooperation includes all thirty-five countries in North and South America. Other regional organizations began forming in the 1950s and 1960s and now cover most of the world (see Map 13-1). Some only hold regular political consultations, such as the Arab League, but most include treaties for economic cooperation as well. Least complex among these are free trade areas like the North American Free Trade Area (NAFTA) between the United States, Canada, and Mexico. Others share fused policies on external tariffs in **customs unions** like Mercosur. Several go further in shared market regulations, making **common markets** like the Commonwealth of Independent States around Russia. A few additionally share the same money, like the Economic and Monetary Community of Central Africa (CEMAC). And one—the EU—goes much further. With a single currency, tightly integrated regulations and policies in many areas, and powerful governing institutions, the EU is by far the strongest international organization the world has seen.

The EU is both the leading example of regional integration and the inspiration for most other regional organizations. It began in the 1950s in pursuit of two goals: peace and prosperity. After two world wars centered on Europe, Europeans sought a way to bind themselves into peaceful cooperation. As these smaller countries had been surpassed economically by the United States, they also aspired to merge into a large, dynamic market. They first integrated key sectors into the European Coal and Steel Community of 1952, expanded it to a broader common market in the European Economic Community of 1958, and

customs union
A preferential trading arrangement that erases tariffs between its members and adopts common tariffs vis-à-vis other countries.

common market
A customs union that also adopts some shared economic regulations across its members.

Map 13-1 Regional Trade Organizations

This map displays selected regional economic organizations around the world. Free trade areas reduce cross-border barriers to trade. Customs unions add coordinated trade policies toward outsiders, and common markets undertake additional internal policy coordination. Monetary unions share a single currency. Economic unions (sometimes combined with monetary unions, as in the EU) adopt many common policies.

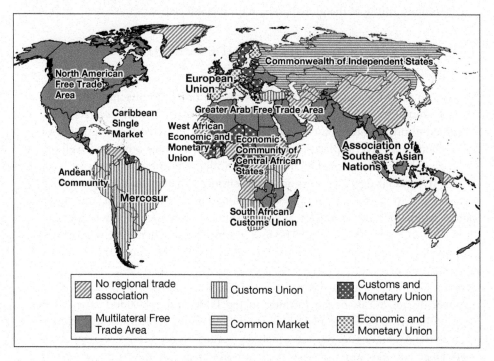

since then have gradually upgraded their shared policies and institutions. Today, most economic regulation and a variety of other policies are formed mainly at the European level. Membership, meanwhile, grew from six original countries to twenty-eight today.

That is not to say that everything is smoothly integrated in Europe. EU states remain far more different than U.S. states, with the Netherlands (GDP per capita at Purchasing Power Parity in 2018: $56,383) about two and a half times richer than Bulgaria (GDP per capita at PPP in 2018: $23,156).[16] With such disparities and huge enduring differences in member-state institutions, culture, and policies, their economies can still diverge very strongly. Certain member-states grow faster or slower than each other, or simply have distinct economic problems, in ways that cause major tensions. Together with widespread concern about how much the EU requires its members to be open to external trade and immigration, these challenges have led to the rise of powerful "Eurosceptical" movements in most member-states. In Britain, a referendum in 2016 led to a narrow vote for exiting the EU—or "Brexit"—and then years of debate about how to implement that mandate. The British were effectively caught between a political desire to run their own affairs and powerful incentives to maintain openness and strong cooperation with their regional neighbors. Extending strongly shared policies across very different countries is not easy, but neither is going it alone in a globalizing world.

Despite its challenges, though, the EU has altered governance in Europe to the point that it would be almost unrecognizable to someone from 1960. Though nowhere else has taken similar shifts quite so far, even the less dramatic changes elsewhere have remade our world considerably in a few generations. Our consumer goods are more likely than not to come from far away. Our employers make decisions about investments—and the location of many of our jobs—as a function of very global considerations. Money shifts around the globe—and in and out of countries—in the blink of an eye. To build and manage such a world, our national policymakers spend more and more of their time interacting with other countries' leaders and the personnel of international organizations. Each of these features of life today was largely absent a few generations ago.

Does that mean that today's young people enjoy fabulous new opportunities—or were their grandparents lucky to live in an earlier golden age? With before/after views of globalization in mind, consider now who gains or loses from it and how.

Globalization's Effects at Home

13.3 **Assess who has gained or lost economically from globalization and evaluate how this has affected democracy at the national level.**

Openness. Cooperation. Loads of cheap stuff. Intercultural connections and free flow of ideas. At a broad level, it may seem hard to dispute that globalization is good overall. Who argues for a more closed world with less cooperation and narrower availability of more expensive goods?

Actually many do, at least to some degree. Few oppose international openness or cooperation in principle, but many worry that the versions of openness and cooperation we see today have costs. In particular, even globalization's champions admit that it produces losers as well as winners. Especially clear is that it produces *relative* winners and losers: some gain a great deal more than others. For a very broad picture of these effects, consider an analysis by several respected economists of changes in income around the world from 1980 to 2016 (see Figure 13-5).

A glance at this chart tells us that two kinds of people have benefitted most clearly from globalization: the global lower middle class and the very wealthy. To see who these people are and where they live—and where we find the relative losers in the dips of the curve—we must look inside developed and developing countries.

Figure 13-5 Change in Income by Percentile of Wealth Worldwide, 1980–2016

This chart presents data about how household incomes grew around the world between 1980 and 2016, depending on how wealthy they were. The richest part of the world's population, above the 99th percentile (situated along the horizontal scale toward the right edge), has become much wealthier—especially the extremely rich, as the chart shows by breaking out the gains of the top one-thousandth of one per cent. The top 1 percent captured 27 percent of all growth in income in this period, more than twice the overall gains of the whole bottom 50 percent (who captured 12 percent). The other segment that has done relatively well could be called the "global lower middle class," between the 20th and 50th percentiles. People between the 60th and 90th percentiles have seen the slowest income growth overall.

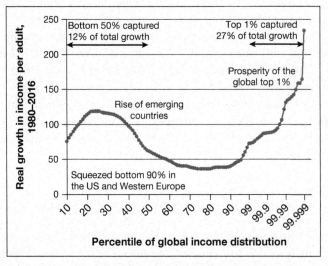

Source: Facundo Alvaredo, Lucas Chancel, Thomas Piketty, Emmanuel Saez, and Gabriel Zucman, "The Elephant Curve of Global Inequality and Growth," *American Economic Association Papers and Proceedings* vol. 108 (2018), pp. 103–108. Used With Permission.

Economic Winners and Losers in the Rich Countries

What does globalization mean for citizens of rich countries? It brings more desirable imports, new markets for exports, and more investment opportunities abroad, including tapping into a huge pool of cheap foreign labor after the "great doubling." People in the developed world have experienced these changes differently, however, as the curve in Figure 13-5 suggests. They stretch roughly from the world's 60th percentile, where income has been stagnant recently, to the top of the scale. Much of the story behind the curve is that wealthy people and skilled workers have gained new frontiers; poorer and less-skilled workers have gained competitors.

Behind the world curve in Figure 13-5 lie national curves of rising inequality in most industrialized countries. Globalization is not the sole source of this

Maximilian/Prisma by Dukas Presseagentur GmbH/Alamy Stock Photo

Once automobile factories had hundreds of workers moving along assembly lines, but now robots do much of the work.

trend; it parallels shifts that economists trace first and foremost to technological change. Machines have altered the jobs available to lower-skilled people more than global trade and FDI. Huge numbers of semiskilled factory or office jobs have disappeared, from car assembly line workers replaced by robots to newspaper typesetters replaced by computers. New jobs have arisen as well, but in economies with less manufacturing and more services, the classic well-paid, stable, semiskilled, middle-class jobs have given way to low-skilled, less-well-paid jobs in areas like retail or food preparation. Globalization has reinforced technological trends by transferring many remaining low- or semiskilled jobs to developing countries. In what economists call "tradable" sectors—goods and some services that can be produced in one country and consumed in another—the United States added *almost no jobs at all* from 1990 to 2008. U.S. businesses in these sectors grew, but without using more U.S.-based labor than in 1990.[17] In recent years, the vast majority of job creation has continued to come in nontradable sectors like education, health care, government, and retail.

Meanwhile, better-educated people in the upper middle class have held their own in the U.S. economy, while the very wealthiest—the top 1 percent—have captured most gains from growth in the past quarter century (see Figure 13-6). Again globalization is only part of this story. Technological change has opened new opportunities for skilled workers: think of the new sector of Internet-based wealth. National political shifts, too, have lowered tax rates on the wealthy. Yet

Figure 13-6 Shares of U.S. National Income after Transfers/Taxes, 1979 and 2017

If we divide the U.S. population into fifths by their income and contrast after-tax income in 1979 and 2017, the share of overall national income going to the lower four-fifths of the population has fallen. Most of the top fifth (from the 81st to the 99th percentile) has gained in relative terms, and most of that gain has gone to the top 5 percent.

Source: U.S. Census, available at https://www.census.gov/data/tables/time-series/demo/income-poverty/historical-income-households.html.

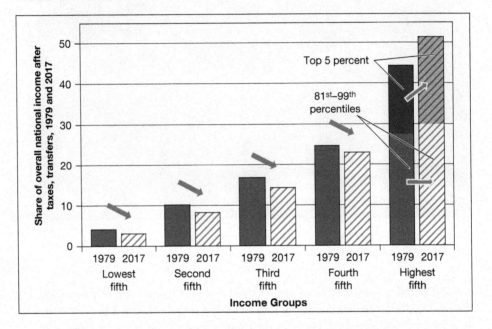

globalization clearly contributes. In enabling money, investments, and production processes to flow more freely around the world, it has increased the profits available to those with money.[18]

The tale of shifting jobs and rising rich-world inequality is partly mitigated by benefits to all citizens as consumers. Prices for manufactured goods have stayed fairly flat in the past several decades, just as we would expect as production shifts toward lower-cost locations. The shelves of Walmart and Target beckon with imported goods that are cheaper today (relative to incomes) than they were a generation ago. Much of the efficiency of globalized production has also gone into making goods better and more varied than they were: nonstick pans are slicker, Nikes have more bounce, and each new iPhone does more than the similarly-priced model before it. Thus consumers get more for their money even if prices remain the same. Since poorer people spend more of their money on consumer goods, they actually feel the most benefit from these shifts. Walmart's "low price guarantee" makes a bigger difference to poorer people than to the rich.

Overall, though, globalization has sharpened economic divergences between relative winners and losers in developed countries. That makes sense: globalization has integrated national economies more into global markets, increasing market opportunities and competitive pressures. People positioned well to be competitive—those with strongly marketable skills or major resources—have gained all around. People with less marketable skills and fewer resources have gained as consumers but lost out as producers, since less-skilled jobs have become so much easier to replace with machines or with cheaper workers abroad.

That said, we do not simply live in one big competitive global market. National economic frameworks still make an enormous difference for our economic fates. These new challenges confront workers within developed economies, within which stable, well-paid jobs for less-skilled workers have become harder to find. For less-skilled workers within the frameworks of developing countries, the consequences of globalization look rather different.

Economic Winners and Losers in the Developing World

Globalization is often ugly in the developing world. Millions work for pennies under bad conditions. In China, Foxconn factories have installed netting in many places to lower the number of suicide jumpers. Disasters also occur frequently in factories, textile sweatshops, or mines. In Bangladesh—second to China for clothes exports—a fire in 2012 trapped and killed 112 T-shirt makers in a crowded building with few exits. In April 2013, more than a thousand Bangladeshi textile workers died when a poorly made building collapsed. In the wake of both tragedies, Walmart and other firms hastily fired suppliers, trying to signal that they insist on better working conditions.[19] But to some degree, Western firms' and consumers' pursuit of lower prices creates incentives for their global suppliers to cut corners wherever they can.

On the other hand, these tragic stories tend to reflect frantic growth in countries with poor regulation, not enslavement of poor workers against their wills. These workers often see such jobs as big improvements in their lives, despite conditions that may seem unacceptable to Westerners. In fact, the hump of income gains seen in Figure 13-5 suggests that workers like these are some of the main economic winners from globalization. Before flooding into factories, they typically earned far less in villages, whether in Bangladesh, China, or Egypt. Now they are part of a remarkable global decrease in poverty. Most of the people moving from poverty to relative comfort have been Chinese, but they also include millions of Indians, Indonesians, Brazilians, and Mexicans. Even poorer people down to lower world percentile have done fairly well on average. Global poverty levels have fallen steadily since the 1990s. Precise data are hard to acquire, but some economists argue that the Millennial Development Goal set for 2015 by the UN—halving the percentage of people worldwide living on less than $1.25 a day—was achieved ahead of schedule.[20] Bill Gates, one of the world's richest people and a leader in international development efforts through the Bill and Melinda Gates Foundation, believes that coming decades will see the most rapid decline in global poverty in world history.[21]

A more pessimistic point about this pattern of gains across poor countries, though, is that it is hugely uneven. Chinese growth accounts for most of the "emerging global middle class," and other Asian countries for most of the rest.[22] Latin American growth has been slower, and the great relative losers of the globalization era are in parts of sub-Saharan Africa (for regional growth rates over time, look back at Figure 10-2 in Chapter 10). As we saw there, experts disagree about why some countries manage to turn globalization more to their citizens' advantage. At a minimum, it seems clear that capturing benefits from foreign investment and trade depends on political stability, limits to corruption, and some well-chosen investments in infrastructure. While some sub-Saharan African countries are doing better on these fronts—as of 2019 Ethiopia had one of the world's fastest growing economies, and Tanzania, Kenya, and Ghana are booming too—others like Nigeria, Angola, and Zambia still face challenges that sap at economic prospects. Many of their people lack fundamental services, and for the moment their governments seem unable to create environments for investment and market-based growth.

Relative winners and losers also stand out within developing countries, not just across them. Growing cities typically exist alongside a poor countryside that economic development has touched far less. In India, programmers in the software-developing capital of Bangalore live much like the glitterati of Los Angeles or San Francisco, but nearly 300 million people in rural villages still live on less than one U.S. dollar a day.[23] China's extreme urban-rural divide is one of the greatest sources of concern for its government. Its Gini index of inequality is now higher than that of the United States. Areas around Shanghai look much like gated communities in rich U.S. suburbs; tens of millions of villagers elsewhere have homes without running water. A constant flow of people leave the countryside for the cities where wages can be ten times higher.[24] Today, as many as 250 million of these labor migrants shift around seeking work—an instable population that worries China's leaders just as much as rural peasants. Other large developing countries such as Brazil, Mexico, Egypt, or Indonesia have versions of the same problems.

The other key qualification of economic gains in developing countries is that they can be volatile, shifting suddenly from boom to bust. The rapid growth of global financial markets has brought waves of new investment money to poorer countries, but money from outside investors can be fickle. For example, in the 1990s, Argentina was making major changes to please foreign investors. Its leaders made painful and contested reforms to respect Washington Consensus-style practices in trade, finance, spending, and governance. When neighboring Brazil's currency had a crisis in 1999, though, spooked investors fled from Argentina just in case something similar happened there. The Argentinian economy collapsed because investors pulled out (not, as we might expect, the other way around).[25] Crises with some similar dynamics hit East Asia in 1997, Russia in 1998, Turkey in 2001, and other places since. As an old economists' joke goes, foreign invest-ment is like an umbrella that can be borrowed but must be returned as soon as it starts to rain. In another metaphor from the editors of *The Economist*—who usually celebrate globalization—developing countries now sail on a "cruel sea of capital" that sometimes swamps even well-steered ships.[26] Globalization may have boosted millions of developing-world citizens out of poverty, but economic openness to the outside world comes with major trade-offs.

Globalization and National Democracy

Whatever economic gains we derive from globalization, it affects our politi-cal choices as well. Assuming, that is, that we have political choices to make. Citizens of authoritarian countries rarely get to make such choices, but in de-mocracies globalization alters the people's political options. On the one hand, globalization may constrain national policies and so make citizens less able to choose their own fates. On the other, openness and international coordination may empower national democracies to obtain results they cannot reach alone.

In a simple sense, it is difficult to deny that globalization puts restrictive pressure on democratic choice. The most consistent theme in antiglobaliza-tion movements around the world, from the United States and Europe to Latin America and elsewhere, is that being open to international markets constrains policy options at the national level. Even if most citizens support raising taxes on the wealthy, for example, or bolstering regulations for labor representation or en-vironmental protection, a globalized context tends to make such policies difficult to choose. The more businesses are free to move across borders, the more they may threaten to take their investment and jobs elsewhere to avoid policies they dislike. Trade can produce the same effect even if businesses stay put, as cheaper imports from less-regulated or less-taxed places outcompete local producers. Critics of globalization worry that trade and FDI force all countries to gravitate toward purely business-friendly policies, dropping other political priorities in a liberalizing "race to the bottom" to make sure that jobs and investment stay in their territory. In effect, this means that democratic governments may offer increasingly narrow choices to voters on economic and social policies. Voters can choose free trade and liberalization with enthusiasm . . . or free trade and liber-alization with reluctance.

This narrowing of choice is sometimes explicit and official because global-ization includes international treaties and organizations, not just economic pres-sures. Not only can the global competition for jobs and investment make it more costly for democracies to choose anything besides free-trade-friendly policies, but global governance often makes it literally illegal to do so. Thus in the "Battle in Seattle" of 1999—the biggest U.S. antiglobalization protest on record—over 40,000 people directed their anger not just against global competition or corpo-rate outsourcing, but more specifically against the WTO. The WTO is, after all, a formal agreement to tie governments' hands on free trade. Signatories bind themselves to economic openness and even authorize WTO panels to disallow national policies that harm free trade. Because all countries agree that international treaties trump domestic laws, governments that ratify the treaty cannot reject a WTO ruling. To do so legally, they would have to withdraw fully from the treaty—a dramatic move that few governments would take without extremely strong political demands at home. Even President Donald Trump has not considered a WTO withdrawal, though his criticisms of globalization have led him to pull out of several other prominent international treaties and to threaten others. Overall, then, national democracy has clearly lost some of its range of choice due to globalization. Pressure from the global mobility of jobs and investment, and formal commitments in the increasingly dense web of international rules, take certain policy options off the national table.

At the same time, the economic openness and international rules of globalization give democracies new capacities. They bring some influence over other countries' choices and enable democratic governments to make long-term commitments that would be hard to imagine otherwise. In periods of low global flows and few international rules, like before World War II, democracies may have been free to choose their own fates, but they also had few tools to steer their neighbors in peaceful, cooperative directions. After the Great Depression and the war, many drew the conclusion that democracies should seek to bind all countries into openness, human rights, and international cooperation. The cost would be to constrain themselves and the range of choices offered to their citizens (especially those who have doubts about the appeal of globalization). But the benefit would be to press other countries—especially, hopefully, those most likely to be threatening—to open themselves up and play within international rules. Arguably, this is roughly what happened with the end of the Cold War, most notably as Russia and China became more integrated and less confrontational with Western democracies. Another benefit was to empower democracies to resist their own internal temptations. By "tying themselves to the mast" with hard-to-reverse openness and international treaties, democracies sought to built a more free-flowing, cooperative world over the long term.

It is clear that today's democracies feel both of these political effects from globalization: they are simultaneously constrained to respect openness and international rules and empowered to push other countries in the same direction. Equally clear is that neither effect is overwhelmingly powerful. In terms of constraining democracies, globalization has not forced all democracies into a "race to the bottom" of liberalization. Some manage to open up and keep jobs and investment while maintaining nonmarket political priorities like redistributive welfare states, powerful labor representation, and strict environmental regulations. Key examples are Sweden, Denmark, Norway, and Finland: countries that are so well governed that businesspeople consistently rank them among the top ten countries for doing business—usually above the United States—despite their fairly interventionist economic and social policies.[27] In terms of advancing global change, the leverage Western democracies gain from openness and global governance to promote change elsewhere has not exactly forced China or Russia (both now WTO members) to become model global citizens in all respects. One of the Trump presidency's central concerns has been that China has continued to engage in a variety of unfair trade practices despite its membership in the WTO.

These points underscore that globalization is a political agenda, not just a set of economic and technological trends, and we must factor in these political effects to think critically about it. The fact that globalization is such a complex blend of economic and political effects, riddled with trade-offs, make it difficult to judge with simple "pro" and "con" views. To even try to work out our own positions on it, we need to draw on the ideologies that help us knit together interpretations of the political world.

Political Ideologies and Globalization

13.4 **Evaluate competing arguments about the costs and benefits of globalization.**

Globalization! Few words evoke such powerfully contradictory responses. We can read into it all our hopes as we gaze out into the wide world: vast new opportunities for business and travel, stimulating encounters with diverse people, new ideas and experiences, stronger cooperation with other peoples. Or we can see it as symbolic of all the ways in which outside forces may threaten what we treasure: fears of harsh competition and exploitation, destabilization of our values and familiar practices, dilution of our communities and identities, a general loss of control. Perhaps we can see it as both at the same time. Or maybe we can work out a stance in support of "just right" policies that capture good aspects of globalization while minimizing what we see as bad.

Why Globalization Means Freedom, Innovation, and Progress

At its core, the normative case for globalization is about the benefits of openness for all individuals. The wider and more open the political, social, and economic framework for our lives, the more opportunities we enjoy to pursue whatever makes us happy. Furthermore, openness is good for us even when it does not directly make us happy. It brings the bracing stimulation of competition to compel us to seek out our own strengths to be more productive. Both directly and indirectly, global openness forges better human beings and better societies.

That case powerfully echoes the core credo of classical liberalism—the goal of politics should be to give individuals the liberty to do as they please—and it is from the liberal tradition that globalization's champions draw their inspiration. Much of this view concerns the case for open trade that we have seen in previous chapters, but the economic benefits of open markets and competition are really just the most well-developed theme within the more general ideological point of view. In all parts of our lives, runs the broader argument, we benefit from having more choices and a wider playing field. To give the greatest number of people the greatest chances to become the most well-realized human being each can be, all should be exposed to the widest possible range of options in all spheres: ideas, religions, music, food, activities, and so on. Such exposure need not mean that people reject their traditional values or practices; it may just bring a more conscious sense of why traditions are valuable. And even if people reaffirm their traditions in an open setting, their encounter with others will tend to make them more understanding and cooperative vis-à-vis people who make other choices. Without being constantly surrounded by open options, by contrast, people tend to become stagnant, unreflective, and fearful of others.

The era of globalization is thus a march toward the worldwide victory of the liberal tradition. With open trade increasingly embedded in international law and organizations at regional and global levels, fewer and fewer barriers shut off pockets of humanity from choices as consumers, as well as from wide outlets and stimulating competition as producers. Together with tourism and migration, trade and other economic flows serve as the conduits for noneconomic opportunities to flow worldwide. They bring us access to everything from the musical acts of Mali and Vietnamese cuisine to Ukrainian martial arts and Argentinian literature. True, some people may complain about both economic and noneconomic flows: they may dislike how a context of global openness may disrupt their local lives, or they may object that worldwide competition is too fierce for people with certain disadvantages. Yet we must resist the temptation to put up barriers as a security blanket. The one choice we should not permit is rejection of an open context of free choice. Even if globalization does have losers—people whose disadvantages or bad luck cause them to lose out—it increases overall productivity and satisfaction so much that the winners should be able to pay off the losers to make them more comfortable.

How many people in the United States or other countries today subscribe to this view? As dominant as the liberal tradition is in the United States and in much of the world, pure enthusiasm for globalization is actually rather rare. As you will see in the next section, even most political thinkers at the center of liberal-democratic politics hold critical views that stem from other traditions.

Why Globalization Means Inequality and Oppression

Our globalizing world is full of objections to classical-liberal-style claims that global openness promises the greatest happiness for the greatest number. Rather than creating a world where everyone gains more choices, globalization may just let the powerful make more choices for others. Alternatively, it may curtail some of the most meaningful choices we could make. It may even generate a world in which many find it difficult to make intelligent or legitimate choices at all.

For devout socialists, the flaw in classical-liberal faith in openness lies in a naïve view of unregulated economic, social, and political interaction as equal and fair. Opening up state borders to free-flowing goods, services, money, and people brings opportunities mainly for people who are positioned to take advantage of them; for those facing poverty or other disadvantages, it brings new threats of being dominated. Economic exploitation of poorer countries by richer ones is one result; another is that lower and middle classes in rich countries are cut out of solid jobs. Alongside economic domination come political and cultural impositions. Weaker countries are subjected to international rules designed to protect the powerful, and Americanization force-feeds cultural change to the whole globe. These problems might be solved if some sort of strong international authority could deliver global (or regional) regulation and redistribution, but no international organization—not even the EU—is powerful enough to do so. In the absence of any such framework that could allow workers to unite across borders, then, globalization must be resisted. Champions of a better society should focus on winning whatever advantages they can within their national contexts.

For those who ideologically oppose Western liberal modernity even more profoundly—fascists in one form, radical Islamists in another—globalization looks even worse. Strong flows across borders threaten national or religious identities and seduce the rich and poor alike into a materialist, individualist, center-less existence that unmoors people from the meaningful foundations of their lives. For fascists, economic openness and especially international migration threaten state security, sovereignty, and cultural homogeneity. The more global flows escape national control, the less the state can safeguard its people and steer the economy to serve the glory of the nation. Migration dilutes national traditions and solidarity, challenging the connection between the state and its culture. Radical Islamists object to roughly the same issues on a regional level. The independence of any particular Islamic state may not be crucial—more important is the *ummah* (community) of believers together—but globalization threatens Islamic societies collectively with ever-greater Western incursions of material goods, Hollywood films, American cultural norms, and notions like women's rights that have no place in radical Islam.

Environmentalists have a somewhat more mixed relationship to globalization, though they still lean heavily in critical directions. In principle, their ideology could be friendly to an open world that moves beyond the territorial state. Major environmental challenges tend to ignore human borders, after all, and so steps to respect the environment tend to call for collaboration across states. Yet the kind of globalization we have so far, roughly matching the vision of classical liberals, tends not to attract environmentalists' support. It privileges economic flows that perpetuate a prioritization of consumerism and moneymaking over more balanced lifestyles. Its international rules, too, bind countries ever more solidly into free trade, effectively steering them away even further from environmentally minded policies. Big polluters—above all China and the United States—tend to block global environmental deals. Further globalization along these lines may create a fluid world economy in which no one has the kind of oversight necessary to respond to environmental challenges.

Even though classical-liberal thinking rejects these arguments, it also contains one parallel theme. Although a free-flowing global context may bring individuals more opportunities and the stimulation of competition, globalization may weaken one tool that people need to protect and pursue their interests: democracy. Individuals need representative government at some level to enforce rules and organize public debate and choice. Since representative world government is unlikely, national democracy is an important pillar of a liberal world. Unfortunately, the same globalizing developments that offer individuals new frontiers of liberty can complicate the boundaries of democratic choice—blurring who "we the people" are and perhaps limiting "our" government's ability to respond to "our" choices. Classical-liberal-style thinkers still tend to see globalization as overwhelmingly positive, but do not see it as flawless.

All these criticisms are active in politics today. Strong attacks are easiest to find, unsurprisingly, outside the democratic mainstream. Socialist and environmentalist critiques dominate antiglobalization rallies. Fascist-style attacks resound in many illiberal democracies and dictatorships. Radical Islamists denounce globalization in many Muslim countries. Even in the core politics of the United States or other democracies, though, we hear versions of all these themes. On the right and left, politicians in the liberal tradition wrestle with how to balance the good and bad in globalization.

Goldilocks Globalization: Can We Get It Just Right?

The liberal tradition remains the core of mainstream political views of globalization in the United States, Europe, and most other democratic arenas—suggesting that global openness is generally a good thing. Still, even moderate figures on left and right voice concerns about it, bringing in toned-down versions of criticisms from other ideologies. In the past decade, these critiques have also been voiced in stronger ways on both extremes of the political spectrum, especially in the United States. Today globalization is more contested in American politics than ever before.

The long-dominant preference among modern liberals is a Goldilocks-style view of globalization: a country should be not too closed but not too open. Their point of departure is the classical-liberal aspiration that all individuals should enjoy opportunities to trade and move across borders. Modern liberal leaders like Presidents Bill Clinton or Barack Obama have generally championed international trade deals like the WTO or NAFTA. At the same time, though, they tend to think that global openness should be managed to mitigate its undesirable consequences. Echoing concerns of socialists and environmentalists, they worry that global competition with low-wage, weakly regulated countries threatens both lower- and middle-class citizens' livelihoods and developed-country environmental standards. Their view of "Goldilocks globalization" thus includes domestic investments to support education and economic opportunities for the disadvantaged—ideally maintaining openness but helping all citizens to compete within it—as well as international agreements to raise environmental standards worldwide.

Traditionally dominant views of globalization among modern conservatives also mix classical-liberal principles with concerns linked to other traditions. Just as conservatives traditionally endorse markets in domestic politics more than modern liberals, so they have usually been stronger proponents of free-trade deals internationally. Ronald Reagan was an outspoken champion of open international trade, and Presidents George H.W. Bush and George W. Bush maintained this stance. Yet conservative enthusiasm for economic openness is also limited by some hesitations. Echoing some themes that fascists would voice in stronger ways, they worry that international openness can threaten national security and identity. A good example of this mix of priorities was the platform of Mitt Romney (now a Senator for Utah) when he was the Republican presidential candidate in 2012. He favored free-trade deals but also wanted to deter immigration, prioritize military spending, and defend cultural identity by making English the sole official language of the United States.[28] Thus, the conservative "Goldilocks globalization" allows business and finance to roam the world freely in search of productive investments while trying to protect a distinct, secure, unified national culture.

In the 2010s, these mostly positive views of globalization on Left and Right came under challenge from their political flanks. On the left wing of the Democratic Party, presidential candidates like Senators Bernie Sanders and Elizabeth Warren attacked globalization as part of their focus on fighting economic inequalities. In Sanders' words, the "increasingly globalized economy, established and maintained by the world's economic elite, is failing people everywhere."[29] Sanders, Warren, and allies do not fully reject openness, but want to do much more to protect American jobs, regulate multinational corporations, and raise international labor and environmental standards. Sanders' 2020 campaign platform summed up their call: "Trade is a good thing, but it has to be fair."[30] The more dramatic shift came on the Right, where President Donald Trump broke sharply with the conservative tradition of support for free-trade deals. Trump agreed with Sanders that trade needed to be "fair," but he posed the problem of fair trade in nationalist terms. He imposed aggressive tariffs to force China, Mexico, and Europe to concede "better deals" for American firms. Arguing that "Tariffs are a beautiful thing," he horrified American business by threatening to block trade with Mexico—with which the U.S. trades almost as much as with China—to leverage Mexican action to prevent immigration into the United States.[31] An agenda of asserting American power and promoting majority national identity had unmistakably come to "trump" the Republican Party's previous support for global openness.

Where do these ideological debates leave us? That is for you to decide. To help you work out your own position, Table 13-1 summarizes the elements of globalization and the most salient arguments about benefits, costs, winners, and losers.

Table 13-1 Summing Up Globalization's Potential Benefits and Costs

Element of Globalization	Apparent Benefits?	Apparent Costs?	Likely Winners?	Likely Losers?
Trade	• More diverse products • Lower prices	• The wider the markets, the more the biggest businesses might dominate?	• All consumers • Competitive producers who now gain wider outlets	• Less skilled or more expensive producers who lose out to foreign competition
Foreign Direct Investment (FDI)	• More investment available to more markets worldwide	• Production is able to move across borders; offshoring and outsourcing may reduce jobs for less skilled people in developed countries	• Investors • Competitive firms who can now produce wherever cost/quality advantages are most appealing • Workers in developing countries	• Less skilled workers in developed countries
Global Financial Flows	• Even more (and more fluid) investment available to more markets worldwide	• Volatility; rapid movements of capital across borders may destabilize vulnerable economies	• Investors • Financial sector • Speculators • Businesses in need of easier access to investment funding	• Countries that may be harmed by sudden outflows of capital
International Law	• More even and predictable global rules and standards • Pressure for spread of human rights, rule of law	• Limits on countries' freedom to choose national policies, perhaps narrowing democracy?	• Proponents of rule of law, human rights, and regional or global cooperation	• Illiberal or authoritarian governments
International Organizations (IOs)	• Increased capacity for cooperation across borders; improved ability to govern businesses and other players who are escaping national oversight	• As above; plus shifts in power from democratic governments to less democratically controlled bodies?	• Different IOs have different winners: some promote free trade, others environmental standards, cultural cooperation, etc.	• Different IOs have different losers, depending on their purpose

Explaining a Case: Uncovering the Whys of U.S. Government Trade Policies

13.5 Identify multiple plausible explanations for the American shift away from supporting open trade.

From World War II until 2016, the U.S. government was widely seen as the most important proponent of open trade in the world. It championed the GATT negotiations, creation of the World Trade Organization, the North American Free Trade Agreement (NAFTA), and many other tariff-reducing deals. Many Americans had misgivings about such policies over time, but the overall orientation of U.S.

The Rational-Material Story

The simplest explanation for the shift is that the position of Americans in the global economy changed over time. For many decades after World War II, Americans were very well positioned to benefit from global openness. The United States had tremendous wealth and resources, and American firms were powerfully dominant in many sectors. Gradually, however, developing countries became more competitive, attracted much of the world's manufacturing activity, and caught up in technology. China in particular became a serious rival. By 2016, American material interests overall reached a tipping point where more people expected losses from global openness than gains.

The Institutional Story

From an institutional point of view, U.S. policy on trade reflects institutions that allow certain interests to influence policy, not a clear material landscape in which most Americans obviously benefit from open trade. This view seems to fit well with earlier support for open trade, since two features of U.S. institutions seem to empower advocates of openness. The strength of Congress in policymaking creates many opportunities for business lobbies to influence trade policy, and the lack of legal limits on giving money to politicians' campaigns allows big businesses to keep the government committed to open trade whether or not it is good for the population overall. The shift against openness was possible because President Trump was more willing than his predecessors to ignore Congresspeople on trade, even those within his own party. An institutionalist thinker would likely predict that U.S. policies will shift back to pro-openness after Trump's departure.

The Ideational Story

An ideational account would trace the U.S. policy change on trade to a cultural or ideological shift. Traditionally, Americans have been more comfortable with open trade than most other peoples. Capitalism and markets are celebrated especially strongly in American society, especially within the white-majority elite that defined the United States as a project in limited government and economic liberties. . These beliefs powerfully shaped U.S. policymaking until the cultural and demographic dominance of the white majority began to weaken. Enough of the white majority became concerned about their status as the traditionally dominant national group that a nationalist political movement to block immigration overwhelmed the political forces that supported globalization.

policy was quite consistent across both Republican and Democratic presidencies. This changed with the election of Donald Trump in 2016. The U.S. government backed out of free-trade deals, renegotiated NAFTA, raised tariffs against both rivals and allies, and was generally seen as unconcerned about impeding international trade. Why the shift?

Once again, it seems plausible that all of these explanations contain some truth, but they are also in competition; the more powerfully one explains U.S. choices, the less the others are crucial to the story. And once again political scientists would use two broad approaches to seek empirical evidence that favors or undercuts each of them:

RESEARCH ON WITHIN-CASE PROCESSES. The most direct strategy to researching the sources of U.S. trade policy is to look at the pressures, incentives, intentions, and decision-making processes on trade in Washington, D.C. Table 13-2 suggests some of what each explanation would expect to find.

Find a news article about American policy on trade from a credible newspaper, magazine, or website, and look for signs that seem to fit best with one version of the story.

Table 13-2 Exploring Within-Case Evidence for Alternative Explanations of Trade Policies in the United States

	Rational-Material Explanation	Institutional Explanation	Ideational Explanation
What is the main dynamic in the shift of U.S. trade policy?	Many American firms gradually lost their dominant positions in international markets and became less favorable to openness	A business-friendly Congress was blocked from shaping trade policy by a newly assertive White House	A large percentage of Americans, especially white Americans, became more concerned with immigration and identity issues than trade
Who should we see calling and lobbying most for open trade?	A wide range of business interests, led by the most competitive big businesses (but these become less numerous and vocal over time)	Big businesses and related lobbying associations (plus the politicians they buy in Congress)	Politicians appealing to images of economic liberty, the "self-made man," and the "American dream"
Who should we see opposing open trade?	Less competitive businesses; labor unions afraid of losing jobs; the poor (and these become more numerous and vocal over time)	Same as box to left—but in this version, they lack institutional access in Congress but have better connections to Trump White House	Politicians appealing to nationalist and racial themes of opposition to immigration and threats to security
Best Evidence to Support Each Explanation	Support for open trade and the intensity of mobilization correlates to each person's place in the economy: more competitively placed people favor open trade, less competitively placed people oppose it	Overall citizen and interest-group preferences on trade look mixed, but pro–openness big business clearly dominates in halls of Congress while anti-openness views are privileged in White House	Whatever people used to think about open trade, their views on openness become increasingly dominated by their positions on issues of nationalism and identity

RESEARCH ON CROSS-CASE PATTERNS. We could also gain explanatory leverage on U.S. trade policies by setting them in patterns across countries. Do countries' degree of openness to trade with the outside world correlate with wealth? Or perhaps countries are more open when they have certain institutional features, or are part of certain regional or cultural groups? Your instructor may be able to help you find data to explore some of these possible cross-case correlations.

Conclusion: Why Understanding Globalization Matters to You

Few elements of our political future are more certain than ongoing globalization in some shape or form. The cross-border flows that have risen so dramatically in recent decades reflect powerful trends in technology, national-level policies, and international law and organizations. These processes are certainly contested, but the politics they evoke tend to focus more on shaping or channeling them than on reversing them. Barring a catastrophic global crisis of war, financial collapse, or something similar (alien invasion?), While the coronovirus pandemic of 2020 stopped the global economy in its tracks, globalization is very likely to continue in future years.

What we do as individuals and nations in a globalizing world, however, is a more open question. We may endorse and try to accelerate economic openness and international governance. We may look for ways to manage, mitigate, or limit our international exposure. We may seek more selective mixes that promote certain kinds of openness and restrict others. In some ways, this will take us into new territory: to pursue our interests and values in a changing global context, we will surely forge new policies, new political movements, and perhaps even whole new political frameworks. To think critically and participate in these politics of the twenty-first century, though, the best preparation is to understand the political alternatives people have built so far. Armed with an organized sense of alternative political arrangements, ideologies, and explanations, you are now on the path to reclaim a conscious role in your own future.

Review of Learning Objectives

13.1   Identify the main ways in which globalization has changed economic patterns in the past fifty years.

The economic parts of the trend we know as globalization—rising flows of goods, services, money, people, and ideas across borders—resulted from technological change and political pursuit of free trade over the past fifty years. International trade rose rapidly and shifted in character, with developing countries taking on more of the world's manufacturing. Governments also increasingly encouraged

FDI, allowing rich-world firms to spread their production processes across borders to take advantage of cheaper labor and other favorable conditions. At the same time, money flowed increasingly rapidly across borders. It brought more freely available investment funds to much of the world, but simultaneously created the potential for unpredictable swings up and down in vast new financial markets.

13.2   Identify several reasons for the growth of international law and international organizations, and cite influential examples in both areas.

Although international law was weak for centuries, it became much stronger in the past hundred years. The horror of industrialized warfare was one cause, provoking the Geneva Conventions and other international treaties that protect human rights of both soldiers and noncombatants and ban chemical and biological weapons. International trade was the other major cause, incentivizing states to make legal commitments to allow freer exchange across borders. Over time, both human rights and trade deals became more multilateral, making participation in such treaties the rule rather than exception, as well as making isolated countries or treaty breakers stand out more from the general pattern. With international law came many international organizations that both propose and manage international rules and policies within them, often with considerable powers. In addition to a global architecture of organizations around the UN, many regional economic organizations have grown up to oversee and foster more intensive pockets of regional cooperation. Of these, by far the strongest is the EU, whose powers extend well beyond those of any other international entity.

13.3   Assess who has gained or lost economically from globalization and evaluate how this has affected democracy at the national level.

Not all economic gains and losses in recent decades are due to globalization, but more free-flowing economic activity has had major effects in the distribution of wealth. In the developed countries, the wealthy have gained new investment opportunities and new markets for their businesses. They have claimed a larger share of national income in almost all cases. Middle-class and poorer citizens have gained as consumers, with wider availability of cheaper and better goods and services, but have gained much less as producers. With more international competition for their jobs, they have lost overall shares in national income. In the developing countries, by contrast, large groups of people have seen substantial gains, but in very uneven ways around the world. As seen more generally in China and Asia, not only have the rich become much richer but millions of poorer people have gained the comforts of the middle class. Similar groups exist in Latin America, the Middle East, and Africa, but their national growth has been thinner and slower and less of the population has become notably richer. Democratic governance, meanwhile, has both gained and lost from globalization. The ability of any democratic government to obey the will of its population has decreased, since governments' options are more constrained by global flows, international law, and international organizations. Yet these same flows, law, and organizational rules have also created more pressure for economic and political liberalization in nondemocracies, encouraging liberal democracy worldwide.

13.4 Evaluate competing arguments about the costs and benefits of globalization.

From a classical-liberal point of view, globalization is almost entirely good. It is, after all, the global version of the openness and individual freedom that classical liberals have long sought at the national level. The more that open markets can be established around the world, with clear but minimalistic rules set up in international law and organizations, the more global liberty will win out. Devout socialists, fascists, and Islamists, on the other hand, see globalization as almost entirely bad. For socialists, it represents the triumph of exploitative big business and global capitalism. For fascists, it dilutes and undercuts national identity and state control. For Islamists, it contaminates Muslim societies with seductive but misguided Western influences. Within the mainstream democratic politics of modern liberals and conservatives, hints of these objections have traditionally been combined with a basic classic-liberal endorsement of globalization. Modern liberals hope to mix a free-flowing world with national policies that allow disadvantaged groups to participate on equal terms. Modern conservatives hope to mix free trade with political and cultural limits, reinforcing national security and identity while gaining from economic exchange. Concerns about globalization have become much sharper on both Left and Right in recent years, especially in the United States, raising doubts about the continued support of democratic governments for global openness.

13.5 Identify multiple plausible explanations for the American shift away from supporting "free trade."

To review for this objective, brainstorm rational-material, institutional, and ideational explanations of varying American support for open trade without looking at Section 13.5. Begin by asking yourself the following questions:

- In a simple rational-material sense, people who are in strong positions presumably like competition because they know they will win it. Why might Americans have been in strongly competitive positions in the past, and why might those positions have weakened in recent decades?

- To take an institutional approach, which features of American political institutions might allow for special influence by the businesses that might champion open trade? How might pro–trade business groups influence policymaking? What or who might get in their way?

- From an ideational point of view, can we see strong themes in past American political culture and identity that place an emphasis on the legitimacy and value of open trade? What reasons would recent skeptics of openness, like supporters of Donald Trump, give for their positions?

After brainstorming your answers to these questions, return to Section 13.5 to see how well you have constructed plausible alternatives to explain this case.

Great Sources to Find Out More

Benjamin Barber, "Jihad vs. McWorld," *The Atlantic Monthly*, 269(3) (March 1992), 53–63. A classic analysis of our era as dominated by conflict between globalizing economic forces and traditional identities.

Branko Milanović, *The Haves and the Have-Nots: A Brief and Idiosyncratic History of Global Inequality* (New York: Basic Books, 2010). The World Bank's chief economist dissects patterns of inequality over time.

Dani Rodrik, *The Globalization Paradox: Why Global Markets, States, and Democracy Can't Coexist* (New York: Oxford University Press, 2011). A development expert at Princeton University breaks down economic and political tensions in a globalizing world.

Ian Bremmer, *Us vs. Them: The Failure of Globalism* (New York: Portfolio, 2018). An insightful public commentator analyzes rising opposition to globalization.

Jagdish Bhagwati, *In Defense of Globalization* (New York: Oxford University Press, 2007). Another renowned economist fires back to defend free markets and globalization.

Joseph Stiglitz, *Globalization and Its Discontents* (New York: Norton, 2002). Criticisms of the Washington Consensus approach to globalization by a Nobel Prize–winning economist.

Mary Ellen O'Connell, *The Power and Purpose of International Law* (New York: Oxford University Press, 2011). An overview of arguments for and against international law that concludes strongly for its value and that strongly criticizes U.S. foreign policy.

Peter Marber, *Seeing the Elephant: Understanding Globalization from Trunk to Tail* (New York: Wiley, 2009). An accessible and well-informed survey of a globalizing world.

Robert Guest, *Borderless Economics: Chinese Sea Turtles, Indian Fridges and the New Fruits of Global Capitalism* (New York: Palgrave Macmillan, 2011). An economic journalist's very positive account of how globalization brings benefits everywhere.

Ronald Rogowski, *Commerce and Coalitions: How Trade Affects Domestic Political Alignments* (New York: Cambridge University Press, 1988). A wide-ranging rationalist-materialist analysis about patterns in support for free trade across history.

Samuel Moyn, *The Last Utopia: Human Rights in History* (Cambridge, MA: Harvard University Press, 2012). A Harvard law professor presents a readable and provocative account of the increasing power of human rights.

Thomas Hale, David Held, and Kevin Young, *Gridlock: Why Global Governance Is Failing When We Need It Most* (Malden, MA: Polity, 2012). This book offers an accessible and passionate plea for the construction of stronger international organizations to sustain global cooperation.

Develop Your Thinking

Use these questions as discussion or short writing exercises to think more deeply about some of the key themes of the chapter.

1. What is the most striking way that globalization has made your life different from that of your grandparents?

2. If you lived in Europe, would you be supportive or worried about the rise of the European Union?

3. Should richer countries such as the United States do anything to protect or support any of their citizens who face new competition thanks to globalization?

4. Are international organizations valuable tools to uphold international cooperation or illegitimate threats to democracy?

5. Do you think the open trade benefits Americans (or some Americans) less than it used to?

6. Is globalization bringing you better chances at a happy life or not? In what ways?

Keywords

bilateral treaty   458
common market   463
containerization   450
creditors   457
debtors   457
customs union   463
diffuse reciprocity   459
diplomatic immunity   458
dumping   459
exchange rate   456
foreign direct investment
   (FDI)   453

globalization   448
global supply chain   454
international nongovernmental
   organization (INGO)   462
multilateral treaty   459
multinational corporations
   (MNCs)   453
nontradables   452
Nuremberg Tribunal   460
preferential trade agreements
   (PTAs)   454
specific reciprocity   459

trade deficit   452
trade surplus   449
trade-to-GDP ratio   449
UN General Assembly   461
UN Security Council   461
value-added   449
volatility   456

Glossary

absolutism   A government that assigns absolute, unchecked power to a single individual.

administrative law   Regulations within a statutory framework that specify how government agencies act and implement policies.

agenda control   In legislatures, the power to schedule what will be debated or voted on and when.

alternative vote (AV)   A modification of an SMP system where voters rank candidates in order of preference.

analytic argument   Argument about how things are or how they change, not about how they ought to be.

anarchism   A political philosophy that calls for erasing government or reducing it to a very small scale.

anticorruption campaigns   Showy government action to convince citizens that corruption is not tolerated.

apathy   A state of indifference and inactivity.

aristocracy   A group of people, usually hereditary, with special legal status that gives them privileges not extended to others.

Aristotle   An Athenian philosopher who saw the study of politics as the "master science" that guides how society in general should proceed and argued for a government balanced between the masses and an educated elite.

austerity   Policies that cut government spending and/or raise interest rates severely.

autarky   Extreme self-reliance and isolation.

authoritarianism   A form of government that claims unlimited authority and is not responsible in any systematic way to citizens' input.

authority   The legitimate right to exercise power.

autonomy   The power or right to act independently from others.

backbenchers   "Normal" legislators who hold no leadership position in their government or party.

balance of power   The distribution of military capability around the world, which realists see as shaping how states act in any given era.

bicameral/unicameral   These terms refer respectively to legislatures consisting of two "houses" (bi-) or one (uni-).

bilateral treaty   A legal agreement between two (and only two) countries.

bipolar   The term for an international system with two centers of power that surpass all others.

bourgeois   The commercial class of people who make money by owning and investing in businesses.

brain drain   The departure of talented people from a location to places with better opportunities.

bureaucracy   A hierarchical organization of salaried professionals who apply systematic rules to accomplish tasks.

cadres   Groups of party officials that supervise and manage a one-party state.

capital   Another word for money, often used with respect to investment.

capitalism   The making of money (or "capital") through ownership or investment in a profit-making enterprise.

capitalists   People who make money with money rather than with labor.

checks and balances   More specific powers assigned to separate branches of government to allow them to prevent each other's abuses.

citizenship   Legal membership in a state, typically giving full access to privileges available to other inhabitants.

civil disobedience   The peaceful but explicit refusal to respect laws or rules.

civil service   Nonmilitary career professionals employed by government, classically with guarantees of neutrality from party politics.

civil society programs   Policies usually funded by Western countries to promote the development of pro-democracy groups in authoritarian countries or illiberal democracies.

civil society   Arenas of action in a country outside direct government influence, such as associations, churches, business affairs, media, and artistic expression.

classical liberalism   A political philosophy and ideology that prioritizes individual political rights, private property, and limited government.

clerics   Members of religious orders, or the clergy.

closed party primaries   Elections to select candidates for a party in which only registered party members can vote.

coalition government   A government in a parliamentary system in which the prime minister and cabinet depend on the support of more than one party in the legislature to form a majority.

code law   The legal system that attempts to create more systematic laws and regulations and leaves less interpretation to judges.

codetermination   A system in which workers have a say in company management.

Cold War   A hostile stand-off in the late 1940s through the late 1980s between the communist USSR and its allies versus the capitalist-democratic United States and its allies.

collective bargaining   The process of determining pay or other conditions of work in negotiations between representatives of workers and representatives of employers.

collective-action problem   A situation in which successful action depends on the involvement of multiple people, but rational individuals would not see sufficient incentives to join in.

colonialism   A form of empire with a state at the center that controls other territories as "colonies."

command economy   A system in which government authorities dictate the production and distribution of goods and services.

common law   The legal system that casts judges as impartial interpreters of unsystematic laws, ruling substantially by precedent.

common market   A customs union that also adopts some shared economic regulations across its members.

communism   The radical version of socialism that calls for revolutionary rejection of capitalism and private property.

comparative advantage   Whatever a person can produce relatively more efficiently than other people.

competition policy   Policies that prevent businesses from avoiding competition, such as the breaking up of monopolies.

computer simulations   The computer-based study of how people might act if placed in certain situations that can be modeled with computer programming

conditionality Offering support such as foreign aid, trade access, or diplomatic recognition on condition that a country adopts specific behaviors.

Confucius A Chinese philosopher who offered rules for virtuous behavior by both subjects and emperors, but also suggested that the people could challenge tyrannical leadership.

conscription A requirement that all young men serve in the military, sometimes called "the draft."

consolidation The process between establishing democracy and making it an unchallenged system of governance.

constituency The voters whom an elected official represents.

constitution A fundamental document that defines rights and processes to limit what government can do.

constitutional law Formal laws included in constitutions.

constitutional monarchies A subset of liberal democracies where a king, queen, or emperor retains a symbolic role, but without substantial political power.

constructivism A version of ideational explanation that suggests that the international arena is shaped primarily by what people believe about international politics.

contagion In a political context, when rising opposition to a government encourages opposition to other governments as well.

containerization Packing goods in trailer boxes that can be easily transported and stacked.

contestation In the context of representative democracy, the principle that more than one candidate must compete seriously in elections for government office.

conventional weapons Classic projectiles and explosives—guns and bombs—that are perceived as "normal" military tools, in contrast to nuclear, chemical, or biological weapons.

correlation A patterned relationship between things that arise and change together.

coup d'état An unconstitutional and sudden removal of a government, usually by small groups of insiders including the military.

creditors/debtors Creditors are people who are owed money; debtors are people who owe money.

cult of personality The use of propaganda to create a God-like charismatic image around a leader, often making absurd claims about her or his virtues and abilities.

customs union A preferential trading arrangement that erases tariffs between its members and adopts common tariffs vis-à-vis other countries.

cycles of protest When small initial protests embolden other people to join them or imitate them elsewhere.

decolonization The rapid process from the 1940s to the 1960s when European states, the United States, and Japan surrendered control of their previous colonies, creating many new states.

deficits The shortfall in a budget when an organization spends more than it takes in.

democracy A Greek-based term for rule by the common people, combining the words demos (for the common people) and kratia (power or rule).

democratic peace The observation that no two democracies have ever fought a war with each other.

dependency theory The Marxist-related theory that sees all of human history in terms of dominance of poor countries by rich countries.

dependency The notion that developing economies are trapped in disadvantaged positions in world markets.

descriptive representation The principle that a group's representatives should proportionally reflect racial, ethnic, gender, and other kinds of diversity within the group.

deterrence The use of threats to deter another party from attacking.

developing/developed countries Labels commonly attached to poor or middle-income countries on the one hand and rich countries on the other.

devolution A transfer of authority to lower levels of government.

dictatorship A form of authoritarianism that lodges authority in a single person, or sometimes in the military overall, in the name of providing stability and security.

diffuse reciprocity The practice of agreeing to broad, general cooperation over time, placing less importance on highly detailed commitments.

diplomatic immunity A status that protects diplomats from mistreatment or prosecution in other countries.

direct democracy A little-used political model in which citizens participate directly in decision making.

dissident Someone who opposes a political system or policy, usually in an authoritarian context where such opposition is not permitted.

dissolution The act of the head of a parliamentary system to resign and call a new election.

divided government A situation in a separation-of-powers system in which representative branches of government are controlled by different parties.

division of labor The specialization of roles in an economy.

double transition When a country simultaneously attempts democratization and major economic reforms.

Downs paradox The idea that the cost of voting in an individual's time usually exceeds the likely benefits, since a single vote rarely affects the outcome.

dumping Selling a product at prices below its cost of production to wipe out the competition.

Duverger's Law The observation that SMP rules encourage two-party systems, since they favor large parties, and that PR rules encourage multiparty systems.

economic development Processes of reorganization in poorer societies that create the conditions for sustained economic growth.

economic growth Expansion in the volume of goods and services exchanged in an economy.

economic stimulus Government action to inject money into a weak economy.

economic voter A theory of voting behavior that expects people to vote in ways that seek economic benefits.

effectiveness The delivery of benefits that can convince citizens to support a regime no matter how it is legitimized.

empire A political system that claims domination over both a central, directly administered territory and other territories that it governs in other ways.

employers' organizations Associations that represent owners or managers of for-profit businesses.

ethnic cleansing The systematic killing or expulsion of an ethnic group from a territory.

exchange rate The cost of one currency in terms of another, such as the number of Japanese yen it takes to buy a U.S. dollar.

executives A government's leading officers, with responsibility for setting a policy agenda, making immediate decisions, and implementing policies.

experiments In political science, the method of evaluating hypotheses by manipulating key relationships across randomized contexts.

exploitation Paying workers less than their labor is worth.

failed state A country where the central government is entirely unable to control the territory, resulting in chaos.

federal state A state in which power is shared between two levels of government with irrevocable authority.

feudalism A social system of obligations in which people provide labor, produce, or service to a lord in return for land and protection.

financial bubble   When prices for something rise very rapidly to implausible levels, typically leading to a sudden collapse.

financial markets   Parts of the economy in which businesses raise money for investment.

first gulf war   The U.S.-led invasion in 1991 to expel Iraq from its small neighbor Kuwait.

fiscal policy   Policies of government budgets, including revenue (taxes) and government spending.

foreign direct investment (FDI)   When foreigners own or fund businesses inside a country.

free rider problem   The category of collective-action problems in which individuals would prefer to let someone else do the work to obtain a collective benefit.

fusion of powers   The organizing principle of parliamentary government, in which the executive depends directly on the support of a legislative majority.

game theory   The mathematical study of strategic decision making that explores how people would logically respond if placed in certain game situations

GDP per capita   The most common measure of average wealth, calculated by dividing GDP by population.

gender quotas   Rules that incentivize or require that a certain portion of candidates or elected officials be women.

Geneva Conventions   Treaties that set rules for warfare and ban the use of chemical and biological weapons.

genocide   The systematic destruction of an ethnic, religious, or national group.

gerrymandering   Within SMP systems, this term means the redrawing of electoral districts to capture certain kinds of voters.

Gini coefficient   The most widely used measure of inequality.

global supply chain   A chain of operations across multiple countries to produce a good.

globalization   Rising flows of goods, services, money, people, and ideas across borders.

government   The organization of political authority within a state.

gross domestic product (GDP)   The total value of goods and services produced in a country.

guerrilla warfare   Irregular warfare that uses highly mobile, surprise-based tactics like ambushes and sabotage.

hegemon   A state that becomes so powerful that it dominates the world (or at least its region).

human development   A concept that sets wealth as one criterion alongside others like health and education as measures of social progress.

human rights   Rights that ostensibly apply to all people simply by virtue of being human.

humanitarian crises   Situations in which the safety or health of large populations are threatened.

hybrid regimes   Governments that incorporate features of both authoritarian and democratic government.

hyperinflation   Extreme drops in the value of money, which are devastating for an economy.

identity politics   Politics in which people emphasize membership in a group as the basis for political action, rather than policies, ideologies, or status that could be shared with other groups.

illiberal democracy   A government in which leaders are selected in regular elections but liberal rights are not strongly respected.

import substitution industrialization (ISI)   An economic strategy to end dependency by limiting imports from rich countries and building up domestic industries for the home market.

independent regulatory agencies   Government bureaucracies that regulate a certain issue area and are deliberately given some independence from politicians' oversight.

industrial policy   Policies that actively seek to strengthen particular local or national industries or firms.

industrialization   The adoption of modes of production that include mechanized technology and the separation of jobs into specific roles for each step in a production process.

inequality   In economic terms, the unequal distribution of wealth; in political terms, the assignment of rights to some people and not to others.

infant industry problems   Challenges relating to creating new firms under pressure from more experienced competition elsewhere.

inflation   A general rise in prices, which means a drop in the value of money.

intellectual property rights   Ownership rules for creative products such as books, music, or inventions.

interest groups   Associations in society that form around shared interests and advocate for them in politics.

interest rate   The additional amount of money a borrower must pay back in addition to the borrowed sum. Interest rates set the price of borrowing money.

interests   In political science, the courses of action that most clearly benefit someone given his or her position in the world.

international law   A set of rules that states generally accept as binding.

international nongovernmental organization (INGO)   Private, nonprofit organizations with operations across multiple countries.

international organizations   Entities created by agreements between states to manage international cooperation or undertake specific tasks.

invisible hand   A free market notion that competition to make money will channel everyone toward their most productive individual strengths, sorting people and resources to their best use even without any government leadership.

judicial review   The ability of judges to question the constitutionality of statutes or regulations and to void them in the event of contradictions.

jus sanguinis   Latin for "right of blood," this principle gives citizenship to those related by blood to other citizens.

jus soli   Latin for "right of soil," this principle awards citizenship to those born on a state's territory.

Kautilya   An Indian philosopher who first suggested reversing the priority of analytic and normative thinking, arguing that virtuous leadership depended on understanding the roots of power and influence in the real world.

kleptocracy   A regime that transparently plunders its country, making no attempt to benefit the population.

labor markets   Parts of the economy in which employers hire (and perhaps fire) employees.

laissez-faire   A French phrase meaning "let them do what they want" that is often used as a synonym for unregulated markets.

left   In politics, progressive groups that advocate social and political reform, usually through government action, to improve society.

legislators   Representatives in an assembly, or legislature, who propose, debate, amend, and approve laws.

legitimacy   The perception of something as rightful and appropriate, regardless of whether it is liked.

liberalization   Policies that encourage market competition in an economy.

libertarianism   The strand of conservative ideology that remains the most focused on classical liberal themes of limited government and individual rights.

majoritarian representation   The principle that a group's representatives should be those who receive the broadest support among the group.

managed accountability When citizens have opportunities to vote or criticize government within parameters managed by leaders whom citizens cannot choose.

market economy An economic system based on private property where people can freely exchange goods and services.

martyrdom A revered status that one obtains by dying for a cause, especially for religious reasons.

mercenaries Soldiers who fight for whomever pays them.

methods The ways in which scientists test or support their hypotheses.

mixed economy An economy that combines market capitalism with various kinds of government policies that shape the market.

mixed-member systems Voting rules in which some seats are won under SMP rules and some seats are won under PR rules.

modernization theory A rational-material theory in the liberal tradition that sees history as a march toward liberal democracy and capitalism.

monarchy A form of authoritarianism that lodges authority in a hereditary ruler.

monetary policy Policies that affect the availability of money, like when the central bank raises or lowers the interest rates it charges to private banks.

mujahedeen An Arabic word meaning "those who struggle for Islam." The term can simply designate very devout Muslims, but has come to be identified with radical Islamists who make that struggle violent.

multilateral treaty A legal agreement between more than two countries.

multinational corporations (MNCs) A business with significant operations in more than one country.

multipolar The term for an international system with multiple major centers of power.

Muslim Brotherhood The largest group of political Islamists in the world, though its Egyptian core has been repressed since 2013.

mutually assured destruction (MAD) A situation of successful deterrence in which adversaries cannot strike without being destroyed in return.

nation A group of people who share a cultural identity and think of themselves as a unit that deserves to govern itself.

nationalism An agenda that seeks political power and control for the members of a perceived cultural group.

nationalists Those who seek unity, recognition, and a distinct state for the members of a nation.

nationalization The shift of businesses from private ownership to public ownership under the government.

nation-states A political model in which inhabitants of a sovereign state share a cultural identity.

natural rights The idea that people are endowed with certain rights simply by virtue of being human beings.

naturalization The process of acquiring citizenship in a state after having citizenship in another state or nation.

negative liberty A conception of freedom centered on protection from abuse or restraint—on what should not be done to citizens.

neoliberalism A political movement since the 1970s to decrease active government intervention in market economies.

noncombatants The legal term for civilians not taking part in an armed conflict.

Nongovernmental Organization (NGO) Any legally created organization that operates independently from any government and does not operate mainly for business profit.

nontradables Things that cannot be sold abroad, such as a haircut.

normative argument Argument about how things ought to be, not about how they are.

North Atlantic Treaty Organization (NATO) The alliance between the United States, Canada, and their European allies established in 1949 against the USSR. It still exists today.

nuclear winter The possibility that nuclear war could cloud the atmosphere with enough dust to block all sunlight and kill all life on Earth.

Nuremberg Tribunal The special court that tried the leadership of Nazi Germany in 1945–1946.

offshoring Relocation of a business practice from one country to another.

one-party regime A form of authoritarianism that lodges authority in a political party that claims special ideological insight into good governance.

overrepresentation A situation when a group receives more offices than its population share suggests, sometimes called disproportionality.

pacifism Opposition to the deliberate use of violence.

pacts Attempts to persuade antidemocratic leaders to accept democratization by allowing them to retain certain privileges or immunity from prosecution.

parliamentary sovereignty The principle that all fundamental authority flows from parliament, implying that judges cannot overturn parliamentary statutes.

participation In the context of representative democracy, the principle that the breadth of eligibility to vote must be as broad as possible.

party base Voters who are most strongly committed to a party.

patronage The allocation of government jobs as rewards for political support.

Pendleton Act of 1883 The U.S. law that created the federal civil service.

personal networks Ties of personal loyalty that can allow leaders to control large groups.

petitioning In China, an ancient practice in which citizens bring complaints or demands to the attention of central authorities.

philosopher-kings Leaders in Plato's *Republic* who deserved to lead because they pursued truth in the study of philosophy and kept on that path by having no private property or families.

Plato An Athenian philosopher and author of The Republic who argued for a system of government led by philosopher-kings.

plenary A full meeting of an assembly.

plurality The largest number of votes cast, whether or not it is a majority.

pocketbook voting Voting choices that focus on direct economic costs or benefits for the voter's household.

policies Series of decisions that establish goals and patterns of government action in an issue area.

political culture Ways of acting, talking and thinking about political topics that people learn to expect as normal for people like them.

political description The task of grasping how political life and action are organized.

political elite People who are knowledgeable about politics, actively participate in it, and are well connected to powerful organizations or groups.

political ideologies The versions of political philosophies that people use to organize political debates and action, like liberalism or conservatism.

political philosophy The project of evaluating the good and bad in politics, addressing both how politics works and how it should work.

political science The systematic effort to explain why politics works as it does.

politicization The selection or promotion in civil service to bureaucratic posts due to political views rather than merit or seniority.

polling Survey processes that pose questions to large numbers of people to identify patterns in their views.

pork-barrel politics The practice of securing government spending for an official's constituency without considering goals of desirable policy.

positive liberty A conception of liberty centered on the capacity and opportunity to develop one's talents—on what citizens should be empowered to do.

post-industrial society A society in which advanced industrialization, mechanization, and trade shift most jobs into service sectors.

power The ability to get someone to do something they would not otherwise have done.

precautionary principle The idea that if our actions may produce catastrophic consequences, we should act now to find solutions rather than wait until the consequences become certain.

precedent A court ruling that suggests how laws should be applied to subsequent cases.

preferential trade agreements (PTAs) Treaties that set trade barriers at especially low levels between certain countries, lower than their trade barriers for others.

privatization Selling of government assets or activities to private owners.

progressive/regressive taxes Taxes are progressive when richer people pay a higher proportion of their income, and regressive when poorer people pay a higher proportion of their income.

proletariat Marx's word for the working class—the people who make money by selling their labor rather than by owning or investing.

proportional representation (PR) voting rules Voting rules in which parties are assigned the same share of offices that they win in votes.

proportional representation The principle that a group's representatives should proportionally speak for diverse views within the group.

prospective voting Voting choices that focus on projecting the likely future actions and policies of political candidates or parties.

protectionism Any policy that provides advantages to local business over outside competitors.

proxy wars Wars fought through representatives, or "proxies," rather than between the main antagonists.

public opinion The patterns of views across a population that can be identified by polling.

qualitative methods Ways to evaluate hypotheses that trace evidence for how an outcome came about in particular cases.

quantitative methods Ways to evaluate hypotheses that look for patterns in data, represented as numbers, across a large number of cases.

rational choice theory A method for sharpening rational-material or institutional arguments that proceeds by imagining how perfectly rational people would act (and interact strategically) within material or institutional constraints.

realism The theory that international relations is always dominated by an anarchical conflict between states.

redistribution The transfer of income from richer people to poorer people, classically through government programs.

rent-seeking In economist lingo, any "excess" payment beyond a reasonable compensation for contributions to production.

reparations Actions or payment to make amends for past harm.

representation Processes in which people select others to speak for them in collective decision making.

representative democracy The much more common political model of indirect democracy in which decision-making power lies with citizens' elected representatives, also known as republicanism.

republic A government that is not governed by a hereditary ruler like a king, but instead assigns power through broad public choice.

retrospective voting Voting choices that focus on evaluating the past record of political candidates or parties.

right In politics, conservative groups that seek to defend current or past political and social practices.

rule of law The principle that laws are systematically and neutrally applied, including to top political leaders, and that law itself regulates how laws are made and changed.

sanctions In international relations, penalties imposed by some countries on others to force changes in behavior.

Second Gulf War The U.S.-led invasion of Iraq that toppled the dictatorship of Saddam Hussein in March 2003.

securitization The practice of taking something that cannot usually be bought or sold, such as a home mortgage, and turning it into a financial product that can be bought and sold.

security dilemma The common problem that one group's defensive moves are seen by others as preparation for an attack.

selective incentives Any individually targeted benefit that attempts to resolve collective-action problems.

semipresidentialism A democratic institutional model with both a directly elected president and a prime minister who is responsible to a legislative majority.

separation of powers The principle that branches of government hold separate authority, keeping each other from abusing their powers.

shari'a A system of law based on the Qur'an and other foundational Islamic texts.

shock therapy In the context of post-communist or very poor economies, government action to suddenly deregulate, liberalize, and privatize to open up markets.

single-member plurality (SMP) Majoritarian voting rules in which individual candidates compete to win the most votes for a single seat representing a district.

social capital A resource gained from making social connections to other people in society.

social contract The notion that legitimate government is based on an agreement among the governed to accept central authority.

social democracy The reformist version of socialism that aimed at winning democratic elections and implementing policies to moderate capitalism's inequalities.

social facts Human-created conditions of action that exist only because people believe in them.

social market economy A mix of market capitalism with policies and institutions that help disadvantaged people in the market.

social movements Short- or medium-term public campaigns that aim to achieve collective goals.

socialism A system where government owns most or all economic activities, with little private property.

socialization The processes in which people learn norms, practices, and ideas from others around them.

sociotropic voting Voting choices that focus on costs or benefits for people with whom the voter identifies.

sovereignty The principle that one organization holds supreme authority over a territory.

specific reciprocity The practice of specifying exactly what each signatory to a treaty offers to others (such as specific tariff reductions).

split-ticket voting   Giving votes to members of different parties in the same election.

stagflation   A condition of simultaneous slow growth (and so unemployment) and inflation.

state of nature   An imagined time prior to the development of society or politics.

state socialism   Political systems run by communist parties that abolished capitalism but then focused far more on enforcing their own power than on improving their citizens' welfare.

state   Organizations that claim a monopoly on the legitimate use of violence in a certain territory.

state-owned enterprises (SOEs)   Commercial businesses owned by government organizations.

statute law   Formal laws passed through legislatures.

subcultures   Groups in society that identify and interact with each other, producing distinct clusters of culture not entirely shared by others.

suffrage   Another word for the right to vote.

surplus value   Marx's idea that since all value came from labor, anyone who profited from selling goods besides the workers who made them (i.e., business owners) must be paying the workers less than their work was worth and taking the "surplus."

Taliban   A radical Islamist group that ruled Afghanistan from 1996 to 2001 and now leads an insurgency against the current government.

tariffs   Taxes levied on goods brought into a country from outside (imports).

Terrorism   Politically motivated violence that aims to terrorize an opponent rather than trying to defeat them militarily.

theocracy   A form of authoritarianism that lodges authority in religious officials.

threshold rule   Under PR voting systems, a rule that parties receive a share of seats only if they receive more than a certain percentage of votes, typically from 2 to 10 percent.

totalitarianism   The extreme form of authoritarianism in which government extends its control to all aspects of citizens' lives.

trade deficit   When a country imports more than it exports, the trade deficit is the difference.

trade surplus   When a country exports more than it imports, the trade surplus is the difference.

trade-to-GDP ratio   The sum of exports and imports as a proportion of a whole economy.

Treaty of Westphalia   The treaty that ended the Thirty Years' War, proclaiming each territorial ruler's right to choose a religion for his or her people.

turnout   The percentage of potential voters who actually vote in an election.

two-round system   A modified version of SMP voting rules, also known as a "runoff system."

tyranny of the majority   The possibility that a democratic majority could vote to harm minorities or political opponents.

UN General Assembly   The main assembly of the United Nations. It lacks major powers.

UN Security Council   The UN's center of power, with ten rotating members and five permanent members (the United States, Russia, China, Britain, and France).

unemployment rate   The percentage of the population seeking a job but unable to find one.

unintended consequences   In institutional thinking, this notion refers to how institutions created for one purpose may channel later politics in unforeseen ways.

unions   Associations that represent employees.

unipolar   This term describes an international system with one state that is so dominant that no other state or combination of states can truly threaten it.

unitary state   A state in which only one level of government has irrevocable authority.

value-added   The worth that a production process adds to its materials; steel has more "value-added" than iron ore and thus sells for a higher price.

veto   The ability to block a law or decision, like a president's refusal to sign a bill passed by the legislature in a presidential system.

volatility   The rate and degree of fluctuation in a market.

vote of no confidence   A vote by a legislative majority to withdraw its support from the executive in a parliamentary system.

Warsaw Pact   The alliance between the USSR and its satellite states in Eastern Europe from 1955 to 1991.

Washington Consensus   The open-market package of advice for developing countries formulated in the 1980s by the International Monetary Fund, the World Bank, and the U.S. government.

weapons of mass destruction (WMD)   Another name for nonconventional weapons: nuclear, chemical and biological.

welfare state   The set of policies that redistribute wealth from rich to poor in market-capitalist systems.

will to power   The philosopher Friedrich Nietzsche's phrase for a supposedly universal human need to assert and exercise power.

Notes

Chapter 1

1. "Local Reaction to Government Shutdown," *Reno-Gazette Journal*, www.rgj.com, posted October 1, 2013, consulted December 22, 2014.
2. U.S. Dept. of Commerce, Bureau of the Census, *Historical Statistics of the United States*.
3. The line is often attributed to the Greek leader Pericles, but no Greek source contains this phrasing. It is close in spirit to parts of Pericles's Funeral Oration as reported by Thucydides, *The History of the Peloponnesian War*, Trans. Thomas Hobbes (Chicago: University of Chicago Press, 1989), pp. 108–115.
4. See the Heritage Foundation's "Index of Economic Freedom" at http://www.heritage.org/Index/.
5. Freedom House's annual rankings of "Freedom in the World" are available at http://www.freedomhouse.org/.
6. As of 2018, Afghanistan was the second-largest source of refugees in the world, after Syria. See the annual report of the United Nations High Commissioner for Refugees, www.unhcr.org.
7. Dareh Gregorian, "Government Shutdown Cost Economy $11 Billion, Budget Office Says," *nbcnews.com*, posted January 28, 2019.
8. Dylan Matthews, "The Shutdown Is the Constitution's Fault," *Washington Post* wonkblog, http://www.washingtonpost.com/blogs/wonkblog/, posted October 2, 2013.
9. For example, Jonathan Tobin, "The One Issue in Our Culture War Is Trump," *NationalReview.com*, posted January 25, 2019.
10. See, among others, https://www.factcheck.org/2019/02/factchecking-trumps-national-emergency-remarks/.
11. We might also call this "ideological explanation," but that can generate confusion, since it makes it sound like the explanation itself is driven by a political ideology. I do not have to be a conservative (or a liberal) to argue that conservatives are motivated by certain beliefs. Here, we are talking about a scientific statement that ideologies shape political action, so the more "science-y"-sounding "ideational explanation" works better.
12. As suggested, for example, by John Alford, Carolyn Funk, and John Hibbing, "Are Political Orientations Genetically Transmitted?," *American Political Science Review*, 99(2) (May 2005), pp. 153–167.

Chapter 2

1. Plato, *The Republic*, 2nd ed., Trans. Desmond Lee (New York: Penguin Books, 1987).
2. Aristotle, *Nicomachean Ethics*, 2nd ed., Trans. Terence Irwin (Indianapolis, IN: Hackett, 1999).
3. Aristotle, *Politics*, Trans. Ernest Barker (New York: Oxford University Press, 1977), vols. 1, 2.
4. Confucius, *The Analects of Confucius*, Trans. S. Leys (New York: Norton, 1997).
5. Actually Kautilya, author of *The Arthashastra* (New Delhi: Penguin Books India, 1992), may not have been the same person who advised emperors (known sometimes as Chanakya)—but most sources treat them as the same person.
6. Niccolò Machiavelli, *The Prince and the Discourses* (New York: McGraw-Hill, 1950 [1513]), p. 56.
7. Leo Strauss, *Thoughts on Machiavelli* (Glencoe, IL: Free Press, 1958), p. 9.
8. Thomas Hobbes, *Leviathan* (San Leandro, CA: Seven Treasures, 2009 [1651]), Book I, Ch. XIII.
9. John Locke, *Two Treaties of Government and a Letter Concerning Toleration*, Ian Shapiro, ed. (New Haven, CT: Yale University Press, 2003).
10. Jean-Jacques Rousseau, "On Social Contract or Principles of Political Right," in Alan Ritter and Julia Conaway Bondanella, eds., *Rousseau's Political Writings* (New York: Norton, 1988), p. 85.
11. Carol Pateman, *The Sexual Contract* (Stanford, CA: Stanford University Press, 1988).
12. Charles W. Mills, *The Racial Contract* (Ithaca, NY: Cornell University Press, 1997).
13. See Karl Marx and Friedrich Engels, *The Marx Engels Reader*, edited by Robert Tucker, 2nd ed. (New York: Norton, 1978).
14. Alexis de Tocqueville, *Democracy in America*, Trans. Gerald Bevan, Isaac Kramnick, ed. (New York: Penguin, 2003 [1840]).
15. Émile Durkheim, *On Suicide*, Trans. Robin Buss, Alexander Riley, ed. (New York: Penguin, 2007 [1897]).
16. Max Weber, "Social Psychology of the World Religions," in H.H. Gerth and C. Wright Mills, eds., *From Max Weber: Essays in Sociology* (New York: Oxford University Press).
17. Max Weber, *The Protestant Ethic and the Spirit of Capitalism*, Richard Swedberg, ed. (New York: Norton, 2008 [1904]).
18. Arthur Bentley, *The Process of Government: A Study of Social Pressures* (Piscataway, NJ: Transaction, 1995 [1908]).
19. Ibid., p. 269.
20. Walter Rostow, *The Stages of Growth: A Non-Communist Manifesto*, 3rd ed. (New York: Cambridge University Press, 1991 [1960]).
21. As in Gabriel Almond, *The Politics of the Developing Areas* (Princeton, NJ: Princeton University Press, 1960).
22. C. Wright Mills, *The Power Elite* (New York: Oxford University Press, 1956).
23. See J. Samuel Valenzuela and Arturo Valenzuela, "Modernization and Dependency: Alternative Perspectives in the Study of Latin American Underdevelopment," *Comparative Politics*, 10(4) (1978), pp. 535–557.
24. Hans Morgenthau, *Politics among Nations: The Struggle for Power* (New York: Knopf, 1948).
25. Kenneth Waltz, *Theory of International Politics* (New York: McGraw-Hill, 1979).
26. Kenneth Shepsle, "Institutional Equilibrium and Equilibrium Institutions," in H.F. Weisberg, ed., *Political Science: The Science of Politics* (New York: Agathon, 1986), pp. 51–81.
27. Robert Wade, *Governing the Market: Economic Theory and the Role of Government in East Asian Industrialization* (Ithaca, NY: Cornell University Press, 1994).
28. Guillermo O'Donnell and Philippe Schmitter, *Transitions from Authoritarian Rule: Tentative Conclusions about Uncertain Democracies* (Baltimore: Johns Hopkins University Press, 1986).
29. As in Stephen Skowronek, *Building a New Administrative State: The*

Expansion of National Administrative Capacities, 1877–1920 (New York: Cambridge University Press, 1982).

30. For one example, see Robert Bates et al., *Analytic Narratives* (Princeton, NJ: Princeton University Press, 1998).

31. Elinor Ostrom, *Governing the Commons: The Evolution of Institutions for Collective Action* (New York: Cambridge University Press, 1990).

32. Alexander Wendt, *Social Theory of International Politics* (New York: Cambridge University Press, 1999).

33. As in Peter Hall, ed., *The Political Power of Economic Ideas: Keynesianism across Nations* (Princeton, NJ: Princeton University Press, 1989).

34. As in Victoria Hattam, *Labor Visions and State Power: The Origins of Business Unionism in the United States* (Princeton, NJ: Princeton University Press, 1993).

35. Philip Converse, "The Nature of Belief Systems in Mass Publics," in David Apter, ed., *Ideology and Discontent* (New York: Free Press, 1964), pp. 206–261.

36. John Alford, Carolyn Funk, and John Hibbing, "Are Political Orientations Genetically Transmitted?," *American Political Science Review*, 99(2) (May 2005), pp. 153–167.

37. See, for example, Rose McDermott, *Political Psychology in International Relations* (Ann Arbor: University of Michigan, 2004).

Chapter 3

1. J.S. Mill, *Considerations on Representative Government* (New York: Prometheus, 1991 [1861]).

2. See the regular Political Quiz surveys of the Pew Research Center for the People and the Press at http://pewresearch.org/.

3. See the results of a July 2017 survey by the Annenberg Public Policy Center of the University of Pennsylvania, "Americans Are Poorly Informed about Basic Constitutional Provisions," available at www.annenbergpublicpolicycenter.org.

4. Thomas E. Patterson, *The Vanishing Voter* (New York: Knopf, 2003).

5. Philip Converse, "The Nature of Belief Systems in Mass Publics," in David Apter, ed., *Ideology and Discontent* (New York: Free Press, 1964).

6. Tom W. Smith, "That Which We Call Welfare by Any Other Name Would Smell Sweeter," *Public Opinion Quarterly*, 51(1) (1987), pp. 75–83.

7. Lydia Saad, "Banking Reform Sells Better When 'Wall Street' Is Mentioned," www.gallup.com, April 20, 2010.

8. Alberto Alesina and Edward Glaeser, *Fighting Poverty in the US and Europe: A World of Difference* (New York: Oxford University Press, 2004), p. 184. Surveys compiled from the World Values Survey, 1983–1997. Pew Research Center, http://www.people-press.org/2015/01/15/publics-policy-priorities-reflect-changing-conditions-at-home-and-abroad/.

9. Jennifer Oser and Marc Hooghe, "Give Me Your Tired, Your Poor? Support for Social Citizenship Rights in the United States and Europe," *Sociological Perspectives*, 61(1) (2018), pp. 14–38.

10. Samuel Huntington, "The Clash of Civilizations," *Foreign Affairs*, 72(3) (Summer 1993), pp. 22–49.

11. For example, Alec MacGillis, "In Obama's New Message, Some Foes See Old Liberalism," *Washington Post*, March 26, 2008; Sarah Huisenga, "Romney: Obama Cares 'More about a Liberal Agenda' than the Economy," *National Journal*, November 4, 2012; Nikil Saval, "Hated by the Right, Mocked by the Left: Who Wants to Be 'Liberal' Anymore?" *New York Times Magazine*, July 5, 2017.

12. See the collection of surveys from 2008 to 2017 discussed at http://www.pewforum.org/2018/06/13/how-religious-commitment-varies-by-country-among-people-of-all-ages/.

13. William Kristol, "The Silent Artillery of Time," *The Weekly Standard*, February 20, 2018.

14. The neutral website Factcheck.org suggests that Trump is substantially less truthful than any major American political figure in recent memory. See, for example, https://www.factcheck.org/2017/12/the-whoppers-of-2017/.

15. For example, Jason Stanley, "If You're Not Scared of Fascism in the U.S., You Should Be," *New York Times*, October 15, 2018; Sean Illig, "Fascism: A Warning from Madeleine Albright," *Vox.com*, February 14, 2019.

16. See Timothy Snyder, "Hitler v. Stalin: Who Killed More?" *New York Review of Books*, March 10, 2011.

17. See Roderick MacFarquhar, "The Worst Man-Made Catastrophe, Ever," *New York Review of Books*, February 10, 2011.

18. Nisha Stickles, "Alexander Ocasio-Cortez Explains What Democratic Socialism Means to Her," businessinsider.com, March 6, 2019.

19. Franz-Josef Bruggemeier, Mark Cioc, and Thomas Zeller, eds., *How Green Were the Nazis? Nature, Environment and Nation in the Third Reich* (Athens: Ohio University Press, 2005).

20. W. Anderegg, "Expert Credibility in Climate Change," *Proceedings of the National Academy of Sciences*, 107(27) (June 21, 2010), pp. 12107–12109.

21. See their website at http://christiansandclimate.org/.

Chapter 4

1. Charles Tilly, "Reflections on the History of European State-Making," in Tilly, ed., *The Formation of National States in Western Europe* (Princeton, NJ: Princeton University Press, 1975), p. 42.

2. See Lowell Barrington, "'Nation' and 'Nationalism': The Misuse of Key Concepts in Political Science," *PS: Political Science and Politics*, 30(4) (1997), pp. 712–716.

3. Michael Pachter, "American Identity: A Political Compact," in Robert Earle and John Wirth, eds., *Identities in North America: The Search for Community* (Stanford, CA: Stanford University Press, 1995), pp. 29–39. Available in abridged form at myamerica.be.

4. See the Afghanistan page in the CIA World Factbook at https://www.cia.gov/library/publications/the-world-factbook/.

5. For one overview, see Irina Ivanova, "What's Immigration's Real Impact on U.S. Wages?" *cbsnews.com*, August 3, 2017.

6. For a concrete discussion, see section 2 of Salman Ahmed et al, "U.S. Foreign Policy for the Middle Class: Perspectives from Ohio," Carnegie Endowment for International Peace, December 10, 2018, available at https://carnegieendowment.org/2018/12/10/how-trade-did-and-did-not-account-for-manufacturing-job-losses-pub-77794

7. Richard McGregor, "China's Bitter Response," *New York Times*, October 10, 2010.

Chapter 5

1. This wording comes from a U.S. State Department daily press briefing, January 18, 2012, http://www.state.gov/r/pa/prs/dpb/index.htm.

2. See prison population statistics at the UN Office on Drugs and Crime, https://dataunodc.un.org/.

3. See the 2018 American Institutional Confidence poll published by the Baker Center for Leadership & Governance, Georgetown University, available at https://bakercenter.georgetown.edu/aicpoll/.

4. See data from the club or rich democracies, the Organization for Economic Cooperation and Development (OECD), at http://www.oecd.org/gov/trust-in-government.htm.

5. For one cross-country comparison that includes China and western democracies, see the "confidence in government" question in the World Values Survey at http://www.worldvaluessurvey.org/wvs.jsp.

6. Max Weber, *The Theory of Social and Economic Organization*, Trans. A.M. Henderson and Talcott Parsons (New York: Free Press, 1947), pp. 324–329.

7. See data from the Stockholm International Peace Research Institute military expenditure database, at https://www.sipri.org/databases/milex.

8. See data at the World Prison Brief, http://www.prisonstudies.org/.

9. Max Weber, *The Theory of Social and Economic Organization*, Trans. A.M. Henderson and Talcott Parsons (New York: Free Press, 1947), p. 328.

10. Annual reports from www.freedomhouse.org.

11. Robert Dahl, *Polyarchy* (New Haven, CT: Yale University Press, 1972).

12. January 20, 1981, http://www.reagan.utexas.edu/archives/speeches/1981/12081a.htm.

13. John Stuart Mill, *On Liberty* (New York: Penguin, 1985 [1859]), p. 70.

14. Inauguration address, January 20, 1961. Video and text available at http://www.jfklibrary.org/.

15. Speech before the French Parliament, June 22, 2009, available in French at www.elysee.fr. Author's translation.

16. Economist Intelligence Unit, "Democracy Index 2018," https://www.eiu.com/topic/democracy-index. World Bank definition of "high income" countries.

17. Adam Przeworski et al., *Democracy and Development* (New York: Cambridge University Press, 2000).

18. Russell Dalton, *Citizen Politics*, 6th ed. (Washington, D.C.: CQ Press, 2014), p. 249.

19. Fareed Zakaria, "The Rise of Illiberal Democracy," *Foreign Affairs*, 76(6) (November 1997), pp. 22–43.

20. "Putin's Russia: Call Back Yesterday," *The Economist*, March 3, 2012.

21. Tom Parfitt, "Russia's Rich Double Their Wealth, but Poor Were Better Off in 1990s," *The Guardian*, April 11, 2011.

22. Anna Politkovskaya, *Putin's Russia: Life in A Failing Democracy* (New York: Holt, 2007).

23. Lynn Berry, "Putin's Macho Image as Nation's Warrior Hero," *San Francisco Chronicle*, August 6, 2009.

24. Ilya Arkhipov, "Putin's Popularity Near 2008 Peak on Ukraine Actions," *Bloomberg.com*, June 26, 2014.

25. See the annual report *Freedom in the World*, available at www.freedomhouse.org.

26. See the annual Rule of Law index at http://worldjusticeproject.org/, and the corruption rankings by Transparency International at http://cpi.transparency.org/cpi/.

27. Text available at http://statutes.agc.gov.sg/.

28. *Straits Times*, April 20, 1987.

29. Fareed Zakaria, "Culture Is Destiny: A Conversation with Lee Kuan Yew," *Foreign Affairs*, 73 (1994), pp. 109–126.

30. For a brief overview, see Ibrahim Kalin, "Islam and the West: Deciphering a Contested History," Oxford Islamic Studies Online, at http://www.oxfordislamicstudies.com/Public/focus/essay0409_west.html.

31. Mara Revkin, "The Egyptian State Unravels: Meet the Gangs and Vigilantes Who Thrive under Morsi," *Foreign Affairs*, June 27, 2013.

32. Josh Gerstein and Jonathan Allen, "Barack Obama's Egypt Coup Conundrum," *Politico.com*, October 19, 2013.

33. Peter Baker and Declan Walsh, "Trump Shifts Course on Egypt, Praising Its Authoritarian Leader," *New York Times*, April 3, 2017.

34. Eugénie Mérieau, "How Thailand Became the World's Last Military Dictatorship," *The Atlantic*, March 20, 2019.

35. "Secret Assad Emails Lift Lid on Life of Leader's Inner Circle," *The Guardian*, March 14, 2012.

36. Damian Tobin, "Inequality in China: Rural Poverty Persists as Urban Wealth Balloons," *BBC News Online*, June 29, 2011.

37. Lisa Wedeen, *Ambiguities of Domination: Politics, Rhetoric and Symbols in Contemporary Syria* (Chicago: University of Chicago Press, 1999).

38. Patrick Clawson, "Post-Assad Syria: Opportunity or Quagmire?," National Defense University Strategic Forum report no. 276, February 2012.

39. Ed Husain, "Life after Assad Could Be Worse," *New York Times*, February 7, 2012.

40. See Anchal Vohra, "Syrians Are Ready to Accept Bashar al-Assad as President," *ForeignPolicy.com*, September 19, 2017.

41. When calculated at "purchasing power parity" (PPP) to adjust for differences in currency purchasing power. World Bank, data available at www.data.worldbank.org.

Chapter 6

1. Grimm, Robert T., Jr., and Nathan Dietz. 2018. "Good Intentions, Gap in Action: The Challenge of Translating Youth's High Interest in Doing Good into Civic Engagement." Research Brief, Do Good Institute, University of Maryland.

2. *Le Figaro*, October 17, 2010.

3. Brian Cowan, *The Social Life of Coffee: The Emergence of the British Coffeehouse* (Yale University Press, 2005).

4. For figures in these two paragraphs and a survey of studies, see Richard Niemi and Herbert Weisberg, eds. *Controversies in Voting Behavior*, 4th ed. (Washington, D.C.: CQ Press, 2001).

5. Timur Kuran, "The Inevitability of Future Revolutionary Surprises," *American Journal of Sociology*, 100(6) (1995), pp. 1528–1551.

6. In 2013, under mounting public pressure, Kenyan parliamentarians agreed to cut their salaries from about $120,000 to $75,000—but gave themselves a $59,000 car allowance at the same time. "Kenyan MPs Gun for Top Global Spot with Pay Raise," *Business Daily Africa*, July 5, 2010; "Kenyan MPs Back Down from Demanding Pay Rise to Accept Pay Cut," *The Guardian*, June 12, 2013.

7. "Obama: I Miss Being Anonymous," *Houston Chronicle*, April 10, 2011.

8. The line originated in a 1975 novel about Irish terrorists, *Harry's Game* by Gerald Seymour (New York: Random House).

9. For this figure and others on turnout from the MIT "Election Lab," see https://electionlab.mit.edu/research/voter-turnout.

10. For one cross-country overview, see Miguel Cainzos and Carmen Voces, "Class Inequalities in Political Participation and the 'Death of Class' Debate," *International Sociology*, 25(3) (2010), pp. 383–418.

11. Dave Gilson, "It's Not the 1 Percent Controlling Politics; It's the 0.01 Percent," *Mother Jones*, April 23, 2015.

12. See Theda Skocpol and Alexander Hertel-Fernandez, "The Koch Network and Republican Party Extremism," *Perspectives on Politics*, 14(3) (September 2016), pp. 681–699.

13. Michael Lewis-Beck and Mary Stegmaier, "Economic Determinants of Electoral Outcomes," *Annual Review of Political Science*, vol. 3 (2000), pp. 183–219. Used with permission.

14. For an overview of debates and challenges, see Timothy Helwig and Dani Marinova, "Dead Ends and New Paths in the Study of

Economic Voting," *Oxford Research Encyclopedia of Politics*, posted January 25, 2017, at http://oxfordre.com/politics/view/10.1093/acrefore/9780190228637.001.0001/acrefore-9780190228637-e-190.

15. A political-science classic that makes this argument is Seymour Martin Lipset and Stein Rokkan, eds. *Cleavage Structures and Party Systems: Cross-National Perspectives* (New York: Free Press, 1967).

16. See the classic by Theda Skocpol, *States and Social Revolutions* (New York: Cambridge University Press, 1979).

17. Robert Pape, *Dying to Win: The Strategic Logic of Suicide Terrorism* (New York: Penguin, 2005).

18. See, for example, the language of his famous "I Have a Dream" speech in August 1963, available at https://www.archives.gov/files/press/exhibits/dream-speech.pdf.

19. Brent Griffiths, "Sanders Slams Identity Politics as Democrats Figure Out Their Future," *politico.com*, November 21, 2016. Used with permission.

20. See German Lopez, "Why You Should Stop Saying 'All Lives Matter,' Explained in Nine Different Ways," vox.com, July 11, 2016, available at https://www.vox.com/2016/7/11/12136140/black-all-lives-matter.

21. Ta-Nehisi Coates, "The Case for Reparations," *The Atlantic*, June 2014, available at https://www.theatlantic.com/magazine/archive/2014/06/the-case-for-reparations/361631/.

22. Audie Cornish, "Cornel West Doesn't Want to Be a Neoliberal Darling," *New York Times Magazine*, November 29, 2017, available at https://www.nytimes.com/2017/11/29/magazine/cornel-west-doesnt-want-to-be-a-neoliberal-darling.html.

23. Farah Stockman, "Women's March on Washington Opens Contentious Dialogues about Race," *New York Times*, January 9, 2017.

24. Robert Kuttner, "Steve Bannon, Unrepentant," *The American Prospect*, August 16, 2017, available at https://prospect.org/article/steve-bannon-unrepentant.

25. Christal Hayes, "Here Are 10 Times President Trump's Comments Have Been Called Racist," *USAtoday.com*, August 14, 2018.

26. For a summary of her research, Perry Bacon Jr., "Why Identity Politics Could Be Good Politics for Democrats in 2020," *fivethirtyeight.com*, April 2, 2019.

27. See Earl Black and Merle Black, *The Rise of Southern Republicans* (Cambridge, MA: Harvard University Press, 2003).

28. Alexis de Tocqueville, *Democracy in America, 1* (New York: Vintage Press, 1945), Chapter 14, p. 259.

29. Laila Kearney, "Smartphone Users Oblivious to Gunman Who Killed Student on Train," *Reuters.com*, October 9, 2013.

30. Russell Dalton, *Citizen Politics: Public Opinion and Political Parties in Advanced Industrial Democracies*, 6th ed. (Washington, D.C.: CQ Press, 2014), p. 49.

31. Lee Rainie, Kristin Purcell, and Aaron Smith, "The Social Side of the Internet," Pew Research Center, January 18, 2011.

32. Neil Howe and William Strauss, *Millennials Rising: The Next Great Generation* (New York: Vintage, 2009).

33. Cécile Bazin et al., "La France associative en mouvement 2018," report by Confédération Nationale des Associations de Protection de l'Enfant, available (in French) at https://www.cnape.fr/documents/rechercheessolidarite_-etude-la-france-associative-2018/.

34. *Le Parisien*, October 18, 2010.

35. "Beijing Blocks Protest Reports," *Wall Street Journal Asia*, January 31, 2011.

36. Elizabeth Economy, "The Great Firewall of China: Xi Jinping's Internet Shutdown," *The Guardian*, June 29, 2018, available at https://www.theguardian.com/news/2018/jun/29/the-great-firewall-of-china-xi-jinpings-internet-shutdown.

37. "China's Homeowners Get Small Taste of Democracy," *USA Today*, April 17, 2006.

38. Li Yongchun, "Number of Government Weibo Accounts Soars," *CaixinOnline*, March 28, 2013.

39. Human Rights Watch, *An Alleyway in Hell: China's Abusive 'Black Jails'*, November 12, 2009.

40. "Why Protests Are So Common in China," *The Economist*, October 4, 2018, available at https://www.economist.com/china/2018/10/04/why-protests-are-so-common-in-china.

41. "China Says It Has 'No Dissidents'," *Agence France Presse*, February 11, 2010.

42. Catherine Porter, "Chinese Dissidents Feel the Heat of Beijing's Wrath—Even in Canada," *New York Times*, April 1, 2019, available at https://www.nytimes.com/2019/04/01/world/canada/china-dissident-harassment-sheng-xue.html.

43. J.S. Mill, *Three Essays* (New York: Oxford University Press, 1975), p. 18.

44. For a pure statement of such views from an influential contemporary political theorist, see Robert Nozick,

Anarchy, State and Utopia (New York: Basic Books, 1974).

45. Michael Sandel, *Liberalism and the Limits of Justice* (New York: Cambridge University Press, 1998).

46. See, for example, William Bennett, *The De-Valuing of America: The Fight for Our Culture and Our Children* (New York: Touchstone, 1992).

47. International Institute for Democracy and Electoral Assistance, http://www.idea.int/. Averages cover years from 1945 to 2018.

Chapter 7

1. David Cameron press conference, February 18, 2011, available on YouTube.

2. These states' system, also known as the "nonpartisan blanket primary," requires a second round even if one candidate wins over 50 percent in the first round.

3. Cynthia Tucker, "Voting Rights Act: I Was Wrong about Racial Gerrymandering," *Atlanta Journal Constitution*, June 1, 2011.

4. George Washington's Farewell Address, September 17, 1796, http://www.digitalhistory.uh.edu/disp_textbook.cfm?smtID=3&psid=160.

5. E.E. Schattschneider, *Party Government*, (New York: Praeger, 1977 [1942]), p. 1.

6. Theresa Amato, *The Grand Illusion: The Myth of Voter Choice in a Two-Party Tyranny* (New York: Free Press, 2009).

7. Comments at debate hosted by *Intelligence Squared*, New York University, February 16, 2011.

8. For extensive data on American fundraising, see the website of the nonpartisan Center for Responsive Politics, https://www.opensecrets.org/.

9. His full name was Charles-Louis de Secondat, Baron de la Brède et de Montesquieu; hence, often referred to as just "Montesquieu."

10 Except in Maine and Nebraska, which can split their votes in more complex ways.

11. If no candidate wins a majority of electoral college votes (270), the House of Representatives selects the president and the Senate selects the vice president.

12. See https://www.nationalpopularvote.com/.

13. James Madison, *Letters and Other Writings* (Philadelphia: J.B. Lippincott, 1865), vol. IV, p. 20.

14. See Joshua Keating, "Why Don't Other Countries Have Government Shutdowns?" *Foreignpolicy.com*, April 7, 2011.

15. John Gerring, Strom Thacker, and Carola Moreno, "Are Parliamentary Systems Better?," *Comparative Political Studies*, 42(3) (2009), pp. 327–359.

16. Woodrow Wilson, *Congressional Government* (New York: Houghton Mifflin, 1901).

Chapter 8

1. Herman Döring, "Parliamentary Agenda Control and Legislative Outcomes in Western Europe," *Legislative Studies Quarterly*, 26(1) (2001), pp. 145–165.

2. Gallup poll, December 3–12, 2018, https://news.gallup.com/poll/245597/nurses-again-outpace-professions-honesty-ethics.aspx.

3. European Social Survey 2016, reported at "Pathways to Political Trust" blog, University of Tampere, Finland, https://blogs.uta.fi/contre/2017/11/02/trust-in-politicians-across-countries-and-over-time/.

4. As summarized by Max Weber in *The Theory of Social and Economic Organization* (New York: Free Press, 1947). These principles condense observations on pages 333–336.

5. Ibid.

6. Peter Haas, "Banning Chlorofluorocarbons: Epistemic Community Efforts to Protect Stratospheric Ozone," *International Organization*, 46(1) (1992), pp. 187–224.

7. Jeffrey Pressman and Aaron Wildavsky, *Implementation* (Berkeley: University of California Press, 1973).

8. Jacint Jordana, David Levi-Faur, and Xavier Fernández-i-Marín, "Global Diffusion of Regulatory Agencies," *Comparative Political Studies*, 44(10) (2011), pp. 1343–1369.

9. B. Guy Peters, *The Politics of Bureaucracy* (New York: Routledge, 2001), p. 94.

10. Cited from Japanese sources in Peter Hartcher, *The Ministry: The Inside Story of Japan's Ministry of Finance* (London: HarperCollins, 1998), p. 12.

11. Pascal Eyt-Dessus, cited in Jean-Louis Barsoux and Peter Lawrence, "The Making of a French Manager," *Harvard Business Review*, 69(4) (1991), pp. 58–67.

12. Merilee Grindle, "Constructing, Deconstructing, and Reconstructing Career Civil Services in Latin America," Harvard Kennedy School Faculty Working Paper No. 10-025 (June 2010), http://www.gsdrc.org/.

13. For an accessible history of the U.S. civil service, see the multimedia materials assembled by the U.S. Office of Personnel Management at http://www.opm.gov/biographyo-fanideal/.

14. B. Guy Peters and Jon Pierre, *Politicization of the Civil Service in Comparative Perspective* (New York: Routledge, 2005).

15. Domenico Montaro, "Ambassadors: Do Patronage Picks Matter?," MSNBC.com, posted August 3, 2009, consulted June 5, 2012.

16. Anne Applebaum, "The Trump White House is Destroying Our Civil Service," *Washington Post*, August 3, 2018.

17. A.V. Dicey, *Introduction to the Study of the Law of the Constitution*, 10th ed. (London: Macmillan, 1959 [1885]), p. 27.

18. Cited in James Holland and Julian Webb, *Learning Legal Rules*, 7th ed. (Oxford: Oxford University Press, 2010), p. 153.

19. Adam Liptak, "American Exception: Rendering Justice, with One Eye on Re-election," *New York Times*, May 25, 2008.

20. See Matthew J. Streb, ed., *Running for Judge: The Rising Political, Financial and Legal Stakes of Judicial Elections* (New York: New York University Press, 2007).

21. See Emily Bazelon, "Arguing Three Strikes," *New York Times Magazine*, May 21, 2010, pp. 40–42.

22. *Marbury v. Madison*, 5 US (1 Cranch) 137 (1803), http://constitution.org/ussc/005-137a.htm.

23. David Law, "Anatomy of a Conservative Court: Judicial Review in Japan," *Texas Law Review*, 87(7) (2009), pp. 1545–1594.

24. "End the Tyranny: No Regulation without Representation," http://wolfhowling.blogspot.com, posted March 16, 2012, June 18, 2012.

25. See the collection of conservative essays in Mark Sutherland et al., *Judicial Tyranny: The New Kings of America?* (St. Louis, MO: National Policy Center, 2005).

26. Jeff Bravin and Geoffrey Fowler, "Gay Marriage Decision Sets Up Next Fight," *Wall Street Journal*, May 31, 2012.

27. Larry Kachimba, "Reversing Citizens United: Stripping the Roberts 5 of Power over Elections," http://www.opednews.com, posted January 13, 2012, June 18, 2012.

Chapter 9

1. Regular studies on student loan balances are available from American Student Assistance, www.asa.org.

2. The World Bank, www.data.world-bank.org.

3. For all countries, see CIA World Factbook, https://www.cia.gov/library/publications/the-world-factbook/. For a detailed American breakdown, see the Bureau of Labor Statistics, https://www.bls.gov/emp/tables/employment-by-major-industry-sector.htm.

4. Frank Ruediger, "North Korea's Economic Policy in 2018 and Beyond," *38north.org*, posted August 8, 2018.

5. The story of the rise of free markets and reactions to limit them is told by Karl Polanyi in his book titled *The Great Transformation* (Boston: Beacon, 1944).

6. Organization for Economic Cooperation and Development (OECD), *Country Statistical Profile: United States 2014*.

7. Sami Bibi and Jean-Yves Duclos, "A Comparison of the Poverty Impact of Transfers, Taxes and Market Income across Five OECD Countries," Institute for the Study of Labor (IZA), Bonn, Discussion Paper No. 3824, November 2008.

8. German Federal Ministry of Education and Research, *Germany's Vocational Education System at a Glance* (Bonn: Federal Ministry of Education and Research, 2003).

9. Stewart Nixon et al., "Fostering Inclusive Growth in Malaysia," OECD Economic Working Paper No. 1371, January 2017.

10. For several views, see "Positive Discrimination: Perspectives on Malaysia," *World Policy*, April 12, 2016, available at https://worldpolicy.org/2016/04/12/positive-discrimination-perspectives-on-malaysia/.

11. See annual reports on their Global Competitiveness Index at http://reports.weforum.org/.

12. See annual figures at CIA World Factbook, https://www.cia.gov/library/publications/the-world-factbook/.

13. For an account of the rise of Petronas, see Andrea Goldstein, "New Multinationals from Emerging Asia: The Case of National Oil Companies," *Asian Development Review*, 26(2) (2009), pp. 26–56.

14. John Locke, *Second Treatise of Government*, ed. C.B. Macpherson (Indianapolis, IN: Hackett, 1988 [1689]), p. 19.

15. See the Occupy website at occupy-wallst.org. Accessed May 6, 2019.

16. Gallup poll, July 30-August 5, 2018. See discussion at https://news.gallup.com/poll/240725/democrats-positive-socialism-capitalism.aspx.

17. Milton Friedman, *Capitalism and Freedom* (Chicago: University of Chicago Press, 1962), p. 7.

Chapter 10

1. Andy Grove, "How America Can Create Jobs," *Businessweek*, July 1, 2010.
2. See http://hdr.undp.org/en/content/human-development-index-hdi.
3. Hernando de Soto, *The Mystery of Capital: Why Capitalism Triumphs in the West and Fails Everywhere Else* (New York: Basic Books, 2000).
4. David Barbosa, "Fast Growth and Inflation Threaten to Overheat Chinese Economy," *New York Times*, April 15, 2011.
5. For this figure and other fascinating comments on inequality from a World Bank economist, see Branko Milanovic, *The Haves and the Have-Nots: A Brief and Idiosyncratic History of Global Inequality* (Philadelphia: Basic Books, 2011).
6. This list paraphrases the article that coined the term "Washington Consensus": John Williamson, "What Washington Means by Policy Reform," in Williamson, ed., *Latin American Adjustment: How Much Has Happened?* (Washington, D.C.: Institute for International Economies, 1990), pp. 7–20.
7. Dani Rodrik, "Development Lessons for Asia from Non-Asian Countries," *Asian Development Review*, 23(1) (2006), pp. 1–15.
8. Alex Dreher, "IMF and Economic Growth: The Effects of Programs, Loans, and Compliance with Conditionality," *World Development*, 34(5) (2006), pp. 769–788; Niels Gilbert and Brigitte Unger, "Do Loans Harm? The Effect of IMF Programs on Inequality," Koopmans Research Institute Discussion Paper No. 09-26, Utrecht University, October 2009.
9. This is a "moving average" that smooths volatile figures into a trend line. On moving averages, see http://www.bbc.co.uk/schools/gcsebitesize/maths/statistics/representingdata3hirev7.shtml.
10. Patrice Franko, *The Puzzle of Latin American Economic Development*, 3rd ed. (Lanham, MD: Rowman & Littlefield, 2007), p. 66.
11. *World Development Report* (Washington, D.C.: World Bank, 1997), p. 27.
12. Dani Rodrik, "Growth Strategies," National Bureau of Economic Research Working Paper No. 10050 (October 2003), p. 21.
13. Andrew Szamosszegi and Cole Kyle, "An Analysis of State-Owned Enterprises and State Capitalism in China," report to U.S.–China Economic and Security Review Commission, October 26, 2011.
14. The most respected argument remains Robert Wade, *Governing the Market: Economic Theory and the Role of Government in East Asian Industrialization* (Princeton, NJ: Princeton University Press, 1990).
15. For an entertaining but extreme version, see Martin Jacques, *When China Rules the World: The Rise of the Middle Kingdom and the End of the Western World* (London: Allen Lane, 2009).
16. Paul Krugman, "The Myth of Asia's Miracle," *Foreign Affairs*, 73(6) (November/December 1994), pp. 62–79.
17. Gordon Chang, "The Coming Collapse of China: 2012 Edition," *ForeignPolicy.com*, December 29, 2011; on China's slowdown in the late 2010s, see Christopher Balding, "What's Causing China's Economic Slowdown," *Foreign Affairs*, March 11, 2019.
18. On the Left since this shift, see James Cronin, George Ross, and James Shoch, eds., *What's Left of the Left: Democrats and Social Democrats in Challenging Times* (Durham, NC: Duke University Press, 2011).
19. Floyd Norris, "It May Be Outrageous, but Wall Street Pay Didn't Cause This Crisis," *New York Times*, July 31, 2009.
20. This figure is adjusted to reflect growth in GDP and inflation. Joy Buchanan, Steve Gjerstad, and Vernon Smith, "There's No Place Like Home," Chapman Economic Science Institute Working Paper No. 3 (2012).
21. "Wall Street and the Financial Crisis: Anatomy of a Collapse," April 13, 2011, http://www.hsgac.senate.gov//imo/media/doc/Financial_Crisis/FinancialCrisisReport.pdf.
22. "Dissenting Statement of Commissioner Keith Hennessy, Commissioner Douglas Holtz-Eakin, and Vice Chairman Bill Thomas," January 26, 2011, http://keithhennessey.com/2011/01/26/the-three-man-fcic-dissent-hennessey-holtz-eakin-thomas/.
23. https://www.forbes.com/sites/dianahembree/2018/05/22/ceo-pay-skyrockets-to-361-times-that-of-the-average-worker/#574a3b7f776d.
24. *Roadmap for America's Future* Version 2.0 (January 2010), p. 1, http://roadmap.republicans.budget.house.gov/plan/#Intro.
25. See Russell Berman, "Donald Trump's Big-Spending Infrastructure Dream," *The Atlantic*, August 9, 2016.
26. The Brookings Institution provides an online tracker of deregulation during the Trump administration at https://www.brookings.edu/interactives/tracking-deregulation-in-the-trump-era/.
27. See Oliver Roeder, "How Kavanaugh Will Change the Supreme Court," *Fivethirtyeight.com*, posted October 6, 2018.
28. See Adam Feldman, "The Big Business Court," *scotusblog.com*, posted August 8, 2018.
29. Ben Casselman, "Why Wages Are Finally Rising, 10 Years after the Recession," *New York Times*, May 2, 2019, available at https://www.nytimes.com/2019/05/02/business/economy/wage-growth-economy.html.
30. See Julia Belluz, "What the Dip in US Life Expectancy Is Really About: Inequality," *vox.com*, posted Noember 30, 2018, available at https://www.vox.com/science-and-health/2018/1/9/16860994/life-expectancy-us-income-inequality. For a breakdown of American life expectancy mapped by neighborhood, see https://qz.com/1462111/map-what-story-does-your-neighborhoods-life-expectancy-tell/.
31. Speech available at http://www.whitehouse.gov/blog/2013/01/21/second-inauguration-barack-obama.
32. Paul Krugman, "Inequality Is a Drag," *New York Times*, August 7, 2014. His claim is cited by IMF research: Jonathan Ostry and Andrew Berg, "Treating Inequality with Redistribution: Is the Cure Worse Than the Disease?," *iMFdirect*, posted February 26, 2014.
33. John Maynard Keynes, *A Tract on Monetary Reform* (London: Macmillan, 1924), p. 80.
34. John Blake, "Ask the Card-Carrying Socialists: Is Obama One of Them?," *CNN Politics Online*, April 15, 2010.
35. See, for example, Clive Thompson, "Nothing Grows Forever: Why Do We Keep Thinking the Economy Will?," *Mother Jones*, May/June 2010, pp. 7–9; Tim Jackson, *Prosperity without Growth* (London: Routledge, 2009).
36. For one accessible and classic statement, Bill Devall and George Sessions, *Deep Ecology: Living as If Nature Mattered* (Layton, UT: Gibbs Smith, 1985).

Chapter 11

1. "'Egypt is Free,' Crowds Cheer after Mubarak Quits," MSNBC.com, February 11, 2011, consulted February 1, 2013.
2. See the annual *Freedom in the World* reports available at www.freedomhouse.org.

3. Sam Dagher, "The Families Who Sacrificed Everything for Assad," *The Atlantic*, April 12, 2018.

4. F. Gregory Gausse III, "Saudi Arabia in the New Middle East," Council on Foreign Relations Special Report No. 63, December 2011, http://www.cfr.org/saudi-arabia/saudi-arabia-new-middle-east/p26663.

5. For an interesting discussion of the Youth League, see Konstantinos Tsimonis, "Keep the Party Assured and the Youth [Not] Satisfied: The Communist Youth League and Chinese University Students," *Modern China*, 44(2) (2018), pp. 170–207.

6. Mehdi Khalaji, "Iran's Regime of Religion," *Journal of International Affairs*, 65(1) (Fall/Winter 2011), pp. 131–147.

7. Ibid.

8. Peter Martonosi, "The Basij: A Major Factor in Iranian Security," *Academic and Applied Research in Military Science*, 11(1) (2012), pp. 27–38.

9. William Dobson, *The Dictator's Learning Curve* (New York: Doubleday, 2012).

10. See, for example, Steven Levitsky and Lucan Way, *Competitive Authoritarianism: Hybrid Regimes after the Cold War* (New York: Cambridge University Press, 2010).

11. See Hooman Majd, *The Ayatollah's Democracy: An Iranian Challenge* (New York: Norton, 2011).

12. Michael Wines, "A Village in Revolt Could Be a Harbinger for China," *New York Times*, December 25, 2011.

13. Mark MacKinnon, "China's 'Little Democracy' Struggles to Maintain Relevance," *The Globe and Mail*, January 9, 2013.

14. Yu Keping, *Democracy Is a Good Thing: Essays on Politics, Society and Culture in Contemporary China* (Washington, D.C.: Brookings Institution, 2009).

15. Dobson, *The Dictator's Learning Curve*, p. 268.

16. Ibid., pp. 269–270.

17. See Jennifer Gandhi, *Political Institutions under Dictatorship* (New York: Cambridge University Press, 2008).

18. On democratic "backsliding" into authoritarianism, see Steven Levitsky and Daniel Ziblatt, *How Democracies Die* (New York: Random House, 2018).

19. Daniel W. Drezner, "Sanctions Sometimes Smart: Targeted Sanctions in Theory and Practice," *International Studies Review*, 13(1) (2011), pp. 96–108.

20. Thomas Carothers, "The Backlash against Democracy Promotion," *Foreign Affairs*, 85(2) (March/April 2006), pp. 55–68.

21. Daniel W. Drezner, *The Sanctions Paradox: Economic Statecraft and International Relations* (New York: Cambridge University Press, 1999).

22. Peter Kenyon, "Iranians Cast Blame as U.S. Sanctions Hurt Iran's Economy," www.npr.org, January 8, 2019.

23. David Herzhenhorn and Ellen Barry, "Russia Demands U.S. Ends Support of Democracy Groups," *New York Times*, September 18, 2012.

24. Adam Przeworski and Fernando Limongi, "Modernization: Theories and Facts," *World Politics*, 49(2) (1997), pp. 155–183.

25. Samuel P. Huntington, *Political Order in Changing Societies* (New Haven, CT: Yale University Press, 1968), p. 43; Przeworski and Limongi, "Modernization," p. 160.

26. Jeffry Frieden, *Debt, Development, and Democracy: Modern Political Economy and Latin America, 1965–1985* (Princeton, NJ: Princeton University Press, 1992).

27. Christoph Neidhart, *Russia's Carnival: The Smells, Sights and Sounds of Transition* (Oxford: Rowman & Littlefield, 2003), p. 184.

28. Clemens Breisinger, Olivier Ecker, and Perrihan Al-Riffai, "Economics of the Arab Awakening," International Food Policy Research Institute Policy Brief 18 (May 2011), www.ifpri.org.

29. Ruth Berins Collier, *Paths toward Democracy: The Working Class and Elites in Western Europe and South America* (New York: Cambridge University Press, 1999).

30. These numbers are debatable, since they depend on how we classify the many regimes that combine some of the features of these categories. See Barbara Geddes, "Authoritarian Breakdown," cited previously.

31. Jeff Martini and Julie Taylor, "Commanding Democracy in Egypt: The Military's Attempt to Manage the Future," *Foreign Affairs*, 90(5) (September 2011), pp. 127–137.

32. Jessica Noll, *Fighting Corruption or Protecting the Regime? Egypt's Administrative Control Authority* (Washington, D.C.: Project on Middle East Democracy, 2019).

33. Roula Khalaf, "Bashar al-Assad: Behind the Mask," *Financial Times*, June 15, 2012.

34. Daniel Steiman, "Military Decision-Making during the Arab Spring," *Muftah*, posted May 29, 2012, www.muftah.org.

35. Sui-Lee Wee, "China's Parliament is a Growing Billionaires' Club," *New York Times*, March 1, 2018; David Hawkings, "Wealth of Congress: Richer Than Ever, But Mostly At the Very Top," *Rollcall.com*, posted February 27, 2018.

36. See Alexandra Fiol-Mahon, "Xi Jinping's Anti-Corruption Campaign: The Hidden Motives of a Modern-Day Mao," Foreign Policy Research Institute report, posted at fpri.org, August 17, 2018.

37. See the overview by Austin Ramzy, "President Xi Jinping's Rise, As Covered by The Times," *New York Times*, February 26, 2018.

38. Dobson, *The Dictator's Learning Curve*, p. 256. Since the Egyptians called their uprising the "Jasmine Revolution," the word "Jasmine" was also blocked, and jasmine flowers disappeared from all Chinese flower markets.

39. Jeff Goodwin, "Why We Were Surprised (Again) by the Arab Spring," *Swiss Journal of Political Science*, 17(4) (2011), pp. 452–456.

40. See Timur Kuran, "The Inevitability of Future Revolutionary Surprises," *American Journal of Sociology*, 100(6) (May 1995), pp. 1528–1551.

41. For a classic discussion, see Robert Dahl, *Polyarchy: Participation and Opposition* (New Haven, CT: Yale University Press, 1972), pp. 62–74.

42. Adam Przeworski and Fernando Limongi, "Modernization: Theories and Facts," *World Politics*, 49(2) (1997), pp. 155–183.

43. Henry S. Rowen, "When Will the Chinese People Be Free?" *Journal of Democracy*, 18(3) (July 2007), pp. 38–52.

44. Minxin Pei, "How Will China Democratize?," *Journal of Democracy*, 18(3) (July 2007), pp. 53–57; or Kellee S. Tsai, *Capitalism without Democracy: The Private Sector in Contemporary China* (Ithaca, NY: Cornell University Press, 2007).

45. Jan Fidrmuc, "Economic Reform, Democracy and Growth during Post-Communist Transition," *European Journal of Political Economy*, 19 (2003), pp. 583–604.

46. Larry Diamond, "What Went Wrong in Iraq," *Foreign Affairs*, 83 (September/October 2004), pp. 34–56.

47. Guillermo O'Donnell and Philippe Schmitter, *Transitions from Authoritarian Rule: Tentative Conclusions about Uncertain Democracies* (Baltimore: Johns Hopkins University Press, 1991), p. 38; Dankwart Rustow, "Transitions to Democracy: Towards a Dynamic Model," *Comparative Politics*, 2(3) (April 1970), pp. 337–363.

48. Adam Przeworski, *Democracy and the Market: Political and Economic Reforms in Eastern Europe and Latin America* (New York: Cambridge University Press, 1991), p. 26.

49. Michael Semple, "Talking to the Taliban," *Foreignpolicy.com*, posted January 10, 2013.

50. Marina Ottaway and Thomas Carothers, eds., *Funding Virtue: Civil Society Aid and Democracy Promotion* (Washington, D.C.: Carnegie Endowment for International Peace, 2000).

51. Thomas Carothers, *Revitalizing Democracy Assistance* (Washington, D.C.: Carnegie Endowment for International Peace, 2009).

52. Sarah Henderson, "Selling Civil Society: Western Aid and the Non-Governmental Organizations Sector in Russia," *Comparative Political Studies*, 35 (March 2002), pp. 136–167.

53. Taedong Lee, Erica Johnson, and Aseem Prakash, "Media Independence and Trust in NGOs: The Case of Postcommunist Countries," *Nonprofit and Voluntary Sector Quarterly*, 41(1) (February 2012), pp. 8–35.

54. Speech to Congress, April 2, 1917. Text available at http://historymatters.gmu.edu/d/4943/.

55. Remarks to the press, March 28, 2011. Text available at http://www.whitehouse.gov/the-press-office.

56. Historian Gregory Hodgson, cited in John R. MacArthur, "The Presidency in Wartime: George W. Bush Discovers Woodrow Wilson," *Harper's*, September 2008.

57. Daniel Larison, "The Enduring Failure of Democracy Promotion Abroad," *The Week*, April 11, 2012.

58. Daniel Drezner, "The Realists versus the Neocons," *TheNationalInterest.org*, posted March 20, 2008.

59. Daniel McCarthy, "Rand Paul's Foreign Policy Speech at Heritage," *Theamericanconservative.com*, posted February 6, 2013.

60. See the excellent profile of Bolton by Graeme Wood, "Will John Bolton Bring on Armageddon—Or Stave It Off?" *The Atlantic*, April 2019, available at https://www.theatlantic.com/magazine/archive/2019/04/john-bolton-trump-national-security-adviser/583246/.

61. David Rieff, "Evangelists of Democracy," *The National Interest* (November/December 2012).

62. Dennis Kucinich, remarks during hearing on "Fostering Democracy in the Middle East," May 20, 2005, *Congressional Record*, 151(Part 8), p. 10710.

Chapter 12

1. Simon Braund, "How Ronald Reagan Learned to Start Worrying and Stop Loving the Bomb," *Empire* (November 2010), pp. 134–140.

2. Bruce Russett and Joel Slemrod, "Diminished Expectations of Nuclear War and Increased Personal Savings: Evidence from Individual Survey Data," *American Economic Review*, 83(4) (September 1993), pp. 1022–1033.

3. "The Odds on a Conflict Between the Great Powers," *The Economist*, January 25, 2018.

4. Matthew White, *The Great Big Book of Horrible Things: The Definitive Chronicle of History's 100 Worst Atrocities* (New York: Norton, 2011).

5. Steven Pinker, *The Better Angels of Our Nature: Why Violence Has Declined* (New York: Allen Lane, 2011), p. xxi.

6. See Jack Levy and William Thompson, *The Arc of War* (Chicago: University of Chicago Press, 2011).

7. Christopher Allmand, "New Weapons, New Tactics 1300–1500," in Geoffrey Parker, ed., *The Cambridge Illustrated History of Warfare* (New York: Cambridge University Press, 1995), pp. 92–105.

8. Stephen Morillo, Jeremy Black, and Paul Lococo, *War in World History*, 2 (Boston: McGraw-Hill, 2009), p. 319.

9. This English version of the French decree comes from Charles D. Hazen, *The French Revolution*, 2 vols. (New York: Holt, 1932), p. 666. (Note that linen was needed to pack around musket balls.)

10. Carl von Clausewitz, *On War*, rev. ed., edited and translated by Michale Howard and Peter Paret (Princeton, NJ: Princeton University Press, 1984 [1832]), pp. 591–592.

11. Richard Sakwa, *The Rise and Fall of the Soviet Union, 1917–1991* (New York: Routledge, 1999).

12. Samuel Glasstone and Phillip Dolan, eds., *The Effects of Nuclear Weapons*, 3rd ed. (Washington, D.C.: U.S. Department of Defense, 1977).

13. Gerard DeGroot, *The Bomb: A Life* (Cambridge, MA: Harvard University Press, 2005).

14. See Peter Kornbluh, ed., *Cuban Missile Crisis Revelations*, National Security Archive Electronic Briefing Book No. 35, http://www.gwu.edu/~nsarchiv/.

15. Carl Berger, ed., *The United States Air Force in Southeast Asia, 1961–1973*, rev. ed. (Washington, D.C.: Office of Air Force History, 1984), p. 368.

16. See the Council on Foreign Relations' annual surveys of foreign policy experts, available at https://www.cfr.org/report/preventive-priorities-survey-2019.

17. John Barry and Evan Thomas, "Dropping the Bomb," *Newsweek*, June 24, 2001. For data on current nuclear forces, see the count by the Federation of American Scientists at https://fas.org/issues/nuclear-weapons/status-world-nuclear-forces/.

18. David Sanger, David Barboza, and Nicole Perlroth, "Chinese Army Unit Is Seen as Tied to Hacking against US," *New York Times*, February 18, 2013.

19. For a tracker of such incidents, including by other countries besides China, see the site of the Center for Strategic & International Studies, at https://www.csis.org/programs/cybersecurity-and-governance/technology-policy-program/other-projects-cybersecurity.

20. Graham Allison, *Destined for War: America, China, and the Thucydides' Trap* (New York: Houghton Mifflin, 2017); Gordon Chang, "Top General Fears War with Russia and China at Same Time," *Dailybeast.com*, posted October 31, 2018.

21. For one very critical review of Allison's book, see Arthur Waldron, "There Is No Thucydides Trap," *Supchina.com*, posted June 12, 2017. The "remote" evaluation comes in Robert Farley, "This Is How Bad a U.S.-China War Would Be (In 2030)," *The National Interest*, September 5, 2018.

22. United States Census Bureau, "Trade in Goods with China," https://www.census.gov/foreign-trade/balance/c5700.html.

23. Yusho Cho, "China Shrinks US Treasury Holdings to 2-Year Low

24. See, for example, Leif-Eric Eisley, "Why China Takes a Middle-of-the-Road Policy toward North Korea," *Washington Post*, February 28, 2019.

25. Robert Jervis, "America and the Twentieth Century: Continuity and Change," in Michael Hogan, ed. *The Ambiguous Legacy: US Foreign Relations in the 'American Century'* (New York: Cambridge University Press, 1999), p. 100.

26. See the Uppsala Conflict Data Program at https://ucdp.uu.se/.

27. See Michelle Starr, "This Chart Says You'll Likely Be Killed by Something You're Not Worried About," *sciencealert.com*, posted April 19, 2018, available at https://www.sciencealert.com/causes-of-death-over-and-underrepresented-in-media-and-google-searches.

28. See the annual Global Terrorism Index reports by the Institute for Economics and Peace, available at visionofhumanity.org/reports/.

29. Tony Harnden, "Bin Laden Didn't Expect New York Towers to Fall," *The Telegraph*, December 10, 2001.

30. According to the American Civil Liberties Union (ACLU), https://www.aclu.org/national-security/guantanamo-numbers.

31. The phrase "The terrorists have won" even has its own Wikipedia entry about how often this notion is invoked. See https://en.wikipedia.org/wiki/The_terrorists_have_won.

32. Bush remarks at Iowa Western Community College, June 21, 2000.

33. Kenneth Waltz, *Man, the State, and War* (New York: Columbia University Press, 1954), p. 3.

34. Mark Twain, *What Is Man? And Other Philosophical Writings* (Berkeley: University of California Press, 1973), p. 84.

35. Robert Wright, "Signing Off," *The Atlantic.com*, January 8, 2013. Original emphasis.

36. Woodrow Wilson speech to joint session of U.S. Congress, April 2, 1917, http://historymatters.gmu.edu/d/4943/.

37. Michael Doyle, "Kant, Liberal Legacies, and Foreign Affairs," *Philosophy and Public Affairs*, 12(3) (1983), pp. 205–235.

38. George W. Bush speech at Whitehall Palace, London, UK, November 19, 2003, http://www.presidentialrhetoric.com/speeches/11.19.03.html.

39. See Erica Chenoweth, "Democratic Competition and Terrorist Activity," *Journal of Politics*, 72(1) (January 2010), pp. 16–30.

40. *The Song of the Girondins*, a French Revolutionary song from 1792 (author's translation).

41. For one account, see Linda Melvern, *A People Betrayed: The Role of the West in Rwanda's Genocide* (London: Zed Books, 2000).

42. Francis Fukuyama, "The End of History," *The National Interest* 16 (Summer 1989).

43. John Mearsheimer, *The Tragedy of Great Power Politics* (New York: Norton, 2001).

44. Kenneth Waltz, "The Stability of a Bipolar World," *Daedalus*, 93(3) (1964), pp. 881–909.

45. William Wohlforth, "The Stability of a Unipolar World," *International Security*, 24(1) (1999), pp. 5–37.

46. Kenneth Waltz, "Structural Realism after the Cold War," *International Security*, 25(1) (2000), pp. 5–41.

47. See Allison, op. cit. (note [get note # above]), or John Mearsheimer, "China's Unpeaceful Rise," *Current History*, 105(690) (2006), pp. 160–162.

48. For cites and an overview, see Robert Delahunty and John Yoo, "The 'Bush Doctrine': Can Preventive War Be Justified?," *Harvard Journal of Law & Public Policy*, 32(3) (2009), pp. 844–865.

49. A useful overview is the *New York Times*' "Guide to the Memos on Torture," available at nytimes.com. Consulted January 28, 2015.

50. Catechism of the Catholic Church of 1992, http://www.usccb.org/beliefs-and-teachings/what-we-believe/catechism/catechism-of-the-catholic-church/epub/index.cfm. The first bullet point paraphrases principles implicit in paragraphs 2302–2317; the others cite paragraph 2309.

51. Remarks by President Obama at the National Defense University, May 23, 2013, http://www.whitehouse.gov/the-press-office/2013/05/23/remarks-president-national-defense-university.

52. Kathleen Parker, "War on Terror Isn't Over Just Because Obama Says So," *Washington Post*, May 28, 2013.

53. Ben Stein, "Declaring End to War on Terror Is Surrender," *CBSNews.com*, posted June 2, 2013.

54. Gerald Seymour, *Harry's Game* (New York: Random House, 1975).

55. Hearings before the Subcommittee on Europe and the Middle East of the Committee on Foreign Affairs, House of Representatives, 101st Congress, First Session, cited in Boaz Ganor, "Defining Terrorism: Is One Man's Terrorist Another Man's Freedom Fighter?," *Police Practice and Research*, 3(4) (2002), pp. 287–304.

56. Chuck Hagel, *America: Our Next Chapter* (New York: HarperCollins, 2008), p. 50.

Chapter 13

1. Thomas Friedman, *The World Is Flat: A Brief History of the Twenty-First Century* (New York: Picador, 2007).

2. For more excellent data, charts, and discussion of patterns of globalization, see Estenan Ortiz-Ospina, Diana Beltekian and Max Roser, "Trade and Globalization," revised version posted October 2018, at https://ourworldindata.org/trade-and-globalization#.

3. International Trade Administration, www.trade.gov.

4. U.S. Bureau of Labor Statistics, *International Comparisons of Manufacturing Productivity and Unit Labor Cost Trends 2011*, www.bls.gov/ilc.

5. Chris Sparks, Theo Bikoi, and Lisa Moglia, "A Perspective on US and Foreign Compensation Costs in Manufacturing," *Monthly Labor Review*, 36 (June 2002), pp. 36–48. In some industries, these differences have even widened since: General Motors' labor costs in 2009 were $55 per hour in the United States, $7 in Mexico, $4.50 in China, and $1 in India for similar types of work. Stephen Rattner, "The Secrets of Germany's Success: What Europe's Manufacturing Powerhouse Can Teach America," *Foreign Affairs*, July 2011, 7–11.

6. See World Trade Organization data on national trade profiles at http://stat.wto.org/CountryProfile/WSDBCountryPFHome.aspx?Language=E.

7. U.S. Bureau of Labor Statistics, May 2018, https://www.bls.gov/oes/current/area_emp_chart/area_emp_chart.htm.

8. See the "American-Made Index" calculated each year on Cars.com on the basis of information supplied by manufacturers, at https://www.cars.com/american-made-index/.

9. United Nations Conference on Trade and Development (UNCTAD) World Investment Report 2012.

10. World Bank, World Development Indicators, data.worldbank.org.

11. Richard Freeman, "The Great Doubling: Labor in the New Global Economy," Usery Lecture in Labor Policy, University of Atlanta, 2005.

12. These quotes are from the *New York Times*' Pulitzer Prize–winning series, "The iEconomy," by Charles Duhigg, Keith Bradsher, and David Barboza, January 21 and 25, 2012.

13. Jon Miller, "Hugo Grotius," *The Stanford Encyclopedia of Philosophy* (Fall 2011 Edition), Edward Zalta, ed., http://plato.stanford.edu/archives/fall2011/entries/grotius/.

14. Ian Hurd, *After Anarchy: Legitimacy and Power in the United Nations Security Council* (Princeton, NJ: Princeton University Press, 2007).

15. Curtis Tate, "IMF's Lagarde: Budget Cuts Are Slowing Down America," *wallstcheatsheet.com*, posted June 5, 2013.

16. International Monetary Fund.

17. Michael Spence and Sandile Hlatshwayo, "The Evolving Structure of the American Economy and the Employment Challenge," Council on Foreign Relations working paper, March 2011.

18. This is a key argument of one of the most celebrated books on economics

in recent decades, Thomas Piketty, *Capital in the Twenty-First Century* (Cambridge, MA: Belknap Press, 2014).

19. Matthew Mosk, "Wal-Mart Fires Supplier After Bangladesh Revelation," *ABCnews.com*, May 15, 2013. Note that "Wal-Mart" is the official name of the firm, though its stores are called "Walmart."

20. Laurence Chandy and Geoffrey Gertz, "With Little Notice, Globalization Reduced Poverty," *Yalegloba-lonline*, July 5, 2011.

21. Simeon Bennett and Laura Marcinek, "Bill Gates Sees Almost No Poor Countries Left by 2035," *bloomberg.com*, posted January 21, 2014.

22. Mario Pezzini, "An Emerging Middle Class," OECDobserver.org, www.oecdobserver.org/news/full-story.php/aid/3681/.

23. See Sintia Radu, "India's Tableau of Inequality," *US News and World Report*, July 26, 2018.

24. Sonali Jain-Chandra et al, "Inequality in China: Trends, Drivers and Policy Remedies," *IMF Working Paper* 18/127 (2018), available at https://www.imf.org/~/media/Files/Publications/WP/2018/wp18127.ashx.

25. See Sebastian Edwards, "Contagion," World Economy Lecture 1999, University of Nottingham, UK, http://www.anderson.ucla.edu/faculty/sebastian.edwards/world_economy5.pdf.

26. "A Cruel Sea of Capital," *The Economist*, May 1, 2003.

27. For example, see *Forbes*'s annual "Best Countries for Business," http://www.forbes.com/best-countries-for-business/list/.

28. See "How Mitt Romney Has Positioned Himself on Abortion and Immigration," *nytimes.com*, posted October 10, 2012; Andrew Rosenthal, "Anything Barack Can Do, Mitt Can Do Tougher," *nytimes.com*, posted July 25, 2012.

29. Bernie Sanders, "Democrats Need to Wake Up," *New York Times*, June 28, 2016.

30. As of June 2019 his platform was available at https://berniesanders.com/issues/fight-for-fair-trade-and-workers/.

31. See, for example, David Jackson and Nicholas Wu, "Donald Trump Rips U.S. Chamber of Commerce for Attacking His Tariff Strategy," *USAtoday.com*, June 10, 2019.

Index

Page numbers followed by "*f*" and "*t*" indicate figure and table, respectively.